√ B
RUBINSTE

Rubinstein

Harvey Sachs

Rubinstein

A Life

With a Discography Compiled and
Edited by Donald Manildi

GROVE PRESS
New York

Printed in the United States of America

FIRST EDITION

Library of Congress Cataloging-in-Publication Data

Sachs, Harvey, 1946–
Rubinstein: a life / Harvey Sachs; with a discography compiled and edited by Donald Manildi.
Includes bibliographical references (p.) and index.
Contents: The life—The recorded legacy.
ISBN 0-8021-1579-9
1. Rubinstein, Artur, 1887–1982. 2. Pianists—Biography.
I. Manildi, Donald. II. Title.
ML417.R79S23 1995   786.2′092—dc20   [B] 95-13539   MN

DESIGN BY LAURA HAMMOND HOUGH

Grove Press
841 Broadway
New York, NY 10003

10 9 8 7 6 5 4 3 2 1

In memory of my grandparents,

Joseph Sachs (1883–1954),
Dora Bloch Sachs (1884–1960),
Carl Bloom (1891–1959),
Blanche May Bloom (1892–1976),

who were all Eastern European Jews,
like the subject of this book,
and of the same generation.

Contents

Preface

Arthur Rubinstein was seven years old in 1894, when he first played the piano in public. By the time his career ended, eighty-two years later, he had performed with extraordinary success in most countries of the world. He was a cosmopolite and world-traveler who spoke eight languages and made his home, at various times, in Poland, Germany, France, England, the United States, Spain, and Switzerland. Members of the international ruling class sought his company, were charmed by his conversation, and conferred honors on him. He enjoyed an unfettered erotic life in his youth, married at the age of forty-five, and fathered four children. When he died, wealthy and esteemed, in the middle of his tenth decade, he left behind high-quality recordings of much of his repertoire and a two-volume autobiography that was an international best-seller. His life appears to have been exceptionally happy and privileged—and in many respects it was.

One need not dig far below the surface of the Rubinstein story, however, to discover unusually strong contradictions. The professional curricula of most celebrated performers follow a pattern: Talent is discovered and cultivated, and recognition is sought and achieved; thereafter, performers either continue to work steadily to maintain their standing or make use of their personae and the power of publicity to the same effect. But Rubinstein was long considered merely one fine keyboard artist among many, especially in northern Europe and North America; not until he was past fifty did he enter his generation's pianistic pantheon. His private life, too, was even bumpier than his autobiography led readers to believe. *My Young Years* and *My Many Years*—thus the volumes were called—are so long (eleven hundred pages in all, as they were originally published by Alfred A. Knopf), and parts of them are so frank that many readers assumed that their author had "told all." This was not the case. He was thorough in providing menus of meals consumed and lists of love affairs consummated, but he gave the misleading impression that the casual erotic encounters of his youth ceased when he married. His relationships with his children were also more troubled, sometimes, than his book revealed. Above all, Rubinstein the author congratulated himself far too

often on his unconditional love of life. The books are often charming but
they are also superficial. Rubinstein the raconteur is very much in evidence—as he ought to be—but many of his observations on music and
musicians are embarrassingly summary or inconsequential, and most of his
encounters with famous, powerful, or just plain wealthy nonmusicians are
related in anecdotal form. Early in the second volume the narrative palls,
and one begins to wonder what was at Arthur Rubinstein's core. By the
end, one wonders whether he had a core. But he did have one. Healthiness
and generosity were the quintessential qualities of his music-making, and
these qualities did not exist in a void: they were a manifestation of elements
in his character, which was much richer and more complicated than his
memoirs revealed. One of my basic tasks, in writing this book, has been to
compare Arthur Rubinstein's official self-portrait with the unofficial portrait
that his papers, the people close to him, and outside observers have created,
cumulatively.

    With respect to autobiographical revelations, Gabriel Astruc, Rubin-
stein's first manager in France, wrote that his own father had taught him an
allegory "borrowed from the Talmud: 'There are three types of memoirs:
funnel-memoirs, *sponge-memoirs*, and *sieve-memoirs*. The first take in everything but let everything escape, the second take in everything and keep it, the
third keep what is good and sift out what is bad.' "[1] Rubinstein's are sieve-
memoirs, except that what they sift out is not so much the "bad" as what their
author consciously or unconsciously wished to conceal. This is a normal-
enough procedure. With the possible exception of money, the desire to use
self-exposure as a form of self-defense must be the most common of the motives that drive celebrities to write autobiographies. Rubinstein's younger son,
John, has pointed out that his father was "able to joke about his failings quite
expansively—but *selectively*."[2] In other words, he would willingly and even
delightedly admit to character defects, but only when he could be the one to
decide what the defects were. I would take John Rubinstein's statement one
step farther: I believe that his father was as unfair to himself in discussing his
virtues as his defects. A small but telling example is his comment about visiting museums. He particularly loved London's National Gallery and British
Museum, he said, because "you can see their masterpieces right away, like
the famous Elgin marbles taken from the Parthenon, or the Venus of Ve-
lázquez . . . , whereas my visits to the Louvre used to exhaust me . . . ; one had
to walk miles to see the Venus de Milo and the Mona Lisa on the same
visit."[3] I imagine that many readers asked themselves, as I did, whether
Rubinstein had ever bothered to look at any of the hundreds or thousands of
works—most of them exceptionally interesting—that line the miles that separate the Venus de Milo from the Mona Lisa in the Louvre. Are not they, too,

worthy of investigation, or is culture merely a Masterpiece Mall? In reality, however, Rubinstein *was* interested in making his own discoveries in art, and over the decades he gave his enthusiastic endorsement and material support to several little-known painters and sculptors simply because their work pleased him. Thus, in his memoirs he attributed to himself a mindless cultural snobbery of which he was not guilty, and in so doing he aroused suspicion about his often-mentioned broad and profound general culture.

Rubinstein's memoirs also generate a more concrete problem: They must be taken as a point of departure on factual matters, but they are unreliable. Rubinstein often complimented himself on his wonderful memory, which, he said, enabled him in old age to reconstruct his life, day by day, without the use of diaries, which he had never kept. But his reconstruction is flawed in the extreme. From the start, it is plagued by a Great Date Confusion and a Great Name Confusion—neither of them intentional, except in a few instances. The date problem has three components. First, the "Old Style" Russian calendar, which was officially in use during Rubinstein's childhood in the part of Poland in which he was born, was twelve days behind the calendar in use elsewhere in Europe and in the Americas. All the dates I give are "New Style," adjusted to agree with the Western calendar. The second component derives from the fact that Rubinstein's birth-year is given differently in different sources: some say 1886, others 1887, still others 1889 (the year that Rubinstein gave for over half a century) or even 1890. The correct year is 1887. It appears on all the early official documents about him, in all the contemporary census registers, and in all the early publicity material and newspaper reports on him, and it is the date to which Rubinstein finally admitted in his memoirs. But by the time he wrote the memoirs, he could no longer remember whether a certain concert had taken place when he was twenty-three—as he had been telling people for decades—or twenty-five, or whether he had met a certain woman when he was thirty-nine or forty-one. The worst source of confusion, however, was Rubinstein's casual attitude toward dates. Entire sections of his memoirs are misdated by a year or a decade or even longer, and in the aftermath of the turbulent events that have taken place during the last hundred years in Poland and Germany, where Rubinstein spent his childhood and adolescence, little relevant documentation remains. In trying to determine dates, I have often had to rely on incomplete information and inductive reasoning, and I hope that I have been correct most of the time.

The name problem begins with Rubinstein's maternal grandfather, who, in the index to *My Young Years*, is called Solomon Heyman. Solomon, however, is the English version of the name of Rubinstein's *great*-grandfather; the grandfather's name was Yechiel. And the spelling of the surname, on

Rubinstein's mother's tombstone, is *Heiman*, which is the spelling that I have used in this book. I have also used the tombstone spellings of the first names of Rubinstein's parents, Felicja and Izaak, which are spelled in other ways in some other sources. Most other names I have given as I found them. The reason for the profusion and confusion of first names in the Rubinstein family is that Jewish babies were usually given, first, a Hebrew name, which, among central and Eastern European Jews, was then adapted into a familiar, Yiddish form, thence into its equivalent—when there was one—in the dominant local language or dialect. Thus, Yitzchak became Itzik in Yiddish and Izaak in Polish. I have, of course, used the traditional Germanic spelling of Rubinstein, rather than the Polish Rubinsztajn or the Russian Rubenshtyain or Rubinshtyain, which appear in some sources, or the not-infrequent Rubenstein, which the pianist disliked. With respect to the spelling of my subject's first name, I have followed his own preference: "In later years, my manager Sol Hurok used the *h*-less 'Artur' for my publicity, but I sign 'Arthur' in countries where it is common practice, 'Arturo' in Spain and Italy, and 'Artur' in the Slav countries."[4] So Arthur it is, here, except in direct quotations from articles, books, and documents in which it is spelled otherwise.

IN A GENERAL sense, this book may have begun to take shape in January 1959, when I first heard Rubinstein play. More specifically, however, I first gave the idea serious thought late in 1986, during a visit to Peter Rosen, a New York–based television producer for whom I had written a documentary on Arturo Toscanini. Rosen had just completed a documentary on Rubinstein, to be shown in conjunction with the upcoming hundredth anniversary of the pianist's birth; he still had several cardboard cartons full of research material at hand, and he said that if I thought I might ever want to write a biography of Rubinstein, I could take any of the material that might prove useful. He also gave me the addresses and telephone numbers of Rubinstein's widow and the couple's older daughter, Eva. I was just finishing a book on the history of music under the fascist regime in Italy, and the thought of starting another book immediately was unappealing. I did phone and write to Eva Rubinstein, but I then let the idea cool until the end of October 1988, when I visited Aniela (Nela) Rubinstein at the Paris home that she and her husband had moved into almost exactly fifty years earlier. Mrs. Rubinstein, who was eighty at the time, was both kind and frank. She told me that she and her husband had had difficulties in his last years—which I already knew—and she said that although she was not opposed to my writing his biography she would prefer that I wait until she was gone. "It won't be long now," she said with a laugh. I told her, equally frankly, that although I was not proposing to write an official, family-authorized biography, I could not attempt to produce a biography of her husband without her cooperation and her permission to examine her husband's papers. Unlike Toscanini, whose biography I had completed ten years earlier, Rubinstein had been a living figure for me — someone whom I had seen and heard many times and had even met. But Toscanini had been a special interest of mine for many years before I was invited to write his biography, and by the time I began that project I already knew, generally speaking, what work had to be done. With Rubinstein, on the contrary, I knew only that his memoirs, which I had read, would have to be carefully reread and checked; the rest was a large question mark. Mrs. Rubinstein agreed to put her memory and papers at my disposal. I wrote up a book proposal, and the following summer I signed a contract.

I knew from the start that the greatest technical difficulty in writing this book would be the scarcity of primary source material from the first fifty-three years of Rubinstein's life. When the Rubinsteins abandoned Paris at the outbreak of World War II, they left behind most of their possessions, including private papers. During the war, their house was occupied by the Germans; items whose cash value was high — paintings and furnishings, for instance — were confiscated and sent to Germany, but correspondence and other documents were destroyed or dispersed and have not been rediscovered. From the time the Rubinsteins arrived in the United States, however, material began to pile up again, and the pile grew to enormous proportions. The material was eventually shipped to their house in Paris, where it occupied considerable shelf-space. Mrs. Rubinstein kindly allowed me to examine the material and to photocopy anything I wished so that I could study the documents thoroughly, at my convenience. I returned home from one of my visits to Paris with approximately two thousand pages of photocopies, and some parts of my book   large stretches of chapters 6 and 7, in particular — are based on a distillation of this material. (Many of the original documents have since been donated to the Library of Congress in Washington, D. C., and the Historical Museum of the City of Lodz, in Poland.) For material on the first 60 percent of Rubinstein's life, however, and for parts of the later years as well, I have had to do a great deal of basic research in Poland, Germany, France, England, Switzerland, Spain, Italy, and the United States. With the exception of Katarzyna Naliwajek, a friend in Warsaw who has helped me to locate and translate a great deal of Polish material, I have had no regular research assistants, and I must therefore assume all responsibility for whatever errors the book may contain.

I AM ESPECIALLY indebted to several people besides Nela Rubinstein and Katarzyna Naliwajek. Eva, Alina, and John Rubinstein — three of Arthur and Nela's four children — have given generously of their time and information,

and so has Annabelle Whitestone, who was Rubinstein's companion in his
last years. They offered sharply divergent opinions of several controversial
matters in the pianist's life, and I have tried to give all of their views a well-
balanced airing. In 1992, a year after the bulk of my consultations with Ms.
Whitestone were finished, she became Lady Weidenfeld—the wife of
George Weidenfeld, who has been my principal publisher in Great Britain
since the 1970s—but this development notwithstanding, there has been no
attempt whatsoever on the part of Lord or Lady Weidenfeld or anyone connected with them to have me change my point of view on any of the controversial matters discussed in this book or in any other respect. And to the best
of my self-knowledge, I have not submitted to self-censorship—the most in-
sidious type of pressure—as a result of the Whitestone-Weidenfeld marriage.
The Rubinsteins and Lady Weidenfeld have all accepted the fact that parts of
the book will make painful reading for each of them, and I thank them all for
their forbearance. I am additionally grateful to Eva Rubinstein, who is a well-
known photographer, for allowing me to use some of the photos that she took
of her father and for helping me to sort through her mother's extensive photo
collection in Paris.

I am enormously indebted to Donald Manildi, curator of the International Piano Archives at Maryland (University of Maryland at College Park),
who has contributed an important Rubinstein discography, located after this
book's final chapter. I feel that Manildi's work greatly increases this book's
usefulness to lay listeners and specialists alike. For research assistance above
and beyond the call of duty or even of friendship, my special thanks go to Dr.
Jonothan Logan of EPG Labs in Manhasset, New York; John Freeman of
Opera News in New York City; Susanne Fontaine of the Hochschule der
Künste in Berlin; María Isabel de Falla, president of the Fundación Archivo
Manuel de Falla in Granada; Ricardo de Quesada of the Dirección Artística
Daniel in Madrid; and to my interviewees, whose names appear in the fol-
lowing list and in the text of the book. Dr. Alex E. Friedlander of Brooklyn,
New York, who has made remarkable investigations into the genealogy of
Polish Jews, provided me with invaluable information about Rubinstein's
ancestors and siblings. Graham Sheffield, music projects director of the
South Bank Centre in London, has been planning a book of his own on
Rubinstein, but has nevertheless been extraordinarily generous not only in
telling me "After you!" but also in sending me tapes and transcripts of his
BBC radio series, *Rubinstein on Record*. Michael Gray of the Voice of Amer-
ica prepared and sent me tapes of some out-of-print Rubinstein recordings.
To Alfred A. Knopf, Inc., publishers, of New York, and especially to Judith
Jones, senior editor and vice-president, thanks for permission to use many
short quotations from Rubinstein's *My Young Years* and *My Many Years*.

I owe special thanks of another sort to James G. Moser, executive editor at Grove/Atlantic in New York; to the publishers/editors Aaron Asher and Alan Williams, who were with Weidenfeld and Nicolson in New York before it became Grove Weidenfeld and/or with Grove Weidenfeld before it became Grove/Atlantic; to Ion Trewin, publisher, and Elsbeth Lindner, my editor, at Weidenfeld and Nicolson in London; and to Ned Leavitt, my remarkably patient literary agent, in New York.

Translations from all languages (French, German, Spanish, Italian, and Portuguese) except Polish and Russian are mine, but I had help with some difficult Spanish expressions from Laura Guasconi Boyer and with some thorny German from Irene Dische, Eva Halstenbach, Angela Paynter, Louise Phoenix-Giedraitis, and Ulla Richter. Eva Hoffman kindly translated from Polish a poem by Jaroslaw Iwaszkiewicz but also persuaded me that it was not worth using, and she kindly gave me permission to quote from her remarkable memoir, *Lost in Translation*.

Other individuals and institutions who have helped me include:

Austria. Vienna: Otto Biba, archive director of the Gesellschaft der Musikfreunde; Randolf Fochler of the L. Bösendorfer Klavierfabrik.

Brazil. Rio de Janeiro: Luli Oswald.

France. Le Havre: Jean-Paul Herbert of the Archives Historiques, Compagnie Générale Maritime. Nice: Odette Golschmann. Orange: Colette Brivet of the Chorégies d'Orange. Paris: Gérald Antoine, biographer of Paul Claudel; Elizabeth Hayes of the Théâtre des Champs-Elysées; Yann Martel; Madeleine Milhaud; Tomasz H. Orlowski and Magda Schnaus, who assisted Nela Rubinstein with her papers; Isabelle and Eric Straram; Alison Wearing. Saint-Jorioz: François-René Duchable.

Germany. Berlin: Daniel Barenboim and his assistant, Frau Topcu, of the Deutsche Staatsoper; Frau Preuss of the Landesarchiv; Dietmar Schenk of the Hochschularchiv at the Hochschule der Künste; Cornelia Praetorius. Hamburg: Gerda and Peter Aistleitner; Klaus Angermann of the Philharmonie; Frau or Herr Möhring of the Staatsarchiv, Senat der Freien und Hansestadt Hamburg. Leipzig: Claudius Böhm of the Gewandhausarchiv; Munich: Dr. Klaus Stadler of R. Piper Verlag.

Great Britain. Hayes, Middlesex: Ruth Edge and Suzanne Lewis of EMI Music Archives. Edinburgh: David Gilmour. London: Robert Baldock of Yale University Press; Nicholas Mosley, 3rd Baron Ravensdale; Libby Rice of the Development Department, London Symphony Orchestra; Jill Shutt of the Wigmore Hall administration.

Israel. Tel Aviv: Nechama Sachar of the Nahum Goldmann Museum of the Jewish Diaspora; Jan J. Bistritzky of the Arthur Rubinstein International Piano Master Competition; Peter E. Gradenwitz.

Italy. Milan: Milena Borromeo of the O.R.I.A. Rome: Annalisa Bini and Laura Ciancio of the Accademia di Santa Cecilia; Fil Pietrangeli and Paolo Rossi of BMG Airola.

Poland. Cracow: Teresa Chylinska and Malgorzata Perkowska-Waszek of the Uniwersytet Jagiellonski. Lodz: Ryszard Czubaczynski, Bozenna Pietraszczyk, Miroslaw Borusiewicz, Iwona Zukowska, and Aleksandra Kocik of the Muzeum Historii Miasta Lodzi (Historical Museum of the City of Lodz). Warsaw: Romano Catalini, Gennaro Camfora, and Paolo Gesumunno of the Istituto Italiano di Cultura; Henryka Kowalczyk and Malgorzata Komorowska of the Akademia Muzyczna im. Fryderyka Chopina; Margaret Jasinska, Elzbieta Jasinska Libera, Jozef Kanski, Maria Kempinska, Marcin Macijewski.

Portugal. Sintra: Marquesa Olga de Cadaval.

Russia. Moscow: Svyatoslav Richter.

Spain. Madrid: Anna Gamazo; Isabela Rua of the Fundación Isaac Albéniz.

Switzerland. Clarens: Nikita Magaloff (deceased). Geneva: Pedro Kranz of the Cæcilia agency. Herrliberg (Zürich): Andor Foldes. Lausanne: Danielle Mincio of the Bibliothèque Cantonale et Universitaire.

USA. Austin: Dell Anne Hollingsworth of the Harry Ransom Humanities Research Center at the University of Texas. Baltimore: Earl Carlyss and Ann Schein of the Peabody Conservatory. Boston: Bridget P. Carr, archivist, Boston Symphony Orchestra. Chicago: Patricia Smolen; Frank Villella, archives assistant, Chicago Symphony Orchestra. Cleveland: Eunice Podis. Concord, Massachusetts: Beatrice Erdely. Hancock, New Hampshire: Cecil B. Lyon. Kansas City, Missouri: Peter Munstedt, conservatory librarian, and Marilyn Burlingame, archivist, of the University of Missouri. Los Angeles: Mathis Chazanov; Orrin Howard, director of publications and archives of the Los Angeles Philharmonic; Jacqueline de Rothschild Piatigorsky. New Haven, Connecticut: Vivian Perlis, Yale University. New York City: Emanuel Ax; Michael Charry; Laura Dubman Fratti (deceased); Barbara Haws, archivist/historian of the New York Philharmonic; Judith Jones of Alfred A. Knopf; Jarmila Novotná (deceased); John Pfeiffer of BMG Classics–RCA Red Seal (Pfeiffer, who produced many of Rubinstein's records, allowed me to go through the company's files on Rubinstein); Alexander Schneider (deceased); Arnold Steinhardt of the Guarneri Quartet; May Stone of the New York Historical Society; Nancy Lee Swift of BMG Classics; Robert Tuggle, director of archives, Metropolitan Opera Association; David Walter, the Juilliard School; Dorothy Warren, biographer of Ruth Draper; Max Wilcox, who was Rubinstein's producer at RCA for the last seventeen years of the pianist's career. San Francisco: Debra Podjed, archivist, San Francisco Symphony.

San Pedro, California: Wendy Knopf Cooper. Washington: Kathie O. Nicastro of the Civil Reference Branch, National Archives; Charles S. Sampson of the Office of the Historian, Bureau of Public Affairs, United States Department of State. Weston, Connecticut: Janina Fialkowska. West Redding, Connecticut: Igor Kipnis.

I also want to thank the many friends who put me up (more than once, in some cases) during my various research trips, and without whose hospitality this book would have been economically unfeasible. They are: Romano and Ted Catalini in Warsaw; Danielle, Henri, and Julie Canonge and Holly Brubach in Paris; Dan Whitman in Madrid; Ruth Bloch and Jonothan Logan in New York; Irene, Nicolas, Emily, and Léon Dische-Becker in Berlin; Sir Anthony (deceased) and Lady Patricia Lousada in London; and Dan Whitman and Asunción Sanz in Washington. Many of these people also helped me in one way or another with my research. And I am especially grateful to my wife, Barbara, and our son, Julian, who put up with me throughout the period in which I was occupied with this project.

I must express one regret. I have been told that in the age of computerized typesetting, the costs of reproducing proper accent marks in the dozens or hundreds of Polish words and names that appear in this book would be prohibitive for an English-language publisher. Thus, the absence of the diagonal slash through the letter *l* in the name Mlynarski (pronounced Mwen-AHR-skee), the acute accent over the *n* in Kochanski (Ko-HIGHN-skee), the dot over the *z* in Rózycki (Roo-ZHIT-skee), the curlicue under the *a* in Dabie (DAHN-byeh), and many related details is not a result of ignorance, but rather of technical exigencies. And as it would be absurd to put in some accents but not others, even those marks that are available—the acute accent over the *o* in Rózycki, for instance—will not appear hereafter, with a few exceptions. I concede diacritical defeat, and my consolation prize is the fact that the name Karol Szymanowski (KAH-roll Sheh-mahn-OHV-skee), which appears frequently in chapters 3, 4, and 5, requires no accent marks.

This biography has never been intended as a replacement for Rubinstein's autobiography. It is an entirely separate, independent entity. With respect to my points of view on various issues in the story, readers may draw their own conclusions, but I declare at the outset that I am opposed to both idolatrous and iconoclastic biographies, born of hypotheses and nourished on material carefully selected to prove them. Martin Gilbert, Churchill's biographer, has justifiably charged that many contemporary biographers attempt to demonstrate their skill "by knocking the subject awry until he becomes a grotesque caricature of the real person."[5] I have tried hard to avoid this damaging form of exhibitionism. I have guided the story along, as every author must do, but I have left a great deal of testimony in the first person, in order to vary the tone and the viewpoint; an extra advantage of this technique is the publication, within the text, of some of the more significant fragments of Rubinstein's correspondence—and since he was not an assiduous letter-writer, there probably will never be a separate volume of his letters. My book does contain a bit of moralizing, here and there, but this has nothing to do with my private standards of behavior. (Kind readers will accept my assurances that I have some standards.) It occurs only at those points at which Rubinstein lied about, covered up, or crudely rationalized deviations from his own declared standards. He was a mixture of selfishness and generosity; so are most other human beings, but his special excellence in a profession that he exercised before a vast international public gave him unusual opportunities to overdevelop both characteristics.

H.S., Loro Ciuffenna, January 1995

NOTE: Nonspecialist readers need pay no attention to numbered reference notes, which contain only source information.

Part I

The Life

1
Talent

N. FOLLMANN   24 December 1890
Lodz
Herrn Prof. Joseph Joachim
Berlin
Highly respected Herr Professor!

Having just returned from a long business trip, I am fulfilling the very pleasant duty of thanking you very humbly, highly esteemed Herr Professor, for the straightforward but no doubt best possible advice that you kindly gave regarding the talented boy, Arthur Rubinstein.

In the meantime, however, this youngster is creating difficulties for us, because in the course of the last six months he has made significant progress, of a sort that you, highly respected Herr Professor, did not expect before his sixth year.

This budding musician not only knows the nomenclature of the individual notes and keys, but is already able to identify all the notes in a chord, even if they have sharps or flats.

It is not unworthy of mention that when the little one plays, he already uses both hands, and so plays everything with an individual yet harmonious accompaniment.

What crowns the whole business, however, is that the cute little fellow declares that he must follow the dictates *of his feelings* and must play his *own symphony*, and so he begins with a passage, which he follows with a pleasant theme and then finishes triumphantly with a cheerful finale; he always plays it the same way, never changing a note, so that everyone around him already knows the theme quite well.

Finally, allow me to repeat, most honored Herr Professor, that I am not exaggerating by one iota and am reporting everything correctly, in accordance with the truth, so that, with the help of my statement, you may now be able to make an important decision. With my best regards, I remain your most humble

Nathan Follmann[1]

Lodz is near the geographical center of Poland, but Nathan Follmann, Arthur Rubinstein's uncle, wrote his letters in German, and in fine old German script. His engraved letterhead gives the town's name without any of the three accent marks that it bears in Polish, to indicate the correct pronunciation: Łódź = Woodzh. Uncle Nathan's stationery was lined, vertically and horizontally, to facilitate the sending of itemized invoices to clients—for Lodz was a manufacturing town, dominated by German- and Jewish-owned factories, and Uncle Nathan was a Jewish factory-owner whose main language was German.

Julian Tuwim, one of twentieth-century Poland's finest poets and a Lodz-born Jew seven years younger than Rubinstein, described his native town with heavy irony: ". . . Lodz / Is legendary Baghdad city / Or Manchester-like La Mancha."[2] More prosaically and morosely, Bronislaw Horowicz, a composer, writer, and opera stage director born in Lodz in 1910, wondered "whether there is another city in the world as sad as the Lodz of my childhood. Perhaps England's Manchester, to which it has often been compared."

> Is it because of the factories' red bricks, which I recall as the dominant color of the years of my youth? . . . The city itself was constructed along a main street, several kilometers long, with which secondary streets converged perpendicularly; these, in turn, were crossed by streets that ran parallel to the central artery. In my mind, I still associate this layout with that of a prison.
>
> As one approached the city by train, one felt strangely oppressed by the view of a veritable forest of factory smokestacks casting their gray and black smoke into the sky. Coal had been feeding the steam-engines since 1839. On many nights, the horizon seemed to have been painted red, and the headlines in the next day's newspapers would say, 'The Cock has Crowed,' which meant that a textile mill had caught fire. Not all the fires were accidental. For a proprietor on the verge of bankruptcy, setting fire to his factory was a relatively easy way of getting hold of an insurance premium. . . .
>
> Cotton, fires, bankruptcy, bank-drafts, stock exchange, budget, profits, losses—these terms were practically the ABC of Lodz's children, even if this child or that later became interested in medicine, architecture, biology, or music. . . . Most of [Lodz's] residents were involved in business and couldn't talk to you without simultaneously touching your jacket or overcoat, to judge the quality of the wool or cotton that you were wearing. . . .[3]

No one knows when a settlement was first established on the site of present-day Lodz, at the northwestern edge of the watershed between the Vistula and Oder rivers, but the hamlet was chartered as a village in 1423. When it gained township rights, 375 years later, it was still little more than a farming settlement within a Poland that had recently been carved up by and parceled out to Prussia, Austria, and Russia; Lodz belonged to Prussia. In 1815, at the Congress of Vienna, the powers that had defeated Napoleonic France repartitioned much of Poland, allowing the same three nations to incorporate large chunks of the country as their own provinces, but the largest sector was made into a nominally autonomous kingdom under the jurisdiction of the tsar of Russia; Lodz, like Warsaw, eighty miles to the northeast, lay within this Russian "Congress Kingdom." In 1820, the kingdom's government began to transform Lodz, which then had a population of only eight hundred, into a center for the manufacture of textiles. Favorable terms for settlement were extended to German weavers, capital began to flow in, and peasants from the surrounding *wojewodztwo* (province) came to the town as laborers. A Saxon industrialist, Geyer, opened the first important factory in 1828, and Lodz's population soon reached four thousand. The growth-rate became frenetic after 1850, when the establishment of free trade between the Congress Kingdom and Russia proper created a vast, new Eurasian market for Lodz's wool and cotton products. Another German magnate, Scheibler, constructed a textile mill that boasted eighteen thousand spindles, and other manufacturers—Heinzl, Kunitzer, Grohman—followed his expansionistic example. In 1877, ten years before Rubinstein's birth, Lodz had fifty-one thousand inhabitants—more than sixty times its population of sixty years earlier; by 1914 the number exceeded half a million. Numerically, Lodz's population was second only to that of Warsaw among Polish cities, and so it has remained.

The most successful of Lodz's entrepreneurs in the last quarter of the nineteenth century was Israel K. Poznanski, whose preeminence reflected the hardiness of Lodz's Jewish population. Even under Prussian rule, there had been a few Jews in the town—eleven in 1793 and ninety-eight in 1809, when a wooden synagogue was built—but after 1820 the Jewish community expanded in tandem with the textile industry. Attempts by local German artisans to limit the Jews' freedom failed: Lodz's Jews, unlike those of Zgierz, a town only six miles away, were allowed to own property, open inns without special permits, and sell liquor. But in 1825 Lodz's town council created what amounted to a ghetto by ruling that as of July 1, 1827, Jews would be allowed to buy property, construct buildings, and reside only within precise boundaries in the town's center. To be allowed to live in the town, Jews had to know Polish, French, or German—a qualification intended, presumably, as a restriction on the immigration of Jews from farther to the east, most of whom spoke Yiddish plus Russian or Ukrainian. Lodz's Jews were not allowed to wear their traditional dress, and Jewish children over the age of seven had to attend local public schools rather than synagogue-run schools. Even Jews who met these requirements were harassed by the authorities, who were hard-pressed by the German community to expel the Jews. The Germans lost the battle in 1848, when the tsar decreed that Jews could live in all Polish cities under Russian jurisdiction; this was not an act of generosity toward the Jews, but rather an incentive for them to leave Russia proper in favor of Russia's Polish territories. Fourteen years later, changes in Lodz's zoning regulations gave Jews permission to live in any of the town's districts, but they continued to keep together, for the most part, either in the quarter they already occupied in the center or in the new industrial suburb of Ibalut (Baluty). Many of them were craftsmen, factory workers, and peddlers; others were wholesale and retail traders, agents, and brokers involved in supplying raw materials to the textile industry. A few, of whom Poznanski was the leading example, became entrepreneurs in their own right, and by 1914 about 175 of the more than 500 large and small factories in Lodz belonged to Jews.

Rubinstein's maternal grandfather, Yechiel (Ichel) Heiman, a bookkeeper, was among the ambitious young Jews who came to Lodz after the tsar's decree of 1848. He was born forty miles to the northwest, in the village of Dabie, in about 1824; his father, Szlame (Solomon), born circa 1795, was the son of Elias (circa 1766–1828) and Czarne. In 1851, Yechiel married Dwojra Dobronicki, who was born in 1830 and was the daughter of Shlomo-David and Rifka Dobronicki. (Rifka's maiden name was Zajdler, or Seidler; her parents were Pinchus and Feiga.) Yechiel must eventually have gone into business on his own or as a partner, because his grandson reported that "he met with success, and raised a family of eight daughters and two sons, my mother being the oldest."[4] Records corroborate Rubinstein's statement that his mother, Blima Feiga (Felicja, in Polish)—was the oldest of at least eight children. She was born in Lodz in 1852—on August 28 according to her tombstone, but November 26 according to municipal records.

Less is known about the family of Arthur's father, Izaak, who was born in Pultusk, about a hundred miles northeast of Lodz, on December 4, 1848; his parents were Szlama (possibly the son of Boruch) and Yenta (Yalta), whose maiden name was also Rubinstein (her father's first name was Szyia). Izaak either did not have any brothers or sisters or was not in contact with them. During the Polish uprising of 1863, his parents were killed by Russian shells, and at some point during the following seven years the young man moved to Lodz—attracted, probably, by its boomtown reputation. According to Arthur Rubinstein, Izaak soon "set up a little plant to make handwoven cloth, and married my mother."[5] The marriage took place in February or March 1870, when Felicja was seventeen and Izaak twenty-one, and during the following ten years Izaak and Felicja had six children. Jadwiga (Jadzia, Yenta, Naomi; later Mrs. Maurycy Landau), born in 1871, was named after

Izaak's mother; Stanislaw (Stas, Szlama), named after Izaak's father, was born on September 5, 1872; Helena (Hela; later Mrs. Adolf Landau) and Franciszka (Frania; later Mrs. Leo Likiernik) made their appearances between 1873 and 1877; Tadeusz (David) was born on June 29, 1878; and Ignacy (Israel, Isidor) on July 31, 1880. On Friday, January 28, 1887, after a lapse of 6½ years, a seventh child "rang the bell at the gate of life as a belated and rather unwanted guest," he was eventually told[6]—for his mother had intended to abort him until her sister Salomea (Salka) dissuaded her. Felicja was thirty-four and Izaak thirty-eight when Arthur was born, thus Rubinstein's oft-repeated statements to the effect that his father was "well over forty"[7] and that both his parents were "quite old"[8] when he was born may have been aimed at supporting a theory dear to him: "Perhaps [their age] had some influence on my musical faculties," he told a Spanish interviewer in 1919. "I read in an English book that the children of older people have a greater intellectual capacity."[9] Felicja had difficulty giving birth to her last child, but once he had emerged his parents decided to call him Leo; they settled upon Arthur only because six-year-old Ignacy knew a talented little violinist named Arthur, and—according to the family story—he wanted his baby brother to grow up to be a great musician.

"LODZ WAS NOT a town of poetry," according to Bronislaw Horowicz, who lived there through his high school years. "Lodz was a working town, a town of workers' struggles, a town of revolts and clandestine socialism at the time of the tsars."[10] But for Rubinstein, who left his hometown for good at the age of ten, memories of Lodz always retained a hint of poetry. He well knew that Lodz in the 1890s had been "the most unhealthy and unhygienic city imaginable," that its air was "infected with gas from the chemical plants," that the sky was obscured by "black smoke from the chimneys," and that the horse-drawn iron tanks used for collecting excrement—there was no sewage system—"filled the streets with an unbearable odor"; but as a child he pretended that the smokestack-crowned factories were "castles with glorious towers, the Russian policemen were ogres, and the people in the streets princes and princesses in disguise!"[11] He remembered "the lugubrious and plaintive shrieks of factory sirens," Gypsies singing, strumming, and dancing, and "the singsong of Jewish old-clothes peddlers, of Russian ice cream sellers, and Polish peasant women chanting the praises of their eggs, vegetables, and fruit. I loved all these noises."[12] In his memory, Lodz *was* childhood, for when his talent uprooted him from Lodz it simultaneously put an end to his childhood.

Unlike Warsaw, Lodz was not physically destroyed during World War II, and when Rubinstein was very old he found it much nicer than it had been when he was a child. "Just like the Augean stables—cleaned up in every nook and cranny," he told a television reporter as he walked along its streets.[13] The Rubinsteins lived in a "spacious, sunny apartment in a nice house on the main street, Piotrkowska ulica"[14]—the long thoroughfare mentioned by Horowicz. The house is a solid structure, three stories high on the street side, four on the internal courtyard side, with large front windows that face south. There are shops on the ground floor of this and the other residential buildings on Piotrkowska Street, as there were a century ago; in old age, Rubinstein particularly remembered a bank and Roszkowski's pastry shop.[15] The main entrance to the building that the Rubinsteins lived in was broad and high enough to have allowed carriages to pass through, and the façade as a whole still reflects the solid, bourgeois values of its time. Rubinstein remembered the home with pleasure, and in 1975 he showed it to a *New York Times* correspondent. " 'Look,' he said, pointing to a long row of second-story windows while reminiscing in the courtyard . . . , 'all these were our windows. That's the kitchen. Every morning there was a battle as my six older brothers and sisters ran off for school and fought for the sandwiches my mother was preparing. And then, every morning, all of a sudden there was silence and I was alone before the small piano.' "[16]

The instrument was an upright that his parents had bought when he was about 2½ years old, not for him, but for Jadzia and Hela, who were expected to learn to "play a little," like other proper middle-class girls. Instead, the purchase quickly and conclusively decided the fate of the girls' difficult little brother, a late talker who communicated by singing disconnected syllables or wordless tunes. Artek (Polish diminutive, like the English "Artie") was spoiled and undisciplined; he enjoyed scaring people, and he learned at an early age to play his parents off against his grandparents and his siblings against one another. He later remembered, or remembered having been told, that from the day the piano was delivered he screamed and wept when anyone attempted to make him leave the drawing room, where the instrument was kept. He listened to Jadzia's lessons with "the obese Madame Kijanska,"[17] and he gradually learned to identify the keys, to distinguish and name all the notes in a chord without looking at the keyboard, and to play—first one hand at a time, then both together—tunes that he had heard.

"When I was three years old I was a musician," the aged Rubinstein told an interviewer. "In fact I could play four hands with my sister then. She played very badly, but I played the four-hand things quite well. . . . There are lots of people who at twenty can't decide if they want to be jewellers or doctors or engineers. I knew at the age of three that I was going to be a musician."[18] His Uncle Nathan Follmann—one of Felicja's brothers-in-law and "a very cultured man," according to Rubinstein, in an interview published nearly three-quarters of a century later—"felt I had no time to lose, that I couldn't begin my career too soon."[19] Follmann sent a letter—a no longer extant letter that predated the one quoted at the beginning of this chapter—to Joseph Joachim, one of the most celebrated violinists of the era. Like Rubinstein, Joachim was the seventh child of Eastern European (Hungarian, in his case) Jewish parents and had been a child prodigy. By the age of fourteen, he had played under Mendelssohn's direction, and he was later associated with Liszt, Schumann, and especially Brahms. In 1890, when Follmann wrote to him, Joachim was fifty-nine years old and at the height of his international career as a soloist, as first violinist with the long-lived Joachim String Quartet, and as a conductor. In addition, Joachim directed Berlin's Hochschule für ausübende Kunst (College of the Performing Arts), which he had founded in 1868. Joachim evidently replied that it was too early to determine the extent of the boy's talent and suggested that he be carefully observed until he was five or six. His cautioning but friendly answer encouraged Follmann to send him a second letter—the one quoted above—a month before Arthur's fourth birthday; it must have solicited a similar reply, but with a concession: Should someone manage to bring the boy to Berlin, Joachim would listen to him. This set off heated discussions in the Rubinstein household and led to the decision to have Felicja and Jadwiga take Arthur to Berlin, where they could also assemble a trousseau for Jadwiga, who was about to be married. They would stay at the home of Felicja's sister, Salka, who had married a Berliner and was now Frau Salomea Meyer.

Of his first trip away from Lodz, the future world-traveler would recall only the bemustached, jackbooted, saber-rattling, pistol-packing Russian border guards and, in Berlin, "the absence of the familiar chimneys and sirens of [Lodz's] factories."[20] In a brief essay written in Spanish ten years before he completed the first volume of his memoirs, Rubinstein wrote: "Joachim ..., who must have been profoundly mistrustful of the parents of more or less prodigious children, seated my mother and sister in the anteroom and took me into his study. Without further preamble, he sang to me, in his throaty bass voice, one of the themes of Schubert's 'Unfinished' Symphony, and he asked me to reproduce it on the piano. For me, it was very easy. Satisfied by my performance, he asked me if I was able to play it again, but this time with its accompanying harmony. I did it without hesitation, and I managed to do it with the same modulations as Schubert's, which seemed evident to me. Extremely pleased, he called my mother and my sister, and he encouraged them to have me begin to study the violin, without further delay, offering to give me all the necessary help and advice. Back home, my father bought me a minuscule violin—which I broke into bits after two weeks. I was decidedly meant to be a pianist, I needed polyphony; a melody without harmonic support meant nothing to me."[21]

This account differs from Rubinstein's later one. According to the memoirs, before Joachim had Arthur play the theme from the "Unfinished" Symphony—which, in the memoirs, Rubinstein identified as the famous second theme of the first movement—he "asked me to call out the notes of many tricky chords he struck on the piano, and then I had to prove my perfect ear in other ways." At the end of the session, "Professor Joachim picked me up from the floor, kissed me, and gave me a big piece of chocolate." The most significant divergence, however, is that in *My Young Years*, the violin-breaking episode takes place before the trip to Berlin, and Joachim, rather than suggesting that Arthur study the violin, says, more generically: " 'This boy may become a very great musician—he certainly has the talent for it. Let him hear some good singing, but do not force music on him. When the time comes for serious study, bring him to me, and I shall be glad to supervise his artistic education.' "[22] The earlier, Spanish version seems more logical, given Joachim's specific interest in the violin. Besides, the direct quotation would necessarily have been reconstructed, at best, from what Arthur's mother and Jadwiga told him when he was considerably older.

What is certain, however, is that there was every reason for Arthur Rubinstein to make something of his talent. Although he was barely four years old, he had already learned that he was special, that he was able to do something that few others could do—something that elicited people's approval and even brought him rewards. The nature of the rewards would change over the years: when he was a child, his parents, aunts, uncles, and older sisters and brothers kissed and applauded him for entertaining them, and Joachim hugged him and gave him chocolate. Later, women would give him other forms of sweetness. ("I still think of chocolates [but] in other terms, you know," he once told an interviewer; his interests had "changed to other subjects," he said, "but there is the same vision of chocolates.")[23] Still later, the rewards were to be admission to the inner precincts of high society, the admiration of fellow musicians, worldwide celebrity, and wealth. But the smiles and sweets and sex, the adulation and all its by-products, were not for Arthur Rubinstein alone: they were for Arthur Rubinstein and his special talent. Talent created "Rubinstein," but it also exacted tribute. There were to be no other gods before it, and every other element in his life would revolve around it.

To do something with one's talent is an achievement; to *have* talent is not—and this may explain why Rubinstein, even in old age, had ambivalent feelings toward his talent. He was understandably proud of having used it to build an enormously successful career—a career that allowed him to lead what he often called a "superb life"—but he knew that the talent itself was a genetic accident, a predisposition that had nothing to do with his work or his willpower. The subject made him uncomfortable. To a junior high school student from Mechanicville, New York—a near beginner at the piano who, in 1962, sent him a comical but absolutely innocent request for advice about how to go about arranging concerts—the seventy-five-year-old master replied sharply: "The only advice I could give you, if you feel you are a genius, is to come to Carnegie Hall and give a recital. If you are not, don't ask such questions."[24] Six years later, when a member of a Northport, New York, teachers' committee tried to enlist his aid in setting up a scholarship fund "for those of our students who show considerable talent for the piano," Rubinstein wrote that "a youngster not only has to have gifts, but extraordinary 'talent' to deserve to be assisted. Don't you think you have used this term a little lightheartedly? 'Considerable talent' for the piano does not occur often. There are few who really have it. . . ."[25] And at ninety, he told an interviewer: "Often I get letters asking me for advice. Some youngster suddenly gets very enthusiastic about music and says I'm studying medicine or my parents want me to be a law student, but I love music, how does one go about becoming a great pianist? I want to tell him to try to be born again with talent. . . . You must have talent and then all you have to do is improve on it."[26]

Throughout his life, however, Rubinstein worried that people loved him only for his talent—for what he was and not for who he was. "WHEREVER did you get that neurosis that people don't love you for yourself????" exclaimed his old friend Mildred Knopf in 1978, after she had received a mournful telephone call from the ninety-one-year-old Rubinstein. "You, with your wit and your loyalty and charm and good looks and, oh, well I could go on and on and you probably wouldn't believe me anyhow, . . . you let this nonsense get to you, which of course *is* absolute nonsense. . . . You must try not to chew on the problem too much, do please try not to live in the past too much but continue to live your own life and know how many people enjoy being with you, just because of YOU," she wrote.[27] But she was right: he never quite believed such reassurances. His son John said, "You couldn't love him enough."[28]

JOACHIM MUST HAVE told Felicja not to have Arthur start formal musical instruction immediately, because the boy's real lessons began only later, at the suggestion of another foreign musician—a Dutch conductor—who visited Lodz at the head of a small, touring orchestra. In his memoirs, Rubinstein calls the conductor Julius Kwast, but the man in question was probably Jan Kwast, a moderately well-known conductor and composer active in Russia and its dominions in those years. Kwast and his orchestra "performed the first suite of Grieg's *Peer Gynt*, which thrilled me so much that when we returned home I was able to play almost all of it—to the amazement of the family," Rubinstein said. "Mr. Kwast was invited to our house, heard me play, and thought it was time for me to take piano lessons. His advice was promptly followed."[29]

Arthur was put under the tutelage of a Mrs. Pawlowska, who wanted the boy to keep his elbows close to his torso and to keep his hands so still that coins could be kept on the back of them during the playing of scales. Fortunately, Arthur instinctively rebelled against this approach, which could have worked against his talent, and a new teacher was engaged. Adolf Prechner was "a strange, slightly demonic person with a pockmarked face and a thick yellowish mustache," according to his most famous pupil. "He would always either speak too softly or shout at the top of his voice, but he knew his job."[30] Beyond this caricature, Rubinstein's memoirs contain no information about Prechner and his approach to technique and interpretation; whatever the approach was, however, and no matter how much it may have been countered or transformed by later teachers, it allowed Arthur to become fluent at the keyboard. He must have studied with Prechner from the age of about 4½ to the age of about 9½—roughly 40 percent of the entire period of his supervised piano studies. "At four," he told an interviewer more than seventy years later, "I played the overture to *Poet and Peasant* four hands with my sister— you know that delightful, melodious piece, so seldom performed nowadays.... On my fifth birthday somebody presented me with calling cards on which was printed 'Arturek [*sic*], pianist virtuoso.' . . . I was, of course, enchanted with the cards and passed them around freely to friends and even strangers. You see, I never had any false modesty. I was sure of myself. I had perfect pitch—indeed, I had everything necessary for a musician."[31]

Concert and opera performances often took place in Lodz; they were not as abundant or, probably, as good as those offered in Warsaw, but they provided Arthur with his first experiences as a listener. When he was still very small, he was taken to the Victoria Theater, opposite the Grand Hotel on Piotrkowska Ulica,[32] for a performance of *Aida* given by a touring Italian company, and he heard several well-known instrumentalists, including the Warsaw-born Jozef Sliwinski—a pupil of the celebrated piano pedagogue Theodor Leschetizky—and the violinist Bronislaw Huberman, a child prodigy who was to become one of the most respected instrumentalists of his generation. Huberman gave two recitals in Lodz in March 1892; one of the accompanists who took part in the second recital was Prechner, Arthur's teacher. "I was delighted by [Huberman's] playing, and my parents invited him to visit us," Rubinstein recalled. "At home, we played for each other, and he was charming to me. We were friends until he died."[33] Rubinstein often told interviewers that the nine-year-old Huberman had advised him, when he was five, "Work hard, my boy, and someday you may become a great musician." But he did not repeat the anecdote in his memoirs.

As an adult, Rubinstein had a few grudges—some of them legitimate—against his parents, but he remained grateful to them for having followed Joachim's advice not to force him into a premature career as a child prodigy. When he was nearly ninety, he wrote to a French interlocutor who was interested in promoting one such infant genius: ". . . as a matter of principle I am against any excessive publicity for child prodigies. Later on (believe what I say, which comes from long experience), they are the first to suffer from it; because in their maturity they often cannot live up to the hopes placed in their talent, and they must suffer the consequences."[34] Only once during his years in Lodz did his parents allow him to perform in public, and only to participate in a charity concert. On December 14, 1894, the seven-year-old artist played a Mozart sonata and pieces by Schubert and Mendelssohn; according to the account he gave in his memoirs, he was "rewarded with a warm ovation from an audience consisting mainly of my family, their friends, and the musical Jews and Germans of Lodz."[35] In old age, he told an interviewer that he remembered having played well at the event, but that, characteristically, his main interest had been in "a huge box of chocolates promised to me, and this fascinated me absolutely. I was playing thinking only of those divine chocolates, which one will I eat first, you know."[36]

At about this time the Rubinsteins moved into a larger, second-floor apartment next door to Felicja's parents, where, Arthur Rubinstein recalled, the proximity to his grandparents "intensified greatly our contact with the rest of mother's large family, who were strict Orthodox Jews. Following the tradition that the children gather around the patriarch every Friday [evening], we began to observe the Sabbath with great solemnity."[37] Arthur's parents, however, were not deeply religious; for them, the Sabbath was "a pretext . . . to bring the family together."[38] Izaak Rubinstein, who had a fine if somewhat pedantic mind and an exceptionally good memory, had been "brought up in a very Orthodox way" and had even studied the Talmud, "but his passion for knowledge was not satisfied, and he managed to learn French and German in order to read the great philosophers." Felicja, unlike her husband, did like to attend synagogue services, but "simply in order to be seen," her son said.[39] The Rubinsteins were "derisively critical" of the Chassidic Jews, "with their long black coats and their sidelocks and beards and their singsong. My father had taken me, once or twice, to a synagogue, but only for musical reasons—to hear a famous cantor perform."[40] Although Lodz in Arthur's day had many Jewish religious schools, from kindergarten through high school levels, and from the Orthodox Talmud-Torah to the Reformed School, Arthur was given virtually no religious education in his native town. As an adult, he referred with pride to his Jewish origins but he called himself an agnostic. (His younger daughter, Dr. Alina Rubinstein, a psychiatrist, has speculated that he was reluctant to call himself an atheist "because it was so hard to accommodate the idea that a musical 'gift' like his could just have come 'out of nowhere.' ") Once, late in Rubinstein's life, Franz Mohr—Steinway's chief concert technician, who was a deeply religious man—attempted to "talk to him about the gospel . . . he cut me off and said, 'Don't worry about me. When I get to heaven, I have no problem. I am Jewish, and if Moses is there at the gate, he will let me in. . . . You know my wife is Catholic—maybe it is St. Peter who is at the gate . . . so *he* will let me in. And I have a son-in-law who is an Episcopalian minister—so how can I lose!' "[41] In short, he did not take the issue very seriously.

John Rubinstein, the youngest of Arthur's four children and a well-known actor, has said that his father spoke "so degradingly, so demeaningly about his closest relatives" that "my sister and I actually used to joke with him" on the subject. "He always made fun of them; he didn't talk about them with any kind of love, and he didn't say, 'I wish you had met my father,' or 'I wish you had been born in time to see my sister.' Never! On the other hand, he didn't speak of them with rage or real anger. One of the things that he respected about his father was that at the dinner table his father would say, 'Shah!' [Ssshh!] and hush everybody—especially when they were eating fish; otherwise, you might choke on the bones. You had to eat quietly and concentrate on removing the bones, on not swallowing them. That image of the paterfamilias hushing his big family is my only real image of his father, because it's the one my father promoted. I know that my father felt some resentment toward his parents; he mentioned it. He used to say that he had had to cloak himself in his precocity, because his parents didn't know what to do with this little boy who seemed to have such a big talent—something that attracted the attention of people from outside his parents' world. His parents were 'haberdashers'; that was the term he used."[42] But Arthur Rubinstein's friend Annabelle Whitestone remembered that in his very last years he spoke of his father "with special tenderness and sympathy" and said that his father "wasn't made for business"—that he preferred to read; he also mentioned that his father had been acquainted with L. L. Zamenhof, the Russo-Polish Jew who invented Esperanto.[43] John Rubinstein said that he was certain that Arthur's parents "loved him to some degree, but I don't think he felt terribly loved by them. I don't want to put words in his mouth, because he never said such a phrase, but whenever he mentioned the subject, over the years, the feeling I got was that he felt he was some kind of object."[44]

As an adult, Arthur Rubinstein knew only a few stock expressions in Yiddish, which was almost certainly his grandparents' best language and his parents' first one. If Polish was spoken in the Rubinstein household, his parents were evidently bent on full-scale assimilation. But in an interview published when Rubinstein was eighty-one, he said that as a child he had been able to learn German easily because "I already knew Yiddish from home."[45] (Yiddish, as it was spoken in Eastern Europe, was essentially an archaic German dialect with a good deal of Hebrew and Slavic vocabulary mixed in.) Perhaps the High German that became his main language when he was ten obliterated most of his Yiddish, which he had few occasions to use thereafter; such phenomena are not uncommon. When, in later years, he said that he spoke eight languages, he did not count Yiddish among them, and in all his languages, his accent was Polish, not Yiddish. Russian was the Congress Kingdom's official language, and Arthur, from the age of seven, had to attend a Russian-language public elementary school. Like other Polish schoolchildren, he resented having to "rattle off the official titles of the Tsar and his family: 'His Imperial Majesty, the Autocrat of all the Russias, King of Poland, Grand Duke of Finland, etc.,' and then sing the Russian national anthem."[46] But as an adult, he was glad that he had mastered Russian. After school hours his sister Frania taught him to read and write Polish; he enjoyed the lessons, he said, and developed a great, enduring love of Poland.

Another influence, however, must have conflicted with his love of Poland. During the 1890s a new, nationalistic sentiment was born in many European Jews who had previously considered the idea of a Jewish homeland utopian, or had not thought about the matter at all. Zionist-oriented newspapers, religious congregations, and cultural societies sprang up in Lodz as elsewhere, and Izaak Rubinstein was among those members of the community who favored the creation, in Palestine, of a state in which Jews would not be at the mercy of an often-hostile Christian world. Arthur was as much influenced by his father's enthusiasm for Zionism as by his indifference to Judaism and to organized religion in general. But his Zionist faith, like his love of Poland, seems to have absorbed him only occasionally, and mainly in his last years.

Apart from music, the only constant element in Rubinstein's life was his adoration of women—a passion that preoccupied him "ninety percent" of the time, he half-jokingly claimed. But no extant testimony would lead a rational biographer to speculate that the preoccupation had been stimulated by unusually strong Oedipal tendencies. His later memories—the only ones we have—of his mother were colored by feelings of resentment and guilt that took hold of him as he entered adolescence and stayed with him for the rest of his life, and in his autobiography he related only a few childhood memories of her, such as her suffering from frequent headaches and other minor ailments that immediately disappeared when her husband or one of her children needed her. His earliest clear recollections of the delights of female company were connected with the fuss made over him by his grown-up or adolescent older sisters; Jadwiga, in particular, adored her little brother, and Rubinstein's wife said that even in later years "Jadzia was practically in love with Arthur."[47] The tenderness and joy that the manifestations of his exceptional talent aroused in his sisters when he was still a child communicated themselves back to Artek and established themselves as one of his basic internal needs. So did the pleasures of his first close friendship, with Noemi, his cousin and contemporary.

Noemi, nicknamed Nemutka, was the daughter of Arthur's uncle Paul Heiman. Her mother had died giving birth to her, and when her father remarried, Noemi was adopted by her adoring Aunt Frandzia Kravets (or Krawetz)—one of Paul and Felicja's three childless sisters—who was married to a moderately well-to-do businessman. According to Rubinstein, Noemi, who lived in the same building that the Rubinsteins and elder Heimans also occupied, "looked like an angel painted by Raphael" and "had a kind and sweet disposition." In part, the pianist's description, written seventy-five years post facto, of his relationship with his cousin was probably an example of retrospective wishful thinking about the relationships that he would have liked to have had with most of the other women in his life—wife, daughters, and lovers: "we loved each other so passionately that we were inseparable. . . . [She] particularly liked playing husband and wife with me. She would obey me blindly, leaving the choicest morsels of food for me, and easily bursting into tears whenever she saw me in trouble. My piano playing made her gasp with admiration."[48] But when the two children were about eight years old, Noemi died of scarlet fever. Rubinstein never forgot either his rage over her death or the onset of his doubt in the existence of God. He was overcome with *zal*, a Polish word that means "sadness, nostalgia, regret, being hurt, and . . . a howling inside you, so unbearable that it breaks your heart."[49] Perhaps he also felt betrayed, as most children would under such circumstances. And yet Noemi remained fixed in his memory as a bride of quietness, adoring, undemanding, untainted by overt libido; perfect. The girls and women who later appeared in his life—the few he fell in love with, the one he married, the dozens he took to bed, the many he tried to dominate—had some flaw: their dispositions weren't always kind and sweet, or they didn't always save their choicest morsels for him and him alone, or they weren't quite so solicitous or so perpetually, unquestioningly admiring. Some had the temerity not to be interested in him at all. Throughout the following eight decades, he searched for another Nemutka.

Not long after Nemutka's death, Grandfather Heiman died, and at about the same time Arthur accidentally witnessed a savage attack by the tsar's local police forces against a crowd of alleged political agitators. This too-rapid succession of terrifying, incomprehensible events made the boy nervous and restless, and weighed him down with thoughts of the disintegration of the body after death. His parents began to worry about him, and his piano teacher could no longer cope with him. Izaak and Felicja decided that Arthur should continue his musical training in Warsaw.

THE EIGHTY-MILE train journey across the wooded plateau and the plains that separate Lodz from the capital now takes a little over an hour and a half; in the autumn of 1896 it took twice as long. However apprehensive Arthur may have been at the prospect of being abandoned by his mother in a strange place, he enjoyed his first trip away from Lodz and its immediate vicinity since the visit to Joachim, 5½ years earlier, and he was delighted with the elegant old Hôtel d'Angleterre—the first of thousands of hotels in Rubinstein's life.

Felicja took Arthur to play for Aleksander Michalowski, the most celebrated pianist and teacher in Warsaw, who had himself had three formidable teachers: Ignaz Moscheles, a Beethoven disciple; Karl Tausig, a Liszt and Wagner disciple; and Carl Reinecke, a noted German composer. He had had a highly successful international career as a pianist and had even been admired by Liszt, who, according to stories that circulated among young Polish pianists, had said that Michalowski's playing was like Chopin's.[50] At the age of forty, Michalowski had decided to give up the life of a wandering virtuoso and had settled in Warsaw, which he loved, and where he was heard and admired by such keyboard masters as Moriz Rosenthal, Ignaz Friedman, and Egon Petri. He became principal piano professor at the Musical Institute, now known as the Fryderyk Chopin Music Academy, where one of his first (and by far the most successful) of his pupils was Wanda Landowska, the future harpsichord virtuoso and early music pioneer. (Landowska told the RCA record producer John Pfeiffer that she was distantly related to Rubinstein, and Rubinstein, too, mentioned this to others. The relationship may have been through his two Landau brothers-in-law, rather than by blood: Landowska was probably a Polish feminine form of Landau.) She left Warsaw at the age of sixteen, one year before Rubinstein arrived, but, like him, she remembered the almost ridiculously opulent furnishings of Michalowski's home, in which even genre paintings of humble peasants were framed in red plush. Rubinstein said of his first and probably only visit to the master, who was forty-five at the time: "The music room . . . looked just like a pantheon, bedecked with dozens of laurel wreaths tied with multicolored silk ribbons—his concert trophies."[51] The dust that had accumulated on the relics gave Arthur a sneezing fit, and either for that reason or as a result of his nervousness, his audition did not go well. Michalowski said that he could not teach so young a pupil and suggested that Felicja have the boy take lessons for a year from Aleksander Rozycki, another well-known local musician.

Felicja made the necessary arrangements with Rozycki, and she also arranged for Arthur, together with a rented upright piano, to occupy a "dark and stuffy room" in the gloomy apartment of a relative—"a widow, Mrs. Glass, who lived with her daughter Isabella, a very pretty young girl."[52] He was to have his meals, too, with the Glasses. Felicja then said good-bye to him and returned to Lodz. "I felt terribly lonely, but within a few days Warsaw had worked its charms on me," he recalled, and he mentioned with particular warmth the "new pleasure" of playing with Polish boys of his age in "the enchanting Saxon Garden,"[53] and the thrill of reading the Russian-prohibited books on Polish history that Mrs. Glass kept in her library. He also began to read Polish literature, especially the works of the national literary star of the moment, Henryk Sienkiewicz, who won the Nobel prize a few years later, and he tried to compose an opera based on the writer's novella *Hania*. Rubinstein rarely mentioned his youthful attempts at composition; when he did, he usually added that, unlike his famous namesake, Anton Rubinstein, he had had the good taste to destroy his works and to consider himself purely a performer. This seems a gratuitous dig: although most of Anton's compositions, which were popular in the late nineteenth and early twentieth centuries, have been forgotten, it is safe to assume that Arthur's compositional skills never approached those of the older Rubinstein.

But the pleasant aspects of life in Warsaw could not have offered adequate compensation to a nine-year-old for the sudden, complete absence of parents and siblings. Rubinstein's glowing memories of the city were probably colored by recollections of the later and considerably wilder periods that he spent there. Fortunately, Arthur was occasionally visited by one or another of his uncles who came to the capital on business. There was Paul Heiman, a kindhearted dandy; Jacob Heiman, a bon vivant who invited Arthur for breakfasts of pressed caviar and taught him risqué popular songs; and Boleslaw Sznek—the husband of one of the Heiman sisters—who was an opera lover and, in particular, a worshiper of Mattia Battistini. Arthur was taken to hear the famous baritone in *La traviata* and in Anton Rubinstein's *The Demon*, and he later declared that Battistini and Caruso had the finest male voices he had ever heard.

But Arthur's piano lessons—the reason for his being in Warsaw—were a disaster. In his memoirs, he laid the blame entirely on his teacher, who, however, had an outstanding reputation as a pedagogue. In 1897, shortly after Arthur came to him, Rozycki published the *ABC Nowa szkola na fortepian (ABC of the New Pianoforte Method)*, which soon became a bible to aspiring Polish pianists; by then, Rozycki had been on the Musical Institute's faculty for thirteen years, and there he would remain for another decade. Arthur, who was not enrolled at the institute, took lessons at his teacher's home. He described the professor as "a big, fat, old man"—Rozycki was fifty-one at the time—"lazy and flabby, with a long gray beard, and the first time we met he received me rather indifferently, making me play a Mozart sonata, at which, to my astonishment, he fell soundly asleep. Awakened by the last chord, he muttered something vague and ordered me to buy some exercises he had published and practice them three hours a day. And we went through the same routine in the lessons that followed."[54] Rozycki claimed that his young pupil was inattentive during lessons, but the only certainty is that teacher and pupil did not get along. On arriving for one of his lessons, Arthur was greeted at Rozycki's door by the professor's twelve-year-old son, Ludomir, who, on his father's behalf, demanded payment in advance. Unfortunately, Mrs. Glass had not given Arthur the money to take to the professor on that occasion; Ludomir slammed the door in the boy's face, and Arthur sat on the stairs and wept over what he later described as his first humiliation. Ludomir Rozycki eventually became one of the best-known Polish composers of his generation, but seventy-five years after the door-slamming incident Rubinstein proudly (and incorrectly) declared that he had never played a note of Ludomir's music.

Arthur wrote to his parents, to inform them of the humiliation and of his teacher's somnolence, and Felicja returned to Warsaw to confront Aleksander Rozycki. When the professor predicted that her son would never become much of a pianist, she took the boy back to Lodz. Luckily for his self-esteem but unluckily in other respects, what Arthur perceived as a personal defeat was soon dwarfed by a family catastrophe: Izaak's handloom mill was driven out of business by more highly mechanized competition. The Rubinstein's factory, home, and other valuable possessions had to be sold to cover debts, and the family was dispersed. Four of the children had already left the nest: Jadwiga and Helena were married, Tadeusz was studying electrical engineering in Berlin, and Ignacy, who had been arrested for revolutionary activities, was in jail in Warsaw—a prelude to banishment to Siberia. But when Izaak and Felicja were forced to move into a spare room in the Follmanns' apartment, Stanislaw, who worked in a bank, and Frania, who was engaged but not yet married, had to move in with one of their aunts. Ten-year-old Arthur went with Jadwiga and her three children to Inowlodz, a summer resort thirty-five miles southeast of Lodz. What with romps in the Pilica River and a daily series of lessons—academic, dancing, and piano (the name of his piano teacher is not known)—he began to feel less overwhelmed by his own and his family's troubles. During the dancing lessons he fell in love with Mania Szer, a twelve-year-old girl; he showed off for her, and he was depressed when she did not pay attention to him and angry when she did. In short, he gave signs of premature adolescence. Usually, however, he behaved like the child he was. He became terribly upset, for instance, when his niece

Maryla, one of Jadwiga's three children, hid a piece of halvah from him; fifty years later, the memory of Maryla's dastardly deed left him ill-disposed toward her. "He was not a forgiving person," said his wife, in telling the story. But he eventually forgave Mania Szer: she phoned him during one of his much-heralded professional visits to Warsaw in the 1920s, and they spent a night together.

Izaak Rubinstein took his bankruptcy philosophically and began to work as an accountant for his brother-in-law, Nathan Follmann, but Felicja's physical and spiritual health was affected by the disaster. When Arthur returned to Lodz in the fall, he found his mother's irritability harder to deal with than the inconveniences of living in the Follmanns' piano-less home and sleeping on a couch in their drawing room. Despite their many problems, however, his parents decided to make another attempt to develop Arthur's pianistic talent. Unfortunately, they had no idea where to send him. Warsaw was out of the question, since the city's two top pedagogues had rejected him. Consideration was given to Vienna, where Leschetizky was turning out pupils of the caliber of Paderewski, Sliwinski, Ignaz Friedman, Artur Schnabel, Ossip Gabrilowitsch, Elly Ney, and Mark Hambourg, "but we had no connections there," Rubinstein recalled.[55]

Now, why not Berlin? The elder Rubinsteins must have reasoned that Joachim might remember little Arthur, and in any case, several well-known teachers—the brilliant Ferruccio Busoni, the Wagner disciple Karl Klindworth, the harsh Heinrich Barth, the methodical Xaver Scharwenka, and others—were based in Kaiser Wilhelm's capital. Felicja's sister Salka would undoubtedly be able to help find a suitable family for Arthur to live with. Once the decision was made, Arthur's few personal effects were quickly packed. He said good-bye to his father, who was "quiet as usual, never showing any emotion,"[56] and left Lodz with his mother. He could hardly have imagined, as the train crossed the border into Germany, that he would never again make his home in Poland.

2

Affection Denied, Affection Pursued

Rubinstein did not perform in Germany during the last sixty-two years of his career, from 1914 onward. As a Pole, a Francophile, and an Anglophile, he felt triple enmity toward Germany during World War I, and he was not inclined to forgive the ex-adversary during the years of the Weimar Republic. After World War II, he described his refusal to perform in the land of Bach, Beethoven, and Brahms as a tribute to the many members of his family who, because they were Jews, had been killed in Germany and German-occupied Europe. But there were additional, less obvious motives behind his uncomfortable relationship with Germany in general and Berlin in particular. Long before the world wars, the country and its capital had become permanently associated in Rubinstein's mind with his strange and difficult adolescence. In Berlin, his home for over six years, he began to recognize the strengths and weaknesses in his talent, intellect, and character; he experienced his first artistic successes and humiliations, enjoyed his first full-fledged sexual relationship, and fell in love for the first time; and he was the protagonist in an episode of double betrayal that would weigh on him for the rest of his life.

Eventually, Berlin also came to represent his ambivalent attitude toward German performing musicians, whose styles he would later describe as too dryly meticulous in comparison with his own more spontaneous and human one—although he admitted that there were exceptions. Such opinions may also have helped him to rationalize his frequent lack of success, in early years, with the German public. The Germans "are not a musical people," he told record producer Fred Gaisberg during the 1930s. "They accept the heavy, pedantic music of Pfitzner, Reger and Bruckner with their long-winded 'developments,' just as they enjoy a stodgy meal of sauerkraut and sausages."[1] The unfair analogy grew out of his profound feelings of inferiority with respect to his Germanic colleagues, whom he thought of as more earnest than himself—however convinced he may have been of his own superior insight and musicality—and even during the last years of his career, he was thrilled with any sign of recognition from "heavy, pedantic" German musicians. Circa 1970, Daniel Barenboim reported to him that Otto Klemperer, who had previously considered Rubinstein "showy" and "superficial," had heard a Rubinstein recording of a Beethoven concerto and had told Barenboim, "I must admit I was wrong—he is really a great musician." Barenboim said, "I told Rubinstein that, and he really got a big kick out of it."[2]

Berlin, in short, is where Rubinstein's conscience—personal and artistic—was formed, and in later years he may have preferred to contemplate this fact from a distance. But the ten-year-old boy whose mother brought him to the German capital in the fall of 1897 did not have such complicated attitudes. What he later remembered most clearly about his arrival in Berlin was the rain. In an early draft of his memoirs, he wrote, in fluent but not always correct English: "There is rain and rain—I love a good spring shower, this creative inspirer of nature, I am grateful for a refreshing summer downpour on a hot day, I enjoy even the violence of a tropical deluge—but nothing can depress me more than the dripping, drizzling, persistent, penetrating, wet rain which freezes your feet and your soul. During a week's time we were the victims, mother and I, of this discouraging meteorological phenomenon; loaded with dozens of letters of introduction to prominent musicians, impresarios, editors and many others, we explored the whole town, wading through ditches, wet to the bone, tired to death. As Aunt Salome[a] was unable to put us up, her apartment being to[o] small, we took a room[.]"[3] This version of the story contrasts with the one in his published memoirs: "We were cordially received by Aunt Salomea, her husband, Siegfried Meyer, and their four children, and stayed with them for some time."[4] The unpublished version continues:

> We were received and I was heard and examined by many teachers
> and pianists; I remember perfectly well a few of these visits. Professor
> [Ernst] Jedliczka, an excellent master, wanted me to work for 2 years
> with a pupil of his before teaching me himself, an idea which did not
> appeal to my mother. The charming and exuberant Xaver Scharwenka, head, with Karl Klindworth, of their famous Conservatory,
> was willing to let me enter his institution, but his terms were unacceptable to us. We had no use for the old academician Prof. [Heinrich] Ehrlich [a pupil of the celebrated virtuosos Adolf von Henselt
> and Sigismond Thalberg], and Mrs. Nicklas[s]-Kempner, who reminded us too much of Mme. Pavlowska and Mr. Prechner. To my
> misfortune, the great Busoni was away on a concert tour, a fact I still
> deeply regret—but we were kindly received by Casimir [or Kazimierz] Hoffman [sic, for Hofmann] and his young son Joseph [Josef],

already famous in Russia as a potential successor to Anton Rubinstein. I remember their apartment in the Joachimsthalerstrasse quite well. Two grand pianos, I think they were Bechsteins, a harmonium and all sort of other instruments filled the musicroom. Joseph Hoffman showed me with pride the present he had received from Thomas Edison, a brandnew phonograph, and thrilled me by making a turning little cylinder perform a loud piece of music. After I had played, his father, an excellent musician himself and, obviously, an expert in child prodigies, gave my mother a whole lecture of invaluable advice. The road to fame was difficult, he said, few were the promising youngsters who became real artists, and great care should be taken of my musical education.

At the end of that rainy week we felt thoroughly disheartened[.][5]

And there the draft fragment ends. Neither in it nor in the published version of his memoirs does Rubinstein say what or how he played at any of his auditions, but in the published version he mentions that his mother was "slightly discouraged by the general lack of interest in me and by the obviously expensive lessons the famous teachers offered."[6]

In *My Young Years* Rubinstein emphasized his regret that he had not become a pupil of Ferruccio Busoni, who was only thirty-one years old in 1897. "He was the one person who might have oriented my talent in a better direction—a man with a broad view, both artistically and culturally, a genuinely great human being."[7] Rubinstein's life and career would indeed have taken a different course had he been influenced by a teacher for whom intellectual curiosity was even more important than keyboard agility, but the course might well have been a less successful one: the boy could easily have come to idolize Busoni, and his own originality might have been suffocated by Busoni's powerful and attractive personality. He needed a teacher who would discipline him, and against whom he could eventually rebel—and he found one when Felicja played her last card: she applied to Joachim, who agreed to hear Arthur again. The session probably took place at the Hochschule für Musik (College of Music, formerly College of the Performing Arts), which Joachim had been directing since its foundation nearly thirty years earlier, and which, in 1897, was a section of the Königliche Akademie der Künste (Royal Academy of the Arts); many of Joachim's intimate acquaintances considered the Hochschule the violinist's greatest interest in life. The institution was housed in the centrally located Fasanenstrasse, in a building that is now the home of the Hochschule der Künste (College of the Arts). In his memoirs, Rubinstein did not mention an important fact that he

had reported in an earlier written account of his second encounter with Joachim: "he looked profoundly disappointed that I had abandoned the violin,
a field in which he was the king, and in which he would therefore have had a
much easier time guiding and helping me."[8] But Joachim received Arthur
with the same cordiality that he had shown him seven years earlier. In this
respect, Rubinstein's recollection was very different from that of young Wilhelm Kempff, another celebrated pianist of Rubinstein's generation, who auditioned for Joachim about seven years later. Kempff recalled having been
dazzled by "the venerable face of the most famous violinist of his time" and
feeling the sternness of the master's glance. "There was good reason for this,
for Joachim liked child prodigies as little as had old Cherubini," Kempff said.
"He himself had had a hard time as a result of such a fate."[9] Arthur, however,
simply played Mozart's Rondo in A Minor, K. 511, to Joachim's "evident satisfaction," he remembered, and he was rewarded with an entire bar of Lindt's
bitter chocolate. He was also rewarded with one of the most successful musical careers of the twentieth century, because on the basis of that brief audition Joachim decided that Arthur had the makings of an outstanding pianist,
and he told the astonished Felicja that he would undertake the supervision of
her son's musical and general education. Since Arthur was too young to be
admitted to the Hochschule, the master decided to have his little protégé
from Lodz study privately with teachers from the school.

Joachim enlisted the support of three Jewish or part-Jewish bankers:
Robert Warschauer, Robert von Mendelssohn, and Martin Levy. Rubinstein
later described Warschauer as "an utterly unmusical man whose wife wor-
shiped Joachim."[10] Mendelssohn, a fine amateur cellist, was the son of Franz
von Mendelssohn (a nephew of the composer) and of Franz's Bordeaux-born
wife, Enole Biarnez, a highly accomplished musician. Martin Levy, an old
friend of Joachim's, was "a retired businessman who made a hobby of com-
posing string quartets,"[11] according to Rubinstein. The three benefactors set
up a fund that covered most of Arthur's educational and living expenses, and
Joachim himself contributed the rest. "What a generous gesture for a great
artist, who was not at all rich himself, to make in behalf of a young foreigner
with merely a promising talent!" wrote Rubinstein. The only condition to
which Joachim held Felicja was not to exploit Arthur as a prodigy. "He insisted that I should get a full education until I was artistically mature. And I
state here with pride that my parents kept this promise in full!"[12]

Felicja's next task was to find Arthur a home with proper middle-class
folk who had an extra room to let, who would allow him to take his meals
with them, and who wouldn't mind hearing him practice for hours every day.
She eventually settled on the well-appointed middle-class apartment of Frau
Johanna Rosentower, a widow who lived with her three grown-up, music-

loving daughters on the third floor of a substantial apartment building at Magdeburgerstrasse 25. The four women took a liking to Arthur: "Right away I was adopted by the whole family, and felt quite happy in this feminine atmosphere."[13] Once he was settled in, his mother arranged for an upright piano to be installed in his room, said good-bye to her youngest child, and returned to Lodz. For the next few years, Arthur would see his parents only during short summer holidays and on special occasions; after that, he would see them even less. His son, John Rubinstein, has said that Arthur "felt abandoned, left on his own at a ridiculously young age. And it made him seek love and acceptance in quarters where a normal little boy wouldn't have had to look. I think that was true of him till his dying day. He was deeply insecure about himself and about his talent and about the public's feelings toward him; it all got mixed together, a *lot*. I *never* felt that he was emotionally secure; I don't say that as a doctor, but as someone close to him, someone who loved him."[14]

MOZART'S RONDO IN A Minor is no showpiece. Its notes can be managed at a logical tempo (it is an Andante in 6/8 time) by anyone who has achieved a moderate degree of keyboard dexterity, and it would not be used in a piano competition to separate true virtuosos from merely competent technicians. But its musical content is profound; it is an exceedingly difficult piece to play well. Written when Mozart was at the zenith of his powers—between *The Marriage of Figaro* and *Don Giovanni*, and shortly before the great String Quintets in C Major and G Minor (K. 515 and 516)—the Rondo is permeated with a melancholy that is occasionally lightened by more sparkling passages but that never disappears. No ten-year-old could have understood the piece, intellectually. One can only suppose that little Arthur Rubinstein was so exceptionally musical that he *instinctively* grasped the Rondo's wrenching but unmournful sadness and translated it into sound, and that this was what astonished Joachim in the boy's playing. The impression was so strong that Joachim, besides looking after the financing of Arthur's education, took the trouble to persuade one of the most celebrated piano pedagogues of the day to accept Arthur as a nonpaying pupil.

Heinrich Barth—or, more properly, Karl Heinrich Barth—was born on July 12, 1847, at Pillau (now Baltijsk), near Königsberg (Kaliningrad), in East Prussia (Russia). Early orphaned, he was raised by his first important piano teacher, one L. Steinmann. During his mid- and late teens, Barth studied with Hans von Bülow, then with Hans von Bronsart, and finally with Karl Tausig—all celebrated virtuosos. He quickly made a name for himself not only as a solo artist but also as a first-rate chamber music performer, and especially as a member of the Berlin Trio, with the violinist Heinrich de Ahna and Brahms's favorite cellist, Robert Hausmann. The three musicians were colleagues on the staff of Joachim's school, where Barth began to teach in 1871. He was later appointed court pianist to the kaiser. By the time Arthur arrived in Berlin, the fifty-year-old Barth was dedicating nearly all of his efforts to teaching; he seldom gave concerts, but according to Wilhelm Kempff, who heard Barth a few years later, "those rare occasions were enough to demonstrate to his public that the white-bearded elf-king could still hold his own with the young knights of the octaves. Although his playing lacked immediacy, evocative power, and charm, the compensation was a wonderful spirituality that illuminated the deepest recesses of a work and allowed it to enter our ears in its most complete form. This presupposed a technique that beggared description. It was said of him that he could do a series of six concerts without dropping a single note under the piano."[15]

Joachim recommended the nine-year-old Kempff to Barth about seven years after Rubinstein's arrival in Berlin, and Barth put him through a difficult audition. Only after the boy had easily transposed down a third the Fugue in G-sharp Minor from Bach's *Well-Tempered Clavier* did "the man with the long beard declare himself ready to undertake the hazardous enterprise, in the name of God," Kempff recalled.[16] For the young Rubinstein, however, Barth not only waived the audition and his fee (he was one of the highest-paid piano teachers in the city) but even agreed to look after collecting and administering the scholarship money. At the end of every school year Barth reminded Arthur to write letters of thanks to his benefactors—a gesture that would have seemed merely tiresome to most youngsters, but that hurt this one's pride; it was "a thorn in my heart," he said later.[17]

Kempff called Barth an "old East Prussian giant" and described him as a stereotypical, old-fashioned music teacher, a foul-tempered taskmaster with a heart of gold. "A sublime purity with respect to technique and perception was Barth's distinguishing mark as a born teacher," he said. "Nothing got past his ear, which was like the legendary ear of the tyrant Dionysius—and woe unto anyone who allowed himself to simplify something, even if it sounded good! . . . When I climbed the four flights to his apartment, I often saw people coming downstairs, sobbing into their fine handkerchiefs—not exactly an encouraging sight for the 'next one.' Was it perhaps one of the hopeless young schoolgirls, during whose playing he would often amuse himself by reading 'Auntie Voss' (the *Vossische Zeitung* [a conservative newspaper])? The person would steadfastly return, and the next time, too, she would sob into her handkerchief; whatever else moved these amusing creatures to seek out Heinrich Barth as their teacher, it was also a sort of musical masochism. But we all knew very well that behind the hard crust there was a soft heart, timidly concealed. It was a child's heart, pure and inviolable. How he enjoyed himself with the youngsters at Ivo Puhonny's marionette theater . . . !"[18]

Barth was an all-or-nothing man who wanted his young pupils to dedicate themselves body and soul to improving their fluency at the keyboard. He cautioned Kempff's father, with respect to the son: "A good school education is certainly worth something, but a good trill can be developed only in the hotbed of youth and not in the muck of old age."[19] Kempff's account corroborates that of Rubinstein, who remembered Barth in his fifties as "a formidable personality. He was more than six feet tall and heavily built, but still quite quick on his feet. His grayish hair showed just a touch of baldness. A long Brahmsian beard, the color of salt and pepper, and a bushy mustache covered a rather weak mouth and chin; but his gold-rimmed glasses gave him a look of uncompromising severity. I was terrified by him." Like Kempff, Rubinstein credited Barth with "a sort of naïve honesty and integrity" as a teacher, and he sensed that Barth respected his talent and eventually even became fond of him. "A tender look in his eyes and a shy, boyish smile would appear now and then in his usually sad, stern face, especially after a satisfactory performance," Rubinstein said. "But God help me if I arrived unprepared for a lesson! I would begin, and as soon as I hit wrong notes, I would notice with horror how his long beard rose bit by bit into a horizontal position, which meant that he was drawing up his lower lip and biting it with rage—and then hell would break loose! He would jump to his feet, shout insults at me, bang his fists on the piano, and disappear for a while. After calming down, he would dismiss me sullenly, without a word."[20]

The young Kempff crumbled under such attacks; although he learned much from Barth and always considered himself a Barth pupil, "the still too tender plant atrophied under the gardener's strong hands," he said,[21] and his parents withdrew him from Barth's class. But the young Rubinstein's parents were three hundred miles away, in Lodz—and perhaps he possessed a tougher psychological fiber than did Kempff. Twice a week for six school-years he returned to his tormentor—a crotchety bachelor who shared an apartment at Kurfürstenstrasse 112 with his fawning, unmarried sister and his irritable adoptive mother, old Steinmann's widow—for a tense session that would last up to ninety minutes.

Studying with Barth may well have been a joyless, mechanical, fear-tinged task, but it turned Arthur into a pianist who, from the age of seventeen on, was able to continue to develop entirely on his own; in later years, Rubinstein occasionally told friends that he credited his training "to one man only, Heinrich Barth."[22] In addition to forcing him to familiarize himself with a great deal of repertoire, Barth built a technique that created a basis for the development of the distinctive "Rubinstein Sound" that was to become familiar to generations of listeners: he taught him to sit calmly at the keyboard, to sit high enough to be able to make full use of the upper-arm, shoulder, and back muscles, to play forte passages with a full sound rather than a harsh one and piano passages with a sustained sound rather than a weak one. And a teacher whose long- and short-term pupils included Rubinstein, Kempff, and the legendary Russian pianist Heinrich Neuhaus (who, in turn, taught Svyatoslav Richter, Emil Gilels, and Radu Lupu, among others) deserves considerable recognition. Several other Barth pupils attained a degree of celebrity in their day: the Germans Elsa Rompe and Theodor Bohlmann; the Russian Mark Günzburg; the Poles Eduard Nowowiejski and Bronislaw Pozniak; the Norwegians Frithjof Backer-Gröndahl, Martin Knutzen, and Dagny Knutsen; the Swede Wilhelm Stenhammar; the Canadian Edward Noyes; and the Americans Leonard Liebling, Rudolph Reuter, and Ernest Schelling. Another Polish-born pianist, Heniot Lévy, who studied with Barth from the winter of 1893–94 to the summer of 1896—and who, like Rubinstein, later won the admiration of the great pianist Leopold Godowsky—eventually became a well-known piano teacher at the American Conservatory in Chicago; his grandson is the American harpsichordist Igor Kipnis. One of Lévy's pupils, the American pianist Beatrice Erdely, said that her teacher, like Rubinstein, made "no excessive movements" at the keyboard and "sat straight and used arm and shoulder to produce a big sound." Lévy told her that "he heard Rubinstein, age eleven, play the Mendelssohn Concerto [in G Minor], spectacularly, in [Barth's] class at the Hochschule." And she added that in reading Rubinstein's memoirs, she "was reminded of the intense loyalty and rigid control that Barth demanded" of his pupils, and that characterized Lévy's behavior toward his own pupils.[23]

At first, Arthur was given preparatory lessons by the thirty-six-year-old Majorcan pianist Miguel Capllonch, a former pupil of Barth and Clara Schumann, and music preceptor to the kaiser's daughters. According to Rubinstein, Capllonch was Barth's opposite: "Music was a pure joy to him— and he knew how to share it with me," he said. "We would play with gusto a Schumann symphony arranged for four hands, or one or two Beethoven quartets, then eat some good chocolates, which he always had on hand, and for a happy finale, Capllonch would play some Spanish popular music." Arthur adored him so much that Barth became jealous, according to Rubinstein, and transferred his new pupil's preparatory studies to the care of "an elderly spinster, Miss Clara Hempel," who was willing "to drown me in drudgery."[24]

Further drudgery was provided by the people who taught Arthur harmony, counterpoint, and other elements of music theory, which Joachim allowed him to study at the Hochschule. Oddly enough, Rubinstein, in his memoirs, barely touched on this important aspect of his musical education, and he named only a Professor Kulemkampff [sic] as his harmony teacher; this was probably Gustav Kulenkampff, Royal Professor of Composition at

Berlin's Stern Conservatory. A 1905 biographical sketch of Rubinstein, prepared by his French manager, states that the young pianist had "worked on harmony with Max Bruch," and this information has been repeated in various reference books and magazine articles. Since Bruch was an illustrious composer who seems to have taught only a master class at the Hochschule— and only from about 1901 on—he would not, in all likelihood, have occupied himself with the instruction of even an exceptionally talented child; Rubinstein, in his memoirs, describes him only as an acquaintance. Other sources mention Robert Kahn, another composer, as one of Arthur's teachers. Kahn, who was thirty-two years old in 1897, had been on Joachim's faculty for three years and was the man to whom other talented young Barth pupils, including Kempff, were sent. But perhaps Arthur had little or no contact with him: Kempff described Kahn as a wonderful teacher and a lovable human being, and Rubinstein would have been unlikely to omit the name of so prestigious a master from his autobiography. Instead, he said only that his theory lessons were "disappointing" and that his teachers annoyed him with "eternal canons and other boring exercises."[25]

Among all of his Berlin teachers, Rubinstein praised unreservedly only the one who had had nothing to do with music. Dr. Theodor Altmann gave him two hours' instruction every day, to prepare him for yearly examinations at the Realgymnasium (secondary school), and the subjects they covered included history, geography, Latin, mathematics, literature, and philosophy. (When Arthur was about fourteen, Joachim allowed him to replace the study of mathematics, which the boy detested, with private lessons in French and English—his fourth and fifth modern languages—the better to be able to cope with the wandering life of a performer; he soon became reasonably fluent in both, and he did advanced work in Latin, which fascinated him.) Altmann, a rotund man of about forty, had the rare gift of making the acquisition of knowledge come alive for youngsters. "You were brilliant at introducing all these different subjects to me, and I was eager to absorb every word you said": thus the aged Rubinstein apostrophized his old mentor's shade. "You used precise, clear terms to express your thought, and it was delightful and exciting to listen to you . . . life became a constant joy in learning."[26] Altmann guided him through Plato, Aristotle, Kant, Schopenhauer, and Nietzsche, and he fostered Arthur's nascent love of reading and directed his literary tastes toward Goethe, Heine, Kleist, Balzac, Maupassant, Dostoyevsky, Gogol, and Tolstoy. Books would remain Rubinstein's closest companions. No matter where he traveled and under what conditions, he usually spent five or six hours a day reading, and he was always happy with his books; at the end of his life, when his eyes could no longer focus on a printed page, he was happy when others read to him. But Barth eventually made Arthur stop studying with Altmann, too—again out of jealousy, according to Rubinstein.

Arthur also adored Joachim, who allowed him to take part in the school's chamber music classes and thus initiated his protégé's lifelong affinity for a segment of the repertoire that many famous pianists neglect. From time to time Arthur was invited to accompany the master's violin classes—an experience that allowed the boy to learn much of the violin repertoire from one of its great, historical exponents. (Rubinstein told his first French manager that when he was still a young boy in Berlin, he went to hear a recital by a violinist named Sussmann, only to discover that the accompanist had been taken ill at the last moment. "A few minutes before the beginning of the session, little Rubinstein offered to replace him and accompanied the violin concertos of Wieniawski and Max Bruch by heart, without rehearsal, and in a way that elicited the audience's admiration," the manager reported.)[27] Joachim expected his pupils to resolve their technical problems with the help of other teachers or by themselves; to resolve interpretive problems, the master would simply point out the problem and then "play the passage or phrase in question himself, in a manner truly divine," according to Leopold Auer, who studied briefly with Joachim.[28] This may or may not have been useful to Joachim's pupils, some of whom must have been seeking more specific types of help, but it made Arthur aware for the first time of the intellectual—as differentiated from the technical—difficulties of musical performance. Joachim also invited the boy to his apartment when the Joachim Quartet, one of the most famous chamber music ensembles of all times, rehearsed there. In those years, its members, besides Joachim (first violin), were the Berlin Philharmonic's concertmaster Karel Halíř (second violin), Emanuel Wirth (viola), and the already-mentioned Robert Hausmann (cello). During one such rehearsal, Arthur, who was sitting in direct sunlight, fell sound asleep. "Professor Joachim took it with his usual kindness, but I felt ashamed for quite awhile," Rubinstein said.[29] He also recalled hearing a performance at Berlin's Singakademie of Brahms's Double Concerto, with Joachim and Hausmann—for whom Brahms had written the work—as soloists, and with the Meiningen Hofkapelle orchestra under Fritz Steinbach, one of Brahms's favorite conductors.[30]

ARTHUR'S TALENT HAD placed him in an abnormal situation, but his day-to-day existence in Berlin followed a pattern—lessons, homework, learning to deal with other human beings—that corresponded to the existences of most other middle-class European children of his and later generations. The lessons took place privately rather than in a classroom, much of the homework was carried out at a keyboard rather than at a desk, and most of the other human beings were outsiders rather than immediate family; Arthur's schedule, however, was fairly regular, and his behavior was monitored by adults. He was by no means a waif abandoned to his own devices.

Often, he was welcomed into the homes of financiers and other successful professional men who patronized the arts. Some of the patrons were sincerely interested in him, but for others he was little more than an ornament to dinner parties—a monstrously gifted child who, for the insignificant cost of an extra meal, would perform for the other guests. This, he recalled, was "a form of exploitation very much in vogue at the time."[31] He cannot have felt entirely at his ease amid such wealth: his parents had not taught him refined manners, and he quickly became aware of his role as the talented but poor little Polish Jew among Berlin's cultivated, assimilated Jewish elite. Fifty years later, a Mrs. Treviranus, the daughter of Martin Levy, one of the patrons who was sponsoring Arthur's studies, sent Rubinstein her recollections of a musical gathering at her parents' home. Her account is sentimentalized, but it demonstrates that some people were aware of the psychological difficulties that the boy had to face.

> On a sunny spring morning, a little musical entertainment takes place in the big music room. . . . But today's artist is . . . still a little man . . . with deep, dark eyes and curly, black hair. The brown velvet suit with white collar . . . is really a little too big on him. The artist mixes with the guests. Artur Rubinstein is just twelve years old, but he is not nervous. Why should he be, since he "only" has to play the piano? . . .
>
> At a sign from the host, the "little man" scrambles onto the piano stool and plays . . . The sounds rush through the air, pearly and pure. One can hardly believe that the tender little hands are big enough to reach the chords. Thus played, the fugue—one of Bach's hardest—is a masterpiece. But the real show of mastery follows. When the little one has finished, Rudorff, a harmony professor at the Berlin College of Music, goes up to the grand piano and asks the youngster: "Can you transpose this fugue?" Since little Artur nods in assent, [Rudorff] says, "Then transpose it for me into A-flat Minor." The child plays an A-flat Minor chord softly, and then plays the fugue again in A-flat Minor, by heart, without a moment's hesitation. This seems incredible. . . . When the little one has finished and has clambered down from the piano stool, he stands alone for a moment next to the tall piano. The light falls on his dark hair and gives it a golden hue. His eyes have an inner liveliness, as if the sounds that he has just played were still echoing inside him. The way the youngster

stands there in the large hall, next to the tall piano, is like a symbol. [He seems] cut off from the people who have just been united with him through the sounds. The little artist still has a long way to go, alone with his art, before he reaches the summit; alone, without children's games, without his parents' home and his friends, in a foreign city.

(According to Eva Rubinstein, Arthur's older daughter, part of Mrs. Treviranus's description of the young pianist is incorrect. "My father had pale blue-gray eyes and auburn hair," she said. And Mrs. Treviranus's description of Rudorff as "a harmony professor" is incomplete. Ernst Friedrich Karl Rudorff, a pupil of Ignaz Moscheles and Clara Schumann, had been teaching at the Hochschule since 1869, and he headed its piano and organ faculty throughout Rubinstein's Berlin years; his pupils included the keyboard wizard Leopold Godowsky. Rudorff was also a choral and orchestral conductor of modest repute, an accomplished if not brilliant composer, and a music editor responsible for portions of Breitkopf & Härtel's complete Mozart and Chopin editions.)

Arthur liked the Levys, and he liked the Rosentowers' kindly doctor, Georg Salomon, who was an enthusiastic amateur pianist. Once, when called in to visit Arthur, who was ill, Salomon told Frau Rosentower that the boy had " 'nothing, just the measles,' " and went on, practically in the same breath, to ask him, " 'What tempo do you take for the F major Organ Toccata of Bach?' . . . He dragged me out of bed, sat me down at my upright piano, and, by Jove, we threw ourselves, with relish, into a performance of the Toccata to the astonishment of everyone," Rubinstein recalled. In retrospect, Salomon and his family seemed to him to typify the German Jewish bourgeoisie: "less Jewish than the Polish Jews, more patriotic than the Germans themselves."[32]

Arthur felt truly comfortable with the family of Lotte Landau Hahn, who was distantly related to a Lodz banker whom the Rubinsteins knew. Rubinstein remembered Mrs. Hahn as "a beautiful and enchanting lady of about thirty-five and a very fine pianist, well equipped for a brilliant career, if it hadn't been for her wealth, her husband, and children."[33] He developed a childish crush on her; she gently deflected it and, at the same time, encouraged a friendship between him and her son, Kurt, who was about two years his senior. For a few years, Arthur, Kurt, and Kurt's school friends Richard Fuchs ("later a successful lawyer," Rubinstein said), Hugo Perls (later "an art dealer in New York"), Franz Pariser (who eventually moved to Washington, where Rubinstein was in touch with him as late as 1970, at least), and Paul Heinitz often got together at one or another's home on Saturday evenings to read through plays by Aeschylus, Sophocles, Shakespeare in the Schlegel and Tieck translations, and the German classics Lessing, Goethe, Schiller, and Kleist, and to have a pleasant supper afterward. Arthur regretted that he was never able to host any of the gatherings, "having neither home nor supper to offer," but he enjoyed being "always elected to play the villains" in the plays, he said.[34] His lifelong love of the theater was born at the meetings of this *Lesekränzchen*, or little reading club, and it flowered when he began to attend performances of classical drama at the Royal Playhouse and of contemporary works by Ibsen, Hauptmann, and others at Otto Brahm's avant-garde Deutsches Theater and at young Max Reinhardt's Neues Theater.

Another, and ultimately more important, of his lifelong loves was born at the Hahns' one afternoon early in his Berlin stay, when Lotte and some friends played the A Major and C Minor Piano Quartets of Brahms, who had died only a few months before Arthur's arrival in Germany. Arthur became "obsessed" with Brahms's music, he said, and his passion grew when, through Joachim—himself the best-known living Brahmsian—he made the acquaintance of Professor Wilhelm Engelmann and his family. Engelmann, director of the University of Berlin's Physiological Institute, had been close to Brahms and was one of Joachim's best friends; his second wife, Emma Brandes, was described by Andreas Moser, Joachim's biographer, as an "excellent pianist, perhaps the best chamber music player since Frau Schumann."[35] Rubinstein said that Emma Brandes Engelmann had been "one of Clara Schumann's best pupils," and this information is supported by an entry in one of Frau Schumann's diaries: "With each piece that she played for me, I was again astonished and overjoyed. When she sits at the piano, the holy seriousness immediately comes over her, she surrenders herself to it completely, and this I have never seen in any of the young girls who arise only to be extinguished."[36] According to Moser, "After her marriage, [Frau Engelmann] withdrew from public musical life," but she often accompanied Joachim in musical evenings for friends, at home, and always "gave proof, notwithstanding everything, that she remained a first-rate artist."[37] She was in her mid-forties when Rubinstein met her, and he said that he "often had the chance to hear her play and to perform with her on two pianos"[38] in the huge music room of the Engelmanns' apartment at the Institute. This further direct connection with the Schumann-Brahms circle was extremely important to his musical development, and it gave him a lifelong respect for female musicians that not all of his male colleagues shared. He also became friendly with Hans, the youngest of the Engelmanns' children; they read each other the adventure stories of Karl May and Jules Verne and they played with Hans's elaborate electric train system.

Musical life in Berlin was rich, and Joachim, Altmann, and even Barth, to some extent, encouraged Arthur to take advantage of it. He attended performances at the Court Opera, which in those years boasted Richard Strauss as its general music director, Carl Muck as its principal conductor, and some of the most famous singers in the world on its roster. In 1900, the thirty-six-year-old Strauss added to his opera duties those of principal conductor of the new Berlin Tonkünstler Orchestra, which specialized in contemporary music, and Arthur may have attended some of the ensemble's concerts. In this case, however, his mentors would not have encouraged him, for they were opposed to the Liszt-Wagner school and its radical progeny, of whom Strauss was the most famous example. The opera orchestra, under the direction of Felix Weingartner, gave many concerts that made a great impression on the young Rubinstein, but he was even more impressed by the Berlin Philharmonic's concerts under Artur Nikisch, whom Rubinstein to his dying day considered "the greatest of all conductors . . . Never since have I heard music played like that. Nikisch . . . stood motionless and erect while conducting; his baton alone dominated the orchestra with short but rhythmically precise strokes. From time to time he would raise his left hand to emphasize a phrase. . . . [I] lived completely under his spell."[39] It was through Nikisch that Arthur became familiar not only with Mozart's and Beethoven's orchestral works, but also with those of Tchaikovsky, Rimsky-Korsakov, Borodin, Mussorgsky, Franck, and Strauss. Arthur must also have attended performances by some of the Hochschule's aspiring young musicians and by Berlin's renowned choral ensembles: the Singakademie under the direction of Martin Blumner and Georg Schumann, the Philharmonic Choir conducted by Siegfried Ochs, and the Cathedral Choir under Albert Becker.

Thanks to Hermann Wolff, the most powerful impresario in Germany, Arthur often received free tickets to the recitals of leading soloists. Eugène Ysaÿe, Fritz Kreisler, and Jacques Thibaud, for instance, opened the boy's ears to new styles of violin playing, more graceful and more intensely sensual than Joachim's approach. Of more immediate importance, however, was his growing familiarity with the playing of many outstanding pianists. Busoni was the measuring stick—"by far the most interesting pianist alive," Rubinstein said in his memoirs,[40]—and he told Fred Gaisberg that the Italo-German master had "poetry and technical equipment in an equal degree."[41] In the 1960s Rubinstein told RCA producer Max Wilcox: "you would react to Busoni probably much in the way you react to [Svyatoslav] Richter. Busoni had an extravagant way of playing. He played more mysteriously than other pianists. He really was a genius. His piano sometimes sounded like magic. We pianists, young and old, were always sitting spellbound by Busoni. Unfortunately, the rest of the public often asked us—'Where is his magic, where is that greatness?' He was above them. He was a man ahead of his time, one of our own time. Today, he would beat us all. . . . I'm sure of that. I've never heard anybody play with such ease, such elegance, and such mastery the most difficult works. I must say sometimes you would be aggravated and annoyed with certain things. He would, for instance, play the Adagio of the Beethoven *Hammerklavier* Sonata with a sort of ironic touch. It didn't have the deep, tearful, and sad feeling which is in it. The Adagio really is the end of life, the end of the world, of everything, those empty chords, those long phrases. Even the consoling mood which comes here and there is desperate. . . . Well, Busoni would give you suddenly a little twinkle of irony: 'I'm doing it, but I don't believe in any of it.' Of course, in every other way, he would do it beautifully, oh yes."[42] Rubinstein also had reservations about Busoni's performances of Chopin, which he described as technically brilliant but lacking in warmth and tenderness, but he adored his interpretations of Liszt and Bach (the latter in Busoni's own arrangements) and always remembered Busoni as "a towering personality, a shining example to all musicians."[43]

Eugen d'Albert was another frequent visitor to Berlin. Rubinstein told Gaisberg that he had admired d'Albert's "exquisite scale-runs and tonal perfection,"[44] and he said in his memoirs that d'Albert had played Beethoven's Fourth concerto "with a nobility and tenderness" that remained a "model performance of this work," which was one of Rubinstein's favorites.[45] To Wilcox, Rubinstein said that d'Albert "would knock off a Beethoven sonata with genius. He would sometimes hew it up brutally and play wrong notes all the way through, as I've heard about Anton Rubinstein, but there was genius and great conviction behind it all."[46] After one of d'Albert's Berlin recitals, Wolff introduced Arthur to him. D'Albert had been chatting with some friends — among them, Engelbert Humperdinck, the composer of *Hänsel und Gretel* — but when he heard Wolff's words of praise for the boy he immediately took him onto the stage of the Beethoven Hall and asked him to play. With all the innocent self-assurance of the prepubescent, Arthur launched into Brahms's Two Rhapsodies, Op. 79; the makeshift audience, which included Humperdinck and some members of the general public who had not yet left the auditorium, applauded warmly, and d'Albert "embraced me, saying, 'Yes, you are a true Rubinstein.' "[47]

Arthur also heard Vladimir de Pachmann, whom he later described as "a miniaturist who enchanted you, who caressed the piano. He would do the most incredible little passages and achieve pedal effects that nobody else would risk."[48] And he heard d'Albert's former wife, "the Walküre-like Teresa Carreño, playing the Tchaikovsky Concerto with the strength and dash of two men; the French pianist Edouard Risler, a wonderful interpreter of Beethoven sonatas; . . . [Ossip] Gabrilowitsch, tender and romantic in the Schu-

mann Concerto; [and the twenty-year-old] Artur Schnabel . . . making his
[Berlin] debut at a Nikisch concert"[49] during the 1902–03 season. Why are
there no complimentary adjectives for Schnabel? In later years, Rubinstein
dismissed his colleague's musical ideas as "intellectual and almost pedantic
. . . He sounded to me as if he were giving lessons to the audience. . . ."[50] This
is a gross misrepresentation of Schnabel's intentions and results, but, coming
from Rubinstein, the description is not surprising. How could two artists who
differed so vastly in temperament and in their approach to music have understood each other? Schnabel was the Anti-Virtuoso par excellence, and he
was in many ways the leading exponent of the "German School" of music-
making, which Rubinstein was always ready to deprecate. ("Wilhelm Backhaus—all this business about Backhaus!" he once exclaimed to Barenboim
about another celebrated pianist, three years Rubinstein's senior.)[51] Schnabel, likewise, had little use for Rubinstein, and, during the 1940s, when both
were living in the United States, he resented Rubinstein's great popularity.
The conductor Carl Bamberger recalled that once, while he, Rubinstein,
and Schnabel were waiting for the same plane out of Havana, a woman
walked up to Rubinstein, told him that she collected autographs of famous
musicians, and persuaded him to sign her autograph book. Schnabel asked to
look at the book; the woman handed it to him and he began to flip through it,
commenting, from time to time, "Ah yes—this one was a pupil of mine. . . .
Oh—also a pupil of mine." When he handed the book back to its owner, she
smiled and asked, "Are you a piano teacher, sir?" Schnabel was not pleased.
And on another occasion, Schnabel offered "a splendid Havana cigar" to the
violinist Henri Temianka, "with the comment, 'You will observe that my cigars are not equipped with gold bands bearing my name. I leave that to my
colleague Artur Rubinstein.' Rubinstein, at that time, was more successful in
America than Schnabel," Temianka said. "That he could even afford his own
personalized cigars was more than the flesh could bear."[52]

ARTHUR'S JEWISHNESS BECAME an issue in his life toward the end of 1899 or
early in January 1900, when his mother arrived in Berlin to supervise preparations for his Bar Mitzvah. "I had to attend a school of the Reformed Jewish
synagogue to learn some Hebrew . . . , and I found this an unexpected moral
attack on me, hard to reconcile with my past and present religious background. . . . But I had to be obedient, and so, for three or four weeks, I was
forced to listen to the bored and monotonous voice of a man who tried to
explain to about fifty of us the intricacies of the Hebrew language and the
biblical interpretation of our existence." Arthur managed to get through the
ceremony without mishap—to his mother's delight—but also without com-
prehension. Afterward, he was taken "to an excellent kosher restaurant,"

where he "received the traditional presents. My mother gave me the tephillin [phylacteries], to be used, presumably, when I would say daily prayers. The Meyers [Aunt Salka and her family] presented me with a silver watch which I found more useful."[53]

The Bar Mitzvah symbolizes a Jewish boy's assumption of the duties and privileges of manhood. And when, in September 1899, only a few months before Arthur's Bar Mitzvah, three young female boarders moved into the Rosentowers' apartment, Arthur began to experience some of the feelings associated with becoming a man. At first, he was miffed because he had had to trade his own room for a much smaller one—and eventually for a cot in the drawing room—so that the young ladies could be accommodated in proper style, but his displeasure was quickly overshadowed by his growing interest in one of the newcomers. Bertha V. Drew was a Bostonian, a recent graduate of Radcliffe College, and a music lover, whose parents had sent her to Berlin for a taste of European social and cultural life. Seventy years later, Rubinstein recalled that Miss Drew's hair was soft and shiny and "not too dark" brown, that her eyes were brown, that she dressed "simply, with excellent taste, and never used a trace of makeup," and that she had "the most ravishing smile I had ever seen."[54] No wonder, then, that instead of practicing on his upright piano, Arthur began to play more often on the grand piano in the drawing room, in the hope of attracting Miss Drew's attention.

Photos taken by Miss Drew early in 1900 show that Arthur still looked very much like a little boy: he hadn't a trace of an adolescent's incipient beard or changing facial features, and he still dressed in a sailor suit—the standard outfit for bourgeois children of his generation and the next. He seems to have known by instinct that only through the piano did he stand a chance of attracting a woman in her early twenties. By coincidence, a great opportunity for impressing her presented itself. Joachim—no doubt with Barth's approval—had decided to have Arthur play Mozart's Concerto in A Major, K. 488, in the Hochschule's main auditorium. The orchestra would be made up of students, but the conductor would be Joachim himself. A trial run took place in nearby Potsdam under the baton of Gustav Kulenkampff, Arthur's theory teacher. "Barth, like a boxing trainer, gave me his last-minute instructions," Rubinstein recalled: " 'When you come out on the platform, make a deep bow to the public, then a shorter one to the orchestra. Fix your piano stool so as to gain perfect control of movement. Don't look at the public. Concentrate on what you are going to play before giving the conductor the sign to begin. . . . Watch your pedal, don't make faces, don't sing while you are playing, never change your fingering—it might get you into trouble.' " So much advice, coming all at once, was a little daunting, but Arthur found that it worked; he followed it for the rest of his life, "and I would rec-

ommend it to every pianist," he said. His performance of the concerto, that
evening, was "not too bad" but "a little dry and scholarly," he recalled, and it
received a tumultuous ovation. But when he attempted to play one of Mendelssohn's *Songs without Words* as an encore, his memory went blank. "All I
knew was that the piece was in A flat, and so, without stopping, my heart
frozen, I began to improvise." The trick worked, and the audience, unaware
that the unfamiliar piece was counterfeit Mendelssohn, applauded Arthur
"with the same enthusiasm as before." He feared that Barth, who was waiting
in the wings, would skin him alive, but instead, the professor exclaimed,
" 'Teufelsjunge [devilish boy], you are a rascal—but a genius! I couldn't have
pulled that trick in a thousand years.' "[55] According to an early publicity
blurb on Rubinstein, this dry-run concert was "a gala attended by the whole
Court. His success was so great that the Society that had engaged him made
him a gift of a Beethoven manuscript and a silver crown."[56] Had any of this
been true, however, Rubinstein would probably have mentioned it in his
memoirs.

The performance at the Hochschule went even better than the trial run
at Potsdam, probably because Joachim prepared it with great care, as was his
custom. Rubinstein recalled, "I played with more warmth and freedom,
while Joachim accompanied beautifully. When we took our bow, he kissed
me on both cheeks in front of the audience. This was a memorable day for
me." There is no record of the event in the Hochschule's concert lists of the
period, but this only means that Arthur's concert was not part of the school's
regular series, probably because he was not enrolled at the school.

Miss Drew began to give him "more of her time, and her smile became
more tender."[57] The Rosentowers put on a party for Arthur on his thirteenth
birthday, and afterward, as he said good night to Miss Drew—everyone else
had already gone to bed—she put her arms around him and kissed him on
the mouth. This was his first adult kiss; he ran off to his room, certain that she
loved him. From that day on, he became a Cherubino, snatching every erotic
crumb that fell his way.

The same French publicity material that described the Potsdam event
as a court-attended gala mentioned that, during the same period, young
Rubinstein played "at the five-o'clocks given by Mr. [Andrew D.] White, the
Ambassador of the United States in Berlin, where he was greeted in the most
flattering manner by the American audience there." This engagement may
well have been arranged at the prompting of Miss Drew, who was being
courted by Morton C. Hartzell, a young minister attached to the American
church in Berlin. Hartzell often took her to the opera in the evening, and
when she arrived back at the Rosentowers' she would slip into the drawing
room—as Arthur had encouraged her to do—and sit down on the boy's cot.

He would "whisper some tender loving words, and she would kiss my mouth, and smile."[58] It seems to have been a textbook case of transference: What she could not or would not do with her adult male friend—whom she married not long after her return to the United States—she did with her willing little fellow boarder, although they never advanced beyond passionate kisses.

These nocturnal encounters continued for about five months, until someone in the house discovered what was happening and reported it to Mrs. Rosentower. The shocked landlady summoned the culprits to her room and accused Miss Drew of debauching Arthur, who was "stunned, not only by this horrible scene, but even more by Miss Drew's violent insistence on her maternal feelings toward me. And I, little fool, had thought it was love!" Miss Drew had the good sense to go directly to Barth, who considered himself Arthur's moral as well as musical guardian; she told him her version of the story before anyone else could recount another, and "to my great astonishment," Rubinstein said, the professor "took her side. I was to discover much later that he, too, had a keen eye for pretty girls." Contrary to the account in his memoirs, however, Arthur was removed immediately from the Rosentowers' apartment and sent to live, temporarily, with his Aunt Salka and her family. At about the same time, Miss Drew's parents arrived from the United States for an already scheduled visit. They, too, dismissed the whole matter, and their daughter moved into their hotel. "They very kindly invited me to lunch with them one day and treated me like one of the family," Rubinstein said.[59] The day before the whole Drew family's departure from Berlin, Bertha's parents made Arthur a gift of a portable writing desk, with stationery, and very early the next morning he used the materials for writing a farewell note (in German) to his friend.

21.7.00.

My dear, dear Miss Drew!
Today, the difficult day of separation has arrived. You cannot imagine how hard it will be to say goodbye to you. But I must try to seem like a man and cannot allow myself to be coddled. But I am sure that you won't forget me, only in one case could I doubt it [if she married Hartzell, presumably]. I myself will certainly never, never forget you. Just imagine how amazed I was yesterday, when I saw this wonderfully beautiful gift at home. It was really so friendly of your parents. Now I can at least write neatly to you and, as you can see, today I am already making use of the stationery. Now I shall always keep the key in my pocket, and then I can really lock things up in it. And how nice it was of you yourself to have made me a present of the beautiful "Meistersinger" [piano-vocal score]. In one respect,

I am happy that you are going away, since people have annoyed you
and me too much. Yesterday I wrote a letter to Frau Rosentower. I
described in it absolutely accurately the outing to Potsdam [with the
Drew family, presumably] and the beautiful things that I have received from your kind parents and yourself. She will be extremely
annoyed. Oh, how nice it would be if I could go to America sometime and to you in Boston. But you mustn't think that already at
that time I will no longer be a child. At sixteen one is of course
grown up, but one can still remain a child at heart, no? If we correspond with each other all the time, you won't notice at all whether
I've grown up. I hope to receive letters from you often, oh how
happy that would make me. My aunt was much delighted by the
wonderful flowers for her. It is only 4 o'clock now, a little early, but
it doesn't matter. I absolutely don't want anyone to see this letter,
and so I got up very early. Your address has already gone into my
nice address book. I've just heard my aunt, so I remain forever your
cordially affectionate friend

                                        Artek

He wrote to her again the next day:

My dear Miss Drew!
Now I am lonely! How sad it is now here in Berlin! Even yesterday,
after I left you, it was terribly hard for me to be courageous. I could
barely keep back my tears, and I was all tear-streaked when I went to
Herr Professor's house. But in the end one must resign oneself. Everyone noticed what a change has taken place in me. I wanted to
amuse myself, but it didn't work. I am already thinking about when
the time will come for me to go to America. I even dreamed about
you, but horrible things that I can't write about. I hope to have your
news soon. Are you having a good time in Eisenach? I am already
playing large parts of the Meistersinger, especially the passages that
you like so much. I can't write much today, because I am going to
the Fledermaus at the theater. I had a bad session with Herr Professor yesterday, because I was of course too agitated to pay close attention. Herr Professor seemed to have noticed it, too, because he
didn't say or ask anything. At my aunt's, however, no one noticed
that I am now so agitated. Were you a little sad, too, while you were
traveling[?] Not much, I hope. Please write to me, too, very soon,
only I'm afraid that my aunt will open the letter, and so I would
rather that she didn't see everything that you write to me. I'm now

being persecuted by my cousins, both of whom want to read my letter. And so I'll now end the letter. Your cordially affectionate friend

Artek

Please say hello to your esteemed parents.[60]

Cherubino's education had been interrupted. In later years, Rubinstein occasionally saw the Hartzell family during his American tours. Fifty years after they had met, Bertha sent Arthur the letters that he had written to her and the album of photos that she had taken during her stay in Berlin; the items were accompanied by a note: "Here are the little keepsakes which I wanted to place in your hands before anything should happen to me. I have not even a copy, but I do have what matters most, the vivid memory of that happy Berlin winter, and the knowledge that all goes well with you now."[61]

AT THE AGE of thirteen, Arthur discovered "something characteristic in my nature—the capacity to work well only if there was something special to work for, like a concert, or, later, my recordings."[62] His attitude was that of the born performer: no use tiring oneself when there is no chance to show off the results. Behind that attitude, however, there lay not only the desire to be admired but also an unquenchable thirst for giving—a feeling that nothing that cannot be shared is worth doing. And despite Miss Drew's disappearance from Berlin, Arthur had a strong incentive to continue to practice during his five-month stay at Aunt Salka's home, because Barth and Joachim had arranged a major concert for him at the height of the following season. This time he would not play at the Hochschule, but rather at the great Beethoven-Saal, with the Berlin Philharmonic under the direction of Josef Rebicek, and the concert would be his official professional debut.

Barth chose a formidable program for the concert, which was to be a mixture of concertos and solo pieces—a genre that was common in those days—and he made his pupil work meticulously. The evening would begin with the same Mozart Concerto in A Major that Arthur had played in Potsdam and at the Hochschule; there would be two difficult solo pieces—Schumann's *Papillons* and Chopin's Scherzo No. 1 in B Minor (in his memoirs, Rubinstein said that he also played a Chopin nocturne, but none is mentioned in either the advance announcements in the newspapers or the reviews)—and the program would end with Saint-Saëns's Concerto No. 2 in G Minor, which remained a staple of Rubinstein's repertoire for the rest of his career. The Berlin newspapers duly announced the young Rubinstein's forthcoming concert, which took place within ten days of appearances by the pianists Godowsky, Jedliczka, de Pachmann, and Fanny Davies, the Joachim

Quartet; the Berlin Philharmonic under Nikisch, with Ysaÿe as soloist; and
the soprano Pauline de Ahna accompanied by her husband, Richard Strauss.
His single rehearsal with orchestra—presumably on the day of the concert,
December 1, 1900—went smoothly, and "the musicians seemed impressed,"
he recalled. Nevertheless, his "nerves were on edge," he said, as he prepared
to walk onto the stage that evening, and it is no wonder: according to Rubinstein's memoirs, the audience included Joachim, Bruch, Godowsky, the impresario Hermann Wolff, and even Arthur's sister Jadwiga and brother
Stanislaw, who had come all the way from Lodz for the event. (Another
source—early but unreliable—says that Humperdinck, Gerhart Hauptmann,
Richard Strauss, and Nikisch were also in attendance.) But, said Rubinstein,
"pulling myself together, honestly I did my best. Every piece was a success,
and after the final Saint-Saëns, the audience jumped from their seats, started
to yell, and stamped their feet. I really must say it was a triumph for me." He
gave four encores, and then Joachim, Bruch, and Godowsky "all came on the
stage to congratulate me, and Professor Joachim embraced me."[63]

His account of the event is no exaggeration. A month later, when Barth
wrote (in stiff English) to Miss Drew, to thank her for a present that she had
sent Arthur, the professor was still basking in his pupil's success. "I handed
over to Arthur your two packages on the 27th [of December]," he wrote,
"when he was removed to his new home Berlin W. Kleiststr. 7 III Care/of
Herr B. Kurt. There was nothing to pay, but his thanks, which he will do
soon, as I hope. His concert the 1. of December was a real splendid success.
Joachim, who attended it from beginning to end, I never saw so excited from
enthousiasm [sic]. May the boy go on in the same way and manner!"[64] Reviews of the concert in the Berlin newspapers were as "excited from enthousiasm" as Joachim had been; they far surpassed the standard remarks,
courteous or admonitory, usually extended to child prodigies. Dr. Leopold
Schmidt, a professor at the Stern Conservatory, wrote in the *Berliner Tageblatt*, of which he was chief music critic: "In the Beethoven-Saal, a thirteen-
year-old boy, *Arthur Rubinstein*, made his appearance, evoking the most vivid
amazement, and rightly so. He played . . . everything not as a child prodigy
but as a mature, adult musician. Only the tone quality revealed, naturally,
the strength of what is still a child's body. The young namesake of the great
Anton (to whom his family is not related) has been formed in Heinrich
Barth's severe school, and this method, which favors artistic legitimacy and
inner musicality over virtuosity, has resulted in Rubinstein's wholesomeness.
The youngster's technique is already brilliant and apparently independent;
the most gratifying thing, however, is that his feeling for sound proved
equally natural. If the necessary human attributes are added to these predis-
positions, as the boy's modest mien allows one to suppose will be the case,

one may hope for the best for his future. The audience encouraged him with hearty manifestations of approbation." In the *Vossische Zeitung,* "W. B." (probably the piano teacher and critic Wilhelm Blanck) wrote: "It was a delight to listen to the little pianist with the big name, the thirteen-year-old Arthur Rubinstein, who gave a concert on Saturday with the Philharmonic Orchestra in the Beethovensaal. The fear that the G Minor Concerto of Saint-Saëns would overwhelm the strength of the handsome little fellow, who gave the audience such an unaffectedly friendly glance, vanished with the very first bars. The listeners' joy and pleasure grew from movement to movement, from piece to piece. May this boy also take care to balance his musical intelligence with his talent for technical mastery, which he possesses in rare abundance; nevertheless, the flawless combination of these artistic strengths is to be considered a result of first-rate teaching. Nowhere were the proportions upset. Everything is so natural, so self-evident, and grows so entirely from within the work itself that it seems it could not go any other way at all. The youngster's wonderful talent revealed itself at its deepest and purest in the rendition of Mozart's Concerto in A Major. He who can play Mozart so successfully is a chosen one among the elect." Rubinstein remembered the last sentence of this review until the end of his life.

Three years of exacting work under Barth's severe guidance had born fruit for Arthur, but success, instead of making him want to continue his step-by-step musical development, made him eager to move on to new triumphs. His reaction was normal for someone his age, but it led to a gradual decline in his relations with Barth. One of the main causes of his dissatisfaction was the repertoire that Barth wanted him to study: not enough Bach and Chopin, too many of what Rubinstein considered the weaker of Beethoven's works—among which he included the Sonata in E Minor, Op. 90—too many outmoded virtuoso pieces by the likes of Henselt, "lots of the minor Mendelssohns, Schumanns, Schuberts, and never the real great works by these masters."[65] In an interview given when he was eighty-nine, Rubinstein also claimed that Barth had not wanted him to study Brahms's First Piano Concerto, and that Joachim had overridden the teacher's opposition.[66] Unfortunately, Barth's views on these and other subjects of contention are not known, but it is clear that Arthur's practicing began to deteriorate when he was about fourteen years old. He would mechanically play through one-handed exercises and use his free hand to feed himself chocolates or cherries, while he read a book that he had propped up on the music stand. "The result was disastrous, of course, and I was always having to make feverish last-minute preparations for my lessons."[67]

For a while, however, the boy's life seemed to proceed unchanged. Shortly after the big concert, Barth found a new home for Arthur in the apart-

ment of Herr B. Kurt and his wife; during at least part of the time that Arthur was living in Berlin a flutist named Kurth (in those days, *t* and *th* were
virtually interchangeable in German names), who held the title of Kammer-
musiker—musician to the Imperial Chamber—lived at Neue Winterfeldtstrasse 42. The imperial musical connection would explain how Barth knew
the Kurths. Barth gives their address as Kleiststrasse 7, but the Kurts could
have moved at some point during Arthur's stay in the city. The streets are near
each other in the pleasant part of town close to the Tiergarten, and they were
within easy walking distance of the homes of some of Arthur's teachers, including Barth himself. It is known that the name Winter, which Rubinstein,
in his memoirs, gave his landlords, was false (it may have been taken from the
name of their street, the Winterfeldtstrasse), but it is not certain that Kurt was
the correct one: he may have changed homes more than once during his
Berlin years. Whatever the correct name may have been, the woman whom
he called Mrs. Winter, and who shall hereafter be referred to as Mrs. Kurt,
"was in her middle thirties, the husband considerably older,"[68] Rubinstein
said in his memoirs; he also said, however, that they had no children,
whereas he told people close to him in later years that there had been a young
son. He remembered that the household atmosphere was peaceful and con-
ducive to study, and as the Berlin concert had led to invitations to perform
elsewhere, there was fresh incentive for him to practice.

According to the minutes of the Hamburg Philharmonic Society's
meeting of January 3, 1901, "For the 10th concert the 14-year-old Arthur
Rubinstein, pupil of Prof Heinr Barth has been invited." He played a Mozart
piano concerto—probably the A Major—and some solo pieces; the conductor, Richard Barth (no relation to Heinrich), a former Joachim pupil, was
well known as a violinist, conductor, composer, teacher, and, later, author of
a biography of Brahms. The minutes of the Philharmonic Society's meeting
of January 19 state, "The child prodigy Arthur Rubinstein was paid an hono-
rarium of 250 marks for his participation in the 10th concert."[69]

A few days later, Arthur performed for the Dowager Grand Duchess
Marie of Mecklenburg-Schwerin, at her palace in Schwerin; the invitation
was sent in care of—and probably also solicited by—Emma Brandes Engelmann, whose patroness the grand duchess had once been. Rubinstein's
memoirs contain a charming account of this first of his many forays into the
world of old-fashioned aristocratic protocol: the court carriage waiting at the
station to take him to his hotel—"a most antiquated hostelry without any
modern comfort"; his frenzied attempts to get ready on time; his embarrassment at not owning a full dress suit with white tie ("I was still wearing short
trousers"); his slightly late arrival at the palace; the rigid formality of the concert, which took place in the ballroom; and his growing feeling of ease at a

dinner in the duchess's apartments. In later years, Rubinstein loved to astonish people by his encyclopedic knowledge of Europe's royal families. "One does not often meet a walking Almanach de Gotha," the pianist Ivor Newton reported, in the 1960s, "but I have heard Rubinstein closely cross-examined on the complicated relationships of Hohenzollerns, Romanoffs and Habsburgs, the families of Hesse and Schleswig-Holstein, the innumerable descendants of Queen Victoria or of King Christian IX of Denmark, and never hesitate for the correct reply. 'How, in your busy life,' I asked, 'did you find time to learn all this?' 'As a boy I played at all their courts,' he said, 'and was patted on the head by most of the kings and queens of Europe.' "[70]

Arthur was invited to return to Schwerin a few days after his first appearance there, to play Chopin's Fantasia on Polish Airs in a concert with orchestra in honor of the grand duchess's birthday. The court's intimidating presence at the single rehearsal was the cause of a poor performance at the concert. "Fortunately, our audience was not musical enough to know the difference, and they applauded politely when they saw the royal persons doing so," said Rubinstein.[71] He had mastered a basic rule of the art of performing: When things don't go well, keep up a good front. The Grand Duchess was evidently impressed, because Arthur was invited shortly thereafter to play Mozart's Concerto in B-flat Major, K. 595, with Dresden's Mozart Society Orchestra under the baton of Aloys Schmitt, who had long been chief conductor at the Mecklenburg-Schwerin Court Opera; his former patroness must have told him about the young pianist. The concert took place early in the spring of 1901, as part of an important Mozart Festival, during which Schmitt conducted the first performance of his own edition of Mozart's incomplete C Minor Mass, K. 427; the edition was widely used in subsequent decades. Schmitt was seventy-four in 1901—thus, the fourteen-year-old Rubinstein was working with a musician born within Beethoven's and Schubert's lifetimes. Joachim had played in the festival the night before Arthur's concert and stayed on to hear his protégé's performance.

News of Arthur's successes in Germany reached Poland, and Albert Reichmann (or Rajchman)—one of the founders of the new Warsaw Philharmonic and administrative director of the city's recently inaugurated concert hall, the Filharmonja—invited him to be a soloist with the orchestra during its first season. (Rubinstein believed that his Warsaw debut had taken place in the spring of 1901, but the correct date is April 1, 1902. He probably had no important engagements during the intervening year.) "I was overjoyed by this offer, and Professor Barth gave his permission without difficulty, stressing only that I was to bring back to him the money I would earn."[72]

The Philharmonic's conductor, Emil Mlynarski, dominated Warsaw's musical life, although he was not yet thirty-two years old. Born in Kibarty, near Suwalki, in the extreme northeast corner of the Russian-ruled sector of Poland, Mlynarski had studied the violin with Leopold Auer and composition with Anatoly Liadov at the St. Petersburg Conservatory, and had become such a fine violinist that Auer—whose later pupils included Mischa Elman, Efrem Zimbalist, and Jascha Heifetz—had made him second violin in the Auer Quartet and concertmaster of the Imperial Music Society's orchestra. At the age of twenty-three, Mlynarski had become professor of violin at Odessa's principal music school, but he had returned to Poland in 1898 to assume the principal conductorship of the Warsaw Opera—a position he still held when the fifteen-year-old Rubinstein played with him for the first time. He had been the driving force behind the creation of the Warsaw Philharmonic, and for the following three decades he would continue to be a leader in Polish musical life. Off the podium, Mlynarski was so mild-mannered that he appeared to have a "soft character," Rubinstein said. "But the minute he walked up to his podium and took the baton in his hand, his whole attitude changed. Erect and quiet, he held his orchestra under complete control with a minimum of gestures, giving the soloist a wonderful feeling of security."[73] Then and later, Rubinstein expressed authentic respect for Mlynarski.

According to a preliminary article in the March 29, 1902, issue of *Echo*, a "musical, theatrical, and artistic" journal published in Warsaw by Reichmann, the first Warsaw concert of "the fifteen-year-old virtuoso" aroused "exceptional interest." The article included a photo of Arthur in a sailor suit and stressed the fact that the people responsible for the boy's education had avoided turning him into an itinerant child prodigy. "He has been strengthened by working seriously and systematically, and his uncommon talent has been developed in such a way that it is now impressive for its complete artistic maturity, which belies the pianist's youth. . . . With a highly developed technique, temperament, and an exceptionally beautiful tone that penetrates to the depths of the listener's soul . . . our compatriot can look forward to a wonderful future." The concert, in which Arthur played two solo pieces (Schumann's *Arabeske* and Brahms's Rhapsody in G Minor, Op. 79, No. 2) in addition to the Saint-Saëns G Minor Concerto, was enthusiastically received by the public, and the leading local critics—Henryk Opienski, Aleksander Polinski, J. Rozenzweig, and W. Miller—praised the young pianist's talent and choice of repertoire. The victory must have been particularly sweet to Arthur, who had not forgotten the shame of slinking away from the city and from the hated Professor Rozycki only five years earlier. And he was proud that his parents and the other members of his family who had come from Lodz for the event were able to witness his success.

Louis Grossman, the Warsaw agent for the Bechstein and Steinway piano companies, invited Arthur to play a few days later at a party in honor of

Edvard Grieg and Pietro Mascagni, who were in town to fulfill conducting engagements. The young pianist jumped at the chance to meet the fifty-nine-year-old composer of the A Minor Piano Concerto (although Rubinstein did not learn to love the work until many years later) and the thirty-nine-year-old composer of *Cavalleria rusticana*, the opera that had seduced audiences all over Europe a decade earlier. The reception probably took place at Grossman's home, which Stefan Spiess, the music-loving son of a wealthy Warsaw chemical manufacturer, described as one of the centers of the city's musical life.

On April 10 or thereabouts, Arthur joined other musicians in a concert held at the Filharmonja to raise money for a Jewish hospital; his portion of the program was a performance of Schubert's "Wanderer" Fantasy. "When I returned to the artists' room I found a young man waiting for me," he recalled. "He had a pale, expressive face, delicate nose, and longish hair that was artificially curled; and he was dressed in a way which suggested the fashion of Chopin's day. I noticed his beautiful hands with fine, long fingers when he grabbed both my hands and showered me with the most flattering compliments."[74] The young man, to whom Rubinstein, throughout his memoirs, gave the false name of Frederic Harman, was Juliusz Edward Wertheim, a promising composer, pianist, and conductor, and the scion of an *haute bourgeoise* family—Jewish in origin but converted to Catholicism—that kept a musical salon even more important than that of Louis Grossman. In 1893, at the age of twelve or thirteen (he was born on September 24, 1880), Juliusz had begun to take piano lessons from Rudolf Strobl, who had previously taught Paderewski, Sliwinski, and Rozycki. The boy had talent, and his parents sent him to Berlin to study composition with Heinrich Urban and piano with the popular pianist-composer Moritz Moszkowski, as well as with Heinrich Barth himself. Shortly before Rubinstein's arrival in Berlin, Wertheim had returned to Warsaw to study composition with Zygmunt Noskowski at the Music Institute. He received the institute's gold medal when he graduated, in 1901; by the time Arthur met him, the following year, he had begun to give piano recitals and lessons, and to Frenchify Juliusz to Jules.

Arthur's first contact with the Wertheims was limited to a brief visit to their beautiful home on the morning after the benefit concert. He listened to Jules play—with "a lovely tone"—on the two fine grand pianos in the "vast salon,"[75] and he met Jules's attractive sister, Joanna (the "Basia" of Rubinstein's memoirs), who was about eighteen. But he was on edge the whole time, he recalled, as if some profound instinct were warning him of something, and he felt both sorry and relieved to have to dash off for a luncheon engagement with his parents and other relatives.

The next day, he left for Lodz, where his family had organized a recital

for him. The Sala Vogla was full for the event; many of those present were
Arthur's near or distant relatives or family friends, and they were understandably enthusiastic. "Afterward, the whole family had supper at home, and we
drank tea and ate fruit until very late hours," he recalled.[76] He returned to
Berlin, warmed by memories of family reunions and of his first professional
successes in his native country, but Barth soon lowered the temperature.
Izaak Rubinstein had instructed his son to tell the professor that the profits
realized from the Lodz recital would be forwarded to Barth as soon as Izaak
had paid the expenses. (Arthur had given his Warsaw fee, like the fees from
his concerts in Germany, directly to Barth, who was in charge of his pupil's
finances.) After having waited about three weeks, Rubinstein recalled, Barth,
who did not understand how easily the boy's pride was offended, exploded in
anger and implied that Rubinstein *père* was trying to cheat him. "This was
too much for me," Rubinstein *fils* recalled. "I picked up my music and ran
for the door, screaming. 'You can't insult my father . . . you'll never see me
again . . . I am leaving for Lodz!' And I dashed home, crying on the way. . . .
I immediately started a letter to my father, telling him the whole story, and
asking him how I might come home. At that, the front door rang, and the
Professor was shown in, breathless after climbing three floors. He shouted at
me: 'I want you to repeat to your father every word I have said. Don't hold
anything back from him.' I said, calmly, 'I have already done exactly that and
shall wait for his instructions.' "[77]

Izaak's answer was reasonable enough: he had had to wait for the accounts of the various expenses; he was sending the money immediately, and
he asked Arthur to apologize to Barth for his not having written to inform him
of the delay. Barth, abashed, apologized to Arthur and, through him, to his
father, but Arthur, in his adolescent pride, failed to understand the difference
between an accusation made in anger—which is all that Barth had been
guilty of—and an intentional insult. "I was stunned, and deeply hurt. I felt
that my father had let me down when I needed him for the first time in my
life! . . . The day I received my father's letter was one of the crucial turning
points in my life. I felt alone, thoroughly alone. After some time of brooding,
I came to the conclusion that I still loved my parents and my family but that
the moral and physical chain which linked me to them was broken forever."[78] Alina Rubinstein speculated that the essence of the problem was her
father's feeling "that he couldn't look up to his father to be the strong guy—
that he was left to do, himself, what had to be done." Previously, he had admired his father as "a patrician who sat in a corner and read the Talmud and
didn't care about what was going on around him," Dr. Rubinstein said, but
the clash with Barth changed his attitude. "It must have been hard to have
been so talented and precocious and to have a father who went out of busi-

ness—and maybe my father felt ashamed of his father. I think he was very ashamed and guilt-ridden about his need to appear to be much stronger than he really was, and to appear to have a much stronger family than he really had."[79] Barth's being an "unavowed anti-Semite"[80] (the description is Arthur Rubinstein's) probably increased the boy's shame over what he saw as grovelling behavior on his father's part. The incident affected Arthur deeply. "In these hard days of decisions, I made up a motto for myself: 'Nie dam sie.' The Polish is not easy to translate . . . but it means vaguely: 'I shall never submit.' I have stuck to this motto all through my life."[81]

But there were consolations. That year, Arthur spent his summer vacation as the guest of his friends, the Salomons, at a villa on a lake in Pomerania, near the town of Lychen, fifty miles north of Berlin; he took walks and went rowing, and gradually came to feel healthy and rested. And, shortly after he had returned to the city, he seduced his landlady.

For some time, Arthur had noticed that he felt jealous of Mr. Kurt when the landlord and his wife indulged in innocently affectionate gestures or kisses. Mrs. Kurt was about twenty years older than Arthur, who was still fifteen, but she had a "pretty figure, good features, and kind, smiling eyes," he said. "In fact, she was really quite attractive."[82] According to his version— the only known one—of the story, he "devised a Machiavellian plan" for getting what he wanted: He told Mrs. Kurt that he could no longer bear to live in her home, but he refused to tell her why, and he made her promise not to mention the matter either to her husband or to Barth. Just as Arthur had intended, his mysteriousness piqued her curiosity. After several days of insistent questioning from her, he calculated that "the right moment had come. 'Well, you see,' I finally stuttered out, 'I feel about you in a way I shouldn't . . . and I cannot take it any longer, living so close to you.' A long, stunned silence. And then, in an artificially light tone, she said, 'This is sheer nonsense, my dear. You will get over it in no time—you really don't have to leave us for such a silly thing!' But I knew—I had won. That same night she came down the dark corridor leading to my room, dressed in a flimsy dressing gown, to wish me a good night's rest. I put my hand shyly on her round, solid breasts, and she let me. Then we kissed. Thus began my first real love affair."[83] Rubinstein later told friends that his first experience of sexual intercourse, that evening, had had a tragicomic aftermath, as a result of his abysmal ignorance of female physiology: Mrs. Kurt was menstruating, and when Arthur saw blood on the bed, he thought that he had mortally wounded her. He was terrified—and one can imagine his partner's amused reaction when she learned why. (He had intended to include the story in his memoirs, but while he was writing them he received, to his surprise, a friendly letter from the Kurts' son, whom he had not seen in nearly seventy years. Rubinstein did not want to offend him—and this probably also explains why he gave the Kurts a pseudonym and said that they were childless.)

His "first real love affair" was no tempestuous passion. It was, rather, an outlet for his sexual needs and a source of emotional comfort—of affection from a woman old enough to be his mother. "I had won," he said, and he probably did think of the affair more as a tournament than as the expression of profound feelings of love. It prepared him, too, for other such tournaments, since Mrs. Kurt must have taught him things about male-female relations in general and about sex in particular that eventually proved useful in his dealings with the approximately three dozen women whom he mentioned, in his memoirs, as bedmates, and with many others whom he chose not to mention. Fortunately for the psyches of both parties, Mrs. Kurt seems to have been using him just as he was using her. She probably lacked diversion and physical fulfillment, and to find both in the arms of a sexually greedy youngster who seemed destined for fame and fortune must have lent additional excitement to the adventure. That the youngster in question happened to be living in her apartment facilitated matters: there was no need for elaborate lies to explain absences from home or for arranging complicated trysts in hotel rooms or in the homes of friends. And Mrs. Kurt seems to have been the sort of person who could enjoy whatever sweetness life offered without compulsively prefiguring regrets. "No wonder [she] was constantly in my room,"[84] remarked the eighty-five-year-old Rubinstein, still delighted with the good luck he had had seven decades earlier.

Practicing in bed—an exhilarating novelty—was much more attractive than practicing the piano. Together with the decline in Arthur's relations with Barth, the long bouts of sexual activity sped up the quantitative and qualitative decline in his keyboard work. Barth was probably too unselfcritical to understand that he bore a share of the blame, but he was sharp enough to suspect that something else was amiss and he felt responsible for his pupil's well-being. In great embarrassment, the gruff bachelor went to see the boy's pretty landlady and told her that he believed Arthur was indulging in excessive masturbation. Barth's suspicions had led him in the right general direction, but he had taken a wrong turn at the last corner. Later, the lovers had a good laugh at Herr Professor's expense.

The first significant result of Arthur's pianistic decline was that he did not do his best at an important recital that had been arranged for him at the Beethoven-Saal on February 12, 1903, under the auspices of the Wolff agency. By his own later admission, the young pianist had "too little understanding" of the second movement of Beethoven's Sonata in E Minor, Op. 90, with which the program opened. Then came Brahms—the Capriccio in B Minor, Op. 76, No. 2, the Intermezzo in B-flat Minor, Op. 117, No. 2, and the terrifyingly difficult second series of Variations on a Theme of Paganini, Op. 35, which Arthur played "in a much too fast tempo," he recalled. "I was nervous and discouraged by then, and hit many wrong notes." As to Schumann's *Davidsbündlertänze*, which followed the Brahms pieces, "Barth had prodded me to exasperation about this or that unimportant detail, and succeeded in extinguishing my last spark of enthusiasm." Rubinstein did not say how he played his Chopin pieces—the Mazurkas in G Major, Op. 50, No. 1, and F Minor, Op. 63, No. 2, and the Nocturne in G Major, Op. 37, No. 2—but the final piece on the program, Liszt's Twelfth Hungarian Rhapsody, "didn't go well, either. I knew the concert was a failure. There was applause but it came mainly from my many friends in the hall, and later, in the artists' room, their words of praise sounded like condolences."[85] He was happy that Joachim had not been present.

The remarks of critic "W. B.," in the *Vossische Zeitung*, correspond to some of Rubinstein's recollections of the event. "Two years have passed since the little pianist *Arthur Rubinstein* first appeared in public and awakened the belief that he had the musical talent associated with his name. . . . At that time, what took one by surprise was his childish, natural joy in playing that had been prepared through painstaking training, and that was so extraordinarily pleasant in the 13-year-old boy. At his piano recital in the Beethovensaal on Thursday, his precocious early ripeness astonished to a similar degree only in the last piece on the program, Liszt's 12th Rhapsody. . . . It is possible that the program was not propitiously chosen for him. The naive [i.e., pre-Romantic] composers were entirely lacking. Instead, the brooding Brahms and the sentimental Schumann and Chopin were given considerable space. This time, too, as two years ago, Arthur Rubinstein has given proof that his exceptional qualities have also been exceptionally well trained, that he is secure in his art. But the capable player's ideas as an artist have not yet enabled him to grow his spiritual wings. We hope that as a young man, which he is on the verge of becoming, he will come to look beyond craftsmanship toward higher goals." But Leopold Schmidt, in the *Berliner Tageblatt*, was altogether more positive and, we now know, more perceptive. "Perhaps he has been called to bring honor once again to the name of Rubinstein, for he is already a most astonishing little virtuoso. It is no wonder that his inner, spiritual development is not yet equal to his mechanical development, or that the delivery of a Beethoven sonata still lies beyond the range of his strength as a performer. What is remarkable, however, is his mastery of the difficulties of a piece like Brahms's Paganini Variations, of which he played the second volume, and it indicates a power as solid as it is early in ripening. The most delightful aspect, however, is the healthy, unaffected way in which he makes music, and which already attracted attention to him at the time of his first appearance. A painstaking education has set the boy on a good path; which rung on the ladder Arthur Rubinstein, whose modest demeanor is so charming, can reach will depend on his development as a man and on the artistic deepening that goes together with that development."

Barth told Arthur in no uncertain terms, "My boy, if you would only work, you could play all the others into the mud." And Rubinstein, in a rare moment of self-revelation in his memoirs, said: "This phrase struck me; it kept ringing in my ears for the rest of my life."[86] He would never be entirely free of the feeling of guilt—the feeling of never having worked sufficiently hard—that casts a pall over the lives of many musicians, and that was humorously underlined by the American pianist Gary Graffman when he gave his autobiography the title, *I Really Should Be Practicing*. There are musicians who regularly diminish their guilt by practicing in a disciplined way, and there are those, like Rubinstein, who irregularly diminish it by practicing only when they feel that they can procrastinate no longer. Among the latter, some pride themselves on how little they work, and even claim to work less than they do. "Practicing is nothing but a bad habit," Fritz Kreisler used to say, but his accompanists reported that although he did not practice the programs he was currently performing he would work carefully on forthcoming programs.

Guilt over not practicing enough was to serve as a constant, mild warning signal to Rubinstein throughout the remainder of his career, but the guilt stirred up by the next memorable episode in his life would be much stronger, although more sporadic—a terrible feeling that would hit him in the gut from time to time until the end of his life. According to his version of the story—which, again, is the only known one—his mother, who had abandoned him to a boarding-house fate when he was ten, suddenly wrote to say that she was coming to Berlin to look after him. She and his father had decided that he needed her care, and since Frania, the youngest of his sisters, was now out of the house (she had married one Leo Likiernik, whom Rubinstein later described as an inveterate gambler and poor provider), the proposition had become feasible. Money would be no problem, Felicja wrote, because the funds provided by Arthur's benefactors could easily be stretched to cover her expenses.

Arthur was horrified: he could not bear the idea of having his benefactors support his mother as well as himself. His benefactors, however, had presumably arranged for their respective banks to provide him with a fixed amount of money at regular intervals, through Barth; whether he used the money to pay for room and board with outsiders—a relatively expensive way of life—or for living in a modest apartment with his mother, who would cook for him and otherwise look after him, would probably have made no difference to the donors. There must have been other reasons for his complete rejection of his mother's plan. Alina Rubinstein suspected that her father "could not tolerate the idea, as he was just coming into adolescence, of living alone with his mother, both because being nurtured and taken care of would have humiliated him, making him feel childish when he was striving to become a man, and to be seen as one, and also because of the obvious Oedipal taboo/guilt that such an arrangement would have imposed. To have the benefactors support such an arrangement would clearly have been intolerable to him."[87] Besides, he almost certainly wanted to continue his exciting relationship with his surrogate mother, Mrs. Kurt. If his real mother came to town, he would have to move out of the Kurts' apartment, and his explorations of the brave new world of sex would end, at least temporarily. He did not mention this factor in his memoirs, nor, it seems, did he speak of it to the friends and family members whom he told, in later years, of his enduring feelings of guilt toward his mother. And yet, even if one allows for his mortification at the prospect of having his mother as well as himself live on the charity of his benefactors, how can one doubt that his sessions with Mrs. Kurt were what steeled his determination to prevent his mother from carrying out her plan?

At first, he sent lame epistolary excuses to Lodz, to dissuade Felicja from coming to Berlin. When they failed, he spoke to virtually all of his important Berlin acquaintances, from Joachim on down, and he was so vehement in opposing his mother's plan that he succeeded in organizing an anti-Felicja conspiracy. She arrived in Berlin in March 1903 (not 1902, as Rubinstein misremembered), toting enough baggage "for a stay of years," according to her son, and she settled into her sister and brother-in-law's apartment, which she intended to use as a base while she looked for a suitable place for Arthur and herself. Before long, however, she realized that Arthur was fiercely determined to make her leave, and that he had enlisted others in his cause. A series of harrowing mother-son discussions took place on park benches and in cafés in and near the Tiergarten: Felicja refused to visit Arthur at the Kurts' place where, she perhaps suspected, something was not quite aboveboard, and he did not have time, what with his studies and other activities, to visit her at the Meyers' place, which was in a different part of town. The encounters served only to deepen his resolve and her rancor. "She would beg, cry, scream at me with rage, but I was stubborn," said Rubinstein. "It did break my heart, though, seeing her in such a state."[88]

The stalemate was resolved by Joachim, the great deus ex machina of Rubinstein's early life, who told Arthur that he had mentioned him to Paderewski and that Paderewski had invited the youngster to play for him at his chalet in the Suisse Romande. Barth expressed misgivings about the venture, on the grounds that Arthur's recent work had not been satisfactory ("he was right," Rubinstein said, in retrospect),[89] but he had to cede to Joachim's will. Martin Levy would finance the trip, said Joachim, and Arthur would have to set out immediately, as Paderewski would be leaving home in a week or so. Thus, one evening in May, Arthur got on a train and abandoned his mother in Berlin, just as she had done to him 5½ years earlier—with the difference that he did not inform her that he was leaving. He stole away.

IGNACY JAN PADEREWSKI'S fame was even greater in his day than Rubinstein's a generation later. Like Rubinstein, he was born in the Russian-dominated sector of Poland (in 1860), but his provenance was Catholic and nationalistic. During his early years he distinguished himself more for his determination to become a pianist than for his keyboard accomplishments, but when, in 1883, Helena Modrzejewska, the world-famous Polish actress, heard and (more important) *saw* him play, in private, she immediately recognized his potential as a stage personality. "Paderewski's head, with its aureole of profuse golden hair and delicate, almost feminine features, looked like one of Botticelli's or Fra Angelico's angels, and he seemed so deeply wrapped up in his muse that this intensity was almost hypnotic," she said. "We had many chats and I advised him to appear in public. His poetic face, combined with his genius, was bound to produce brilliant results."[90] With Modrzejewska's financial assistance, Paderewski went to Vienna to study with Leschetizky, who helped him to solve some of his technical problems—although Paderewski was already far too old, in his mid-twenties, to learn to feel at ease at the keyboard. His professional debut, at Paris's Salle Erard in 1888, was a triumph for which he was unprepared, as he later reported: "It was a landslide of applause, a landslide of success if you like—and a catastrophe, the responsibility! . . . There followed immediately, in the wake of my debut, a great public demand for a second concert. And I had nothing! I had no other program."[91]

Within four years, however, Paderewski had conquered most of Europe and the United States, and from the turn of the century until his death, in 1941, his name was truly an international household word. Riond-Bosson, his chalet near Morges, in Canton Vaud, had been purchased in 1889 with the fruits of the pianist's first great successes. Ten years later, he moved in with his longtime mistress and new bride, Helena de Rosen Gorska, and his palsied, nineteen-year-old son, Alfred—the child of his first wife, who had died in childbirth. Not many months before Arthur's visit to Riond-Bosson, young Alfred Paderewski had died there.

The chalet and its grounds were run like the country estate of a monarch. When Paderewski was home, the entire household—family, guests, and staff—would assemble at noon in the great hall. "At one o'clock the Master descended the staircase smiling, and greeted each person present with a few apt enquiries about their health and activities," Fred Gaisberg said. "It resembled a small court. He then led the way to the dining-room where, seated at the head of the table, he saw that everyone was cared for."[92] Arthur, on arriving at Riond-Bosson, was immediately shown into the music room and told to wait. He was intimidated by the grandiosity of the surroundings and by the off-putting manner of Madame Paderewska and her ancient aunt, who passed through the room before the master entered. "I was really on the verge of running away, when—a miracle happened: the center door went wide open and there appeared the Sun—yes, the Sun," Rubinstein recalled. "It was Paderewski, the still young Paderewski in his middle forties, dressed in a white suit, white shirt, and a white lavallière tie; a shock of golden hair, a mustache of the same color, and a little bush of hair between his mouth and his chin gave him the look of a lion. But it was his smile and his charm which made him appear so incredibly sunny."[93]

Despite the natural warmth and kindness of Paderewski's welcome, Arthur made a mess of the second volume of Brahms's "Paganini" Variations when he played for his host. Paderewski sensed that his young colleague was ill at ease, and he invited him to stay at Riond-Bosson for the next few days. After supper that evening, Paderewski asked him to play for his other house guests and himself. "This time I was in the right mood," Rubinstein said. "After I had played with all my heart my favorite pieces by Brahms, two rhapsodies and an intermezzo, and an impromptu of Chopin, Paderewski jumped to his feet and embraced me, saying, 'I knew right away that you had great talent. I shall write Professor Joachim about this performance.' "[94]

Arthur passed several enchanted days at Riond-Bosson. He bowled in the garden and played billiards in the billiard room with his host, chatted with him at length, and observed him playing one-handed bridge after supper. Because Paderewski's piano technique was unnatural, he was a slave to the keyboard—the opposite of Rubinstein, whose natural keyboard ability was almost boundless, but who was often disinclined to refine what he could do reasonably well without much effort. Arthur heard his host practicing assiduously for hours and hours every day. On the last evening of the boy's stay, Paderewski played for him "for about two hours, showing me all sorts of pianistic difficulties, pointing out brilliant fingerings, tricky pedaling, and other interesting sidelights." Arthur was thrilled by certain details in his senior colleague's playing and by his tone, but he did not like his "exaggerated rubato and frequently broken chords," he said in his memoirs.[95] Some of Rubinstein's later, off-the-cuff observations about Paderewski's playing and its effect on the musical taste of his time were a good deal more cutting. "In Poland in my 20s they liked me very much, but they thought my Chopin was cold.

Why? Because Paderewski was the major exponent of Chopin and he was overly romantic. He was a great musician but not really gifted for the piano. He had an overwhelming personality—his greatest success was in bowing. He played Chopin in a very sentimental way. He used to break chords, for example. I fought that style because I knew that Chopin was better than that."[96]

When the time came for Arthur to say good-bye, Paderewski invited him to be his guest at Riond-Bosson during the summer holidays. The prospect of repeating so delightful an experience kept Arthur happy during most of the return trip, but as the train neared Berlin he began to worry about confronting his mother again. He was not prepared for the news that awaited him: Felicja had given up the fight and returned to Lodz. Thus he learned, all in a rush, that the realization of a desire is often accompanied by a strongly negative component. "Something broke in me," he remembered; "I felt suddenly so desperately sorry for my poor mother I was on the verge of begging her to come back."[97] But he did no such thing. His plan had worked, and the balance of guilt was now his.

NO SOONER HAD Felicja Rubinstein disappeared than Arthur had to decide how to deal with Paderewski's invitation, which had been reiterated in a letter from the celebrated pianist to Joachim. Paderewski's praise for Arthur must have pleased Barth, when he was informed of it, but the invitation alarmed him: he feared that his most promising pupil was about to be stolen from him, and that a globe-trotting celebrity performer would eventually take the credit for the hard work of a teacher who could only hope to achieve glory through his disciples. Martin Levy, ever concerned for Arthur's future, wrote to Paderewski on the boy's behalf and persuaded him to send Barth a diplomatically phrased request to release Arthur for the period in question. The request arrived, and Arthur's mentor-tormentor had no choice but to give his assent, however unwillingly.

That summer, Arthur spent three weeks with Levy and his family at a villa near Marburg and then returned to Riond-Bosson, where he discovered that he was not Paderewski's only house guest. His companions included the poet Alfred Nossig, a Zionist from Lvov who had written the libretto (in German) of Paderewski's opera, *Manru*, which had had its premiere in Dresden two years earlier; Nossig's wife, "a woman in her thirties, rather good-looking, a little too fat, with a sparkle in her eyes," according to Rubinstein[98] ("ogni donna mi fa palpitar" says Cherubino); and three concert agents—one French, one British, and one Russian-based Pole. Occasional visitors included the Polish pianist, composer, and teacher Zygmunt (Sigismond) Stojowski (a former Paderewski pupil, eighteen years Arthur's senior) and the

American piano manufacturer Charles Steinway. Paderewski was nervously preparing for a forthcoming tour of Russia—a country he hated almost as much as he hated Germany, where he rarely performed—and he had little time for his guests; Arthur was able to practice, but rarely to play for his host. Some unpleasant moments were caused by the overbearing Madame Paderewska, who would ostentatiously and condescendingly compliment him on his manners, as much as to say, "How remarkable in a child of Jewish merchants!" (Ninety years later, Daniel Barenboim commented, "I think that this story is very indicative of Rubinstein's thinking about being Jewish: 'I, too, can meet high society; I, too, can meet Queen This and Lady That.' He didn't articulate this to me, but it's the impression I got. He had an absolutely clear knowledge of his position in society—a real enjoyment, not just of the social graces but of the social one-upmanship, too."[99] Still, Arthur spent a largely enjoyable summer in the Suisse Romande and returned to Berlin feeling refreshed.

Barth was pleased that his most promising pupil had not taken lessons, as such, from Paderewski, and he began to treat him more humanely. It was a propitious moment in Barth's life: His cranky old stepmother had died; he and his sister had moved to a pleasant apartment in the Tauenzienstrasse; and his reputation as a pedagogue was at its zenith—which enabled him to earn twenty marks an hour for lessons. (By way of comparison, the top price for a concert ticket in those years was five marks.) But Barth inadvertently shocked Arthur by proposing to adopt him in order to facilitate the boy's career and by suggesting that the pupil follow in the master's footsteps by obtaining, in due course, a teaching post at Joachim's school. How an adoption would have helped is not clear, except inasmuch as it would probably have comprised conversion to Christianity and thus enabled Arthur to occupy positions and obtain forms of recognition that were not available to Jews. He was too intimidated to reply that all he really wanted was to be independent and to perform, and as neither possibility seemed to be on the verge of materializing he began to feel trapped. He was lucky enough to receive frequent invitations to the home of Max Friedlandler, the University of Berlin's leading musicologist and a pioneer in research on German folk songs and lieder; there Arthur played chamber music with such accomplished artists as the violinists Carl Flesch and Huberman and gave piano lessons to Mrs. Friedländer who, in her youth, had been a Leschetizky pupil. But despite these and other moments of respite, the peace of mind that he had achieved during his weeks at Marburg and Riond-Bosson quickly faded.

On the street one day, Arthur bumped into Jules Wertheim, who had come to town to organize a concert in which he would play and conduct his own compositions with the Berlin Philharmonic. Arthur and Jules agreed to get together the next day at Wertheim's pension; there, Jules's "intelligence and vitality, his interesting compositions so well played, the pleasure of speaking Polish with him, and the warm comfort of his room left the immature boy I still was entirely defenseless," said Rubinstein.[100] The statement is strangely ambiguous in itself, and it appears just before the revelation that Jules was homosexual. According to everyone who knew Rubinstein intimately in later years, however, the statement's ambiguity was entirely unintentional: although homosexual men were attracted to him at various times in his life, he is not known to have had sexual relationships with any of them. And his ambiguous statement was followed by the story of "a very attractive young woman, just divorced from a famous playwright"[101] and hotly pursuing Jules, who readily took up Jules's suggestion to let Arthur do for her what the object of her infatuation was unwilling to do. (She was "endowed with an uncommon flexibility of morals,"[102] Rubinstein recalled.) Arthur began to understand that the number of penetrable bedrooms in the world was virtually infinite; his interest in Mrs. Kurt began to wane, and once this process was under way, Berlin itself began to loosen its hold on him.

For the moment, however, he was caught up in Wertheim's plans. "I was helping him prepare for his concert and taking an active part in his life. With a large allowance from home, he could afford to have me often for meals at his place, or invite me to theaters and concerts, or take me to expensive restaurants."[103] This heady way of life proved to be habit-forming, and the habit was to be responsible for Arthur's frequent economic woes over the following three decades. Jules was a cosmopolite and a good conversationalist, and in these respects, too, he served as a model for Arthur. But the most important effect that Jules had on Arthur was to reveal to him "the real authentic Chopin," Rubinstein said. "I cannot stress enough the great debt I owe him for that. . . . He was not a great pianist, he was even handicapped by a lack of memory and some technical defects, but his Chopin sounded right because he possessed the true accent for this music. . . . I drew to a great extent my own inspiration for the Polish master from [Wertheim's] deep and intuitive understanding of his genius."[104]

Rubinstein's opinions of Wertheim's playing were much kinder than those of some other observers. In *Meister des Klaviers*, a book published in Berlin in 1919, Walter Niemann, a well-known composer and writer on music, said: "Jules Wertheim would like to be thought of as representing the modern Polish school. This Warsaw-born artist, a nephew of Tausig's, sweeps no one away by his élan or personality. Musically good and technically respectable—although neither polished to the highest degree nor endowed with real control—he is a player whose emotional temperature never rises above lukewarm. A certain rigidity and club-footed dragging, a bar-by-bar approach, clings to his playing. It would be more than advisable for him to do something about the extreme lack of internal development, of natural exposition of the bits and pieces of a work's structure, of the outlining contours and clarity, especially in the neglected inner voices. Indifference to spirit and sound, however, completes the picture of a way of playing that doesn't make the grade even by academic, by-the-book standards."[105] In the same year, on the other hand, a critic in the *Gazeta Warszawska* described Wertheim with words that closely correspond to Rubinstein's view: "To give back to Chopin the dignity of the great musician, worthy of standing beside . . . the greatest titans of music is the duty and the task that Wertheim has set himself and carried out, thanks to hard work governed by deep thought and no less deep feelings. . . . Nothing is done for effect, everything for art. This is not a [mere] pianist who speaks to us, but always the great human spirit that manifests its achievement through him."[106]

Wertheim's mother and the younger of his two sisters came to Berlin a few days before his concert; Arthur spent much time in their company, and so did Josef Hofmann, who was eleven years older than Arthur and who had been Anton Rubinstein's last private pupil. In the six years that had passed since they had first met—when Arthur had auditioned for Josef's father, Casimir—Hofmann had developed a reputation as one of the world's great piano virtuosos. Arthur was much impressed by his older colleague's phenomenal memory and left-hand technique, but what really kept Hofmann on his mind was the growing awareness that they both were fascinated by the delicate, dark-eyed, full-lipped, and exceedingly flirtatious Joanna (Joasia) Wertheim. Nor was Arthur immune to the charms of the mother, Aleksandra—"a tall brunette, vivacious of manner, with a touch of coquetry."[107]

Jules's concert took place at the Beethoven-Saal, under Hermann Wolff's auspices, on January 2, 1904. He conducted his symphony, *Per aspera ad astra*, played and conducted his fantasy for piano and orchestra, and accompanied the soprano Selma Nicklass-Kempner in some of his songs. According to Rubinstein, Wertheim's conducting was as insecure as his playing, his compositional style was too heavily influenced by Tchaikovsky, and his instrumentation was "heavy and gauche . . . but the specifically Polish, naïve freshness was his own."[108] Rubinstein described the event as moderately successful, but the review in the *Vossische Zeitung* could hardly have been more negative: the critic called Wertheim "pretentious" in his attempt to appear before the public. "Had he at least allowed his wee little song's melody to sing out, one could perhaps have said that a modest talent was under consideration. . . . But as Herr Wertheim also produced big orchestral works . . . it is necessary to advise him seriously to go back to his place at the school desk, in order to make him understand what a vast amount of technical preparation and spiritual maturity is required for the construction of large forms." Jules stayed on in Berlin, in the hope that his self-financed debut would lead to other engagements, but Joasia and Aleksandra returned to Warsaw. Their departure made Arthur feel that he was in love with Joasia, and he began to send her impassioned letters that she did not answer. At last—probably late in January—she wrote to her brother, asking him to invite Arthur to go quickly to Warsaw, to play at a large reception at their home. Her father would pay a decent fee plus travelling expenses, and Arthur could stay at their home. "All of this sounded like a typical business letter written by a secretary," Rubinstein recalled. "But there was a postscript! 'Namów Artura'—Persuade Arthur—and these two words were to change the course of my whole life."[109]

Arthur raced to Warsaw, only to discover that Joasia was having an affair with a painter twice her age. She further humiliated him by enlisting his help in bringing off her trysts, and he claimed, nearly seventy years later, that her "cold egoism was contagious. . . . nothing, in later years, had such an impact on my character. From the love-lorn 'Werther' I was when I arrived, I had turned into a cynical bad-boy."[110] But wasn't this love-lorn Werther embroiled, just then, in erotic affairs with at least two other women—Mrs. Kurt and the playwright's former wife—and possibly with Jules? Is it not conceivable that Joasia would have known from her brother about Arthur's affairs? If she did know, might she not have been insulted by Arthur's proclamations of undying love for her alone, and only too happy to pay him back in kind? So ingrained was the double standard in sexual behavior, in men of Rubinstein's generation, that none of these questions seems to have crossed his mind, either at the time the events took place or in subsequent decades. He considered himself the sole injured party, and he used the injury to excuse—to himself—all of his future misbehavior toward women. He would be an *homme à femmes* and a Don Juan—and this would be his right, he believed, because he had been maltreated by Joasia Wertheim.

Despite his disillusionment, he played at the Wertheims' dinner party and was much applauded. He also enjoyed the family's active, bohemian social life, around which much of Warsaw's musical culture revolved. Jules's paternal grandfather, also named Jules (Juliusz), had been an owner of the Warsaw Sugar Company, in partnership with Leopold Julian Kronenberg, who, with Reichmann and Mlynarski, was a cofounder of the Warsaw Philharmonic. Jules's father, the fifty-two-year-old Piotr (Pierre) Wertheim, whom Rubinstein called "Paul Harman," was a successful banker and the stepbrother of Karl Tausig, who had been Liszt's favorite pupil and a leading Wagner disciple. According to Stefan Spiess, Piotr was a well-known Warsaw eccentric. He was blind in one eye and very short—"grotesque looking," said Maria Kempinska, Jules's first cousin once removed, who, in 1991, still remembered the family as it had been during World War I.[111] Piotr was easily provoked to wrath, and he terrorized his family.

His wife, Aleksandra Klementyna, née Leo—Magdalena Harman, in Rubinstein's memoirs—was the daughter of Ferdinand Leo, editor of the *Gazeta Polska*, a leading newspaper, and a close friend of Henryk Sienkiewicz. Mrs. Wertheim had a fine voice and great artistic sensitivity, according to Spiess, and she even sang with the celebrated Battistini in a performance of Verdi's Requiem. Arthur sometimes accompanied her at impromptu musical soirées. (On one page of his autobiography Rubinstein said that she "had a pleasant voice and sang with the right feeling," but two pages later he said that "her voice was not very good and her performance amateurish."[112] He was consistent, however, in declaring that although her technique was faulty he was grateful to her for introducing him to the Polish, Russian, and French song repertoires and even to the rarely performed *Lieder eines fahrenden Gesellen* of Gustav Mahler, who was then, at forty-three, much better known as the conductor of the Vienna Court Opera than as a composer.) She was physically attractive, "witty if a bit hysterical"—the description is Spiess's— and inordinately proud of her son and two daughters. (Lily, nicknamed Lilka—the "Pola" of Rubinstein's memoirs—was older than Joasia and already married when Rubinstein became acquainted with the Wertheims.) "The members of the family, given to mutual admiration, melted in delight over each other, and financial independence favored their over-refined natures and unconventional behavior,"[113] Spiess said. According to Marian Fuks, a historian of Warsaw's Jewish community, nearly all the Wertheims "were somehow connected to music by strong and diverse ties," and Jules, in particular, "lived music in a permanent state of exaltation . . . which, for that matter, was not at all unusual at the Wertheims' home."[114]

At Jules's prompting, Arthur praised his friend's musical abilities to Piotr; his show of confidence in the son evidently impressed the previously skeptical father, for shortly after Arthur had returned to Berlin Piotr showed up there with plans to engage the Warsaw Philharmonic for a special, end-of-season concert that would be conducted by Jules. Arthur would be the soloist; he would stay with the Wertheims in Warsaw, then move with them to a villa that they had rented for the summer at Zakopane, a resort in the Tatra Mountains. Had the decision been entirely his to make, Arthur would have shouted yes, immediately; instead, however, he first had to obtain Barth's permission. He carefully prepared his rationalizations: If he could launch his Polish career in a big way, he would more easily be able to make a name for himself in Russia; he needed a substantial uplift after the downward spin that his career had entered following his unsuccessful Berlin recital, a year earlier; and he would spend the summer extending his repertoire. But Barth would have none of it. " 'Lazy as you are, living in luxury without any supervision would ruin your future completely,' " he said, according to Rubinstein—and there were times during the following decades when Barth's prediction almost came true. But the professor had the psychological finesse of a bulldozer. He argued his case by reiterating the hope that Arthur would eventually join the faculty of Joachim's school—a prospect that terrified the boy—and he threatened to tell Arthur's benefactors to withdraw their financial support, a remark that wounded his pupil's pride. Arthur, in one of the blind rages to which he was susceptible throughout his life, told Barth that he no longer wanted to be supported by anyone and did not want to live a dull and joyless life like Barth's; better to live blissfully for one week and then die. ("It was one of the worst and most cruel things I have ever done," said Rubinstein, in retrospect.) He spent the following days writing letters of thanks to his benefactors, saying farewell to Joachim ("who, as usual, showed a complete understanding")[115] and to his friends, most of whom seem to have disappeared from his life the moment he left Berlin. He and Mrs. Kurt wept together, he reported, but he did not say how he took leave of his other lady friend—the one who used him as a sexual proxy for Jules.

When all was ready, Arthur, Piotr, and Jules boarded a Warsaw-bound train. It was February 1904; Arthur Rubinstein had just turned seventeen, but his formal education had ended. Now he wanted to *live*.

3

High Life, Low Life

In *L'antagonista*, a novel published in 1976 by the Italian writer Carlo Cassola, the main character's childhood is suggested, rather than described, in a few introductory pages of impressions—a sort of prelude to the book—and his adulthood is summarized at the end, in what amounts to a postlude. The bulk of the story, which is a long one, takes place during the protagonist's adolescence, and Cassola gives the reader to understand that the patterns of thought and behavior that take shape during those years will become lines of demarcation within which the protagonist's adult life will inevitably unfold. After adolescence, the author seems to be saying, life is a matter of what one does with what one is—a set of variations on an already-stated theme.

L'antagonista's main character is destined to lead a "normal" life—an unobtrusive life—whereas the accomplishments and events that form the career of a celebrated performer are abnormal and exceptionally visible. But a celebrity's life, too, unfolds within limits established early on. Arthur Rubinstein, for instance, was already an odd mixture of a human being when he left Berlin for Warsaw early in February 1904, shortly after his seventeenth birthday: he was proud of his exceptional talent but not especially assiduous—and not at all systematic—in cultivating it; sure of his musicality but unsure of his ability to develop it without further coaching; determined to minimize contact with his parents but full of feelings of guilt toward them; delighted over his success with women twice his age but worried about his lack of success with a sophisticated girl of his own generation; accustomed to frequenting the *haute bourgeoisie* but ashamed of his lack of money. None of these problems defeated him, and some of them he eventually overcame, but their side effects remained part of him forever.

Rubinstein's performance of Jules Wertheim's Fantasy and Brahms's First Concerto with the Warsaw Philharmonic under Wertheim's baton—a somewhat unsteady baton, the pianist recalled—took place on February 13 and won him an invitation to give a solo recital at the conservatory shortly thereafter. He did not mention in his memoirs that on March 10, with the

Philharmonic under Mlynarski's direction, he played Chopin's Concerto in F Minor as well as a Liszt rhapsody and, as an encore, a Chopin étude.

The mastery and maintenance of such difficult repertoire requires considerable effort. Rubinstein may not have spent as much time at the keyboard as he ought to have done, but he probably worked harder than he let on in his book, if for no other reason—and there is no better one—than that he loved music, loved to play Brahms and Chopin and all the others. At the same time, however, life at the Wertheim home offered irresistible distractions: excitingly bohemian social life, fine and abundant food and drink, and frequent trips to the city's main theaters. He later recalled hearing the Italians Mattia Battistini, Gemma Bellincioni, Giuseppe Anselmi, and Enrico Caruso, and the Poles Jean and Edouard de Reszke, Marcella Sembrich, Salomea Kruszelnicka, and Janina Korolewicz-Waydowa at the Teatr Wielki—the main opera house—and seeing wonderful actors and singers in plays and operettas at other theaters.

One evening, Jules took Arthur to a supper at the home of his friends the Styczynski family, to introduce him to a brilliant young violinist who was a house guest there. Paul (also Pawel or Pol) Kochanski, only a few months younger than Rubinstein, was a native of Odessa, the city that later produced Nathan Milstein and David Oistrakh, too. Kochanski began to play the violin as a small child, and at the age of seven he entered the Odessa Conservatory, where Mlynarski was his teacher. Mlynarski left Odessa in 1898, but three years later, when he founded the Warsaw Philharmonic, he summoned the barely fourteen-year-old Kochanski to become the orchestra's concertmaster; he also took charge of the boy's upbringing and general education and "treated him like a son," as Rubinstein said. Mlynarski believed that Paul was destined to become a world-class soloist, and in 1903 he persuaded some wealthy Poles, including the Styczynskis, to sponsor the boy's studies with the celebrated Belgian violin pedagogue, César Thomson, at the Brussels Conservatory. After only four months in Thomson's class, the sixteen-year-old Kochanski won the conservatory's first prize and embarked on the life of an itinerant virtuoso. It was then, at the start of his career, that he and Rubinstein met.

The two boys shared not only their Eastern European Jewish background but also the fate of having been "practically uprooted from our own families and thrown into the hazardous artistic world a little too soon for our own good," as Rubinstein put it. At their first encounter the young pianist was fascinated by the young violinist's "square and strong" face, with its pointed chin and delicate nose, and especially by his eyes, which were "coal black, formed like oblique almonds, with a velvety deep expression which could be very moving, especially while he was playing." And play they did—immediately, before supper at the Styczynskis' that evening. They read through Beethoven's Sonata in C Minor "as if we had always played together," Rubinstein said. It was the first of many social and artistic get-togethers. "Our friendship fortified, embellished, and ennobled our lives," he recalled.[1]

Rubinstein's stay in Warsaw was further enlivened by sexual adventures. As had happened in Berlin, women who showed interest in Jules were often passed on to Arthur, who "would assault [them] with amorous declarations, and in a few instances, where I found a passionate temperament, the battle was won. . . . all I ever had on my mind was to get in touch with this or that lady—and I wanted them all."[2] Among his liaisons, the one that most surprised himself and others featured his hostess, Aleksandra Wertheim, as coprotagonist. Rubinstein would eventually claim that Jules had made him notice that his mother was in love with him and that he himself had merely taken advantage of the situation. One may legitimately surmise, however, that her "love" for him was pro forma. She must have been flattered, above all, by the attentions of a seventeen-year-old who was evidently one of Poland's up-and-coming musicians—as flattered as he was by the attentions of a beautiful, wealthy, prominent woman thirty years his senior who was known to lead what used to be called a fast life. Her age and the fact that she was his friend's mother made her suitable for the maternal role that he seemed to require his principal lovers to fill, in those years, and he may have wanted to have an affair with the mother in order to get back at her daughter Joanna, who had rejected him. He seems to have had a fundamentally healthy attitude toward sex: When it was good, it was good, no matter with whom. Besides, in this as in all his later erotic attachments, his deep conviction that he was ugly and that he had to prove to himself that he could overcome this obstacle by any means at his disposal played a large part. "I am not a good-looking man," he told an interviewer in 1962, "so naturally in the past the piano played an important part in convincing a woman I really cared. You must remember that to win a woman you do not need looks. All you need to do is convince her that you adore her above anything else in the world. I'll admit it's easier to say it with music. Don't you know the old saying, 'Mothers always dread piano teachers and husbands of sopranos always dread tenors'?" Thus he explained the fact that he had "always had the greatest luck with women."[3]

Had the Rubinstein-Wertheim story been published a few years earlier than it was, one might have suspected that Pier Paolo Pasolini made use of it in his 1968 film, *Teorema*, in which a young man eventually becomes the lover of all the members of a well-to-do family. Although it is unlikely that the ambiguity of Rubinstein's remark about his relationship with Jules was significant, the relationship was in any case a close one. He also said, in *My Young*

Years, that when Jules had told him that Aleksandra was probably in love with him, his mocking reply had been, "I bet one of these days you will tell me that your father is also in love with me!" He had already been in love with young Joasia Wertheim, although there is no information to indicate that they ever became lovers; now it was the turn of the mother—and hers was not the last. But the most remarkable aspect of Rubinstein's account of his affair with Aleksandra is his complaint that his parents did not intervene, force him to come home, and then make "a real effort to find the means to send me to some Leschetizky in Vienna, or to Busoni himself."[4] As he had intentionally excluded his parents from his life and had not even taken the trouble to visit them in nearby Lodz since his return to Warsaw, his protest brings to mind the example that is sometimes used (and that Rubinstein loved) to explain the Yiddish word *chutzpah*, which means brazen nerviness or cheek: A young man kills his parents, then asks the court for clemency on the grounds that he is an orphan. That's *chutzpah!*—and so was Rubinstein's complaint against *his* parents. He had not killed them, but he had sent them unmistakable signals that he wanted to have as little to do with them as possible. His sisters Jadzia and Hela found out about his Warsaw concerts, attended some of them, and reprimanded him for ignoring his family; they were mollified, he said, when they learned that he was a guest in the home of the rich and prominent Wertheims, and he claimed to have been more offended by their hypocrisy than by their initial show of anger. ("I saw as little as possible of them," he said.)[5] More likely, however, he feared that his family would discover what was really going on at the Wertheim home. And an ever-present undertone in his statements about members of his family indicates that he considered them unpresentable, by the Wertheims' standards. He was beginning to think of himself as an urbane young fellow, accustomed to frequenting the cream of cultivated, assimilated, upper-middle-class Jewish society in Berlin and Warsaw, whereas the Lodz Rubinsteins and Heimans were small-time merchants, provincial Yids. Such an attitude on the part of a seventeen-year-old is not surprising; more unsettling is the fact that the octogenarian who was writing the story down appeared to be defending the same point of view.

Joasia Wertheim and her older sister, Lily, resented Rubinstein's new position of power in their family, and they battled, verbally, with their mother. Jules, on the contrary, seems to have encouraged the affair, and Papa Wertheim, who spent much of his free time with a young ballerina, either didn't know about his wife's latest fling or, more likely, didn't much care about it. Gradually, Mrs. Wertheim's "constant attentions" began to make Rubinstein feel "acutely uncomfortable,"[6] he said. She wanted him in her bed all the time, and this he didn't like. He told his daughter Eva that "never, in his days of running around before he got married, did he ever *go to sleep* in the bed of the woman he was with, because he couldn't stand the idea that he might snore, or his hair might go awry, or he might make some rumbling noises, or look unkempt. He would just lie there with his eyes wide open until morning, because he had to be in control. This always struck me as terribly sad—to be so untrusting, so insecure with people. And once, many years later, when he had a hernia operation at the American Hospital in Paris, he didn't let my mother visit him for three or four days because he didn't want her to see him not in control or looking a little gray."[7] During his long summer holiday with the Wertheims at Zakopane, he avoided Aleksandra, when he so chose, by practicing the piano at night. In an early draft of his memoirs, he wrote, in fluent but occasionally awkward English:

> When everyone in the house was asleep, I used to go down to the drawing-room, there I would open the piano entirely, light two candles, place them on both sides of the music desk and start to work. The candles and the opened piano-lid in the dead of the night gave the room an air of solemnity and ghostliness; I felt at times the presence of the creators, whose works I was playing.
>
> Being now free from the pedantic tyranny of Prof. Barth, I wanted to absorb the whole piano literature at once, played every piece of music I loved, knowing it by heart after a few readings and giving it life and shape by intense intuition, but neglecting sadly the detail of technique and text. If a passage refused to yield promptly to my fingers, I would alter it to my convenience and my memory, refusing to look back at the score, would not halt at inaccuracies filtering into my performances.
>
> Thus, the silent and solemn nights of Zakopane laid the base of my future repertoire. I played much Bach and Beethoven, most of Chopin and Brahms, some Schumann and not too much Liszt, also a few modern Russian composers, Medtner, Scriabine, Liadov, yet not one of these works could I claim to play well, although my audiences were easily persuaded by my enthusiasm and my temperament.[8]

The repertoire list that Rubinstein presented to a concert agent a few months later demonstrates that, for a seventeen-year-old, he had memorized a great deal of music indeed: Beethoven's Third and Fourth Concertos, Thirty-two Variations in C Minor, and Sonatas Op. 28, 31 (Nos. 2 and 3), 53, 57, 90, 101, and 111; Mozart's Concertos K. 453 and 488 (oddly, the list does not include K. 595, which Rubinstein claimed to have played in Dresden in 1901); Chopin's two piano concertos, Second and Third Sonatas, F Minor Fantasy, Fantasy-Impromptu, Barcarolle, three impromptus, First and Third Scherzos, last three ballades, four polonaises, seventeen of the twenty-four preludes, all of the études (although many of them he never played in public), six mazurkas, and two waltzes; Brahms's two piano concertos, Sonata in F Minor, Two Rhapsodies (Op. 79), Variations in D Major, Handel Variations, "Paganini" Variations, five intermezzos, two ballades, and three capriccios; Schumann's Concerto, *Carnaval*, Symphonic Etudes, Fantasy, *Faschingsschwank aus Wien, Fantasiestücke, Davidsbündlertänze, Papillons*, two Nachtstücke, three Novelettes, and the Sonatas in G Minor and F-sharp Minor; the Saint-Saëns G Minor Concerto; Tchaikovsky's First Concerto and a *Song without Words*; Anton Rubinstein's Concerto in D Minor; three Scarlatti sonatas; four pieces by Bach (arranged by Liszt, Busoni, and Tausig); Liszt's Twelfth Hungarian Rhapsody, *Au bord d'une source, Leggerezza*, and Valse-Impromptu; Tausig's arrangement of a Strauss waltz; Giovanni Sgambati's Toccata; Grieg's Lyric Pieces and Ballades; Alexander Glazunov's Sonata in E Minor; Nikolai Medtner's Sonata in F Minor; and Paul Juon's Humoresque.

The list also included some works by Karol Szymanowski, a practically unknown, twenty-two-year-old composer who entered Rubinstein's life during that Zakopane summer of 1904. In the draft of his memoirs, Rubinstein wrote:

> While playing, one night, I was aware of being watched from the outside. Feeling uncomfortable, I went to the next room, and there, in the darkness, through the window, I saw a stranger standing under a tree, close to the drawing-room. He was wrapped in a cape of loden, with the hood attached to it covering his head and giving him a sinister look. Somewhat frightened, but proudly conscious of being the only man in the house (Jules did not count), I opened bruskly [sic] the window and shouted, with a slightly trembling voice: "What are you doing here, who are you, leave at once or I shall call the watchman! (there was none). A soft, singing voice replied: "My name is Gromadzki, I am a student and love music,—I hope I did not disturb your work." My frightened anger changed with relief into an exuberant cordiality: "Please come to-morrow at tea time and meet my friends—I am sure they will be delighted to know such a real musiclover."
>
> He would come with pleasure, he said, and bring some music composed by his schoolmate, to which I acquiesced with mixed feelings, disliking immature productions.
>
> The next day Bronislaw Gromadzki turned out to be a man in

the early twenties, shy and a little awkward, speaking jerkily and abruptly as if a hot potato were jumping in his mouth. He was a dreamer and moved us by his tender description of his wandering in the mountains and his warm affection for his composer-schoolfriend, and so I put reluctantly the music he brought on the piano desk and started to read it.

There were some etudes and preludes, a piano sonata, a violin sonata and songs by one *Karol Korwin Szymanowski*, pieces of true genius.

This, indeed, was music which stirred my deepest emotions; not since the revelation of Chopin did I experience anything like this. Who is this man? Where does he live? Where is he now? I must know him!

Gromadzki told us with a happy smile all he knew.[9]

Szymanowski came from a family of Polish landowners who had lived for generations at Tymoszowka, an estate near the largely Jewish-inhabited town of Elisavetgrad (renamed Kirovgrad under the Soviet regime) in the Ukraine. The family was musical: both of Karol's parents were competent amateur pianists, and his father also played the cello; his older brother, Feliks, eventually became a pianist and a composer of light music, and their younger sister Stanislawa became a professional soprano. Another sister was a poet, and yet another a painter. The Szymanowskis were closely related to the pianists Felix Blumenfeld, who later taught Vladimir Horowitz, and Heinrich Neuhaus, who still later taught Emil Gilels and Svyatoslav Richter. Karol began to compose at the age of ten, but he did not study composition systematically until he was eighteen, when he went to Warsaw. Contrary to Rubinstein's account, Szymanowski was not enrolled at the Warsaw Conservatory, but rather studied privately under Zygmunt Noskowski and Marek Zawirski, who were professors at the Conservatory.

Gromadzki, a medical student who later described himself as "mad about music, especially good music," and a good violinist, had been introduced to the Szymanowskis by an uncle who was vice president of the regional court that sat in Elisavetgrad. The Szymanowski home was "an isolated oasis of elevated and highly refined culture," Gromadzki said, and he had immediately become close to the whole family. Rubinstein recalled that after having played through all the music of Szymanowski that Gromadzki had brought to Zakopane,

> I wrote a long letter to Szymanowski, of which I do not remember a word, all I know, it had to be written. A few days later he arrived

in Zakopane. I saw descending from the train a young man, rather tall, slightly limping; he wore a bowler hat and dark overcoat. His face was pale, his mouth sensitive but somewhat feminine, he had a straight, good nose and finely shaped ears. The most remarkable about him [sic] were his eyes: they were very large, of a beautiful greyish blue, and there was a dreamy sadness in them, an infinite charm, which betrayed his true self, the rest of his appearance giving rather the impression (and he liked it) of an embassy attaché.

Szymanowski and Gromadzki were joined by another striking personality, Stanislaw Witkiewicz [known as Witkacy], son of a painter and art critic, himself a painter, writer, philosopher, musician, greatly influenced by Nietzsche and Strindberg, decadent, pessimistic and a bit mephistophelic [sic], gifted with a superior intelligence and a keen sense of humour. The four of us became inseparable. For the next two weeks we roamed the valley around Zakopane, drove along the silvery, clear Dunajec river, falling in a rapid, gay cascade from the mountains, under huge, majestic pines lining the roads, the air fresh and sweet as a kiss of a child.

We would start endless discussions on every subject, deciding finally on the future of mankind, we quar[r]elled bitterly about art, music, literature and felt intensely happy. In the evening, back in Zakopane, we used to settle at a piano and played whole acts from Wagner operas, Chopin and Brahms; Szymanowski played his latest songs, his violin sonata with Gromadzki, and music took us late into the night.

I saw nothing more of Jules, who became interested in a young, talented sculptor, a "góral" [mountain dweller] of exceptional beauty. Mrs. W. was bewildered by the change in my life without understanding the deeper meaning of it and the sisters continued in their hostile attitude towards me.[10]

In his published memoirs, Rubinstein said that Jules shared his enthusiasm for Szymanowski's music but was jealous of Rubinstein's growing friendship with their new acquaintance. Like Jules, Szymanowski was homosexual, although he was sometimes strongly attracted to women.

While Rubinstein was at Zakopane, a letter from Count Konstanty Skarzynski, a friend of the Wertheims who lived near Paris, surprised the household with the news that Skarzynski wanted to introduce Arthur to one Gabriel Astruc, who was organizing a concert agency in the French capital. The count and his wife, a retired opera singer, had heard and admired Rubinstein's playing in Warsaw and wanted to help him in his career. If the young man could make the trip to Paris, Skarzynski said, he would be welcome to stay with him and his wife while he auditioned for Astruc. Rubinstein was thrilled by the opportunity to broaden his professional horizons, and he wrote, in the draft of his memoirs:

> All during the time, after my break with Berlin, when asked by friends or family about my plans, I used to answer boastfully, but without any reason or hope, just for the hell of it: "Oh, next winter I am going to play in Paris[.]" And now this letter! I began to realize how desperately I tried to become free of the spell the family W. had thrown on me, how much I felt myself organically alien to Jules' conception of music, to the hothouse atmosphere of the W.'s home, to their self adulation, to their constant quarrels; how they had affected the weakest points of my character, pushing me into a life of luxury to which I had no right and, wors[t] of all, making me dislike myself intensely.
>
> The appearance of Karol in the shape of his behooded friend that night under the window, and this unexpected invitation to Paris gave my 15 [*sic*] years the blissful and romantic consciousness of protection by a guardian angel. I arranged hastily a concert in Zakopane [at the Morskie Oko Hotel] and, forcing with energy the tickets on friends and acquaintances, made enough money to be able to leave for France.[11]

Together, Rubinstein and Szymanowski made the slow, sixty-mile, overnight train trip from Zakopane to Cracow, and during the journey Rubinstein broke into a long fit of uncontrollable weeping—a result of the complications in his life, which were too great for a seventeen-year-old to deal with calmly. Szymanowski was discreetly solicitous, and Rubinstein said that their lifelong friendship really began that night. They parted in the morning, and twenty-four hours later Rubinstein arrived for the first time in what quickly became his favorite city in the world.

GABRIEL ASTRUC, BORN in 1864 into a family of Sephardic Jews, had worked in his mid-teens for his cousin and future father-in-law, the music publisher Wilhelm Enoch, who brought out the works of such important composers as César Franck, Emmanuel Chabrier, and André Messager. At seventeen, Astruc was taken on as a junior editor at the book publishing house of Paul Ollendorff, where he became acquainted with Guy de Maupassant and Octave Mirbeau. Four years later, he began a career as a journalist, first for *l'Evénement* and later for *Le Figaro, Liberté,* and the *Journal des Débats.*

Through Enoch he eventually returned to music and was the publisher, for a while, of Maurice Ravel and Georges Enesco, among others, as well as the founder-editor of the mass-circulation magazine *Musica*. He founded the Racing-Club and was one of the first people in France to fall in love with jazz and to engage professional African-American musicians in Paris.

At the age of forty, Astruc, who dreamt of creating a Parisian lyric theater that would outstrip the Opéra by presenting an up-to-date repertoire with the finest performers, took the first step by opening a concert agency. During the following eight years, he built up his credibility as an impresario through his "Grandes Saisons de Paris," and in so doing he gave the city nearly a thousand performances—operas and ballets, vocal and instrumental recitals, and chamber and symphonic concerts. He organized a series of Italian opera performances with Caruso and Melba in 1905, the first great season of Sergei Diaghilev's Ballets-Russes in 1909, an historic guest appearance by New York's Metropolitan Opera ensemble under Toscanini in 1910, the world première of the D'Annunzio-Debussy "mystery play" *Le Martyre de Saint-Sébastien* in 1911, and much, much more. These successes at last allowed Astruc to organize the construction of the Théâtre des Champs-Elysées, near the avenue of the same name. The theater opened in the spring of 1913, and its first three months of activity included the world premieres of Debussy's *Jeux* and Stravinsky's *The Rite of Spring*, which altered the course of music history. But such events did not appeal to the "people who counted" in Paris. Astruc ran up terrific debts; he was attacked by Action Française, a right-wing, anti-Semitic organization, and he was forced to relinquish the direction of the theater that he had created. Marcel Proust wrote to him: "I have read the letter that you sent to *Le Figaro* and in which you are too modest, for you leave out much about what you have done for art and about the monument that you have given Paris. The difficulties that your project has met with will give you a place in the history of the arts more surely than an immediate success would have done."[12] And Debussy told Astruc, in a letter: "You've inspired so much devotion in the past; it must be possible for you to go on doing so!"[13] But it was not possible. The débâcle was a terrific blow to Astruc; although he later helped his friend Proust to correct the proofs of *A la recherche du temps perdu* and wrote his own memoirs, he never completely recovered from his defeat at the Champs-Elysées. Maurice Martin du Gard said, in reviewing Astruc's memoirs, in 1929, that "we owe him unforgettable productions and concerts of unequalled excellence," and he described Astruc as "a great example of devotion to the interests of art."[14] Astruc died in 1938, at the age of seventy-four. But in September 1904, when Rubinstein first saw him, Astruc was just setting out on his career as an impresario. He had recently rented offices in the Pavillon de Hanovre (33 Boulevard des Italiens, at the corner of Rue Louis-le-Grand), and the only artist to have signed up with his fledgling Société Musicale was the twenty-five-year-old Wanda Landowska.

Rubinstein and Skarzynski set out from the count's residence in suburban Chaville to meet Astruc at the Pavillon; Astruc, after having exchanged a few brief, friendly words with them, asked the count to bring the young pianist to an audition at the Pleyel piano manufacturer's headquarters in Boulevard Rochechouart the following afternoon. There, Rubinstein's examiners were Ravel, who was only twenty-nine years old; Paul Dukas (now remembered as the composer of *The Sorcerer's Apprentice*, above all), who was ten years older; and the twenty-four-year-old violin virtuoso Jacques Thibaud, whom Rubinstein had heard and met in Berlin. Rubinstein sat down at the piano and played by heart the bits of the Bruch and Mendelssohn violin concertos that he felt Thibaud had played especially well on that occasion, and Ravel and Dukas got the message: This boy was not just a key-pusher, but rather a real musician of wide-ranging interests. He then played keyboard pieces by Bach, Beethoven, and Chopin; the examiners were "unanimous in their praise of my talent . . . and advised Monsieur Astruc in strong terms to take me in hand."[15] Rubinstein's account of the event must be correct, for Astruc brought Rubinstein and Skarzynski back to his office to discuss and draft a contract (dated September 22, 1904) that still exists in the pianist's archives. The contract's essential clauses are worth quoting:

> 1st—Starting with the signature of the present contract, Mr. Arthur Rubinstein places exclusively in the hands of the Société Musicale all his concerts and all his engagements both for France and for the five continents of the world.
>
> 2nd—For all the concerts it organizes the Société Musicale will pay Mr. Arthur Rubinstein's travel expenses, round trip to and from Paris, the publicity that concerns him, and the costs of moving instruments. For this category of concerts, both in France and abroad, Mr. Arthur Rubinstein will receive 40% (forty per cent) of the gross receipts after the deduction of authors' and poor people's royalties.
>
> 3rd—For all engagements for which the Société Musicale [merely] represents Mr. Arthur Rubinstein, the latter will receive 60% (sixty per cent) of the receipts offered by the organizing Societies. In this case, the Soc. Musicale will not be required to cover any expenses.
>
> 4th—For all private soirées, official or private meetings, the honoraria paid will be split half and half, 50% (fifty per cent) to Mr. Arthur Rubinstein and 50% (fifty per cent) to the Soc. Musicale.
>
> 5th—The Soc. Musicale guarantees Mr. Arthur Rubinstein a

minimum gross salary of 6,000 frs. (six thousand francs) per year, pay-
able at the rate of 500 frs. (five hundred francs) per month, starting on
November 30, 1904.

6th—Mr. Arthur Rubinstein undertakes never to negotiate
concerts or engagements without using the Soc. Musicale as inter-
mediary and without communicating to the latter all the proposi-
tions that are addressed to him directly or indirectly from France or
abroad.

7th—Mr. Arthur Rubinstein undertakes to play the instruments
that the Soc. Musicale will designate for his use; the Soc. Musicale,
on its side, undertakes to present only first-rate instruments.

8th—The Soc. Musicale does not have the right to make Mr.
Arthur Rubinstein play any specific piece; he will propose a certain
number of programs, among which the Soc. Musicale will have the
right to choose those which seem to it most suitable for the various
concerts to be organized.

9th—Mr. Arthur Rubinstein will pay the Soc. Musicale a for-
feiture of 50,000 frs. (fifty thousand francs) if he breaks any of the
above agreements.

10th—The present contract is to last five years, starting with the
date given below. It may be ended sooner if Mr. Arthur Rubinstein
becomes incapable of working.

11th—As Mr. Arthur Rubinstein is a minor, the present contract requires, after his signature, those of his father Mr. Isaak Rubinstein and his mother Mrs. Félicie Rubinstein, née Heymann. . . .

In his memoirs, Rubinstein said that Astruc's terms were exorbitant,
and that he had signed the contract because of the guaranteed monthly income ("these five hundred francs . . . shone like five hundred stars in heaven!").[16] But the terms were not bad at all. Today, concert artists charge
concert organizers a fee for their performances; the artists' managers take 20
percent of the fee and do not pay their clients' traveling expenses or provide
them with pianos. In those days, artists' managers often organized the engagements and ran the risk of losing money on them. Forty percent of the net take
was a standard fee for artists, and indeed a few years later, when Rubinstein
was thinking of signing what seemed to him a more favorable contract with
another manager, he was willing to accept the same percentage. Besides, Astruc was running the unusual additional risk of granting Rubinstein a
monthly salary—a sort of ongoing advance—on which the young man could
live decently, although not luxuriously, even if he proved to be a complete
failure. Debussy, whose opinions of most impresarios were uncomplimen-

tary, described Astruc as "infinitely more disinterested" than others of his acquaintance.[17]

At the bottom of the typed contract, Rubinstein wrote: "read and approved what is written above[.] This agreement will be replaced by a final agreement bearing my parents' guarantee. September 23, 1904 Arthur Rubinstein." After having spent a few days as the guest of the "agreeable and hospitable" Skarzynskis (whom he did not mention again in his memoirs), Rubinstein traveled to Poland—first to Warsaw, to stay with the Wertheims, who had returned from Zakopane, and then to Lodz, to his parents. He was worried that Izaak and Felicja might not approve of his plan, and his anxiety increased when "something unbearable happened: my father burst into tears, crying like a child. I had never seen him in such a state, and it made me feel like a criminal. And I try in vain to forget it," wrote the octogenarian Rubinstein.[18] He did not say, in the memoirs, what had provoked his father's emotional outburst, but he told Annabelle Whitestone that his father had wept because his pride was being undermined: he felt that he had always been impotent with respect to his gifted son. ("I always felt that Arthur felt terribly sorry for his parents—which of course was always connected to the guilt he felt towards them," Annabelle said.)[19] But Izaak signed the contract and persuaded the reluctant Felicja to do the same. Arthur, who now had virtually sole control over his own finances, returned to Warsaw, and from there he continued on to Paris in the company of Piotr and Joasia Wertheim; the father was taking the daughter to the French capital to study singing with Jean de Reszke.

Astruc lived with his wife and their five-year-old daughter, Lucienne, in Rue Cardinet, not far from the Arc de Triomphe, and he helped Rubinstein to find a room in a *pension de famille*, owned by a Monsieur Cordovinus, in the same street, at No. 42; Rubinstein's room—barely large enough to contain a small bed and an upright piano—cost seven francs a day, including complete board, thus nearly 60 percent of his guaranteed monthly income remained for other expenses. He was often invited to the Astrucs' for meals, and little Lucienne developed a crush on him. (Sixty-five years later, she wrote to remind him that she had been "among the first" people who "admired you passionately—and loved you.")[20]

The impresario quickly arranged a debut in the grandest style for his new artist: at the Nouveau-Théâtre, on December 19, Rubinstein would be the soloist with the celebrated Lamoureux Orchestra under the baton of its well-known conductor, Camille Chevillard. Mary Garden, the thirty-year-old Scottish soprano who, two years earlier, had performed the role of Mélisande at the world premiere of Debussy's *Pelléas et Mélisande*, would also participate in Rubinstein's concert, and the event's official patrons were to be Saint-

Saëns, whose Second Piano Concerto would be on the program, and Elisabeth de Caramon-Chimay, Countess Greffulhe, who was the arbiter of musical taste in Parisian high society and a model for Proust's duchess of Guermantes. ("At Parisian galas, the aristocratic silhouette of Countess Greffulhe reigns wherever it appears," Astruc wrote in his memoirs.)[21] The young artist was expected to pay homage to each of his patrons. He enjoyed his encounter with the sixty-nine-year-old Saint-Saëns—who, on learning that Rubinstein was a Pole, played him Chopin's E Major Scherzo ("a little too quickly for my taste, but technically perfect," Rubinstein recalled)[22]—but he was intimidated by the countess, whom he visited at the Château du Bois Boudran, her country estate. She "greeted me in a haughty manner, without a smile, introduced me to her companion, Don Roffredo Caetani, and asked me right away to play something. Her Pleyel was in bad shape and out of tune, but I somehow managed to rattle off the A flat Polonaise of Chopin."[23] The young, Rome-born Caetani, prince of Bassiano, was an accomplished composer—a pupil of Giovanni Sgambati, who, in turn, was a Liszt pupil. When Caetani mentioned that he was an ardent Wagnerite, Rubinstein returned to the piano and played the *Meistersinger* Prelude by heart; this so impressed the prince that the countess immediately promised Rubinstein that the Grandes Auditions de France, her association of music-supporting blue bloods, would turn out for his debut.

"When I announced the first concert of Arthur Rubinstein, in articles in which I had taken care to underline his first name, the public persisted in confusing him with the great [Anton] Rubinstein," Astruc said, in his memoirs. "The grandson of the illustrious tenor Tamburini, glory of the Italian theater, told me, 'I thought that Rubinstein was dead!' And [the impresario] Raoul Gunsbourg, who . . . knew no obstacle to success, coldly advised me to say that it was the Other One."[24] Rubinstein's name was the first matter that concerned *Le Figaro*'s chief music critic, Charles Joly, in an article about the young pianist that appeared five days before the concert.

> "A pianist called Rubinstein! It's impossible! He must change his name immediately!"
>
> This was the on-the-spot reaction of a very refined and shrewd person to whom I recently mentioned the arrival in Paris of a young virtuoso who bears this redoubtable name. . . .
>
> A meeting was immediately arranged, and a few days later, the young Rubinstein filled his listeners with admiration and astonishment for two hours, under the inspiration of his own imagination, or obeying the wishes of the people present, who wanted to test his technique, his memory, and above all his abilities as an in-

terpreter. The admiration was for the sureness and the majestic
simplicity of his art, which seems to know no technical difficulty
and in which the spirit of the masters is reflected as in a mirror; the
astonishment was for his truly prodigious level of culture, which allows him to play not only all the masters of the classical and modern piano literature, but also the symphonies of Haydn, Mozart,
Beethoven, Schumann, and Brahms, the symphonic poems of
Richard Strauss, and the lyric dramas of Wagner—all by heart and
always with the proper expression.

The privileged few who had the opportunity of listening to the
young Rubinstein received the same surprising impression. Edouard
Colonne [a famous conductor], Camille Chevillard, Paul Dukas, Ernest Van Dyck [a Belgian tenor], Gaston Salvayre [a composer and
critic], and a few others—all marveled as much at the extent of his
musical knowledge as at his masterly performance.

"What strikes me about this artist," said Monsieur Pierre Lalo,
Le Temps' highly distinguished critic, after having listened to him,
"is that despite his extreme youth, he is so accustomed to dealing
with all the technical problems that he is able to look beyond the
details of the work he is interpreting in order to give it a comprehensive performance. His view is large and so is his playing. He doesn't
lose himself in those details in which others take pleasure, because
the technical problems take care of themselves. This serenity allows
him to give himself wholly to the interpretation of the masters, and
this is why he is to be counted, right off, among the greatest."

This is the young artist—he is not yet eighteen years old—
whom Paris will hear for the first time on Monday evening. . . . He is
of medium height, slender and naturally elegant; his hair is characteristically abundant, and he is of a proud bearing that softens into a
charming timidity. Rubinstein's young face is a mask of the passions
that he interprets. His eyes, which are sometimes crossed by a flash of
disquiet, acknowledge the emotion that his fingers are translating.

Joly provided a brief biographical sketch of Rubinstein, then continued:
"during a recent interview, Rubinstein made a great impression on the witti-
est of music critics, namely Henry Gauthier-Villars: 'His art as an interpreter
is so great,' said the latter, after having heard the young artist play several
pieces by Brahms, 'that he even manages to give color to, and to make enjoyable, music that I consider extremely arid, and to which French musical life
has not yet accorded a position comparable to that of Beethoven and other
great masters.' And this is why Arthur Rubinstein won't change his name!"[25]

Rubinstein's memories of early-twentieth-century Parisian music critics were candid and sordid: The journalists were routinely bribed by artists' managers either to write complimentary reviews of their clients' work or to sign and publish reviews that the managers provided. But Joly's article, which was not a review, has a ring of authenticity to it. Gauthier-Villars, whom Joly quoted, was better known as Willy, one of his many noms de plume, and was one of Paris's great bohemian figures. When Rubinstein met him he was also the husband and literary collaborator of Colette, who, at the age of thirty-one had just published *Dialogues de bêtes*, the first of her independently written novels; Rubinstein got to know her, too.

His preparations for the debut concert were disrupted by Aleksandra Wertheim's arrival in Paris, ostensibly to be near Joasia—Piotr had had to return to Warsaw—but really to be near Arthur, whom she expected to accompany her everywhere and, of course, to spend a great deal of time in bed with her, at the Hôtel d'Iéna. He "enjoyed the food in the fine restaurants and, most of all, the theaters," he said, but he felt embarrassed "to be her eternal guest"—and the high living was "detrimental to my work."[26] The concert was sponsored by Etienne Gaveau, a well-known piano manufacturer, and this meant that Rubinstein had to play a Gaveau piano, which he found cold in tone, weak in the treble, and inferior in other ways to the Bechsteins to which he was accustomed. Two days before the concert, an announcement in *Le Figaro* mentioned that the program of Rubinstein's concert, "about which so much has been said in recent days," would include "the Concerto in F Minor by Chopin; the Rhapsody in B Minor [Op. 79, No. 1] by Brahms and the Etude in A Minor [Op. 25, No. 11] by Chopin," in addition to the Saint-Saëns Concerto, the pieces for orchestra without piano, and Miss Garden in Debussy's recently published *Ariettes oubliées*. "A few tickets are still available at Durand's [the music publisher] and at the Nouveau-Théâtre."[27]

Rubinstein was extremely nervous on the day of the concert, which was a mixed success. In the Chopin concerto, "my usually good and full piano tone was lost" as a result of the Gaveau's sound, he said; "the delicate filigree of the Larghetto was hardly audible, and in the third movement I actually stumbled once or twice," he recalled. Rubinstein also reported that Chevillard, the conductor, "couldn't understand the meaning of a rubato" and that "the unearthly beauty of the Larghetto escaped him altogether,"[28] but in an interview published before his memoirs he admitted that he himself had not yet learned the work adequately.[29] French audiences of the day were largely allergic to Brahms, and the B Minor Rhapsody (not an intermezzo, as Rubinstein mistakenly recalled) "was received with icy indifference." He said that he had not yet mastered the difficulties of Chopin's A Minor Etude (the so-called "Winter Wind") and that he had "banged out the heroic theme in the left hand with all my might, and smeared up, with the help of the pedal, the difficult passage work in the treble, and finished the piece in a brilliant flash! This provoked an ovation, even some 'Bravo' shouts from the gallery." (He admitted, to his shame, that during the next few decades he often resorted to similar ploys.) He ended the concert with the Saint-Saëns concerto; it "went very well," he said, "but I was again cruelly handicapped by the defects of the piano." The audience greeted the performance with enthusiasm, and even demanded an encore. Saint-Saëns, who did not like to go out in the evening, had attended Rubinstein's rehearsal earlier in the day and had complimented the young pianist on his playing of the piece; he later sent him a photograph of himself, inscribed "For A.R., with admiration for his great talent. C. S.-S."[30] After the concert, Astruc dragged Rubinstein to *Le Figaro*'s offices, to tell Charles Joly how he was to review the event. (The review is fulsome indeed, and not worth reprinting.) There, Rubinstein said, he ran into the playwright Henry Bernstein—already celebrated at the age of twenty-seven—who had come to dictate a review of his latest play. Rubinstein then rushed off for a late supper with Aleksandra and Joasia Werthcim; Aleksandra gave him a gold watch—"my first," he recalled[31]—as a memento of his Paris debut.

The three solo recitals that Astruc scheduled for Rubinstein took place at the Salle des Agriculteurs, a popular Paris auditorium in Rue d'Athènes, on January 17 and 26 and February 2, 1905. The first of them included Beethoven's "Waldstein" Sonata, Schumann's *Carnaval*, and a group of Chopin pieces, and was duly praised in *Le Figaro* by Alfred Delilia.[32] A shorter, unsigned review of the second recital mentioned that Rubinstein had "played Schumann's *Symphonic Etudes* and some works of Brahms admirably, but it was in his fiery and passionate interpretations of Chopin's Sonata [probably the 'Funeral March'], preludes, and etudes that he really showed his mettle. Arthur Rubinstein's last recital will take place on February 2nd at the auditorium in Rue d'Athènes, after which he will leave Paris for the South of France, where he has been invited for some brilliant engagements."[33] The final recital was not reviewed.

Astruc was satisfied, and he later recalled that "the success of my two stars"—Landowska and Rubinstein—"attracted proposals from every French and foreign musical center. The Wolff agency in Berlin and impresarios from Italy, England, and Monte Carlo were alarmed."[34] These proposals meant that Astruc was asked to manage ever more numerous and important musical events, but Rubinstein, according to his own testimony, gained no particular advantage from the situation: his first Paris appearances had not won him many invitations to play in public either in Paris or elsewhere. Astruc, however, seems to have been genuinely fond of his young client. Shortly after Rubinstein's eighteenth birthday, the impresario accompanied him to Nice, where Rubinstein gave a little recital before a tiny and inattentive audience at the Salon Rumpelmayer, a tearoom; this seems to have been the full extent of the "brilliant engagements in the South of France" to which Le Figaro had referred. Although the event cannot have covered Astruc's costs, he treated Rubinstein to a trip to nearby Monte Carlo, to attend the world premiere of Jules Massenet's opera Chérubin, on February 14, 1905. The production, with the beautiful, thirty-year-old soprano Lina Cavalieri and the tenor Charles Rousselière in the principal roles, was organized by the well-known impresario Raoul Gunsbourg. With Gunsbourg's connivance, Rubinstein, who was a minor, entered the gambling casino and bet the money that Astruc had given him for the occasion. He won a fair amount, he later claimed, but then lost it all when Colette, who was also visiting the casino, gave him a tip that didn't work. He held this against her for the rest of his life.[35]

On his return to Paris, Rubinstein was surprised to find that his sister Jadwiga had come to visit him and was occupying the room next to his in Monsieur Cordovinus's pension. He suspected that his family "assumed that my career was made" and wanted to partake of the economic bounty, thus he determinedly kept Jadwiga "away from my new friends and acquaintances."[36] But her visit was propitious: he came down with a severe case of scarlet fever, and she nursed him devotedly for three weeks. During his slow recovery, he developed abscesses in his ears and had to have them lanced; what he did not mention in his memoirs but did tell people close to him is that his hearing in his right ear remained permanently and considerably impaired. The Canadian pianist Janina Fialkowska, who knew Rubinstein well in his last years, believed that this explained "why he played so resoundingly, why he projected a multicolored sound so well, and why he developed his great, wonderful, unique sound," she said.[37] The piece of good fortune within the piece of bad fortune, Eva Rubinstein pointed out, is that the damage affected the ear that was directed toward the audience, rather than the one that was directed toward the orchestra in concerto performances.

Paris's musical life was not nearly as rich as Berlin's, in those days, according to Rubinstein, but in most other respects he found his new base much more congenial than the old one—probably too congenial. Frequent attendance at grand dinners given by wealthy acquaintances increased his taste for high living, but his modest monthly salary did not allow him to indulge the taste when he was not a guest. He was well aware of the "discrepancy between the daily struggle for survival and the frequent escapes into these most refined luxuries," he said, and he began "to live the excruciating life of someone constantly short of money, constantly in debt."[38] Paris was also a wonderful place for pursuing women. At a dinner party at Lina Cavalieri's home, for instance, he met a sexy young actress, and he took her to bed that night. He nearly seduced a "Mrs. Dettelbach"—probably a pseudonym—after having dared to kiss her bare back while they were sitting in her wealthy husband's darkened box at the Opéra, but logistical problems intervened. Similar occasions with other women arose from time to time. Although Rubinstein did not suggest, in his memoirs, that anything serious ever transpired between himself and Joasia Wertheim, whose lover was frequently with her in Paris, he often visited her at the apartment that she had rented in the fashionable Avenue Victor-Hugo and that she shared with two English girls who, like herself, were studying with Jean de Reszke: Olga Lynn, later a well-known voice teacher in London, and Margaret Tate, a sixteen-year-old who would soon become famous—under the slightly altered *nom d'art* of Maggie Teyte—as an interpreter of Debussy's vocal works, including the role of Mélisande. The three young ladies provided pleasant company, at least, and when Joasia—whom Maggie called Jane—suddenly needed extra money for which she couldn't ask her parents (Rubinstein implied, in his memoirs, that she had decided to have an abortion), he obtained an advance on his salary and gave it to her.

At Joasia Wertheim's one evening, Rubinstein met Jozef (Jozio) Jaroszynski, a wealthy young Polish landowner, music lover, amateur pianist, and bon vivant, who took a liking to the young musician and began to treat him to first-rate meals and concert and theater tickets. Astruc, too, was generous with Rubinstein: he continued to invite him often to dinner, and helped him to regain his strength following his bout with scarlet fever. In exchange, Rubinstein tricked him. He went off to Lodz, ostensibly to regain his health, but really to give two concerts that he had lined up secretly, to avoid having to pay Astruc his commission. During a stop in Warsaw, however, he sent his manager a friendly note:

> Dear Mr. Astruc!
> I am happier than I can say to be in Warsaw. They are now creating difficulties about passports here, but I think that I'll have mine in 3 days. My health is in a fine state, I am working a lot, and I am ready to give concerts. I think that I forgot to leave my address with you; here it is:
> > c/o Mr. Wertheim
> > Warsaw, 9 Aleja Ujazdowska 9 [*sic*].
>
> I shall have some magnificent engagements in Warsaw and Lodz next winter. How are you? And Mrs. Astruc?

When you absolutely need me, would you please be so good
as to telegraph me? I am so grateful to you for your permission!
A thousand grateful greetings from your
                                    Arthur Rubinstein
                                    Best regards to Mrs. Astruc.[39]

Rubinstein was having difficulty obtaining a passport because Polish
nationalists, taking advantage of the revolutionary situation that was developing within Russia that spring, were pushing for independence. On May 3,
1905—probably only a short time after he had written the above letter—
Rubinstein wired a desperate message to Astruc: "Danger of not being able to
leave[,] awaiting permission[,] suffering terribly[.] Telegraph some reassur-
ing words—Arthur."[40]

Eventually, however, he returned to Paris, where a radiant Astruc
greeted him with the news that an agent of William Knabe, a Baltimore-
based piano manufacturer, had invited the young pianist to make his first visit
to North America the following season, under his company's auspices. The
Knabe & Gaehle piano company had been established in Baltimore in 1837
by two German-born and -trained piano makers; after Gaehle's death, the
business had continued as Knabe & Co. Early in the twentieth century, the
firm's directors were William and Ernest Knabe, grandsons of the founder.
William had heard about Rubinstein from a Boston-based music critic who
had heard him play at Paderewski's villa two years earlier, and he was offering
Rubinstein a three-month, forty-concert tour. The pianist's transportation
would be paid by his sponsors, but he would cover his own living expenses
out of his total fee of four thousand dollars—of which sixteen hundred dollars
would go to Astruc. But twenty-four hundred dollars was a fair amount of
money in those days—the equivalent of two years of Rubinstein's monthly
salary from Astruc—and news of this major engagement brought Rubinstein's name back before the Parisian public. The twenty-year-old Sacha
Guitry, who was just beginning to make a name for himself as a playwright
and actor and was supplementing his income by drawing caricatures, made a
silhouette of Rubinstein that appeared in the papers; the original he sold to
Astruc, who, in the 1920s, described its "swelling torso, pointed nose, and
curly hair" and said that it resembled Rubinstein "almost as much today as
twenty years ago."[41] It disappeared during World War II.

In August 1905, Rubinstein went to the South of France as the guest of
Astruc and Gunsbourg at the Festival d'Orange, which Gunsbourg directed.
In the town's Roman amphitheater Rubinstein attended performances of
Boito's *Mefistofele*, Berlioz's *Les Troyens*, and the Comédie Française's pro-
ductions of Sophocles's *Oedipus Rex* and Corneille's *Le Cid*. The rarely per-

formed *Troyens* and the acting of the celebrated Mounet-Sully in the title role of *Oedipus* impressed him more than anything else. Although Cavalieri was the female lead in *Mefistofele*, the real star of the production was the thirty-two-year-old Russian basso Fyodor Chaliapin, who had already befriended Rubinstein in Paris. Since the pianist was one of the few people in Orange who spoke Russian, he and Chaliapin spent a great deal of time together, and Rubinstein lived what he later described as "the most riotous ten days of my life,"[42] taking to bed surplus women from the handsome singer's extensive entourage. From Orange, Rubinstein went to a resort in Switzerland, where he was to be the Wertheims' guest; Astruc accompanied him as far as Lyons and treated him to a night at "the finest bordello in town"[43] — Rubinstein's first visit to a prostitute, he said. The Wertheim party was staying at a hotel above Montreux, at Caux. Toward the end of their holiday, they regaled the hotel's other guests and visitors from nearby towns with a performance of Oscar Wilde's *Salome*, in a German translation and with musical accompaniment. The work was evidently in the air in 1905: Richard Strauss's new opera on the same text had its first performance in December.

During the fall, in Paris, Rubinstein met the thirty-three-year-old Alexander Scriabin—a composer he admired—but angered him by declaring that he loved the music of Brahms, which Scriabin detested. The Russian composer was in Paris to attend the world premiere, under Nikisch's direction, of his Third Symphony (the *Divine Poem* and not, as Rubinstein says in his memoirs, the *Poem of Ecstasy*, which was still unwritten); Rubinstein was present, and he later recalled that the piece "was received with boos and shouts of disgust . . . I saw Dukas, [the composer and critic Alfred] Bruneau, and Fauré climbing up on their seats and whistling into their latchkeys with gusto. But I, on the contrary, admit that I was impressed by the work, and some parts of it pleased me immensely."[44]

Among the people who had attended the Wertheim entourage's makeshift *Salome* performance in the Suisse Romande the previous summer were a Colonel Clayton, aide-de-camp of the Duke of Connaught, who was King Edward VII's brother, and the colonel's French wife, the Baroness de Fouquières. They evidently enjoyed Rubinstein's playing because they invited him to be their houseguest in London for a few days in November, to "play at a great reception they were giving in honor of the Duke and his daughter, Princess Patricia. I was to receive a fee and traveling expenses,"[45] Rubinstein said. This first trip to England, during which he was introduced to upper crust society, whetted his appetite for further visits. "Claytons leaving for Switzerland[,] I am returning [to Paris] tomorrow[.] Great success," he cabled Astruc on November 6, 1905.[46] Immediately after his return to Paris, he succumbed to an invitation from two prostitutes at the Folies-Bergère; as he did not have enough money to pay for their expert services, he left the valuable cufflinks that the Claytons had given him as collateral, but by the time he had collected enough money to redeem the cufflinks, the brothelkeeper had sold them.

ON DECEMBER 22, 1905, Astruc accompanied Rubinstein to the Gare Saint-Lazare, where the pianist boarded a train for Le Havre. There, the next morning, he embarked on the French steamship *La Touraine*, bound for New York. The crossing was exceptionally rough, and when, on New Year's Eve, Rubinstein gave a concert for those of the passengers who were not too seasick to emerge from their cabins, he had to be strapped to the piano stool—which, in turn, was hooked to the floor. He made friends with a pretty, middle-aged widow from Los Angeles and with a young French count, Armand de Gontaut-Biron, whose mission was to do discreet publicity among wealthy Americans for Panhard-Levassor, a French automobile company. The inexpert Rubinstein lost all the money he had brought along to other shipboard companions, who beat him at poker, and when Bernard Ulrich, the tour manager, met him at the dock on January 2, 1906, the pianist introduced himself by asking for a ten-dollar advance, so that he could tip the ship's staff.

Ulrich had reserved a four-dollar-a-night room for Rubinstein at the respectable Netherland Hotel, but Gontaut persuaded him to stay instead at the luxurious Waldorf-Astoria, which cost more than five times as much. "What enchanted me most was the bathroom, the first bathroom I had ever had all to myself," Rubinstein recalled.[47] He soon had his first encounters with American journalists, who, in those days, made their French counterparts look like paragons of accuracy and objectivity. One assumes that to the question, "Do you compose?" Rubinstein answered that he had written some music but nothing of consequence, and that he never performed any of his compositions. But the statement that appeared in the January 6, 1906, issue of *Musical America* said: " 'I shall use very few of my own compositions in my programmes.' " He was also quoted as having said that he and Paderewski, with whom he had spent " 'many summers,' " were " 'great friends,' " and that "in Warsaw . . . he lost a brother and two cousins through the Russian massacre. . . . 'I cannot forget the terrible scenes of those outrages. It depresses me constantly and my only relief seems to be my piano. I have improvised a sonata under the influence of this depression and perhaps I shall play it at one of my concerts.' "[48]

Rubinstein's debut in the Western Hemisphere was scheduled for Monday evening, January 8, 1906, at Carnegie Hall, with the Philadelphia Orchestra; he was not yet nineteen years old, Carnegie Hall was not yet fif-

teen years old, and the Philadelphia Orchestra had celebrated its fifth birthday only two months earlier. He had chosen the trusty Saint-Saëns G Minor
Concerto as his debut piece, but he was not delighted with the Knabe
pianos—or so he said many years later ("their tone was muffled, the action
was hard, and the bass was weak").[49] His worst fears had been allayed only by
the arrival of George Hochman, a capable technician who made the instrument that Rubinstein had selected sound better. But the letter that he wrote
(on Waldorf-Astoria stationery) to Astruc the day before his debut demonstrates that at the time he had not been dissatisfied with the Knabe pianos.

> Dear Mr. Astruc,
> It was completely impossible to write a word, each day I've had at
> least 15 interviews, 10 visits, and every evening dinner, the theater,
> supper, etc. Have you received my telegram? I am writing today to
> tell you that I have been introduced all around in a most extraordi-
> nary way. I am altogether famous here. Tomorrow is my first con-
> cert. I hope that you will be thinking of me, I want to play well, the
> pianos are good, the Steinway is of course better but not a great
> deal. I was with [Heinrich] Conried [General Manager of the Met-
> ropolitan Opera] who received me for *an entire hour* and he chatted
> with me very, very kindly, afterward he gave me a box for Tristan, I
> have also met Mrs. Vanderbilt and Astor, and Gould. Enough for
> today. I'll telegraph tomorrow, I am very nervous.
> So goodbye! Tomorrow!!!!
> Best greetings
>
>   Your
>   Arthur
>
> Give my regards to everyone. To Mrs. Astruc, to [Robert] Brussel
> [Astruc's secretary, later a music critic for *Le Figaro*], etc.[50]

(The *Tristan und Isolde* performance at the Metropolitan, to which Rubinstein referred, took place on January 5, with Alois Burgstaller and Lillian Nor-
dica in the title roles; Alfred Hertz conducted. In 1906, the descendants of the
nineteenth-century tycoons Cornelius Vanderbilt, John Jacob Astor, and Jay
Gould were among the wealthiest and most talked-about people in America.)
    Rubinstein met Fritz Scheel, who was to conduct his debut perfor-
mance, at their first and only joint rehearsal, on the morning of the concert
day. Rubinstein described Scheel, the Philadelphia Orchestra's German-
born founder, as "the typical German musician, well trained, solid, but cold
. . . efficient and indifferent."[51] And yet, that evening Rubinstein pleased his

audience in the concerto. The American pianist Arthur Loesser—not yet twelve years old at the time—was present, and he recalled many years later that "the impression produced by Rubinstein was indelible. He played the Saint-Saëns Concerto in g minor, and I had never heard it before. I was enchanted with the shapely tunes of the Scherzo, and can remember, when the pianist came to the last strain of the end of the third movement, with its extraordinary ascending triplet passage in alternating octaves and single notes, that father [the pianist Henry Loesser] poked me in the side to make sure that I was appreciating the extraordinary brilliance of the performance. The applause was vigorous and Rubinstein was recalled to take bows. He didn't let the audience wait too long, but sat down again to play, of all things, Liszt's *Mephisto Waltz!* Quite a strenuous encore, right on top of a major concerto." Rubinstein remembered the encore and told Loesser that " 'at the time I didn't know that encores were tabu in American symphonic programs. But when I came back-stage again Scheel, the conductor, was deeply offended. He wouldn't speak to me at all.' "[52] Rubinstein may not have known that Scheel's petulance toward him was part of a pattern of increasingly erratic behavior on the conductor's part; he had a mental breakdown not many months later, and he died only fourteen months after Rubinstein's debut concert.

The Knabe brothers and their wives were delighted with Rubinstein's playing and with the audience's enthusiasm, and they took him and Gontaut to a lively supper at Delmonico's restaurant after the concert. The critics, however, were less pleased than the Knabes. Richard Aldrich, for instance, wrote in the *New York Times* that Rubinstein's arrival "had been preceded by circumstantial stories of his past and present prowess. He was an infant prodigy but was preserved from the fate of infant prodigies and is now a mature artist, though he is still a youth. This young Rubinstein is undoubtedly a talented youth, but his talent at present seems to reside chiefly in his fingers. . . . [In the Saint-Saëns concerto] a mature artist can exhibit a certain weight and dignity and many of the finer graces of style. Mr. Rubinstein has scarcely arrived at these qualities. He is full of the exuberance and exaggeration of youth, and he is at present concerned chiefly with the exploitation of his dexterity and with impressing not only the ears but also the eyes of his hearers with his personality and the brilliancy of the effects he can produce. For this he is well equipped. He has a crisp and brilliant touch, remarkable facility and fleetness of technique—though this is not altogether flawless—and much strength of finger and arm. He knows how to make all these things count for the utmost; and his performance . . . was imposing, if there was no thought of any deeper significance that lay behind the notes. . . . There is little warmth of beauty in Rubinstein's tone and little variety in his effects. . . .

He was much applauded after the concerto, and played again, a piece of pure display, an arrangement . . . of Liszt's orchestral piece, *The Mephisto waltz*. . . ."⁵³

Richard Schickel, in his history of Carnegie Hall, suggested that Rubinstein's "austere virtuosity ran counter to the current of the time." The young man was, after all, a product of the antispectacular musical school of Brahms, Joachim, and Barth, and his natural approach to phrasing was considered "unpoetic" in comparison with the more freely Romantic virtuosos who had subjugated the American public. "Let the next five years bring him some genuine heartache," the silly and presumptuous reviewer for a music magazine wished for Rubinstein. "Let some American girl twist his heartstrings around her dainty little finger and then break the alleged seat of affection and—Arthur Rubinstein will be the greatest of all pianists." When the keyboard firebrand Josef Lhévinne made his Carnegie Hall debut later that month, he practically obliterated the impression that Rubinstein had left. Lhévinne's success was "immediate and really sensational," according to Henry T. Finck of the *New York Post*. "An attempt has been made lately to introduce a new 'Rubinstein' to local audiences, but the real Rubinstein II is Mr. Lhévinne," Finck continued. "He has the great Anton's technique, his dash and bravura, his brilliancy and a good deal of his leonine power. He can make a piano sing, too."⁵⁴

Together with Scheel and the Philadelphians, Rubinstein repeated his Carnegie Hall program in Brooklyn and then in Baltimore, the Knabes' hometown, where he was fêted at the home of one of the brothers. When Rubinstein returned to New York, Gontaut and his friend the Marquis Melchior de Polignac—the owner of the Pommery et Greno champagne-producing firm—introduced Rubinstein to a good-looking, middle-aged socialite whom he called Dorothy in his memoirs, and who was his bed-partner during his various stops in the city. He was also visited by Adolf Neumark, a first cousin from Lodz, who had immigrated to America when Rubinstein was a small child.

From the Waldorf, Rubinstein wrote another letter to Astruc, to bring him up to date.

Dear Mr. Astruc,
Everything is going marvelously. My first concert was a triumph!! I was called out for perhaps 12 bows, I gave 2 encores, and the audience gave me an ovation. The next day in Brooklin [*sic*] the same thing happened, perhaps even better. [William] Knabe is delighted, he adores me, I think, as he is so kind to me. And it was horribly difficult to have a success, because it seems that since Paderewski no

one has had such publicity before a concert. A thousand tall tales about me, whole pages, reproduced throughout America, the walls covered with me, ah, it's immense. Every day I receive a great number of people, pianists who play for me, women——Yesterday I played in Baltimore with Mme. [Johanna] Gadski [a celebrated soprano] with great success. Afterward, Knabe gave a big reception for 200 people, and I played again, the people were in an enthusiastic state; what I'm writing isn't modest, but it is true and I think I'm giving you pleasure in writing you this. The newspapers (reviews) are varied, there are bad, good, and superb ones. But not one of them has dared to say that the publicity was excessive—and this means a great deal. If they are nasty and malevolent, they talk about my personality; that I am a Jew or that I am a poseur etc.

In a few days I'll write more to you—Goodbye

Your friend Arthur

Best wishes to Mrs. Astruc and please tell everybody everything.

On January 15 he played his first New York solo recital—Bach's Toccata and Fugue in D Minor, Beethoven's "Waldstein" Sonata, and Schumann's *Carnaval*, and a Chopin group—at the Casino Theater on Thirty-ninth Street. ("Why this unlikely little locale was chosen no one knows," Arthur Loesser said. "I am pretty sure that there never had been a piano recital there before, nor ever since." But it seems that the Knabes had signed with the young Shubert brothers, Lee, Sam, and Jacob, who were beginning to dominate the American stage industry, and that many of Rubinstein's tour recitals were to take place at Shubert-owned or -leased theaters. Rubinstein disliked the Casino Theater, one of the Shuberts' New York venues, but he found some of its counterparts in other cities less objectionable.) Loesser was present at the recital and remembered being "startled, in fact alarmed, at the terrific speed and sizzle with which he plunged into the [Waldstein's] final *prestissimo!!* Another incident of that recital has helped fix it in my memory. During the intermission one of the ushers carried down one of the aisles a floral tribute to Rubinstein and set it on the stage. But what an object! It was in the shape of a wooden cross, as tall as a man, covered all over with roses, I believe, except in the middle, at the junction of the arms, where there was a photograph of a portrait of Mozart! Rubinstein took no notice of this irrelevant item as it stood on the stage during the entire latter half of his program, or even after making his first bows at the end. Finally, when he decided to take no more recalls, he looked at it, a little hesitantly, picked it up and carried it out, gingerly. Years later he told me that it had come from an eccentric 'admirer,' who had borrowed money from him and never paid it back."[55] A few days later, he gave another recital at the Casino Theater; this time, he played Schumann's Fantasy, Chopin's Sonata in B Minor, Brahms's Variations (presumably Book Two of the Paganini Variations), and Liszt's Twelfth Rhapsody.

Rubinstein made his Philadelphia debut with Scheel and the orchestra at the Academy of Music, in a pair of concerts (January 23 and 24) in which he played the Chopin Second Concerto. In Chicago two weeks later he was delighted to play at the nearly new Orchestra Hall with the local orchestra under thirty-three-year-old Frederick Stock; Theodore Thomas, the orchestra's founder-conductor and a pioneer in American musical life, had died a year earlier. Reviewers' comments in four Chicago newspapers ranged in tone from generally negative to exuberantly positive, but all agreed that the audience was exceptionally enthusiastic about the young pianist. On February 11, the day after his second Chicago performance, he cabled Astruc: "Success assured[,] triumph Chicago[,] prejudiced New York critics will change[.]"[56] During his stay in Chicago, he attended a vaudeville show, toured the brothels ("without touching the objects on display,"[57] he said), and made the acquaintance of the Swiss-born pianist Rudolph Ganz, a Busoni pupil ten years Rubinstein's senior who was to remain a leading figure in Chicago's musical life for the rest of his ninety-five years. As Rubinstein crisscrossed much of the eastern half of the United States—accompanied by Hochman, who was an amusing companion—he experienced for the first time a phenomenon known to many traveling performers before and since: exhaustion during the first few days, followed by a manic pleasure in keeping up the pace, pressing on from one destination to another, getting to the next train station, the next hotel, the next restaurant, the next auditorium, the next audience's demonstrations of approval, and then boarding the next train. Moving across great distances, constantly facing new situations, and performing every second night, on the average (in addition to his forty prescheduled concerts, he was invited back to Baltimore, Washington, Providence, and Cincinnati for extra performances), Rubinstein found himself enjoying the tour "more and more," he said.[58]

In Boston's Jordan Hall, on March 16, he played the Bach-Tausig Organ Toccata in D Minor, Chopin's Third Sonata, the second volume of Brahms's "Paganini" Variations, some shorter pieces by Chopin and Brahms, and Liszt's Mephisto Waltz. Earlier that day he had sent Astruc a letter in which he replied to criticism of his irresponsible handling of money.

My dear Mr. Astruc,
In everything you say in your last letter, you are absolutely right. I

have allowed myself to be exploited in an ignoble way; I myself
don't know how it was possible, but 900 dollars were swallowed up
in the first month, in part through the fault of my new friends (who
of course are becoming very numerous here) and also a lot through
my weakness and my lack of experience with money. In any case I
cannot excuse myself for not having paid greater attention to your
advice, which was so just and so fatherly and which I shall certainly
follow better the next time; as to this experience, it will remain a
good lesson for me and I myself am the one who is suffering the
most from it.

My silence was caused by the immense amount of work that I
had throughout the month of February and thus far in March. I
have given 32 concerts in all (this is really a lot) and during the
month of February alone (28 days) 17 concerts and 3 open rehearsals with orchestra. From this you can see that I am traveling almost
every day.

I can tell you frankly and without exaggerating that my success in America is very great, above all for a first tour, which is difficult. I carried away my audience nearly everywhere and the reviews
are magnificent, there are some that put me in a class by myself,
even in very important newspapers. In Chicago, in Toronto, Montreal, Washington, Buffalo, St. Louis, Cleveland, Detroit, and Philadelphia I had real triumphs. The Theodore Thomas orchestra in
Chicago [i.e., Chicago Symphony Orchestra] and the philharmonic orchestra of Philadelphia are asking me back all the time
and all the cities in which I've played again want to have me for a
second tour.

Everyone says that since Paderewski no one has been so
fought over as I—and I am now very well known in America. The
New York critics were in part very nasty, at first through prejudice
and then because they were furious about my great success with the
public. But each of them admits that I know something and finds
me worthy of such nastiness. [Rubinstein may have meant that even
the critics who were nasty to him took him seriously.]

. . . As to Ulrich, he is very kind and very happy with me, we
have even become great friends, but I don't think he is giving you
very correct information about me, he is a very cunning "businessman", and I suppose that he wants to have me very cheaply for a future tour. But don't let yourself be influenced by him, after the tour
you will see the results. I have only 8 or 6 more concerts to give,
today in Boston, afterward in Cincinnati, Indianopolis [sic], etc.

In Washington Mrs. Roosevelt [wife of Theodore Roosevelt, who was then president] was at my concert and sent me a superb box of flowers with a charming note.

Don't believe that this stupid money business has harmed me with respect to the Knabes. They know me and know that it is the fault of my weakness of character, which we all so deeply deplore.

Thousands and thousands of thanks for all the friendship that you are demonstrating toward me and do believe, dear Mr. Astruc, in my gratitude and warm feelings. Your
Arthur

Don't be so distressed!!! Things are going well.[59]

Newspaper feature writers in American cities and towns had a good time following Rubinstein's doings. "Girls Dash for the Polish Pianist," read a headline in the *Cincinnati Post* on March 27; and the article stated (one wonders how accurately):

Young Rubinstein, who plays at the Grand Opera House on Tuesday afternoon, gave an impromptu and entirely unpremeditated recital at the Conservatory of Music Saturday afternoon. . . . A number of visits to celebrated local institutions brought the youthful player to the Conservatory of Music, where a pupils' recital had drawn a large crowd of students and their admiring mamas.

Shortly the rumor spread through the corridors that the Polish pianist was calling on Miss Baur [one of the conservatory's directors, presumably], and ceremony was immediately cast to the winds by about 400 girls, who gathered at the library door, and with vehement hand clappings, invited the ardent little pianist to come forth and be admired. . . . Rubinstein finally relented from a determination to play only in regular concerts and, in company with Miss Baur, proceeded to the recital hall, where he played half a dozen selections to an audience of girls, who cheered him to the echo.

In *My Young Years*, Rubinstein claimed that he had arranged an engagement in San Francisco, so that he could cross the Rocky Mountains and see the Pacific, and that the Knabes, in cancelling it—because they were unwilling to incur substantial additional travel expenses, according to Rubinstein—may have saved his life: his stay in the city would have included the date of the great earthquake and fire. Instead, he returned to Chicago for an extra recital and received a visit from Bertha Drew Hartzell, who was living in

the suburbs with her minister husband. Rubinstein lunched with them the
next day and gave them a prudently edited version of the story of his life during the six years that had passed since Bertha had left Berlin. But the dramatic tale of his narrowly avoided brush with death in San Francisco seems
highly unlikely. Rubinstein was booked to return—and did indeed return—
to France aboard *La Touraine*, which left New York on April 5, thirteen days
before the disaster in California.

By the time he boarded ship he had spent nearly all of his earnings
on expensive hotels and other extravagances. The Knabes were kind enough
to pay the last of his whopping bills at the Waldorf, but he was going back
to Europe with hardly any money in his pocket and with no new tour contract in hand. The voyage was much calmer, meteorologically speaking,
than the outbound one had been, but for Rubinstein it was enlivened by
the presence of two pianists whose celebrity in those days was much greater
than his: the fifty-four-year-old Frenchman Raoul Pugno, well known for
his playing of Mozart and Chopin, and the thirty-four-year-old Russian
Josef Lhévinne, who had outshone him in New York, and whose marvelous
left-hand technique Rubinstein described as the envy of all other pianists.
On the last night at sea, the three virtuosos gave a concert to raise money
for sailors' orphans; they were joined by Charles Gilibert, a French baritone—formerly with the Metropolitan but at that time with the rival Manhattan Opera—and his wife, a soprano. The ship docked at Le Havre at 1
A.M. on April 13.

In Paris, Rubinstein had to admit to Astruc that his tour had been only a
qualified success and that the Knabes had not invited him back for the following year. But instead of trying to improve his prospects by practicing and
studying harder, Rubinstein became lazier and lazier. An opportunity for
high living arrived in the form of an invitation from Armand de Gontaut-
Biron, who had returned to Paris before him. The young count said that his
brother had temporarily moved out of the luxurious apartment they shared in
Avenue Kléber, and he easily persuaded Rubinstein to leave his cheap pension and move in with him. Not only did Rubinstein no longer have to worry
about paying rent: Gontaut and his friends—the flower of young Parisian society—usually treated him to fine meals, too, and made sure that he was invited to the best homes. He was free to spend nearly all of his salary from
Astruc on stylish clothes and accessories for himself, gifts for his wealthy
friends, and flowers for the women he pursued. In a photo taken of him in the
Bois de Boulogne early that summer, with Mr. and Mrs. William Knabe and
their daughter, he is quite the dandy, wearing a short, dark jacket, white trousers, and a straw hat, and carrying a fashionable cane.

His social connections led to engagements to play at soirées, which Astruc arranged at a charge of a thousand francs each. No sooner would Rubinstein begin to play than the "elegant audience" would break into "lively conversations, interrupting them from time to time by a 'Bravo,' usually after a loud passage," Rubinstein recalled.[60] But at five hundred francs (his share of the "take") per performance, he could not afford to turn down such work offers. Occasionally, however, he played for more attentive private audiences, one of which included the composer Gabriel Fauré, the much talked about young poet Anne de Noailles, and the still little-known, thirty-five-year-old Marcel Proust.

Gontaut departed for another business trip to America; Rubinstein stayed on at Avenue Kléber and kept up the other habits that he had acquired in the count's company, but he began to realize that his life was becoming terribly empty and that his career was going nowhere. "I had become thin and pale, with hollow cheeks and rings under my eyes," Rubinstein recalled.[61] One day, Dukas, who had listened to him rattle on about his fun-filled, naughty life, invited him to his apartment and showed him his collection of pornographic pictures. Rubinstein believed—not necessarily correctly—that the composer was making fun of his stupid behavior, and he decided to follow Dukas's advice to get away from Paris for a while in order to rest, gain back his health, and recover his desire to work. For some time, Jules Wertheim had been sending Rubinstein invitations to spend the following July with him at the home of friends, in the country near Warsaw, but Arthur had not answered. After his encounter with Dukas, however, Rubinstein decided to accept Wertheim's invitation, but July was still a few weeks away and, as usual, he had no money. "Dear Mr. Astruc," he began an undated letter written during that difficult period,

> I spent 2 hours at the office today, to ask Mr. Becasse [who looked after the Société Musicale's accounts] for 20 or even only 10 francs, to be able to have something to eat, I haven't eaten anything since yesterday.
>
> Apart from the tips I gave, I had to pay a laundry bill of 20 f. and I owed a few francs to my friend [Gontaut].
>
> My friend has put his apartment at my disposal until I leave, but of course I have to eat in town.
>
> I didn't ask you personally for money because there were people around, and I can't talk about it in front of people.
>
> I hope to be able to leave on July 1st, and once I have left, I will no longer need money, but until then I need it for food and for small expenses. Will you please have the great kindness, Mr. Astruc, to have the money sent to me at Avenue Kléber 53? I would be very

grateful for this; I am really suffering too much in going all the time
to ask Mr. Becasse, as if I wanted to take something away from him.

> With my great thanks in advance
> Your grateful
> Arthur Rubinstein

I know very well that Mr. Becasse refuses to give me money out of
duty and not out of ill will, but all the same it is horrible for me.[62]

Whether or not Astruc complied is not known, but his young client
survived. Before Rubinstein left Paris, he paid several visits to Dukas, to play
through the four-hand piano reduction of the composer's nearly completed
opera, *Ariane et Barbe-bleue*. Like Debussy's *Pelléas*, *Ariane* is a setting of a
text by Maurice Maeterlinck; it was given its first performance the following
May, at the Opéra-Comique in Paris. Although it was much admired by
musicians of such divergent aesthetic convictions as Schoenberg, Messiaen,
and Toscanini (who conducted its American premiere at the Metropolitan in
1911), it has never achieved a secure place in the repertoire. Rubinstein loved
it, but he was even more grateful for the fatherly solicitude of its composer,
whom Astruc, in his memoirs, described as a man of broad spirit, high soul,
exquisite modesty, and noble character.

WERTHEIM MET RUBINSTEIN at the station in Warsaw, and together they proceeded to the manor and farm of a Mr. Barylski, a music-loving insurance
executive, and his wife and four sons. Thanks to walks in the country, mush-
room hunts, and fresh local food, Rubinstein gradually recovered his strength
and, with it, as Dukas had predicted, his desire to work. He learned new repertoire, practiced the old, and played for his eager and appreciative hosts. His
gratitude to them for their hospitality was probably equalled by their delight
at having him as a guest, because in Poland he had become a celebrity in
absentia: his French and North American successes, however qualified, had
been noticed at home. Thus, when he returned to Warsaw to spend the early
fall with the Wertheims (minus Jules, who had gone to Paris in the hope of
finally making a name for himself), he quickly managed to secure engagements at the Filharmonja—not three, as he said in his memoirs, but six. He
informed Astruc:

> I haven't written to you in all this time, because I was sure that you
> didn't much care. Now I don't know at all what I ought to do. I
> thought you would give me instructions on September 15th. During
> this time I have been working extremely hard, while resting at the
> same time.
>   You know, my dear Mr. Astruc, instead of having you send

me money, I am going to bring some back to you; I accepted here
(in Warsaw) some concerts, for which they will give me 600 rubles
(1600 f.). It is a huge sum these days and in the current terrible political situation, and that is why I accepted immediately. Have I
done the right thing? I'll bring you the contract written in French
and the money.

Would you be so kind as to inform me when I *absolutely* must
return[?]

I feel much gratitude and friendship for you, but I think you
hate me.

> Best wishes from your very
> devoted
> Arthur Rubinstein

My friend Wertheim is in Paris.[63]

With Mlynarski and the Philharmonic he played five concertos, all in minor
keys: the Chopin F Minor, the Saint-Saëns G Minor, the Rubinstein D
Minor, the Rimsky-Korsakov C-sharp Minor, and Wertheim's Concerto in B
Minor. His large solo repertoire for those concerts included one of Beethoven's Sonatas in C Major—probably the "Waldstein"; Chopin's Third
Sonata, Second Ballade, and one of the C Minor études; the Schumann Fantasy; a Hungarian Rhapsody, the Mephisto Waltz, and other pieces by Liszt;
Paderewski's Sonata in E-flat Minor; Debussy's *Jardins sous la pluie* from *Estampes*; Scriabin's Nocturne for the Left Hand; and four early (1902) études
by Szymanowski. According to the Filharmonja's annals, these concerts were
among "the biggest successes of 1906–07" in Warsaw,[64] and news of them,
along with the legend of his triumphs abroad, attracted the attention of his
family. First, his sister Jadwiga arrived from Lodz, enlisted his support in getting their brother Ignacy—recently returned from prison camp in Siberia but
again involved in revolutionary activities—safely out of the tsar's domains,
and persuaded him to pay a dressmaker's bill that she did not want her husband to see. Then, in Lodz, where he played two recitals, he "felt morally
obliged"[65] to give half of his fee to his parents. Added to his own needs and
extravagances, the other expenditures made his earnings disappear as quickly
as ever. His professional successes led to invitations to the homes of the leaders of Warsaw society, both Gentile (for instance, the Marchioness Wielopol-
ska, whom Rubinstein called "the uncrowned queen of the city") and Jewish
(Rubinstein singled out for mention Mr. and Mrs. Mieczyslaw Epstein,
"close relations of the Rothschilds of Paris"), and in such surroundings he felt
obliged to keep up a show of well-being.[66]

The success of his Warsaw concerts must have renewed his artistic self-confidence, because he decided to return to Paris and Astruc, to seek further engagements. Late one afternoon, however, before he left Warsaw, he found himself sitting and talking with Lily Wertheim (the "Pola Harman" of his memoirs), alone "at the tea table" in her parents' house, "when suddenly, compulsively, we became silent. My heart began to beat faster. I searched her eyes questioningly, intently; she did not withdraw hers. Then we both knew; we were in love, deeply and passionately in love."[67] Thus began the last, the longest, the most profound, and, ultimately, the saddest of Rubinstein's Wertheim affairs.

Lily, or Lilka, was in her mid- to late twenties—six to ten years older than the nineteen-year-old Rubinstein. She was married to a Mr. Ràdwan (the "Mr. K." of Rubinstein's memoirs), and they had two small daughters. In 1991, Lilka's aged cousin Maria Kempinska described her as "not very beautiful but absolutely charming, a very fine musician, intelligent, refined, sweet, and marvelous."[68] If one reads between the lines of Rubinstein's descriptions of her, one comes to the conclusion that she was the least ambitious and demanding member of the Wertheim family, considerate of others and fragile herself. All his life, he sought and often found women who would pose no threat to his ego—beautiful and/or charming women who admired his talent and whose attachment to him redounded to his credit. He liked intelligent women, but not so talented that they might steal some of the limelight. (During the following few years, he had affairs with singers as famous as or more famous than himself, at the time, but he considered them his musical and intellectual inferiors.) Lilka came closer to meeting his unstated and probably unacknowledged criteria than had anyone else since the death of his little cousin Noemi, a dozen years earlier. The affair posed logistical problems, not only because Lilka lived with her husband and daughters, but also because word of the new development had to be kept from her mother, who may still have been having sexual relations with Rubinstein from time to time, and who, in any case, would not have been happy with the news. Lilka confided in her good friend Zofia (Zosia) Kohn, the young daughter of Jozef Leon Kohn, a prominent local lawyer; Zosia—eager to please the sister of Jules Wertheim, with whom she was frustratedly in love—invited Lilka and Arthur to meet in her boudoir, which contained a Bechstein concert grand; there, however, the couple felt too intimidated to do anything but hold hands and talk.

From Paris, Jules wrote to tell Rubinstein that he had rented a room in an English widow's flat at 25 Rue Lauriston, in the fashionable sixteenth district, not far from Gontaut's apartment, and to say that another pleasant room was vacant in the same flat. Rubinstein overcame his regret at leaving Lilka and returned to Paris, probably in January 1907. Astruc must have come to the conclusion, in the meantime, that no matter how disappointed he was in Rubinstein's showing so far, and no matter how worried over his young client's extravagant way of life, there was no sense in keeping him on a salary without trying to find him more engagements. He arranged for him to participate in a gala benefit concert at the Théâtre Sarah-Bernhardt, in honor of Francis Planté, the sixty-eight-year-old (not eighty-six-year-old, as Rubinstein stated in his memoirs) doyen of French pianists—a former protégé of Liszt and Rossini; the event included recitations by Bernhardt herself as well as by Lucien Guitry, Mounet-Sully, Benoît-Constant Coquelin, and other actors, as well as vocal numbers performed by the sopranos Félia Litvinne, Aline Vallandri, and Lucienne Bréval, and short piano pieces played by Rubinstein and Planté. Rubinstein almost ruined the evening by inadvertently choosing, as an encore, the piece that Planté was to have played as his main number; the older pianist angrily played something else instead. At another gala, Rubinstein shared the stage of the old Trocadéro with Caruso and the soprano Geraldine Farrar. "I had the good idea to play as my last piece the 'Liebestod' from *Tristan and Isolde* in the Liszt transcription; it brought the house down," Rubinstein recalled. "Saint-Saëns, who was present, complimented me very warmly."[69]

Rubinstein resumed his performances at private soirées, most of which he undertook purely to earn money, and he became involved in the preparations for the French premiere of Richard Strauss's *Salome*. Indeed, he was indirectly responsible for the event, according to Astruc, who one day "heard the piano sing the introductory phrase of the Dance of the Seven Veils" through the half-opened door to his office. "It was too much for me," Astruc recalled. "I left my refuge and went to lean on the piano on which Arthur Rubinstein, who knew my weakness for this piece, was playing it with incomparable mastery. The result of that session was two-fold: first, I took out of my pocket a banknote that Arthur—who is today [late 1920s] a rich man and who has remained very generous—immediately spent on munificent tips for the waiters at the Café Américain. And then I went back to my office saying to myself: 'No one but you can be the first to have *Salome* in Paris.'"[70] The Opéra had already reserved the rights to the French premiere of the work, which was receiving widespread international attention—even more for its scandalous subject than for its musical innovations—but Astruc used a legal technicality to circumvent the obstacle: the Opéra, if and when it produced the work, would present it in a French translation, whereas Astruc secured the rights to the original German version for the performances that he organized at the Théâtre du Châtelet. Thus, the premiere took place under his auspices in May 1907, with Strauss on the podium and the twenty-nine-year-old Czech soprano Emmy Destinn in the title role, which she had already sung in Berlin the previous year. Rubinstein helped to rehearse "various groups and some of the soloists," he said, and "Destinn herself asked me to run through the last scene with her."[71] She also asked him to sleep with her—or at least he later claimed that the invitation had come from her—and he duly did what was expected of him, although Lily was "in my heart and on my mind." Destinn was fairly beefy-looking, in those years (Toscanini, who worked with her at the Metropolitan Opera between 1908 and 1915, is reported to have said that on stage " 'she looked like a cook, but she sang like an angel' "),[72] and Rubinstein was shocked to see "a bright-colored tattoo of a boa encircling her leg from the ankle to the upper thigh . . . I am afraid I was not at my best that night, but she seemed not to mind."[73]

In his memoirs, Rubinstein depicted Destinn as a female Don Juan interested in totting up new, young conquests, whereas he was merely being nice to her while keeping his thoughts fixed on his great love in Warsaw. Destinn's version of the story is not known, nor is it possible to know how much her affair with Rubinstein, which continued sporadically for a few months, meant to her. Astruc said that he remembered hearing the couple perform Schumann's *Dichterliebe* cycle and the aria "Un bel dì" from Puccini's latest opera, *Madama Butterfly*, at the Baroness Gustave de Rothschild's salon; he may, however, have been confusing two events: a *Dichterliebe* performance that Rubinstein and Félia Litvinne had given at the Countess de Béarn's, and a performance of two arias from *Carmen* and the final scene from *Salome* that Rubinstein and Destinn gave at the Baroness de Rothschild's, "at a soirée which marked the end of the *saison* and was considered the most important social function of the year," Rubinstein said.[74]

Salome made a great impression on musical Paris. Debussy summed up musicians' reactions in a letter to Astruc: "I don't see how anyone can be other than enthusiastic about this work—an absolute masterpiece . . . almost as rare a phenomenon as the appearance of a comet."[75] Curiosity about Strauss's controversial score led to several private engagements for Rubinstein, who had committed the entire opera to memory: for five hundred francs, he would play it to gatherings of people who wanted to familiarize themselves with what was, at the time, a work of great harmonic and dramatic audacity. And for the considerably larger fee of one hundred guineas he went to London early in June to play the "Dance of the Seven Veils" and to accompany the American soprano Olive Fremstad in the final scene of the opera—which had been banned from the British stage—at two private gatherings, one of which was attended by King Edward VII. The hostess of the events was Mrs. Potter Palmer, a wealthy American woman who, in 1893, had been president of the ladies' section of the Chicago World's Fair, and whom Astruc knew. Rubinstein recalled that afterward the king remarked to him, " 'I did not notice anything shocking in what I heard, and I cannot understand why our censors objected to it.' . . . Obviously, he expected to be a little scandalized and was secretly disappointed."[76] The visit to London gave Rubinstein a chance to spend a few days with Destinn, who was one of the stars of the 1906–07 Covent Garden season (she sang in performances of *The Flying Dutchman, Madama Butterfly*, and *Cavalleria rusticana* while he was there), and he enjoyed himself so much that on June 5 he wrote to Astruc, from the Hotel Victoria on Northumberland Avenue: "Do I have to go back? I would very much like to stay a few more days! You would be enormously kind to drop me a line if you need me! The soirée at Mrs. Potter's was charming—the next day we did the same thing before the king who was charming. Mr. Boosey [concert agent] wants to engage me with Destinn for next winter—I'll see him again."[77] The engagement did not materialize.

It is strange that Rubinstein did not find an excuse for returning to Lily in Warsaw as soon as Paris's musical and social season had ended, especially since he was out of pocket, homeless (his landlady had closed her apartment for the summer), and even, on one occasion, reduced to spending a night on a bench near the Arc de Triomphe. Although a demand—made by Joasia through Jules—to return the letters that Lily had sent him (Jules had been privy to the Lily-Arthur story from the start, and Rubinstein complied with the demand) had given him "several sleepless nights,"[78] he made no attempt to find out what was happening. His reason for not rushing to Warsaw is clarified, in part, by a letter that Astruc made him write in July, when a tailor to whom Rubinstein owed money tried to sue the Société Musicale.

Messieurs G. Astruc et C.ie
32 rue Louis le Grand
Paris
Gentlemen,
I herewith accept that Mr. Franck, tailor, has unjustly demanded that you pay the sum of one thousand fifty francs (1050 fr.) which I personally owe him.
    In drawing on your account the drafts of 500 and 550 fr. last February 15th and March 5th, I had thought that I had this sum to my credit in your account. But I declare that on the contrary I am your debtor for a considerable sum.
    Mr. Franck cannot therefore have any legal recourse against you.

Sincerely yours,
Arthur Rubinstein[79]

Rubinstein must have been forced to stay close to Paris until he could pay his bills. But he was able to accept an invitation from Count Nicolas

Potocki, scion of a family of Polish patriots, to spend the holiday period at
Potocki's country estate at Grange Colombe, near Rambouillet, fifty miles
southwest of the capital. Rubinstein had met Potocki earlier that year
through Count Recopé, Armand de Gontaut's friend. Potocki kept an open
lunch table for his friends, at his Paris home, and Rubinstein had become an
assiduous partaker. Widely read and a great lover of music and women, Potocki had much to discuss with his young compatriot. Rubinstein frequently
played for him, in private, and he even played for a gathering of actresses,
courtesans, and their lovers that the count arranged at his palace. Through
much of August and September 1907, Rubinstein stayed at Rambouillet,
practicing on the Pleyel grand piano that the count had rented for him, learning to ride under the count's expert guidance, going on fishing expeditions
(he once injured a finger on a fishhook and had to undergo a painful operation), and enjoying good meals with Potocki and his mistress as well as several other hangers-on. He became friendly with the count's cousin, Stanislaw
Rembielinski, an adventurer and sage whom Rubinstein, to the end of his
life, considered one of the most intelligent men he had ever met, and he
managed to exchange passionate kisses, one evening, with Potocki's beautiful
young goddaughter, who had been moved by his playing. (He claimed to
have elicited a similar reaction the previous year from the exquisitely beautiful niece of another Polish count, Jan Zamoyski.) The incident angered the
count's secretary, Biernacki, who was hoping to marry the goddaughter—or
so Rubinstein said in his memoirs, to explain the deterioration in his relations
with Biernacki. A letter (September 1) from Biernacki to the long-suffering
Astruc provides a different explanation.

> Sir
> I have had the pleasure of visiting you on behalf of Count Potocki.
>   I am writing to you today completely confidentially, counting
> on your total discretion.
>   The business is as follows:
>   I have perhaps played too great a part in having Mr. Rubin-
> stein admitted here, or rather in allowing him to put down roots
> here.
>   I told the Count that he [Rubinstein] had a lucrative contract
> with you and that Mr. R. had only good things to say about you.
>   Unfortunately, there was soon a complete reversal with re-
> spect to yourself: [Rubinstein said that] the contract was broken in
> order that he not be *exploited*, [that] you were going to be com-
> pletely indemnified, [that] a debt would be paid and a new contract
> signed with Baron Hochwächter (who is associated with 2 Ameri-

cans in this enterprise), [that Hochwächter would give Rubinstein]
a 5-year contract—3000 fr. a month as a fixed fee—guarantee of at
least 50 concerts [a year]—40% of the gross earnings—travel paid—
installation in lodgings in Paris! But today, 4 weeks after the new
contract, Mr. R. declares that he wants to break it! that he doesn't
want to be tied down for such a long time! and I can see that all this
will lead to a request for a subsidy from my boss in order to avoid
the exploiters. Of course the Count will have none of it—but I
could be reproached for having been too credulous. I would like to
be certain that all this is simply fantasy and that the true story is
different.

    Answer me frankly if my hunches are incorrect—you can
count on my complete discretion and if you don't want to put too
much in writing phone me. . . .

Sincerely yours,

Z. Biernacki

P.S. Who is Mr. Hochwächter[?] . . .[80]

Who was Mr. Hochwächter? Rubinstein had become involved in a wild
adventure with Olive White, a former chorus girl from America who had
married a wealthy New Yorker and was touring Europe in the company of
another young American woman; the entourage was completed by a German
baron—Hochwächter—who had fallen in love with Olive. Rubinstein spent
much time with them, it seems, in order to take advantage of Olive's apparently bottomless purse and of the second woman's willingness to be fondled
day and night. (In his memoirs, Rubinstein placed this episode in the summer of 1906, but it is clear from Biernacki's letter that the correct year was
1907.) The details of the foursome's story can no longer be determined, but
Rubinstein's version of it was carefully edited. He depicted Hochwächter as a
fortune hunter who loaned him money that really belonged to Olive (who,
Rubinstein said, had intended to make him a present of it) and that Hochwächter demanded back after World War I, at prewar rates. But he made no
mention of his short-lived client-manager relationship with the baron.

    Biernacki may have been trying to sully Rubinstein's reputation for rea-
sons of his own, but there seems little reason to doubt his accusations. Astruc
might not have been inclined to involve himself at all in the Rubinstein-
Potocki-Biernacki affair had he not already used Rubinstein as go-between in
his initially successful attempt to enlist Potocki as one of the financial backers
for his dream project, the creation of the Théâtre des Champs-Elysées. Thus,
the innocent-sounding first sentence of Biernacki's letter—"I have had the

pleasure of visiting you on behalf of Count Potocki" — carried a great deal of weight with Astruc. On September 5, Astruc telegraphed Biernacki: "Situation revealed by letter very unexpected. Shall finish assembling information Tuesday. Above all be careful. Regards & thanks. Astruc."[81] And Biernacki replied, two days later: "I'm not lacking in prudence. I don't like having people mock me by telling me lies, I have turned to you knowing in advance that everything that I suspected would be confirmed by you."[82]

No further documents on the matter have been found. But Biernacki's version of the story explains why, in Astruc's memoirs, Potocki does not figure among the people who ultimately came through with money for the Champs-Elysées project; it explains the sudden and total disappearance from Rubinstein's memoirs of his great friends Potocki and Rembielinski; it explains Rubinstein's strange animus against Hochwächter; and, most important, it explains Astruc's absence — apart from some casual references — from the remainder of Rubinstein's memoirs, which never reveal that the five-year contract between impresario and pianist was broken before the third year had ended. Many years later, Rubinstein, in expansive moments, would speak admiringly of Astruc: he was "the biggest impresario Paris ever had . . . not the usual impresario who just lives on commissions," but a man with "a big vision, . . . a genius in his own way," he told one interviewer. He would go so far as to say that Astruc had treated him as "the son of the house," and to blame himself for his lack of success in Paris: "I was not mature myself, and unfortunately Astruc thought I was."[83] But when it came to putting black on white in *My Young Years*, he evidently decided that he had to make Astruc look a smidgen less admirable and himself a smidgen less unadmirable than he had admitted in less guarded moments.

BACK IN PARIS after his hasty departure from Rambouillet, with no cash in hand, no manager, no paid work in view, and creditors in hot pursuit, Rubinstein prepared for a depressing autumn. Temporary relief came in the form of an invitation to participate in a gala charity concert in Warsaw, for which he would be decently paid; the other soloists were to be Kochanski and Joanna Wertheim, who, under the stage name Joanna Devera, eventually performed in various operas and as an interpreter of her brother's songs; and the orchestra would be directed by an up-and-coming young composer-conductor, Gregor Fitelberg. Rubinstein accepted three hundred francs from Rembielinski — the occasion furnished the last mention of the man in Rubinstein's memoirs — and took a train to Warsaw. As he did not want to stay at the Wertheims', he settled into the Hotel Victoria, where Kochanski, Fitelberg, and Szymanowski were also staying. At the concert, he played the Chopin F Minor Concerto, Paul played the Tchaikovsky Concerto, and Joasia sang some Mahler and

Strauss songs with orchestra. Rubinstein, who sat in the audience while the others performed, later claimed that he had managed to catch Joasia's eye while she was singing, and that this had made her miss one of her entrances; Fitelberg had had to restart the piece, and Rubinstein was "well-pleased with my private little mesmerism."[84]

His already-excellent professional reputation in Poland was further enhanced by his fine showing at the benefit concert, which led to numerous engagements for him in various Polish cities and towns. He also began to perform in a duo with Kochanski; the programs of their concerts at Warsaw's Filharmonja, on November 9 and 23, 1907, included Beethoven's "Kreutzer" Sonata, the Tchaikovsky Trio in A Minor—with the participation of the cellist J. Sabelik—and, for Rubinstein alone, works by Chopin, Schumann, Liszt, and Szymanowski (the Four Etudes, again, although Szymanowski had already dedicated the Variations, Op. 3, to him). Rubinstein's growing friendship with Kochanski was one of the most pleasant aspects of his life in those years. Besides being outstanding musicians, both were great talkers, joke-tellers, and mimics. They were gifted Jewish boys, upwardly mobile with a vengeance, in love with success, possessed of strong instincts for enjoying it, and tough enough to withstand setbacks. Rubinstein's daughter Eva recalled that long after Kochanski's death, her father "always talked about how much he adored and loved him," but she added: "I wish I had seen it, because I always had the impression, from the stories my father told, that it was the kind of relationship you would have when you were sixteen—playing jokes on each other and that sort of thing. I never heard anything that made me think there was some depth of contact, and I really don't know whether my father was capable of it. Other men were a threat to him, and I don't think any of his relationships, with his family or other people, were totally straightforward."[85] This is a much tougher judgment than others have made; certainly Rubinstein, for the rest of his life—which lasted nearly half a century longer than Kochanski's—always referred to his friend with great emotion, and considered him more of a brother than his own brothers had been to him.

Rubinstein met Lilka Wertheim several times in Zosia Kohn's bedroom, but Lilka's behavior was awkwardly formal. This puzzled him until he received a threatening note from her husband: Leave Warsaw or expect to be given a good thrashing, the message said. Radwan had evidently caught his wife writing to Rubinstein the previous spring; it was he who had spoken to the Wertheims, demanding that they ask his young rival to return Lilka's letters and that they help him to put an end to the affair. After having received the intimidating note, Rubinstein, with the help of aristocratic friends who knew how to arrange such things properly, challenged Radwan to a duel. Radwan had not anticipated such a reaction and was as frightened as his challenger by the very idea of physical combat; when the protagonists and their seconds met, at the designated time and place, Radwan signed a retraction, to everyone's relief. During the remaining weeks of Rubinstein's stay in Warsaw, he consoled himself in the company of one Genia Chmielnik, the mistress of an elderly count. She was "a tall, statuesque, gorgeous creature with a spectacularly curvaceous figure," Rubinstein said, and she was another of the many women who pursued the handsome Jules Wertheim but were willing to accept Rubinstein as a substitute. After his first night with Genia, Rubinstein "felt like a graduate from a college of the art of making love," he said.[86]

When Aleksandra Wertheim asked Rubinstein just what turn his friendship with Lily had taken the previous year and in the intervening months, he answered evasively—and indeed, he no longer knew how things stood between his beloved and himself. Observant readers of Rubinstein's memoirs will have noticed that his account of the affair is full of strange gaps, for which there were several reasons. One of them, certainly, was Rubinstein's understandable inability to remember the exact sequence of events more than sixty years after they had taken place. Another was his equally understandable reluctance to admit how badly he had later behaved toward Lilka, in some respects, and to describe the effect that his behavior had had on her. And he was unwilling to mention a tangential mess that continued to have repercussions for the rest of his life.

In about 1911 Paul Kochanski married Zosia Kohn, and Rubinstein, to the end of his days, believed that their decision to wed had been a grave error. Although Zosia had apparently long since gotten over her hopeless love for Jules Wertheim, not long before she married Paul she had told Rubinstein that she was in love with one of the Barylski boys, at whose parents' farm Rubinstein and Wertheim had stayed during the summer of 1906. Besides, "Zosia Kochanska was always a snob," Rubinstein's wife recalled. "To her, Paul was a little bit 'too Jewish,' not refined enough. Paul liked simple people. He liked to play cards and to speak a little roughly." (Many years later Rubinstein told a young friend that Kochanski "did not have a way with people. . . . He was impatient and sometimes rude. He would get angry and walk out on people and slam the door behind him.")[87] Nela Rubinstein added that "Zosia was charming, oversexed, and more pretentious. She would have loved to marry Arthur. That was her idea of a Jew."[88] Paul, for his part, had always laughed with Rubinstein about Zosia's ugly nose; although she was good looking in other respects and always elegantly dressed, her nose was huge, red, and misshapen: "it looked like a penis," one person who knew her commented. And Rubinstein knew that three years earlier, in Berlin, Paul had taken Zosia's mother to bed one night; he knew it because he himself had been to bed with Mrs. Kohn the following night, and he and Paul had joked together about their dual escapade. (She was the woman whom Rubinstein misleadingly described in his memoirs as the "wife of a banker" from Warsaw.) For all these reasons, he suspected that Zosia and Paul did not marry for love—that she wanted to become the wife of a famous musician and that he wanted to become the son-in-law of a wealthy, generous, music-loving lawyer who would, and did, buy him a Stradivarius as a wedding present. Rubinstein refused to attend their wedding; outwardly, the offense was soon forgiven, but Zosia used it as an excuse for stirring up trouble more than once in later years. On one occasion, Zosia "seduced" Arthur (so he claimed), and made him hate himself afterward for what he saw as a betrayal of Paul, his best friend, and presumably also of Lilka, his beloved and Zosia's friend. In short, both Paul and Arthur had sexual relations with both Zosia and her mother, and Arthur was the only member of the strange foursome who knew about all the sides of the quadrangle. Even to Rubinstein, the episode seemed a bit much to confess publicly.

RUBINSTEIN INNOCENTLY ASKED himself, in his memoirs, why he had decided to go to Berlin when he left Warsaw in January 1908; he could, after all, have gone back to Paris—or he could have remained in Warsaw. "I have tried in vain to find a logical answer to this question," he wrote.[89] But there were at least two logical answers: his rift with Astruc, which he did not wish to mention to his readers, and his desire to reencounter the Berlin-based Emmy Destinn, which he did mention, but casually, presumably so as not to appear less than completely caught up in his passion for Lily Wertheim. Destinn greeted him amicably, but she was traveling in the company of a new fiancé In *My Young Years*, Rubinstein made merciless fun of the couple—Destinn, he said, was a collector of Napoleonic memorabilia, and her boyfriend was a Napoleon look-alike, with the exception of his unintelligent and unexpressive face—but he was probably more upset by the situation than he let on: he must have been a little jealous of the new man, naturally, and disappointed at not being able to count on Destinn to help him with his living expenses. He stayed at the Hotel Bellevue in the Potsdamerplatz, practicing—when he could think of nothing more interesting to do—on a Bechstein baby grand provided by the manufacturer, and watching his modest reserve of money dwindle. Embarrassed over what he considered his lack of professional success, he avoided his old friends and acquaintances, not to mention Barth; Joachim, his generous deus ex machina, had died five months earlier. Rubinstein did, however, make the acquaintance of the thirty-year-old Ossip Gabrilowitsch, "who, besides being a fine pianist, was a lovable human being," Rubinstein said.[90] The two of them passed an enjoyable evening of music-making at the home of Josef Lhévinne and his wife, Rosina, who was later the most sought-after piano pedagogue of her day.

For the most part, however, Rubinstein saw only his relatives—the

Meyers, of course, and his sister Jadwiga, who arrived from Lodz to take part in what she had thought would be her brother's madcap social life, but who departed after having pawned her jewelry in order to lend him three hundred marks. (He redeemed the items during a subsequent visit to the city, he said.) When that money, too, was on the verge of disappearing, Rubinstein wired his friend Jozef Jaroszynski for help. Jaroszynski, however, had just given a considerable sum of money to Kochanski, who was as irresponsible, economically, as Rubinstein; the wealthy landowner assumed that Rubinstein, who often asked him for money—and usually got it—was crying crocodile tears while enjoying himself in Berlin, and he let the request pass.

On January 28, 1908, Rubinstein turned twenty-one, an age at which most middle-class young people are just preparing or beginning to do without parental guidance, but Rubinstein had done without it for more than half of his life. He had already seen more of the world than most people ever do; he had experienced extremes of praise and discouragement, lust and disgust, high life and low life. And yet he felt desperate. His career was at a standstill; he had alienated Astruc and concluded nothing with Lily; Destinn had thrown him over; and he had only enough money to pay for one sausage-roll, twice a day. He could not even check out of his hotel, because he could not pay the ever-mounting bill. One afternoon, he tried to hang himself, using a noose that he had made out of a frayed dressing-gown tie and attached to a clothes hook in his bathroom. But "as I pushed the chair away with my foot the belt tore apart and I fell on the floor with a crash." He admitted that the story seemed silly, but he insisted that it was true—and he would get angry when, many years later, his children would point out that he must have known that the old dressing-gown belt couldn't hold his weight. The moral of the story, for him, was that in the "chaos of thoughts" that followed, he "discovered the secret of happiness. . . . Love life for better or for worse, without conditions."[91] He repeated this principle publicly a bit too often for comfort in later years, but he also lived by it, to the best of his ability.

RUBINSTEIN'S BROTHER STANISLAW and brother-in-law Maurycy Landau sent him the money he needed to pay half of his Berlin hotel bill and return to Warsaw, where he initiated several months of delightful idleness by visiting Kochanski, Fitelberg, the Kohns, and the Wertheims—except Lily, to whom he evidently did not give a great deal of thought. He and Jaroszynski had a long chat, by the end of which the landowner felt so guilty for having inadvertently contributed to his young friend's suicide attempt that he invited him to spend a week with him, first at his family's estate in the Ukraine and then at their townhouse in Kiev, where he made him a princely gift of four thousand rubles—about two thousand dollars. Rubinstein immediately suggested that the two of them and Kochanski spend the money on a tour of European capitals—Berlin, Paris, and London; Jaroszynski, although taken aback, agreed to the proposal, and Kochanski was easily persuaded to join. In the end, Jaroszynski covered half the expenses out of his own pocket, and they all had a marvelous time. (A decade later, in the aftermath of the Bolshevik revolution, Jaroszynski and his family lost all their possessions, and Rubinstein was able to reciprocate his generous friend's former largesse.) Their last stop together was Karlsbad—present-day Karlovy Vary, in the Czech Republic—where Jaroszynski had arranged to take the cure, and where Rubinstein and Kochanski raised about six hundred dollars for themselves by putting on a concert at the Kursaal. Rubinstein made two excursions to Bayreuth, about sixty-five miles away, to hear *Parsifal*; the experience overwhelmed him, and he followed it up by going to Munich to hear *Tristan* and the entire *Ring* cycle conducted by Felix Mottl, one of Wagner's disciples. These events were the high point of Rubinstein's love affair with Wagner's music.

On his return to Warsaw, he concentrated on strengthening his relations with two people whom he had met during previous stays in the city. The first, a Russian colonel, Stremoukhov, was a melomane for whom Rubinstein and Kochanski played frequently, to encourage him to help them avoid the Russian draft, to which they both became subject on turning twenty-one. The draft was one of the worst of the many problems that haunted Russia's Jewish communities, as Paul Johnson explained in his *A History of the Jews*: "The government demanded fixed quotas of Jewish conscripts from the local communities. But these took no account of [mass] emigration. Jews should have provided no more than 4.13 per cent of recruits. The government demanded 6.2 per cent. Some 5.7 per cent were actually produced, and this led to official complaints about the 'Jewish deficit'—provoking, in turn, anti-Semitic clamour that Jews evaded conscription. In fact they furnished between 20 and 35 per cent more than their fair share. From 1886 families were held legally responsible for non-service of conscripts and fined heavily; there was no possibility of successful evasion without massive bribes." In addition, the category of Jews that was deemed professionally "useless" to the State was subjected to triple conscription quotas.[92] Polish Jews, moreover, were required to serve in the army that not only persecuted their ethnic group but also occupied their country; their desire to avoid the draft was doubly strong, and Rubinstein had to grapple with the problem for a long time.

The other man whose goodwill Rubinstein sought during the fall of 1908 was Prince Wladyslaw (or Ladislas) Lubomirski, who had become a leading benefactor in Warsaw's musical life. While studying composition under Fitelberg, he had created the Polish Composers' Press and had begun to promote performances of music by Fitelberg, Szymanowski, Ludomir Ro-

zycki, Mieczyslaw Karlowicz, and Apolinary Szeluto—a group that became
known as Mloda Polska, or Young Poland. These young men—all in their
twenties at the time of their first, successful concert, in February 1906—
wished to open musical Warsaw's ears to new musical trends from abroad as
well as to promote their own works. In 1908, Lubomirski decided to rescue
the young Warsaw Philharmonic, which had fallen on bad times in the three
years since Mlynarski had resigned its conductorship, and the ensemble was
put back on the rails thanks to the prince's financial backing and under Fitelberg's baton. Nela Rubinstein, who met Lubomirski many years later, described him as "a wonderful music-lover, a great aristocrat, and a charming
man."[93]

Rubinstein said that he played the Saint-Saëns G Minor Concerto,
without fee, at a gala event that launched the newly transformed ensemble,
but the Philharmonic's records do not mention such a performance—which
is not to say with certainty that the performance did not take place. The
records do, however, list four Rubinstein appearances with the orchestra
between November 13, 1908, and March 5, 1909; Fitelberg and Henryk
Opienski conducted, and their soloist played Beethoven's Fourth, Chopin's
First, and Brahms's Second Concertos, and what was probably his first performance of a work that soon became a staple of his repertoire—the Concerto No. 2 in C Minor of the thirty-five-year-old Sergei Rachmaninoff.
Rubinstein had already played Rachmaninoff's Elegy and Prelude from the
Fantasy Pieces, Op. 3, in a recital at the Filharmonja in October 1908, at
about the same time that he gave Warsaw its first public performance of the
Brahms "Paganini" Variations, a rare performance of Franck's First Piano
Sonata, and, with Kochanski, a performance of Franck's celebrated Violin
and Piano Sonata. Throughout the season, he performed in various Polish
cities and towns, and on March 23, 1909, back in Warsaw for a special
benefit concert for the School Enrollment Society, he played Beethoven's
"Kreutzer" Sonata with Kochanski, a Brahms trio with Kochanski and his
brother Eli, who was a fine cellist, and solo pieces by Chopin. On April 19,
Kochanski and Rubinstein gave the first public performance of Szymanowski's Sonata in D Minor for Violin and Piano. "Pawel and Artur gave a splendid interpretation of my 'Violin Sonata' Op. 9, yet the reviews were dim and
uninspiring," Szymanowski reported, in a letter.[94]

For Rubinstein, however, the great event of those months was the flow-
ering, at last, of his love affair with Lily Wertheim Radwan. They secretly
exchanged a few words one evening, at her parents' home, and plotted how to
meet. Rubinstein bribed the watchman at the Hotel Victoria, where he was
living, to leave the delivery entrance unlocked on certain afternoons, from
four to five. "Twice, three times a week I would wait in my room, my ears

trained to the soft squeak of the side door," he said. "An instant later my [Lily] was in my arms. We made love and we talked and talked and we made love again. It was heaven."[95] Before long, however, her parents and husband learned what was happening; according to Rubinstein, Piotr and Aleksandra Wertheim went to Lily's home, beat her, took her two little girls away from her, and threatened to have her shut up in a mental hospital. Rubinstein quickly arranged for her to be sheltered by his sisters Jadzia and Hela, who were staying at a resort in the German-ruled part of Poland, and he accompanied her as far as the border but not beyond: his passport had been taken away because his military status had not yet been resolved.

Rubinstein's relations with the Wertheim family—"mother, daughter, brother, sister," he said—quickly became a favorite subject of Warsaw gossip and satire, and he was depicted as a fortune hunter. But when Kochanski and Szymanowski tried to persuade him to settle the question by marrying Lily, he pointed out that as she was Catholic, she could not get a divorce, and that he was not yet able to support a wife. And he admitted that "it is not in my nature to marry a woman who is older than I and who has children by somebody else." When Szymanowski accused him of not really loving Lily, he protested vehemently. According to Rubinstein—and once again, his version of the events seems to be the only extant one—Piotr Wertheim tricked Lily into meeting him in Berlin, to talk things over, and then had her confined to a madhouse. She wrote a desperate note to Rubinstein and a kind guard mailed it for her; Rubinstein immediately procured a false passport, borrowed some money from Kochanski, and dashed to Berlin. The same guard helped Lily to escape, and she and Rubinstein returned to Warsaw, much to the surprise of her parents. "From then on she had no access to her home or to her children," Rubinstein said, "but at least she did have a small monthly allowance,"[96] thanks to a legacy from her grandfather.

Lily and Arthur were lovers for four or five years, intermittently. He mentioned having spent some weeks with her at the country estate of the Warsaw socialite Pauline Narbut during the summer of 1909, but he left her there when he returned to Warsaw to make ready for his forthcoming season. By his own account, he took her on some of his Polish tours, and they were often together in Warsaw between 1909 and 1914; he introduced her to his parents, who welcomed her warmly, he said; he was with her in Vienna, Berlin, and Rome in 1910; and they stayed together in London for a time in 1912, in Vienna in March 1913, and at Zakopane during part of the summer of 1913. Maria Kempinska, Lily's cousin, said that Rubinstein and Lily "may have had children of their own,"[97] but according to all other intimate sources, inside and outside the family, this was not the case. In *My Young Years* he mentioned having paid for an "urgent" operation for Lily, and he told Annabelle

Whitestone that the operation was an abortion—illegal, of course, in those days.

If one strings together the references to Lily in his memoirs, Rubinstein comes off looking like a cad, mainly because he took care not to be seen in her company whenever and wherever he thought his career or important social relations might be damaged thereby. But standards of officially acceptable behavior were much more rigid then than they are today, and Lily, too, tried to be seen in public with Rubinstein as little as possible, in the hope of regaining access to her daughters. Besides, it is unrealistic, unreasonable, and probably downright idiotic to expect a person of great talent not to do everything possible to protect his or her right and ability to exercise that talent. And yet, there is more than one hint in the memoirs that one of Rubinstein's reasons for not wanting to be seen with Lily, let alone marry her, was the fact that she was the older partner. In discussing another matter, he had admitted that he was always full of "vanity and pride, and a certain lack of humility. I simply couldn't bear to be seen in a state of weakness or inferiority; the façade of success had to be kept intact, even when my affairs were at their lowest—which is a rather unpleasant trait of my character, I admit."[98] This applied to his relations with Lily, too.

By the beginning of the First World War their love story had palled, and by the end of the war—throughout which they were completely out of touch with each other—it was finished. "He really was in love with her, but he also dropped her like a hot potato," Rubinstein's wife said, many years later.[99] Still, there had been much tender love between them for several years, and the aftermath of their affair was not rancorous. Lily and Arthur met once again, in Paris in the mid-1920s, after her husband's death, and she introduced him to her daughters, to whom she had long since regained access. A few years later, at about the age of fifty, she developed breast cancer; she refused to undergo surgery and went instead to a quack doctor who did nothing for her. She died in 1932—the year of Rubinstein's marriage. Someone reported to him that "her sad comment was: 'He begins his life when I finish mine.' "[100] Maneta Radwan, one of her daughters, later lived with Count Zamoyski, a sculptor, and the other, Jadwiga, eventually married Bronislaw Mlynarski, Rubinstein's future brother-in-law. Both daughters were upset by the publication of the first volume of Rubinstein's memoirs, in 1973—although Rubinstein had carefully changed all the Wertheims' names—but he maintained friendly contact with them as late as the end of the decade. Maria Kempinska recalled that when Maneta Radwan, who had developed into a "charming woman, like her mother," was sick and dying, "Nela Rubinstein was very kind to her."[101]

***

A GOOD DEAL of information and a few significant innuendos emerge from a letter that Rubinstein sent from Warsaw on August 7, 1909, to Astruc, of all people.

> You must think I'm dead! I was completely absorbed in the business of my military service, which has kept me from leaving Russia [and territories]. Also, I could not play outside of Russia and I have played 20 times in Warsaw alone. In St. Petersburg I was invited by Mr. Glazunov to play before members of the press and musicians and I have been engaged for a symphonic concert this winter.
>
> Now then, this winter I am going to do some nice things, and it is Prince Ladislas Lubomirski who is looking after my affairs and who wants to launch me at last! I have already made an arrangement with [Karl] Fernow [a director of the Wolff concert agency] in Berlin; on February 3rd [1910] I am giving a concert with orchestra there at the Philharmonie and then two recitals. At the beginning of November (1909) I have engagements at Cracow, Lvov, Prague, Budapest, and probably Vienna (I'll know in six days). So in December I would like to play in Paris. My wish is of course to play with orchestra first and to give two recitals on my own afterward. Is it possible to arrange something with Chevillard or Colonne? I would be willing to play with them even without fee. Or is it better for me to engage the hall and orchestra myself? Do you want to make an arrangement with me? In that case, we could work out something for the different categories of concerts. I will probably go to Paris in two weeks to set all this up, but before that I would be grateful if you would answer my queries, as I want to talk about all this with the prince. I am very keen on the month of December (or the end of November) because afterward I want to play in Germany and Russia. In London I'll do some work with the Polish conductor, Mr. Mlynarski, but this hasn't yet been decided.
>
> Prince Lubomirski has now taken over the Warsaw Philharmonic hall with the orchestra for two seasons. My great friend G. Fitelberg (a brilliant composer and conductor) is its director; he will conduct my concert in Berlin.
>
> Well, goodbye, my dear Mr. Astruc, I look forward to your answer, tell me if I ought to go to Paris now. With best wishes from your devoted
>
> Arthur Rubinstein
>
> If you have reviews and newspaper items about me, please do send them to me. I am living at the Hotel Victoria.[102]

In *My Young Years,* Rubinstein explained that Alexander Glazunov's invitation to him to play in St. Petersburg—his first appearance in Russia proper—had been arranged by Maurycy Landau during a business trip to the Russian capital. Landau had met Glazunov, who was one of Russia's best-known composers and the director of the celebrated St. Petersburg Conservatory; the merchant from Lodz had spoken in glowing terms of his young brother-in-law's accomplishments, and Glazunov had agreed to let Rubinstein perform before an invited audience. As a Jew without a special permit, Rubinstein was allowed only a twenty-four-hour stay in St. Petersburg, but this gave him enough time to check into a hotel, practice at the hall, perform for a highly enthusiastic audience (although Glazunov pointed out that wild demonstrations of esteem were common at Russian concerts), catch a little sleep, and depart.

Although the Paris events that Rubinstein tried to organize for the 1909–10 season did not materialize, he had indeed managed to make Prince Lubomirski "persuade" him to accept his support, which took the form of the equivalent of five thousand dollars, put at Rubinstein's disposal to cover the expenses of the concerts he wished to give in the great European capitals. In his letter to Astruc, Rubinstein implied that Lubomirski was doing for him what Astruc had been unable to do, but a second letter to Astruc demonstrates that the French impresario had reacted positively to his former client's proposal. "I have received your letter of September 30th and I've shown it to the prince," Rubinstein wrote on October 13. "I would be extremely happy to make this arrangement with you, and the assurance of your friendship toward me has given me the greatest pleasure. The amount for the Paris and London concerts seems a little high to me; I have only 8000 frs. at my disposal, as I am spending quite a bit already for Berlin and Vienna and I want to have some more concerts in Russia."[103]

Shortly afterward, however, Fitelberg, the prince's main protégé, persuaded Lubomirski that Rubinstein could not be trusted with money; Rubinstein believed that Fitelberg was jealous of other musicians who showed themselves capable of dipping into Lubomirski's purse without Fitelberg's mediation. (Nela Rubinstein, who knew Fitelberg much later, said, "He was a gifted conductor, but he would kill out of ambition.")[104] Not until some weeks later did Rubinstein have a chance to talk to the prince and straighten out their relations. Once that had happened, Rubinstein found a Warsaw-based manager—a Mr. Dropiowski—to set up his debut in Vienna, which was enjoying what were to be its last years as Europe's unofficial musical capital. In the Great Hall of the Musikverein, on Sunday, December 12, 1909, Rubinstein played the Beethoven Fourth, Brahms Second, and Saint-Saëns Second Concertos with the three-year-old Tonkünstler Orchestra (now called the Vienna Symphony Orchestra) under the direction of its founder, the thirty-five-year-old Oskar Nedbal, a Czech who had studied composition under Dvořák, and who was on the verge of achieving success as a composer of Viennese operettas. Rubinstein was upset, at first, that he was expected to play a Bösendorfer piano instead of a Bechstein, but in the end he found the instrument "quite good." The *Neue Freie Presse* announced the concert ("Artur Rubinstein, who is playing in Vienna for the first time, has had great success in America, Paris, and London," a tiny article said),[105] but the newspaper's music critic, Julius Korngold, did not review the event, which was but one among many musical performances that took place in the city every day. And yet the concert, given under the aegis of Hugo Knepler, of Gutmann's Concert Management, was so successful that it induced the seventy-four-year-old (not eighty-six, as Rubinstein stated in *My Young Years*) Ludwig Bösendorfer, recently retired head of the piano factory, to invite Rubinstein to give a solo recital on December 22 at the firm's auditorium, a major Viennese concert venue in those years. This event, too, was a success, although Rubinstein was understandably disconcerted by the eighty-year-old Theodor Leschetizky, the doyen of piano teachers, who focused "a huge pair of binoculars on my fingers"[106] throughout the performance. Also present at the Bösendorfer-Saal that evening, Rubinstein recalled, were two celebrated Liszt pupils, Moriz Rosenthal and Emil Sauer—each of them twenty-five years older than Rubinstein; Franz Schalk, principal conductor of the Vienna Court Opera and a former pupil of Bruckner; and the well-known violinist Arnold Rosé.

Before Rubinstein had left Poland for Vienna, Lubomirski had introduced him to Count Aleksander Skrzynski, a wealthy and cultivated Galician Pole whom Rubinstein described as "one of the most popular bachelors in Europe."[107] Nela Rubinstein, who knew Skrzynski in the mid-1920s, when she was in her teens and when the count was prime minister of an independent Poland, said that she had been "infatuated" with him: "He was a most attractive man," she recalled.[108] In 1909 or 1910, when Rubinstein got to know him, Skrzynski was a twenty-seven- or twenty-eight-year-old attaché at Austria's Vatican embassy; he was well introduced in the upper echelons of Roman society, and after he had heard Rubinstein play he offered to help launch the young pianist's Italian career. He invited Rubinstein to Rome, arranged and sponsored a private recital in the ballroom of the Grand Hotel, and invited many powerful people, including Count Enrico San Martino di Valperga, president of the Accademia di Santa Cecilia, Rome's main musical institution, to attend. This private performance, which probably took place in the spring of 1910, aroused great enthusiasm, and Rubinstein was engaged to give highly paid private recitals at the homes of the Marchionesses Dora di

Rudinì and Luisa Casati. Better still, San Martino invited him to give a public concert with orchestra the following season.

Rubinstein fell in love with Italy. He took advantage of every free moment to sightsee in Rome and to visit other celebrated cities—Florence, Venice, and especially Naples and vicinity, where he was bilked by a guide, invited to take advantage of the services of a ten-year-old prostitute, and pursued by a homosexual English writer, whom he did not name. During his first Italian visit, he also became acquainted with Giovanni Sgambati, one of the best-known Italian pianists and composers of instrumental music of his day (Rubinstein already had a Sgambati toccata in his repertoire), and with Modest Ilyich Tchaikovsky, one of the composer's younger brothers, who lived in Rome.

Prince Lubomirski did indeed sponsor the Berlin concert at the Philharmonie on February 3, 1910, to which Rubinstein had referred in his letter to Astruc. Rubinstein played Beethoven's Fourth and Brahms's Second Concertos with the Berlin Philharmonic under Fitelberg, who then conducted Mahler's Fourth Symphony—a rarely heard work, in those days. (Four days earlier, he and Fitelberg had performed the same program in Warsaw with the local Philharmonic.) "The knowledge that I had to perform this heavenly music accompanied by a man I loathed kept me in a state bordering on hysteria," Rubinstein recalled, but the Berlin critics "found more to praise than to blame. All in all, it was not a *great* success, but an 'honorable' one."[109] Barth, who attended the concert, sent Rubinstein a letter in which he pointed out the virtues and defects in his playing. Six weeks later, when Rubinstein returned to Berlin for a recital at the Beethoven-Saal, he visited Barth, who, he said, shouted at him for including "filthy" music by Debussy on his program; Rubinstein's memory, however, was incorrect on this point, because the program consisted of Beethoven's "Waldstein" Sonata, Brahms's Two Rhapsodies, Op. 79, Szymanowski's Variations on a Polish Folk Theme, and a Chopin group. Of this recital, the *Vossische Zeitung*'s critic wrote:

> Mr. Arthur Rubinstein showed himself to be an excellent technician in the six Chopin pieces that I was able to hear. [On the evening of Rubinstein's recital—March 14, 1910—Nikisch had conducted the Berlin Philharmonic, Mahler's disciple Oskar Fried had conducted a concert for the Society of the Friends of Music, and the outstanding young American violinist Albert Spalding had given a recital at the Bechstein Hall; the reviewer had evidently been obliged to attend bits of each event.] He is undoubtedly a talented pianist who, being young, has yet to mature spiritually. The immediate impression is that rational coolness dominates his playing, even his touch com-

municates to us no hearty or juicy sounds, he is a little weak-toned in the soft parts and often somewhat harsh in the loud ones, which certainly penetrate but lack greatness. The Barcarolle and the F-sharp Major Impromptu, in particular, were dealt with more conventionally than lovingly by the performer. Mr. Rubinstein still has time to become more profound, and it is to be hoped that he will manage to do so.[110]

This was precisely the sort of German review that Rubinstein always remembered with anger: He plays well, technically, but his music-making isn't deep enough. His estimate of himself was exactly the opposite, and, like most other human beings, he did not like others to doubt his estimate of himself. Barth, however, reportedly told another pupil that Rubinstein, despite his treasonous departure from Berlin, seemed to have "worked a little" during the intervening years. And Rubinstein recalled that his postrecital visitors included Emma Engelmann and her son Hans, Max Friedländer and his family, and even Mrs. Kurt, who, however, became "a little shy" when she saw Lily, who was traveling with him.

Thanks to Dropiowski's efficiency, Rubinstein began to play more often in cities in all three sectors of Poland, and he frequently made use of one or another of Warsaw's numerous passport forgers in order to cross borders. One of the most unusual events of the season was an all-Chopin recital in Lvov, to commemorate the centenary of the composer's birth. Rubinstein shared the program with Ignaz Friedman, another remarkable Polish-Jewish piano virtuoso, five years his senior: Friedman played the Second Sonata, Rubinstein played the Third Sonata, and together they played the two-piano version of the Rondo in C Major, Op. 73. Thanks to introductions from Lubomirski to some of the local nobility—Count and Countess Roman Potocki, Princess Radziwill, and Countess Tarnowska—Rubinstein enjoyed a spectacular success in Lvov and outshone Friedman. He long remained a local favorite.

IN 1890, FOUR years before his death, Anton Rubinstein had founded and generously endowed a competition for composers and pianists that was to take place once every five years. When, toward the end of 1910, Arthur Rubinstein participated in the fifth running of the competition, the Rubinstein Prize had already been bestowed on some remarkable talents: the twenty-four-year-old Ferruccio Busoni had won the composition prize in 1890; twenty-year-old Nikolai Medtner had won the piano prize in 1900; and twenty-one-year-old Wilhelm Backhaus had won the piano prize in 1905. Initially, when Kochanski and Antek Moszkowski—a member of a cultivated, well-off Warsaw Jewish family with which Rubinstein had become friendly—had tried to persuade him to enter the competition, he had refused on the grounds that his technique was not polished enough. Only when he read that Tsar Nicholas II's prime minister, Piotr Arkadievich Stolypin, had turned down a request from Glazunov and the competition's jury to allow nonresident Jewish competitors to stay in St. Petersburg for longer than the twenty-four hours permitted by law, did he decide to go, he said, because the ruling angered him. In the end, the government avoided embarrassing itself by ignoring the matter until the competition was over, at which time the authorities "remembered" to order Rubinstein to leave.

At least one detail of his account of the competition was incorrect: He claimed to have learned his great namesake's Concerto in D Minor—a required piece—only a few days before the event, whereas it figured on the repertoire list he had given Astruc six years earlier, and he is known to have performed it in public at least as early as the 1906–07 season. He played it again, in Warsaw, on December 16, 1910, at about the time of the competition. The rest of the story is hard to verify. Rubinstein remembered that the other pianists—all born between 1885 and 1891—included the Russians Alexander Borovsky, Julius Isserlis, Lev Pouishnov, and Leo Sirota; the Swiss Edwin Fischer and Emil Frey; and the German Alfred Hoehn. All of them eventually had successful careers, but the only one besides Rubinstein who achieved lasting fame was Fischer. The most important member of the jury, besides Glazunov, who headed it, was Anna Nikolayeva Esipova (also called Annette Essipova), a magnificent pianist in her own right. She was one of the numerous former pupils and almost as numerous former wives of Leschetizky, and she had been professor of piano at the St. Petersburg Conservatory until her retirement in 1908; her musical progeny included Sergei Prokofiev.

Some aspects of Rubinstein's description of the impression he made at the competition seem inflated: The audience went wild with enthusiasm, the jury stood up and applauded his performance of the first movement of the Rubinstein Concerto, Esipova wept over his Chopin, and everyone was certain that he would win. But the description may well be accurate, not only because Rubinstein tended to understate rather than exaggerate his musical successes but also because he frankly declared that some of the other participants had played better than he, at least in one part or another of the competition. He was highly complimentary about Hoehn's playing of Beethoven's "Hammerklavier" Sonata, and even more generous in his account of Frey's work ("quite marvelous . . . the whole program he played was a sheer delight").[111] Frey was official pianist to the Rumanian court and a composer of promise, and he won the composition prize as well as one of the piano prizes.

The first piano prize went to Hoehn; Rubinstein believed that he himself had not won it because Hoehn's patron, the grand duke of Hesse, had requested it for his protégé as a favor from his sister, the Tsarina Alexandra. But, Rubinstein added, "after hearing Hoehn's performance of the *Hammerklavier* Sonata, a work so much more important than my short E Minor one [Beethoven's Op. 90], and, on top of it, after the fine recital of Frey, I became less confident of actually deserving the prize." In the end, "a special first prize, a document of praise, [was] unanimously conceded" to him;[112] this meant that the jury regarded him as an *ex aequo* first-prize winner but gave him no portion of the two thousand rubles (one thousand dollars), which went entirely to Hoehn. Rubinstein's partisans, who included Stefan Grostern—Zosia Kohn's cousin, at whose apartment Rubinstein was staying—and André Diedrichs, the local Bechstein representative, were upset, but the story of what had happened at the competition aroused the curiosity of Sergei Koussevitzky, a thirty-six-year-old Russian double-bass virtuoso of Jewish origin who had made his debut as a conductor two years earlier. Since then, he and his wife, an heiress, had founded an important music publishing company, a concert agency, and the Koussevitzky Orchestra. Koussevitzky wired Diedrichs and asked Rubinstein to visit him immediately at his home in Kharkov; Rubinstein made the eight-hundred-mile train journey from St. Petersburg, played for Koussevitzky and his wife, was engaged on the spot as soloist for a series of concerts that the Koussevitzkys' agency was to sponsor later that season in various Russian cities, accepted a generous advance against his fee and a ticket to Warsaw, and got back on the train for another eight-hundred-mile journey.

On January 4, 1911, Rubinstein played Chopin's Second and Brahms's First Concertos with the Warsaw Philharmonic. Fifteen days later, in Rome, he made his official Italian debut at the Augusteum, a concert hall that had been built atop the ruins of Emperor Augustus's tomb. He played the Saint-Saëns G Minor and Rubinstein D Minor Concertos (not the Beethoven Fourth, as he incorrectly recalled) with the Santa Cecilia Orchestra under the direction of Bernardino Molinari, as well as the Chopin A-flat Ballade and A-flat Polonaise and—thanks to the wildly enthusiastic response of the Roman audience—numerous encores. As he had not yet resolved the question of his Russian military service, he was still afflicted with passport problems, and he begged Modest Tchaikovsky to intervene with the Russian diplomatic corps in Rome. Tchaikovsky introduced him to the ambassador, Prince Dolgoruki, one of Lina Cavalieri's lovers and a scion of one of the oldest Russian aristocratic families; Rubinstein volunteered to play a few pieces at an embassy gathering, and the following day the prince gave him an impressive safe-conduct pass, but asked him to destroy it after he reached

Warsaw. Rubinstein, however, soon discovered that when he showed it to the Russian border police they all but gave him a twenty-one-gun salute, and he decided to continue to flash it at anyone on whom he felt it might have a similar effect. And yet a mystery is connected to the story of the pass: Rubinstein claimed that he had given 1889, rather than 1887, as his birth year, when asked by the ambassador's secretary, thereby "making myself younger than the draft age,"[113] and he continued to use the later date for many years thereafter. But the minimum draft age was twenty-one, and in 1911 a person born in 1889 would have been twenty-two. The tactic would have been pointless. Either the story was untrue or, more likely, the date of its occurrence was incorrect. In any case, the lie about his age, plus the fact that Riemann's *Musikalische-Lexikon* eventually picked it up and then mistakenly printed the 9 as a 6, meant that for the rest of Rubinstein's life friends, colleagues, and orchestra managers were forever sending him incorrect birthday greetings— for his fiftieth in 1936 and 1939 but not in 1937; for his seventy-fifth in 1961 and 1964 but not in 1962; and so on, even after he had straightened the matter out in *My Young Years*.

Shortly after his return to Warsaw, Rubinstein traveled to Russia to fulfill his contract with Koussevitzky. In Moscow and St. Petersburg he played the Rubinstein D Minor Concerto with the conductor and his orchestra (he did not think much of Koussevitzky's abilities as an accompanist) and gave solo recitals that included Beethoven's "Hammerklavier" Sonata; by his own account, his success with the public was better than satisfactory but not sensational, and he found more "genuine enthusiasm"[114] among his audiences at Kharkov and Rostov-on-Don. In Kiev, the final stop on the tour, he was received lukewarmly, at first, but he eventually gave three more recitals and achieved a brilliant success, thanks to the interest of new friends, Dmitri Lvovitch Davydov and his wife, Natalya. Dmitri's mother, Alexandra, was Tchaikovsky's sister, and when, in 1878, Tchaikovsky had written to Alexandra's husband to tell him that he was dedicating his *Children's Album*, Op. 39, to the Davydovs' younger son, Vladimir, he had added: "The only thing that worries me is that Mitiuk [Dmitri, who was eight years old] might get offended. But how can one dedicate music to him when he says he does not like it?"[115] By 1911, however, Dmitri's attitude toward music had evidently changed—and besides, Rubinstein, as a friend of Dmitri's uncle, Modest Tchaikovsky, had an excellent entrée with the Davydovs. In addition, Verbovka, the Davydovs' estate, was not far from Tymoszowka, the Szymanowskis' estate, and the two families knew each other well. Karol Szymanowski had always spoken warmly of Natalya Mikhailovna Davydova, and Rubinstein found himself in full agreement: he described her as "one of those rare human beings one cannot forget—a person who emanated a luminosity, a nobility of heart and intelligence."[116] The Davydovs had long been leading figures among the Ukrainian nobility—although Dmitri's grandfather had spent several years in Siberia following his participation in the Decembrist uprising of 1825—and Dmitri was able to persuade the cream of Kiev society to attend Rubinstein's recitals. (One of the people who came for purely musical reasons was a seven-year-old pianist, Vladimir Horowitz, who lived in Kiev.) And the Davydovs invited their new young friend to spend part of the following summer with them at Verbovka.

Much has been written about anti-Semitism in Eastern Europe, and Paul Johnson has explained why the Russian government's anti-Jewish code exacerbated the problem: "While baptized and smart Jews did well, the code impoverished or criminalized others, so ethnic Russians ended by both envying and despising the race, accusing Jews of being, at one and the same time, perfumed and filthy, profiteers and beggars, greedy and starving, unscrupulous and stupid, useless and too 'useful' by half. . . . Russia was the only country in Europe, at this time, where anti-Semitism was the official policy of the government."[117] Anti-Semitism was virulent in Eastern Europe, and not least in Poland, where Jews accounted for over 10 percent of the population; the percentage was much higher in the cities. And yet, as the young Rubinstein's story has already demonstrated, there was also a great deal of productive cross-pollination between Gentile and Jewish secular cultures. Cultivated Poles, many of them members of the nobility, generously helped to foster his talent and considered him a full fledged Pole, worthy of representing Polish music before the world, regardless of his ethnic origins. Paderewski, the Skarzynskis, Jaroszynski, Mlynarski, the Szymanowskis, the Barylskis, Skrzynski, two branches of the Potocki family, Rembielinski, Lubomirski, and many others gave him moral and material support that was of the greatest possible use to him, and he also won the sympathies of Prince Dolgoruki and the Davydovs, high-standing members of the Russian nobility—which, traditionally, was even more anti-Semitic than its Polish counterpart. (Natalya Davydova, however, whose maiden name was Gudim- or Hudim-Levkovichovna, may have had Jewish or partly Jewish origins.)

Some of these people were interested in Rubinstein only because he possessed a special talent. Their open-mindedness might not have extended to an Arthur Rubinstein who ran a clothing factory in Lodz or plucked chickens in Pultusk—but then, similar attitudes were common among the Jews themselves. Rubinstein admitted that when he was young, he had thought of his people as, on the one hand, "masses of meek little men with their beards and side curls," in the ghettos, and had asked himself why they didn't use their "gifts and intelligence for something better than buying and selling old clothes"; on the other hand, he said, there were the "rich Jews and their wives

. . . showing off their wealth, . . . pushing themselves forward," and he had considered them responsible for "the indignation of the Gentiles." He knew that there was also a "highly cultured Jewish elite," but he felt that it was "too small . . . to offset the bad effect of the rest." Once, however, when he expressed these opinions to a well-known Jewish doctor in Warsaw, he was asked, " 'Have you ever tried to think about the causes of all these phenomena which you criticize so harshly?' " Dr. Goldflam lent him Heinrich Graetz's mammoth, epoch-making *History of the Jews*, which had been published between 1853 and 1876, and by the time Rubinstein finished reading it he had become "acutely conscious of being proud to be a Jew"—a member of a community that had maintained its identity despite "ostracism, persecutions, inquisitions, tortures, killings, expulsions."[118] Although he never became religious, he maintained his ethnic pride for the rest of his life.

RUBINSTEIN SPENT AT least part of the spring of 1911 in Warsaw. On April 17 he played the Ballade of Ludomir Rozycki—who had humiliated him at the door of his father's piano studio fourteen years earlier—with the Warsaw Philharmonic under Fitelberg, on a program that included the premiere of Szymanowski's Second Symphony. Nine days later he played Szymanowski's Variations on a Polish Folk Theme, Op. 10, for solo piano, on a mixed program during which the first performance of Mlynarski's Symphony in F Major ("Polonia") took place. He spent part of the summer at Verbovka, the Davydovs' estate, sleeping in the very room and bed that Tchaikovsky had used during his summer visits, and frequently exchanging visits with Szymanowski, who was at nearby Tymoszowka. Rubinstein thought that he detected serious feelings between his hostess and Szymanowski; in any case, Natalya Mikhailovna "never left the room" when Rubinstein was studying Szymanowski's just-completed Second Sonata in A Major, Op. 21, which the pianist described as "a very complicated and difficult work, but a masterpiece, full of new ideas and irresistible élan and passion."[119] He recalled having been fascinated by his reading of Stefan Zeromski's novel *Popioly (Ashes)*, but he was incorrect in describing it as a new book—it was published in 1904—and in saying that it "later" inspired part of Szymanowski's Second Symphony, which had been finished in 1910.

     In the fall, Rubinstein gave concerts in Cracow, Lvov, and other Galician towns and returned to Russia for recitals in Moscow, Kharkov, Rostov, Saratov, and—thanks to a special invitation from a caviar merchant who was a friend of Chaliapin's—also in Astrakhan, some fifteen hundred rail miles from Warsaw. On December 1, 1911, he gave the world premiere of Szymanowski's Second Sonata at the Philharmonie in Berlin; the work occupied the second part of a program whose first part had consisted of the same com-

poser's Second Symphony, with Fitelberg conducting the Berlin Philharmonic. The concert and the tour that followed were sponsored by the
wealthy, widowed mother of Szymanowski's friend Stefan Spiess. After the
successful Berlin concert, Rubinstein returned to Warsaw to play Brahms's
Second Concerto under the Philharmonic's new conductor, Zdzislaw Birn-
baum, whom the pianist Wiktor Labunski, Rubinstein's future brother-in-
law, described as "a man of many gifts, a prodigious memory . . . but no
particular talent for conducting."[120]

From Warsaw, Rubinstein proceeded to Leipzig for a performance of
the Szymanowski program on December 15. The negative account of the
event that he gave in his memoirs does not correspond to the account given
by Bronislaw Gromadzki, who was in the audience: "The Alberthalle was
full. The 'chief' of musical life was Artur Nikisch [conductor of Leipzig's
Gewandhaus Orchestra], who, as everybody knew, never attended the concerts he did not conduct. His appearance at Szymanowski's concert provoked
astonishment and jealousy. Fitelberg was already standing before the orchestra when Nikisch entered a box by the pit. A geyser or volcano wouldn't have
caused greater astonishment. 'Nikisch! Nikisch! Nikisch-sch-sch-sch!' you
could hear the amazed audience whisper. Nikisch calmed them and applauded Fitelberg, and the audience joined him. The concert began. After
the overture [first movement of the symphony?], there was another surprise.
Nikisch got up and entered the box in which Szymanowski was sitting, quiet
and embarrassed. The audience shouted. Nikisch listened to the rest of the
concert from Szymanowski's box."[121] It is odd that Rubinstein, who idolized
Nikisch, did not mention this single, documented occasion on which the
celebrated conductor heard him play. The Leipzig critics' reactions to
Szymanowski's works were mixed, but they were unanimous in their praise of
Rubinstein. "Mr. Artur Rubinstein displayed rich artistry in gradation of tone
coloration and virtuosity," the Neue Zeitschrift für Musik reported. "Arthur
Rubinstein played the young Warsaw composer's more than slightly orches-
tral second Piano Sonata with bravura and vigorous temperament," said the
Signale für die musikalische Welt. And Eugen Segnitz wrote, in the All-
gemeine Musikzeitung: "the composer's second Piano Sonata (Op. 21, A
Major) [is] a technically very difficult and complicated work, which Arthur
Rubinstein communicated excellently and above all with great temperament. . . . The audience gave both compositions its approval and bestowed
much honor on the performing artists in particular."[122]

On January 18, 1912, the same program was given in Vienna, where
Szymanowski had recently signed a contract with Universal-Edition, one of
the most important publishers of new music. The concert took place in the
Great Hall of the Musikverein, with the Konzertverein Orchestra under

Fitelberg, and the twenty-nine-year-old composer was accorded a triumph. During Rubinstein's stay in Vienna, he and Stanislawa Szymanowska, the singer among the composer's sisters, gave a joint recital of Karol's music at the auditorium of a private club, and on February 9 he played Brahms's Second Concerto with the Tonkünstler Orchestra under Fitelberg. According to the Austrian composer Joseph Marx, Rubinstein performed the Brahms "with wonderful imagination" and with "the same hard-to-define personal touch" that he brought to bear on "the Second Sonata of Szymanowski and later on Spanish music." Marx spent a good deal of time with his Polish colleagues—who "enjoyed the city's musical life"—and he reported that "at the hotel [Krantz], a truly artistic idyll reigned. One got up about noon, spent time in dressing-gown discussing art and life, smoked great quantities of cigarettes, drank vermouth, and got Rubinstein to play Strauss's *Salome*, which he did with the skill of a master." (Marx also said that Rubinstein "tried to interest Richard Strauss in conducting Szymanowski's Second Symphony, and Szymanowski hoped it would happen, but Strauss didn't keep the promise he had made to Rubinstein in Rome and said, 'I know nothing about it.' ")[123] Max von Oberleithner, a Viennese department store owner and accomplished amateur composer, invited Rubinstein to dinner and then asked him to play for his guests; although this was a nasty trick to play on an artist, Rubinstein readily acceded because, he said, many of the other guests were well-known musicians. Afterward, however, he asked Oberleithner to loan him a thousand crowns; Oberleithner loaned him eight hundred and made him sign a note (April 28, 1912) in which Rubinstein promised to pay him back by the following January 15. The promise was not kept, and fifty-seven years later a Viennese woman, Frau Renee von Bronneck-Uhlenhut, who was Oberleithner's sole surviving heiress, had a lawyer try (unsuccessfully, it seems) to make Rubinstein pay her three thousand dollars—the approximate equivalent, in 1969 buying power, of eight hundred pre–World War I Austrian crowns.

Rubinstein enjoyed a frenetic social life in Vienna—so frenetic that Szymanowski and Fitelberg were nearly driven out of their minds. The composer wrote to Spiess: "you knew our style of life, for example in Berlin. Well, there are now about four times as many people, more noise, and general pandemonium around us. . . . we are exhausted and even bored by this way of life. . . . I am beginning to long more and more for real work. But on the other hand, both Ficio [Fitelberg] and I see and feel the positive results of what we are doing here, so that one has to continue patiently through these wanderings. The concerts in Vienna and even in Leipzig were a great success. . . . Ficio and I are so seldom alone that we communicate with some kind of signs rather than with words. Our only real 'family home' is that of the Godowskys!! who shower us with violent affection."[124]

Leopold Godowsky was among those who heard the Szymanowski concerts in Vienna and liked both the music and the performers. At the age of forty-two, Godowsky—a Vilna-born Jew—was among the most celebrated piano virtuosos in the world, and he spent part of each year teaching advanced students at Vienna's Akademie der Tonkunst. He, his American wife, and their four teenage children quickly made Szymanowski, Fitelberg, and Rubinstein feel at home. Rubinstein felt honored by an invitation from Godowsky to take over the preparatory class at the Akademie, but he wished to preserve his freedom, he said. He and Szymanowski were strongly attracted to Dagmar, Godowsky's fourteen-year-old daughter, who, Rubinstein said, "looked like a Persian miniature. . . . Her heavy black braids, almond-shaped eyes, pretty nose, and full, red, arched mouth made her look older than her age . . . and she was coquettish and provocative toward us." The precocious siren led her guests to believe that she had already had more than casual friendships with Josef Hofmann, who was more than twenty years her senior, and with the composer Franz Lehár, who was six years older than Hofmann. "She was quite a girl, this Dagmar," Rubinstein said.[125] Szymanowski wrote to Spiess, "The main trouble [is] that I am taken with [the Godowskys'] young daughter whom I simply adore, and I do not know why, I am a little afraid of having some unpleasantness with this charming family."[126] Dagmar, however, was taken with Rubinstein. Many years later, in her apparently uninhibited but in fact heavily self-censored memoirs, she wrote:

> Artur was all I ever dreamed of and all I ever wanted. . . . I didn't know how I could attract him more—as a nun or harem dancer. . . . I visualized myself in the alternate roles, and Artur didn't visualize me at all. He saw me as I was—a baby with braids, braces on my teeth, and a big bow at my back that became creased whenever I sat down.
>
> It is impossible to describe my adoration for Artur. I worshiped him as a god. I loved him so that I even loved his sweethearts. If they were worthy of his love then it followed that they must be goddesses. I had more goddesses than Mr. Bulfinch. Artur's head was grotesque, his hands magnificent, and I always expected his feet to be cloven. He looked just like Pan. He was my torment and my dream.
>
> When he played our Bechstein, I would leave my bed and hide on the steps in the hall and weep. While he was at dinner with the parents, I would find his coat in the entrance hall and put my cheek against it. After dinner, I would lie in wait, and before the servants could clear the table I would find his place and take his spoon to my room as a souvenir. I put it under my pillow. My diary was stained

with tears and macaroons. Didn't Artur know that I would die for him? All he had to do was ask it.

Somehow, this was the most graphic way of showing my love—sacrificing my life to him. . . . I played the scene daily as other children played hopscotch. . . . I expired in a hundred different settings; and somewhere vaguely in the frame of my vision was Artur brilliantly playing Chopin's "funeral march" in a storm of self-reproach as he gazed at my white-clad, shattered little body. . . .

The attentions of other men embarrassed me and made them seem silly. . . . With these admirers, I was a bright young lady; with Artur I was a self-conscious, tongue-tied little girl. He didn't know I was alive!

It was true that Artur took me—on Sundays—for walks. Ah, Vienna! . . . The happiness, just walking through that dream city with Artur!

He would take me to the [Kunsthistorisches] Museum where he guided my taste in painting. He taught me to love Velasquez, which was easy, and to think of Murillo as saccharine, which was difficult. I adored Holbein so much that I never mentioned it. I was afraid that Artur, with his great influence over me, might spoil him for me. His word was law.

His best friend, composer Karol Szymonowski [sic], was as beautiful as Byron. He limped, too, ever so slightly. Karol wanted to marry me, and was willing to wait through a long betrothal. One day he came to the house with white gloves and a silk hat and asked Pa for my hand. That's all he got. . . . I preferred a man I couldn't have.[127]

Eventually, Szymanowski accused Rubinstein of flirting with Dagmar, and the enraged Rubinstein decided to flirt with her seriously, he said. "Karol and I ceased speaking to each other for a whole year, [until] Dagmar herself brought us together again."[128] Dagmar said that even years later, after she had been married and divorced, Rubinstein "still treated me like a child."[129] But Rubinstein's wife said, "Arthur must have slept with Dagmar Godowsky when she was fifteen." In later years, according to Nela Rubinstein, Dagmar was "a filthy sort of person. She was huge. She looked like a madam." Dagmar possessed "great vitality," Mrs. Rubinstein said, but "she asked Arthur for money, and he gave it to her."[130]

DURING HIS STAY in Vienna, Rubinstein heard the already-celebrated Pablo Casals make his local debut playing a cello concerto by Emanuel Moór. Or

so he said. Once again, the facts do not correspond to Rubinstein's story: Casals's Viennese debut had taken place in 1910; when the cellist returned to the
city early in 1912 he did not repeat the Moór Concerto. Perhaps Rubinstein
was present at both events and eventually combined them in his memory.
The two musicians had met in Paris a few years earlier, and each had been
delighted by the other's love of Brahms: Rubinstein, who was ten years
younger than Casals, had impressed the cellist by rushing to a piano and playing through much of Brahms's First Piano Concerto, which, according to
Rubinstein, Casals had never heard. Now, in Vienna, the cellist introduced
the pianist to his British manager, Montague Vert Chester, of the well-
established N. Vert Concert Agency, and Chester suggested that Rubinstein
make his official London debut under the Vert aegis; Prince Lubomirski,
who was also in Vienna, agreed to act as financial guarantor. According to
Rubinstein, Casals suggested that the pianist's solo debut be preceded by a
duo recital: the cellist was already a favorite in Britain, and the event would
bring Rubinstein's name before the public in a special way. In reality, however, Rubinstein's first two solo recitals took place before the joint one with
Casals.

Rubinstein wrote to Lily and persuaded her to join him in London,
where they took a furnished flat in Hanover Square. On May 1, 1912, at the
550-seat Bechstein (later Wigmore) Hall, he made his official British debut.
The *Times*'s anonymous critic liked Rubinstein's "vivid and poetical performance" of Schumann's *Carnaval*, although he had a few reservations:
"The Valse noble was a trifle too heavy and deliberate and the Papillons
rather too rapid to enable the figures to be heard; otherwise there was hardly
anything which one would have had different. The player has a varied and
well-controlled tone, ranging from a very delicate *piano* to a full and sono-
rous (sometimes almost too noisy) *fortissimo*. In rapid passages yesterday his
touch was exceedingly clear and brilliant, and generally speaking his technique is sufficiently complete to enable him to take no account of difficulties. The Studies by Liszt included in his programme would, however, have
been sufficient to prove this without the insertion of a long and turgid Sonata
in A major by Karol Szymanowski, almost the only interest of which was the
way in which it enabled Mr. Rubinstein to show off his bravura playing."[131]

Rubinstein's second recital took place on May 6, and he and Casals
gave their joint concert on May 16 at the 2,300-seat Queen's Hall. "Señor
Casals opened his programme with Brahms's Sonata in E minor for violoncello and piano with Mr. Arthur Rubinstein to play the piano part," the *Times*
reported. "The phrasing of both players in the Allegretto was beyond praise.
Except in the trio of this movement, where there was a slight difference of
understanding in the pace adopted, the two players were in close touch with

each other the whole time." Casals was accompanied by Coenraad v. Bos in a few virtuoso pieces, and then "the concert came to an end with a brilliant performance of Grieg's somewhat mannered Sonata in A minor for violoncello and piano, in which Señor Casals was once more joined by Mr. Rubinstein."[132] Rubinstein later recalled how grateful he was to Casals for treating him, throughout the performance, as a partner rather than as an accompanist. Although the pianist described the cellist's way with the Brahms Sonata as "too sweetly romantic," he said that he was "proud to play with this great master. . . . We received a great ovation with shouts of approval, and finally we had to repeat the last movement" of the Grieg sonata.[133] Not much later, Rubinstein and Casals had a falling-out over an insignificant amount of money; the rights and wrongs of this remarkably petty story are impossible to determine, but the incident cooled their friendship for the duration of their long lives.

Rubinstein had attracted so much praise for his solo recitals and his performance with Casals that two extra solo appearances were scheduled for him at the Bechstein Hall, on May 24 and June 4. In addition, Jacques Thibaud, who had attended Rubinstein's first solo recital, persuaded him to join him in two of the three recitals that the violinist was scheduled to give during the following weeks at the Bechstein Hall. The first of them took place on May 23; they played Guillaume Lekeu's Sonata, and the *Times's* critic reported that "the combination was a very happy one, for both players caught exactly the intimate and yet rhapsodic character of the music, and both, while giving the music the greatest freedom, did not allow the pace . . . to run away with them."[134] Rubinstein's participation in the last of Thibaud's recitals, on June 5, was more extensive: "M. Thibaud had the co-operation of Mr. Arthur Rubinstein, and very fine performances of Beethoven's Sonata in F, Op. 24 ["Spring"], and Franck's only Sonata for violin and piano were given," according to the *Times.* "The two players were splendidly matched; they understood the music and each other so well that there was little temptation to draw distinctions between them further than to suggest that the keenly intellectual phrasing of the pianist gave special distinction to the Beethoven Sonata, and that the emotional warmth and fervour of M. Thibaud's style dominated the interpretation of Franck's work. . . . Beethoven's Romance in F added to the pleasure of the concert. . . ."[135]

This sealed the success of Rubinstein's London season, the greatest moment of which had taken place the previous evening, at the second of his two extra solo recitals at the Bechstein Hall. His performance of Schumann's Symphonic Etudes, according to the *Times's* critic, was technically brilliant and musically original, but Scriabin's Sonata, Op. 53, which was being heard for the first time in London, "so baffled the audience that the abrupt end was received in dead silence, not from any ill-will, but because no one supposed that it could be the end. Among other things in a programme which was full of variety were some charming and delicate pieces by Karol Szymanowski, which were played with perfect taste and finish."[136]

The three London performances that Rubinstein had originally been scheduled to give during his five-week stay had become seven, and yet he discovered, to his regret, that he had earned nothing from them; Prince Lubomirski had had to make up the losses, Rubinstein said, and he implied that Chester had cheated Lubomirski and himself. But this visit to London was important to him: it launched his career in Britain and gave birth to friendships with two very different couples—the elderly Bergheims and the young Drapers. John Bergheim, a well-to-do, Jerusalem-born Jewish businessman, and Clara, his English Protestant wife, had heard about Rubinstein through a common Viennese acquaintance; they attended his performances, entertained him at their home, and helped him to survive economically by engaging him to play at their dinner parties. John Bergheim wished to take the management of Rubinstein's British career into his own hands, but he died in an automobile accident a few months later; for several years, however, Rubinstein was often Mrs. Bergheim's houseguest when he visited London, and his stays there were often extended.

Rubinstein felt that he could not introduce Lily to the elderly and conventional-minded Bergheims, but he brought her to the home of Paul and Muriel Draper, young New England blue bloods of moderately bohemian ways and considerable means. Paul was an aspiring singer, talented and devoted to music, who had been studying in Florence but had moved to London in the fall of 1911 to escape from a love affair and to study with the gifted tenor and teacher Raimund Zur Mühlen; his progress was hindered by alcoholism. Muriel, née Sanders, was an intelligent and outspoken woman who prided herself on being a keen observer. According to a friend of theirs,

> Paul was always a "gentleman" no matter how drunk he was; the night he ran down the corridor without a stitch on, his arms high, his [hair] startled from his forehead, he looked like a weak Blake drawing, but at the same time indubitably a gentleman.
>
> But Muriel was not only a lady in the quaint, old-fashioned sense of that word which connotes long, slender arms and legs, and a sweep and a satisfaction of mien that only ladies ever have; she always had, in addition, an infinitely elegant and royal air that permitted her any license of speech or gesture that she cared to indulge; no matter what she said or did she could not escape the limitation of her ivory ladyhood.[137]

During their Florence days the Drapers had had little money to spare, but in London they suddenly "became rich and fashionable," according to the same friend, because of Paul's "almost uncanny luck" in betting on horses. "Soon—really quite soon—they appeared to have several hundred thousands, a large house, and Muriel was sitting in a box at the opera in ivory satin with an entire pair of jet black raven's wings found upon her small, pale head."[138] Husband and wife were determined to transform the home they had rented in Holland Street, Kensington, into a musical gathering place for the best talent that lived in or visited London, and they had approached Montague Chester for help. Muriel said that Chester "cautioned us not to miss the début of a young Polish pianist, Arthur Rubinstein, who was at that time practically unknown."[139] Rubinstein recalled having met the Drapers after his solo recital series had ended, but Muriel's version of the story is different. One evening, she said, Chester brought the young pianist to dinner.

> When Rubinstein entered the room it became suddenly smaller. He had a young, short body and broad shoulders, from which long arms ended in the most powerfully sensitive hands I have ever seen. Above those shoulders appeared an ageless, grotesquely ugly face at the prow of a beautiful head. This head was topped with a crop of gracelessly crimped dun-blond [sic] hair that sprang aggressively from a high concentrated forehead. Eyes pale with intensity seemed more like hieroglyphics of intelligence than eyes in a face and a sombre Semitic nose carved with chastening Polish delicacy supported them. Pale firmly-full lips smiled with nervous sadness over strange teeth, and only the chin was allowed to rest a little from the forward-moving pace of his vitality. It afforded a slight pause in the breathless race to take in the rest. The next minute you realized that its backward movement was controlled with a fierceness that could defeat a Napoleon. . . .
>
> It was difficult to converse with this dynamo: words withered in the blast. We just dined, four of us. Afterward we went into the large high room and that nervous thing began in all of us, at any rate three of us, as to whether or not this pianist was going to play without being asked or whether he *would* play if asked. Even Chester began to talk politics with me, and that needed harsh treatment. Finally I turned to Rubinstein desperately, and said: "If you play the way you *are*, please begin."
>
> So with beautiful Polish courtesy, he rose, bowed, thanked me, and went to the piano. He sat down and plunged at once into the Hammer Klavier sonata of Beethoven . . . as it was meant to be played

and as it must have been essentially conceived. It became a work of monumental splendour through his fingers. Such was the young Polish pianist in 1911 [*sic*].[140]

In this published account of her first meeting with Rubinstein, Muriel Draper omitted Lily, perhaps out of discretion—which, however, she did not always display in her book—or perhaps out of a posteriori jealousy. Her nasty and exaggerated description of Rubinstein's face as "grotesquely ugly"— worse, even, than Dagmar Godowsky's reference to his "grotesque head"— cannot have pleased him (he was forty-one when her book, *Music at Midnight*, was published by Harper & Brothers in New York and London), and it may explain why, in his much later memoirs, he took the trouble to describe her in what he considered a not wholly complimentary way: "her narrow, long head, topped by hair that she kept closely under a net"—a net made of silk stockings, according to another friend—"her high cheekbones, her short, slightly flat nose, and exuberantly large mouth with thick red lips made her look like a white Negress."[141] But he may have plagiarized his description from one published more than thirty-five years earlier by Mabel Dodge Luhan: Muriel's "blonde negroid profile, with its crushed, long nose, met the circumference of the jutting bony jaw with its thick, protuberant, intelligent lips, painted scarlet," Luhan said.[142] And yet, something attracted Rubinstein to the Drapers; he was not sure, for a while, just what that something was, but he and Lily often visited Holland Street. When Lily returned to Poland, he continued to frequent the house by himself or in the company of other musicians. Casals, Thibaud, and the pianist Harold Bauer followed Rubinstein's lead in visiting what Muriel described as a "large high sky-lighted room" that housed "a Steinway piano, all the sofas we could move in from the rest of the house, [and] books of written words and written sounds."[143] They played solo or chamber works for the Drapers and a variety of guests, most of whom had monstrous musical appetites. "All other arts are more or less dimensionally confined. . . . Music forces you to recognize that there is more beyond, to which we have lost the key," Muriel wrote, to try to explain her appetite to herself.[144] But she did not mention either her husband's appetite for strong drink or the fact that she had chosen the twenty-five-year-old pianist as her confidant in the matter.

After the London season had ended, Rubinstein spent much of the summer of 1912 as a guest of the Davydovs in the Ukraine. He did not visit the Szymanowskis at Tymoszowka that year, he said, because he and Karol had not yet patched up their friendship after their rift over Dagmar Godowsky, but his statement is challenged by a memoir written in 1947 by a prominent Polish writer. Jaroslaw Iwaszkiewicz, who was distantly related to the Szymanowskis, spent part of the summer of 1912 with them, and recalled that Rubinstein was "a frequent guest at Tymoszowka, and I had the good luck of hearing him play. In those days he was not yet the interpreter of Spanish music—he played Chopin and Beethoven, but also the works of his friend Karol; later, he almost entirely neglected his music."[145] (Iwaszkiewicz would have been more correct had he said that by the 1940s Rubinstein was playing only a few of Szymanowski's compositions but with reasonable frequency.) The composer was working on his opera *Hagith*, and he invited Rubinstein over to hear the parts that he had already written. Iwaszkiewicz "grabbed the opportunity and asked Karol to be allowed to listen. Quiet as a mouse, I sat on the sofa in a corner of the salon, without stirring at all. Thus, I heard everything that Karol played for his friend. . . . But how great was my surprise when Rubinstein, after listening to the music, which had lasted a good hour, said to Karol: 'You know, my dear, I don't understand a bit of it!' . . . Karol then began to comment on the themes and to tell the story of the opera. Thus, I discovered that the part of the young king was intended for a soprano, so that the duet with Hagith, the opera's high-point, would be a duet for two sopranos. Rubinstein got Karol to give up this idea by using an argument that seems rather funny today: 'My dear, it would be like *Der Rosenkavalier!* This "travesti" is unbearable, I recently heard the piece in Dresden [where the opera had had its premiere the previous year]. The finale is so boring that you can't stand it.' "[146] Iwaszkiewicz also recalled that at a gathering at Tymoszowka that summer, Rubinstein was to have accompanied Szymanowski's brother, Feliks, in a performance—in drag—of the "Dance of the Seven Veils" from *Salome*, but the car that was taking the pianist from Verbovka to Tymoszowka got stuck in a large mud puddle during a storm. Karol had to do the playing.

Early in the 1912–13 concert season, Rubinstein acquired a new manager; why he and Dropiowski, his previous manager, parted ways is not known. Rudolf Ignaz Eisenbach—Ignaz Friedman's cousin, secretary to the manager of Cracow's concert hall, and a true admirer of Rubinstein's playing—proposed to arrange Rubinstein's tours in an orderly way, look after his publicity, obtain higher fees, and, in cities in which Rubinstein was already well known, organize concerts without the assistance of local managers, who always kept large portions of the proceeds for themselves. For these services, Eisenbach asked for 10 percent of Rubinstein's net earnings, and agreed to cover his own travel expenses " 'until the time comes when it will be easy for you to pay me back.' "[147] In other words, he wished to function as a modern concert manager and, in addition, to look after Rubinstein during his tours. After having consulted Eisenbach's boss, who spoke well of his employee and said that he was sorry to lose him, Rubinstein and Eisenbach drew up a three-year contract that satisfied both of them. The new manager proved to be efficient and effective; Rubinstein remembered that Eisenbach had "some neat little brochures printed with my picture and excerpts from reviews,"[148] and a still-extant letter from the manager to Astruc (about a prospective Rubinstein recital in Paris in 1913—a recital that never took place) bears the printed heading:

RODOLPHE IGN. EISENBACH

SECRÉTAIRE

ET REPRÉSENTANT UNIQUE

d'ARTHUR RUBINSTEIN

PIANISTE[149]

Rubinstein's engagements in the fall of 1912 took him to Lodz and elsewhere in Russian Poland, to Cracow and elsewhere in Galicia, and to Kiev, St. Petersburg, and smaller centers in the Ukraine and Russia. He spent the holiday season in Warsaw, then went via Vienna to Rome, where, he recalled, his concert at the Augusteum "was well attended, the public acclaimed me, but the fee was so derisively small that it barely covered my traveling and living expenses."[150] According to the records of the Accademia di Santa Cecilia, however, he played at neither the Augusteum nor the Accademia's own auditorium between his debut appearance in 1911 and 1924. Rubinstein spent a few days in Venice, he said, before he returned to Vienna for two successful recitals at the Musikvereinssaal; Godowsky praised his playing of the "Hammerklavier" Sonata but urged him to practice harder. The recently widowed Clara Bergheim was also in Vienna and, with her niece Madge and the niece's husband, Fred McGarvey, put money at Rubinstein's disposal, "to promote my concerts in London, Vienna, Berlin, and other important cities," he said.[151] Szymanowski was also staying in Vienna, and so was the Polish musicologist Zdzislaw Jachimecki, who wrote to his wife on March 12, 1913:

> Yesterday, about 7 . . . I went to Karol's place. Arthur Rubinstein and Mrs. Radwan were present. Karol played *Hagith*. . . . I had supper with Rubinstein and Mrs. Radwan alone, in the Kaiserbar we met Karol and Ficio [Fitelberg]. . . .
>
> [March 13th:] Yesterday afternoon . . . we played a bit of roulette. Arturek fell in, too, and gambled. With my system, I won three crowns and then, against the system, I lost them. A librettist [of operettas], Karol Feliks [Felix] Dörmann, then arrived, and the romantic Dr. Effenberger, who once was bearded like Christ, but

now—since he was expelled from the Imperial Library for having seduced someone's wife—is shaven and tragically sad. [Hans Effenberger, alias Sliwinski, was a music critic and a friend of Rubinstein, Szymanowski, and Fitelberg. When Rubinstein knew him, he was trying to make ends meet by surreptitiously preparing an international catalogue of pornographic literature.] . . . In the evening we ate supper together at Dreher's. Arturek vanished, to the sorrow of Mrs. Radwan. For these people even 30,000 crowns a month wouldn't be enough. Nowadays, Rubinstein must spend at least 100 crowns a day for his own expenses and those of Mr. and Mrs. Radwan and Eisenbach. They are always discontented and modestly desire millions, without them they cannot find the strength to work or the courage to live. I advised them to take a lesson from the modest way in which I have arranged my own life.[152]

It is hardly surprising that Rubinstein, who hated to be on the receiving end of lectures, vanished from the restaurant. The mystery is why Mr. Radwan, Lily's husband, was traveling with his wife and her lover. Jachimecki's letter sheds no light on the matter.

Rubinstein moved on to Berlin for a recital at the Singakademie, but the highlight of his stay there, he said, was an afternoon of playing four-hand arrangements of Beethoven and Schubert quartets with Emma Brandes Engelmann, at whose home he stayed. This was the last encounter with the Engelmanns that he mentioned in his memoirs. More concerts in Galicia and another trip to Vienna followed—he was seen at a concert of Szymanowski's works at Vienna's Tonkünstlerverein Hall in April—and then, in May 1913, he returned to London. He stayed at Mrs. Bergheim's home while he prepared for two recitals at the Bechstein Hall under the auspices of Daniel Mayer, with whom Eisenbach had replaced Montague Chester as correspondent agent. The first program, on May 20, included an arrangement of a Bach Toccata and Fugue, Beethoven's Sonata in E Minor, Op. 90, Szymanowski's Variations on a Polish Theme, Chopin's Polonaise-Fantasy, and other pieces by Chopin and Liszt. The *Times*'s critic said that the Szymanowski piece was "interesting for the wealth of ingenious ornament which is loaded upon the simple theme, and such ornament . . . gives the pianist an admirable chance of showing his technical ability, and he was particularly successful in building up the climax of tone in the *coda*." The critic described Rubinstein's playing of the Polonaise-Fantasy as "sympathetic and thoughtful in addition to being technically strong."[153] The success of this and the following recital, on June 6, led to an engagement in July with the well-known conductor Henry Wood and his orchestra. Chaliapin was in town to make what proved to be a phenomenally successful London debut in *Boris Godunov*, and at a dinner that he gave for his English admirers—Chaliapin later recalled—"my friend, Artur Rubinstein, played."[154] Fred Gaisberg of the Gramophone Company met Rubinstein in Chaliapin's Jermyn Street flat; the pianist impressed him as a "Gay Lothario," and Gaisberg said that he had been "struck by his precocity and satiric wit. He seemed a young edition of my good friend, Landon Ronald [composer, conductor, and pianist], whom he greatly resembled."[155]

A few months earlier, the Drapers had moved to a double house at 19 and 19A Edith Grove, off Fulham Road just north of the Thames, and there Muriel created a real music room. "By pulling out all the insides of 19A, I made out of a house a room big enough for the Mendelssohn octet," she wrote. "I left nothing but the brick walls, which I pierced with windows and a fireplace, and the roof of the house, in which I put a skylight and across which I stretched iron rods for support. By knocking a hole in one wall, I pushed a staircase through from 19A to 19, taking down a solid little stone fence that had separated them. And then we moved in. . . . Arthur Rubinstein . . . found us a matchless Bechstein piano. A Kien Lung screen unfolded itself on one side of the room and a huge sofa was built to fit another side. Plenty of small chairs for the players and plenty of big ones for the listeners were chosen: floor cushions, of a size that made it possible for a half dozen people to sit, or one tired artist to sleep if he arrived exhausted from a performance, were piled high in the corners of the room. . . ."[156] Besides Rubinstein and Harold Bauer, the pianists who participated in the Drapers' all-night bouts of music-making included, that year, Benno Moiseiwitsch, Irene Scharrer, and Landon Ronald; the violinists, in addition to Thibaud, were Kochanski (brought along by Rubinstein—"an act for which I am forever in his debt," Muriel said), Pedro García Morales, Louis Persinger (teacher-to-be of the not-yet-born Yehudi Menuhin), and another conductor, Enrique Fernández Arbós; the violists Lionel Tertis—who made Rubinstein appreciate how strong and refined an instrument the viola can be—Rebecca Clarke (wife of the composer and pianist James Friskin), and Gertrude Bauer, Harold's sister; the cellists Augustín Rubio and Felix Salmond, in addition to Casals; the flutist Georges Barrère; and the young members of the promising new London String Quartet. Once, the nineteen-year-old violist and aspiring conductor Eugene Goossens managed to squeeze seventeen musicians into the room for a performance of Wagner's *Siegfried Idyll*. In his memoirs, published nearly forty years later, Goossens said that all of his other chamber-music playing "paled beside" the "sequence of musical thrills" that he experienced at Edith Grove.[157] And Tertis declared, in his own memoirs, that "no public performances could ever have reached such a pitch of carefree, rapturous inspiration. There were no rehearsals; the music came fresh, and the executants were no duffers."[158]

Rubinstein recalled playing, on various occasions and with various partners, Brahms's F Minor Quintet and C Minor Quartet, Schumann's Quintet, Schubert's Trio in E-flat Major and *Winterreise* song cycle, the Franck Sonata for violin and piano, excerpts from *Die Götterdämmerung*, and miscellaneous lieder by several composers. Muriel remembered Arthur playing Schubert's "Trout" Quintet with Thibaud, Tertis, Casals, and Salmond and accompanying Paul Draper in Szymanowski's recent *Love Songs of Hafiz*.

Occasionally, Muriel brought Henry James, a new acquaintance, to Edith Grove. Of James's reaction to one performance, Muriel reported: "During the last [movement], when Arthur Rubinstein was burning the music out of the piano with an accumulating speed that left even those great artists somewhat breathless as he rushed them up to the high climax of the trio, H. J. turned the attention of his listening eyes toward him and kept it there until the performance came to a close."[159] After the performance, as the musicians came up one by one to converse with James, Muriel imagined that the novelist was making mental notes on each one's distinguishing characteristics, including "the life-defying speed with which Arthur Rubinstein managed to stand still."[160] Goossens said that on one occasion, "between quartets Henry James held forth on the virtues and beauties of great classic music, and most of us listened intently to his quiet eloquence of speech. He ruminated rather than orated, which makes it difficult to recall his words over a stretch of years."[161] Rubinstein felt that James had no particular liking for music but visited Edith Grove because he enjoyed Muriel's company, and perhaps James's monumental reputation intimidated him. Among the nonmusicians who came to the Drapers' at homes, Rubinstein found James's fellow American expatriate, the painter John Singer Sargent, and the English writer Norman Douglas more congenial.

The soirées at Edith Grove were not his only reason for staying on in London after he had given his concert with Sir Henry Wood. As he had no immediate professional engagements, he was able to save money by continuing to live at Mrs. Bergheim's house, with its ample staff of servants. Then, at Covent Garden, he attended what proved to be an epoch-making season of Diaghilev's Ballets Russes, during which he experienced "the revelation of a great composer, Igor Stravinsky." The company gave the British premiere of *The Rite of Spring* only a few weeks after the work's scandal-provoking world premiere in Paris; afterward, Rubinstein needed "weeks of study to understand the greatness of this work," but *The Firebird* and *Petrushka* appealed to him immediately. Most of all, however, he wanted to avoid going back to Warsaw—to Lily—because a few months earlier, after Muriel had revealed

to him the full extent of her distress over Paul, he discovered that his feelings
for her had intensified. "I took her in my arms, I kissed her. I spoke to her
soothingly and stroked her hair tenderly. I fell in love."[162]

In *Music at Midnight*, Muriel Draper commented on the private crises
and entanglements of many of her friends, but not on her own or those of her
husband, who is a cardboard cutout figure in her account. She seems to have
lived for the tributes of the celebrities who visited her home, but she never let
on which ones were her assiduous admirers, let alone whether or not she fell
in love or had affairs with any of them. Rubinstein, in *My Young Years*, is
unusually unforthcoming with details and explanations of his affair with
Muriel—and it was a full-scale affair—probably because he never thoroughly
figured the matter out for himself. Muriel was an unsettling woman. When
she suddenly announced that she and Paul were going to visit a friend in
Florence, during that summer of 1913, and asked Rubinstein if he wanted to
go along, he "accepted without the slightest hesitation,"[163] he said, although
he had promised to meet Lily in Zakopane. Muriel, in her book, merely said,
"At the end of the season Paul and I went to Florence for a brief visit with
Mabel Dodge. Robin de la Condamine [an actor], who divided his life between London and Florence, came along with us, and we took Arthur Rubinstein and John McMullin ['a young, good-looking amateur interior decorator
and Muriel's pet friend,' according to Rubinstein][164]—Mabel having told us
to bring anyone we liked."[165] Mabel Ganson—who had been married, in succession, to Messrs. Evans and Dodge, and who later married, in succession,
Messrs. Sterne and Luhan—was a thirty-four-year-old American expatriate
who had chosen Florence as her home. She dabbled in radical art and radical politics: her friends, then or later, included Gertrude Stein, D. H. Lawrence, Max Eastman, and John Reed, and she gave considerable financial
support to Cubist painters and the Freudian psychoanalytical movement.
Mabel was the woman with whom Paul Draper had had an affair in Florence
two years earlier—an affair that had driven the apparently tough Muriel to
attempt suicide—but Mabel found Muriel the more interesting member of
the Draper couple. At the Renaissance Villa Curonia, which she had taken
over, she played hostess to, or at least put up with, dozens upon dozens
of houseguests, some of whom were harder to accommodate than others.
Muriel recalled:

> Lunch . . . was not an easy meal. Arthur Rubinstein and Paul would
> come in late from playing and singing some new Sczymanowski [sic]
> songs. As his songs are incomparably difficult, these two would stand
> up for minutes by the chairs we were waiting for them to sit down in,
> and dispute a musical interval. Arthur's voice was in the category of

composers' voices, but his musical memory was unimpeachable, and he could sing very loud. He was usually right, and Draper would finally sit down, amicably defeated, and begin his belated spaghetti. Arthur would hum in unquenchable musical enthusiasm as he ate. This would be the crowning touch for Mabel . . . she would order the car, walk out of the room into it and go to Bologna. Small wonder, poor dear, turned out of her own house.

    An afternoon of sleep would pacify us, and dinner had even chances of success. Of course, Carl [Van Vechten, the novelist and music and drama critic] did not care for Bach, and Arthur played it as often as I asked him to, which was every night.[166]

    Rubinstein described Van Vechten as "a genius at arguing" and Reed—"Mabel's choice companion"—as "sullen and very aggressive." All he said of the thirty-nine-year-old Gertrude Stein, who dropped in from time to time, was that she "engaged in some interminable vocal battles with Van Vechten." Norman Douglas, who had come along to observe the human circus, swore at everyone, and Rubinstein, by his own account, was "persistently jealous and irritable."[167] Paul returned to London after a few days, and Muriel, McMullin, and Rubinstein went to Venice to recover their equilibrium, Rubinstein said. One day, however, Muriel told her companions that she was pregnant (the Drapers already had one young son—Paul Jr., who later became a well-known dancer) and was returning immediately to London to tell Paul Sr. As her train started to move, Rubinstein jumped aboard; he accompanied Muriel as far as Paris, then returned, depressed, to Venice. Although he did not say so in My Young Years, he was depressed because Muriel had told him that the child she was carrying might be his, but that she intended to remain Mrs. Paul Draper and to assume, correctly or incorrectly, that her second child was as much a Draper as her first. In Music at Midnight, however, she very carefully referred to her children as "my sons," rather than our sons.

    In Venice, Rubinstein picked up his luggage and departed for Zakopane, via Vienna and Cracow. He and Lily passed "six or seven weeks" at Zakopane, "in perfect harmony, happy in each other's company," he said, although he had told her about Muriel's strange hold over him: " 'I simply couldn't help falling in love with that woman, but I don't like her!' " Did he tell her that he might have been the father of the child Muriel was expecting? Probably not. A few weeks earlier, he had agreed with Norman Douglas, who had persuaded him (probably without much difficulty) that if Lily had lost his love, " 'it is her fault; she is not strong enough to hold you.' " But he now told Lily, " 'I love you more than ever, my darling, and I admire you!' " According to Rubinstein, Lily answered, " 'I have seen it coming for a long time, Arthur. I really am too old for you, and I gave you nothing but trouble.' " They stayed at the home of a Madame Zagorska, a cousin of Joseph Conrad. Her daughter, Aniela, had translated some of Conrad's works into Polish, and the Zagorska supper table was usually graced by some of the leading Polish literary figures of the day: Witkacy, whom Rubinstein had met at Zakopane in 1904; the novelist Stefan Zeromski; and the poet Leopold Staff. Another paying supper guest was Poland's future liberator and dictator, Jozef Pilsudski, whom the pianist remembered as "somber" and "uncommunicative." Rubinstein, when he was not enjoying convivial dinners, pleasant walks, and "lovely nights of love" with Lily, used the Zagorskas' piano to prepare his programs for the forthcoming concert season.[168]

He did not mention in his memoirs, and may not have remembered, that at the end of the summer he left Zakopane and revisited the Davydovs and Szymanowskis in the Ukraine. Iwaszkiewicz reported that at the very moment at which he himself was leaving Tymoszowka, at the end of his summer holiday, Rubinstein, full of enthusiasm for the music of Stravinsky—his new discovery—arrived in the Davydovs' car to play through the score of *Petrushka* with Karol. This was Szymanowski's first encounter with the work, and he wrote to Stefan Spiess: "Artur is here now, but he will leave shortly. We are making masses of music. Stravinsky (the one of the Russian ballets) is quite a genius, I am very impressed by him and par conséquence [*sic*] I am beginning to hate the Germans (I don't mean the old ones, of course!)."[169] For Szymanowski, those sessions at the piano with Rubinstein were the beginning of a new musical era, but for Iwaszkiewicz, the episode, as he thought back on it more than thirty years later, had been a farewell hymn to a world on the verge of self-annihilation. "From the distance a wild 'Trepak,' played by the two artists, reached my ears. I couldn't have suspected that this had been my last stay at Tymoszowka. . . . A few years later, most of the house's contents, including the grand piano, had been thrown into the pond, the house itself burned down, and its groves chopped down. How it looks today, I don't know."[170] Natalya Davydova, writing to Szymanowski in October 1919, remembered "with great tenderness our years spent together, Artur and all that was beautiful and great!" She added, "I used to be very happy, now I can be unhappy. There is still some reservoir, some remnant of happiness that can't be torn out of me. There is still some part of me that is alive."[171]

IN THE AUTUMN of 1913, not even the canniest politicians, let alone the crowd of self-absorbed artists and socialites that Rubinstein frequented, imagined that a disaster of unprecedented magnitude was about to engulf Europe.

When Rubinstein set off on his busy round of concerts, his main worry was that he had undertaken to play too much repertoire—some of it incompletely mastered; later, he blamed Eisenbach's greed for his own irresponsibility. His fall seasons included a tour in Galicia, his first appearances in Rumania (a public concert in Bucharest was followed by a private performance for the old Queen Elizabeth at the royal palace), and further concerts in Poland. On November 21, he played Beethoven's Third and Fourth Concertos with the Warsaw Philharmonic under J. Oziminski, and twelve days later he returned to the Filharmonja to give a recital that included works of Bach, Chopin, and Schumann, as well as Szymanowski's Second Sonata. In between (and not in January 1914, as he said in his memoirs), he played in Russia and the Ukraine. His recital in Kiev on November 24 was not well attended, according to Anna Szymanowska, the composer's mother, who was there, and who wrote to her son, in Vienna, that an appearance by Scriabin a few days later had had a fuller house: "there were lots of people, and I was envious on behalf of Arthur, who earned only 50 silver rubles."[172] This corroborates Rubinstein's statement that his fees on that tour were "barely sufficient for the travel and hotel expenses."[173] Karol Szymanowski was wintering at Zakopane, where Rubinstein visited him early in the new year. "Artur was with me until today and I was happy, but he has just left," the composer wrote to Spiess on January 20, 1914. "It's a beautiful and pleasant place, but I don't know how long I will be able to stand it."[174]

In Vienna on February 20, Rubinstein gave a solo recital in the Middle Hall of the Konzerthaus; his program consisted of Beethoven's "Waldstein" Sonata; Brahms's G Minor Ballade, B-flat Minor Capriccio, six waltzes from Op. 39, and Rhapsody in E-flat Major; Szymanowski's Etude in B-flat Minor and two preludes; Debussy's *Poissons d'or*; two *Goyescas* by Enrique Granados (this was one of the earliest of Rubinstein's public performances of Spanish music); and Chopin's Barcarolle, Ballade in A-flat Major, Nocturne in F-sharp Major, Scherzo in C-sharp Minor, and Polonaise in A-flat Major. A correspondent of the *Kurjer Warszawski* (*Warsaw Courier*) reported that Rubinstein's success in Vienna was increasing: "The number of his admirers grows here with his every appearance. The enormous Musikvereinssaal was sold out a week before the concert."[175] Rubinstein said that during the same visit to Vienna he performed the Brahms and Schumann piano quintets with the Rosé Quartet at the Musikvereinssaal, but their joint concert probably took place at some other time, as it is not listed in the *Neue Freie Presse*'s 1914 concert advertisements. The Rosé Quartet was then at the peak of its continent-wide fame. Its first violin, the fifty-year-old, Rumanian-born Arnold Rosé, was also concertmaster of the Vienna Philharmonic and Court Opera orchestra, and was married to Mahler's sister; he had followed Rubinstein's development since the young pianist's Vienna debut. The ensemble's first joint concert with Rubinstein must have convinced Rosé that the partnership worked, because he invited the pianist to participate in their projected tour of Spain during the 1914–15 season. "Nothing could have pleased me more," Rubinstein recalled, because he had long felt attracted to Spain and things Spanish, but political events soon rendered the plan unrealizable.

From Vienna, Rubinstein went to Budapest for a recital (Bach-Liszt, Brahms, Chopin, Szymanowski, Scriabin, and Liszt) at the Royal Hall on February 24, then to Rome, to play at a soirée given by the Marchesa Casati. (Once again, he recalled having given a concert at the Augusteum with the Santa Cecilia Orchestra under Bernardino Molinari, as well as a recital in the lovely hall of the Accademia di Santa Cecilia, but the Accademia's records list no such events.) He then traveled to Berlin, to give a recital at the Beethoven Saal; the critics liked it better than his performances the previous year, and they—not to mention Rubinstein himself—would have been surprised to learn that he would never again perform in Germany.

In London—the next stop on his tour—he had a talk with Paul Draper, who had figured out that Rubinstein was in love with Muriel; Rubinstein assured him that nothing compromising had happened and that he considered the matter closed, and Paul acquiesced. Something compromising had happened, however, and the matter was not closed, but Rubinstein began to frequent Edith Grove again. Sanders ("Smudge") Draper, who may have been his son, had been born the previous December, and Muriel reported that when the baby "was three days old he went to his first [musical] party. I was carried downstairs and installed on the big sofa, and I tucked him under my arm in a corner of it where he lay quite peaceably, waking and sleeping at his leisure and supping when he was hungry. This particularly pleased Casals, whose reverence for birth and children mounted to a passion almost tribal in its intensity. . . . Casals played a Bach suite and Arthur Rubinstein the Chopin B flat [Minor] sonata and some Scriabin."[176] But Rubinstein's first contribution to Smudge's musical education cannot have taken place before the baby was three *months* old and probably did not take place until late April or early May 1914.

One of the friends whom he brought along to the Drapers' that spring was Chaliapin, who had returned to London to perform the roles of Konchak and Galitsky in Borodin's *Prince Igor*. "He adored Arthur Rubinstein," Muriel recalled, "and the field of chamber music being relatively unfamiliar to his ear, it gave him intense pleasure to watch it unfold under his eyes, so to speak. Grand man!"[177] Rubinstein said, in his memoirs, that he also brought Stravinsky—whom he had met that spring—to Edith Grove, but the fact that a name-dropper like Muriel Draper said nothing on the subject in her book

raises one's doubts. It is known, however, that Rubinstein introduced Stravinsky to Kochanski in London in June 1914; Stravinsky became an admirer
of Kochanski's playing and dedicated to him a transcription for violin and
piano of three pieces from *The Firebird*.[178] More generally, there can be no
doubt that a friendship between Stravinsky and Rubinstein really existed during the nineteen-teens and -twenties, and indeed Rubinstein was one of the
few friends with whom Stravinsky used the intimate "tu" form of address,
in Russian and French.[179] After Stravinsky's death, the aged Rubinstein
described the composer as "a strange personage but full of genius"—an un-
derstatement if ever there was one. "He wasn't good-looking, but he had
enormous charm. I remember that he used his nose a lot, in our conversations. It was a very important nose that seemed to be almost independent of
him, and that preceded him before each sentence that he wished to emphasize: it was the nose first and then Stravinsky who appeared behind it, as if to
approve what the nose had declared."[180]

Rubinstein made five appearances in London that spring, all of them at
the Bechstein Hall. His two solo recitals took place on May 5 and 19, again
under Daniel Mayer's auspices; at the first, he played Scriabin's Sonata, Op.
53, of which he had given the London premiere two years earlier. The
Times's critic reported: "There is something in Mr. Rubinstein's playing
which reminds us strongly of M. Scriabin's . . .—something in the quick perception of the real import of each phrase and the certainty with which its
character is conveyed to the hearers in strongly cut outlines and brilliant
tone."[181] The second recital was also well received, and so were the two joint
recitals that Rubinstein gave with Kochanski. The first of these, on May 13,
consisted entirely of contemporary music. In the opinion of the *Times*'s
critic, "It was impossible for the players to feel that Korngold's Op. 6"—the
Sonata in D Minor by the sixteen-year-old prodigy, Erich Wolfgang Korngold—"was beautiful music, and they were too honest to pretend to what
they did not feel. The sonata was played in a take-it-or-leave-it manner. . . ."
In the middle piece on the program, Rubinstein was joined not by Kochanski
but by Paul Draper, for the first London performance of Szymanowski's *Love
Songs of Hafiz* (1911), in German. "Mr. Paul Draper [has] a clean and true
voice, one of those which may be classified as a tenor with baritone quality. . . .
The manner was refined and the articulation both clear and beautiful. The
songs . . . are cameos . . .—anything but set pieces." And the recital ended
with Kochanski and Rubinstein playing Max Reger's Sonata in F-sharp
Minor, Op. 84 (1905). Rubinstein's final London appearance that season was
at a benefit concert for a Mr. C. Karlyle, a voice teacher and music critic who
had fallen on hard times. Rubinstein played Debussy's *Poissons d'or*, Chopin's A Major Polonaise, and, with Kochanski, Mozart's Sonata in E Minor;

among the many other artists who participated were Rubinstein's old friend Emmy Destinn, the French baritone Dinh Gilly—who was reputed to be another of Destinn's many lovers—and the English tenor Frank Mullings.

Paul Draper's successful performance of Szymanowski's *Hafiz* songs coincided, approximately, with his financial ruin. He had entered upon a disastrous losing streak at the racetrack, and he took Rubinstein and another friend with him—for good luck, he hoped—to the 1914 running of the Epsom Derby, where he bet all his remaining assets. Muriel recalled the trio's return home:

> Sozia [*sic*] Kochanska was with me when Paul [Draper] came in with Arthur Rubinstein and a quiet, humorous little cleric from that temple of distinguished failure, Groton School. Paul was greyly pale. Arthur was strangely flushed: the little cleric less quiet than usual. All three emanated a disturbed alarm. . . . Dear Sozia's protecting friendliness sensed an imminent gloom descending, and so she took the clerical gentleman and Rubinstein up the stairs from 19A to the small drawing-room of number 19 Edith Grove. Paul and I were alone.
>
> He grew greyer and then said:
>
> "All the money is gone. It has been going for a long while. The last went this afternoon—*all* of it."
>
> "Will you have a cup of tea?" I asked.[182]

According to Mabel Dodge Luhan, the Drapers "had the house on a long lease paid in advance; they had the furniture and all the beautiful clothes. But it was not long before they had nothing else. The telephone company presently took out the telephone, the gas company cut off the gas; the servants left, except one or two gallant, devoted ones with the gambling spirit as strong in them as in their master. . . . Just the same, the imperturbable, brilliant London crowd continued to come to the Drapers' where Muriel, in her Worth frocks, gave them boiled rice and the laughter they needed and adored. . . ."[183] Rubinstein said that Muriel and Paul were saved from complete ruin only through the deus ex machina–like intervention of Paul's twenty-nine-year-old sister, Ruth Draper, who was soon to become famous throughout the English-speaking world as a monologist and monodramatist. Ruth gave Paul "the bulk of her inherited capital to deliver him from the most urgent debts," Rubinstein said; Paul was "deeply affected by her gesture, but Muriel played the queen who receives a gift from her vassal."[184] Indeed, in her memoirs Muriel rarely mentioned her famous sister-in-law.

For a while, the musical orgies at Edith Grove went on as before.

Muriel remembered the evening on which Arthur, together with Paul and Zosia Kochanski, almost carried the shy Szymanowski into the house for his first visit; she placed the event in 1913, but it happened in the summer of 1914. "From the moment [Szymanowski] arrived at Edith Grove he became one of the most dearly loved people in it," she wrote. "Rubinstein played the score [of *Hagith*] through for us that night."[185] (Either his opinion of it had changed since the summer of 1912, or he was being a good sport.) On another evening, in the presence of Kochanski, Casals, Tertis, and Pierre Monteux— Monteux often came to play the viola in chamber ensembles after having conducted performances of the Ballets Russes—Thibaud said that he would play the Brahms Violin Concerto if Rubinstein would accompany him. Unfortunately, there was no score of it in the house, but, as Muriel recalled, "Arthur accepted the challenge. . . . Arthur became an orchestra. . . . In the unlighted corner of the studio, they played the work through, without slip or unwritten pause. Needless to say, they had never played it together before. Arthur had never played it at all."[186]

Rubinstein eventually abandoned Mrs. Bergheim's home to stay with the Drapers, who, before the horses let them down, had leased another house connected to their own; they had knocked through yet another wall and had converted part of the new space into what Muriel called "amicably separate guest apartments."[187] Szymanowski, whom Rubinstein had introduced to Stravinsky, was also a houseguest, and when Jaroszynski arrived in London he, too, became a frequent visitor, much to Muriel's dismay. Szymanowski and Rubinstein had described him to her as a shy, sensitive connoisseur of the arts, but she found him to be a clumsy, rude, and demanding guest. He even committed the sin of sleeping through performances of a Mozart quartet and a Beethoven trio by an ensemble that included Rubinstein, Kochanski, and Casals, although he woke up when Rubinstein began to play a Chopin polonaise. "He listened attentively as Arthur tore brilliantly through it," Muriel recalled, "and at the end turned smilingly, sleepily to me and said, 'He plays well, my friend, does he not?' 'He does,' I answered."[188] Only when she fed him large quantities of *pêches Melba* and discussed pig-breeding with him did hostess and guest begin to understand each other.

Rubinstein's final prewar public appearance, it seems, was a performance of Beethoven's Third Concerto with the London Symphony under the Belgian conductor Henri Verbrugghen, at the Queen's Hall on April 25, 1914, as part of a Beethoven Festival organized by Daniel Mayer; the other piano concertos were played by Frederic Lamond, Ernö Dohnányi, and Max Pauer, and the series also included all nine symphonies, and the Violin Concerto with Efrem Zimbalist.[189] (Rubinstein placed this event a year and a half later in his memoirs.) As tension mounted between the Germanic powers, on

the one side, and the Russo-Franco-British alliance, on the other, Paul Dra-
per suddenly departed for Germany, ostensibly in order to study at first hand
the culture from which the German lied had sprung, but more likely, as
Rubinstein said, "to escape from the mess he had created" at home.[190]
Szymanowski departed for Tymoszowka on the day of the assassination of the
Austrian Archduke Franz Ferdinand at Sarajevo, but Rubinstein stayed on.
Muriel recalled that he was with her when she learned that England had
declared war, and that he went to the piano and played the shepherd's melancholy theme from *Tristan*. But her account of his part in the war effort differs
greatly from his version. She implied that he was stirred into action by exter-
nal considerations: "John McMullin brought [to Edith Grove] a young man
who made hats out of feather dusters and faded window curtains. For a day,
he sat cross-legged on the Chinese daybed in a corner of the studio, and un-
perturbed by wars . . . , fashioned lovely nonsense to put on my head. . . . It
infuriated Rubinstein so that he left for Russia, preferring death to such indig-
nity. Unfortunately, he could not get across the Russian frontier, and might
better have borne with millinery for a day, for he had only to come back
again."[191] But Rubinstein said, "I could read in [Muriel's] eyes that she disapproved of me for not joining the war. It was of no use explaining to her that
in the three divided parts of Poland brothers were forced to fight against
brothers, that I would like nothing better than to fight the Germans, but not
on the Russian side." Only when word came that Russian Poles would be
allowed to fight under their own flag, and that an independent Polish Legion
was being formed within the French army, did he decide "to leave for Paris
without delay and enroll in the Legion of my compatriots," he said.[192]

Rubinstein did go to Paris, where, after many ups and downs in his
luck—corresponding to changes in Russia's and France's official attitudes toward Poland—he found work, through Gabriel Astruc's good offices, as a civilian translator of documents confiscated from German prisoners of war. He
was reunited with his brother Ignacy, and the two of them, together with
other Polish exiles, often congregated at the Café de la Rotonde in Montpar-
nasse. He also frequented a Rumanian couple whose lovely young daughter
played the piano; he paid her "polite little attentions," kissed her "when we
were alone for a second," and held her hand under the table. But when she
showed up at his hotel one day, hoping to elope with him, he was upset by
her recklessness and, above all, her thoughtlessness in disturbing him. "A
strange girl, this Marguerite. Rather sweet and lovely, but she poisoned the
air of Paris for me on that long day," he commented, like Don Giovanni
commenting on Donna Elvira.[193] Soon afterward, he said, he saw in a London newspaper that he had been engaged to play Beethoven's Fourth Piano
Concerto with the London Symphony in January 1915 (really Brahms's Sec-

ond Concerto on December 7, 1914, with Verbrugghen conducting). He claimed that the notice surprised him, but this seems unlikely. Either the engagement had been arranged directly after his performance with the same orchestra and conductor earlier that year, or he himself had sought it, independently or through an agent, at a later date. Eisenbach, who was a Galician Pole and therefore an Austrian subject, had returned home with members of the Austrian embassy's London staff immediately after the outbreak of war, and there is no further mention of him in Rubinstein's memoirs; no other agent would have tried, unasked, to secure a concert for Rubinstein or any other artist, let alone an artist whose whereabouts were unknown. Whatever the truth of the matter, Rubinstein persuaded a Russian colonel of his acquaintance to provide him with "a signed legal document stating that my artistic work was a useful contribution to the war as propaganda for the Allies,"[194] he said, and he returned to London no later than the first days of December 1914. Thus ended Rubinstein's war, which had lasted only three months.

With the violinist Sylvia Sparrow—a former pupil of Kochanski and Thibaud, and the girlfriend of Albert Sammons, the first violin of the London String Quartet—Rubinstein rented a studio and began to give piano lessons. He also rented a cheap room in the Fulham Road that was close to the studio and to Edith Grove, where neither war nor financial disaster could dampen musical spirits—for a while, at least. Lionel Tertis recalled that it was precisely during those months that he "took part in some of the most delightful chamber music making imaginable" in "Mrs. Draper's cellar," where "the meetings lasted as a rule from midnight till daybreak!"[195] One evening, Thibaud brought along his esteemed older colleague, Eugène Ysaÿe, who, at fifty-seven, was one of the most celebrated violinists in the world. "Thibaud played a Mozart sonata with Arthur," Muriel recalled, "and when Warwick Evans, Albert Sammons, [and] Waldo Warner [all members of the London String Quartet] . . . arrived an hour later, they played the Brahms piano and string quartet in C Minor. Ysaÿe wept with pleasure at this performance."[196] He loved the environment so much that on more than one occasion he returned to play in what he referred to as *la cave*. "Out of the innumerable works performed, ranging from duets to octets, one in particular stands out in my memory," said Tertis:

> Brahms's C minor piano quartet, played by Ysaÿe, Casals, Rubinstein and myself. Prodigious, the lusciousness and wealth of sound! Ysaÿe with his great volume of tone and glorious phrasing, Casals playing in the slow movement with divinely pure expression, Rubinstein with his demoniacal command of the keyboard (his ferocity in the

Scherzo was frightening)—what an experience for me to be associated with such giants.

It was my good fortune to meet Rubinstein when he was a young man in his twenties and I was in my thirties. He was a wonderful pianist at that time but had more leisure than in later years to devote to his friends, and I had the joy of making music with him on many occasions. From the numerous parties at which we gathered, a memory that is particularly impressed on my mind is of his extraordinary gift for playing excerpts from any symphony or opera that you cared to mention—a marvellous feat at which he never faltered.[197]

Tertis also reported that during the same period "a message came to Ysaÿe from Lord Curzon," the formidable former viceroy of India who was then privy seal in Asquith's emergency coalition government. The war-beleaguered Belgian king and queen had sent one of their little daughters to live at Curzon's country home, Hackwood, near Basingstoke, and Curzon invited Ysaÿe, the child's compatriot, to "come and make some music," Tertis said. "Arthur Rubinstein was in London, and Ysaÿe collected three others to form a quintet—Albert Sammons, Emile Doehaerd [a Belgian cellist] and myself. We went down for the day and were greeted and delightfully entertained by Lady Ravensdale, Lord Curzon's daughter. We played chamber music galore but so engrossed were we all (including our host [who, however, fell asleep during the performance, according to Rubinstein]) that we overlooked the clock and missed the last London train. So at Hackwood we spent the night, kitless. Lord Curzon produced one unused toothbrush which he put up for auction among the five of us. He lent me a suit of his pyjamas—the pyjamas of a much taller man than myself, and of far greater girth. . . . How the other members of the quintet fared, history does not relate."[198] Irene, Lady Ravensdale, was twenty years old, pretty, poised, and charming. Rubinstein took note.

The burden of maintaining the house at Edith Grove eventually became too great for Muriel, who decided to return to America with her two little boys. Paul had already gone back, after his ill-advised German jaunt. Rubinstein claimed not to have been present when Muriel actually departed, and indeed that his unhappiness at not being able to help her out, economically, had given him "an acute sense of inferiority."[199] But by her account he did attend the all-night party that took place at Edith Grove just before she left:

[Norman] Douglas was with me. People arrived. Arthur, back from Russia [sic], had come for dinner. . . . Ysaÿe . . . soon followed. The

London String Quartet arrived. Barrère, in London by happy chance, hurried in with his flute. . . .

Ysaÿe played the first movement of the Mozart E Minor sonata with Arthur. . . . Sammons and Arthur followed with my favourite A Major violin sonata of Brahms, and then Arthur played Bach. . . . Barrère, Ysaÿe, and Arthur played the exquisite serenade for violin, piano, and flute that is one of Beethoven's earliest and loveliest accomplishments. When it was over, Arthur played the Chopin B flat [Minor] Sonata. . . .

I walked down and called the others from the studio for breakfast. We lighted the faithful old percolator once again, and broke eggs for the last time in the dining-room of Edith Grove. Arthur and I made a search in the kitchen for some butter to scramble them in, and discovered two small bottles of champagne and a little yellow terrine of paté-de-fois-gras [sic]. . . .

It was time to go. . . . I turned to look. And there in the door they stood, Ysaÿe, Barrère, Rubio, Sammons, Warner, Petrie, and Evans, their instruments miraculously at hand, playing divinely. I do not know what they played, but as it carried me across the sidewalk and into the waiting cab, I heard from the open window in the roof of 19A the splendid chords of the Hammer Klavier Sonata.[200]

For a while, however, musical life went on at Edith Grove: Muriel had suggested that Sylvia Sparrow occupy the house until the lease expired, and the soirées continued thanks to the financial assistance of Juanita Gandarillas, a young Chilean woman whose family had begun to play a major role in Rubinstein's life. Juanita's husband, José Antonio (Tony) Gandarillas, had an aunt, Eugenia Errazuriz—the wealthy, beautiful, middle-aged former wife of a Chilean diplomat—who had met and heard Rubinstein play at the Paris home of the American artist Romaine Brooks in 1906, and she had been singularly impressed by him. Late in 1914 or very early in 1915—shortly after Rubinstein had returned from his brief war effort in Paris—Errazuriz learned, through John Singer Sargent, that the pianist was living in London, and she immediately invited him to her home. Sargent told him that although Errazuriz spoke in a strange and at times unintelligible mixture of Spanish, French, and English, she had " 'unfailing, uncanny taste' " in the arts, major and minor.[201] Rubinstein was soon in full agreement; moreover, the Chileans quickly conquered his heart, and he theirs. They gave him costly gifts and invited him to their dinner parties, at which he met and sometimes played for Augustus John, Harold Nicolson, and many other well-known guests, British and foreign. Before long, Errazuriz, who enjoyed being a patroness of the arts, had installed Rubinstein in a beautiful, elegantly furnished little flat—complete with butler and Bechstein concert grand—in the Royal Hospital Road at the corner of Tite Street, in Chelsea; his new home was close to Edith Grove, to the studio that he shared with Sylvia Sparrow, to Sargent's studio, and, most important, to the Chileans' own, larger apartment at the corner of Tite Street and Chelsea Embankment.

On August 5, 1915, the Russians abandoned Warsaw, Lodz, and the rest of their sector of Poland to the Germans. Rubinstein's concern over the fate of Lily, his family, and his many friends back home must have been intense, but it was tempered by the prospect of a new adventure: Through the conductor Enrique Fernández Arbós, whom he knew from the music room at Edith Grove, and who had just given up his position as professor of violin at London's Royal College of Music, Rubinstein had received his first invitation to perform in Spain. He recalled the circumstances in a short essay that he wrote in Madrid nearly half a century later:

> With his [Madrid] Symphony Orchestra, [Arbós] organized magnificent seasons every summer at the Casino in San Sebastián. In 1915 he had the strange idea of organizing a Brahms festival, and I call the idea strange because in those days, the Spanish—like audiences in many other countries—ferociously hated the music of the great composer from Hamburg. Within the framework of this Festival, the French pianist Maurice Dumesnil was supposed to play the Concerto in D Minor. But the war was on and Dumesnil found it impossible to abandon his country. The desperate Arbós wrote to an agent in London and asked him to send a pianist capable of playing the Concerto in question, giving my name as one of the Brahms interpreters he most esteemed. Naturally, the agent—who wasn't my own—negotiated first to offer the opportunity to one of the artists he represented, but none of them was prepared for such a difficult task and, at the very last instant, he called me.
>
> How can I describe my happiness? All my life I had had a tremendous wish to see Spain. Even when I was only seven or eight years old I felt that I was under the spell of Spanish music, of its obsessive rhythms with their irresistible power. I was told at the time that over in Mexico they had played the Spanish song *La Paloma* while they were executing Emperor Maximillian and, profoundly impressed by the story, I got tears in my eyes every time I heard the song's sweet habanera rhythm.
>
> Unfortunately, my joy over the trip to Spain was soon dimmed. Although Polish, I was a Russian subject, and I could by no means

leave England without the permission of the [Russian] Embassy, which I didn't dare to approach. What if, when I had presented my-self, they sent me to Russia to fight? . . . At the last moment, when I was on the verge of giving up, I managed to win out over that inde-scribable mass of difficulties thanks to a lady [Errazuriz] who was the friend of the [Russian] ambassador, and to a special permit from the English Ministry of War.[202]

Early in August 1915 Rubinstein embarked on an English warship bound for Bilbao. The trip was slow and uncomfortable—everyone aboard had to wear life jackets at all times, in case of an attack by enemy U-boats— but it proved exceptionally worthwhile. At the age of twenty-eight, Arthur Rubinstein was about to meet the nation of his dreams, and to add a new and important dimension to his career.

4

The Latino from Lodz

Each summer during the Belle Epoque, many of Madrid's prominent citizens migrated two hundred miles northeastward to vacation at San Sebastián, on the Bay of Biscay. When Rubinstein arrived there on August 9, 1915, only twenty-four hours before his first concert with Arbós, the temporary local residents included the prime minister, Eduardo Dato; the minister of the interior, José Sánchez Guerra; the minister of education and fine arts, Count Esteban de Collantes; the government's chief of staff, Marquess de Lema; the queen mother, María Cristina; and hundreds of other representatives of the Spanish aristocracy, government, and *haute bourgeoisie*. Beachcombing was insufficient diversion for some of the members of these echelons of society: to keep everyone happy, plays, vaudeville shows, ballets, movies (silent, of course), and other forms of entertainment were presented in four theaters and two cinemas. And the center of social life was the Gran Casino, which offered gambling, an excellent restaurant, a café "con afternoon tea todos los días," and a theater in which, along with plays like the then-running *Nieta y abuela (Granddaughter and Grandmother)* by Jacinto Benavente—Spain's future Nobel prize–winner—many concerts were given by internationally known musicians.

In his memoirs, Rubinstein wrote with understandable pleasure and pride of the warm reception he was accorded in San Sebastián, but his report was excessively modest. His Spanish debut performances were no mere success: they were a triumph more immediate and more immense than any he had known. The first concert, an all-Brahms program, began at 5 P.M. on August 10 with the "Academic Festival" Overture, after which Rubinstein entered to play the First Piano Concerto. In the next day's issue of *La Voz de Guipúzcoa*, one of the local newspapers, the critic (Shabiroya) wrote: "From the first moment, we could perceive that we had before us a great pianist, a great artist, a complete musician. His stupendous gifts as a pianist with a gigantic and perfectly balanced technique, his beautiful sound and great musicality, took hold of the listeners. They gave the great artist a warm ovation at the end of the 'maestoso' [first movement], and so on throughout the work, which made a profound impression. . . ." Lushe Mendi, the music critic of the other local paper, *El Pueblo Vasco*, wrote of the "magnificent effects" that the "distinguished pianist" achieved, and went on: "Mr. Rubinstein is a complete artist. He possesses a stupendous technique . . . [and] he feels the music he interprets. . . ." But these reactions were put in the shade by the response to the following day's concert, in which Rubinstein played his trusty Saint-Saëns G Minor Concerto and three solo pieces by Chopin. Mendi reported that the concert was "one of those listening sessions the memory of which cannot easily be forgotten," and that Rubinstein had played the Saint-Saëns concerto "in a more prodigious manner than we have ever—I repeat, ever—heard, and don't forget that we have heard this work played several times by the distinguished French composer himself!" Shabiroya's account of the concert was even more enthusiastic:

> The grandiose success that this extraordinary artist achieved yesterday was epoch-making. We do not have words adequate for describing the impression we received while listening to this colossal pianist. He has everything: musical talent of the highest order, a formidable and perfect technique, an extremely beautiful tone that sings and that is related to the emotion of the voice, bravura, imagination, fine taste in everything he interprets, and the temperament of an exceptional artist.
>
> Rarely have we heard so great and unanimous an ovation as the one that this highly noteworthy artist received yesterday. After the first movement of Saint-Saëns's Concerto in G Minor the audience burst into bravos and loud applause that obliged him to bow time after time; then, after the Scherzo, the ovation exceeded all limits, and the audience, fascinated by this marvelous way of playing, so musical and so extraordinarily spiritual, applauded with mad enthusiasm.
>
> Finally, the concluding Presto of Saint-Saëns's delightful concerto was brought off with such great speed and feeling for rhythm that the audience was left amazed, stupefied, and as if subjugated by the colossal artist's hypnotic power, and before the end of the number people broke into shouts of enthusiasm, creating a general ovation; Maestro Arbós, the orchestra, and the entire audience paid homage to the young pianist, whose natural smile could not have been more winning.
>
> In the second part—the solos—we heard a Chopin such as we had never heard before, a Chopin beyond dispute. This is the way it must be, this is Chopin! What poetry, what intense sentiment, what

imagination! Even those who are most demanding with respect to Chopin interpretation applauded frenetically, won over by the conquering talent of Arthur Rubinstein. . . . To say that the audience applauded the distinguished artist madly is to say little indeed. After repeated returns to the stage, he gave us as an encore Chopin's Etude in A-flat Major, and it was ideal, leaving everyone under the impression of this extraordinary pianist's supreme art. As he is young and prodigiously talented, he will know days of glory and have a triumphal career.[1]

The queen mother received Rubinstein at Miramar Palace, and, according to Arbós's memoirs, "intervened so that he would give two recitals."[2] Arbós probably misremembered: in addition to a third concert with orchestra, which may have been added at María Cristina's request and/or by public demand, there was only one solo recital, which could not be scheduled until August 30; Rubinstein must have attached great importance to this event, because he cancelled a performance at Henry Wood's Promenade Concerts in London in order to stay on. (According to Wood, the English pianist William Murdoch "played the 'Emperor' concerto at very short notice . . . when Arthur Rubinstein was detained in Portugal [sic].")[3] Rubinstein's third orchestral concert in San Sebastián took place on August 13; he played Beethoven's Fourth Piano Concerto and, in his solo interlude, Debussy's *Poissons d'or*, Scriabin's Nocturne for the Left Hand, and Liszt's Twelfth Hungarian Rhapsody. Then he spent two weeks as a tourist in Madrid, Toledo, Córdoba, Seville, and Granada. Far from exhausting him, the eleven-hundred-mile train journey refreshed him, and the recital he gave in San Sebastián on his return could hardly have gone better. When Lushe Mendi arrived at the Casino, forty minutes before the performance was scheduled to begin, "an immense mob, crowded together impatiently and invading the grand staircase of the main entrance and the small staircases of the side doors, was waiting for the moment when it could enter the hall. There we waited a good quarter of an hour, thrown together, putting up with more or less violent pushing and shoving until the order was given to open the doors. The row that followed was highly irregular. It was a matter of every man for himself . . . in the midst of a giant wave like those in the most furious storms."[4]

The program consisted of the Bach-Tausig Toccata and Fugue in D Minor, a Brahms capriccio, a Chopin group (the Barcarolle, F-sharp Minor Polonaise, some preludes, the Berceuse, and the B-flat Minor Scherzo), Debussy's *La Soirée dans Grenade*, Rachmaninoff's Prelude in G Minor, an étude by Szymanowski, and, once again, the Liszt Rhapsody. As an encore, Rubinstein played Chopin's A-flat Major Polonaise. Audience and critics

were again ecstatic, and even Francisco Gáscue y Murga, the well-known
Basque musicologist who was the local correspondent of the *Revista Musical
Hispano-Americana*—a much more important publication, for musicians,
than San Sebastián's newspapers—declared that Rubinstein belonged "in
the front rank" of pianists.[5] Still more important was an offer, which Rubinstein accepted, to give twenty concerts in various Spanish cities during the
following winter. After a farewell dinner that Arbós gave in his honor, Rubinstein returned to England, more than satisfied.

He could hardly have made a greater cultural and climatic leap within
Europe than the one from Spain to northern Scotland—the town of Forres,
on Moray Firth, where he spent the late summer and early fall as a guest in a
large house that Eugenia Errazuriz and Juanita and Tony Gandarillas had
rented. He practiced, performed for his hosts, went riding, played billiards,
read, and enjoyed being entertained in lordly fashion. En route back to London, Rubinstein stopped at Leeds to give a recital—his local debut—but after
a joint concert with Ysaÿe, in London, he returned to Scotland: on November 13, 1915, at St. Andrew's Hall in Glasgow, he made his Scottish debut and,
simultaneously, gave his first performance of Tchaikovsky's First Concerto.
The Scottish Orchestra was conducted by Emil Mlynarski, who had escaped
to Russia with his family when the war began and thus had no news of their
friends in German-occupied Poland. Rubinstein recalled that "many imper-
fections" in his playing of the Tchaikovsky Concerto had been evident during the rehearsal with orchestra, on the morning preceding the concert, and
that Mlynarski had given him "precious advice on how to handle, musically
and technically, this exacting score. . . ." The conductor replaced some of the
all-too-frequent fortissimo indications in the piano part with piano-crescendo
marks, "thus refreshing and heightening the effect of the whole," and he
warned Rubinstein not to play the waltz sequence in the second movement
too quickly. "I never play this work without being conscious of his words.
And, thanks to him, I had a real success in Glasgow and Edinburgh."[6] The
story was somewhat different, however, as Mlynarski recounted it to Wiktor
Labunski, one of his future sons-in-law. "Artur came to the rehearsal obviously unprepared, got mixed up in several places, and sounded quite vague,"
Labunski reported. "Upon returning to the hotel Emil asked Artur what was
the matter with him; Artur Rubinstein hesitatingly conceded that he never
saw the printed copy of the concerto before, and thought that he knew it well
enough to play. Emil handed him the score. . . . 'Here,' he said, 'you will now
practice until you learn it.' Artur spent all afternoon at the keyboard, with the
result that he gave a brilliant performance that night, much to the delight of
the audience and of his severe mentor. When Emil told me this story, he
added: 'If Artur only wanted to work really hard, he would be the greatest
pianist in the world.' "[7]

Sixteen days after his Scottish debut, Rubinstein played the Saint-Saëns Concerto at the Queen's Hall, London, for the Royal Philharmonic Society; this was his first appearance with the conductor Thomas (later Sir Thomas) Beecham, who was eight years his senior.

In *My Young Years,* Rubinstein incorrectly stated that his first major Spanish tour began early in January 1916 and that he signed a contract with young Ernesto de Quesada and his Madrid-based Daniel Concert Agency when the tour was already well along. The tour really began in the second half of February 1916 and was organized from the start by the Cuban-born Quesada, who had studied in Boston at the turn of the century and had worked for the Wolff concert agency in Berlin before going to Spain. He had met Rubinstein at San Sebastián the previous summer and had immediately begun to organize his 1916 Spanish itinerary. Indeed, the directors of the local Philharmonic Society in Bilbao, where Rubinstein made two of his earliest appearances on the tour, on February 23 and 24, had complained that Quesada was sending them Rubinstein instead of the more celebrated Teresa Carreño or Busoni. But after the first concert, their protests dissipated. "Last night we heard for the first time this prodigious pianist named Rubinstein," wrote the critic of the local paper, *El Nervión,* after the first concert, "and we humbly confess that he seduced us through his domination of the keyboard, his amazing capacity to assimilate, perform, and interpret. . . . Rubinstein received formidable ovations, which will be repeated today, and rightly so."[8] He shared his second and equally successful recital in Bilbao with the eighteen year old cellist Gaspar Cassadó. In Oviedo, on the twenty-sixth, he played Beethoven's "Waldstein" Sonata, Liszt's Twelfth Rhapsody, and four Chopin pieces; two days later, in another recital shared with Cassadó, he performed Chopin's Third Sonata—a local premiere—Brahms's Rhapsody in E-flat Major, and *Navarra* by Isaac Albéniz. This contradicts the pianist's claim that he did not dare to play Spanish music in Spain until later in the tour, after Albéniz's widow and daughter had encouraged him to do so. He played a similar program in Santander, again sharing the stage with Cassadó and again including music of Albéniz.

After having performed in other cities, Rubinstein made his first appearances in Madrid, at the Teatro Lara, on March 10, 13, 15, and 17; his programs included the pieces he had played in Oviedo as well as works by Debussy, Ravel, Scriabin, Szymanowski, Liszt, and others. The recitals were enormously successful, but there was also some negative criticism, as a defensive article by Miguel Salvador in the *Revista Musical Hispano-Americana* indicates. Salvador was president of the Philharmonic Society, the National Music Society, and the musical section of the Cultural Society. "We are battling indignantly . . . against those who wished to make him seem a *pianolaist,* that is to say, a great technician, all speed and lots of noise, but completely mechanical and lacking in brains; luckily, we were right when we declared that they would change their opinion, since they have all recanted in the meantime. But the defeated didn't admit their inconstancy without listing the real or imagined defects they perceived in him: the majority referred to an *excess* of speed . . . , *excessive romanticism* in certain works, lack of mastery in the use of the pedals, the messing up of some passages, and equivocal interpretations." Some of these negative descriptions were remarkably similar to the criticisms that Rubinstein had received in Germany, where he had occasionally been described as a superficial virtuoso, and they were the opposite of what was often said about Rubinstein during the latter half of his career: From the late 1930s on, his technique was often described as unexceptional but his musicianship was usually considered profound—an opinion that corresponded to his own. Salvador, however, was convinced from the start that Rubinstein's virtues, technical and musical, far outweighed his defects. "I concede that he is sometimes too fast, that some passages are sloppy, and that the pedalling could be improved," he said, "but even in those passages he keeps the main outline safe and maintains what in my opinion is his greatest quality as a pianist, that is, a sensitivity to levels or gradations in the quantity of sound."

Salvador's defense of Rubinstein was not meant to fend off an army of enemies, but merely to dust away a sprinkling of dissenters in the midst of what was an overall triumph. In the course of the tour—whose twenty planned concerts kept growing in number—Rubinstein returned to Madrid to play the Saint-Saëns Concerto with Arbós and the Madrid Symphony Orchestra on March 27 and to give a solo recital, on April 14, that included Szymanowski's Variations on a Polish Folk Theme, Op. 10, and Scriabin's Fifth Sonata. Salvador reported that although some of the pieces played were "very advanced," the audience of the Sociedad Nacional de Música, "which is made up of real music lovers, was fascinated by the program and the works."[9] Indeed, in those years Rubinstein was a dedicated performer of contemporary music—not the music of Schoenberg, Berg, Webern, or other avant-garde German-school composers, but of many French, Slavic, and Hispanic moderns. Among the composers whose works he played during the 1916 Spanish tour, Debussy was fifty-four, Rachmaninoff forty-three, Ravel forty-one, Medtner thirty-six, and Szymanowski thirty-four; Albéniz had died seven years earlier at the age of forty-nine and Scriabin in 1915 at the age of forty-three.

A recital in Barcelona on March 24, 1916, included "La Maja y el Ruiseñor" ("The Maiden and the Nightingale") from *Goyescas* by the forty-nine-year-old Enrique Granados, whose children were present. They were awaiting their parents' return from America, where the operatic version of

Goyescas had just had a successful premiere at the Metropolitan Opera. Earlier that day, however, the boat on which the composer and his wife were crossing the English Channel had been torpedoed by the Germans; Granados had been picked up by a lifeboat, but when he saw his wife struggling in the water he dived back in to save her, and drowned with her. The children, as they listened to Rubinstein play their father's music, did not know about the not-yet-confirmed disaster, and the performance, as Granados's daughter, Natalia, later wrote, turned out to be a "posthumous homage to Maestro Granados." She was probably incorrect, however, in describing Rubinstein and Granados as "cordial and affectionate, if not intimate" friends, because there is no record of their ever having met, and Granados's name does not even appear in Rubinstein's memoirs.

Rubinstein returned to Barcelona's Palau de la Musica Catalana at the end of April to perform a Spanish work that he had recently learned and that remained close to his heart: *Iberia*, a piano suite written by Albéniz between 1906 and 1909. He had met Albéniz in Paris in 1904 or 1905, but he had not been aware that the "chubby and very cheerful Spaniard"—thus Rubinstein described him in 1963—was an accomplished composer. A year or two later, "Paul Dukas handed me a volume of music, saying, 'Look at this; this will certainly interest you, since you're so crazy about Spanish music.' It was the first volume of Isaac Albéniz's *Iberia*. Although I considered myself a good sight-reader, it seemed to me fearfully difficult to play. Its essence, however, which was so purely Spanish, immediately aroused my enthusiasm."[10] During a stop at Palma de Mallorca during his 1916 Spanish tour (not the following season, as his memoirs suggest), he played parts of the work for the composer's widow and daughters, who lived there; they told him that he played it very much as Albéniz had done—including the omission of " 'a lot of the nonessential accompaniment,' "[11] he said—and they encouraged him to perform the work. "I was no Andalusian, but I imagined that this was how Albéniz had conceived the piece," he told an interviewer, more than forty years later. "Albéniz was an extraordinary creative genius, but he never learned the art of musical construction and almost all of his work retains its popular roots. People said this about it, and so when he wrote the *Iberia* Suite he belabored it to such a point that he made it exaggeratedly difficult. It came out almost unplayable, and this prevented it from being a success in its day."[12]

Rubinstein evidently believed that the encounter with Albéniz's family had authorized him to make whatever changes he saw fit. "I studied a way of freeing Albéniz from some technical obstacles through which the composer sought an international accent," he told another interviewer. "I've done this in order to make him, on the contrary, more genuinely Spanish."[13] And to still another interviewer, he said, "Albéniz did not know the resources of the piano too well, and he often wrote in an awkward way. So I had to fix up his music to suit my fingers and to make his unpianistic Spanish vignettes 'sound,' as we say. Have you tried to play *Navarra* as Albéniz wrote it? You'll find it impossible. It is not only finger-breaking, it is ineffective. . . . I learned things very quickly in those days. It took me three weeks to learn all the twelve pieces of Albéniz's *Iberia*."[14] When he felt ready, he programmed the work in Madrid and Barcelona, splitting it into three groups of four pieces, to be played in a series of three recitals that also contained works by other composers. The Madrid performances he described as "without exaggeration the real turning point in my career. After every one of the pieces there was a roar. 'Bis, bis, bis,' shouted the audience, forcing me to repeat one after another. At the end they gave me the greatest ovation of my life; I had to bow a dozen times, I was showered with flowers, and out in the street a crowd accompanied me to my hotel and continued shouting 'Bravo.' Señora Albéniz, Laura [one of her daughters], Arbós, de Falla, and other musicians embraced me. . . ."[15]

The reaction was similar when he repeated the feat in Barcelona, on April 22, 26, and 29, 1916 (the programs also included music by Beethoven, Schumann, Chopin, Liszt, Schubert-Tausig, Rachmaninoff, Debussy, and Medtner), but a few observers expressed reservations. "Although he is always prodigal of his outstanding qualities as a performer, we have never seen Artur Rubinstein give of himself in such a total, youthful, and generous way as in the interpretation of *Iberia*," Federico Lliurat reported in the *Revista Musical Catalana*. "In general, he seemed sensitive above all to the brilliant, sunny aspect of *Iberia*, of which he certainly gave an admirable reading. . . . But is this . . . the most important aspect of *Iberia*?" The critic thought it was not, and he went on to compare Rubinstein's performance to that of a Catalan pianist, Joaquim Malats, who, Lliurat felt, played the work more subtly than Rubinstein. He complained, too—rather churlishly, one can hardly help feeling—that Rubinstein's performance of each piece was "so madly applauded that one lost sight of . . . the previous one and of *Iberia*'s continuity."[16] But Lliurat was himself a Catalan pianist and may simply have been cheering for the home team. Some musicians, then and later, found Rubinstein's simplifications of the work objectionable. The pianist Gaby Casadesus heard Rubinstein play *Navarra* during the 1920s and was "astonished," she said, "to notice that he did not play all the notes. As I was working on it at the time, I knew it well, and I was really surprised that a pianist of his magnitude could have this sort of gap. He played the theme in a marvelous way, with incredible style, but apparently this did not prevent him from skipping a few notes."[17] In Spain, however, Rubinstein's name became so closely associated with this music that in 1958 an interviewer for Barcelona's *La Vanguardia* asked him, "Who owes more to whom: you to Albéniz or Albéniz to you?" Rubinstein replied, "I did no more for Albéniz than diffuse his work through my interpretation."[18] Five years later, he wrote: "I had met the composer who made me give the best of myself as an interpreter. From then on, my greatest successes were inseparably connected with the name of dear and illustrious Isaac Albéniz."[19]

Rubinstein was present at the premiere of Manuel de Falla's *Nights in the Gardens of Spain*, in Madrid on April 9, 1916 (not in 1917, as he incorrectly recalled); the piece fascinated him, and later, in Argentina, he gave the first performance of it in the Western Hemisphere. He soon became friendly with Falla, who took him to a cabaret to hear the gypsy singer and dancer Pastora Imperio perform "a trifle that he had written for her," as Rubinstein told an interviewer many years later. "Do you know what it was? *El amor brujo*, whose theme Pastora had suggested to him. She had hummed it to the composer, saying, 'I heard this at home from my mother and grandmother.' As soon as it was written down, she said to Falla: 'Give me a scrap of paper and I'll change it to fit my style.' "[20] In his memoirs, Rubinstein recalled asking for and receiving Falla's permission to make a piano version of the "Ritual Fire Dance" from *El amor brujo*, and he delightedly reported the wild success that he achieved with this arrangement. In an earlier interview, however, he revealed that there was another side to the story. "I still now [circa 1960] have to live to a great extent on the 'Fire Dance' of Falla, which I made into a piano piece on one unfortunate night in Spain. You see, I heard that piece played by a little quartet for dancing. It was danced by a famous gypsy dancer, and I said to Falla, who was a friend of mine, 'This is a good piano piece.' He said, 'Nonsense.' Well, I arranged it . . . comfortably for the piano and played it in Madrid, and you know, if I hadn't repeated it for the third time I might have been killed. The audience wouldn't let me go on. They shrieked and yelled. I was unwilling to play three times the same piece, but they wouldn't let me off. Then I discovered that that was a piece which absolutely fascinated all the audiences of the world, including Chinese, Japanese, wherever you can imagine. I think when the moon will be open for concerts I will play right away the 'Fire Dance' and I might get away with it."[21]

There was considerable ambivalence in Rubinstein's attitude toward playing not only the "Fire Dance" but Spanish music in general. On the one hand, he was understandably proud of his achievement: "Very early in my career I showed an affinity for Spanish music," he told Samuel Chotzinoff, an American music critic, nearly half a century later. But, Rubinstein continued, "I must confess that, while I was happy to give pleasure with Spanish music, my heart really belonged more to the classics, old and new—to Bach,

Mozart, Beethoven, Schubert, Schumann, Chopin. It also belonged to the
impressionists, to Debussy, Ravel and our Polish Szymanowski. . . . I played
Spanish music in such a way that my audiences found it hard to resist me.
And that, my dear fellow, was a tragedy for me. . . . I gave [people] what they
wanted in the way they wanted, and I had a big success. But there was a void
in my heart. Musically speaking, I was leading a double life."22

EARLY IN HIS stay in Madrid, Rubinstein had made the acquaintance of the
Infanta Isabel, the king's aunt, and then of the young King Alfonso XIII and
Queen Victoria Eugenia. Rumor had it that he and the queen had an affair;
forty years later, when his wife and older daughter questioned him on the
matter, he angrily denied the accusation, and his anger seemed to them confirmation that the story was true. But at the end of his life, when he often
talked openly about his earlier erotic adventures, he said that although the
queen had been fond of him they had not had a love affair. Through the
royals, however, and through the well-introduced Errazuriz-Gandarillas family—who arrived in Madrid during Rubinstein's first stay there—he met a
whole slew of dukes and duchesses, counts and countesses, marquesses and
marchionesses. At first, he communicated with the Spanish grandees in one
or another of his five languages, but he quickly began to improve his fluency
in Spanish, the last language that he learned to speak well—so well that he
could imitate the accent of Madrid's working-class suburbs. (He was eventually able to express himself in Portuguese and Italian, but he did not speak
them well. Late in life, when he was praised for his knowledge of eight languages, he said that he would gladly "give away seven for one good one.")23
Rubinstein adored high society and high society adored him. During Holy
Week 1916, he went to Seville via Toledo and Córdoba in the company of the
Duke and Duchess of Fernán-Núñez and their largely aristocratic entourage.
Before returning to Madrid, via Málaga, Granada, and Ronda, the well-
heeled company stopped in Algeciras, from which Rubinstein and a few of
the others made a day-excursion across the Strait of Gibraltar to Tangiers,
Morocco. On his return to Algeciras he met a beautiful but unhappy young
war widow with whom he managed to have sexual intercourse on a park
bench that overlooked the Rock of Gibraltar. She ran off immediately afterward, and he never saw her again.

　　The combination of public acclaim and acceptance into the highest
aristocratic circles not only gave Rubinstein's ego a boost: it also demonstrated to him that a lifelong career as a pianist might have more to recom-
mend it than he had previously thought. "I'll tell you quite frankly," he said,
during an interview taped some forty years later, "at the beginning of my career I had a rather dreadful, distasteful disdain for the standing of a pianist. I

thought it was an inferior matter. You see, I was of course born a musician. I adored music, I lived by music—it is a sixth sense of mine. But the actual piano playing—I was irritated by this sort of way of cleaning the teeth of the piano, you know; I mean, up and down the scales—it looked to me exactly like a [tooth]brush. . . . You are compelled to do that for hours, and of course it's very necessary. But I hated it. And then I thought about it: the greatest pianist sometimes doesn't convince an audience because they say he's dry, or he is this way, or he is that way, you know. The critics—criticizing. I remarked that the one thing which matters is to have a magic hold on the audience. You see what I mean? To have a sort of antenna established with your audience. And there, to my surprise, I saw, sometimes, inferior technicians, you know—I mean, pianists who played all the wrong notes in the world—I was among them, you see—singers who didn't have the best voices— . . . with a tremendous hold on the audience. Some sort of magic way. A sort of . . . nervous contact. The audience felt at once compelled to listen to them. . . . The thing is to convey, to force our kind of emotion on our audience. Our emotion must be overwhelming, in order to give that feeling to the audience."[24] In Spain in 1916, the intensity of the public's response to his work demonstrated to Rubinstein that his attempt to communicate big emotions was *consistently* succeeding for the first time, and consequently he was treated not as an appurtenance to life—an amusing trifle—but as an essential part of it.

This feeling of belonging, at last, to society, and of having a useful function to fulfill is what has attracted countless foreign musicians to the Latin countries for hundreds of years, despite the fact that concert life is usually more haphazardly organized in southern Europe and South America than in northern Europe and North America. Most Latin orchestras, in particular, are less reliable and accomplished than their northern counterparts. But when things go well a performer can get a thrill, a kick, a "high" out of an audience in even a small or medium-sized town in Spain or Italy, Argentina or Brazil, such as can rarely be obtained in New York or London, Berlin or Vienna. The prolongation of the war probably also played a part in what must eventually have become a conscious decision on Rubinstein's part to stay away from England for the duration, but it probably was not his only consideration. The pleasure, the satisfaction of performing before Latin audiences was what made Rubinstein put up with the unsatisfactory pianos, the acoustically inadequate auditoriums, and the low fees that he often complained about in Spain.

Unlike many other performers—even performers many degrees less celebrated than himself—Rubinstein was not especially fussy about the conditions under which he had to play; even in his last active years, when he could easily have limited his appearances to the world's cultural capitals, he continued to play in provincial towns, too, and he usually used "the pianos—and the piano tuners—available at each location," said Franz Mohr, Steinway's chief concert technician.[25] The admirable, lovable side of what Rubinstein described as his "perfect egotism" was his thirst for communication, for sharing whatever was best in himself. In Spain, he could slake this thirst to his heart's content. "In 1916 Spain adopted me, you know, in the way America adopted Paderewski," he told an American interviewer nearly half a century later,[26] and a journalist in Barcelona suggested an explanation for the phenomenon: "Nos quiere y España le corresponde." He loves us and Spain reciprocates.[27]

Rubinstein demonstrated his love not only by playing *in* Spain but also by playing the music *of* Spain—works of Albéniz, Falla, and, to a lesser extent, Granados, Federico Mompou, Joaquín Turina, and Ernesto Halffter—around the world. And he communicated his enthusiasm for Spanish music to other non-Spanish musicians, including Szymanowski, as the Polish musicologist Jachimecki pointed out in 1927: "A temporary inclination toward the characteristic features of Spanish music appeared in Szymanowski's work at the same time as the influence of Debussy and the tone-painting aesthetics of the French School. This interest in Spanish music was undoubtedly created by his frequent contacts with the brilliant pianist Artur Rubinstein, who, at the very time when he was enthusiastically leading the propagandistic and performing campaign on behalf of Szymanowski's work, was also charming everyone with incomparable interpretations of the hot-blooded music, rich in southern fragrances, of Isaac Albéniz and Enrique Granados."[28]

IN *MY YOUNG YEARS*, Rubinstein mentioned that he had encountered Diaghilev and his Ballets Russes ensemble—including the *primo ballerino* and choreographer Leonid Massine—in San Sebastián at the beginning of June 1916. The company, however, was performing in Madrid at the time, and Rubinstein was present: he even gave a private performance of a piano reduction of *The Firebird*, among other works, for an invited audience (at the home of the duchess of Montellanos) that included Stravinsky himself and Queen Victoria Eugenia. The previous day, Stravinsky had had his first encounter—probably through Rubinstein's good offices—with Eugenia Errazuriz, who immediately undertook to provide the financially hard-pressed composer with one thousand francs a month until the end of the war; a few months later, she arranged a first encounter between Stravinsky and Pablo Picasso, who was another occasional beneficiary of her largesse. The Errazuriz connection also led to a brief affair between Stravinsky and Juanita Gandarillas in London five years later; Rubinstein probably knew about it, just as he must have been privy to the fact that, at the time of his Madrid encounter with Stravinsky, the composer was having an affair with the twenty-five-year-old Lydia Lopoukhova, who was dancing the title role in the Ballets Russes's production of *The Firebird*. In his memoirs, however, Rubinstein mentioned only that Lopoukhova later married the economist John Maynard Keynes. At some point, Rubinstein may have had an affair with Tamara Karsavina, Nijinsky's partner during the Ballets Russes' heyday and one of the most celebrated ballerinas in history. Nela and Eva Rubinstein believed that this was the case, but Arthur did not mention the story in his memoirs; his reticence could be attributed to the fact that Karsavina—two years his senior—was still alive when *My Young Years* was published, but as he also did not mention any such affair to other intimates, the story is suspect.

Rubinstein saw Diaghilev and Massine in San Sebastián, too, but not until early July, when impresario and choreographer arrived to organize the performances that were to take place there at the end of the following month. The whole company arrived in August, and Rubinstein, who was holidaying at the resort town, recalled getting to know the dancers Lila Kashouba, Adolph Bolm, and the Shabelski sisters, in addition to Lopoukhova; the thirty-three-year-old conductor Ernest Ansermet, whom Rubinstein later described as "a man of great personal charm and vast erudition";[29] "two Russian painters"—probably the celebrated husband-wife team Michel Larionov and Natalya Gontcharova, who were there that summer; and the now legendary muse and patroness of the arts, Misia Godebska Sert, half sister of Ravel's friend Cyprien (Cipa) Godebski and wife of the painter José María Sert. The war was creating dreadful financial difficulties for the members of Diaghilev's company—as for everyone else who was not directly or indirectly involved in the armaments industry—and Rubinstein lent two helping hands by playing in a benefit concert under Ansermet's direction. The money that he raised paid the dancers' hotel bills, Rubinstein said, and Diaghilev, who had been in London to try to extract funds from old and new patrons, brought him two handsome ties as a thank-you gift. During his stay in San Sebastián, Rubinstein also heard Falla play to the skeptical Diaghilev some preliminary sketches for the ballet *El Sombrero de tres picos (The Three-Cornered Hat)*; three years later, the premiere of the work, in London, launched one of the Ballets Russes' greatest successes. On September 20, 1916, Diaghilev, Massine, and Misia Sert attended a concert in which Rubinstein played the Tchaikovsky Concerto with Arbós; they "loved the Concerto and the way I performed it, and it was on that day that I really won Diaghilev's friendship," he said.[30]

Rubinstein's 1916–17 season began where his 1915–16 season had ended:

in Spain. He crisscrossed the country from the Canary Islands in the Atlantic to the Balearic Islands in the Mediterranean, from the Basque countries in the north to Andalusia in the south. More than fifty years later he said that he could not think of any Spanish city in which he had not played during that tour, in the middle of which he reached his thirtieth birthday. On June 2, 1917, he attended the opening gala of a brief Ballets Russes season in Madrid, with Nijinsky in the role of the slave in Rimsky-Korsakov's *Schéhérazade*, and during the intermission he had his first encounter with Pablo Picasso, who had designed the sets for the company's new ballet, *Parade*. Rubinstein and Picasso remained friends for the rest of their lives, despite or perhaps because of the fact that they rarely saw each other. (A Picasso portrait of Rubinstein was lost during World War II—"it was done before he was 'Picasso' and I was 'Rubinstein,' " the pianist used to say—but twenty-seven portrait drawings of the pianist, made by the artist in 1958, still exist.)

By the time the Ballets Russes' two-and-a-half-week season ended, on June 19, Rubinstein, accompanied by Ernesto de Quesada, was making his way to South America for the first time, aboard the steamship *Infanta Isabel*: he had been offered the princely fee of £4,500 (about $22,500) for fifteen concerts in Buenos Aires and Montevideo. His departure (in mid-June, not mid-May, as he stated in his memoirs) had been in doubt until the last moment because the cataclysmic political changes that were taking place in Russia had rendered his passport worthless. In the end, King Alfonso had arranged for him to be given a special Spanish passport as a citizen of Poland—a country that did not yet exist in international law—" 'but with my personal guarantee of your identity,' " the king had told him. " 'I think that this document will give you the freedom to enter any country.' "[31] (Two years later, when he traded the document for a passport from what was by then a truly independent Poland, the surprised Polish official who handled his case told him that he—Rubinstein—had been "the first person to be recognized as a citizen of free Poland.")[32] On the Argentina-bound ship, Rubinstein met Regina Badet, a French actress who had also been engaged for a South American tour, and she became his bedmate for the duration of the voyage, he said.

As in Spain, so in Hispanic America success arrived quickly for Rubinstein and proved to be enduring. A letter of introduction from Pastora Imperio to her admirer Luis Mitre, the owner of *La Nación*, Buenos Aires's most important newspaper, assured the pianist of excellent advance publicity. His first concert—on July 2, 1917, at the Teatro Odeón, under the auspices of Faustino da Rosa, the city's leading impresario—was warmly received by the audience and the critics. In an article entitled "A Brilliant Pianist—Mr. A. Rubenstein's [sic] Debut at the Odeon," the anonymous critic of the *Buenos Aires Herald*, an English-language newspaper, wrote:

During the past twelve months there have been various pianists of distinct merit who have played before Buenos Aires audiences, but it is doubtful whether music lovers have as yet had such a treat of combined sympathy and technique as was presented to them yesterday by Mr. A. Rubenstein at the Odeon theatre. That the house should be full was perhaps but a natural tribute to the fame of the pianist, whose reputation in London and Paris is unquestioned, but it is safe to say that few there present who had not the opportunity of hearing the artiste in private realized how completely his performance was in accord with his reputation. A young man, with no exaggerated mannerisms, he sat down before the Steinway Grand and played. . . . His programme was very well chosen for a Buenos Aires debut. Opening with the Bach-Tausig Toccata . . . and following with Beethoven's Sonata Op. 53 ["Waldstein"], his second part was all Chopin. But such Chopin! A scherzo, a nocturne, a ballade, a waltz, a polonaise. How could one choose between them, given such perfect rendering? . . . A perfect storm of applause greeted the conclusion of Albéniz' "Navarra" in the third part. The nocturne of Scriabine for the left hand was perhaps Mr. Rubenstein's greatest triumph from the point of view of *fingerfestigkeit* [finger dexterity] and expression combined. . . . Liszt's Twelfth Rhapsody closed a most attractive programme, and the warmth of Mr. Rubenstein's reception was certainly well deserved. . . . For without wishing to make any comparisons it is safe to say that such piano-music on this side of the Atlantic is very much the exception.[37]

As the series progressed, Rubinstein's popularity grew. In addition to the works specified by the *Herald*'s critic, the pianist's remarkably extensive repertoire that season included Beethoven's "Tempest," E-flat Major (Op. 31, No. 3), "Appassionata," and "Hammerklavier" Sonatas; about thirty pieces by Chopin, including the Second and Third Sonatas; Albéniz's *Iberia* (complete); Scriabin's Fantasy, Op. 28; "Ondine" from Ravel's *Gaspard de la nuit*; and various works of Liszt, Szymanowski, Rachmaninoff, Schumann, Mendelssohn, Brahms, Medtner, Debussy, Falla, and Granados, and Liszt's arrangement of the Liebestod from *Tristan und Isolde*.

Thanks to Argentina's minister in Spain, who had enthusiastically attended Rubinstein's Madrid concerts and who was the son-in-law of Manuel Quintana, a former Argentine president, the pianist was immediately invited to dinner at the home of Quintana's widow, Susana, who introduced him into the highest echelons of Argentine society. "This remarkable lady behaved like a mother to me," he recalled, "inviting me almost daily for meals with her family, presiding proudly at my concerts, and even coming surreptitiously in the early morning to my hotel to see if my laundry and clothes were being well cared for. She recommended the finest Italian tailor in town, who dressed me in the best concert clothes of my life. She made me put the bulk of the money I had earned into the excellent bonds of the Crédito Argentino, which was state-guaranteed and yielded 6 percent." Doña Susana also gave him "a pearl with the most beautiful iris which had belonged to her husband. . . . I have worn her pearl in my tie every day up to this moment," he said, sixty years later.[34] Rubinstein also got to know several important local musicians—among them, the composer, conductor, pianist, and teacher Alberto Williams, who had studied composition with César Franck and Charles Wilfrid de Bériot; the composer Carlos López Buchardo, whom Rubinstein considered highly talented but lazy; and the pianist Ernesto Drangosch, who had studied under Barth in Berlin at the same time as Rubinstein. In Montevideo, where he gave his first recital on July 21 at the Teatro Solís, he met Eduardo Fabini, an Uruguayan composer and violinist, and Joaquín Mora, a violinist who had been a roommate of Paul Kochanski's during their student days in Brussels, and he renewed an acquaintanceship with Wilhelm (Guillermo) Kolischer, a fellow Polish Jew and former Barth pupil who was becoming an influential figure in Uruguayan musical life.

Rubinstein enjoyed an even greater success in Montevideo than in Buenos Aires. His first program there consisted largely of the same pieces that he had played on his first Buenos Aires recital, except that *Navarra* was replaced by Debussy's *L'Isle joyeuse* and Ravel's "Ondine." "The concert to be given this evening has aroused truly high expectations among musicians and aficionados, given the fame of the great interpreter," *El Día* announced,[35] and a review, signed "Enne" and published two days later, demonstrated that the expectations had been surpassed. "Last night," he wrote, "in the first part of the recital . . . , this concert artist played Beethoven's Sonata Op. 53 ["Waldstein"]. The extraordinary interpreter found . . . an appropriate outlet for revealing, without holding back, the uncommon power of intensity of sound and prodigious agility that seem at first blush to be the fundamental characteristics of this great artist. At times Rubinstein's formidable playing reaches such a level of impetuousness that one has the impression of listening to a concert of several pianos in combat. . . ." The reviewer wrote at such length and so excitedly about the Beethoven performance that, after barely one enthusiastic sentence about Rubinstein's Chopin, he was forced to stop: "Enough for today, so that perhaps tomorrow lack of paper will not stop me from detailing other thoughts on the great Polish interpreter who is now a guest in Montevideo."[36] The same critic reported that at the end of the second recital, which included Schumann's *Carnaval*, excerpts from Albéniz's *Iberia*, Chopin's Polonaise, Op. 44, and Liszt's Twelfth Rhapsody and *Tristan* arrangement, "a numerous group of admirers carried him on their shoulders to his lodgings."[37] An article in the following day's paper reassured readers that Rubinstein had "formally promised to return to Montevideo this coming September, stating that never had he been received by any other audience with the affection and enthusiasm showered on him here, because everywhere else he had had to perform several times before achieving a success such as he has had in Montevideo."[38]

In addition to his brilliant playing, Rubinstein's many highly placed musical and social contacts helped him to establish an unshakable position in Latin America, and Quesada did a fine job of looking after the technicalities. In later years, there was disagreement between Rubinstein and Quesada as to which of them had launched the other's South American career. Although Rubinstein admitted that Quesada's "managerial talent" secured five concerts for him in Santiago and Valparaiso, Chile, and many extra concerts in Buenos Aires and Montevideo, he also complained that Quesada had taken advantage of the trip—for which Rubinstein had paid him a fee plus expenses—to set up branch agencies in Buenos Aires and other South American cities. Manager-artist relationships are often difficult: The managers whine about the egomaniacal pretensions of their artists, and the artists whine about being exploited by their managers. Often, both complaints are correct. Rubinstein was suspicious of most of the people on whom he relied—managers and agents, piano company executives and piano technicians, secretaries and valets—and sometimes with good reason. In his dealings with nearly all of his managers and agents, from Barth (who had handled the business arrangements for his earliest concerts) to Astruc, from Eisenbach to Quesada, and on and on through the years, there were frequent moments of tension and more than a few temporary or permanent breaks. The fact that his professional relationship and warm personal friendship with Quesada and, later, Quesada's sons, endured for six decades speaks well of the family, and Rubinstein benefited from having a single agency function as a clearinghouse for his affairs throughout the Spanish- and Portuguese-speaking world.

The extremely warm welcome that he had received in Montevideo made Rubinstein decide to return there even earlier than he had promised, and the recitals that he gave at the city's Teatro Urquiza on August 8 and 12 quickly reinforced his success. "Under circumstances like yesterday's," wrote "Enne" after the second recital, "one cannot speak of an 'interpreter' of Chopin and Albéniz: it is necessary to refer to a 'collaborator,' who infuses the life that the creators gave to their immortal works. . . ."[39] Following a *gran con-*

cierto extraordinario at the Odeón in Buenos Aires on August 17, Rubinstein boarded a train for the long and exhausting trip to Chile, where, within four weeks, he gave not only his scheduled concerts but also several extra ones in Santiago. The cover of the program of the *último concierto extraordinario*, which began at the unusual hour of 4:30 P.M. on September 13 (a Thursday), includes a printed message: "The artist has chosen this hour in order to be able to return to Buenos Aires on the connecting train that is leaving this very day at 7:30 P.M." In the Argentine capital once again, he added high-paying recitals for such private organizations as the Sociedad Wagneriana, the Sociedad Hebraïca, and the exclusive Jockey Club to his already-busy schedule of public *conciertos extraordinarios*; the Jockey Club engagement alone brought him the astonishing fee of 20,000 pesos ($10,000). In mid-September he returned to Montevideo for performances at the Teatro Solís; the last of these was billed as a "farewell" performance, but on October 1 Rubinstein was back in the Uruguayan capital, playing again and "at no moment showing any sign of physical fatigue or interpretive weakness, despite having played . . . eight encores," *El Día* reported. "We don't have enough space for describing the emotions that we experienced last night. . . . The enthusiasm that the audience expressed throughout the evening reached extraordinary proportions, and the great Polish concert artist was accorded the most intense acclamations that even the most celebrated performers have ever heard among us. And the audience was not exaggerating this time, because Rubinstein deserves the greatest applause. . . ."[40]

In mid-October Rubinstein gave two concerts with a sixty-piece orchestra under Drangosch's baton at Buenos Aires's Teatro de la Opera: on the thirteenth, he played Beethoven's Fourth and Tchaikovsky's First Concertos, and on the seventeenth he played the Brahms and Saint-Saëns Second Concertos and Franck's *Les Djinns*. Then he returned to Montevideo, where, at the Teatro Solís on October 26, he and Nijinsky shared top billing in an absurdly disorganized gala event that proved to be the twenty-seven-year-old dancer's last public performance before mental illness forced him to retire. At the Teatro La Lira on the twenty-fifth, twenty-eighth, and thirtieth, Rubinstein gave three solo recitals. The last of them was a mammoth program that consisted of the "Hammerklavier" Sonata, *Carnaval*, and a series of pieces that he had not preannounced in his program, but chose instead on the spot—pieces by Albéniz, Debussy, Scriabin, Liszt, Mendelssohn, and Chopin. Rubinstein took his leave of the Montevidean public with the A-flat Polonaise, and *El Día*'s critic wrote: "The acclamations that greeted this Polish hymn seemed interminable, and amid the spontaneous embraces of the men and the effusive handshakes of the women, the famous artist left La Lira a little later, while, in the street, for a long stretch he was accompanied by the enthusiastic applause of his admirers."[41]

Warmed by memories of his South American successes, Rubinstein returned to Spain, where he met the new Steinway concert grand that he had ordered from New York through the company's Buenos Aires branch. Although its action was "a little too heavy," the instrument had a "beautiful tone," he told Vivian Perlis in 1979, and it must have inspired him to do some hard practicing: the programs of his recitals at Madrid's Teatro Odeón on April 6, 8, and 10, 1918, indicate that he had added to his repertoire the difficult Liszt Sonata, the "Alborada del gracioso" from Ravel's *Miroirs*, and *Vers la flamme*, one of Scriabin's last works. He passed the 1917–18 season as he had passed the 1916–17 season—entirely in Spain. A special event took place at the University of Madrid on April 27, when he played in a memorial tribute to Debussy, who had died on March 25; other participants included the Polish singer Aga Lachowska, the Madrid Philharmonic, and Falla, who read a speech, "The Profound Art of Claude Debussy." At the end of the season, Rubinstein asked Joaquín Peña, his manager in Barcelona, to find a buyer for the Steinway; Peña, who had debts to pay off, "sold it in my absence and kept the money," according to the pianist.[42] But memories of the fun he had had during the previous months may have provided balm for the loss, because the bulging wallet that he had brought back from South America had allowed him to play the "role of the parvenu," he recalled. In Madrid, "I spent night after night with my young aristocratic friends, fooling the bill more often than not." One member of the crowd was "a bright and witty young man" whom Rubinstein, in *My Many Years*, called Juan Avila, but whose real name was Jaime Zulueta. When the pianist told his friends that he was looking for a secretary to accompany him on his forthcoming return trip to South America, Zulueta—whose passion for adventure was stronger than either his sense of responsibility toward his wife and children or his pride in his aristocratic lineage—took the job, much to Rubinstein's surprise.[43]

Rubinstein often used his money with real generosity, and not merely for showing off or for his own convenience. In the course of the same season, for instance, he learned that Stravinsky was more hard-pressed than ever for money, because the new Bolshevik regime in Russia had deprived the composer of the right to royalties on most of his compositions, including the increasingly popular *Firebird*, *Petrushka*, and *Rite of Spring*. Rubinstein immediately offered to help. "Thank Rubinstein warmly," Stravinsky said in a telegram to Errazuriz on March 23, 1918. "I will compose an important piano piece especially for him."[44] And on May 1, Falla wrote to Stravinsky: "Dear friend, Arthur Rubinstein has entrusted me to send you the enclosed letter of exchange of 5,000 francs (through the Agence de Crédit Lyonnais in Geneva). Time was short, and [Rubinstein] was unable to send it himself before his departure from Madrid. He also asked me to relay his best wishes and to inform you that he is at your disposal, at the

Plaza Hotel, Buenos Aires, until August, should you come to some decision about the composition (which he leaves entirely up to you). . . . You know already that your good friend [Rubinstein] had a veritable triumph in Spain, and his popularity increases every day. Now he will spend several months in the Argentine Republic."[45]

The piece that Stravinsky decided to write for Rubinstein "became the *Piano-Rag Music*," said Robert Craft, the composer's assistant during his last decades. "The dedication to him in Stravinsky's sketchbook for the work (the pianist's name with a frame drawn around it) antedates all of the musical notations." On July 23, 1919, Stravinsky, in Morges, Switzerland, wrote to Ansermet: "Show Kling [director of J. & W. Chester, Stravinsky's London-based publishers] my new piece for piano solo called Piano-Rag Music, which I composed recently for Art. Rubinstein."[46] But Craft has also pointed out that Rubinstein, in *My Many Years*, muddled the composition's history. In reality, "The pianist cabled to Stravinsky from London, October 15, 1919, requesting a year's exclusivity to perform the *Rag*. Stravinsky cabled back the same day, ignoring the request, saying that he had already sent the manuscript to New York, in care of a mutual friend and advising Rubinstein to obtain a copy from J. & W. Chester before leaving London. Rubinstein did not understand the music, and he never played it."[47] In his memoirs, the pianist wrote: "To me it sounded like an exercise for percussion and had nothing to do with any rag music, or with any other music in my sense. I must admit I was bitterly, bitterly disappointed."[48] There is good reason to believe that he was offended, and not merely disappointed, over Stravinsky's decision to thank him with a jazz-inspired composition: by the time the *Rag* was finished, the pianist's feelings toward the United States were becoming profoundly negative, for reasons that will soon emerge, and jazz had become one of his favorite symbols of American degeneracy. Toward the end of his life, Rubinstein said of Stravinsky, " 'His first works were very Russian and especially beautiful. But later, he lost contact with Russia. You know, every composer needs his old country and its folklore: unfortunately, he had been distanced from his.' "[49] But what is one to make, then, of composers—from Josquin Desprès to Handel to Chopin—who composed most of their important works far from their native lands? For that matter, most of Stravinsky's important "Russian" works were written when he was already spending most of his time abroad. Rubinstein was simply indulging in the common pastime of rationalizing his instinctive likes and dislikes.

He shared some of his new wealth with Falla, too, during the 1917–18 season, by commissioning him to write a piano piece for him. The composer duly set to work, and in 1919 he completed the *Fantasía Bætica* (or *Bética*), which was to remain his most extensive and complicated solo keyboard work. *Bætica* is the Latin name of the ancient Roman province that approximately corresponded to modern Andalusia, and *Betis* is the poetic name for the Guadalquivir River, which runs through Seville, Córdoba, and much of the rest of the region. In a letter to a friend, Falla described the piece as "the only one written by me with 'purely pianistic' intentions, with respect to its instrumental technique. Another thing: the title *Bætica* has no specific 'special Sevillian' reference. I have only intended to render homage through it to our Latin-Andalusian race."[50] According to the Falla scholar Susanne Demarquez, "A work dedicated to *Bética* and to an illustrious pianist had to celebrate the region and, at the same time, the art of the dedicatee. Thus it follows that folk melodies, flamenco rhythms, and guitar effects are transferred to the piano. . . . From the start, the composer manages to emphasize a feeling of enchantment, through thematic repetitions that correspond to the work's Gypsy-like essence."[51] Rubinstein intended to give the work its premiere in Spain in 1919, but he was unable to learn it in time and instead gave the first performance in New York in 1920. Early in the *Fantasía*'s life, the musicologist Vladimir Jankélévitch ranked it among Falla's masterpieces, and Jankélévitch's colleague Henry Prunières described it as "direct, profound music born in the heart and expressed in a form as beautiful as it is original."

"Unfortunately, time has not confirmed these enthusiastic judgements," Demarquez commented half a century later,"[52] but in recent years the *Fantasía* has become a repertoire piece for most Spanish pianists. Rubinstein was unhappy with it, and after having performed it several times—in London in 1922, Madrid, Málaga, and Barcelona in 1923, Buenos Aires in 1924, Paris in 1925, and Cádiz in 1926—he dropped the piece from his repertoire.[53] A few years later, said Jaime Pahissa, an expert on Falla's music, "Falla met Rubinstein near Versailles in the house of an Italian prince, and as they were leaving Rubinstein asked him to write a work for him. Falla replied by pointing out that he had already written the *Fantasía Bætica* for him, and that he never played it, besides which he did not want to write any more works for piano. . . . Rubinstein justified himself by saying that [the piece] had been too long and added other excuses. Falla then told him that he had thought of arranging the *Fantasía Bætica* for piano and orchestra. This seemed an excellent idea to Rubinstein and also to [Eugene] Cools [manager of Eschig, Falla's publisher], when he was told of it later. However, it was never carried out."[54] Late in life, Rubinstein scathingly described the *Fantasía* as "a vastly enlarged *Fire Dance* but without the impact of its model, interrupted unnecessarily by a short intermezzo which sounded as if it belonged to another piece. To make it worse, the coda, which [Falla] tried to make as brilliant as the end of the *Fire Dance*, is badly written for the piano."[55]

Rubinstein's lack of enthusiasm for the *Fantasía* did not damage his friendship with its composer. They got together whenever they were in the same city at the same time, and some of their correspondence still exists. In one letter (February 21, 1921), Falla vehemently demanded to know "What has been the fate of the Fantasía?" But he also said, "I have learned with joy that you are in London. This gives me the hope of having some news from you and of seeing you soon. . . . How long will you be in Europe? I have been living in Granada for some months. My health hasn't been very good but, thank God, I'm beginning to get better. A long time ago I asked Eschig to send the proofs of the Spanish Songs to you in New York—Have you received them? Send me news of your doings. . . ."[56] And there is a note from Rubinstein to Falla, written on the stationery of the Gramophone Building, Hayes, Middlesex, England, on January 24, 1929: "Dear Friend—I would very much like to play for 'The Gramophone Company Limited' your two dances (ritual fire and terror [both from El amor brujo]), with the little changes that I've taken the liberty of inserting—I hope that this idea isn't disagreeable to you— if you are willing, please drop a line to this company—(Copyright Department) naturally you will receive all the royalties that are your due. . . . A thousand friendly greetings from your most fervent admirer and friend Arthur Rubinstein." The truth is that Rubinstein had recorded the pieces the day before he wrote the letter, and was merely writing, at the insistence of the Gramophone, for routine permission from the composer. A week later, Falla sent his authorization "with great joy (and honor)."[57] On July 10, 1940, from his last home, at Villa del Lago in Argentina, the ailing composer wrote to the pianist: "Dear and esteemed Arturo Rubinstein: Just a word (and dictated, at that, since I have just undergone an operation) to tell you how very sorry I am not to be with you and not to be able to enjoy your concerts [in Buenos Aires]! Will you come here? How I would like it! I embrace you with all my heart."[58] Rubinstein did visit his old friend, for what proved to be the last time (Falla died in 1946), and gave him a photo of himself with his two young children.

AT MADRID'S TEATRO REAL early in 1918, Rubinstein heard Gabriella Besanzoni sing the title role in Carmen. Besanzoni, an Italian mezzo-soprano who was on the threshold of what was to be a major international career, was "the greatest Carmen I ever heard," Rubinstein said in his memoirs[59]—although, earlier in the memoirs, he had written that he "never heard Carmen sung better" than by Emmy Destinn.[60] Besanzoni's "lowest notes sounded like those of a baritone although she could reach with perfect ease the highest notes," he reported, and indeed, she was a mezzo-soprano with the vocal depth of a contralto—a marvelous type of voice that is nearly extinct today. "There was something of a wild sensuous animal in her," Rubinstein said.

"Though not exactly beautiful, she was the perfect incarnation of Mérimée's gypsy. The thunderstruck audience gave her the greatest ovation I have ever witnessed in Madrid." According to Rubinstein, Besanzoni was having an affair with Faustino da Rosa, who had come to Spain "to engage her for the [Teatro] Colón in Buenos Aires and to make the final arrangements for my own [South American] tour." Da Rosa assiduously avoided introducing Besanzoni to Rubinstein, but one evening, when the two performers' paths crossed in the corridor of the Hotel Palace, where they were both staying, "she clutched my head with both hands and kissed me so violently that she drew blood from my lip," Rubinstein said. The next day—the first day of Carnival—they went for a drive together along the crowded Paseo de la Castellana; back at the hotel, "Gabriella took my hand, led me to her room, and said, 'Caro, let us lie down and rest.' Three hours later, I left her room, tired but exuberantly happy. . . . I thought of it as the passing whim of a passionate woman. I was wrong. It rapidly turned into something serious. Gabriella behaved like a woman in love."[61]

But Rubinstein was not in love. He was "proud of this lovely adventure, of having had Carmen in my arms," but he was not about to play Don José as *un homme ivre, jaloux et troublé dans l'âme.* Carmen would either do things his way or leave him in peace. He was horrified when, after they had said good-bye to each other in Madrid and agreed to meet in Buenos Aires, Besanzoni surprised him by showing up at a recital that he gave in Valencia, where she announced that she had changed her departure date for Buenos Aires so that they could sail on the same boat. " 'If da Rosa sees us arriving together he might break off his contract with both of us,' " he told her. "Fortunately there was an Italian steamer from Genoa that stopped in Barcelona on the way to Buenos Aires. I forced her to take it."[62] According to another source, Besanzoni made the trip, as originally scheduled, with the rest of the Italian troupe with which she was to perform in Buenos Aires,[63] but in either case, Rubinstein and Zulueta took a different ship. During the crossing the pianist and his secretary shared the erotic services of a "lovely young French demimondaine . . . I would enjoy her charms in the niches between the lifeboats on the upper deck when there was nobody around," Rubinstein recalled.[64]

His descriptions of Besanzoni are even less detailed and revealing than his descriptions of most of the other women whom he loved and/or had affairs with. He portrayed her as a sexually uninhibited but stereotypically featherbrained singer, and he detested the cute nickname—Tutullo—that she had invented for him. But the fact that she was fluent only in Italian—which, when their affair began, he hardly spoke at all—would have prevented hightoned exchanges between them even if they had both been brilliant philosophers.[65] The great tenor Aureliano Pertile, one of Besanzoni's colleagues, told his son that her morals were so light that she would go to bed with any-one who might have been able to help her career, and Pertile *fils* could hardly believe "that so refined a man as Rubinstein could have had an affair with Besanzoni."[66] Even if this is true, however, it does not necessarily mean that her feelings toward Rubinstein were not serious.

Little information about Besanzoni is available. She was born in Rome, but she was vague about her age; the most likely of the various birth dates given for her is September 20, 1888, in which case she was twenty-nine in February 1918, when she met the thirty-one-year-old Rubinstein. She had studied in her native city, made her debut as a soprano in 1911, then devel-oped her lower register and redebuted two years later as a contralto, at the Teatro Costanzi in Rome. Her 1918 seasons in Madrid and Buenos Aires initi-ated a decade and a half during which she was one of the most sought-after lyric mezzos in the world. And she was one of those uncommon singers who are loved, and not merely admired, by their colleagues. Lina Pagliughi, the celebrated soprano, described Besanzoni's singing as "formidable" and added that she was "a divine human being—warm, understanding."[67] Gilda Dalla Rizza, a great soprano of Besanzoni's generation, admitted that she her-self had refused to attempt the role of Carmen because "Gabriella Besanzoni was around in those days, and no one could equal the velvet in her voice and the verve of her personality."[68] Gianna Pederzini, who became the most pop-ular Carmen at La Scala after Besanzoni's retirement, described her prede-cessor as "the most *simpatica* person one could meet"[69]—and anyone who has spent much time in opera houses knows that pleasant behavior on the part of divas in decline toward divas on the rise is, as the Italians say, "more unique than rare."

The Teatro Colón's 1918 opera season, in which many popular works were performed by outstanding Italian artists, including Besanzoni, was in part a gift to Argentina from the Italian government, which was lining up international support for projected postwar claims to certain border areas of the crumbling Habsburg empire. According to Rubinstein, da Rosa kept a close watch on Besanzoni in Buenos Aires, and the pianist and singer were able to see each other only once before Rubinstein had to make a long and unpleasant journey by train to São Paulo and thence to Rio de Janeiro. His Brazilian debut, on June 11, 1918, was also the opening event of the season at Rio's Theatro Municipal. "Great curiosity prevails about this artist, who has been preceded by excellent recommendations and results in various capitals, and who, although not yet known here, is already the source of arguments," the *Jornal do Commercio* announced.[70] The cause of the arguments was clarified in the next day's review by the city's leading music critic, Oscar Guanabarino.

No pianist, among those who have visited us, has provoked as many arguments as Mr. Arthur Rubinstein before being known here, and this is on account of his name's being the same as that of the celebrated Russian pianist and composer Antonio Rubinstein. . . .

The recital began with the *Toccata and Fugue in D Minor* by Bach-Tausig; but it should be noted, in the first place, that the atmosphere of frivolity that had been created around the unknown artist led to uncertainty and lack of confidence, so that the reaction was unforeseen and unexpected; and immediately, with the first passages of the *Toccata*, the whole auditorium was taken, subjugated by the extraordinary qualities of this truly amazing pianist. . . . We had believed the great [Portuguese] pianist [José] Vianna da Motta to be a model of fugue-playing, but Mr. Arthur Rubinstein completely exceeded our expectations.

Our amazement still persisted when the great artist launched into the "Waldstein" of Beethoven, a sonata that until yesterday no one had ever revealed to us in this way, as full of detail as it is diverse in phrases that, when repeated, emerge individually as different and distinct factors.

The program, which included a Chopin group and pieces by Albéniz, Ravel, Scriabin, and Liszt, continued to astonish Guanabarino and the other listeners, and the critic reported: "When the recital ended with Liszt's Twelfth Rhapsody, played as we had never heard it, we left the theater in order to have time to write this article; and there we left him, still doing the bidding of his audience"[71]—playing encore after encore, in other words. A second appearance by Rubinstein, two nights after the first, caused Guanabarino to report: "Another recital and another victory, which will continue to grow, because the galleries of the Theatro Municipal, full of artists, are going crazy over the amazing pianist who, besides offering Rio society unequalled evenings of pianistic art, is teaching lessons of great usefulness to new generations. . . . Mr. Rubinstein was more applauded yesterday than at his first recital; it seems impossible, but it is a fact."[72]

Two days later, Guanabarino wrote: "Third recital, yesterday, and third triumph."[73] This performance was followed by an extra Sunday afternoon recital; then came a fourth subscription concert, a "special concert," a fifth subscription concert, a second Sunday afternoon concert, a "grand popular concert," a "final subscription concert," a "final evening concert," and a "farewell matinée," for a total of twelve recitals in nineteen days. The Rio public couldn't get enough of Rubinstein, and the enthusiasm demonstrated at his last recital bordered on hysteria. He played encore after encore, and then "the stage was overrun with *senhoras e senhoritas*," Guanabarino reported; "the artist was besieged to autograph programs and postcards; but so great was the number of claimants that it was not possible to satisfy all of them. Mr. Rubinstein asked for light and air; a space opened up and the prisoner escaped to shut himself in his dressing room. But it was not so easy to beat those who resisted; they were waiting at the exit door at the rear of the theater, and they carried him to his automobile, amid the applause of about three hundred people who accompanied the car all the way to the Avenue. He left, and the group, waving handkerchiefs or clapping their hands, shouted 'Goodbye! Goodbye!' . . . 'I have never seen,' he told us, 'an audience as attentive, as kind, or as enthusiastic as this one. I am extremely grateful, and I shall always keep a profound recollection of these concerts.' "[74] The unnamed critic of the *Correio da Manha*, another Rio newspaper, said: "If, as we believe, Arthur Rubinstein will carry off some nostalgia for the Rio public, the public will certainly keep the most pleasant memories, for a long time, of the elect artist and his interpretations, which are models for the masters of the art of music."[75]

The success of these concerts paved the way for Rubinstein's enduring popularity in Brazil and for his love of Rio and its beautiful natural setting. During his first visit, he made the acquaintance of the well-established Brazilian composers Alberto Nepomuceno and Francisco Braga (a pupil of Massenet) and the "brilliant" (so he described them) pianists Antonietta Rudge and Guiomar Novaës; Rudge is known today mainly as the sister of Ezra Pound's companion, the violinist Olga Rudge, but Novaës, who was twenty-two in 1918, enjoyed a long and successful international career. Rubinstein paid tribute, in his memoirs, to Luigi Chiafarelli (although he misnamed him "Schiafarelli"), the São Paulo–based teacher of Rudge and Novaës, whom he described as "a great piano teacher . . . a man of great intelligence, [who] spoke four languages fluently, was well read, and had a vast understanding of human problems and world affairs . . . [and] a superb sense of humor. We became friends on my first visit . . . and remained so for years to come."[76]

A friendship with Darius Milhaud was also formed during Rubinstein's weeks in Rio. Severe rheumatoid arthritis had rendered the young French composer unfit for wartime military service; instead, he had been engaged as secretary to the French minister in Brazil—his friend Paul Claudel, the poet and playwright, who earned his living as a diplomat. Five years earlier, at the age of twenty-one, Milhaud had begun to write incidental music for performances of the *Oresteia* in Claudel's French translation; in 1918 they were collaborating on the ballet *L'Homme et son désir*. By then, the fifty-year-old Claudel's most lasting literary work—especially the plays *Tête d'or, Partage*

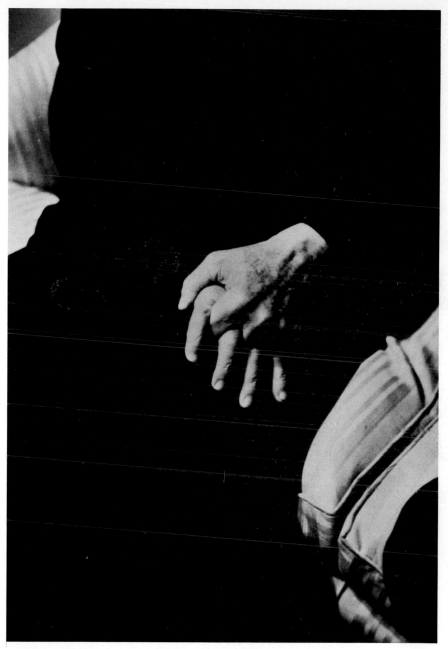

A typical Rubinstein hand position — away from the keyboard.

Except where otherwise noted, all photographs and caricatures are courtesy of the collection of Nela Rubinstein.

Top left: Arthur in the Tiergarten, Berlin, early 1900.

Top right: Arthur in the Tiergarten, Berlin, spring 1900.

Bottom right: The 17-year-old Rubinstein at the time of his Paris debut, 1904.

Lodz, 1912: Arthur's parents, Izaak and Felicja Heiman Rubinstein.

Rubinstein with Pastora Imperio and Manuel de Falla in Madrid, 1917. (Archivo Manuel de Falla)

Rio de Janeiro, 1918. From left to right: Rubinstein, Darius Milhaud, Paul Claudel, and Henri Hoppenot.

An undated caricature from the 1930s.

Geneva, 1920s; the jury of a piano competition. From left to right: Rubinstein (with his head bandaged after a minor traffic accident), Alfred Cortot, an unidentified man, Ernest Schelling, Professor Pembauer.

With Zosia and Paul Kochanski and (far right) Maurice Ravel, 1920s.

Paris, c. 1930. From left to right: Alexander Steinert, Paul Kochanski, Vladimir Horowitz, Rubinstein.

London, July 1932. Nela and Arthur at their wedding reception with their hostess, Sybil, Lady Cholmondeley.

A 1940s publicity photograph.

Nela and Arthur in California in the 1940s, with the painter Elias Kanarek and part of the triptych he was painting for them.

With Andrés Segovia, 1940s.

A bust done by Nela Rubinstein,
mid-1940s.

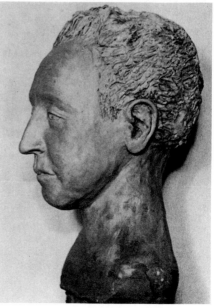

Arriving in Buenos Aires in 1940: Eva, Nela, Paul, Arthur.

*Amused by someone else's story?
Rubinstein in 1941.*

*The Rubinsteins in front of their
newly acquired home in Tower
Road, Beverly Hills, 1948. From left
to right: Arthur holding Johnny,
Paul, Nela holding Alina, Eva.*

Rehearsing with Heifetz and Piatigorsky at Ravinia, Chicago, 1949.

In Piazza San Marco, Venice, 1950s.

A caricature by Kantor.

On a ski lift at Aspen, Colorado, 1950s.

With Charlie Chaplin and a young admirer aboard the ship that was taking Chaplin away from the United States forever, 1952.

de midi, and *L'Annonce faite à Marie*—was behind him, whereas the works by which Milhaud is mainly remembered, such as *Le Boeuf sur le toit* and *La Création du monde*, were not yet written. In *My Many Years*, Rubinstein described a riotous dinner with Milhaud and Claudel at a rooftop restaurant: The writer put away considerable quantities of wine, loudly recited bits of Rimbaud's poetry and his own by heart, and then threw grapes at passersby in the street below. Throughout the rest of Rubinstein's stay in Rio, he and Zulueta frequented the French embassy—where the pianist also met Henri Hoppenot, another career diplomat and future Milhaud librettist—and Claudel and Milhaud attended Rubinstein's concerts. The lack of diplomatic tact on the part of Claudel the diplomat impressed the pianist: Claudel slapped the hand of a music critic who tried to read the note that accompanied a bouquet of flowers in Rubinstein's dressing room after a concert; he told the Brazilian foreign minister's wife that she was "talking rubbish" after she had criticized some popular contemporary French authors; and while he was taking a portrait photo of Rubinstein (Claudel was an assiduous amateur photographer) he told him that he sat "like a dead body!"[77] But Claudel was impressed by Rubinstein's artistry. "We have here right now a truly astonishing pianist named Arthur Rubinstein," he wrote to his sister-in-law, Elisabeth Sainte-Marie Perrin, on June 21, 1918. "Do you know him?"[78]

Throughout the South American tour, Zulueta kept an eye on the box office receipts of potentially unscrupulous managers, persuaded a few unfriendly music critics to change their minds, and looked after travel arrangements and social engagements. After Rubinstein's concerts in Rio and São Paulo, Zulueta booked his boss and himself on a boat that took them back to Buenos Aires, where Rubinstein won fresh triumphs, renewed old friendships, spent a little time with Besanzoni—when da Rosa's back was turned—and followed Zulueta's advice to hire a valet. Rubinstein and his two-man entourage then traveled to Chile by train, and after another successful group of concerts they sailed from Valparaiso to Lima, Peru, where, in the middle of a Rubinstein recital on November 11, shouts of "*Armisticio! Armisticio!*" spread through the audience. Like everyone else, Rubinstein rushed into the street to cheer and weep; then he went from tavern to tavern, banging out the *Marseillaise* "on the nearest broken-down piano" and ending up with "the biggest hangover of my life." Did the end of the war make him want to return quickly to Europe, to find out how his parents and siblings, Lily and her children, the Kochanskis and Szymanowskis, and countless other friends and acquaintances on both sides of the German lines had fared during the war and the Bolshevik revolution, and to assist them if necessary? He made no mention of any such feelings until later in his narrative, and indeed he admitted that he was upset when Zulueta decided to abandon him and return immediately to Europe. His fellow-adventurer's departure was "a great blow to me," he said. "Our combined vitality gave me a curious feeling of power."[79] But the tour proceeded. After having given a gala benefit concert to raise funds for the French, English, and American Red Cross organizations, Rubinstein left Lima in the company of Enrique, his valet, and a Mr. Biancamano, da Rosa's representative. They boarded a ship at nearby Callao and headed for Cuba, where Rubinstein had lined up some recitals.

Upon his arrival in Panama City or Balboa (not Colón, as he said in his book: Colón is on the Caribbean side of the canal), he received a telegram from Besanzoni, who told him to wait for her there so that they could proceed to Cuba together. Her message worried him: he had not had a regular female companion since his affair with Lily had petered out five years earlier, and he was not sure that he wanted one. "There is no denying that my masculine vanity was highly flattered but at the same time I was rather cowardly before new and complicated responsibilities. I had no intention of marrying Gabriella and I was terribly afraid that that was her goal."[80] Join him she did, however, and Rubinstein related at length and amusingly, in his memoirs, the vicissitudes of the rest of their trip: Besanzoni's fury when the American military guards at their Panamanian hotel refused to let an unmarried couple share a room ("Since when do they stop a man and a woman from being happy?" she demanded); the pianist's plea to the American civilian governor to find space for them on one of the few available Cuba-bound boats—most of which were overcrowded with military personnel—and the governor's surprise on realizing that this was the same Arthur Rubinstein who, as a fourteen-year-old prodigy, had given him his autograph aboard a Berlin-to-Dresden train in 1901; the governor's granting of U.S. visas to Rubinstein, Besanzoni, and Enrique, with the proviso that the two artists give an open-air concert for the troops; Biancamano's abandonment of the tour; and the passage through the Panama Canal and the stop in Colón (not Balboa, as he said in his memoirs) to change ships. Rubinstein also remembered the murderous-looking crew on the second boat; the stop in Santa Marta, Colombia, to take on a shipment of bananas—with swarms of insects—in unimaginably intense heat; his and Besanzoni's decision to disembark from the infernal vessel when it stopped in New Orleans; his trouble in getting through U.S. immigration with his Hispano-Polish passport; the long train trip from New Orleans to Miami; and finally, the boat trip to Havana, where Rubinstein collapsed and slept for sixteen hours.

His account of their Cuban adventure is exceptionally confused with respect to dates, names, and even the events described. The local impresario, whom he called Antonio Braccale, was Adolfo Bracale. The performances of *Carmen* and *Aida*, which, Rubinstein claimed, Besanzoni sang with Caruso in Havana at that time—the end of 1918 or early in 1919—really took place in May and June 1920; the great tenor was in New York throughout the earlier period. Even more puzzling is Rubinstein's recollection that it was Maria Barrientos, the celebrated Catalan soprano, who, in Havana, alerted him to the fact that he was announced as soloist with several major orchestras in the United States during the following few weeks: Barrientos also took part in Caruso's 1920 Havana season, but was not in Cuba during the 1918–19 season, so far as I have been able to determine. It was true, however, that before he left Buenos Aires, Rubinstein had received an offer from R. E. Johnson, an important New York agent, to make a fifteen-concert tour of the United States; the fees—four hundred dollars per concert—were far lower than those he received in Latin America, but he was eager to return to North America thirteen years after his debut tour, and he was pleased to learn that "it was not my South American success but Eugène Ysaÿe's warm recommendation that was responsible for this offer."[81] He had let Johnson know that he was interested in the proposal, and he had requested contracts and an advance. As neither had come through he had proceeded with his South American tour. Although his first two concerts in Havana were highly successful and led Bracale to schedule others, Rubinstein cabled Johnson to ask for confirmation of what—he claimed—Barrientos had told him; the answer, according to Rubinstein, was somewhat vague, but the possibility of engagements with the Boston Symphony and other important ensembles made him decide to take the risk.

Besanzoni wanted to cancel her Cuban performances and accompany Rubinstein to New York, but he persuaded her to fulfill her contract in Havana first and to join him later. He did not admit, in his memoirs, that his reason for persuading her to stay behind was his hope of seeing Muriel Draper in New York, but he did say, further on: "I loved Gabriella but was not in love with her, while with Muriel Draper I felt exactly the contrary; I did not like her but was in love with her. And I was terribly afraid of falling again under her spell." The spell ended, he said, within twenty-four hours of his arrival in New York: he accidentally (or so he claimed) bumped into Muriel in the lobby of the Ritz-Carlton Hotel, where he had arranged to meet Dagmar Godowsky for lunch. "When I kissed [Muriel's] hand the strangest phenomenon occurred. I felt free. Free. As if I had never known her."[82] He learned that she and Paul had divorced; on subsequent visits to America he occasionally saw them, separately, and probably also saw little Sanders Draper, who may have been his son. Paul's early death, in 1925, affected him deeply, although he did not say so in his memoirs. In October of that year, Ruth Draper, who was staying in Oxford, wrote to a friend in America: "Arthur has just turned up in London and I'm lunching with him tomorrow—he is so afraid to see me—I'm afraid too. He is terrified of emotion and of seeing pain, you know—it's a strange cowardice on his part. . . . He really adored Paul and knew him so well and you know what Paul felt for him."[83] In 1932, Arthur met Muriel in Moscow: he was there to give a concert, and she was there as "an envoy of the Communist Party of the United States," he said. "As Muriel insisted on speaking Russian, she made me laugh and that angered her. I never saw her again, nor did I wish to."[84] Sanders Draper was killed in action during World War II.

Like his accounts of his relations with other agents, Rubinstein's tale of his relations with R. E. Johnson is a mixture of mild praise and harsh blame, and in this case the manager is verbally caricatured (lame, vulgar, hard-drinking, and inseparable from his large-breasted lady assistant) as well as criticized. The pianist's Boston Symphony engagement had been lost as a result of delay—Johnson's delay in providing a contract, according to Rubinstein; Rubinstein's delay in committing himself to the tour, according to Johnson—but performances in New York, Chicago, and Cincinnati were still available. Rubinstein's second New York debut took place at Carnegie Hall on February 20, 1919, and was attended by Sergei Prokofiev, Josef Hofmann, Josef Lhévinne, Jacques Thibaud, and Besanzoni, whose arrival in New York the previous day had thrown Rubinstein into a nervous state, he said. John Galsworthy also attended, according to an entry in the diary of the twenty-seven-year-old publisher Alfred A. Knopf, who met the writer and his wife "at Carnegie for Artur Rubinstein's debut. Truly a master pianist. Splendid Bach [Organ Toccata and Fugue in D Minor, arranged by Tausig] and Beethoven Waldstein. Then Chopin [A-flat Ballade] and the finest rendering of the F Sharp Minor Polonaise I've ever heard. [The Berceuse and Nocturne in F-sharp were also played.] Mrs. Galsworthy was 'thrilled' by the C Sharp Minor Scherzo and the C Minor Etude given as an encore. The Twelfth Liszt Rhapsody was absolutely transcendental. I predict an enormous popularity for this young man. He has a presence and you never forget he is a *man*. No mannerisms of any kind—a wonderful left hand and a fine staccato. Astonishing accuracy in runs and great chords—also a notable ability to outline the broad contours of an intricate composition. Only in the A flat Ballade did he key his pitch so to speak too low so that the tremendous climax he might have evoked from the keyboard never really came. His Debussy was splendid especially l'Ile Joyeuse: also the Triana of Albéniz. A superb program—the most well chosen and interesting piano recital I ever remember to have attended. The Galsworthys had a really good time."[85]

Not everyone was as enthusiastic as Knopf about the recital, which drew mixed reactions from the critics. "A pianist of charm and technical finesse is Arthur Rubinstein, who gave his first pianoforte recital at Carnegie

Hall yesterday afternoon," Richard Aldrich said in the *New York Times*. "The newcomer played here before, ten or twelve years ago, it is said. . . ." Aldrich evidently did not recall having written a review—largely negative—of Rubinstein's United States debut in 1906. The rest of his awkwardly written, condescending article is based on hard-to-reconcile comparisons and technical twaddle.

> Rubinstein is a miniaturist; he is more affiliated in style to Emil Sauer . . . or even to the magical de Pachmann, than to the first and only Anton of his name, or to Josef Hofmann and Ethel Leginska [an English-born Leschetizky pupil a few months older than Rubinstein]. But, while his scale of dynamics is not wide within its compass he admirably succeeds. He is a trifle old-fashioned in style; the Viennese school, with its light action keyboard, the lack of depth in his chordal playing, the too rapid scales, also superficial in tone; above all his pedalling after, instead of before, his attack. The triceps play a minor role. Finger velocity and a staccato, brilliant incisive with a splendid left hand, are undeniable qualities coupled with a sweet singing touch and a musical temperament; traits sufficient to equip a half dozen pianists. Strangely his tone was occasionally hard and his phrasing not ductile, but slightly angular. After all, a début with its concomitant nervousness. . . . It may be said of this Rubinstein that he came, played and was liked. But a miniaturist.[86]

According to Arnold T. Schwab, biographer of the well-known musician, writer, bohemian aesthete, and music critic James Gibbons Huneker, this review was written by Huneker—who also wrote for the *New York Times*—rather than by Aldrich, but since it appears in Aldrich's published collection of reviews, *Concert Life in New York, 1902–1923*, I have assumed that Aldrich wrote it. A *Times* review of a second Rubinstein recital, three weeks later, appealed much more to Aldrich (or Huneker), whose review bore the headline "A Brilliant Piano Recital." "Rubinstein still tended to play Beethoven too fast"—so Schwab summarized the critic's reactions—"but he had found his triceps and, consequently, a deeper, larger, and more varied tone. In Debussy, Ravel, and Albéniz, Rubinstein was 'simply fascinating.' The Spanish music was 'positively electrifying,' the reviewer declared, and the 'diabolic verve, color scheme, and dash would alone make the reputation of a less musical artist.' "[87]

Between his two Carnegie Hall recitals, Rubinstein played the Brahms Second Concerto with the New York Symphony under Walter Damrosch (on February 22, at Carnegie) and traveled to Cincinnati, in Besanzoni's company, to play the Beethoven Fourth Concerto with the Cincinnati Symphony under Ysaÿe—who was in the second year of a four-year engagement as the orchestra's music director—and to give a joint sonata recital (Beethoven's "Kreutzer," the Brahms D Minor, and the Fauré A Major) with the Belgian master. Back in New York, at the Commodore Hotel's Grand Ballroom on April 2 (not the following season, as he incorrectly recalled), he played Chopin's A Major Polonaise, Liszt's "Liebestraum," Mendelssohn's "Spinning Song," the "Triana" from Albéniz's *Iberia*, Debussy's *Le Plus que lente*, and the Schubert-Tausig *Marche militaire* as part of a program—"The First Pershing Square Musicale"—in which Mary Garden, Mischa Elman, and Caruso also performed.

During the same period Rubinstein began to make piano rolls. From 1904, when Welte-Mignon refined the "player piano," until the late 1920s, when the quality of phonograph recordings began to improve dramatically as a result of new electronic recording techniques, piano rolls were a popular means of musical reproduction. Mahler, Debussy, Richard Strauss, and almost every famous pianist of the day made piano rolls. Most pianists were not happy with the results—tempi and dynamic nuances could not be reproduced with complete accuracy—but few could resist the money that the companies offered. Rubinstein made most of his rolls for the New York-based Aeolian Duo-Art company, which gave him a five-year, six-thousand-dollar-per-year contract to make three rolls annually; Aeolian also gave him a release to make three rolls, once only, for the Ampico Pianola company, a competitor. Aeolian's publicity material on Rubinstein emphasized the fact that "he made his first visit to America in 1906, and displayed an amazing dexterity of finger and other technical acquirements remarkable in an adolescent. After thirteen years he returned to us as a finished artist and a musical interpreter of rare powers. He has been a great traveler and has concertized in all parts of the civilized world with brilliant success."[88] In retrospect, Rubinstein was embarrassed about having participated with Godowsky, the young virtuoso Mischa Levitzki, and the composer-pianist Leo Ornstein in a six-city series of demonstration recitals, about which he reminisced in an answer to a letter from Ornstein's son, Severo, in 1977. "Your letter was both a pleasure and a wonderful surprise that your father is alive and well," Rubinstein said. "I remember him better than you would believe because besides my admiration for his work and playing in the early Twenties, we had a funny and a little shameful concert tour together, Godowsky, Lewicki [sic], your father and myself. We were obliged to listen on the stage to a piece played by us on the pianola and then repeated by a live performance. Your father's piece, as I well remember, was the Nocturne in F sharp by Chopin." Some of Rubinstein's rolls—originally released between 1920 and 1925—were reissued on compact discs in the early 1990s.

Decades after his 1919 American tour, Rubinstein told Samuel Chotzinoff that it had been "a personal triumph and an artistic disaster. I knew everybody, I dined out, I was sidetracked by pretty girls and beautiful women, and all this took up so much of my time and energy that I neglected the piano. The critics sensed this and were critical. . . . I was distinctly *not* a success in my second American venture, and I assumed that I should never return."[89] "Disaster" is, of course, an exaggeration: Rubinstein was merely considered one gifted and interesting pianist among many, rather than a great one. "I came back to America with my huge South American success, Spanish success," he remarked to another interviewer more than forty years after the event. "Well, they conceded me playing Spanish music to perfection. But they always criticized everything else, including Chopin—they always had preferences for others. Well, I had three dangerous colleagues: there were Paderewski, Hofmann, and Rachmaninoff. You must admit, they deserved [their success]!"[90] At a practical level, the main problem was that "engagements did not flow in," he recalled.[91] On the other hand, he had a marvelous time in New York, as his remarks to Chotzinoff indicate. He got together more than once with Adolph Bolm, one of Diaghilev's star dancers, whom he had met in Spain in 1916, and with Richard (originally Ryszard) Ordynski, a Polish stage director who had been Max Reinhardt's assistant during Rubinstein's Berlin days, and who, between 1916 and 1920, staged more than fifty productions at the Metropolitan Opera. Rubinstein also met the eighteen-year-old Jascha Heifetz, who had made an astonishingly successful New York debut the previous season and was already considered one of the greatest violinists in history. "My playing did not impress him particularly," Rubinstein admitted, "but he was wildly interested in the shops where I bought my ties and shoes."[92] Dagmar Godowsky, who had introduced the two musicians, was also good for a gossip session now and then—they both stayed at the Biltmore Hotel—although probably not when the jealous Besanzoni was around. And of course he mixed with high society: Mr. and Mrs. Charles Lanier, great patrons of music; Bob Chanler, the millionaire who had been married to Lina Cavalieri; and Adolf Ochs, the publisher of the *New York Times*, among others.

Of all his new acquaintances, the one he valued most was Sergei Prokofiev, who was spending much of the season in and near the city. Rubinstein was greatly impressed with the new works that the not-yet-twenty-eight-year-old composer played for him, and Prokofiev's delight in Rubinstein's playing made the pianist feel happier than "the success of my whole tour in South America."[93] They were coparticipants (Prokofiev as conductor of one of his own works), together with Mary Garden, in a Red Cross benefit concert at the Metropolitan Opera House; the event had been organized by young Elsa Maxwell, the well-known social butterfly and do-gooder, in the best sense of

the term, according to Rubinstein. Once, Rubinstein and Prokofiev bumped
into each other at a dinner of "The Bohemians"—the nickname of the New
York Musicians' Club; on that occasion Prokofiev was escorting Carolina
(Lina) Codina, a beautiful twenty-one-year-old woman of mixed Castilian,
Catalan, French Huguenot, and Polish background who was living in New
York with her mother and studying singing. At the dinner, Codina (whose
stage name, later, was Llubera) heard Rubinstein ask Prokofiev, "Where did
you hook such a beauty?" He had taken her for an American girl and hadn't
realized that she spoke Russian, among many other languages. "I got so red in
the face that I wanted to run away," she recalled, late in life. "When I saw
Rubinstein sixty years later, he reminded me of that dinner."[94] Rubinstein
remained friendly with them both and often saw them in New York during
the early 1920s and in Paris after their marriage, in 1923. In his memoirs,
Rubinstein said that he had attended the world premiere, in New York early
in 1921, of Prokofiev's Third Piano Concerto, with the composer as soloist and
Walter Damrosch conducting, but the world premiere took place in Chicago
eight months later, with Frederick Stock conducting; Rubinstein may have
been remembering the New York premiere on January 26, 1922—when he
was again in the United States—with the composer as soloist but with Albert
Coates conducting. He was probably present, however, at one of the first performances of Prokofiev's opera The Love for Three Oranges in Chicago at the
end of 1921, and he attended the premiere of the composer's First Violin Concerto at the Paris Opéra on October 18, 1923, with Marcel Darrieux as soloist
and Koussevitzky conducting.

Oddly enough, Rubinstein performed only some short pieces, among
Prokofiev's abundant piano works, and ignored the sonatas and concertos. He
liked the big works—especially the later sonatas—and often went out of his
way to hear other pianists play them, but he probably believed that his own
keyboard equipment did not include the brilliantly percussive techniques
that much of Prokofiev's music requires. "I was too lazy to learn them sufficiently for a public performance but I read them at home, played them often
in my head with great perfection, and remained satisfied with that," he said
in his memoirs.[95] And during his last active season, he told an interviewer, "I
will die with the feeling that there are at least a hundred works that I might
have played—the Sixth Sonata of Prokofiev, for instance, also the First and
Third concertos."[96] The composer returned to the Soviet Union in the mid-
1930s and never again received permission to leave; although he and Rubinstein did not meet again, Rubinstein, to the end of his life, considered
Prokofiev not only an "authentically great composer" but, surprisingly, "the
most important Russian composer"—even more important than Stravinsky,
in other words.[97] In an autograph album that belonged to Prokofiev, Rubin-

stein wrote: "The Roi-Soleil said: 'L'état c'est moi.' You, my dear Prokofiev, could say: 'Le soleil c'est moi.' "[98]

Although Rubinstein and Besanzoni stayed in separate suites at the Biltmore Hotel, musical New York knew that they were a couple, and Rubinstein found himself dealing with managers, agents, and recording company executives on behalf of his companion, rather than on his own behalf. The situation cannot have done their relationship any good. Besanzoni signed a contract to sing at the Metropolitan Opera the following season, to make records for the Victor Talking Machine Company, and to give a series of ten concerts for three thousand dollars each—7½ times the fee that Rubinstein was receiving for his performances. But both performers were invited to Mexico City for late-spring and early-summer engagements that proved to be lucrative for each of them: Besanzoni sang in *Carmen* and other operas with a company that included Pertile and the soprano Rosa Raisa, and Rubinstein played four recitals a week—twenty-six performances in all—in order to satisfy the apparently maniacal pianistic appetites of the local public. Chotzinoff, who was visiting Mexico that summer, could hardly believe his eyes and ears: "The house was packed and the audience rose in a body and cheered when [Rubinstein] came on the stage. At the end of the program there were shouts for *Navarra*, *Sevilla*, *Córdoba* and other pieces by Albéniz, all new to me then but favorites with the Mexican audience. . . . He was made to play countless encores, and when the concert was finally over, he was carried to his hotel on the shoulders of hysterical Mexicans. When I returned to New York and reported this astonishing triumph, someone jokingly remarked that the Mexicans probably thought they were hearing Anton Rubinstein, not Artur."[99]

All this took place in the midst of the bloody revolution that Pancho Villa was leading against the government of Venustiano Carranza. The rebel-hero Emiliano Zapata had been killed only a few weeks earlier; guns were visible everywhere, atrocities were committed, "trains were assaulted and bandits roamed the country," Rubinstein said. "But nothing could dampen the incredible vitality of these people." He later recalled that his and Besanzoni's fees were paid "after every show . . . in beautiful twenty-peso gold pieces. We used to amuse ourselves building piles of gold on the table and looking at them with wonder."[100] More and more recitals were added to the twenty-six, and the gold piles rose. Rubinstein went to Guadalajara for some concerts, gave joint recitals with Besanzoni in San Luis Potosí and Monterrey, then returned to New York to make arrangements with Johnson for engagements in the United States the following season and to board a ship bound for England, while Besanzoni went back to Mexico City "for her appearances with Caruso," he said.[101] Those appearances, however, did not take place until October; Besanzoni probably returned to Mexico for other performances and stayed on through the summer, in anticipation of the special fall season with Caruso. The performances with the most celebrated tenor of all times were held in the Plaza de Toros, which seated twenty thousand. Howard Greenfield, Caruso's biographer, wrote that "though the supporting cast was . . . poor, the tenor was fortunate enough to sing opposite the Carmen of Gabriella Besanzoni, the only singer in the company worthy of the occasion."[102]

THE ARTHUR RUBINSTEIN who arrived at Clara Bergheim's home in Hampstead in the summer of 1919, with trunks, valises, and a valet in tow, was bent on wiping out the memory of the impecunious Arthur Rubinstein who had set out for Spain 3½ years earlier. This new Rubinstein was an international success, a man of means, and well pleased to be able to make what he frankly described as "a great display of personal vanity . . . after my ever-miserable, penniless past in London. . . . Overnight I became 'the rich friend' "[103] who shopped at Aspreys' and gave costly gifts to the people who had been kind to him. But he also played chamber music with his old friends Sammons, Tertis, and Evans at Sylvia Sparrow's studio, and he gave Ordynski, who was passing through London en route from New York to Warsaw, some money and a food parcel for his parents and siblings, in the hope that they were still alive and well. Then he set out for a tour of Spain, stopping in Paris to visit his brother Ignacy, the revolutionary, who had spent the war years working as a journalist—astrology columnist, to be precise—for the left-wing newspaper La Dépêche de Toulouse. Ignacy related whatever family news he had managed to glean: their father and mother had survived the war and were in Lodz, as were most of Ignacy and Arthur's uncles and aunts, brothers and sisters, and nieces and nephews. Their sister Hela and her children were in Warsaw, but there was no news of Jadwiga and her family, except that they had fled to Russia during the German invasion. Arthur could not be troubled, then or for some time thereafter, to visit his family, and he was offended when he discovered that they had been offended by the food parcel that he had sent (along with costlier gifts), even though it had been "nicely packed by Fortnum and Mason."[104]

His Spanish tour was "as successful as the previous ones," he said.[105] In the course of it, he was interviewed in Madrid by a journalist who used the pseudonym El Caballero Audaz (The Bold Gentleman). Unlike most newspaper interviews, this one provides at least the outlines of an interesting portrait of its subject, not long before his thirty-third birthday.

> I looked around the room [said the interviewer]; a luxurious
> apartment at the Hotel Palace, which differed from all the other

apartments in that the bed was covered and decorated with several magnificent, large, embroidered Manila shawls, and on the tables there were some twenty studio photographs of beautiful women: in the passionate dedications, each declared herself very much in love with our eminent interviewee. . . .

"Good grief, Rubinstein! This is quite a harem," I murmured.

"Don't let it surprise you. It's of no importance. They're keepsakes. I want to live surrounded by things that are pleasant to look at. I feel less lonely when, on opening my eyes in the morning, I encounter the charming physiognomies of these angelic little friends. Besides, please note that they are all smiling at us, that none of them is troubling us with complaints."

"Does each of them remind you of a moment of love?"

He smiled and replied: "If not of love, of a pleasant moment in my life. And, put together, they provide me with divine happiness. They are of all different nationalities."

"Except Spanish?"

"No, also Spanish; and how! You see"—and he showed me the portrait of a beautiful popular artist, whose name he hid, out of natural discretion. He resumed talking: "With these shawls, which I bought in Seville, and with these photographs, I manage to sweeten the hostile coldness of hotel rooms and to fill them with my personality, to give them character; the suites stop looking so severe and transform themselves into peaceful little nooks. Don't you think so?"

I agreed and took my seat. Meanwhile, Rubinstein groped in the pockets of his magnificent, silk dressing-gown . . . pulled out a cigarette-box, and offered me an Egyptian cigarillo. He is young, slender, and elegant. His profile is sharp; his nose is broad and a little crooked; his eyes gray with sparkling irises; his hair fair and very curly; his manners gentlemanly. He is like a prince of legend. What is most interesting about Arturo Rubinstein is his conversation, which is original and most delightful. His Spanish is nearly correct. . . . I asked him: "What is your biggest vice?"

He thought for a moment. "I don't know," he said at last. "I'm a man of small vices. I love women tremendously; however, I don't consider this a vice, but rather, on the contrary, a virtue to be encouraged. If I had sons, I would tell them: 'Love without respite; love until you die.' Because to me this is the most important mission in life."

"What was the saddest moment you've been through?"

"I haven't lived even a single day in a way that I didn't wish to live it; as a result, I've never had a sad moment. One can regret hav-

ing done things out of convenience, but those that were dictated by
one's being, by one's heart—never!"

"And your happiest moment?"

"Oh, I have had so many! As you can see for yourself, I'm not
well today; I have a terrible headache. I have to leave for Barcelona
this afternoon, and yet, at this moment, as I chat with you, I am
happy."

"So am I," I replied, thanking him with a smile for his kind
gentlemanliness. "And tell me, Rubinstein: what in life upsets you
most?" . . .

"Everything and nothing makes me impatient. Sometimes
I'm a little upset by the thought that on no given day am I my own
master."

"And death?"

"Oh, far from upsetting me, it's something that attracts me!"

"What gives you the greatest pleasure during your concerts?"

"Listening to the music I'm playing. And then, when I feel that
I have the audience under my control. How strange is the way in
which an artist forms, out of three thousand spectators, a single soul
that surrenders itself to him! And what we call a soul turns out to be
somewhat like an electric current, a fluid, an x-ray. Seated before the
piano, concentrated within myself, I am precisely aware of all the
movements that are going on in the auditorium; once, I felt in my
hands and my nerves, at the exact moment when he entered the hall,
the arrival of an artist who is a friend of mine and whom I wasn't
expecting. Without having seen him, I said to myself: "Smith is
there." And in fact, Smith had arrived at that moment and I felt him
looking at me." . . .

"How much money have you made through your art?"

"Ugh! I've *earned* about three million [old Spanish] dollars,
which I've spent well, living as I please, and surely no millionaire can
have made use of his money as I do with the fruits of my labors. Because to me, money begins to be worth something at the moment
that one begins to spend it wisely. Just as a sheet of your notebook
acquires no value until you've begun to write on it. Of what use are
sheets of paper if one has no ideas? Morgan, Rothschild, and Rockefeller are slaves of their money, servants of their gold. I remember a
noteworthy incident in my life, à propos this subject. I was staying in
Rome with a much loved, pretty little lady [Lily Wertheim], but we
were penniless! One night, the American ambassador invited me to a
banquet and introduced me to the famous millionaire [J. P.] Mor-

gan. He was a frightful, repugnant-looking man. He had an enormous, beet-colored nose, spattered with spots of pus; tiny, watery grey eyes; some of his teeth were covered with a greenish-black coating; and he had a flabby paunch. I looked at him with pity; he was a poor fellow. Of what use was his money? None at all. Because I, from my artistic abundance, could give him a few pleasant moments by making music; in exchange, despite all his wealth, he couldn't offer me a penny's-worth of spiritual value. So I turned out to be a lot more useful in life than Morgan the millionaire, no?"

I agreed. . . . "Which country would you like to live in?"

"London for living; Italy for looking at; Andalusia and Rio de Janeiro for loving."

"Who is the musician you most admire?"

"Among virtuosos, Pablo Casals."

"And among composers?"

"Stravinsky."

"Do you want to talk about a disagreeable incident that involved you and the Madrid public?"

"Oh, everything is all right now; yesterday peace was made between the public and me, with great enthusiasm. . . . I adore the Madrid public; it spoils me more and more every time, and amid all this reciprocal affection I wanted my friends to be friends of the Madrid public, too. Well then: one evening I played Ravel's famous waltzes [the *Valses nobles et sentimentales*], which are favorites of mine. I was surprised and embittered to discover that the audience received my friend Ravel rather inconsiderately. This was not possible, and in return I repeated the composition, putting all my soul into it. I was trying to convince the audience that it had been unjust; the audience then rejected my attitude. but [yesterday] there was great joy, reconciliation. I played whatever they asked and they showered me with ovations. It was moving, affectionate applause."[106]

From Spain Rubinstein went back to England late in the fall of 1919, stopping again in Paris en route. It was probably during this stay, and not a year later, as his memoirs suggest, that he looked up Milhaud, who took him to the Bar Gaya on Rue Duphot and introduced him to the other five members of "Les Six"—Georges Auric, Francis Poulenc, Arthur Honegger, Louis Durey (the oldest, at the age of thirty-one), and "the lovely Germaine Tailleferre."[107] Under the influence of Erik Satie and Jean Cocteau—both of whom Rubinstein met—these young composers were beginning to make a mark on French musical life. Poulenc was barely twenty years old, but his

piano music interested Rubinstein more than that of any of the others; he
soon began to play some of it in public, and Poulenc dedicated his *Promenades* to Rubinstein. According to James Harding, who wrote about Les Six,
Rubinstein "once joined Milhaud and Auric to play a piano arrangement of
Le Boeuf sur le toit." (The title of one of Milhaud's best-known orchestral
compositions was the name of one of the group's favorite hangouts.)
"Though originally intended for four hands only, Rubinstein's impromptu
assistance turned it into a thoroughly convincing arrangement for six."[108]
Falla, too, was in Paris, and Rubinstein sent him a note (on stationery of the
Hôtel Meurice, Rue de Rivoli): "My dear friend—I must leave for London in
great haste and I have a great favor to ask of you—Would you be so kind as to
send me (if possible) in New-York (Hotel Ritz) the copy of your Spanish
songs. Besanzoni absolutely wants to sing them and this would be a triumph
for you—the other copies are at Vallin-Pardo's as I told you—don't worry
about giving them to me, nothing bad will happen to them. A thousand greetings! Your most devoted Arthur Rubinstein. My address in London Hotel
Ritz."[109] (Eugénie Vallin-Pardo, better known as Ninon Vallin, was a noted
French soprano.) Falla sent the songs, but what came of Rubinstein's proposal is not known.

Before he left for America, Rubinstein gave a short series of joint recitals with Emma Calvé and Jacques Thibaud in the English provinces. The
sixty-one-year-old French soprano—one of the great divas of her generation,
and the "creator" of major roles by Mascagni and Massenet—had long since
retired from the opera stage, but she was still appearing on the concert platform. Although her voice was no longer in good shape, she was an old trouper
and a pleasant companion, and she enjoyed carrying on mock flirtations with
her two costars, both of whom were young enough to be her sons. An accompanist played her numbers and most of Thibaud's, but Rubinstein and Thibaud joined forces in Beethoven's "Spring" Sonata and Rubinstein played a
group of solo pieces. This, at least, is how Rubinstein remembered the episode. Ivor Newton, a well-known English accompanist, said, in his memoirs,
that he took part in a provincial tour at that time as accompanist for the Russian tenor Vladimir Rosing, and "in the scintillating company of Calvé and
Artur Rubinstein." Thibaud's name was not mentioned. If Newton's version
is correct, Rubinstein may have been confusing two different tours.[110] In
London, on December 30, 1919, Rubinstein gave a well-publicized recital at
the Wigmore Hall. "Mr. E. A. Michell has the honour of presenting Arthur
Rubinstein whom he has been fortunate enough to secure on his way from
Spain to the United States," the advance material read. "As Mr. Rubinstein is
due to open extended tours of North and South America early in January, the
present occasion will positively be his only recital in London for a consider-

able time."[111] The event was successful, and Michell remained Rubinstein's London agent until well into the 1930s.

During his stay in London, Rubinstein frequented Lord Asquith, the former prime minister; his famously headstrong and sharp-tongued wife, Margot; their musically inclined son, Anthony ("Puff"), who later became a film director; the duke and duchess of Rutland and their daughter, the actress Diana Cooper; and Tony and Juanita Gandarillas and their highly placed friends. He got to know Christabel McLaren, née Macnaghten, the wife of Henry Duncan McLaren, Baron Aberconway, and he also became friendly with William Jowitt, a barrister two years his senior—and friendlier still with Jowitt's wife. In *My Many Years,* Lesley Jowitt (née McIntyre) is mentioned several times, en passant, as a pleasant, casual acquaintance, but Rubinstein told Annabelle Whitestone that he had loved and had an affair with Mrs. Jowitt; he avoided saying this in his book to avoid hurting the feelings of the Jowitts' daughter, Penelope—their only child—and also, perhaps, to avoid admitting to his readers that his interest in Besanzoni, whatever it had meant to him initially, was by then almost entirely a matter of vanity. He described Lesley as one of the sweetest, most adorable people imaginable, and he added that her husband preferred to spend his nonworking hours reading the *Times* rather than paying attention to his wife, whom he had married in 1913. (After the 1945 elections, Jowitt became lord chancellor in the Labour government, as Baron Jowitt of Stevenage; he died in 1957.) He also said that William Jowitt "used to go to Paris every so often, to some special maison, and get himself beaten up. Something sort of kinky. And yet he had this indifference that most Englishmen have," reported Whitestone, who is English. "Englishmen really understand women very little. There's nothing worse, for a woman, than indifference. Arthur was one of the very few men who really knew how to treat women, how to make a woman feel good—to make her feel that she's the only woman who exists. Even if it isn't true, you feel while you're with him that there is no other woman, that you're the most divine creature on earth. And he had that incredible way, without making any effort. The feeling emanated from him. He didn't sit there paying cheap compliments, and he wasn't one of these men who have 'techniques' for getting hold of a woman. It was as natural as his playing: calm."[112]

Rubinstein certainly would not have won many points with feminists, and in some respects his attitude toward women seems to have been downright adolescent. At the age of ninety he told an interviewer, "Women have always attracted me for a whole mass of reasons. I don't know whether you've ever noticed, but they are very different from us, no? Their hair, their eyes, their mouth, their chest, their waist—the further down one goes, the more one realizes that they are different. And it's this difference that I love above all else. Look well: you'll see that I'm not mistaken. And then, women don't have to be intelligent to be seductive, and in this, too, they are very different from men. It's always been more important to me that women be feminine than spiritual. With due respect for the scale of importance, they sometimes make me think of my passion for cigars: they're absolutely delightful, but you have to keep relighting them!"[113]

About Rubinstein's relationship to Lesley Jowitt, Whitestone said, "Lord Jowitt didn't mind Arthur taking his wife to the theatre and taking her to dinner; whether he knew that there was anything else going on, I don't know." After the publication of the first volume of Rubinstein's memoirs, Penelope Jowitt came to him after a concert and asked him to write a dedication in her copy. According to Ms. Whitestone, Rubinstein commented afterward, " 'Perhaps I've put it very badly, but I wrote, "To Penelope, whom I loved before she was born." It looks as if she might have been my illegitimate daughter, which wasn't the case at all.' What he meant was that he loved her mother. And he did love her mother tremendously."[114]

It is safe to assume that Rubinstein did not mention this fact to Besanzoni when they met, on his return to New York in January 1920. Two months earlier she had made a highly successful debut—as Amneris in *Aida*—at the Metropolitan Opera, but subsequently, she told "Tutullo," her work had been sabotaged by the Hungarian-born contralto-turned-soprano Margarete Matzenauer and the American soprano Geraldine Farrar, both of whom were determined to keep Besanzoni out of their repertoire-territory—the role of Carmen, in particular, but other roles as well. In a letter written the previous August, however, Giulio Gatti-Casazza, the Met's general manager, had described Besanzoni as "a bizarre and unpredictable woman," and she herself may have contributed as much as her rivals to her downfall. Whatever the reasons may have been, in ten weeks at the Met Besanzoni sang only fifteen performances; her contract was not renewed, and the concert tour and most of the recording sessions that had been planned the previous year were cancelled, although she was invited to sing at Chicago's Lyric Opera the following season. According to Rubinstein, "Caruso was indignant" at the treatment that Besanzoni had received in New York, and the great tenor's confidence in her was vindicated three years later, when Toscanini engaged her to sing leading roles at La Scala, where she became a favorite. But at the time of her Met defeat, she was angry and depressed. Rubinstein "stayed with her for hours, and tried to restore her courage and vitality," he said, but he was relieved when she departed for Italy after her last Met performance, which took place on January 26: "I recovered my full freedom and concerned myself more with my career."[115]

The combined evidence of all the references to Besanzoni in Rubin-

stein's book indicates that he put much more effort into avoiding her, especially as a bedmate, than in trying to be with her. Perhaps he didn't perform
well, sexually, with her, and thus found their encounters embarrassing.
(Besanzoni was very tiring and demanding, after the initial excitement, he
told Whitestone, who pointed out that "few of Arthur's serious lovers were
fellow artists, and Besanzoni was so temperamental.")[116] They did see each
other again in Havana, approximately four months after the singer's far-from-
triumphal departure from New York, and the following year they were again
together quite often in New York—a fact that Rubinstein did not mention in
his memoirs. Later in 1921 they met in Paris where, Rubinstein claimed, an
emergency telephone call from Stravinsky, who was depressed over financial
and sexual problems (impotence in bed with Lopoukhova, Rubinstein told
Whitestone), prevented him from meeting Besanzoni at the station when her
train arrived. He sent a reluctant Szymanowski in his stead, to escort her and
her sister to the Folies-Bergère that evening. Rubinstein's lack of attention
infuriated Besanzoni. She accused him of being Szymanowski's lover and
told him that she never wanted to see him again, he reported, and he also
claimed that Besanzoni's sister had once tried unsuccessfully to seduce him.
Two years later Gabriella married Enrique Lage, a wealthy Brazilian industrialist. After her retirement from the stage she ran the Theatro Municipal in
Rio de Janeiro—very ably, according to Lina Pagliughi.[117] Rubinstein and
Besanzoni eventually made their peace, and they saw each other occasionally
during his concert tours. Ricardo de Quesada, Ernesto's son, recalled that in
1947 or thereabouts, "when I was a child, my parents and I were in Rio with
Rubinstein—Hotel Gloria—and besides the usual concerts, he was awarded
an important medal by the Minister of Culture; so he organized a cocktail at
the new building of the Ministry designed by Oscar Niemeyer—and I had
the opportunity there to meet an old (now I wouldn't say she was old at that
time) and beautiful lady: la Besanzoni."[118] Nela Rubinstein recalled that
Besanzoni remained "very fond of Arthur. When she was dying, I think she
wanted to will him some jewels or something like that, and her family was
absolutely after her not to let him near her."[119] Besanzoni died in her native
Rome on June 8, 1962, at the age of seventy-three.

ON JANUARY 25, 1920—the day before Besanzoni's last performance at the
Met—Rubinstein played there, in a concert with the house orchestra conducted by Richard Hageman; the pianist's part of the program consisted of
the Saint-Saëns G Minor Concerto, Chopin's Scherzo in C-sharp Minor and
Berceuse, and Liszt's Tenth Hungarian Rhapsody; other participants included the soprano Marie Sundelius and the bass Giovanni Martino. At this
concert and others in the course of his tour, Rubinstein was warmly received,

but he did not become a major celebrity in North America. He may well have been relieved to depart for concerts in South America, where he knew that he would be welcomed as a returning hero, and where his fees reflected his special standing. On his arrival in Rio de Janeiro, however, he was not pleased to discover that Ernesto de Quesada was having him split a recital series with Georges Boskoff, a Paris-based Rumanian pianist five years his senior whom Rubinstein liked as a person but did not esteem as an artist. But he was happy to give concerts of music for two pianos with Edouard Risler—a Frenchman whose Beethoven performances Rubinstein greatly admired—and he enjoyed meeting Artur Napoleao dos Santos, a music publisher and "a onetime famous pianist who at the ripe age of ninety-eight played for me, with astonishing precision, a piece by Gottschalk," Rubinstein said.[120] (The Italo-Portuguese-Brazilian musician had evidently been pulling Rubinstein's leg: he was only seventy-seven.)

This may have been the visit to Rio during which Rubinstein had an attack of guilt over his inadequate practicing. "Once, in Rio," he told Chotzinoff, "I ran into the great pianist Godowsky in the lobby of my hotel. 'I'm coming to hear you tonight,' Godowsky said, beaming. I blanched. 'Please, please don't come,' I implored. 'It is impossible to fake in front of you.' " And Rubinstein admitted: "Like all persons who lead a double life, I was happy only on the surface. Outwardly I was a man to be envied. My facility on the piano was incredible, but my technique was questionable."[121] What made his 1920 visit to Brazil especially memorable for him, however, was an episode that he described a few years later in an article for *Muzyka*, a Warsaw-based magazine.

> During a stay in Rio, the name of [Heitor] Villa-Lobos, which was unknown to me until that moment, came to my attention. . . . He was poor, life's difficulties had made him take a job in a third-rate movie house orchestra. . . . He played the cello and many other instruments; he had such an instinct for instruments that once, when he had to replace a friend who was ill—a violinist—he grabbed the violin without thinking twice, set it in front of him like a cello, and played the friend's whole part. But stories of this sort interested me less than the fact that this brilliant player was also a composer who had an individual creative style. All the professional musicians with whom I had a chance to talk about Villa-Lobos described him only in brusque, disdainful terms, but in their descriptions I sensed the sort of confusion that always characterizes our opinions of what lies beyond the realm of common and readily understandable ideas.
>
> On my first free evening I went to the cinema where Villa-

Lobos worked. The orchestra was playing some pieces from the international repertoire. . . . I was starting to get bored when something unexpected happened. One of the orchestra members, looking around the auditorium during the intermission, noticed me in the audience. When the next part began, I heard music that was completely unlike what had been played in the previous part. It was a furious, exotic dance, crazy in its ceaseless rhythmic impulse, extraordinarily colorful, clear in its harmony and instrumentation. I immediately felt a breeze of uncommon talent in this music. . . . I made my way to the wings, introduced myself to him, and asked for further details about the piece that had just been performed. The answer was unexpected: "Such things cannot be of any interest to you," Villa-Lobos said abruptly. He turned his back on me and disappeared into the backstage darkness.

A couple of days passed. One morning, I was awakened by footsteps and noise in the vestibule of my [hotel] suite. . . . I found more than ten musicians with instruments under their arms, and with Villa-Lobos standing in front of them. In a few words he announced to me that he had made up his mind and had decided to perform some of his compositions for me. "These are my friends," he said, "lovely people who have agreed to give me the only free time they have in the working day."

. . . In order to set the whole orchestra up, the living room had to be transformed into a concert hall. The wardrobe, tables, arm chairs, and sofas were pushed aside. Finally, the whole orchestra was in place and the "concert" could begin. I don't think I'll ever forget it for the rest of my life. Villa-Lobos's music was not only ravishingly beautiful, it also had a feature that one rarely finds. That feature was the total uniqueness of his style, and it characterizes Villa-Lobos's music right up to the present day. There was nothing to compare it to. The color, sonority, and form were unknown to us Europeans. . . . You would have had to be deaf not to sense the scope of this music. I surrendered myself to its charm, and listened to it with delight and sincere joy.

Villa-Lobos contains within himself all the elements that suit our epoch's definition of beauty and aesthetic requirements. For us musicians, the tragedy of our times is the chaos and disorder within the discipline of musical aesthetics. Dangerous, fatal elements have entered our music from the arena of world politics. In the political constellation we see old, aristocratic Europe on its knees before omnipotent America, home of the dollar, athletic records, the cult of brute strength, and plebeian self-satisfaction. In music, we see high culture, refined and subtle, handed down by the great masters of the past, pursuing the brutal effects of American primitivism, full of dull concepts.

Irony of fortune! I want to laugh when I hear the various sorts of "jazz" compositions born in Europe, when I see how many attempts and how many talents are wasted, how much inspiration is burned up year after year on the pagan altar of jazz, which is so popular in Europe nowadays. According to the opinions of some determined "modernists," jazz is the most characteristic expression of our day, the richest declaration of the Yankee race's spirit. This is what is said in Europe. Yet in America it is common knowledge that the three composers who are the creators and prophets of modern jazz—Irving Berlin, [George] Gershwin, and Jerome Kern—are not ethnically connected to America; and the most capable propagator of jazz in Europe is Jean Wiener [or Wiéner, a French composer; Rubinstein's implication is that all were Jews of Eastern European origin]. These are young people, not without talent, witty, skillful, and—most important—capable of compromise. If Mr. Wiener puts the touching words, "To you, the American Negroes," as the dedication on his compositions, he follows his destiny and intentions. But when the powerful talent of a Stravinsky shrinks, makes itself small, and tries to bend itself to the pigmy-like ideals of jazz; when, by dint of hard effort, he produces *Rag-Time*, an imitation of jazz—this makes a pitiful impression. It reminds one of all the subterfuge and cowardice of European politicians, in order to flatter the potentates of the land of the Dollar.

Villa-Lobos hasn't the slightest intention of flattering anybody. He creates with the brilliance and power of genius; as to fertility and ease of self-expression, he reminds one of Schubert. . . .

. . . The enduring power of primitive peoples is to be heard in every measure of Villa-Lobos's music. It is not destructive and brutal but rather creative, rushing forward in unbridled movement. Furthermore, Villa-Lobos is a son of South America. An abyss separates him from the facile fashions and words, full of Negromania, of the countries of North America. He brings new creative values to modern music because he draws upon the rich folklore of his wonderful native country, and his strong and original individualism is reflected in every bar of his music.

. . . When I met Villa-Lobos, he was reputed to be a "madman." I did everything I could for him. I commissioned three of his

larger pieces from him, to give him at least partial financial independence. I included Villa-Lobos's compositions in my repertoire and
supported him with whatever authority I had managed to achieve in
his country. When I visited Rio de Janeiro two years later, Villa-
Lobos was much talked about and his artistic tendencies were discussed. A few years later, he was considered a "master," and the
most famous musicians called him their "colleague." Two years ago,
during a dinner at the home of one of Rio de Janeiro's biggest indus-
trialists, the guests were speaking about Villa-Lobos. I said that I considered him one of the greatest composers of our century and that he
would be enthusiastically welcomed in Europe, where he would be
able to have his bigger works performed. The host interrupted me
and laconically asked the question: "And how much money is
needed for this?" I named a fantastic amount. A little while later, I
held in my hand a check for that amount. Villa-Lobos organized
some concerts in Paris with the participation of his exotic orchestra.
It was an artistic event that will not soon be erased from the minds of
Parisian musicians. They were hearing, for the very first time, a truly
new musical art-form that unites the sincerity and impulsiveness of
inspiration with perfect mastery of technique; it is very special and
full of a new kind of charm.

Villa-Lobos is now forty-three and at the height of his creative
development. We strongly hope that this powerful artist will cure our
sick modern music, which is losing itself in its search for goals.[122]

Rubinstein's interest in Villa-Lobos—his junior by only five weeks—did indeed help to launch the international career of the composer, whose exotic
music enjoyed great popularity among Parisian musicians in the second half
of the 1920s. Rubinstein's article demonstrates not only his faith in Villa-
Lobos but also his intense anger at the United States for not having taken
him, Rubinstein, to its collective heart. The same Europe that had just given
the world the worst war in history was selling its delicate, refined soul to those
vulgar Americans, and in so doing was being tainted with "Negromania," according to Rubinstein. (His article was written just as many conservative
musicians in Germany were writing about the pernicious influence of Jews
on European musical life. But Rubinstein's anger dissipated a few years later,
when America began to accept him as one of the pianistic giants of his time;
his children were raised to abhor racial prejudice.) The article also reveals his
less intense but no less real anger at Stravinsky for having dedicated to him a
piece—the *Piano-Rag Music,* which is related to *Rag-Time*—that Rubinstein
considered unworthy of himself. Besides considering jazz "low art," he evi-

dently did not understand that for eclectic geniuses, everything is grist for the mill. Just as Picasso could feel compelled to transform a broken construction brick into a highly personal representation of a human head, so Stravinsky would become fascinated by types of music much simpler than his own and feel compelled, not to copy them, but to transform them, to put his imprimatur on them. Stravinsky remains the greatest force in the history of music in the twentieth century, whereas Villa-Lobos was one gifted, original composer among many—which does not detract a whit from Rubinstein's perspicacity in recognizing the Brazilian composer's eccentric talent or from his generosity in helping the talent to flourish.

Between 1921 and 1926 Villa-Lobos wrote what Rubinstein later described as a "very long and very complicated" piano work, to show his gratitude toward the pianist. "*Rudepoêma*, for piano solo, to Arthur Rubinstein," begins the dedication on the manuscript; it continues: "My true friend, I don't know whether I have been able wholly to absorb your soul with this Rudepoêma, but I swear with all my heart that I feel, in my spirit, that I have engraved your temperament and that, machine-like, I have written it on paper, like an internal Kodak. As a result, if I succeed, you will always be the real author of this work." *Rudepoêma* means rough (or unpolished) poem, and Rubinstein said that Villa-Lobos had told him, on giving him the piece, that he felt that neither of them " 'cares much for pedantic detail. I compose and you play, off the heart, making the music live. . . .' " To Rubinstein, the piece seemed to be "a monumental attempt to express the origins of the native Brazilian *caboclos*, their sorrows and joys, their wars and peace, finishing with a savage dance. . . . a vast improvisation . . . [Villa-Lobos's] immense gift for musical invention often compensated for the lack of form and his refusal of discipline."[123] Rubinstein learned the work and performed it for many years thereafter, although infrequently. (Eva Rubinstein remembered hearing her father practice it in the late 1940s or early 1950s. "He struggled and fretted over it," she said, "and once, referring to its savage rhythm, he exclaimed, 'Does Villa-Lobos *really* think this music is like me?' ") The only pieces by Villa-Lobos that appeared often on his programs throughout the rest of his career were selections from the solo piano suite that the composer called *Prole do bêbê* (*The Baby's Children*, or dolls).

FROM BRAZIL RUBINSTEIN went to Montevideo, where, on July 28, 1920, he played the Saint-Saëns Second Concerto and Falla's *Nights in the Gardens of Spain* with an orchestra under the direction of Maurice Dumesnil. (Dumesnil, better known as a pianist, was the man whose cancellation of a concert in San Sebastián in 1915 had led to Rubinstein's all-important Spanish debut.) In Buenos Aires—another stop on his tour—he became involved with the wife of "a wealthy and well-known landowner," he said,[124] who lived in the Hotel Plaza, where Rubinstein was staying; the affair was difficult to arrange, logistically, but the intrepid couple succeeded. Aboard the boat that took him back to England, he lost a considerable sum of money, at cards, to his colleague and compatriot Ignaz Friedman. Some piano historians consider Friedman to have been a better pianist, technically, than Rubinstein; the opinion is debatable, but the fact that Friedman was the better poker player seems incontrovertible.

On arriving in London Rubinstein was met at the station by Paul and Zosia Kochanski—"one of the most beautiful reunions of my life," he recalled.[125] They caught up on each other's news, after a separation of more than six years, and when the Kochanskis rented a flat at 3 Cork Street, near Piccadilly, Rubinstein decided to take a flat for himself in the same building. Paul and Arthur gave a joint recital at the Wigmore Hall on December 2; they played the Bach Sonata in E Major, the Beethoven Sonata in C Minor, and the Brahms Sonata in D Minor. Rubinstein made a short English tour in which he shared programs with the outstanding soprano Elisabeth Schumann, one of Richard Strauss's favorite artists; he always remembered "the joy of hearing her beautiful singing brilliantly accompanied by Ivor Newton."[126] Rubinstein also gave three important solo recitals at the Wigmore Hall, and among the series's reviewers was Ezra Pound, who was living in London and occasionally writing music criticism for *The New Age*, under the pseudonym of William Atheling. Although he was not a professional musician, he grasped more readily than did most of the professional English music critics of the day that Rubinstein was a major performing artist. Some of his remarks are eccentric to the point of exasperation, but they are worth a glance. In an article published on December 9, 1920, Pound wrote:

Arthur Rubinstein (Wigmore, November 11) began with Bach-D'Albert Toccata in F maj.: a solidity of rhythm, the whole like a set of taut steel cables whirling, seizing and holding the auditor; a barbaric noise, splendidly structural, fit for a decade that has taken up African sculpture. Rubinstein then relapsed into the sickly opening of the Franck prelude, with enormous waste of technique; he showed himself a hopeless sentimentalist pyrotechnic in the Chopin barcarolle, gave the Etude as a speed test, and whatever one may say in praise of his Polonaise, it was anything but an interpretation of Chopin.

. . . Rubinstein came back in the rather shallow alerte of Poulenc, did well in the Prokofieff "Marche" and in the Falla "Dance." The other two Prokofieff numbers were omissible, and as for "Suggestion diabolique," the poor old devil is such a worn out stage prop that one is ashamed to heave rocks at him any longer. "Diabolique" fiddle-sticks.

As Rubinstein is so great a pianist that all the other star-players come out to listen to him, we may as well analyse his "art"; sic. [The "sic" is in the original text.] For him the piano is not an abbreviation of the orchestra; it is not the means whereby one performer can express his orchestral thought. His technique is adequate; it is that abundant technique which is required of a master-pianist or a trapeze virtuoso. Beyond a certain point any great concentration of technique is bound to be interesting. But Rubinstein's personality is ordinary; only at one point is he a super performer; i.e., in his rhythm. And the compelling power of this excites the audience, for the same reason that a really great drummer or even a normally good tom-tom player excites. For Rubinstein the piano is a Schlaginstrument [percussion instrument]; it is not a little orchestra; it is a gorgeously varied drum or series of drums. . . .

. . . That part of music which can be expressed by sheer rhythm he gets—the toccata, the March, the Dance; but music to interpret human passion, or reverie, or psychology, no. He expresses either perfectly ordinary and common-place nullities, or sentimental tosh; he does not "interpret" anything of interest. . . .

. . . in his Bach, Rubinstein is perhaps the only musician who has succeeded in bringing into musical performance the qualities which Vlaminck and Picasso have admired in African carving. But not Chopin, and certainly not Debussy.

Rubinstein probably never saw Pound's reviews; if he did, he must have been horrified by a description of his playing that was the exact opposite of what he wanted and believed it to be—and of what it was. He considered himself above all else a communicator of human emotion on an instrument that had to be made to sing rather than to sound percussive. And the fact that the poet gave the pianist higher marks for his Bach than for his Chopin is either a tribute to the revolutionary characteristics of Rubinstein's Chopin playing or a proof of the sheer zaniness of Pound's tastes, if not both.

In a review published on December 23, Pound said: "*Arthur Rubinstein* compels me to eat my words, or rather one word, Debussy, for at the Wigmore (December 7) he gave one of the best *public* performances of a Debussy group that I have heard in England. The rest of my criticism of his work still seems to me correct. . . ." And in a review that appeared on January 6, 1921, Pound wrote: "Arthur Rubinstein is . . . wholly the performer; he was magnificent in Bach (Dec. 18) and despicable in Chopin. The rest of the concert is already covered by our previous criticism of his previous concerts, save that he got more orchestral colour into the Fugue, and needed, possibly, more severe condemnation for the Chopin."[127]

On the part of the London public and press at large, Rubinstein was received well but without special enthusiasm. In *My Many Years* he attributed the situation to his "popularity in the finest drawing rooms" of the capital,[128] which marked him as a dandy rather than a serious artist. Twenty years before the memoirs were published, however, he had told an American interviewer: "In England I received large fees for playing in private houses — two hundred pounds [about one thousand dollars], in fact, which in those days was a large fee indeed. But I was too lazy, too comfortable to practice, and I dropped as many notes as I played."[129] Fred Gaisberg, the record producer, felt that in those years it was Rubinstein who "more or less neglected England," rather than the other way around, but Gaisberg added that "except for a few socialites who faithfully patronized his Wigmore Hall recitals, he had no real following in the popular sense."[130]

En route to Spain again — probably between the first and second Wigmore Hall recitals — Rubinstein made what had become a customary stop in Paris. He looked up Ignacy, who told him that their mother was gravely ill, but he did not go to Poland to see her. Jaime Zulueta, too, was in Paris; Rubinstein bumped into him at Maxim's, and the pianist and his former secretary were soon enjoying a rollicking night life with a seemingly endless supply of beautiful women. Rubinstein also saw Stravinsky, who was angered by the pianist's lack of appreciation of the *Piano-Rag Music,* but who "immediately forgot all that had been said,"[131] according to Rubinstein, when the pianist played part of *Petrushka* to him. The following year Stravinsky made a now celebrated full-fledged piano arrangement of three pieces from the ballet — the so-called "Petrushka" Sonata ("I have finished *Petrushka* for Rubinstein, a very virtuoso transcription," the composer wrote to Ansermet on September 10, 1921.[132] Like many other pianists since, Rubinstein found the arrangement "very difficult to perform." In later years, he said that Stravinsky had told him to make whatever changes he saw fit in order to render it playable without having to "retard the dynamic progress of the piece,"[133] and for decades his playing of this retouched arrangement brought him great success in many countries.

Rubinstein said that he had seen Szymanowski, too, in Paris in the fall of 1920, after a 6½-year separation, but, according to the composer's letters of the period, the reunion took place in London, after Rubinstein had returned from his Spanish tour. Szymanowski had agreed to work with Jan Sliwinski (alias Hans Effenberger), his and Rubinstein's old friend from Vienna, to help organize concerts in various countries under the aegis of the Polish government's Office for Foreign Propaganda. "When I arrived [in London]," Szymanowski wrote on December 26 to his family in Warsaw, "I found Pawelkowie [diminutive meaning the 'dear little Pauls'—Paul and Zosia Kochanski] and Arturek on the platform at Victoria Station—the same place where we parted company seven years ago—we all were very touched—but soon it was as if we hadn't seen each other in only a couple of weeks or months."[134] According to Rubinstein, Szymanowski soon revealed that his homosexuality had become more active and even told him about an important affair that he was having. During a meeting that Rubinstein had arranged between Diaghilev and Szymanowski, in the hope—fruitless, in the end—that the impresario would commission the composer to write something, Szymanowski made the terrible discovery that Diaghilev's companion was the young man whom he had considered his own partner. The "traitor"—whose name Rubinstein did not give—was Boris Kochno, who, shortly thereafter, wrote the libretto for Stravinsky's Mavra.

Szymanowski probably did not tell Rubinstein that during the alternately terrible and tedious war years, he had written a novel in which the pianist was one of the characters. Ephebos was never published and the manuscript was destroyed early in World War II, but Iwaszkiewicz, who had read it, recalled many years later that it had included a description of Kochanski and Rubinstein playing his music. "With great precision, [Szymanowski] described the manner and style of their playing, and not only the internal interpretation but also their outward aspect (Rubinstein's highjinks at the piano, for instance)," Iwaszkiewicz said. "Szymanowski lovingly portrayed the performance of Korab's sonata." Korab was the composer's name for himself. "If I regret the loss of the whole manuscript, I regret most of all the loss of this concert episode," Iwaszkiewicz concluded.[135]

Szymanowski's friendship with Rubinstein and the Kochanskis deepened considerably during the weeks they spent together in London. In a letter to his own family, whose money and Ukrainian estate had been lost as a result of the Bolshevik revolution, the composer described the pianist as "so kind now—always full of life, joy, interest in and sympathy for people, only he's got some position and money behind him now (not so much, to tell you the truth, as they say—entre nous!)—and handing it out left and right to all who need it and never refusing to help. This is an extremely nice quality of his, all the more so as he does it with extraordinary delicacy. This happened with me, too—of course I didn't ask him for money, but he forced me to take a checkbook which I could use to draw on several hundred pounds, he took me to the tailor, prepared things, etc., etc. The money I sent to Mama is of course also from him, and the thing that enchanted me in him was that he handed me all the checks directly so that I would be completely free in my *faits et gestes* and would not feel any impediment in sending money to my family, for instance; in this regard he is really delicate in an elegant way. By the way, he is very much attached to Mama—and he laughed a lot when I read him the bit about 'remember me to Arturek' in Mama's letter, and he asked me to kiss Mama's hands tenderly."[136]

Arthur and Zosia couldn't live without abundant socializing, and Paul and Karol let themselves be seduced by whatever society was offered them, although not without complaining. "For the second time I've been to the sea near Brighton at Lady Leavis's home with Arturek," Szymanowski continued, in the above-quoted letter to his family. "It's very beautiful there, although sad and gloomy at this season. . . . Almost every day, the 'club'—as Pawelek calls it—comes to our apartment (we have two tiny three-room 'flats,' one for the Pawelkowie, and I'm in the second one with Arturek and his Spanish servant) at about twelve noon—that is: various very nice and pretty ladies, friends of Arturek, of the Pawelkowie, of mine, etc., and in the end it's too much—I admit—Pawel and I curse, one would like to have some peace and quiet. We almost never frequent the theaters—because there's always some full-dress dinner in the evening. There is now a sort of tiny fad for us here. . . . I've forgotten to write that Arturek is now really thoroughly first class as a pianist! He has completely rid himself of his old characteristics (a certain negligence, etc.), he knows everything very well by heart, has a formidable technique—an unbelievable repertoire, and really is a completely first-rate artist. . . . Arturek is going to come with me to Poland, where he absolutely wants to give public benefit concerts. This patriotism of his is a fine quality. . . ."[137]

Before long, Karol reported, Arthur, Paul, and Zosia were "very firmly" trying to persuade him "to resign my diplomatic tasks," which were to have taken him to Scandinavia, "and simply stay with them and try to develop a good name abroad. This is the basis of the plan for a joint journey to America, where Arturek has great connections and a good name. Since Hans Effenb. was also inciting me to do this, I finally made up my mind, despite the apprehension that I feel about the journey and America in general." Rubinstein had several concerts lined up on the other side of the Atlantic, and Kochanski was scheduled to make his American debut with the New York Symphony Orchestra under Walter Damrosch. The friends hoped that Szymanowski would meet important people and score a success that would give him a much-needed economic boost. On January 8, 1921, Kochanski and Szymanowski played a joint violin and piano recital, under Michell's aegis, at the Wigmore Hall, and on the fifteenth the foursome boarded the *Carmania* at Liverpool and departed for New York. "We have excellent cabins connected to a private bathroom," Szymanowski wrote in his diary—a fine guide to what was in many ways a typically Rubinsteinian tour—and he noted that while he and Zosia busied themselves by trying to ignore symptoms of seasickness, Paul and Arthur played piquet. On the nineteenth Szymanowski wrote, "Arturek played [the piano] a lot. Among other things, my *Maski*" (*Masks*), a set of three piano pieces written in 1915–16. On the twenty-second, two days before their arrival in New York, the three Polish artists gave a shipboard concert for the benefit of sailors' orphans. At the dock, Paul Draper and George Engels—Kochanski's American manager—and his wife were waiting for the travelers, who were soon settled into rooms on the twentieth floor of the Biltmore Hotel. The same evening, they attended a performance given by the visiting Chicago Lyric Opera at the Manhattan Opera House and were visited by Muriel Draper. Rubinstein also introduced his friends to Besanzoni, with whom he had not yet broken, and who was singing with the Chicago company.

The next day, January 25, there was a "morning excursion to Arthur's bank in the city," Szymanowski reported. "Breakfast at the Ritz with Besanzoni; she is very nice. After breakfast hunt for an apartment. Visit to Muriel's place. She was not at home." They returned to the Manhattan Opera House that evening, and Rubinstein introduced Szymanowski to Mary Garden, the Chicago ensemble's director and an "awful crone," according to the composer. Afterward, there was "a supper together at the Ritz," with Muriel. The following morning the friends received Paul Draper in their suite and then breakfasted at the Ritz Grill with Prokofiev, who "makes a very good impression," according to Szymanowski. They then proceeded to the conductor Kurt Schindler's "for wonderful liquor," Szymanowski said—Prohibition was in effect and he had evidently been feeling deprived—and they spent the evening at the apartment of Bob Chanler, the millionaire painter, who, it seems, provided prostitutes for those who wished to indulge. On the twenty-seventh, they attended an early afternoon performance by Ruth Draper at the Princess Theater ("Nothing new," Szymanowski commented), a late afternoon concert given by Fritz Kreisler at Carnegie Hall ("Disenchantment!"), and a movie at the Capitol Theater, and they managed to squeeze in a tea at the home of Mrs. Linzee Blagden, who was Ruth and Paul's sister, Dorothea; there, they saw the pianist-composer-conductor Ernest Schelling and Otto Kahn, the Metropolitan Opera's Maecenas, whom Rubinstein unsuccessfully attempted to persuade to support Szymanowski's work in some way. The following Saturday evening, they attended a large party at the Laniers' home, and on Sunday evening they visited Chanler's for an even wilder party than the previous one. "Arthur played charmingly. I got a little drunk and behaved rather badly," Szymanowski said. On the thirty-first they had supper with Besanzoni at the Restaurant des Beaux Arts, "where a wonderful jazz [ensemble played] (Haitian-Blues that we adore, with Arthur)." At a dinner at the home of Rubinstein's friend Hoyty Wiborg on February 1, Szymanowski talked to Prokofiev and Ruth Draper again and made the acquaintance of Prince Battenberg, brother of the queen of Spain; Lord Allington, whom he described as "young—extremely nice and handsome"; and Mrs. Cornelius Vanderbilt, who, he said, was "W. K."—which, in Polish, can mean either a "great duchess" or a "great whore."

On February 2, Szymanowski sent his family his general impressions of America: "All four of us are already aware (Arthur always used to tell us this before) that this may be a good place to visit, for dollars—but to live here, no, not for all the treasure in the world! . . . So far we are living here more or less as in London, visiting a lot and getting to know people. This is even more important here than in Europe, as the entire artistic and cultural life seems to be in the hands of various wealthy crones. . . ." The next day, the friends moved into a six-room apartment that they had rented at 145 East Thirty-fifth Street, and on February 4 Szymanowski mentioned having had an excellent breakfast with Rubinstein and Besanzoni and having gone to see *Way Down East*, D. W. Griffith's latest film ("a wonderful picture," he said), in the evening. "Breakfast at Mrs. Lanier's" on the fifth, for "Arthur, Paul, and me. After breakfast playing of my pieces. She liked them a lot." The following day, R. E. Johnson and Paul Draper came to tea at the Poles' apartment. Rubinstein, Kochanski, and Szymanowski played; then, while Kochanski and Szymanowski were performing the composer's *Mity* (*Myths*, three poems for violin and piano, written in 1915), the Swiss composer Ernest Bloch arrived with the score of his First Sonata for Violin and Piano, whose world premiere was to be given later that season by Kochanski and Rubinstein. "Arthur and Paul are torturing that damned Bloch's *Sonate* all the time," Szymanowski wrote in his diary on February 18, and the next day he reported that the whole Bloch family—including the "quite charming" little daughter (Suzanne, then thirteen, later well known as an early music specialist)—had been over to listen to the two performers give the piece a trial run. The family was moved, and Szymanowski remarked that Rubinstein and Kochanski had "both played wonderfully."[138]

On February 7, after a breakfast with his apartment-mates plus Besanzoni, Johnson, and Johnson's assistant, Rubinstein left for Chicago, where he was to give a recital. On the tenth Szymanowski wrote in his diary: "Artur came in this morning. He had a great success in Chicago. Raves from critics."[139] Rubinstein did not mention this in *My Many Years*; what he did mention—and what obviously gave him the most memorable pleasure during his fourth visit to North America—was Kochanski's debut in the Brahms Concerto, at Carnegie Hall. Paul "had horrible stage-fright!"

Szymanowski wrote in his diary, on February 14, but "he played wonderfully and—he was extraordinarily well received. *Il est fait*—it seems, thank God. A mass of people in the artists' room.—All the friends, general enthusiasm." Rubinstein described Kochanski's debut as "a sensation. . . . I had never heard him as inspired as on this evening. . . . Paul was right away in great demand by the most important orchestras."[140] But Szymanowski's first American visit was not as successful. Iwaszkiewicz reported that the composer's "sojourn in the USA, about which he had nothing good to say and to which he could not become acclimatized, led to absolutely no concrete results, contrary to the expectations of Rubinstein and Kochanski, who had had high economic hopes for Karol."[141] But Stanislaw Golachowski, another friend, pointed out that Szymanowski "made numerous contacts in [New York's] international musical community and met many conductors and virtuosos, and this was an advantage later in the popularizing of his work throughout the world."[142]

On February 21 Szymanowski noted in his diary, "In the evening Arthur's concert with [Willem] Mengelberg [and the short-lived National Philharmonic Orchestra] at Carnegie Hall. *D minor Concerto* of Brahms. Arthur played fabulously and had a great success." Szymanowski returned to Carnegie Hall to hear Rubinstein repeat the concerto two days later; it was an afternoon performance, and afterward they had tea at Ruth Draper's home.

Szymanowski enjoyed a trip to Florida and the Caribbean with Rubinstein, who had lined up a few concerts in Havana. They left New York by train on February 26 and arrived in Miami two days later. There, according to Szymanowski's diary, they took a boat ride, went fishing, and saw *The Kid*, Charlie Chaplin's latest movie. From Key West they took a boat to Havana, about which Szymanowski noted with enthusiasm:

[March 7] It's altogether wonderful, wonderful here! It's not like the U.S.—villainous! Typical charm of the South and of the Latin races! I am in heaven! We drink a good deal! The Hotel Inglaterra is a joy— so old fashioned. The two of us have breakfast. We meet the agent, Brenly. (Nice man.) Visit with Fontanill (critic). We wander by automobile. We visit the "Romeo y Julieta" cigar factory. . . . In the evening a Spanish comedy at the Teatro Nacional. . . .

[March 8] We wander through the city all day, enjoying the sun, the sea, and Latin life. . . . Breakfast at "Dos Hermanos"—we have a photograph taken. Siesta in the afternoon, because the heat is terrible. In the evening the first act of a Spanish operetta (nothing special) and one or two [acts] of a Spanish drama at the Nacional. . . .

[March 9] . . . Arthur practiced a little, concert at 5 with extraordinary success, shouting, etc., etc. Supper at "Dos Hermanos." . . . Then some nighttime wandering.

[March 10] . . . In the evening with Arthur at jai-allai (pellote basque). Quite a wonderful game! I even got nervous. Arthur won about fifty dollars. Then we went with Choué and two other guys to the Casino, where Arthur lost at roulette. . . .

[March 11] . . . After lunch Arthur went to play and I arranged passport and tickets. Concert at five. A lot of people, great enthusiasm!! Arthur played excellently. After the concert dinner with [the impresario Adolfo] Bracale—his wife and two other people (an old Italian maestro—nice). A merry dinner. A lot of drinking. Excellent Spanish food. Then I went with Arthur to the Casino, where there was a ball for the Americans. Arthur played roulette till four—He lost about one hundred dollars. . . .

[March 12] We get up tired at 7. Packing. Friends come to say good-bye. At eleven we board ship. Alas, we have to leave lovely Havana! . . . We are so exhausted that we have to lie down in our cabins. At 5 p.m. we arrive in detestable Key West. Right away there are aggravations with Americans at the station. God, how annoying they are! Before lunch we drink in secret the last bottle of cognac.

The two musicians returned to New York late on March 14; the next morning Besanzoni came to breakfast with them, but "poor Arthur left for Chicago right after breakfast," Szymanowski wrote in his diary. On the twenty-first, "unexpectedly, to our great joy, Arturek arrived (in the evening)," and the two musicians "went to Naps's [Lord Allington], who was sad and lonely, for a glass of wine. The three of us had a nice chat." The next evening, they visited Hoyty Wiborg and "Arthur played Spanish music delightfully. Unexpected feeling of happiness and fulfillment. Naps came. The four of us went to his place for a cocktail." A few days later Rubinstein traveled to Chicago yet again; he returned on the evening of the twenty-eighth, having had "yet another success. . . . We played *Petrushka* four-hands. Then Arthur imitated the Ballets Russes (he played wonderfully), *Tamara*, *Scheherazade*, etc."[143]

For Rubinstein, one of the most important events of the 1921 American tour was his first appearance as soloist with the Boston Symphony Orchestra. Under Monteux's baton, he played Beethoven's Fourth Concerto (not the

Chopin F Minor, as he said in his memoirs) on April 1 and 2, and was highly praised by most of the critics. "Mr. Rubinstein . . . gave an excellent performance of the Concerto," wrote the veteran commentator Philip Hale, in the *Herald*. "The Andante is one of Beethoven's supreme conceptions. Its very simplicity is a stumbling block to many. . . . Mr. Rubinstein's technical ability, conspicuous as it is, was not ostentatiously displayed; it served gladly the composer." In the *Post*, the young Olin Downes, future principal critic of the *New York Times*, described the performance as "delightful" and said that Rubinstein's playing was "brilliant without being metallic or superficial. He was imaginative, poetic, without losing for a moment that note of underlying virility and force which is felt in the most tender passage of Beethoven. We do not remember a finer performance of the concerto in G major. Mr. Rubinstein was repeatedly recalled." Only H. T. Parker, Charles Ives's former teacher, dissented, in the *Transcript*: he described Rubinstein as an old-fashioned, mannered virtuoso, declared that the pianist had "expertly skimmed" the surface of the first and last movements, and admonished that the second movement "runs deeper than his virtuoso-shallows, and such quality, quite missed yesterday by both conductor and pianist, is the one and only reason for this Concerto in concert-halls of 1921."[144] Rubinstein said that during his Boston stay, his old friend John Singer Sargent had shown him the murals depicting the history of religious thought that he was working on at the Boston Public Library, but the paintings had been finished about ten years earlier. He took the night train to New York after his second Boston concert and arrived at the apartment at seven the next morning with two pieces of good news: His Boston appearances had been a "triumph," he said, and Monteux wanted to program Szymanowski's Second Symphony in Boston the following season. That evening, at "a very nice dinner" at Hoyty Wiborg's, "Arthur played very beautifully," Karol wrote. "I listened again with delight." Composer and pianist spent part of the weekend of April 9–10 at Wiborg's country home at East Hampton, on Long Island. ("Ocean enchanting. A pleasant house. All frolicked," Szymanowski reported.) On April 12, "Arthur left for Minneapolis and elsewhere, for concerts."

As soon as Rubinstein had returned to New York, the four Poles sailed for England aboard the same ship that had brought them to New York. Early in May, Szymanowski and Rubinstein were in Paris, where the composer wrote a letter, in English, to a Mr. Ben Friedman, whom he had met in New York: "You know Arthur well enough and this tremendous life is swinging everywhere with him! In a few days I knew with him Paris better as I did ever before. . . . Arthur does not want to play here. He is right saying he must rest for some time and he is enjoying Paris in his way—which is a very good one; he is surrounded by many interesting people, going with us to exhibitions,

museums—theatres, buying all the new editions of poetry and music. . . ."145
Within a few weeks, Rubinstein was back in London, where Stravinsky was
his and the Kochanskis' houseguest at their flat in Cork Street. Rubinstein
probably attended the unsuccessful London premiere of Stravinsky's Symphonies of Wind Instruments on June 10, 1921, and certainly became involved, although only peripherally, in the recriminations that the fiasco
unleashed. Stravinsky told an interviewer that he blamed the failure on Koussevitzky, who had conducted the performance, and Koussevitzky replied by
sending the *Times* a letter in which he insulted the piece. Stravinsky wondered why Rubinstein had done nothing to help defend him from Koussevitzky's attack, and late in July he wrote to Ansermet: "Artur says that
Koussevitzky has even discredited himself with my enemies, thanks to this
letter. But how can it be that none of my friends has answered him? Are they
all cowards?"146 (In *My Many Years*, Rubinstein incorrectly placed Stravinsky's Octet, rather than the Symphonies of Wind Instruments, at the
center of the story.) This was the episode over which Diaghilev warned Stravinsky not to trust his Jewish friends—although the remark was aimed at
Koussevitzky, not Rubinstein, whose friendship with Stravinsky remained
intact.

At the same time, however, another composer was reexamining his relationship to Rubinstein. Early in August, Szymanowski wrote an extraordinary
letter to his pianist friend:

> I would also like to talk about some personal matters—knowing
> your pen-aversion, I won't wait for your answer to them—until we
> see each other—orally. It's difficult for me to write about this—and
> speaking about it was impossible, and the worst of it is that I seem to
> have lost access to you of late. I would like to set this matter forth
> clearly, at once. As you know, Artek, you don't belong to the class of
> people with whom one can casually remain friendly and equally ca-
> sually part company forever. So it seems to me, at least. I would like
> you to understand, at last, who you are to me. It is not a question of
> either friendship or attachment or even of love. It is, if you will,
> none of these things or all of them together. You simply "exist" in
> my life, and that's the most important thing. You will certainly un-
> derstand what I mean. This is why, during the winter and spring [in
> England and America], in spite of all that you've done for me, in
> spite of your quite extraordinary goodness and delicacy, it seemed to
> me several times that you "ceased to exist," and then I suffered
> more horribly than I would ever suffer if my dearest lover had be-
> trayed me. Because in the end, erotic matters are a question of *Un-*

terleib [the stomach—i.e., physical needs] and are directed by the
logic proper to them. But in this case everything personal, the highest logic in life rebels and suffers. Don't think, Arturek, that I'm raving and chasing after *Hirngespenste* [bogeymen]. At a certain level
(a very deep one) of life, solitude becomes an unbearable blow. And
at this level, partings and farewells are much worse than in the mad-
dest love affair. I am writing this to you today quite calmly and logi-
cally—for I have the peculiarity of being better at remembering
good things than bad ones from the past—and this is why I still
think of you with the old warmth and emotion. However, I couldn't
bear another winter like this [past] one—I can't explain to you what
I mean in writing any more concretely than this. Believe me, this
feeling has never taken the form of resentment toward you (maybe
at certain moments and in a very specific way). Nevertheless, I felt
something not explicit, something half-way, some continual danger
(that I would lose you entirely). I know that you can't stand it when
anyone lays a burden on you. However, a most profound instinct
makes me write to you about all this, and I am sure that it had to be
done. It's possible that I'm the guilty one in the whole matter. In recent years I have still been lacking in self-confidence, such disgust-
ing self-skepticism oppresses me that it keeps intimidating me and
me rend gauche [makes me awkward] in life. It may be that these
characteristics of mine were responsible for my attitude toward your
possession of precisely that mastery of life. When I rushed toward
my "solitude" or could not express overwhelming feelings toward
you, you just couldn't understand what I had become during all
those long years during which we hadn't seen each other.—At this
point, I could say so much about this that I prefer not to start, even
though sometime, when I see you, I *will have to do it*. Don't worry,
Artuszka [Russian-style diminutive], there will be no "putting upon
you"—it is not a question of complaining about my fate, nor is it a
call for moral support—properly speaking, I feel very *strong* toward
life—it is only because you somehow enter *organically* into my
most profound concept of life, and not having you—or rather, having you somewhere far away—behind some door or beyond some
mountains or rivers, would mean unbearable suffering for me. You
can be absolutely sure that no one *in the world* understands you as
deeply, completely, [and] in such a specific way as I do, and that's
also why your opinion is more important to me than anyone else's.
For me, you are the weight and measure of what is valuable in life,
next to this, what importance do trivia or differences of opinion or

anything of the sort have[?] I don't know how you will take this letter, but I am sure that you feel how *deep* are the feelings that it
reflects.

Once again, I repeat that I'm not waiting for an answer—we'll
probably see each other anyway—but I'm enclosing my address [in
the town of Bydgoszcz] and I am asking Zosienka [Zosia Kochan-
ska] for a short, informative letter—whether they've already decided
when they'll leave [for America, again], where we are to meet, etc.
etc. Meanwhile, I embrace you with love, as well as the dear
Pauls—And kindest greetings to [our] friends, especially Elsie [not
further identified], who sent me such a nice letter, and I—swine
that I am—haven't answered—as usual.

Good-bye, à bientôt

Your Karol[147]

Szymanowski never sent this letter, and Rubinstein did not know of its existence until Teresa Chylinska, the leading Szymanowski scholar, sent him a
copy of it when he was ninety-three years old. With the assistance of his
friend Roman Jasinski, Rubinstein explained some of the letter's contents to
Chylinska. At that time, Jasinski wrote, "even though Arthur still considered
Karol as his nearest and dearest friend, and continued to help him according
to his means, he did feel a certain weakening of his faith in Szymanowski's
great talent. As he was close at the time to composers of the stature of Stravinsky and Prokofiev, and very much admired their exceptional originality,
he believed that Szymanowski submitted too often to various influences
(Scriabin, Reger, and the French Impressionists, in succession), rather than
taking possession of his own original style. Arthur said, verbatim, 'I would
have liked him to demonstrate some of his own Polishness, and not to continue in the same way, which was unoriginal, to some extent.' Arthur did
not like either the German song-texts or the German libretto of the opera *Hagith*, which, he says, could have been set by a German composer. It was disagreeable, and it had a certain cooling effect on Arthur's attitude toward
Szymanowski's music. Besides, it was the period in which the internal
transformation of Szymanowski (Kochno, etc.)"—the reference is to Szymanowski's increasingly open homosexuality and to his above-mentioned relationship with Boris Kochno—"was creating a certain distance between [him
and] Rubinstein, a man of very normal instincts. And Szymanowski was too
subtle, by nature, not to have felt these things. He probably grieved over it,
and, as he wished to clear the air completely, he wrote this letter. At any rate,
they never had any 'basic' discussion on this subject, afterward, and Arthur
was happy that his friend soon found himself and created so many truly Pol-

ish compositions that were 'his own.' " Jasinski added that Szymanowski's letter had had "a great effect" on the aged Rubinstein.[148]

Despite his complicated feelings toward Rubinstein, Szymanowski began to plan a return trip to America with him and the Kochanskis; the trip
would take place that fall. On August 21, Zosia wrote to Karol: "We've had a
few words from Stravinsky. . . . he writes that Arthur is gambling at the Biar-
ritz Casino, I don't know whether successfully or not.—You know, I will tell
you *secretly* that I am resting from Arthur's rushing around. Just as I adore
him in many ways—in many others his superficiality, which is often childlike but horribly empty—bores me terribly. Please don't let this sincere sentence pass your lips—because Arthur would never forgive me for it."[149]

Rubinstein's fifth trip to the United States included his first visit to California, to play the Saint-Saëns G Minor Concerto with Alfred Hertz and the
San Francisco Symphony on November 25 and 27. But his New York appearances had a longer-range effect on his career, because among those who
heard him play there that fall was Solomon Israelovich Hurok, a flamboyant,
Russian-born impresario one year younger than Rubinstein. Hurok had immigrated to the United States in 1906—the year of Rubinstein's first American tour—and had soon begun to organize concerts for Jewish workers'
clubs. After World War I he began to function as an agent for a few major
performing artists, and before long he was a major force in the performing
arts in America. "Rubinstein's volcanic personality struck me no less than his
colossal artistry at the piano when I first heard him in Carnegie Hall during
the season of 1921–22," Hurok recalled in his memoirs. "He was unique in
every way: in his dynamic approach to his instrument, in the grandeur of his
interpretations, in the charm which left a train of adorers wherever he passed
by. . . . I wooed him that season, borrowing him from his manager, R. E.
Johnson, for concerts in Philadelphia and in the Brooklyn Academy of Music."[150] According to Rubinstein, in a statement to the *New York Times* in
1976, his first encounter with Hurok had come about when "Chaliapin, who
was my dear friend—my big brother almost, I adored him—invited me to his
hotel here in New York for breakfast. And there was a little man sitting in the
corner. Chaliapin treated him terribly, told him to sit there, don't speak,
things like that. I played 'Petroushka' on the piano and the little man—who,
of course, was Hurok—thought it was fine. . . . Hurok, at that time [was]
putting on low-priced concerts here in the Hippodrome. Mischa Elman, the
circus, horse shows, [the soprano Amelita] Galli-Curci, everything—oh, how
it smelled. Hurok remembered me from Chaliapin's and came to see me. 'I
have Titta Ruffo for a concert but he is able to sing only a few arias, so would
you play two items on his program?' Yes, I would. As it happened, Ruffo was
not in voice, but I was in voice and the audience made me give two encores
in the middle of the concert. Hurok was very impressed."[151]

Rubinstein's American "adorers," as Hurok put it, were not sufficiently numerous to bring him complete success at the highest level. George Engels—Kochanski's manager, for whom Rubinstein had abandoned Johnson—lined up some important engagements for him for the fall of 1922, including debut appearances with the New York Philharmonic (he played Mozart's A Major Concerto, K. 488, on November 24 and Beethoven's Fourth Concerto on November 28, both under the baton of Josef Stransky), and performances of the Tchaikovsky Concerto with Frederick Stock and the Chicago Symphony on December 1 and 2, but "he was not happy in America," Hurok said. Among the causes of his unhappiness was a run-in with the Steinway Company. Speaking about his relationships with pianos, Rubinstein late in life told the American music historian Vivian Perlis that he was "born with Bechstein," which was "really my piano" during his early days in Berlin. "It was mechanically perfect," he said. "I could play my best. I was absolutely happy. There was nothing like it." Later, however, he was overwhelmed by the Steinway, which he heard Busoni play and which had a "deeper sound," he said. He played some Hamburg-made German Steinways in the homes of friends in Berlin, "and I found that they have a beautiful tone, much deeper than Bechstein, but the mechanism was very difficult for me, [it] was made for very strong fingers," whereas his young fingers were accustomed to the old-fashioned, lighter Bechstein action.[152] After his departure from Berlin, he played a variety of pianos—the Gaveau at his Paris debut, the Knabe during his first tour of the United States, the Bösendorfer at the time of his first Viennese appearances—but by 1917, when he was able to acquire a good piano for himself, he chose the Steinway, and the Steinway was the piano he played during his first post–World War I visits to North America. During the 1921–22 tour, however, he found that the Steinway company had provided what he described as an inadequate, medium-sized grand piano for a recital that he was to give at Chicago's Kimball Hall, and he decided to play, instead, a full-sized Mason & Hamlin concert grand that happened to be in the hall. It was "one of the most beautiful pianos I ever had the chance to play," he recalled. When the Steinway people found out they told him that he could not use their pianos for the duration of his tour. He had to make do with Knabe instruments—"a heavy fight with a reluctant keyboard," according to Rubinstein.[153] The dispute was eventually made up, but at least as late as 1932 Rubinstein's testimonials in favor of Gaveau pianos were appearing in European concert programs.

The tour occasionally brought him small compensations, however. Once, for instance, in New York, he was introduced to a "beautiful little blonde"—an aspiring, nineteen-year-old actress, Tallulah Bankhead, who asked him to play for her. When he refused, she did a handstand for him, "exposing her bare secrets."[154] Rubinstein played. Nevertheless, "after the

1922[–23] season he did not return [to the United States] until 1927," Hurok
reported. "Then he forswore this country forever."[155]

"And so I abandoned finally America, came back to Europe and started
to fight Europe on my terms," Rubinstein told an interviewer in Paris many
years later. "And I won out, I was very successful here."[156]

THE EXPRESSION "Paris in the Twenties" has become a cliché in our time,
but during the years that followed World War I the *Ville Lumière* was indeed
one of the greatest crucibles of intellectual and artistic activity that Western
civilization has known. Marcel Proust and Piet Mondrian, Marie Curie and
Jean Renoir, James Joyce and Pierre Teilhard de Chardin, Paul Valéry and
Pablo Picasso, Henri Bergson and Colette, Gaetano Salvemini and Jose-
phine Baker, Gertrude Stein and Salvador Dalí, André Gide and Ernest
Hemingway, Alberto Giacometti and F. Scott Fitzgerald, Joan Miró and
Blaise Cendrars—the list goes on and on—lived in Paris through some or all
of that decade. Among composers, Ravel, "Les Six," Stravinsky, Prokofiev,
Falla, Szymanowski, Villa-Lobos, and others either made the city their home
or frequented it assiduously, and so did many of the world's most acclaimed
performing musicians. Rubinstein, who had not lived in Paris since his break
with Astruc in 1907, began to gravitate toward it again, and his joyful account,
in *My Many Years*, of the rich social life of Paris's aristocratic and artistic
classes, and of the recklessness of its demimonde, indicates that as early as
1920 he was beginning to dream again, as he had dreamed in 1904, of making
the French capital his base of operations. Not later than June 1922 he moved
into the city's Hôtel Villa Majestic, which remained his headquarters for a
few years. (In April, Rubinstein had again toured South America. Kochanski
was playing in Buenos Aires at the same time, and Zosia passed to Szymanowski some information that Paul had sent her: "Arthur is in love with an
Argentinean woman whom he met—Paul doesn't approve of his taste—
Besanzoni left a day before their arrival—they say she led an impossible life,
getting drunk till 5 A.M. in the hotel bar—Arthur learned that she has scandalous affairs with everyone.")[157] He was especially happy to plunge headlong
into Parisian night life, and Chotzinoff recalled having seen him "in a Paris
restaurant . . . [on] the night of the famous Quatre Arts [Quat'z Arts] ball. On
that night . . . all the accumulated restraints of civilization may be discarded,
the celebrants permitting themselves freedoms normally prohibited or
frowned on. Rubinstein (accompanied by Jascha Heifetz [Chotzinoff's
brother-in-law]) wore a bizarre armless, full-length garment, underneath
which one caught glimpses of his white skin. Persons equally unrobed or dis-
robed wandered in, seemingly unconscious of their strange appearance.
Unorthodox behavior by the students and their guests at the ball was hinted at

in the next morning's papers." Rubinstein described the event as an orgy: men and women who didn't know each other copulated on the floor and false rapes were enacted. Heifetz, he said, could not believe his eyes and feared a police raid, which did not take place. According to Chotzinoff, "in the early hours of the morning, Rubinstein and Heifetz stopped on their way home at a night spot in Montmartre, took over the chores of the establishment's violinist and pianist and played for hours, to the patrons' delight." This took place at the Abbaye de Thélème restaurant in the Place Pigalle; the principal members of the audience were Domingo Merry del Val, brother of a cardinal and of the Chilean ambassador to Britain, and the two prostitutes who were his table companions. Rubinstein told Chotzinoff, forty years later: "Those were happy times. . . . How different from the strained gaiety of today. When we dance these days, it is in desperation, as if over a volcano, really a *danse macabre*. An uneasy dance like Ravel's *La Valse*."[158]

As to making professional appearances in Paris, however, Rubinstein continued to bide his time. A breakthrough came in the spring of 1923. Zulueta had become friendly with Jacques Hébertot, the director of the Théâtre des Champs-Elysées—Astruc's creation—and had "hypnotized Hébertot into believing that my appearance there would be the greatest thing which could happen to him," Rubinstein said.[159] His first postwar Paris performances took place on May 2, 7, and 13, shortly before one of his Spanish tours. "Rubinstein in Paris," *Le Figaro* announced the day before the first recital. "The great Polish artist, the ideal interpreter of Chopin, hasn't played in Paris since his career was just beginning, seventeen years ago."[160] His first program included works by Chopin, Debussy, and Albéniz; the second, works by Bach, Beethoven, Poulenc, Prokofiev, Ravel, Szymanowski, and Liszt; and the third, works by Franck, Schumann, Falla, Villa-Lobos, and Chopin. The performances were acclaimed by the public and much of the press, although there were dissenters—notably Jean Marnold, to whom Ravel had dedicated "Le Gibet," the second piece in his piano suite *Gaspard de la nuit*. Marnold used one-quarter of his long, gratuitously snide review in the influential *Mercure de France* to castigate the pianist for the poster on the Théâtre des Champs-Elysées that announced "Concerts Rubinstein" instead of specifying "Concerts Arthur Rubinstein," as if potential ticket-buyers might have confused Arthur with Anton, who had died twenty-nine years earlier. Marnold, who attended the second recital, also took Rubinstein to task for not having had the name of the arranger of the Bach Organ Toccata in F, with which the concert began, printed on the program, and he dismissed his performance of it: "Mr. Arthur Rubinstein dashed it off at a gallop; that's the best one can say about it. The 'Appassionata' Sonata followed. It shows its age, the 'Appassionata' Sonata does. . . . Mr. A. Rubinstein evidently per-

ceived this and treated it accordingly. He even carried it to its extreme consequences. . . . he seemed to bestride it as if it were a ghostly horse whose sides
he would suddenly pierce with his spurs, or that he would lash with a stroke
of the whip, rein in, and then immediately allow its head again. . . ."

But Marnold allowed that Rubinstein's "musicality is infinitely more
open and his culture more refined. This is probably why he plays Beethoven so badly [sic!]. One feels that he loves and understands contemporary
music, and, when he resists beefing it up with effects of his own production, he attains perfection. The 'Alborada del Gracioso' [by Ravel] wasn't
bad at all, but in the 'Vallée des Cloches' [by Debussy], interpreted with
scrupulous fervor, he was wholly admirable. And his far-reaching curiosity
doesn't stop with Mr. Maurice Ravel. He is one of the most valuable propa-
gandists of 'new musics,' to use Caccini's term. In addition to three charming little pieces by Mr. Serge Prokofiev, he played Mr. Francis Poulenc's
'Promenades'—a premiere, I believe. . . . Mr. Arthur Rubinstein, who interpreted it superbly, is much to be thanked and praised for having made it
part of his repertoire. . . ."[161]

Most other reviewers, however, were kinder than Marnold about
Rubinstein's way with Bach and Beethoven, and at least as enthusiastic about
his performances of modern music. Henry Prunières, one of the most au-
thoritative musicologists and critics of his generation, summed up the general reaction: "Rubinstein has one of the most extraordinary minds with
which any of today's virtuosos is endowed," he wrote in La Revue musicale,
"and we cannot be grateful enough to this great artist for not being satisfied
with achieving triumphs through the usual virtuoso pieces, but for giving
substantial room in his programs to the young composers whose works he
defends and spreads around the world."[162] The success of these recitals led to
a contract between Rubinstein and Marcel de Valmalète, a French manager,
who organized most of his domestic and some of his foreign appearances for
many years. From 1923 until the end of his career Rubinstein was a great
favorite with the Parisian public, and during the remainder of the 1920s the
Salle Gaveau was one of his preferred performing venues. There he played
the Bach-Busoni Chaconne, Schumann's Fantasy, Stravinsky's "Petrushka"
Sonata, and pieces by Debussy, Szymanowski, and Chopin on October 23,
1924; on November 12, 1925, his program included Beethoven's "Waldstein"
Sonata and shorter works by Brahms, Ravel, Scriabin, Busoni, Szymanowski,
Prokofiev, Chopin, and Liszt; on December 6, 1925, there were substantial
groups of pieces by Chopin, Debussy, and Albéniz; on January 20, 1927, Beethoven's "Waldstein" and "Appassionata" Sonatas were separated by seven
Chopin pieces; and four days later, Rubinstein gave a potpourri recital made
up of short works by Bach-Tausig, Brahms, Beethoven, Prokofiev, Villa-
Lobos, Poulenc, Albéniz, Mompou, Turina, and Falla.

By the time Rubinstein came to the story of his Paris success, when he was dictating *My Many Years*, his narrative had degenerated into what were described in the introduction to this biography as, primarily, menus of meals consumed and lists of love affairs consummated, in addition to detailed accounts of his disputes with concert managers. The change in tone was inevitable: once he had achieved substantial international fame, his professional life became a series of trips from one city and country to another; an account, chronological or otherwise, of even 5 or 10 percent of the approximately six thousand performances that he gave during the following half-century would have made exceedingly dull reading, and he did well to avoid the pitfall. Another cause of the change in tone was the gradual ossification of Rubinstein's repertoire. As late as the mid-1920s, he was still performing a remarkable amount of contemporary music, as the programs of some of his Wigmore Hall appearances in London testify: on May 14, 1924, he played Ravel's *Valses nobles et sentimentales*, two pieces by Falla, three pieces by Debussy, and two pieces by Albéniz; on July 9, 1924, his program included Milhaud's *Saudades do Brazil (Sumaré, Leme,* and *Ipanema)*, Szymanowski's Four Mazurkas (the world premiere of what eventually became part of the Twenty Mazurkas, Op. 50), Stravinsky's "Petrushka" Sonata, and two pieces by Albéniz; on November 1, 1924, in a special recital for the Pianoforte Society, he played two pieces by Debussy and repeated the "Petrushka" Sonata and Szymanowski's Four Mazurkas; on November 11, 1924, he presented works by Albéniz, Granados, and Falla; on January 24, 1925, he played pieces by Ravel, Milhaud, Debussy, Prokofiev, and Albéniz; and on October 31, 1925, his program included four pieces from Villa-Lobos's *Prole do bêbê,* Ravel's "Vallée des cluclies," Debussy's *L'Isle joyeuse,* Busoni's *Turandots Frauengemach,* Scriabin's *Vers la flamme,* and Prokofiev's *Suggestion diabolique.* When he was invited to appear on the Royal Philharmonic Society's prestigious concert series at the Queen's Hall (October 28, 1926, with Sir Henry Wood conducting), Rubinstein chose to play Falla's *Nights in the Gardens of Spain* rather than a more familiar eighteenth- or nineteenth-century concerto.

And yet, although he continued from time to time to learn and play new works by already-mentioned contemporary composers as well as by the Poles Alfred Gradstein (Three Mazurkas) and Roman Maciejewski (Two Mazurkas), the Polish-American Karol Rathaus *(Kujawiak),* the Hungarian Béla Bartók *(Allegro barbaro),* the Englishmen Arthur Bliss (Viola and Piano Sonata, with Lionel Tertis) and John Ireland (Piano Concerto in E-flat Major, with Sir Henry Wood), the Soviets Dmitri Shostakovich (Fourteenth Prelude, Polka) and Aram Khachaturian (Piano Concerto in D-flat Major), the American George Gershwin (Second Prelude), and the Yugoslav Marko Tajcevic (Six Balkan Pieces), his interest in new music slowed down as he approached middle age and found himself increasingly in demand as a performer of repertoire in which he had already been heard. "I think he was swallowed by his reputation and by the number of concerts he gave," Madeleine Milhaud, the composer's widow, commented in 1991. "You have to have time to discover music that is not the type that you are asked to play every night. Once, in Florence, we saw him at the Maggio Musicale, and he said to me: 'I haven't done what I ought to have done.' I quite forgot about the sentence until twenty years later, when he said it to me again, and then I thought about it. I think he meant that although he had done much for Villa-Lobos and played Stravinsky's *Petrushka* and some music by Milhaud and others, there were dozens and dozens of [contemporary] composers to be discovered. I don't think he had the courage for that. But what is moving is the fact that he felt this and regretted it."[163]

Rubinstein knew that the musical story of the last two-thirds of his career was far less variegated than that of the first third, and he evidently felt obliged to compensate, in his memoirs, by providing ever more abundant anecdotal accounts of amusing incidents, dinner parties, erotic escapades, and superficial encounters (or so he recounted them) with famous, powerful, or just plain wealthy people. The women—almost all unnamed, in his memoirs—whom he took to bed in those years included an American actress who threw herself at him in Paris; a young acquaintance who was waiting for her boyfriend at Evian, where Rubinstein was vacationing; a Chilean friend, also at Evian; a dancer who was a friend of Vera Soudeikine (Stravinsky's companion and future wife); "some lively young married women" in Paris; a young Parisian piano student, with whom he made love in a private room at a fashionable couturière's atelier, for the price of a dress that her husband could not afford to buy her; two otherwise unspecified "friends"; and dear old Mania Szer from Lodz. But he had little of interest to say about the aristocrats, politicians, magnates, philanthropists, musicians, writers, and painters whose names appear in *My Many Years*.

Moreover, at this point in his narrative Rubinstein threw to the winds what little chronological caution he had previously used. Events that took place in the early 1920s are sometimes lumped together with others from the 1930s—no dates given—and accounts of concerts that took place in a given year are followed many pages later by accounts of concerts performed several years earlier. For instance, on page 164 of the English-language editions of *My Many Years* he placed the premiere of Marcel Achard's play *Jean de la lune* (1929) among events that took place in 1921–22; on page 176, he described events that took place at Venice's International Music Festival in 1932; two pages later he described the premiere of Stravinsky's *Pulcinella*, which had taken place in 1920; and on page 195, in talking about his life in 1924, Rubinstein included his recollection of a two-piano recital by Saint-

Saëns, who had died in 1921, and Planté, who had retired in 1922. Except in a few special cases, the mistakes were unintentional: Rubinstein merely mis-remembered sequences of events or made tenuous mental connections between events without bothering to explain himself. Casual readers may not even notice the leaps, but careful readers sometimes find themselves clutching at straws.

My Many Years also contains one bit of chronological confusion that may politely be described as the result of a profound psychological need to reinvent history. Rubinstein claimed that shortly after his return to Europe from the United States in the spring of 1921 he had gone to Paris, where "very, very sad news awaited me . . . Ignacy told me that both of my parents had died. My poor mother had died of cancer and my father, whom I had never seen ill, survived her only by two months. He had died from pneumonia, which seemed to be only a pretext. He simply couldn't survive the death of his wife after fifty-two years of marriage. I was very unhappy. I had been looking forward to being able to send them on some cure but all this was shattered."[164] Perhaps Rubinstein chose his words badly; as the statement stands, the message it conveys is that he was upset about not having had time to make the grand gesture of sending his parents on a cure, rather than about their deaths. But whatever his feelings on the matter may have been, much of the story is untrue. Felicja Rubinstein did not die early in 1921 but rather on March 25, 1922, which means that an additional year went by in which she was gravely ill and in which her youngest son did not take the trouble to visit her. And Izaak Rubinstein died on April 27, 1924 — more than two *years*, not two months, after his wife. In all the intervening time Arthur had not managed to see him. He had not seen either of his parents since the autumn of 1913, at the latest, and so far as is known, he had not even written to them. The gifts that he had sent through Ryszard Ordynski in 1919 seem to have been his only contact with them during the last years of their lives.

Why had he avoided his parents so completely after the war? Surely not for lack of time or money: his European concert schedule was not tightly packed in those years, and he had earned so much money in Latin America that he was able to stay in the best hotels everywhere he went and to pay a valet to travel with him. But if Arthur had considered Felicja and Izaak unpresentable to the Wertheims, at the outset of his career, how much less presentable they must have seemed to him fifteen and twenty years later, when he was a celebrity who hobnobbed with the king of Spain, the Asquiths, and the Rothschilds. Nela Rubinstein, who did not meet Arthur until after his parents' deaths, got the impression from her husband that he had felt "no warmth" for them. "I think they just didn't have much in common." ("Haberdashers," he called them, dismissively, according to his son John.)[165]

"They were close, but only as far as Artek and talent and money and all that," Mrs. Rubinstein said. "It always ended in 'What will you give to Auntie So-and-so?' They were very nice people," she recalled—referring to her husband's siblings, whom she did meet, as well as to his parents—"but also extremely ungifted for doing anything for themselves."[166] Even these factors, however, would not have made him cut off all contact with his parents. It is more likely that he acted as he did because he was "terrified of emotion and of seeing pain," as Ruth Draper said of him. "It's a strange cowardice on his part."[167] And as some of his parents' pain had been caused by his neglect of them, his terror and cowardice were reinforced by feelings of guilt. Perhaps he had more and better reasons than he was willing to declare publicly or privately for his resentment of them, but the only certainty is that until their deaths—indeed, until his own death—his feelings toward them remained a mixture of love, anger, and guilt, just as they had been in his Berlin days, when his strategy to force his mother to return to Lodz had worked so well that his conscience had been bothered.

So strong was his fear of confronting his parents in their last years that it even prevented him from returning to newly independent Poland, of which he claimed to be so proud, throughout the first five years of its nationhood. No sooner were the older Rubinsteins dead, however, than Arthur rushed back home. And even then, the man who saw himself as a Polish patriot and an opponent of the "flatterers of the potentates of the land of the Dollar" insisted on being paid in dollars, because "the new Polish zloty was dangerously fluctuating," he said. And he added, cynically: "I knew my Varsovians well; they remained the snobs they were during the Russian times. They admired me for taking so long to play in my own country."[168] But Mlynarski had written to the Kochanskis, as early as March 1921: "The news of Artek makes me happy [i.e., news of his successes], greet him warmly. Have him come here, too, with dollars, and help me somehow with artistic life."[169] Of course Mlynarski, who was running the Warsaw Opera, was joking about asking Rubinstein to help subsidize the financially beleaguered company, but it is clear that Rubinstein the performer would have been welcomed heartily.

That Rubinstein adored Poland—the people's strength in the face of adversity, the city of Warsaw, its culture, the natural elegance of its women— is beyond doubt; that he was willing, in later years, to take a stand on behalf of Poland's rights in the family of nations, even when the country was governed by a communist regime that he detested, is demonstrable. But Rubinstein was a cosmopolite and internationalist, and he ought to have said so. (He did on at least one occasion: "I hate all the *nations* in the world—except maybe Switzerland, who could always stay neutral because the others could use her," he told a *New York Times* interviewer in 1972. "Can you believe one word your leaders say? Hypocrites!")[170] He loved Poland, he loved Paris, he loved Spain, he loved Rome and Venice, he loved London, and he eventually came to love Israel and many aspects of life in the United States; but he was, truly, a citizen of the world, and one who had the diffidence toward nationalism that comes naturally to Jews, who, as a group, have been maltreated at one time or another by most of the nations in which they have found themselves.

And yet, Rubinstein's basic feelings toward Poland were so positive that in his memoirs he did not even mention the anti-Semitic remarks to which he was sometimes subjected by the conservative sector of the Polish press. As the history of the twentieth century so dramatically demonstrates, cosmopolites in general and Jewish cosmopolites in particular are not much loved by vehement nationalists, and anti-Semitism was endemic to the ultranationalist and ultra-Catholic segments of Polish society in the 1920s. In the fall of 1924, only a few months after the pianist's first postwar performance in Poland, Iwaszkiewicz—a Gentile Pole—felt called upon to defend him. "Publicity about Rubinstein, that dandy who reigns over all the courts of Europe and the drawing rooms of America, has not necessarily left people favorably disposed toward his music-making," he wrote in a Warsaw literary journal. "[But] one should admire the titanic power with which Rubinstein, at the piano, purifies himself of any hint of snobbery. There is no pose, nothing is done for effect or for the public—there is only great, noble, excellent music.... And whether Rubinstein comes from Lodz or Pacanow [i.e., cities with large Jewish populations] makes as much difference to me as the question of whether Mickiewicz's or Chopin's mother was Jewish. For me, it is sufficient that [Mickiewicz and Chopin] have given us the greatest treasures of Polish culture and that [Rubinstein] is one of the greatest interpreters of such treasures. And the fact that Rubinstein has managed to reveal, for a moment, Chopin's great face, a face that had been covered with so many masks by so many of his other interpreters, is enough to give him an official certificate of the noblest Polish origins. The fact that some Poles do not understand this cannot be helped! As well as 'dreadful Jews' there are also 'dreadful Poles,' who have much in common with them—especially *irritability*."[171]

On the whole, however, during the 1920s and '30s Rubinstein was a great favorite of Polish music-lovers, regardless of their ethnic extraction. In Cracow, for instance, he gave at least twenty-three solo recitals between October 1924 and January 1936, and there are similar statistics for other Polish cities. Wiktor Labunski, who headed the Cracow Conservatory's piano department during the 1920s, said of Rubinstein's playing in those years: "His talent and personality were overwhelming, and left you breathless. He had something quite unique ..., in spite of the fact that he sometimes was underpracticed, and not very sure of his notes. As Nicolas Orloff [a brilliant Russian pianist five years younger than Rubinstein] once said: 'His talent bursts out of his every pore.' "[172] Nor did Rubinstein neglect Polish artistic society. He would arrive in Warsaw, settle into Ryszard Ordynski's home—where he slept on a couch that was too short for him—and immediately enter the social whirl, in which his host was a protagonist. "Arthur's stay here was rather meteoric because so short (here in Warsaw only a week, then in the provinces)," Szymanowski wrote from Warsaw to the Kochanskis in New York on December 12, 1924, "but I *didn't travel* with him. His concerts were a great success—the Filharmonja was full both times. Arturek played excellently and he made a great impression. He was so moved by his arrival in Warsaw that even I did not expect it of him."[173]

"Meteoric" describes not only Rubinstein's visits to Poland: throughout the 1920s, he undertook one international tour after another; he crisscrossed Europe and vicinity, discovering new venues—the Balkans, Turkey, North Africa, and the Middle East—and returning to favorite (or not-so-favorite) old ones. He remembered with special pride his first visit to Palestine, where he played gratis in an airplane hangar—the only sufficiently large space—for an enthusiastic audience of native and immigrant Jews who had to stand through the entire program, as chairs were not available. Spain, of course, welcomed Rubinstein year after year: he would rush from town to town, but he nearly always managed to squeeze delight and enjoyment out of every situation and to share his pleasure with his audiences. Paco Aguilar, a member of the Aguilar Family Lute Quartet, left a memorable description of a Rubinstein recital in Granada—probably the one that took place on May 8, 1925, and certainly not during the 1919–20 season, as Rubinstein misremembered. The pianist had been delayed on the road from Almería, one hundred miles away, and the audience was already beginning to leave when Rubinstein's car suddenly pulled up at the theater.

> A black bundle, a big coat with a little hat . . . crossed the vestibule en route to [the stage]. It was Rubinstein. He didn't walk, he precipitated. The bang of the car-door, heard when the man was already halfway across the vestibule, gave an idea of the sort of hand that had shut it. . . . By the time [Ernesto de Quesada] managed to get to the stage, [Rubinstein] had already bowed to the audience, whose members had gone back to their seats, and was sizing up the keyboard. . . . His tails were impeccable. He had gotten dressed in the car, while traveling at sixty miles an hour. . . .
>
> [Rubinstein played Chopin and Spanish music.] A miracle? Yes. The greatest Spanish pianist to have a grasp of Polish music was born in Poland.
>
> During the first intermission, there were greetings, embraces, and introductions. The quartet members were chatting with the pi-

anist, who was enthusiastic about them. He had to celebrate the encounter.

"Let's get together—what do you say?"

"Tomorrow?"

"Tonight!"

"Won't you be tired?"

"From what?"

"The concert, the trip."

"Oh, I traveled sitting down! And as to the concert, yes; I'll change the Stravinsky piece for something else, and quickly."

"You're not going to play *Petrushka*?"

"It's not worth it. You've already seen that the audience prefers 'Romantic' music. It isn't prepared to listen to this 'hurricane.' Keep my secret: I'm not really ready to confront the piece tonight. You know what *Petrushka* is—a giant, a cyclone!"

"We know the work, but not the version that Stravinsky made for you." The quartet's spokesperson was Elisa, who added: "It was the piece that most interested us on the program." The pianist's kindness in promising to play it for the quartet at the earliest opportunity, and the decision to get together after the concert, to pass the evening together, led to unanimous approval of the program change.

When Rubinstein was again seated before the piano, his glance settled on the Aguilars' box. Their smiles were answered with a slight but expressive nod of the head. The pianist had to speak—he was obliged to announce the program change. The four lutenists didn't breathe. Rubinstein looked in their direction.

"I am going to play. . . ." He looked pensive for a few seconds. He was searching, mentally, for the right piece to play. His hands changed position on the keyboard two or three times. At last he decided. He had had an idea. A magnanimous gesture was accompanied by a sly look in his eye. "I am going to play *Petrushka*."

The four Aguilars, propelled by a spiritual spring, jumped to their feet and broke the silence with frenetic applause. The audience didn't understand; the pianist had announced what was already printed in the program. But the quartet's attitude and personality, which brooked no opposition, moved the listeners to follow suit, while one spectator's comment spread through the hall: "He has dedicated it to the Aguilars."[174]

During the 1920s and well into the 1930s, Italy was almost as wild about Rubinstein as Spain was. The Italian public "never let me down," he often said in later years. Rome, in particular, was "his" city: between March 1924 and February 1937 he gave eight recitals for the Accademia di Santa Cecilia and nine concerts with the Santa Cecilia Orchestra under Bernardino Molinari, Mario Rossi, and Ferruccio Calusio, in concertos by Beethoven, Falla, Mozart, Saint-Saëns, Tchaikovsky, Chopin, Brahms, and Liszt. He also formed a liaison with a Roman noblewoman whom he called Princess Carla Palladini, in *My Many Years*, but who was really Marchioness Paola Medici. Born in 1895, Princess Paola di Viggiano, Marchioness Sanfelice di Monteforte was the daughter of Prince Ludovico Sanfelice di Viggiano Monteforte and the Franco-Belgian Princess Jeanne Marie Emilie de Bauffremont, lady-in-waiting to the Queen of Italy. In 1917 she married Marquess Luigi Medici del Vascello, a lawyer and parliamentarian who, in the 1920s, became an ardent fascist. Rubinstein described the marchioness as exceptionally beautiful, "with a delicate round face and a pale complexion. She parted her shiny black hair on one side and let it fall freely to cover her ears in a curl. Her dark eyes were shadowed by long lashes and heavy eyebrows and they looked at you with a bit of haughtiness but with a touch of humor as well."[175] He found her somewhat unpleasant when they first met, in Venice, but she fell in love with him, it seems. According to his account—which, once again, is the only one available—she virtually threw herself at him the next time they met, in Paris, and thus their affair began, possibly as early as the fall of 1923 or the following winter; it continued, off and on, at least until the summer of 1928. The Vatican eventually annulled the Medicis' marriage, but even before that the marchioness managed not only to spend time with Rubinstein in Italy and France but also to travel with him to South America, Eastern Europe, the Balkans, and North Africa, although he could rarely take her with him to the various receptions and dinners to which he was invited during his tours. A noblewoman who enjoyed high society but would put up with being left in a hotel room while her man—a commoner, and a Jewish commoner, at that—hobnobbed with the aristocracy may indeed have been deeply in love. She even asked Rubinstein whether he would marry her if she could obtain a divorce, and he embarrassedly made a series of excuses—after which she apparently treated him as one lover among several, one diversion among many in a life with no center of gravity.

But according to Luli Oswald, a pianist who lives in Rio de Janeiro, the affair had another result: herself. She is the daughter of Rubinstein and Paola Medici, she has said, and is not sure of the exact year of her birth. In 1967, her nominal parents, Odoardo and Maria Oswald Marchesini, and Mrs. Marchesini's sister, Enrichetta Margherita Oswald Alfieri, signed an affidavit in which they declared that Luli had been entrusted to them by her "real biological parents," Paola Medici, princess of Viggiano, and Arthur Rubinstein, the "young Polish pianist," because she was the "fruit of a forbidden love."

Her real name was Luisa Maria Theresia; her legal name is Margarida Henriqueta Marchesini—the name of a deceased child of her nominal parents—and she took the professional surname Oswald from her adoptive mother, whose father, Henrique Oswald, was a well-known Brazilian musician whom Rubinstein had known since his first visit to the country. As a baby, Luli had at first "stayed with her real parents, but had to be hidden from the time of her birth," the affidavit states. When she was entrusted to the Marchesinis, the baby wore a gold necklace that had the name Lulli (double *l*, in Italian) engraved on it and that bore "a marvelous . . . star made of the finest diamonds. . . . We promised to keep the secret and to give the child all our love." The Marchesinis, people of means, brought Luli up in comfort and made sure that she studied music, at home and abroad. She has written that as a young woman she often met Rubinstein at the Drake hotel in New York, where their friend Felicja Blumental, a Polish-Brazilian pianist, lived (and where Rubinstein himself lived in later years). "There I received excellent but few lessons from him," she said. "But without Nela's knowledge. And this was a disagreeable situation for me. Another time we met in Dallas (Texas). He invited me to Houston, where he was going to play with Barbirolli. . . . There we stayed in the Rice Hotel and once more he said that no one should know it, except my manager Mrs. Lankford and a friend who was travelling with him. I never knew who [the friend] was." (It was probably Louis Bender, who was employed to accompany Rubinstein on his North American tours in later decades.) "Arthur sent me then to Budapest to study with Prof. Josef Gatz [*sic*; presumably Gát, a Bartók pupil and well-known piano pedagogue], and afterwards for a few weeks in Warsaw with Prof. Margherita Trombini Kazuro, to learn the [special] interpretation of Polish music, and so avoiding an imitation of his own style, already visible in my spontaneous way of playing." She married a Mr. Teixeira de Freitas; they raised seven children and were later divorced. Luli Oswald performed in North and South America, withdrew from concert life in 1972, and resumed performing in 1986. All of this information, including a photocopy of the Marchesini affidavit, was revealed to me in correspondence with Ms. Oswald between November 1994 and March 1995, and I revealed it to members of Rubinstein's family and Annabelle Whitestone, Lady Weidenfeld. Eva Rubinstein said that she, her sister, Alina, and her brother John thought the story of Luli's parentage "more than probably true, fairly likely" and that Alina remembered her father's telling her about an illegitimate child of his in South America; Nela Rubinstein and Lady Weidenfeld were more skeptical but did not exclude the possibility.

SOMETIME IN THE mid-1920s, Rubinstein the Parisian gave up his suite at the Villa Majestic and rented a bungalow in Montmartre. His decision may have been a signal from a nesting instinct that had long lain dormant but that would soon make its presence felt in a more decisive way. Jeanne de Marjerie, a friend, had told him about the availability of the house, at No. 15 on the sharply inclined Rue Ravignan, at the corner of Rue d'Orchampt; its previous occupant had been Pierre Fresnay, the actor. In the early decades of the twentieth century, Montmartre was one of Paris's liveliest quarters—lively with respect to artistic and intellectual life as well as to the demimonde that Rubinstein adored. He was happy with his home and delighted to have Madame de Marjerie and his old friend Eugenia Errazuriz assist him in decorating it. As he had long since had a falling out with Enrique, his Argentinean valet, Madame de Marjerie found him a French valet, François Delalande, who gave him outstanding service for many years, Rubinstein said, and made home maintenance feasible for a busy bachelor who had no domestic skills. Wiktor Labunski and his brother Feliks visited Rubinstein in Rue Ravignan, and Wiktor later described the bungalow as "not large, but . . . furnished in fine taste. All the items in the house—furniture, glassware, china—were the best, seemingly the most expensive kind. Of course, there was a grand piano, and a number of interesting paintings mostly by contemporary artists. And then—books—hundreds of them in book cases, including some rare books, first editions, etc. Artur is a perfect host, and he made us feel as if our call was of tremendous importance to him, and as if we were the most important people in the world. I think that he makes everyone feel this way, and this is perhaps one of the secrets of his tremendous popularity among people of all ages and of all countries. He charmed us both to the highest degree." Labunski gave a successful Paris recital, after which Rubinstein congratulated him by hosting "a lavish party for about eighteen to twenty people in one of the best Paris restaurants," Labunski recalled. "There was marvellous food, champagne, a congenial group of people, interesting conversations. Throughout the more than thirty years since that first Rubinstein party, I have been invited many times by Artur to take part in small and large gatherings, at his homes and in restaurants, and each time I admired his largesse, elegance, and good taste in everything: food, wine, cigars, clothes. I have never known another person whose habits were in such perfect harmony with his personality."[176]

Fifteen Rue Ravignan was perfect for Rubinstein: he could play the piano or entertain whenever he pleased, and when he needed rest he could get it. But early in 1926, the Paris debut of a twenty-two-year-old pianist from Kiev made him lose some sleep. Vladimir Horowitz, a refugee from the newborn Soviet Union, created a public and critical furor of vast dimensions. Only three years after Rubinstein's decisive triumph in the city, someone had arrived to steal the champion's title. Or at least this is the impression that Rubinstein gave in his book. The truth is that there was plenty of room for both artists, as well as for Alfred Cortot, Walter Gieseking, and all the other outstanding pianists of the period. Each had a following, and the admirers of one were not necessarily detractors of the others. But when Rubinstein first heard Horowitz play, his initial reactions were wonderment and self-disgust: "There was much more than sheer brilliance and technique; there was an easy elegance—the magic something which defies description," Rubinstein said, but what he perceived as Horowitz's attitude of superiority to him "caused me to begin to feel a deep artistic depression. Deep within myself, I felt I was the better musician. My conception of the sense of music was more mature, but at the same time, I was conscious of my terrible defects—of my negligence for detail."[177] The two pianists often got together—usually at the home of their friend Alexander Steinert, an American composer—to play two-piano repertoire and arrangements of orchestral music, and sometimes they were joined by the young French pianist Jacques Février, whom Rubinstein regarded as the best keyboard sight-reader he ever met. In the end, Rubinstein's hold on Paris proved to be just as enduring as Horowitz's, and the older pianist certainly played there far more often than the younger one did.

Later in life, Rubinstein must have realized that the most significant occurrence in his career during the 1920s was not his conquest of Paris, the extension of his frontiers to countries in which he had never played before, the worrying competition that Horowitz represented on the international scene, or any of the other ups and downs in his life as a concert artist, but rather his first professional encounter with Fred Gaisberg. Born in Washington, D.C., in 1873, Gaisberg had been involved in the infant recording industry from the age of sixteen, and in 1898 he had gone to England to promote Emil Berliner's flat phonograph discs, whose popularity soon outstripped that of Thomas Edison's cylindrical recordings. In 1925 Gaisberg became artistic director of the Gramophone Company, which owned the His Master's Voice (HMV) label. Walter Legge, who dominated the British classical music recording industry a generation later, said that Gaisberg "believed that his job was to get the best artists into the studio and get onto wax the best sound pictures of what those artists habitually did in public, intermittently using his persuasive diplomatic skill as nurse-maid and tranquilizer to temperaments."[178] In 1928, when he used his diplomatic skill to persuade Rubinstein to make a few discs, the electrical recording process, which involved the use of microphones, had only recently replaced the old acoustical method, which had required performers to play or sing into large horns.* The devel-

---

*It is now believed that Rubinstein made at least one record for the Polish Favorit label in about 1910; the extant disc contains Liszt's Twelfth Hungarian Rhapsody

opment had brought about an enormous leap forward in the quality of recorded sound.

Rubinstein said that Gaisberg, after having attended his performance, in London, of John Ireland's new piano concerto, had taken him to lunch at the Gramophone Company's headquarters in Hayes, Middlesex—in the outskirts of London—and had then sworn that if Rubinstein would make a test recording it would not be issued without the artist's permission. Rubinstein agreed to try; Gaisberg led him to a recording studio, where a Blüthner piano awaited him. Rubinstein objected that the instrument was not a full-size concert grand, but Gaisberg persuaded him to try it. "Well, this Blüthner had the most beautiful singing tone I had ever found," he recalled. "Suddenly I became quite enthusiastic and decided to play my beloved Barcarolle of Chopin. The piano inspired me. I don't think I ever played better in my life. And then the miracle happened; they played it back to me and I must confess that I had tears in my eyes. . . . Gaisberg had won."[179] In reality, the session took place on March 9, 1928, two years before the premiere of Ireland's concerto, and not at Hayes but in central London, in "C" Studio of the Small Queen's Hall. The lunch-plus-recording session at Hayes probably took place in 1930, when the Gramophone Company successfully persuaded Rubinstein to make his records at their headquarters, where acoustic conditions were better than at their rented studios in London.

Rubinstein's first test recordings included not only the Barcarolle but also Debussy's "La Cathédrale engloutie," Brahms's Capriccio in B Minor, Op. 76, No. 2; Schubert's Impromptu in A-flat Major, Op. 90, No. 4; Chopin's Waltz in A-flat Major, Op. 34, No. 1; and Falla's "Ritual Fire Dance" and "Dance of Terror" from El amor brujo. All except the Falla excerpts were recorded twice that day—once on the Blüthner and once on a Steinway; the Falla pieces were recorded only on the Steinway. Among these recordings, only the Chopin waltz and the Brahms capriccio were released; the Steinway version of the waltz was used, but the company's records are unclear as to which version of the Brahms was used. Rubinstein returned to the Small Queen's Hall on April 18 to rerecord, in "C" and "D" Studios, the versions of the Chopin Barcarolle and the Schubert impromptu that were eventually published, and versions of other pieces that were not; at this second session, he used only the Blüthner piano. Subsequent sessions took place on January

---

and an arrangement of the "Blue Danube" Waltz. Donald Manildi, the author of this book's discography, heard a tape dub of the record and reported: "The playing is quite casual and slapdash, the recorded sound pretty bad." In his memoirs, Rubinstein did not mention this early venture into the recording studio.

23 and 24 and February 1, 1929, with a Bechstein piano, and yielded successful recordings of four pieces by Albéniz and the "Cathédrale engloutie," plus unsuccessful versions of two Brahms pieces. And on October 22 and 23, 1929, he made his first large-scale recording: Brahms's Second Concerto with the London Symphony Orchestra conducted by Albert Coates. In his memoirs, Rubinstein incorrectly stated that the sessions took place a few days before he left for a tour of South America (his next trip to South America did not take place until 1931), that he did not like the results, and that Gaisberg "had betrayed me" by having the records issued.[180] There is no reason to doubt his negative opinion of the recording, but in the Gramophone Company's files there is no trace of an objection, at the time, from Rubinstein. "The Brahms Concerto passed all our tests, and a very fine set of records has been obtained," a letter from the house's Artistes' Department routinely informed Rubinstein in January 1930. "The work is being issued in England in a month or two's time."[181] Rubinstein did not reply—at least not in writing—and the company's correspondence indicates that before long he was eager to have the recording released in France.

By the summer of 1932, Rubinstein had added to his recorded repertoire a substantial number of Chopin pieces; short works by Falla, Liszt, Granados, Villa-Lobos, Debussy, and Albéniz; the last (D Minor, Op. 108) of Brahms's violin and piano sonatas, with Kochanski; and three important concertos (Chopin Second, Mozart A Major, K. 488, and Tchaikovsky First) with the London Symphony Orchestra conducted by the young John Barbirolli. The economic benefits of recording were low, at first, for Rubinstein, but they multiplied quickly. In 1930, for instance, the Gramophone Company paid him only £30 (about $144) per 78 rpm side as an advance royalty, and for the second half of 1930 he earned only about £130 ($624) in royalties beyond advances. But during the first half of 1931 the royalties beyond advances reached £450 ($2,160); although this was not a vast sum, it was an enormous increase over the previous payment. He seems to have understood the need for patience, and his only major dissatisfaction with the Gramophone Company, at the time, had to do with the way his recordings were being distributed and advertised in France. In general, the Gramophone Company stood by Rubinstein: its people kept in touch with the pianist's managers and did their best to alert their agents in foreign countries to forthcoming Rubinstein tours in their respective territories, so that his live appearances would help to increase record sales. Thus, the EMI Music Archives provide a good vantage point from which to survey Rubinstein's professional travels; the following incomplete, bare-bones list, for instance, demonstrates that although he was not as busy then as he eventually became, his concert schedule from the late summer of 1929 to the early spring of 1932 was anything but empty.

France (resorts), August 1–20, 1929

France, October 1–10, 1929

Italy, November 1–8 and December 11–31, 1929

Rumania, January 1–9, 1930

Poland, January 12–31, 1930

France (south), March 7–15, 1930

Spain, March 16–31, 1930

(South America, May to ? 1930: cancelled)

Belgium (Antwerp), May 28, 1930

Poland, June 2–4, 1930 (Warsaw, with Kochanski, June 2; Lodz, June 4)

France, December 8–12, 1930; January 11–16, 1931 (including Monte Carlo)

Vienna, Mittlerer Musikvereinssaal, January 21, 1931

Poland, January 27–February 9, 1931 (During this trip Rubinstein visited Szymanowski at the home the composer had rented at Zakopane while he was completing his ballet pantomime, *Harnasie*.)[182]

Vienna, Grosser Musikvereinssaal, February 11, 1931

Budapest, February 13, 1931

Belgium (Liège), February 28, 1931

South America (Brazil, Chile, Argentina, Uruguay), May–October 1931

Paris, October 10, 1931

Poland, Budapest, October 28–November 29, 1931

Belgium, December 18–19, 1931

Paris, December 26–27, 1931

Poland, early January 1932

Vienna, Prague, February 18–19, 1932

Belgium, February 21–24, 1932

Paris, February 25, 1932 (Rubinstein played Brahms's Second Concerto with the Orchestre Symphonique de Paris, conducted by Nicolas Slonimsky, who is better known today as a musical lexicographer than as a conductor. "Rubinstein was very popular in Paris, and the applause greeting his appearance on the stage was tumultuous," Slonimsky said in his memoirs. "Immediately after his number he disappeared.")[183]

France, February 27–March 3, 1932

Rome, March 18–20, 1932

North Africa, March 30–April 5, 1932

The list does not include Rubinstein's many British engagements, one of the most important of which took place on October 29, 1930, when he played the

Tchaikovsky Concerto on the second concert of the promising new BBC Symphony Orchestra, under its chief conductor, Adrian Boult; this was one of Rubinstein's first ventures into the medium of radio. Two days later, he gave a major recital at the Queen's Hall, London.

After each extended trip, Rubinstein returned to Paris, where his friends included Eve Curie, the musical younger daughter of the celebrated scientists Marie and Pierre Curie (Rubinstein also met Marie Curie, who, as a Polish communist, was put off by her compatriot's dandyish ways); Moïse Kisling, a well-known Polish painter who had long made his home in Paris; and the patroness of the arts Princess Edmond de Polignac, née Winnaretta Singer, of the Singer Sewing Machines family. Old friends, too, showed up in Paris from time to time, and in 1932 Rubinstein saw Ruth Draper for the first time in several years. Since they had last met, she had had a life-transfiguring love affair with Lauro De Bosis, an Italian intellectual seventeen years her junior who was living in exile in France as a result of his anti-fascist beliefs. In 1931 he had piloted a solo suicide flight from the south of France to Rome, to drop anti-fascist leaflets over the capital; he had accomplished his mission without difficulty but his plane had run out of fuel on the return flight and he had perished in the Mediterranean, at the age of thirty. Now, a year later, Draper wrote to a friend: "Arthur's concert was wonderful and I've had lovely talks with him—he remains the vital, faithful friend that one can find again after years of silence and indifference. He grasped at once the significance and beauty of Lauro; and all that enthusiasm and energy of life that I always found in both of them did me good to feel again in him. His music was like a torrent of sparkling sound—healing and strong—divinely beautiful in the andantes and wildly alive in the Spanish things—God—how he plays them! . . . I went to a party at Mme. [Misia] Sert's afterward, and recited and it took me back to Edith Grove days and Paul's delight in Arthur's genius."[184] Under the circumstances, Rubinstein probably refrained from telling Draper that during a recent trip to Rome he had had a cordial private audience with Benito Mussolini; the encounter may have been arranged through Paola Medici or one of her friends in the Roman aristocracy—a group of people who, for the most part, privately made fun of the fascists but took advantage of whatever benefits the regime offered them. Although the meeting took place long before the fascist government adopted anti-Semitic policies, Mussolini had long since demonstrated that his regime was dictatorial and militaristic. For the time being, however, Rubinstein, like most other foreign visitors—including the politically astute Winston Churchill—was convinced that Mussolini was Italy's Man of Destiny.

Another old friend who occasionally looked Rubinstein up in Paris in those years was Dagmar Godowsky. "Pa and [Artur] showed me the city—Pa by day, Artur by night," she recalled. "Andrés Segovia was showing me Paris too. . . . But it was Artur who was most wonderful to be with. He introduced me to Maurice Ravel at *Le Boeuf sur le Toit,* Ravel's favorite place. We met him there often and one night he showed me photographs of his beloved cats. . . . But Artur, still flawless to me, was the one man in the world who was unimpressed! Here I was, a woman divorced, a woman annulled, and he still treated me like a child. All he had to do was look at me and I acted like one. . . . When he showed me photographs he had just brought back from Poland—pictures of a lovely girl—I wasn't in the least jealous. It was the old pattern. If Artur loved someone, she must be marvelous. Her name was Aniela Mlynarski and her father was Director of the Warsaw Opera. She was exquisite."[185]

So exquisite that Rubinstein wanted to marry her.

5

Unite and Conquer

In the course of an interview that took place in Madrid toward the end of 1919, a journalist drew Rubinstein out on the subject of love and marriage.

"All my women, the adorable women with whom I have dreamed, have interested me. The naughty attraction that Nature has set between the two sexes, to perpetuate the species, is excessively strong in me. But the idea of marriage horrifies me; if you hear someday that I have married, you'll know that I've gone mad. For an artist, marriage is a misfortune. I want to get up every day in a different state of mind, ready for new sensations; to marry would be to give up everything else in life. I've been around enough to have observed all the married artists in the world; well then, ninety-eight out of a hundred are wretched, and the other two cease to be artists. . . .

"Do you know what I like best? To make a collection of happy moments, eternities, without ever stopping, so that they could replace the moments of disappointment. I don't know whether I'm making myself clear. I would like to take leave of every woman and of every friend at the highest moment of affection, and never wait until the disenchantment comes. Some women strive for the impossible, for a permanent love, and in their stubbornness they merely attenuate love and happy memories, which are what one ought to aspire to. How long two people love each other is unimportant. What is unforgettable is the intensity with which they love. You can love a woman for forty years, but how? The divine part of that love, the only part that endures, is the terrible and exalted madness of the first three weeks. All that remains are leftovers. One day in Venice, in perfect freedom, in the company of a woman you've dreamt of, is worth more than the whole, prosaic lifetime of a marriage of convenience."[1]

Millions of people with similar attitudes toward marriage have married, and so did Rubinstein. His change of mind came in Warsaw in 1926. During a concert intermission, after he had played Beethoven's Fourth Concerto with the Philharmonic under Mlynarski, he received in his dressing room the two youngest of the conductor's three daughters and one of Mlynarski's nieces, who had come to congratulate him. He later described them as the "three Graces, three Polish beauties. . . . The tallest, who was very blond, showed great vitality and charm. . . . [She] was the only one I looked at, as if the other two were not in the room."[2]

Aniela—Nela, for short—Mlynarska was the youngest of Emil's five children. "The oldest was Wanda, who married the pianist Wiktor Labunski," Nela Rubinstein related many years later. "She was twelve years older than I, and she was my godmother, even. Then there was Bronek—Bronislaw—who was eight years older than I; then there was another brother, six years older—Feliks; and then there was Ala [Alina], four years older. And then me, born on July 30, 1908. My father had five brothers; they all married and had children, and we were seventeen cousins. I was the youngest of the whole clan, the whole mass of Mlynarskis."[3] During World War I, Nela and most of her family had lived at Ilgowo, a Lithuanian estate on the Niemen River that had belonged to her mother's family, the Hryncewiczes, since the eighteenth century. Immediately after the war, her father was named general director of Warsaw's Teatr Wielki (Grand Theater), one of the most important opera companies in Eastern Europe. Much of the east wing of the grandiose opera house was occupied by the director's apartment, where Nela took up residence when she returned to Warsaw from Ilgowo late in 1920 or early in 1921. She was immediately enrolled at the Kowalczykowna-Jawurkowna School, an outstanding private institution for girls that her sister Alina was already attending. A friend of Alina's recalled meeting Nela there shortly after her arrival: "Two big blue eyes, a pair of tight, curly blond pigtails, and a beige homespun woolen dress 'skated' the length of the waxed corridor in a pair of felt slippers right into my arms. Alina had spoken so often and lovingly about her 'baby sister' that I knew it must be she. Apparently, Alina also had talked of me to Nela. We embraced each other effusively, and from that moment on our friendship was sealed for life." The new friend, Halina Lilpop, was the daughter of one of Warsaw's leading architects, grandniece of the great violinist Henryk (Henri) Wieniawski, great-granddaughter of the celebrated basso Wilhelm Troszel, and future wife of the conductor Artur Rodzinski. Later in life, she remembered the twelve-year-old Nela as "tiny for her age, and very, very graceful. Without any formal instruction, she had already begun to dance beautifully and had hopes of becoming a ballerina. . . . I was at this time aspiring to be either a portrait painter or an architect. Ironically, we both ended in the same line of work, and helped each other get our 'jobs.' "[4]

About her aspirations as a dancer, Nela Rubinstein said, seventy years later: "I was always pretty lazy. I was very gifted, so whenever I did something it looked very good. But life was too complicated for me as a young girl in Warsaw. I was going to school, then I was taking ballet lessons, then I was going to all the concerts and plays and operas. We led a much richer life than I should have. I should have sat and studied mathematics, for instance, but I went to the opera every day, and my father, who loved me, asked my opinion about the singers. They sang in the living room, and my bedroom was next to it. When I was supposed to work I was often disturbed; I was anything but a good student. I somehow sweated myself through here and there, and there were some subjects that I was good at, but mathematics and things like that were catastrophic. You could never even study properly, because the phone rang—people wanting tickets to the opera—and it was like a mill." Nela's mother spent most of her time at Ilgowo, for the management of which she was responsible. When Mrs. Mlynarska was away, her husband was left in charge of his daughters in Warsaw. "It often seemed, however, that the girls were in charge of him, functioning as his hostesses and watching over the complex details of an opera director's household," Halina Rodzinska recalled.[5] Nela agreed. "Poor Daddy!" she said. "We tried to help him as much as possible. At the age of fourteen, fifteen, I was already sort of hostessing for him and defending him. Stokowski came, or Backhaus, or Battistini; they had to be entertained and we daughters had to be there. And my brothers and my cousins—always a mass of boys around! It was not easy. But of course that's what I loved."

The unusually heady life that Alina and Nela led in those years gave them what Mrs. Rodzinska later described as "an attractive poise far beyond their years."[6] There was a great gap in life-experience between Nela Mlynarska and Rubinstein when they met—she had turned eighteen only a few months earlier and had always lived in the bosom of her adored and adoring family, whereas he was approaching his fortieth birthday and had lived nomadically since he was ten—but he immediately felt attracted to her, that evening in his dressing room. He would have liked Nela and the other two "Graces"—her sister Alina and their cousin Hela—to accompany him to a party that his friends Stanislaw and Zofia Bernstein Meyer were giving for him after the concert, but the Meyers said that the Mlynarska girls were too young to attend. ("They didn't want it because they were jealous of anybody who would approach Arthur," Nela said.) He was angry with his hosts, but felt that he could not fail them. The next day, he left to give concerts in Cracow and Lvov, but as soon as he got back to Warsaw he phoned Szymanowski and successfully "begged Karol to telephone Nela Mlynarska and ask if the two of us could come for tea," he said. ("That's true," Nela recalled; "they came together.") And it was on that occasion, which he compared to a similar one with Lily Wertheim nearly twenty years earlier, that "both of us, Nela and I, felt the *coup de foudre.*"[7] ("Yes, I remember it," Nela concurred, with a smile.)

One evening, soon afterward, Nela attended a concert that her father and Rubinstein were giving in Lodz with the local orchestra, and the next morning, on the train back to Warsaw, "we talked and talked, standing in the corridor, and exchanged our first words of love,"[8] Rubinstein recalled. Nela said that during the trip she had "a sort of vision. I really fell in love with him, and somehow I saw my life with him as it was going to be." They agreed to meet in a park the next morning, next to the Chopin monument; there he told her that he wanted to marry her but that her extreme youth and the difference in their ages made him hesitate. He had never before felt that he wanted to marry, he said, although the issue had come up twice, with Englishwomen. ("He told me about them," Nela said. "One was a Pamela Something-or-other, but it never really got off the ground.") He suggested that they wait to see whether they were both sure that this was what they really wanted, and she agreed. Apart from the enormous difference in their ages, Nela and Arthur seemed ideally matched as a result of their Polish and musical backgrounds, naturalness in bohemian artistic society, love of good food, adaptability in travel, and even linguistic facility: Nela already spoke Polish, Russian, Lithuanian, and French, and she eventually became fluent in English and Spanish and capable of getting along in German.

Rubinstein left to continue his concert tour. Months went by. He and Nela waited to hear from each other, but neither wanted to be the first to write a letter. "Not hearing from her disquieted me terribly," he said in his memoirs, but he added that "a letter from me would only have repeated what I had said last time in the park."[9] She said: "When Arthur left and never wrote to me, he expected that I would write to him, and I was really honestly in love with him then, so I started to. First of all, everybody laughed at me: 'Look how foolish Nela is—she believes that Arthur is really serious.' Because even then in Warsaw he had always one woman and then another and another, always somebody. And so I sort of began to give up on it." The person who took advantage of the misunderstanding was Zosia Kochanska, who still nourished complicated feelings toward Arthur; when she learned that the man whom she had preferred to her own husband had proposed to little Nela Mlynarska, she became jealous. Once, during those months, Nela's brother Bronek went to Paris; the Kochanskis were there, too, and he went to visit them. Bronek "adored Zosia and Paul," Nela said. "They were like a sister and brother to him. A big trust he had with her, but she was a viper, she was not to be trusted. And Bronek, in the innocence of his love for me—because he worshipped me—said, 'Zosia, look, you know Arthur so much better than I. Do you think that he is really interested in Nela, seriously? Because she sometimes cries a little bit and she is sad.' Well, instead of making it sound like it really was, Zosia then told Arthur, 'You know, the Mlynarskis want to know whether you will declare yourself." And it was just like pouring a pail of cold water on him. He was already very self-conscious about the matter."

Enter the third party—Mieczyslaw (also called Miecio or Mietek) Münz, a twenty-seven-year-old, Cracow-born pianist who had studied with Busoni and had made a successful debut in Berlin in 1920. According to Labunski, who knew him well, Münz had "exceptional talent and personal charm. . . . He came from a middle-class Jewish family (his father was a not very prosperous lawyer), made his studies in Cracow and Vienna, and at an early age made a niche for himself in Viennese musical circles. His ambition was reaching higher, however, and he decided to try for luck in the United States. He went there [in 1922] with a very modest sum of money. . . . Good luck was with him—within one season he made a name for himself on the so-called 'big circuit.' The return to Cracow of the local boy who made good was a triumph, he was fêted and wined and dined. He never forgot that we were his friends even before he had had his first successes in Vienna, and during summertime he often visited us, or invited us to parties at his home. . . . It so happened that Wanda's sister Nela visited us from time to time, and became acquainted with Münz."[10]

Enter, or rather reenter, the fourth party. Paola Medici showed up in Paris while Arthur was there, and when he returned to Warsaw to give a concert, after a full year during which he and Nela had not communicated, Paola went with him—against his wishes, he claimed. Once there, he "did not dare to get in touch with Nela . . . without knowing if I would be received." Instead, he accepted an invitation to a reception that was to be given at the British embassy by Ambassador Max Muller and his wife, whom Rubinstein had met in Rome. The Mullers invited Princess Medici, too—unbeknownst to Rubinstein, he said, because he was staying at Ordynski's home and she at a hotel. But she phoned and asked him to escort her to the reception, and he gallantly accepted. "When [Paola] and I entered the great reception room, the first people I saw were Emil Mlynarski and his daughter," Rubinstein said. "My heart froze. . . . [He] gave me a warm handshake but Nela turned her back. It was one of the rare moments in my life when I felt miserably unhappy." Later in the evening Rubinstein "almost forced Nela to follow me to a corner where I could talk to her. She looked at me with icy indignation . . . but agreed to receive me" at her home the next day.[11]

Nela said that her brother, not her father, had been with her at the party, but she agreed with the rest of Arthur's account of what happened that evening and of their meeting the next day. He told her the story of his affair with Paola, and "we began to exchange our doubts and our disappointments, our indignation about the interference of others and all the suffering it had created for both of us," he said. She told him—he later reported—that she would have ignored all the gossip that she had heard about him " 'if you had written a single word. You asked me to wait for you but do you realize what it is for a young girl to wait for a man of your reputation who doesn't take the trouble, over such a long time, to reassure me that he meant what he said, that he *was* the man I had begun to love?' " Nela said that the essence of this quotation, too, is correct, and she added: "That was the whole thing, you see. He expected *me* to write flowing letters, but I was not raised like that. I was too proud." A thaw occurred between them that day, but Arthur was greatly alarmed when Nela told him about Münz, who had asked her to marry him: " 'He is terribly in love with me. He sends me flowers and letters. . . . I told him that I was in love with you but I admitted that I do not believe you mean to marry me.' " Arthur tried to persuade Nela that this was not so. His concert that evening was "a disaster," he said. Paola "sat placidly next to the Mullers and I could see Nela sitting next to some girl friends of hers, whispering to them, paying little attention. . . ." (Nela later denied that she had been inattentive.) The next day, he revealed to her a plan that he had formulated: He would return to Brazil and Argentina the following year, to "pile up enough money to be able to provide my future wife with a comfortable living, because . . . I was still the spendthrift of old and always lived luxuriously on the last concert I had given, so that my bank account was always nearly empty. . . . I used all the tender words I knew to tell her my love and she finally consented to wait for me."[12] Then he departed for travels in Rumania, Greece, and Egypt—with Paola Medici! (Nela recalled that after World War II, "when Arthur played in Rome he would send a car to take Paola Medici to his concerts. It was a grand gesture: he liked to see himself as a Don Juan. He was doing it more for himself than for her—to satisfy his vision of himself. She ended up working as a saleswoman in a shop, and the last time we saw her she had only one tooth. It was my revenge," Nela added, self-mockingly.)

About Arthur's statement to the effect that Nela had consented to wait for him, she later commented: "Consented, yes, but I was deeply disturbed by his visit. I wrote to Münz then that I was not ready yet, that I had seen Rubinstein and he had made such a confession, and in any case I was not finished with it. So [Münz] immediately dropped his whole tour [in the United States] and arrived [in Warsaw] a week or so later. And then nothing happened from Arthur, still! I thought, now! Now, perhaps! But no, nothing! I don't know what he was counting on: he went to Buenos Aires to make money—all of a sudden he had an idea that he had to make money, as if I was

some millionaire who needed money. I didn't need anything, I was very un-
spoiled." Once again, she did not write to him because he did not write to
her, and he did not write to her because she did not write to him.

If Odoardo Marchesini's and Luli Oswald's statements are correct,
however, Rubinstein may well have had an additional and more pressing objective in going to South America in 1928: to arrange, with Paola Medici—
who may have accompanied him on the trip—to give their young daughter to
the Marchesinis. The story is entirely plausible. If he really knew, as he
claimed, that he wanted to marry Nela, and that she had another serious
suitor, younger than himself, why did he not marry her immediately? Although he was not a vastly wealthy man in the late 1920s, his financial circumstances were better than decent, and one more South American tour,
however lucrative, would not have resolved whatever long-range economic
problems he may have had. Arthur's and Paola's need to get the child off their
hands, far from Europe, would explain his "sudden" decision, as Nela described it, to go off to South America without first having married Nela.

Whatever the truth of the matter, two great shock-waves from Warsaw
hit Rubinstein in South America in 1928. In a café in Pernambuco, Brazil, he
read in a newspaper that forty-seven-year-old Jules Wertheim had had a fatal
heart attack while conducting Wagner's *Meistersinger* Prelude during a concert with the Warsaw Philharmonic on May 6; Aleksandra, his mother, who
was seventy-one, had been listening to the concert on the radio. Rubinstein's
complicated affair with Lily Wertheim, followed by his decade-long absence
from Poland, had virtually put an end to his friendship with Jules, although
they had seen each other once, briefly, after a Rubinstein recital in Warsaw.
Wertheim had been assistant conductor of the Warsaw Philharmonic during
the 1915–16 season and a frequent guest conductor thereafter. From 1919 to
1921 he had been professor of instrumentation, conducting, and score-
reading at the State Conservatory in Warsaw, and he taught piano at the Karlowicz School of Music. But Jules died without having established himself as
an important composer, and the destruction that World War II wreaked on
Poland not many years later obliterated, physically, most of what had remained of his work as well as many of the people who had cared about it.

The other shock hit Rubinstein in Buenos Aires. One evening, when
he was not performing, he attended a concert conducted by Fitelberg, his old
friend and enemy. Backstage, Fitelberg "smiled at me," Rubinstein recalled,
"and said, 'I have news for you, Arthur: Nela Mlynarska married Mieczyslaw
Münz in Warsaw. I thought that might interest you. . . .' For a moment I
froze, but the news did not surprise me. For months I had been weighing that
possibility constantly in my mind. But it finished something in me. . . . I just
didn't care about anything. I . . . decided to return [to France] on the next

boat. . . ." If the Oswald-Marchesini story is correct, however, this declaration of Rubinstein's rings particularly hollow, and it rings slightly hollow in any case since, by his own admission, during his stay in Buenos Aires he had resumed his "old friendly relations" with the wealthy landowner's wife—the woman of the logistically difficult affair of eight years earlier. (Whether or not Paola Medici had accompanied him to Brazil on this trip, she obviously did not accompany him to Argentina.) No, the lovelorn Werther was not a role tailored to Rubinstein.

On his return to Europe he made several visits to Deauville, lost more than half a million francs gambling, and considered the money "my wedding present to Nela," he said.[13] She, however, has cautioned that his story must be taken "with a grain of salt. Because he always exaggerated, in those respects. The story sounds so dramatic—of leaving [Argentina] immediately, and he comes here [to France] and loses all his money—having a wonderful time at the same time, you know! I don't want to deny him all that he felt: he felt it, he was cross, he was furious, but he never went deeply into the reasons—that a girl like me needed a little more than just talking his head off in the living room. I was *very* young and inexperienced, and he had all the experiences possible. And I was faced with this boy [Münz] who was really very sweet, good-hearted, completely in love—he really lost his head over me."

Nela described Münz as a very fine pianist but not as daring as Rubinstein; despite his success in the United States he began to concentrate on teaching instead of developing a major career. "He had a heart of gold—he was much nicer than Arthur," she said, and she pointed out that the age gap between Münz and herself—he was her senior by eight years—was more "normal" than the 21½ years that separated her from Rubinstein. "I was so very naive then. I thought, my God, nobody is ever going to love me again like that. I cannot refuse such a love. I liked him. It wasn't like with Arthur— with Arthur my feeling was particularly strong—but I was swept with Münz's love. It's very contagious." Labunski described "a spectacular courtship, which included flowers by telegraph from New York, San Francisco, and Yokohama. . . . Some of the close and distant [Mlynarski] relatives had their objections to Nela marrying a Jew. To the immediate family this fact was of no concern: musicians on the whole do not have that absurd notion, especially in the Mlynarski household, where a Jewish boy [Kochanski] was brought up as a member of the family."[14] In order for the couple to marry, however, one or the other had to convert, and Münz was the one who did it. "I hate to speak about it," Nela said, "but he had to have himself baptized, because in those days, still, the church and the civil marriage were together—you couldn't separate them." Neither party was religious, and the problem seems not to have troubled them much at the time. They were married in August 1928, shortly after Nela's twentieth birthday; Halina Rodzinska remembered that Miecio drove his bride to the church in his big, shiny red Cadillac, but Nela said, "It's funny, some things get completely out of one's mind: I can't remember my wedding. And where did we go? Back to the Opera, where we lived. There must have been a lunch or something—nothing fancy. And I never was married in a white dress. I regret it now, because it's pretty." The young couple moved to Cincinnati, where Münz had accepted a teaching position at the Conservatory. Nela, however, soon began to feel as if she and Miecio were on a desert island together: she was accustomed to Warsaw's active cultural life, whereas her husband's nonmusical interests were limited mainly to playing bridge, she recalled. Labunski said, "On the surface Nela and Mietek were a happy couple. But not everything went well between them, and it was getting worse as the years went by."[15]

Since Rubinstein had not let his engagement get in the way of his erotic life, it is no surprise that his disappointment over the loss of Nela Mlynarska did not affect his libido. In his memoirs, he mentioned an affair with "a pretty and charming young lady" from Chile and another with "a very beautiful Polish lady";[16] he took both of them to Spain—separately. Among the affairs and one-night stands of the years 1928–32 that he did not mention, there was a love story with Juliette Achard, the beautiful young wife of the well-known playwright Marcel Achard. Rubinstein had met the couple after the premiere of Achard's *Jean de la lune*, in 1929, when the writer was thirty, and the affair with Juliette probably began soon thereafter. Rubinstein told friends that Marcel had affairs with many other women, and it is not impossible that the writer knew of and accepted Juliette's affair with one of Paris's favorite pianists.

In the fall of 1931, Rubinstein was in Warsaw for a concert; he stayed at Ordynski's, as usual, and the host gave a party in his honor. Halina Lilpop, who was present, wrote, forty-five years later:

> I went . . . in the company of my neighbors and Rubinstein's friends, the Meyers. . . . When Rubinstein entered, there was a respectful hush, a parting of people like the waters of the Red Sea, then applause. . . . In moments he made his way to where the Meyers and I stood, and we met for the first time. . . . By the end of the evening he asked me to join him the next night for dinner and dancing at a Warsaw nightclub, Oaza (the Oasis), along with the actress Marysia Modzelewska and our host, Ordynski. . . .
>
> The four of us enjoyed ourselves and each other's company that night. As anyone who has ever known Rubinstein in the role of a host will attest, he picked a superb menu and the best wines to go

with it. After we finished dining, Artur invited me to dance. On the dance floor, where our feet slid through the aimless steps of a fox-trot, he announced that he had had "enough of the single life."

"And so?" I asked.

"And so I am looking for a wife, a Polish girl. The French, the Spanish, the Italians—they are all fickle. I want one heart, a faithful, loyal, Polish heart," he concluded.

Dimly, faintly, a conversation hoarded away in a back cupboard of memory echoed in my ears.

"I do know of a beautiful girl. She used to be very much in love with you."

"Could I have missed one? Who?"

"Nela Mlynarska."

"Ah. But she is married to Münz and is in America."

"Wrong," I came back at him. "She is divorcing Münz. . . ."

Artur's pleasure was reflected in that electric and compelling smile of his.[17]

(Although the Münzes had already parted company, divorce procedures had not yet been initiated.)

During the same stay in Warsaw, at the end of October or in November, Arthur saw Nela at a concert at the Filharmonja, at which he heard the cellist Gregor Piatigorsky ("the best . . . since Casals," Rubinstein said) for the first time. After the concert, Arthur and Nela went to the Adria dance hall, where they met Halina Lilpop and Ordynski. Rubinstein said that as he and Nela danced, "she asked me half seriously, half jokingly, 'Well, would you marry me now?' I answered in the same tone, 'Certainly, you should know that.' From that moment on . . . we began a serious flirtation. I took her home. . . . Before she left me, we kissed for the first time."[18] Back in Paris, after he had concluded his fall tour, Arthur received a postcard from Nela. She was in Zakopane, and she invited him to join her and her sister Alina there for New Year's Eve. He made the long journey, only to discover on the morning after his arrival that Nela had plans to spend the day (December 31) skiing with friends. Thus began a holiday full of bickering, pouting, and mutual recriminations. According to Rubinstein, he ordered a bottle of expensive champagne for their first dinner together and Nela refused to drink it. While she was out skiing, he passed his time with "a very good-looking lady with beautiful dark hair" who was a Rubinstein fan and happened to be staying in the room next to his at the pension; the dark-haired lady stared at him throughout the New Year's Eve festivities and Nela resented it. He tried to learn to ski and Nela laughed at him; he decided to prove his ability by skiing down the same steep hill that she and her party had just descended, and he almost killed himself in the attempt. ("When I reached the bottom my vertiginous speed did not allow me to put on the brakes, so my whole body shot into the air. My head and half of my trunk were buried in the snow with my legs sticking out. . . . When my face emerged it was covered with blood. . . . [but only because] the impact had burst the skin. Everybody took great care of me. . . .")[19]

According to Nela, however, there is "a lot of crookedness" in Arthur's version of the story. "Of course, when I look at it now, from his point of view, maybe it looked different. The fact is that he came there to be with me, but I had already my arrangements. My beloved brother, Feliks, had TB and had to live in Zakopane," which is in a mountain valley. "And his life was saved"—albeit temporarily—"by a wonderful Dr. Sokolowski. . . . He was a very busy doctor, the head of [Zakopane's] big sanatorium, and before Arthur came I had arranged to go skiing with him; I had to keep that pledge. Arthur could not get it through his head: nothing was as important as him! So when I said that I am going to go with the doctor, Arthur absolutely resented that. He tried to get revenge—I think he immediately tried to sleep with some woman who was there in that same pension. He says that he flirted with her, and flirting means right away more, probably; and I must say that after everything that had happened, I didn't yet feel I could trust him all the way. [His version of] the Zakopane story was a little confused because he was getting back at me, because I went on that ski outing. So he immediately learned to ski in one day, and nearly broke his neck. I never was so scared in my life—I saw him shooting down, his head pointing down under the snow. Ach, he was a character! Always there was the vindictive side along with the loving side. He was fantastically suspicious of everything. He hardly ever took anything at face value, and always liked to look for a hidden motive. That tired me so much! Because I was not like that—I was much more straightforward. It was very difficult. And sometimes, late in life, it became even quite complicated.

"It was very difficult to get back to where we had been," Nela Rubinstein continued, referring to her three-year estrangement from Arthur. "I had sometimes a little sharp quality, and I had my pride, always present. It was not simple, and I was still married. But then we discussed that I was going to divorce. Münz's father was a dear old lawyer who arranged it all painlessly. . . . I had to change religion in order to get a divorce, because Catholics couldn't. I think I am a Lutheran—which I like very much, by the way. But that is not a very pretty page, because I did it strictly to get the divorce. . . . When I left Münz, he never quite knew what had hit him, but he wrote me a long, wonderful letter, thanking me for the most wonderful years of his life." Rubin-

stein said, "Münz behaved in the most noble way; in spite of the deep unhappiness he felt about losing [Nela], he did all in his power to give her her
freedom."[20] Nearly five decades later, he said that he believed that Nela had
left Münz because Münz had lost his money in the wake of the 1929 stock
market crash. Münz, however, would not have behaved as nobly as he did
toward his wife had she abandoned him for such a reason, and Rubinstein
would have been exceedingly stupid to have married a woman whom he believed had acted in such a way.

EARLY IN THE new year, 1932, Nela went to Dresden to study with the
Hanover-born dancer and choreographer Mary Wigman, a pioneer in the
modern dance movement in Europe, and Arthur set off on a tour that took
him to Turkey, Greece, and Egypt. In Cairo, just before he was to give a
concert, he received a telegram from Nela. According to his statement in *My
Many Years*, it read: " 'Am ill in the hospital [she gave the name and address],
please send urgently some money, Nela.' "[21] He played the concert, then he
wired the money and departed for Dresden. But he told Annabelle Whitestone that the telegram had begun with the words, "You have infected me."
Whitestone said, "He felt terribly guilty and responsible. He thought that
maybe it was some ghastly venereal disease, and he really felt like committing
suicide. He thought, 'My goodness, this young girl—what have I done to
her?' So he went to Dresden, to the hospital, and found out that Nela was
home again. He found her perfectly fine. She said, 'I was afraid of some
dreadful symptoms,' which turned out to be nothing at all." In his memoirs,
he ended the tale by saying merely that "we feasted the good news with a
warm embrace and right away made plans for the evening,"[22] but Ms. Whitestone said that he held this incident against Nela for the rest of his life. "He
said, 'Any woman who loved me would never have sent me that kind of telegram. How could she accuse me like that and make me feel guilty?' This was
something they used to argue and scream at each other about till the last
days. She'd say, 'Well what did you expect me to do? I thought that that was
what it was.' "[23]

Back and forth go the accusations. Arthur recalled having attended a
performance of *Parsifal* with Nela while they were both in Dresden but having to leave during the second act because "the fat German flower girls who
tried to seduce poor Parsifal made us laugh,"[24] whereas Nela said, indignantly, "When I was young I went six times and *stood* to hear *Parsifal*, but
when I went with him, he was so impatient that after two hours we left."
Arthur said that he "received a cold handshake"[25] from Mrs. Mlynarska when
he and Nela told her parents that they were going to be married, but Nela
said that it was "not a cold handshake. My mother was shy—and then that

ogre, that Don Juan, with her beloved little daughter all of a sudden. . . . And don't forget, after the things that had happened in Warsaw—my mother was aware of all his doings there. She did actually exclaim 'That's all we need!' when she heard I was going to marry Arthur. But Father was never against it because he respected Arthur, he admired his talent tremendously, and he knew that I was not just a little girl, that I needed something else, and it was just fine. He had no misgivings about it." Later, when Nela and Arthur were traveling to Prague and the train stopped at Plzen, he wolfed down sausages at a stand next to the railroad tracks until he "saw Nela's face at the window showing stern disapproval," he said. "I quickly dropped the third pair back on the stand like a boy caught in a little mischief. An ominous sign of my marriage!"[26] Nela commented, "That's not fair! It's a remark just for the sake of making a remark. He ate what he wanted; I might have shaken a finger and smiled, in a nice way, but not seriously."

From mid-April through the first five days of May 1932, Nela accompanied Arthur on a tour that took him to Rome, Palermo, and even Tunis; she then had to leave him, but they arranged to meet in Spain, where he was to play a series of concerts later that month. When she arrived in Barcelona, he was waiting for her with flowers, he said, but she told him immediately that she had a terrible toothache and—horror of horrors—she even showed him the bad tooth. "This Arthur never forgot," Whitestone said. "It was something he used to go back to time and time again—how they were supposed to be meeting, romantically, in Barcelona, and all that she could think of was finding a dentist. Then he wanted to show her the dawn over Granada," as they approached the town in a chauffeur-driven car that he had hired, "but she was fast asleep—too tired. They fought over stupid little things like this. Even before they were married, they had an incredible talent for hitting each other's raw nerves."[27] But Nela wanted to correct this story "because it makes me so mad. . . . They had started root-canal work on me [in Warsaw], and they said, 'When you get to Barcelona you have to see a dentist about finishing it.' Well, he said he met me with roses and things in his arms, and I arrived and I didn't even kiss him, but just said: 'Where is a dentist here?' or something like that. . . . But of course I fell into his arms and I kissed him. But probably he asked me, because he knew that the tooth was in that terrible state. He might also have said that I was suffering—but that didn't count. His version hurt me, because I know it was not so. I was so happy! And to have twisted it so, making it look as if I was only occupied with myself, ignoring his poetic flowers. I ignored nothing; I saw everything and appreciated it." Despite the bad start, most of Nela's first visit to Spain was pleasant, and more than half a century later she wrote: "On the same day that I met Arthur I learned from him to love

Spain—because of the enthusiasm with which he spoke to me of its beauty, of the variety of its countryside, of the humanity of its people, of the Spanish public that demonstrated real love for him. . . . I was able to see for myself that during his concerts an extraordinary electric current was created between Arthur and the audience, and the enthusiasm followed him out onto the street."[28] She also remembered, about that trip, that Arthur "was a wonderful guide, he always showed everything that he had seen himself and liked."

From Spain, Nela went to Vilna to obtain her divorce papers. She had given up her studies with Mary Wigman, partly because of her forthcoming marriage and partly because of the deteriorating political situation in Germany. From Vilna she proceeded via Warsaw to Paris, where she and Arthur were to get married. He, meanwhile, had stopped briefly in Paris, had then gone to London to make some records, and had returned to Paris, where Jacqueline de Rothschild—the daughter of Baron Edouard and Baroness Germaine de Rothschild—saw him before Nela's arrival.

> One day Artur Rubinstein, who was a close friend of my mother's when I was young, came to visit at the studio. I had never considered him any other way than as a friend of my mother's. From time to time he spoke to me, but he was intensely concentrated on himself. . . .
>
> Rubinstein and I had tea, and sat talking. I confessed how poorly my [first] marriage was working out.
>
> "Is there someone else?" Rubinstein asked.
>
> "Yes, I do love someone else, but it is crazy." He was quiet. I continued, "He happens to be a musician, but he is very much older than I. . . ." Silence. "I think you know him."
>
> He perked up; his expression showed some interest. Then, changing the subject, he spoke about his concerts, his successes, his glory.
>
> I came back to my problem. "You know him," I repeated. "Maybe you have guessed who he is?"
>
> "No, I haven't," he said, and he got up as if ready to leave.
>
> "I'm sure you know," I insisted as I followed him to the door.
>
> "No, really." He turned, looked at me, his bulging eyes seeming to say, "Tell me." He repeated, "No," with a slight hesitation.
>
> Finally I said, "Alfred Cortot."
>
> His expression shrank, as if he had been slapped in the face. He said good-bye nicely. Shortly after, I heard that he married a young Polish woman, Nela. . . . The possibility of considering him other than my mother's friend would never have entered my head. Con-

versely, the possibility of someone not being in love with him would never have entered *his* head. What a misunderstanding![29]

Arthur and Nela were reunited in Paris; he put her up at the Hotel Scribe, but she was usually with him in Rue Ravignan, where he introduced her to many of his friends. (Nearly thirty years later, Arthur and Nela visited the house with their two younger children and Joseph Roddy, a writer who was working on a story about the pianist for *Look* magazine. Roddy later recalled, in a letter to Rubinstein: "Bolted to the door was a knocker you knew well, and Mrs. Rubinstein was particularly delighted to find it still there after so many years. She pointed out to the children that she had given it to you before you were married because a lot of Montmartre sports kept walking in on the two of you without stopping to knock. 'All of them piano tuners, my dears,' you assured your son and daughter." With his letter, Roddy sent Rubinstein the knocker, which he had managed to buy from the house's proprietor and ship back to New York. Rubinstein was tickled to have it. "I think it was a deed of a great gentleman and also of a man with a sense of humor," he wrote. "I shall keep this knocker as a relic of one of the best times of my life. . . .")[30] Among their visitors were the Achards and the Kochanskis. Nela remembered, "Paul loved Arthur so much that he said to me, 'Promise me that you're not going to hurt him.' And I didn't hurt him. I took it as a sacred oath."

Arthur and Nela discovered that, under French law, obtaining a marriage license required a longer residence period than they were prepared to wait. Instead, they decided to go to England, where a two-week stay was sufficient. In London, Rubinstein said, "My friends opened their warm and generous hearts to Nela in that true English way." Lady Cholmondeley offered to give the wedding reception, and Lesley Jowitt, his former lover, "helped Nela in every way, just as a mother would have done." She gave Arthur an antique gold watch chain as a present. Christabel McLaren gave him an autographed letter of Chopin's, and Sylvia Sparrow—who had married a Mr. Caunter—made them what Rubinstein described as "a regal present" of "two whole nights" of "all the chamber music we loved best."[31] The participants were Jacques Thibaud, Lionel Tertis, Felix Salmond, and, of course, the hostess and the groom. During the week prior to the wedding, Rubinstein recorded Chopin's Berceuse and two mazurkas (Op. 63, No. 1, and Op. 33, No. 2) for HMV; all three discs were approved and released.

The wedding took place on July 27, 1932, three days before Nela's twenty-fourth birthday; Arthur was forty-five and a half, minus one day. In his memoirs, he described going to Aspreys' early in the morning to pick up the wedding rings, then dressing in his "elegant cutaway . . . , top hat, [and] white gloves," and taking Nela's brother Bronislaw—whom Rubinstein had brought over from Poland to be best man—"to lunch at Quaglino's restaurant in Bury Street." (In those years, Rubinstein used to stay at Georgian House in Bury Street when he visited London.) "I was suddenly panic-stricken at the thought of losing my freedom," he said. But he and Bronislaw went to the registry office to meet Nela, who showed up a little late: "I was so nervous that I had forgotten to go to the hairdresser and had had to use curling irons," she said. "Arthur and Nela, his 23 year old bride, were married on Wednesday at a Registry Office, and had a lovely reception later at Lady Cholmondeley's," Ruth Draper wrote to a friend. "I saw a lot of them the days before and shopped and helped her pack, and was quite helpful! She is a sweet little thing, frail and flowerlike, very young (tho' already divorced), and loveable. . . . He's very serious, and really seems to want marriage and children. I was so happy to be there—only the [Polish] Ambassador—the girl's brother, two other old friends [including Lesley Jowitt] and I were present at the ceremony—which is, by the way, very nice—so swift and simple. . . . We had wonderful music two nights running, before—at an old friend's studio— and it took me back to Edith Grove days."[32] After the ceremony, the newly-weds went to Lesley's "for a rest and a glass of champagne," Rubinstein recalled, thence to Lady Cholmondeley's reception, which included "all the available ambassadors and their wives . . . , many members of the British government, . . . famous musicians, writers, actors, and painters." ("There were so many important people, and all on first-name terms," Nela remembered.) Unfortunately, Paul and Zosia Kochanski were not there, and Rubinstein believed that Zosia "was responsible. It might have been a belated revenge for my refusal to be at her wedding," twenty years earlier; "but I did not miss her, I only missed him."[33]

Rubinstein then gave a dinner at Quaglino's, "where I was really drunk for the first and last time of my life," he recalled.[34] (Nela said that Arthur was drunk even before the dinner, because he and her brother had been sipping champagne for hours.) But he chose not to mention in his memoirs that he abandoned the dinner "to go see one of his ex-loves," Nela recalled. "To this day I haven't forgiven him that. He went to console her, because she was so desperate that he was getting married. He always wanted to be extremely elegant with his 'exes.' He thought that this was more important than being with me, and he left me in the middle of London on our wedding day—yes sir!" The woman was Irene, Lady Ravensdale, Lord Curzon's thirty-six-year-old daughter, whom Rubinstein had first seen during World War I, and with whom he had later had an affair. (Nicholas Mosley, the novelist and biographer, who inherited the title of Lord Ravensdale through his aunt, Irene, wrote to this author, in a letter dated February 27, 1995, that although he had seen no written evidence to demonstrate that Rubinstein and Lady Ravensdale had been lovers, he knew that they were close friends and assumed that they had also been lovers. He described his aunt as a warmhearted person who would have been generous to anyone she loved.) "I remember her very well," Nela continued; "she was biggish—handsome but sort of manly." Rubinstein did not tell his wife but eventually confessed to others that "he slept with his ex-girl friend" that afternoon, "and the reason he did it was to prove to himself that he wasn't trapped by his marriage," Eva Rubinstein said.[35]

"Arthur has never been so nice," Ruth Draper said, in a letter written two days after the Rubinstein wedding. "It's brought out all his sweetness and I really think the chances are—at least—even!"[36]

AT THE AGE of eighty-eight, Rubinstein told an interviewer: "She [Nela] is very much younger than I—21 years. When I married her, I was afraid of that, I knew very well it was all right when I was 45 and very strong. But when I would be 75 and she would only be 50-something, it would make a great difference. So we talked about it and we made a lovely plan, like Russia's five-year-plan. We said we would take five years at a time. Laughingly, of course.... I was always shy of being seen by my wife in an ugly way. I comb my hair while she is still asleep so she will never see me disheveled."[37] A few years later still, he set down his ideas on love and marriage a little more extensively. "My long experience with women proved to me that a lover has the advantage [over a husband]; he shows himself to the object of his love in the best light and only at moments chosen by himself. He need stay with her neither too long nor too little; his courtship can remain fresh, he sends her flowers at the right time. He succeeds by being discreet, and, whenever the right moment comes, passionate.

"Now look at the fate of a husband. He is always around even if she wants to see less of him. Or else he is never home when she needs him most. Perhaps he snores at night, or looks tired and disheveled in the morning, or has bad bathroom manners. He has to share with her her worries, make her share his own; they have to discuss money matters, the cost of living, children, servants, etc. I see love life and married life in this way."[38] One can hardly help wondering whether Rubinstein noticed how remarkably selfish these words seem: "he shows himself . . . moments chosen by himself . . . He need stay . . . his courtship . . . he sends her flowers . . . He succeeds . . ." Is this the impression that he really intended to convey? Can one calculate "the right moment" at which to be passionate? Is a person in love capable of thinking about maintaining his or her control over the situation? Should long-term partners resent the sharing of life's difficulties with each other? That

Rubinstein considered love affairs more attractive than marriage is not the issue; the issue is whether, as he implied, the most important aspect of a love relationship—be it a short, madly intense affair, a long, steady partnership, or anything in between—is the superficial impression that one partner makes on the other, rather than what each of them feels toward and thinks of the other. If Rubinstein's statement truly represented his thoughts and feelings on these subjects, one can only assume that the need to be in control must have made an entire sector of his emotional life terribly opaque. On the other hand, the musical-emotional sector of his life was exceptionally rich; when he made music he was probably capable of letting his guard down to a degree that few people can even imagine.

And yet, despite what seems, today, to have been a fundamentally muddled attitude toward marriage, Rubinstein adjusted to his new condition as well as it is possible for a traveling virtuoso to do, and especially a traveling virtuoso who has spent forty-five years as a bachelor. As he did not want to hurt Nela, he carried out his philandering surreptitiously. He was delighted that his friends found Nela charming, and his friends were as delighted as he that she quickly developed into an outstanding cook. "Being a famous 'gourmet,' " Nela wrote of Arthur, in the introduction to a cookbook that she published after his death, "he knew the best restaurants all over the world. Then I discovered that I had an odd but very useful talent: much as one might have a musical ear, I had the ability to decipher and identify the ingredients in even fairly elaborate dishes—and made a sort of game (and challenge!) of reproducing them at home without asking for recipes. Succeeding was great fun and gave me confidence to add or change or improvise, and finally to invent!"[39] The Rubinsteins were soon entertaining frequently, and Nela's cooking was the mainstay of their parties' successes.

At the same time, Arthur's career was again expanding: he played in Holland, Scandinavia, Switzerland, and other countries in which he had not previously been heard, and later in the fall of 1932 he went to Russia and the Ukraine to give his first performances in what had become the Soviet Union. He and Nela found the country dingy, depressing, and frightening, but the concerts in Moscow, Leningrad, Odessa, Kiev, and Kharkov were a great success. Rubinstein's Odessa concert was attended by the seventeen-year-old Svyatoslav Richter, who told him, many years later, that the event had convinced him to pursue a career as a musician; he had previously been undecided. In the same city, the sixteen-year-old Emil Gilels played for Rubinstein, who was so impressed that he recommended the youngster to his old friend Harry (Heinrich) Neuhaus, who was the leading piano teacher at the Moscow Conservatory. Neuhaus later accepted Gilels as an advanced pupil.

In London earlier that season, Rubinstein had recorded the four Chopin scherzos. His popularity as a recording artist was growing, but for some reason the Gramophone Company's directors "decided not to exercise our option but to record with this artiste without a contract on a royalty basis only in future," according to an interdepartmental memorandum written at the end of October. Rubinstein, possibly acting on the advice of E. A. Michell, his British manager, may have opted for an item-by-item agreement rather than an annual contract, in the hope of keeping the company on its collective toes, but not later than 1934 he was again recording by annual contract. Throughout the decade he received a 10 percent royalty with no advance on his solo and concerto recordings, and a 5 percent royalty on his chamber music recordings; this part of the arrangement was satisfactory, but Rubinstein felt that his records were not given adequate publicity. "I wish you would indulge in a little special press advertising for Rubinstein," Michell wrote to Gaisberg early in 1933. "You gave our friend Schnabel a wonderful show: cannot Rubinstein have the same in his turn for the Tschaikowsky Concerto?" Gaisberg replied, "You make a mistake about the colossal advertising given to Schnabel. This kind of thing multiplies itself, and for the most part it was given gratis by various critics and music writers. We assure you that our special advertising of Schnabel has been the very minimum. In any case, Rubinstein has been very well treated, and our English Company have made frequent issues of his records in their supplements, and given him important positions. Also the titles he has recorded are among the most popular in piano literature. Rubinstein is a particular favourite of ours, and we would not see him neglected." (Three months later, Michell informed Gaisberg that Rubinstein had "fixed up a world contract with de Koos of Holland, who has seen fit to transfer the English concert business to [Wilfrid] Van Wyck," but Michell continued to deal with the Gramophone business.)[40]

When the Rubinsteins returned to Paris from the Soviet Union, Nela knew that she was pregnant; the baby had been conceived in Moscow on the day of the big military parade in honor of the fifteenth anniversary of the Bolshevik revolution, she said. The birth was predicted for the end of August 1933—just after the Rubinsteins were due back in Europe after a South American tour, for which they departed early in April. Arthur enjoyed showing Nela the points of interest in Brazil and Argentina, just as he had enjoyed showing them to Paola Medici a few years earlier. In Buenos Aires, however, Nela realized that a trip back to Europe during the last weeks of pregnancy would be too much of a strain for her. They decided to stay on in the Argentine capital; Arthur gave extra concerts, and Nela gave birth—to a baby girl, on August 18. The following evening, Rubinstein attended a performance of *Die Meistersinger* at the Teatro Colón, after which he and his wife decided to name their daughter Eva (originally Ewa, in Polish), after the opera's female protagonist. In retrospect, it seems odd that a Jew chose to name his little girl after a Wagnerian heroine seven months after Hitler's assumption of power in Germany, but at the time few people would have made a mental connection between Wagner and active persecution of the Jews. Besides, Eva is the only entirely human and lovable heroine in all of Wagner's operas, and the name comes from the Hebrew *Chavah*—"she who gives life."

In reminiscing about his first thoughts of marriage, Rubinstein told an interviewer in the 1960s, "I began to dream of having a wife and daughter of my own."[41] Later, when he wrote his memoirs, he recalled having told Nela at the time of his first proposal of marriage to her: " 'you are the only woman in the whole wide world with whom I would like to have a daughter.' "[42] And in commenting on Nela's announcement that she was pregnant, he said: "Ever since adolescence I had felt a deep desire to have a daughter, as I have in my nature a passion for women. A daughter is your own daughter, even if she hates you, and this very fact of *belonging* calms a possessive mind."[43] In retrospect, Nela said: "He thought that a daughter was going to be his property. It's not going to be just any child. This is a woman that he's going to own, because all the others were just temporary. The possessiveness! It was tremendously egocentric! Arthur should really have been put on a psychiatrist's couch to tell." His attitude does seem to have been derived from a manual for amateur psychologists: A son is a rival for the mother's affection; a daughter gives her affection to the father. A son would assert his independence, Rubinstein thought, whereas a daughter would in some way devote herself to her father until his dying day.

Paul and Zosia Kochanski were among the first friends to see little Eva in September, when the Rubinsteins returned to Paris. Paul, who had recently helped Szymanowski to complete his Second Violin Concerto and had then played the premiere, was dying of cancer, and Rubinstein was shocked by his wasted appearance. "Paul gave Eva a long sad look, took my hand, and we both had tears in our eyes," Rubinstein recalled. "They left the next day for New York and that was the last time I saw him." Kochanski died on January 12, 1934, at the age of forty-six. A nonreligious funeral, held at the Juilliard School—whose violin faculty Paul had headed for several years— was attended by fifteen hundred people; the pallbearers included Toscanini, Frank and Walter Damrosch, Heifetz, Horowitz, Fritz Kreisler, Koussevitzky, Stokowski, and Efrem Zimbalist. When Szymanowski's concerto was published, it bore the dedication: "In memory of the great musician, my dear and unforgettable friend Paul Kochanski." And forty-five years after Kochanski's death, Rubinstein wrote, "I have had to survive all these long years since deprived of a friend I could never replace."[44]

In February 1934 Rubinstein was in London to play Rachmaninoff's Second Concerto with the London Symphony under Sir Hamilton Harty and to record short pieces by Ravel, Liszt, Scriabin, Chopin, and Albéniz. At another London engagement that season, Lionel Tertis and Rubinstein played Arthur Bliss's recently completed Sonata for Viola and Piano. "Rubinstein only had the score a day or so before the concert, but despite that he gave an electrifyingly assured performance," the composer reported. "It is a wonderful moment for a composer when he hears his music given a deeper significance than he himself thought it could bear, and then, with two superlative players there is the certainty that for each and every section the right tempo will be found. I have come to the conclusion that I do not so much mind wrong notes or a disregard of dynamics provided the basic tempo is right. I have heard performances of this Sonata that have taken fully three minutes too long."[45]

In addition to the usual western European venues, Rubinstein's concert schedule in the spring of 1934 included Turkey, Syria, Palestine, Greece, and Egypt, as well as return engagements in Moscow and Leningrad. In the Soviet capital—where he gave a concert that included works of Chopin, Liszt, Poulenc, Ravel, and the anti-Communist exile Stravinsky—Rubinstein bumped into Artur Rodzinski, and together they attended a performance of young Dmitri Shostakovich's opera *Lady Macbeth of the Mtsensk District,* which had had its premiere in Leningrad only four months earlier. Both Polish musicians were enthusiastic about the work, and the pianist used his connections and his fluency in Russian to help the conductor secure for the Cleveland Orchestra—of which Rodzinski was musical director—the right to give the first performances outside the USSR; these took place in Cleveland the following January. On his way back to Paris, Rubinstein stopped in Warsaw to collect Nela, Eva, and Karola, Eva's Polish nursemaid; all three had been staying with the Mlynarski family. No sooner had they returned to Rue Ravignan than Nela discovered that she was pregnant again.

Rubinstein's attitude toward practicing the piano had changed dramatically during the summer of 1934, he said. "I didn't want my kids to grow up thinking of their father as either a second-string pianist or a has-been," he told an interviewer in 1958. "So . . . I bundled my wife and baby into a small Citroën and we drove up to Saint-Nicolas-de-Véroce, a tiny village in the Haute-Savoie . . . where we stayed in a modest *pension de famille.* I rented the only piano in the community—an old upright—and moved it into an empty, windowless garage just below our room. That became my studio. It had no electric light, so I put a candle on top of the piano, and then I buckled down to work—six hours, eight hours, nine hours a day. And a strange thing happened. By the time we returned to

Paris, after spending the whole summer in that village, I'd begun to discover new meanings, new qualities, new possibilities in music that I'd been playing regularly for more than thirty years."[46] This version of the story differs in a few details from the version that Rubinstein gave in *My Many Years*, in which the garage was a barn, the single candle became four candles, the practicing took place not by day but by night, and the piano was not rented but rather borrowed from the Polish composer Michel Kondracki, whose mother-in-law ran the pension. In essence, however, the story was the same. "I felt suddenly an intense physical pleasure when I succeeded in playing the étude in thirds by Chopin in a clear decent way without pedal and without getting too tired," he said. "I repeated endlessly an unimportant passage simply to gain more respect and confidence in my poor left hand, feeling the fourth finger becoming alive and independent."[47]

In later years, Rubinstein often exaggerated the extent of his dilatoriness before 1934: one need only listen to his 1928 recording of the Chopin Barcarolle to realize that his technique was already superb, despite his admirable refusal to make it his primary concern. His internal insecurity, born when he had fled from Barth's tutelage, was probably what made him speak deprecatingly about his technique and what made him balk at some of the Chopin études, Rachmaninoff's Third Concerto, and many other virtuoso pieces. He simply couldn't convince himself that his mastery of the keyboard was up to tasks of that sort. As to the change in Rubinstein's attitude, Labunski may have been on the right track when he said that once his brother-in-law had married, he "abandoned excessive preoccupation with social affairs, concentrated within himself, and fully devoted himself to self-improvement." It was not a matter of irresponsible playing suddenly becoming responsible playing; it was a matter of a somewhat calmer way of life making greater concentration possible. "The change in his performances was spectacular," Labunski recalled in the 1960s: "in place of an enormously gifted, promising young artist, he became the great master . . . he is now, grew in depth and in precision. . . . The astonishing thing about it was that he never stopped growing, and these days each new performance is a revelation."[48]

During the 1934–35 season Rubinstein recorded all of the Chopin polonaises in London. He told Labunski "what a terrific job it was to make all these recordings in the course of just a few days. 'And some of the Polonaises,' he said, 'I had never played in my life. For example, this Andante Spianato and Polonaise—I spent a whole three hours learning it.' Three hours!"[49] One of the polonaises—the F-sharp Minor, Op. 44—was recorded on January 29, 1935, the day on which Rubinstein's first son was born in Warsaw, where Nela was staying with her parents; although Rubinstein played some wrong notes, he approved the record for release because he felt it was an exceptionally good performance, overall, and "because it was fun for my son to know what his father was doing while he was born."[50] By making complicated flight arrangements, Rubinstein, who was in mid-tour, managed to stop in Warsaw three days later, to see his little boy. The baby was given the name Paul, after Kochanski.

In mid-February, Arthur and Nela said good-bye to both of their children and began a long Oriental tour, most of which had been organized by A. Strok, the leading sponsor of Western artists' relatively rare appearances in the East. "Seventeen days after Paul was born, I left that baby," Nela Rubinstein recalled. "I had no choice, because Arthur was not somebody you could let go for six months. It was very hard, it was the hardest thing to do. To part with a newborn baby is a terrible thing to do, for a woman. We could not communicate: there were only telegrams, no telephones. It was a tremendous distance, and it lasted six months." The tour began with concerts in Moscow and Leningrad, after which Arthur and Nela spent eight days and nights in a filthy, bug-infested car on the Trans-Siberian railroad, which took them to Japanese-occupied Manchuria. They continued by train via Harbin to Seoul, Korea—which had also been occupied by Japan—and onward to the port of Pusan, where they boarded a boat that crossed the Strait of Korea to Shimonoseki, Japan. Another long train ride brought them to Tokyo, where Rubinstein gave concerts with orchestra and solo recitals. He also performed in Osaka, Nagoya, Kobe, and Kyoto. As usual, he was an intrepid sightseer everywhere he went, although he found the Shinto temples, geisha "waitresses," Kabuki theater, tea ceremony, and other manifestations of Japanese culture incomprehensible and often boring. His concerts were a success, but a telegram from Warsaw left Arthur upset and Nela grieving: Emil Mlynarski had died on April 5, at the age of sixty-four, after years of suffering from an acute form of arthritis that had forced him to give up first the directorship of the Warsaw Opera and then a professorship at the Curtis Institute of Music in Philadelphia. But Rubinstein's tour proceeded.

He remembered having gone from Japan to Shanghai, China, by boat, and then by train to Tientsin and Beijing. In each city he was disappointed to discover that the vast majority of his audience was Caucasian, but in Beijing he was pleased to reencounter the American composer John Alden Carpenter, with whom he had become acquainted in Chicago, and the French diplomat and writer Henri Hoppenot, whom he had met with Milhaud and Claudel in Rio seventeen years earlier. Cecil B. Lyon, then third secretary of the American legation in the Chinese capital, recalled more than half a century later that Rubinstein had been unhappy with the piano that had been provided for him and had asked to borrow the Blüthner grand that belonged to

Lyon's wife, Elsie, who was the daughter of Joseph Grew, the United States' ambassador to Japan. In later years, when the Rubinsteins met the Lyons elsewhere around the world, the pianist "would give a dramatic, much exaggerated account of the Blüthner being transported by dozens of coolies, slipping and stumbling in the snow, from our house to the Peking Hotel," Lyon said.[51]

By Rubinstein's account, he and Nela went directly from Beijing to Singapore, but it is known that they went at least as far north as Mukden, in the Japanese-annexed sector of China. From that city's Yamato Hotel, on May 2, Rubinstein wrote a letter to Gaisberg:

> I received the new one-year agreement of the Gramophone Company for the year 1935–36 which I duly signed and hereby send to you—as to the option for a further year which the Company wants me to sign, I am not yet decided, as really I am not satisfied with the advertisement done for my records! There has never been any newspaper line on them, and no envelop [sic] of any record has my picture, while many quite unknown artists are widely propagated in this in that [sic] way! Here in Japan all of my records have been sold out after the first 2 concerts, without one word of advertisement, so you can easily imagine how the sale would be raised in many countries with a slight effort on your behalf!
>
> Dear Mr. Gaisberg, this is not a personal grievance against you, as I know you to be a good friend—but you must bring this to the knowledge of those concerned—because I am rather warmly approached by another Company, who is disposed to make a big effort. . . .
>
> Japan has been a great triumph![52]

In replying, Gaisberg expressed delight over "your great success" and regret because "you are not satisfied with the amount of publicity given to your records in the East . . . as you are personally on the spot, we would advise you to call on our representatives wherever it is possible. . . . Of course, we have taken up the matter ourselves by correspondence, but I feel that a personal visit from you will be much more effective. Your recent record of the 'Toccata' (Bach-Busoni) has been very well received—it is a wonderful record. . . . I am enclosing one of our recent record envelopes, which reproduces your photograph." Two weeks later, Gaisberg elaborated on his earlier answer. The Victor Talking Machine Company, which represented the Gramophone Company in Japan, "inform us that as soon as your tour was announced they approached your impresario, Mr. A. Strok, in order to arrange an effective co-operative publicity campaign," he said. "Victor offered to undertake joint newspaper advertising, to print all the concert programmes and to arrange a reception for you as soon as you arrived. Mr. Strok insisted that a toilet company should participate in the joint newspaper advertising and the Victor Co. did not consider this to be compatible either with your position or with their standing in Japan. In addition Mr. Strok demanded that he should receive 200 Yen for the privilege of distributing the programmes at the concerts. This they would not agree to as, while willing to co-operate, they did not see why they should contribute towards an impresario's legitimate expenses. Apparently Victor have had a similar experience with Mr. Strok when other foreign artistes have visited Japan. Nevertheless, Victor claim that they advertised your records in the concert programmes and in all the leading Japanese daily newspapers on the days of your concerts, but as the advertising was done in Japanese they think that possibly this escaped your attention. Samples are enclosed of the advertising that was undertaken."[53] Rubinstein continued to record for the Gramophone Company until the war.

The Rubinsteins took a boat to Singapore, where the most enthusiastic member of the audience at Arthur's concert was Noël Coward, who knew him from London. The next day Arthur and Nela embarked for Batavia (now Jakarta) on the island of Java; the Kunstkring (Arts Club) of the Dutch East Indies (now Indonesia) had set up some twenty concerts for him in Batavia, Bandung, Surabaya, Malang, and other towns. Once, during a lull in their wanderings, he and Nela were playing cards, "and he was losing and losing and losing, and making fun of it," Nela said. "But he lost one time too many, and all of a sudden he threw the table over. The cards went on the floor, and he banged the door and left. Like a child. I laughed so hard that he burst out laughing, too." They also managed to squeeze in a three-day sightseeing tour of Bali before they embarked for Hong Kong, en route to the Philippine Islands. During the Rubinsteins' Hong Kong stopover, Arthur was induced by a hotel manager—a Russian—to give a concert that had not been part of his schedule; the heat and humidity in the hotel's ballroom, where he played, were so oppressive that he passed out afterward, but the event brought him "a good pile of English pounds."[54] Another steamer took the couple to Manila, where Arthur was much fêted by the Spanish-speaking community. Before leaving the Philippines he also played in the town of Iloilo on the island of Panay. After having survived a variety of discomforts, including a typhoon at sea, the Rubinsteins arrived back in Hong Kong; the Russian hotel manager had arranged two more concerts for Arthur—a return event in the hotel's ballroom and a performance before university students in Canton—which proved to be the last appearances of the tour. They made their return journey in a frenzy of determination to reach Otwock, the resort near Warsaw where their children were staying, in time to celebrate Eva's second birthday. And they managed it: they arrived just before midnight on August 18. Eva, awakened by the light, "sat up with a start, looked at us with suspicion, studied our photo on the wall next to her cot, and only then recognized that we were we," Rubinstein said. "When Nela threw her arms around her, the child said with a reproachful voice, 'Will you leave again?' "[55]

In Paris, Rubinstein managed to rent additional rooms in the building at the corner of Rue Ravignan and Rue d'Orchampt, to accommodate his growing family and domestic staff. But no sooner had they settled in than he was off on another round of touring in Europe. Fortunately, he said at the end of his life, he enjoyed not only playing in public but "all that it involved; the traveling, even uncomfortably, the constant change of cities, hotels, food, climate, I simply adored it all. . . . [And] whenever I was obliged to stay in the same place for more than two or three months . . . I began to get irritated."[56] Besides his concert appearances, the important events of the 1935–36 season, for him, included his first encounter with Marian Anderson's singing, which he loved; the premiere at the Paris Opéra of Szymanowski's ballet-pantomime *Harnasie*, starring Serge Lifar; and the first recording sessions for a complete set of Chopin's nocturnes. These sessions may have been the ones that Gaisberg was recalling when he said that Rubinstein would bring little Eva "to our studio, where she would sit on his knee and pound the piano, his eyes meanwhile popping out of his head with admiration." Gaisberg reported the "amazement" of Rubinstein's friends over the fact that "this confirmed bachelor . . . became the idolizing father. He must have wasted many precious practice hours dandling the child on his lap."[57]

Szymanowski was pleased by *Harnasie*'s success, at and after its Paris premiere, but he was dying of tuberculosis. Over the years, Rubinstein's friendship had remained important to him, and as early as June 1926 he had written to Zosia Kochanska that he had recently found the pianist not only "extremely nice" and generous, as always, but also "somewhat more serious and profound" than he had previously been, and he had quoted a "letter— the first one in a hundred years—" that Rubinstein had sent him from aboard a ship that was taking him from Lisbon to Rio de Janeiro: " 'You know very well that in the whole world it is only to you and Paul that I have a feeling of completely belonging—as to something absolutely my own. All the rest of humanity plays a bit-part. . . .' "[58] Late in January 1937, Rubinstein, who was to give a recital at Cannes, saw Szymanowski at nearby Grasse, where the composer was living in a clinic. Karol managed to attend Arthur's recital, after which they said good-bye for the last time. On March 29—Easter Sunday—the fifty-five-year-old composer died at a sanatorium in Lausanne. Wertheim, Kochanski, Mlynarski, and Szymanowski: all were gone. Two months after his fiftieth birthday, Rubinstein had already lost all of the close Polish musician friends of his early years.

THERE WAS LITTLE respite in Rubinstein's professional life between the fall of 1936 and the spring of 1938. Among many other engagements, he played in Copenhagen early in October 1936, in Helsinki late in November, in Poland early in December, and in Lausanne and the South of France late in January 1937. From February 12 to 14 he recorded more Chopin nocturnes in London; from February 19 to March 1 he played in Italy; and from March 3 to 13 he played in North Africa. Early in April he returned to London to complete his recordings of the nocturnes and to make other records, including the Chopin First Concerto with Barbirolli and the Franck Violin and Piano Sonata with Heifetz. By mid-April Rubinstein and his family had embarked at Marseilles, bound for South America, where he gave many concerts in Argentina, Uruguay, and Chile. They returned to Paris in August, but Rubinstein immediately left by himself for his first tour of Australia. (He did not mention in his memoirs that the tour had originally been planned for Horowitz, who, however, had entered a period of withdrawal from public life.) The trip began with a nine-day series of flights from Amsterdam to Sydney via Athens, Cairo, Basra, Allahabad, Calcutta, Kuala Lumpur, Timor, and Port Darwin; it continued with concerts in Sydney, Melbourne, Adelaide, Perth, Melbourne again, Canberra, Sydney again, and Brisbane; and it concluded with another long series of flights, one of which stopped in Rangoon, Burma. All in all, the Australian tour lasted from August 22 to October 15 and, like the Oriental tour, it gave Rubinstein many new impressions and thousands of new fans. No sooner had he returned to Paris than he and Nela packed the children and their nursemaid off to Poland and departed for the United States, where Rubinstein was to play for the first time in a decade.

Sol Hurok, the impresario who had engaged Rubinstein for a few concerts during the 1921–22 season, had been actively pursuing the pianist since 1928. "To me his decision to remain away from the United States was not final," Hurok recalled. "I talked to his European managers each time I went abroad, and at last one day in Paris I cajoled him into a conference. We talked an hour or more, and in the end I had convinced him that America was ready for him at last. In November, 1937, he and his lovely wife stepped off the *Queen Mary*. . . . Dozens of his friends came . . . to see them step off the boat, bundled in furs, onto the soil of America for the first time in ten years. . . . His first concert [November 17th] was with the New York Philharmonic, John Barbirolli conducting. He played the Brahms B flat Major concerto brilliantly, but Daniel Gregory Mason's *Lincoln Symphony* had its first performance on the same program, and the critics devoted their principal attention to this event. . . . I was disappointed, but not discouraged. . . . He played seventeen concerts in those nine weeks, appearing with seven leading symphony orchestras. By the time he reached Carnegie Hall [on January 7, 1938] for his first of two solo performances the critics were writing of his 'triumphant return,' his 'inflammatory' playing. . . ."[59]

Hurok was not exaggerating. "The event of the 1937–38 season was the return and—at last—the triumph of Artur Rubinstein," said Richard Schickel, in his history of Carnegie Hall. The reviews of Rubinstein's first recital were "ecstatic," Schickel said. "Wrote Olin Downes: 'Mr. Rubinstein must have possessed six hands and thirty fingers on his person, perhaps an orchestra as well, concealed in the vicinity of his sounding board.' Seconded Louis Biancolli: 'Mr. Rubinstein left his audience cheering and his piano limp.' "[60] The New York Times's critic, "N. S.," said, "Power and verve, phenomenal dynamic range and rare imagination for the production of color effects gave the artist's performances an allure which brought him many demonstrations of hectic acclaim in the course of the long and formidable program," which comprised the Bach-Busoni Toccata in C Major; Franck's Prelude, Choral, and Fugue; Poulenc's Mouvements perpétuels; three pieces by Debussy; the "Forlane" from Ravel's Le Tombeau de Couperin; Stravinsky's "Petrushka" Sonata; and Chopin's Barcarolle, Mazurkas in C Minor (Op. 56, No. 3) and D Major (Op. 33, No. 2), Nocturne in F-sharp Major, and Polonaise in A-flat Major. The Times's critic noted that the audience had contained "a large number of the city's leading musicians,"[61] and indeed, according to Rubinstein, the pianists present included Rachmaninoff, Godowsky, and Josef and Rosina Lhévinne.

Schickel described the vindication of Rubinstein's artistic value as "the surest indication of the decade that there had been some growth in the musical public's ability to distinguish the meritorious from the meretricious."[62] Rubinstein's long-sought American triumph had become a reality, and the reality would endure for the rest of his career. Although he conceded that Hurok had been "instrumental in bringing me back," a good deal of sarcasm about the impresario is implicit and at times explicit in My Many Years. Nela Rubinstein said that "Hurok was a wonderful man" and that "Arthur doesn't say enough good about him" in his memoirs. "Hurok loved Arthur from the bottom of his heart. He made his American career. It's true that he made his own at the same time, but still!" In 1973, when Hurok was terminally ill, "there was a big tribute to him at the Met, and all his artists performed," Mrs. Rubinstein continued. "Arthur didn't, and it hurt Hurok. Arthur didn't find it in himself. I think maybe he was a little jealous of the other artists. He should have done something; it hurt me that he didn't." But pride probably played a larger part than jealousy, not only in his attitude toward Hurok but also in his attitude toward his popularity in the United States. Rubinstein never quite got over the fact that he did not achieve full recognition there until he was fifty, and this is demonstrated by his reaction to a letter that the Recordak Corporation in New York sent him in March 1965. He had been asked to allow his name to be used at the business's pavilion at the forthcoming World's Fair, and the descriptive sentence about him read: "Although he made his concert debut in Warsaw at the age of five, this internationally renowned pianist did not achieve his present eminence until forty-three years later." Rubinstein replied: "First of all, my concert debut was at the age of six [really seven going on eight, and in Lodz, not Warsaw], and I do not think that at that age any debut matters much from a career or generally musical point of view. As to achieving my present eminence, as you put it, after forty-three years, reached at the ripe age of forty-eight [really fifty], that is not quite accurate. You might say I have achieved a certain amount of eminence in the United States, but I was lucky enough to achieve a completely predominant situation as a pianist in 1916 during the First World War, in Spain, and subsequently in all the Spanish-speaking countries of South America, and all over the world. I must say, with great pride, that I still hold this situation unchanged. So it would be rather frustrating for me to have people informed that the time between my debut at five until forty-three years later was of no account."[63]

Rubinstein followed his successes in the United States with successes in Latin America: while his wife was en route back to Paris and the children, he played concerts that Ernesto de Quesada had arranged for him in Mexico City, Bogotá (where he bought a bag of emeralds for Nela), Caracas, and Kingston, Jamaica. Then he flew back to New York and boarded the *Normandie* for his return voyage to France in February 1938. Shortly afterward, Nela and Arthur learned that a house was for sale in the Square de l'Avenue du Bois de Boulogne (now Avenue Foch), in Paris's elegant sixteenth arrondissement, next door to the house in which Debussy had spent his last years and died. "Our Montmartre house was much too small," Nela recalled: "My mother was staying with us and there were the two children and the nanny. The house for sale belonged to the Singer family, and we bought it for peanuts. It had to be re-done, and it was all fixed up beautifully." While the house was being renovated, the Rubinsteins spent the summer of 1938 at Aix-les-Bains; they moved into their lovely new home in September.

Rubinstein gave concerts in France and the Baltic states during the fall of 1938; then, having left Eva and Paul in the care of Mrs. Mlynarska and the household staff, Nela and Arthur traveled to North America for a four-month tour during which the previous year's triumphs were repeated and reinforced. According to Hurok, the box-office receipts from Rubinstein's first American season had not been good. "I had complete confidence, however, and presently the bookings that began to come in for the next season bore me out." From then on, he said, Rubinstein's American tours were "a record of sold-out houses. He rushes back and forth between California . . . and New York two or three times a season, selling out consistently all over the country, breaking box-office records. He plays two or three times a season in Carnegie Hall in solo and with orchestra besides. He is a busy, happy man, fulfilling his artistic and his personal life in a seemingly endless round of study and concerts and people from early morning far into the night."[64]

Almost immediately after his return to Paris in the spring of 1939, Rubinstein recorded his dear old Saint-Saëns Second Concerto with the Orchestre de la Société des Concerts du Conservatoire conducted by Philippe Gaubert, and then dashed to London to complete a major recording project that he had begun the previous November and December: the Chopin mazurkas. Gaisberg reported that when Rubinstein had been approached about this project, his reaction was "none too enthusiastic. Although he had always played many of the most popular ones, he was not intimately acquainted with the bulk of the series and was inclined to think that, recorded as a whole, they would prove monotonous. However, he got to work and soon found that in every one there was some beauty hitherto unrealized." According to Gaisberg, "Rubinstein insists that the Mazurkas more than any of Chopin's other music express the Polish nationality. . . . In recording these dances, he would often get up and illustrate the steps of various types of mazurka, all in different tempi. Outstanding was his interpretation of Nijinsky in the famous C Major. . . ." After having recorded the set, Rubinstein wrote to the Gramophone Company:

> I have always considered that the Mazurkas are the most original, if not the most beautiful, of Chopin's works. . . .
>
> It is very difficult to get into the mood of 52 different Mazurkas, and I viewed the job with apprehension, thinking it would be difficult to cast myself into just the right expression of so many works, every one of which has a distinct characteristic. To my great joy I found that both Mr. Gaisberg and myself became more and more enthusiastic with every new Mazurka. I only hope that . . . the listeners will hear at least some of the love I have felt whilst recording this work.
>
> I do not know if I have succeeded in what I tried to do, but I hope that my records of these Mazurkas will help to convey to the vast audience of the gramophone, all the world over, a little of what Chopin's music means to the Poles.

Gaisberg believed that the great improvement in Rubinstein's professional fortunes in the English-speaking world immediately prior to World War II was directly tied to "his large and interesting repertory of gramophone records. . . . Perhaps of all his titles the Scherzi, Nocturnes, Polonaises and last, but not least, the Mazurkas of Chopin are chiefly responsible for his popularity in British and American concert-halls."[65] "Chiefly" may be an exaggeration, but the records certainly helped his reputation.

The completion of the mazurka project in May 1939 was by no means Rubinstein's last task of the season. In June he traveled by steamer to South Africa, where he gave well-received concerts in Cape Town, Johannesburg, Kimberley, and Durban; bought a diamond for Nela; and flew back to France via Angola, Dar es Salaam, Victoria Nyanza, Khartoum, Cairo, Piraeus, and Brindisi. During his absence, Ruth Draper had stopped in Paris and visited Nela and the children, whom she described in a letter as "*dreams* of charm, personality and beauty, exquisite and darling. [Nela's] mother is an angel, and the atmosphere is charged with all the things one loves to find in a house. Little Paul grabbed my hand and pulled me upstairs to see his toys— never having seen me before—so dear and frank and friendly and gay with humor—and to hear them chatter Polish and then French to me was intoxicating—those baby lips framing the words of those two languages—with equal ease."[66] After Arthur's return, the Rubinsteins spent the remainder of the summer on the coast of Normandy, at Germaine de Rothschild's villa— between Deauville and Pont-l'Evêque—and, for a time, at Maison Blanche, Bonneville-sur-Toucques (Calvados). There they followed radio broadcasts that kept them abreast of the ominous events of August and September 1939.

BY THE TIME Rubinstein's recordings of the mazurkas were released, his declared hope that they would help foreign listeners to understand "a little of what Chopin's music means to the Poles" had taken on tragic connotations, because the young, independent Polish nation had been wiped out by Hitler's Wehrmacht and World War II had begun. Although Rubinstein, like most other non-Germanic Europeans and especially European Jews, had long been horrified by Nazi Germany's rearmament, racism, and belligerence, he was not politically sophisticated. He greatly admired Léon Blum, France's socialist leader and the architect of the Popular Front, but he adopted a public attitude of strict neutrality on the subject of the Spanish Civil War, since he had admirers on both—or rather all—sides in the conflict. "After the war they all came back to him," Nela Rubinstein said. Whatever admiration he had felt for Mussolini was shaken by the Italian invasion of Ethiopia in 1935 and destroyed in the fall of 1938, when Mussolini promulgated anti-Semitic laws, with the intention of bringing Italian policies into line with those of the Germans. Rubinstein was enraged. He told Gaisberg

shortly afterward that he had "happened to be in the South of France" when
he learned of the new decrees, "and went straight to a telegraph office where
he wrote out a strongly worded telegram to the Duce. When asked to send it,
the clerk was panic-stricken and begged the pianist to wait. Meantime he
would consult his superior officer, and in a couple of hours would be able to
obtain a ruling as to whether such a message could be transmitted to a foreign
country. Three hours later, Rubinstein returned and was told it had been
passed for dispatch. As he left the office, after paying the fee, newsboys were
already running down the street with an extra featuring the story. Although it
was the French who had double-crossed him by their unauthorized disclo-
sure of a private message prior to its actual dispatch, this only made him an-
grier than ever with the Italians."[67] Rubinstein returned the decoration that
Mussolini had bestowed on him and was promptly banned from Italy's musical life—which would have happened in any case, thanks to his ethnic
origins.

News of his action was reported all over the world. On September 20,
1938, the Warsaw newspaper *Warszawski Dziennik Narodowy* ran a story on
the subject: "On September 7 the English radio presented its listeners with
the following Reuters wire-service message: 'The distinguished Polish pianist
Artur Rubinstein has cancelled all his concerts in Italy and sent back to Mussolini all his Italian medals as a protest against Italy's anti-Semitic laws.' In
quoting this, *Merkuriusz Polski* [a right-wing daily] ironically asks the 'distinguished Polish Rubinstein why, as a Pole, he is interfering in matters that
interest only Jews and Italians,' and adds: 'The honorable gentleman need
not bother answering. We know enough about Rubinstein's origins, and this
knowledge is better than any answer. But you remember, Mr. Rubinstein,
that what you have perpetrated by calling things by incorrect names is a nasty
offense against a nation [Italy] that Poles respect, and an abominable transgression. You have passed yourself off as a Pole, and you have acted with no
right whatsoever to do so, and against Poles' intentions, which are the diamet-
ric opposite [of yours]. This transgression will not be forgiven. Remember
that well. You can say goodbye forever to concerts in Poland. In Poland you
won't play, of that you can be sure.' We may add that the Polish Wire Service
has been making publicity out of Rubinstein's being a Pole—a fact to which
we quite often used to call the public's attention."[68]

But the fact that Rubinstein's love for the Polish people and Polish culture was not reciprocated by some of his compatriots did not diminish the
love. When the Rubinstein family—still staying near Deauville—heard that
Germany had completely conquered Poland, "Nela and I were watching the
sea from the beach and I felt an irresistible urge to disappear in it," Rubinstein recalled. "Nela and Anatole [Mühlstein, Diana de Rothschild's hus-

band] must have been aware of it, for they suddenly dragged me away from there."[69] Asked many years later whether this was true, Nela Rubinstein said, "I think he wants to dramatize it a little—I don't believe that he would have drowned himself—but we were absolutely in despair." Nela was now cut off from her mother, sister Alina, brother Bronek, and most other relatives, who were in Poland or Lithuania, and most of Arthur's brothers and sisters and their families were in Warsaw or Lodz.

Rubinstein had two concerts scheduled in Amsterdam early in October; he booked passage on a Dutch boat that would take him and his family from Holland to the Americas, where he was to begin to play in mid-November, but "our friends here in Paris were frantic and wanted us to leave sooner, not to wait for the concerts," Nela recalled. "I was of course rather anxious not to wait and be caught with the two children, but rather to go. So I tried to persuade him to go earlier, and he disliked the idea because it didn't look right; he wanted to be a grand fellow and wait until the last moment. He didn't want to look as if he was running away. But we were really forced by the American ambassador, William Bullitt, who was a friend of ours and a great friend of the Polish ambassador. He arranged a visa for us, although we were not Americans, so that we could go on the boat on which Americans in France were being evacuated." Arthur cancelled his Dutch concerts, and he, Nela, the children, their French governess, and Zosia Kochańska caught a train to Bordeaux, where they prepared to board the overcrowded, New York–bound SS *Washington.* On October 3, 1939, from the Hôtel Gascogne in Bordeaux, Rubinstein sent Rex Palmer of the Gramophone Company in London what was probably the last letter he wrote in Europe until after the war: "My dear Rex—We are just sailing for New York, where I shall stay for quite a long while—Will you kindly give orders to the Victor Company to pay my half-year account in dollars in New-York? My address there will be: Hurok Attractions[,] 30, Rockefeller Plaza, New York[.] I hope the Mazurkas of Chopin are out, or at least they will be out in America. I have a tour in C. America (Porto [*sic*] Rico, Cuba, Jamaica, Venezuela) during November, December, from January till end of May the United States, then South America. Please write me a few words. Yours very sincerely Arthur Rubinstein. I hope everything is allright in England."

Fred Gaisberg, who was just retiring from the company (he died in 1951), answered the letter six days later: "Dear Arthur, Your letter to Rex Palmer has been passed over to me as he is on Active Service. Regarding the accounts, these are somewhat delayed because of the war and reduced staff. Also we are waiting for a ruling as to how the payments can be made in view of the various Government restrictions. . . . The first half of the Mazurkas were issued in September and the Victor Company have received matrices of the entire set. . . . I hope you will have a successful tour and now and again give a thought to we [sic] poor devils over here, who will soon be on rations and food coupons. . . ."[70]

Rubinstein received Gaisberg's letter in New York, where he and his family were staying at the Buckingham Hotel on West Fifty-seventh Street. "The children made themselves at home right away," Rubinstein said,[71] but the adjustment was less easy than he thought: four-year-old Paul believed that he was being pursued by cruel Nazi soldiers, and both he and six-year-old Eva, in different ways, found the transition to a new language and a new environment—or, rather, the first in a series of new environments—difficult. But one way or another, the Rubinsteins were about to become Americans.

6

"Rubinstein"

The War and Immediate Postwar Years

From the fall of 1939 to the fall of 1947, Rubinstein's activities were confined
to the Americas and—for the duration of the United States' involvement in
the war—to North America. (Until 1946, when he became a citizen of the
United States, his legal status was that of a "resident alien," albeit a highly
regarded one.) The pleasure that he took in his professional successes during
the first two of those years was dampened by his worry over Germany's conquest of one European country after another and the United States' reluctance to enter the conflict, and the worry was never stronger than during the
ocean voyage that he and his family made to Brazil and Argentina in May
1940, while the Germans were overrunning France. Ruth Draper, Henri
Focillon, a well-known art historian, and Madame Focillon were also aboard
the SS *Uruguay*, and they and the Rubinsteins constituted a glum, anxious
little community. From shipboard, Draper wrote to her sister Martha on May
14: "The Focillons and Rubinsteins and, I must admit, I, all felt the great
indifference [to Hitler's conquests] among Americans all thro' the West. No
re-action at the horrors portrayed in cinema 'news'—little comment or expression of disapproval. Admiration rather for Hitler's skill and success. The
parachute landings are amazing, but when Arthur asked the Captain if he
didn't think the wearing of fake uniforms was dreadful, he said: 'Well, they
got away with it'! It's all so terribly sad—but I do hope that the attacks on
Belgium and Holland have aroused the country. . . . But the stars and moon
and these calm blue seas, and the two enchanting children [Eva and Paul]
who come to my room every morning on their way from breakfast, are a great
comfort. They are perfectly adorable, and correct my French, and run to me
whenever they see me—with radiant faces. Nothing is so healing as the innocence and gaiety of children."[1]

Rubinstein was active in Polish relief projects in the United States. In
New York in November 1939, for instance, he and the Polish tenor Jan
Kiepura raised forty thousand dollars in the first of a series of joint benefit

concerts for Polish refugees, and the following year Rubinstein was in touch with many Polish diplomats about his continuing relief work. He also took part in efforts to induce Americans to prepare for war, and one of his most significant pre–Pearl Harbor contributions to this cause was a radio address that he delivered on June 13, 1941, under the auspices of the United States Treasury Defense Savings Staff. His talk contained a fair number of platitudes, but they were virtually inevitable under the circumstances.

> Those of us musicians . . . who travel continuously around the world, who speak many languages, who perform in almost every town of every country, have a quite unique opportunity to get into close contact with thousands of people of all races and creeds, all classes and opinions, who would gladly confide to us their most intimate thoughts for the simple reason that in return for their response and understanding of our Art, they take it for granted that we respond just as completely to their conviction and sympathize with their ideas. I would like to give you a vivid proof of this assertion. While giving concerts in Madrid just before the outbreak of the antimonarchic revolution in Spain, I received the visit of the Chamberlain of Queen Victoria Eugenia, to convey Her Majesty's regret at being unable to attend my concert as she always used to do, because of the growing unrest among the revolutionaries. The chamberlain while delivering this message addressed me as if I were a convinced monarchist. A half-hour later a young Spaniard of my acquaintance came to present me with the first copy of the new hymn of the Revolution having no doubt that I was at heart with their cause. This example repeating itself everywhere in the world, has enabled me to watch closely the different reactions of each nation towards the developments which slowly led up to this greatest tragedy of mankind.
>
> I saw, heard and felt the underground work of disintegration and the attack on the unity, strength and faith done by the Germans since years in my own country. The Poles would have bravely resisted their enemy much longer if it were not for these abominable methods of fifth column activities which proved so successful in the recent Spanish war. The rapid collapse of powerful France showed to the highest extent what a mighty weapon this diabolical warfare from the inside proves to be. All the other unfortunate, noble and peaceful countries who naively believed Hitler's word and felt safe behind the wall of neutrality, have to pay for their innocence and good faith with the loss of their freedom, destruction of their homes and a slow hunger-death. . . .

Americans, in these most tragic times the world has known you have found again an inspired leader [President Franklin D. Roosevelt] who realizes the terrible danger his country is facing—who will go the utmost to defend its freedom, its constitution and the life of its people. He wants you to buy the Defense Savings Bonds and Stamps, they are the means for your safety. Many well-intentioned usually sincere people among you believe and try to make you believe that you are well protected against any hostile army, navy or planes by the distance of thousands of miles which separate your hemisphere from your potential enemies. This is a great, a complete mistake. Please remember what I told you about the German warfare. There are many rats, many white termites who gnaw unceasingly at the bases of your national structure, and in South and Central America, all countries which I have visited extensively a few months ago, I was aware of how the pernicious scourges of humanity have eaten quite important bits of this structure already. I can assure you, the danger is right here, right everywhere. . . .

You are the most generous people on earth. You were and you are helping relentlessly every free nation under the stars. But what I ask you this time is to buy Government Defense Savings Bonds and Stamps, because each one of them represents a weapon in your hand to defend your family and your great country—and perhaps to restore eventually a peaceful and free life to the rest of the suffering humanity.[2]

With Eleanor Roosevelt, Mrs. Vincent Astor, soprano Lucrezia Bori, Walter Damrosch, Ruth Draper, New York's Mayor Fiorello H. La Guardia, New York's Governor Herbert H. Lehman, Secretary of the Treasury Henry Morgenthau, pianist Sigismond Stojowski, and other celebrities, Rubinstein was a member of the New York–based Paderewski Fund for Polish Relief, and on July 3, 1941, four days after Paderewski's death, Rubinstein participated gratis in a memorial radio broadcast, in which he played Paderewski's popular Minuet and the Funeral March from Chopin's Second Sonata. On December 7, 1941, Rubinstein was about to walk onto the stage at Carnegie Hall to play the Brahms B-flat Major Concerto with the New York Philharmonic and Rodzinski when the news arrived that Japan had attacked Pearl Harbor; Rodzinski made the announcement to the audience, and the concert proceeded. But even after the United States had entered the war, Poland remained one of Rubinstein's primary concerns. He accepted, for instance, an invitation—"in the cause of Poland's freedom"—from Edgar A. Mowrer, a well-known journalist who was serving as deputy director of the

Office of Facts and Figures in Washington, to play "Polish music . . . as only you can play it" in a "broadcast to the world on Polish Constitution Day, the third of May. . . . If you consent, the broadcast will be relayed by shortwave to the heroic people of Poland. . . .³ Two months later, Charlotte Kellogg, who chaired the Paderewski Testimonial Fund—the new name of the former Paderewski Fund for Polish Relief—wrote to Rubinstein: "Your part in the C B S Paderewski Memorial program last night [July 8, 1942] was not only a nobly impressive tribute to Mr Paderewski, as you expressed it through Chopin's music, but an important contribution to our organization, which is trying to keep alive his memory and the ideals for which he stood, and to carry forward those undertakings which he and we began together. . . . we should not have been able to have this program had you not so generously offered to play. We are deeply grateful to you."⁴ In September of the following year, Rubinstein made another radio broadcast, this one for the Friends of Poland committee during its "Tribute to Poland" week. In March 1945, as the war was coming to an end, the United States Office of War Information invited him to record an intermission talk to be broadcast in Poland along with a recording of a concert that he had recently given with the New York Philharmonic. And as late as 1976, Rubinstein made a contribution to the London-based memorial fund that sought to shed light on the wartime massacre of Polish officers by the Russians at Katyn; Bronislaw Mlynarski, Nela Rubinstein's brother, had been one of the survivors of that slaughter.

Rubinstein also helped many individual Poles—Christians and Jews—who were living in exile in America. One of them, the painter Moïse ("Kiki") Kisling, had been a friend of his in Paris, where he had moved from his native Cracow in 1910, at the age of nineteen. The generous, exuberant Kisling had joined the French army during World War I and had reenlisted in 1939, but he had been forced to flee the following year. He had made his way to New York, where he was involved in helping fellow artists-turned-refugees from all over Europe, although his own finances were shaky. Kisling was often in touch with the Rubinsteins and stayed with them in California for a while. In the spring of 1944 he informed them that the Polish government in exile in London had withdrawn the pension it had granted Julian Tuwim—one of Poland's finest poets and a Lodz-born Jew, like Rubinstein. The cutoff had come about because Tuwim supported a Polish-Soviet alliance and spoke out against what he described as anti-Semites and fascists within the government in exile. Kisling said, "I don't want to enter into the question of whether the government in London has acted correctly or incorrectly—I only know that Tuwim is a great poet and that he and his wife are headed toward complete poverty."⁵ Rubinstein must immediately have sent Kisling a substantial amount of money for Tuwim, because the painter wrote to thank him for his "magnificent response. . . . you can imagine Tuwim's joy at hearing that he was being helped by you."[6]

In the spring of 1945, just before the war ended, Rubinstein gave a recital at San Francisco's War Memorial Opera House for an audience that included many of the delegates who had assembled to create the United Nations. "A long range of multicolored flags represented the nations which had convened for the historic act of signing the charter," Rubinstein recalled. "I tried to find the Polish flag but there was no sign of it." After he had played "The Star-Spangled Banner," which was required at the beginning of all wartime public events in the United States, "a blind fury took hold of me," he said. "I addressed the audience in a loud, angry voice: 'In this hall where the great nations gather to make a better world, I miss the flag of Poland, for which this cruel war was fought.' And now I shouted, 'I shall play the Polish anthem. . . . I played it with a tremendous impact and very slowly and repeated the last phrase with a big resounding forte. The audience stood up as one man when I finished and gave me a great ovation."[7] The story is "authentic," said Nela Rubinstein, who was present, and she added that "Poles all over the globe were moved" by her husband's gesture.

Rubinstein's contributions to the war effort and to postwar relief appeals were by no means limited to Polish-related events. With no remuneration, he performed for American soldiers, participated in concerts and broadcasts that raised funds on behalf of Russian and French relief societies, played at a fund-raising dinner given by Elsa Maxwell in Beverly Hills to celebrate the liberation of France, was heard in special broadcasts that marked the Allied victories over Germany and Japan, and responded positively to dozens of other requests for donations of his services or money.

AFTER HAVING MADE the Buckingham Hotel in New York their base of operations for a while, the Rubinsteins rented a house in Manhattan's Turtle Bay—a complex on East Forty-eighth Street where Ruth Draper also lived. During the summer of 1941 they rented a house at 428 North Carmalina Avenue, in Brentwood, West Los Angeles, for what they thought would be a short stay, but they liked the relaxed way of life in California so much that the following year they bought a house in Brentwood—12921 Marlboro Street— from the actor Pat O'Brien, who had had a new house built next door for himself and his family. In true Californian spirit, Rubinstein decided that he had to learn to drive, although two earlier attempts in France had ended in near disasters. His wife described his effort as "not fortunate. Actually, it was an act of revenge, because I was driving all my life and I was always driving him and the children and whatnot. It was a protest: He didn't want to be the one who didn't know how to drive. So he struggled and struggled, and finally he did pass the exam. He was always petrifying all of us when he was at the wheel, because it was too late—he didn't have good reactions and it was really a very dangerous thing. The children and I tried all the tricks—we pretended that he didn't like to drive, that it wasn't healthy, that it was tiresome, and so on, and he resented that."[8] In truth, he did not enjoy driving; he proved his point by getting his license, drove once in a while for a few years, and eventually stopped altogether. Before he gave up the wheel, however, his driving provided him with one good story that involved Sir Thomas Beecham, the celebrated English conductor. Beecham "was once mean to me," Rubinstein told the American journalist Art Buchwald twenty years after the event. "I was playing at the Hollywood Bowl with him and he was very rude. After the rehearsal he asked me if I could give him a lift home. I said I would be glad to, but when he got in my car I told him, 'This is a great occasion. You are the first passenger I've ever driven. I just received my license yesterday.' I never saw a man so frightened in my life."[9]

Beecham was one among many excellent European conductors who lived and worked in America during the war years, and who helped to create a great era in the history of American orchestral life. Most conductors enjoyed making music with Rubinstein, not only because of his outstanding playing and the luster that his name brought to their rosters of soloists, but also because he was easy to work with. Many famous soloists of Rubinstein's and earlier generations established a single approach to each concerto in their respective repertoires and would not or could not deviate from that approach: "This is how I play it," they would say, when questioned about a basic tempo, a small nuance, or anything in between. Others, on the contrary, were erratic, capable of producing in performance a drastically different version of the piece than the version that they had produced in rehearsal a few hours earlier, on the assumption that conductor and orchestra would simply follow them; if the end result sometimes resembled a cat-and-mouse chase, that was just too bad. Rubinstein, like other outstanding musicians, had strong ideas about the interpretation of the pieces he played, but he was always ready to reexamine his approach and to take seriously the points of view of other musicians whom he respected. For all these reasons, many conductors refused to limit themselves to customary managerial channels in their efforts to secure Rubinstein as soloist, but also wrote to or phoned him directly to say how eager they were to have him perform with their orchestras. His files contain alluring letters of this sort from Dimitri Mitropoulos, Eugene Ormandy, Charles Munch, Erich Leinsdorf, Sir Malcolm Sargent, and many others.

Leopold Stokowski repeatedly invited Rubinstein to be his soloist, especially in later years, but his requests were politely turned down. Rubinstein had admired Stokowski until 1945, when they had a serious disagreement about the interpretation of Chopin's F Minor Concerto; thereafter, the pianist avoided the conductor like the plague. Stokowski "embarrassed me in front of the orchestra," Rubinstein recalled more than fifteen years later. "I got so mad I walked off the stage during a recording and refused to come back. But we made up recently when he became sick and I sent him some flowers."[10]

Rubinstein played only once with Arturo Toscanini, the most celebrated of all the conductors of his day, but Toscanini was so pleased with their performance of Beethoven's Third Piano Concerto that he insisted that Victor publish a live recording of it. Rubinstein said, in his memoirs and elsewhere, that during a first run-through of the piece at their single rehearsal for that performance, he and the orchestra had been completely at odds, but a second run-through had gone perfectly because during the first one Toscanini had memorized Rubinstein's every nuance and now followed him without missing a detail. The results, however, as heard in the recording, do not demonstrate such unity of intent; maybe the two musicians enjoyed working together and, on listening to the playback of their joint effort, heard their own enjoyment rather than what was really happening musically. Toscanini gave Rubinstein an autographed photo "in remembrance of the unforgettable date (October 29–1944) of our first artistic meeting."[11] But by 1944 the seventy-seven-year-old Toscanini was conducting only a dozen or so concerts a year and was little inclined to perform concertos; although his personal relations with Rubinstein remained cordial, their "first artistic meeting" was also their last.

Rubinstein had a more productive professional relationship with George Szell, whom he had seen conduct in Prague as early as 1932. When they first performed together, in the Hague in 1933, they disagreed over the interpretation of Beethoven's Fourth Piano Concerto, but their relationship soon warmed up and they often played together in America in the early 1940s. "I have been engaged by the New York Philharmonic as Guest Conductor for next season," Szell wrote to Rubinstein in February 1944. "You can imagine how happy I am. I consider this a very important milestone in my career and of course I shall try to prove worthy of the occasion and to make my concerts as brilliant as possible. Consequently, the *only* Soloist I have *asked* for are [sic] YOU, and you have been granted me at once. Unfortunately, however, I was given to understand a few days later that you have decided to 'jump' the Philharmonic for one year. This is a bitter disappointment that I am not going to take lying down. I wish to ask you therefore to reconsider your decision in the light of the fact that you would play with me if you accepted and in consideration of our friendship and the many happy occasions on which we were associated in making music, here and abroad, which I always enjoyed more than I can say. . . . your affectionate friend George. P. S. I am not going to take 'no' for an answer."[12] Rubinstein did return to the Philharmonic at the end of the following season, but only for a special concert with Bruno Walter. Eight years letter, Szell left a note for Rubinstein at the St. Regis Hotel in New York: "My *Dear* Artur, I was here trying to catch you on the fly but, alas, failed—. I have a great request: the Cleveland Orchestra [of which Szell had been musical director since 1946] has a Jubilee Season 1952–53 and I *must* have you as Soloist, as the crowning glory of a list of distinguished artists, not only for the usual pair of concerts in Cleveland but also for the Cleveland Orchestra's *New York* Concert. The Orchestra is now really *TOPS*[.] I mean it and, as you know, I am not in the habit of kidding myself.—Mr. Hurok is informed of my plans and my heart's desire and promised to talk to you; I just wanted to talk to you directly as well. It is *much* too long since we have seen each other! I embrace you and Nela in affectionate love—George."[13]

Rubinstein said that the Cleveland Orchestra reached so high a level of excellence under Szell "that it put in the shade the Philadelphia and Boston orchestras, which had previously reigned for decades."[14] He played many times in Cleveland during Szell's tenure. According to Klaus G. Roy, the Cleveland Orchestra's program annotator, "During most of the twenty-four-year tenure of George Szell in Cleveland, a visiting pianist, violinist, or singer was listed on the program page as 'Assisting Artist.' One day there was an emphatic phone call from Mr. Szell: 'Arthur Rubinstein says he is not an assisting artist. He is a soloist. Please designate him as such from now on.' "[15] Rubinstein told many people, and repeated in his memoirs, that he greatly regretted not having been able to make recordings with Szell and the Cleveland Orchestra because Szell was not a Victor artist, and intercompany loans of well-known performers were less common in the 1950s and '60s than they are today. Temperamentally, the autocratic, ultra-self-disciplined Szell seemed Rubinstein's opposite, but Daniel Barenboim has voiced the opinion that "Rubinstein's great attachment to Szell, musically, had to do with his upbringing in or his relationship to the 'German style.' "[16] The Szells and Rubinsteins remained the best of friends (Szell was quite taken with Nela Rubinstein), and when Szell died, in 1970, at the age of seventy-three, his widow, Helene, wrote to the Rubinsteins, "Thank you for your friendship, which he valued so highly, please keep some for myself."[17] Years later, Rubinstein said that he still lamented the loss of Szell, but he added: "fortunately, some splendid records are available which allow me to hear in the intimacy of my room symphonies by Schumann, Brahms, and Beethoven conducted by the great, one and only George Szell."[18]

Rubinstein also enjoyed working with John (later Sir John) Barbirolli, to whose career as a recording artist he gave a significant push. Their first joint effort, in January 1931, produced recordings of Chopin's Concerto in F Minor and Mozart's Concerto in A Major, K. 488, but it was the recording of the Tchaikovsky Concerto, in June 1932, that sealed their artistic entente and made their partnership a great commercial success. "We started on a run-through before making tests," the conductor recalled. "We had only played a few bars when he jumped up and shouted, 'Oh, what a man! At last I can *play* this concerto.' . . . It wasn't that I was 'following' him. . . . I felt the music in the same way as Artur felt it. I had the same *warm* approach as his. . . . After that I started accompanying other big artists. They had either heard what Rubinstein had said about me at the run-through, or they had heard the recording itself."[19]

Another conductor whom Rubinstein is known to have admired was Vladimir Golschmann, a Paris-born Russian, later naturalized American. David Walter, a double-bassist in the NBC Symphony Orchestra in the 1940s, recalled a recording session with Rubinstein and Golschmann in 1946. Golschmann had asked the strings to play a certain melodic embellishment in a specific way, but later in the movement Rubinstein played the same figure differently. According to Walter, the "startled Golschmann said: 'Strings, please note we will play the turn as Mr. Rubinstein did.' Rubinstein, [likewise] startled . . . , tried [it] right side up and upside down, decided, 'Oh, no, Maestro, we will do it your way!' Mr. G.: 'No, Mr. Rubinstein, you are the soloist.' Mr. R.: 'No, my dear Golschmann, let's do it *your* way.' Mr. G. (adamant): 'No, I insist we do it *your* way.' Mr. R.: 'But I like it better your way.' An impasse. What to do? Rubinstein reached into his pocket, took out a quarter, said, 'There's only one way to settle this properly. What do you say: heads or tails?' Mr. G., now in the spirit: 'Heads!' Rubinstein peered closely at the coin, not allowing Golschmann to see it, and triumphantly pronounced, 'Tails! You lose! We do it your way!' And we did. I often wonder about young pianists, in the 21st century, citing Rubinstein as their musicological authority . . . unaware of the power of a coin-flip."[20]

Nela Rubinstein said that her husband considered Koussevitzky "a great talent and a great organizer, but limited in his tastes." Monteux, on the other hand, was "a wonderful fellow. Arthur loved playing with him, but his wife was a bore." Rubinstein played several times with Fritz Reiner and made several recordings with him (including a magnificent Brahms D Minor Concerto) when Reiner was the Chicago Symphony Orchestra's conductor, but they quarrelled over Chopin: "Reiner tried to insinuate something about Chopin—I don't remember what—and Arthur almost overturned the table where we were sitting," Mrs. Rubinstein said. (The issue may have had to do with Chopin's sexual tastes: Rubinstein became angry when anyone implied that Chopin might have been homosexual or bisexual, and he spoke badly of the Chopin scholar Arthur Hedley because he thought—incorrectly—that Hedley held that opinion. Rubinstein could also work himself into a rage when he heard people say that Chopin's musical genius came from the French, rather than the Polish, side of his family.) But Frank Miller, who was for many years the Chicago Symphony's principal cellist, told the pianist Emanuel Ax that the real break between Rubinstein and Reiner had occurred when they were recording the Tchaikovsky Concerto together. At the end of the first movement, one of the orchestra's solo wind players had asked Reiner if a certain passage could be rerecorded, because he felt that he hadn't played it as well as he could have. Reiner grumbled but acceded to the request. When another player asked to record the previous passage as well, for a similar reason, Rubinstein spoke up: " 'If we are going back that far, let's go back a bit further still, because I played a few wrong notes just before that.' "

" 'Well!' " said the notoriously sour and sarcastic Reiner. " 'If we're going to correct all of *your* wrong notes we'll be here all day!' " Rubinstein stood up and walked off the stage, without saying a word. The recording session ended abruptly, and so did Rubinstein's relationship with Reiner.[21]

Rubinstein could be cruel to incompetent conductors, or to those who wished to show off at the expense of the music. One conductor, in trying to impress the audience at a Rubinstein concert by conducting the concerto accompaniment by heart, made a mistake that led to a disastrous patch in the performance. André Previn was in the audience and reported, "Rubinstein instantly mimed to the audience: 'This is not my fault, ladies and gentlemen.' Which of course was ruthless of him. Still, I can't see why [conductors] accompany from memory. . . ."[22] Once, late in his life, Rubinstein himself tried to conduct. At the end of a concerto rehearsal with Zubin Mehta and the Israel Philharmonic, he said, "All my life I have wanted to conduct a Brahms symphony." Mehta handed Rubinstein his baton and the private read-through of the Brahms Third began. "Apparently unaware that it was his own ponderous beat the musicians were following, Rubinstein urged them on," reported Martin Bookspan and Ross Yockey, Mehta's biographers. " 'Gentlemen, gentlemen, can't you play a little faster?' . . . 'As far as I know,' recalls Zubin, laughing, 'it was the first and last time Mr. Rubinstein ever conducted. But I tell you, it was a treasured experience for all of us who were there.' "[23]

Outstanding playing and flexible and intelligent musicianship: the same qualities that made Rubinstein a great concerto player, beloved of most of the major conductors of his day, also made him a great chamber music player. First under the tutelage of Joachim—one of the most celebrated

chamber musicians in history—and then as partner to some of the finest soloists and ensemble players of the twentieth century, Rubinstein had developed
his capacity as a member of duos, trios, quartets, and quintets to a degree that
most famous soloists never even attempt, let alone achieve. One of the most
important fruits of his efforts in this area was born early in his American years,
when he partnered Jascha Heifetz and the Polish-born cellist Emanuel Feuermann in a series of trio recordings that have become classics in the field.
That the idea had originated with Heifetz in 1935 is clear from a letter that
Gaisberg sent Rubinstein in September of that year: "I have had a letter from
Heifetz, who will be in London during the month of November. I also note
that you will be here during the same month. Heifetz would very much like
to do the Concerto of Chausson for piano, violin and string quartet with the
Pro Arte Quartet, who will also be in London during November. I put forward the idea to you. Also there is another idea which Heifetz favours, that is
trios, preferably Tchaikovsky or the Schubert Op. 100 with Feuerman[n],
who will be in London, and yourself. I hope you will give this serious
attention."[24]

There seems to have been no immediate follow-up to this query, although Heifetz and Rubinstein did record Franck's Violin and Piano Sonata
in 1937. In December of that year, someone at the Gramophone Company—
probably Gaisberg again—returned to the attack and wrote to Rubinstein,
who was in America: "I just want to remind you of the conversation we had
about making TRIOS with Heifetz and Piatigorsky. I am hoping that you will
see Heifetz whilst you are in America and arrange some dates mutually con-
venient. I think we said that perhaps Heifetz would be in Paris about May
and rehearsals might then be arranged. Trio recording is the one blank left in
our catalogues and this field promises excellent sales. Ten years ago, we
made a few Trios with Cortot-Thibaud-Casals, but since then no attempt has
been made to continue this recording." Rubinstein cabled back, lamenting
what he interpreted as lackadaisical behavior on the part of RCA Victor,
HMV's American correspondent, in selling his already-extant recordings:
"State absolute lack interest cooperation[.] Victor constantly misses advertising in spite exceptional success enormous possibilities improving sales."[25]

Once Rubinstein had moved to the United States, however, conditions
changed. In April 1940, he asked for and obtained from the Gramophone
Company a release to record with Victor, and despite wartime restrictions on
the export of capital the Bank of England allowed him to receive in America
the royalties owed him in Britain.[26] The trio project was revived, again with
Feuermann, who, like Rubinstein and Heifetz, was a European Jew who had
found refuge in the United States. Although the initial proposal had come
from Heifetz, before the sessions began the violinist was "worried" over

whether or not Rubinstein would "fit in" with Feuermann and himself—at least according to Heifetz's biographer, Artur Weschler-Vered. Brahms's Trio in B Major, Op. 8, Beethoven's Trio in B-flat Major, Op. 97 ("Archduke"), and Schubert's Trio in B-flat Major, Op. 99, were recorded in only three days—September 11–13, 1941 (the final day's sessions lasted eleven hours)—but "right from the beginning of the recording sessions, there was a certain tension between Heifetz and Rubinstein," Weschler-Vered wrote. "The pianist often complained that the violinist missed no opportunity to direct the microphone towards himself. [Charles] O'Connell [RCA's producer], on the other hand, felt that only too often Feuermann's cello was muted by the lower register of the piano and the excessive use of the pedal by Rubinstein. On several occasions the recording engineers had for brief periods of time to turn off the microphone near the pianist in order to allow the cello to be heard. . . . Heifetz complained that Rubinstein liked to linger over romantic passages. The pianist found the violinist too aggressive in his playing, always thrusting ahead. The violinist felt the pianist to be superficial. The other felt the former to be too cold. . . . When all the recording sessions were over, O'Connell, seated in the control room with the two artists, would witness another sort of argument. Heifetz and Rubinstein were arguing over which 'takes' should be included in the final releases. Each felt that the other opted for passages which were favoring their respective instruments to the detriment of the other. When, however, everything was decided upon, along came Feuermann and the same problem arose again."[27] Of Heifetz's playing at those sessions, Rubinstein wrote that "nobody could touch his perfection. There was always the beautiful tone, the impeccable technique, and the pure intonation, but when it came to the interpretation proper there was often a fundamental discord between us." Feuermann, on the other hand, was "an artist after my heart. A supreme master of his instrument, he was a source of inspiration throughout our recordings. In the Schubert and the Beethoven, I had constant arguments with Heifetz, never with Feuermann."[28]

The celebrated violist William Primrose, who was in Los Angeles to record other chamber works with Heifetz, turned pages for Rubinstein during those sessions. He recalled that during a rehearsal of the last movement of the "Archduke," "with its jaunty, lilting theme in the piano, Rubinstein injected more than a modicum of Polish espièglerie. I was standing behind him . . . and he turned to me and winked. Heifetz just stopped playing, and everything else stopped. . . . [Heifetz] didn't say anything at first, but faced Rubinstein and gave him the sort of look he reserves for the undue prankster. Then he said in a very precise, somewhat martinet manner, 'Do you mind if we do that again?' Artur just shrugged his shoulders and 'played it straight.' With all my soul I wish Artur had insisted on his own version. I don't remember any other occasion when Heifetz imposed himself even to that extent."[29]

Despite the difficulties, the results came reasonably close to satisfying all three artists, as is evident from a series of letters (written mainly in German) from Feuermann to Rubinstein.

[October 24, 1941] Dr. [Paul] Schiff [a concert manager] related to me on the telephone that you told him you were enchanted with our trio recordings. . . . From Heifetz and Florence [née Vidor, Heifetz's wife] I had "raving wires" about the trios. You can imagine how we [Feuermann and his wife] are burning to hear the records at last. Since you seem to agree that they should be published, I can now anticipate the pleasure of hearing them.

[November 18, 1941] I have played our trios over and over again on the phonograph, I found some passages wonderful, in others I found fault with this or that, I found my own playing good at best (and no better), was overwhelmed by your and Heifetz's playing, but in some phrases I felt that what you do is not so right, in others what Heifetz does isn't [right], as to myself I was, as I said, disappointed—altogether I found the trios magnificent, but I was listening critically. By chance, I was in town [New York] this afternoon, had a little free time, and went into a phonograph shop where the Beethoven trio was being played by Cortot-Thibaud-Casals. Now I am absolutely enchanted by US, I am overwhelmed. I find our trio-playing—individually and as an ensemble—perfect, beautifully phrased, and aside from a few too rapid tempi, I can think of nothing more beautiful. I had to tell you this, and if you are here and have some time, do let yourself listen to the Beethoven trio, too. I know after my experience of this afternoon *how* good our trio is.

[November 24, 1941] Heifetz did *not* let me know what choice [of takes] the two of you hit upon. I sent him mine. . . . What do we do now? It seems that these three numbers deviate from those chosen by you. There seems to be more of a hurry than I had thought, and it would be appropriate if we could talk about it tomorrow.[30]

Feuermann's choice of takes was eventually accepted by Heifetz and Rubinstein, but a hitch developed with respect to the issuing of the records. On December 15, 1941, Feuermann wrote to Rubinstein: "You are having a personal quarrel with Victor, and the question of our trio is once again or rather perpetually unsettled. I assume that your controversy with Victor has now been settled, and naturally along your lines. And now, what about the trios? . . ." This problem, too, was soon settled, and according to Weschler-

Vered, when the records were ready for issue RCA arranged a concert "in which the trio would make its début as part of advance publicity."[31] But the performance never took place, because on May 25, 1942, Feuermann—the trio's youngest member—died at the age of thirty-nine, following minor surgery.

Seven years after Feuermann's death, Rubinstein and Heifetz formed a trio with Piatigorsky. In the summer of 1949 the group gave four concerts at Chicago's Ravinia Park, and Weschler-Vered reported that the "triumvirate was so successful that one of the critics called it 'The Million Dollar Trio' . . . Rubinstein [said that he] resented the fact that this nickname was quickly attached to them and . . . [that he] immediately ceased to appear with the formation. Historically, however, Rubinstein's assertion was a little premature," because he subsequently made some recordings and even a film with his partners. The rehearsals for these sessions, which took place in 1950, "were reported to be dominated by frequent, interminable musical 'squabbles' between Heifetz and Rubinstein," Weschler-Vered said. "Divergences of opinion would occur over the most minute phrase, their respective tempos, and almost every other facet of musical interpretation. At times the 'discussions' became so stormy that the artists were compelled to interrupt the rehearsals."[32] They even fought over whether the trio should be called Heifetz-Rubinstein-Piatigorsky or Rubinstein-Heifetz-Piatigorsky; the poor cellist didn't have a chance—and not only about the name. Piatigorsky told Ivor Newton that at one rehearsal, Heifetz had stopped playing to say, " 'The balance is all wrong. I can hear the cello.' " And when Newton asked Rubinstein "how he had enjoyed this episode in his career, he simply replied, 'They wanted me to play like a mouse!' "[33]

Rubinstein and Heifetz never again played together, and Weschler-Vered's guess that their musical differences also affected their social relations was right. "Dear Jascha—Thank you for having asked your secretary to phone us your refusal to come to our dinner," begins the draft of a note that the pianist sent to the violinist. (The document is undated, but was found among papers dating from 1952.) ". . . you proved beyond doubt that your manners did not change since our last outspoken conversation in Chicago, on the contrary, if possible, they are getting worse. You resented my not answering a printed new year's card, but ignore for a month a formal invitation to dinner. For some unknown reason you seem to think you are entitled to special privileges. I always wonder why? Is it the fact that you play in tune and quicker than other violinists? In any case and if you do feel yourself to be such a great man, accept this last friendly advice, dear Jascha: try to acquire some manners, because, as the French say, 'noblesse oblige.' "[34]

Rubinstein's "personal quarrel with Victor," to which Feuermann had referred in his last note to the pianist, concerned the company's favoring a new Horowitz-Toscanini recording of the Tchaikovsky Concerto No. 1 over Rubinstein's earlier recording of the work with Barbirolli. But it also had to do with his dislike of the bossy, I-know-better-than-you working methods of RCA's Charles O'Connell (not O'Connor, as Rubinstein called him in *My Many Years*), whom Toscanini and several other major Victor artists had also found difficult. O'Connell was eventually dismissed, and Rubinstein's recording of the Tchaikovsky Concerto was given renewed attention. Shortly thereafter, with RCA's and Nela's encouragement, Rubinstein studied, fell in love with, and recorded the Grieg Concerto—a popular work that had not previously interested him. His partners in the venture were Eugene Ormandy and the Philadelphia Orchestra. "Let me tell you how glad I am that you also agree that the Grieg Concerto recordings are excellent," Ormandy wrote to Rubinstein in June 1942, after having listened to the test pressings from the sessions, which had taken place three months earlier. "They really are, and even though some of the wind instruments could still be more audible in places (in spite of my having taken the liberty of reorchestrating these weak parts) the general effect is without any question outstanding. In fact, if I think of the records we listened to the day before our recording date, I must enthusiastically yell to you, 'Bravo, Arthur'. I only hope that you will use your influence with the Victor Company and have these records released now while this concerto is 'popular.'" The records were soon released, and in mid-August Ormandy wrote again to Rubinstein: "The Grieg records are selling like hot cakes. I am so glad for us both."[35] Shortly after the records were issued, Rachmaninoff, who loved the Grieg Concerto, was visiting Rubinstein, and the younger pianist could not resist the temptation to play part of his new release, of which he was very proud, for his senior colleague. At the end of the first movement, Rachmaninoff was silent for a while. At last he said, "I need a record player. Where can I find one like yours?" In later years, Rubinstein enjoyed telling this story at his own expense.[36]

As a result of the Grieg "hit" and of the more favored status that he was enjoying at Victor, Rubinstein's RCA earnings, which had been approximately $2,000 in 1940, $3,000 in 1941, and $4,000 in 1942, jumped to $14,000 in 1943; then slipped back slightly to $12,000 in 1944 but leapt forward to $27,000 in 1945, to $67,000 in 1946, and to the astonishing figure, for its day, of $90,000 in 1947.[37]

THE WAR-ENFORCED RESTRICTIONS on travel abroad and the relative scarcity of summertime musical activities in America in those years kept Rubinstein at home with his family during long vacation periods. One of the few important summer concert venues, at the time, was the nearby Hollywood Bowl, where he played twelve times—not including repeat performances—between July 1941 and August 1951, with the Los Angeles Philharmonic under Szell, Barbirolli, Beecham, Otto Klemperer, William Steinberg, Izler Solomon, Ormandy, Koussevitzky, Alfred Wallenstein, and Rodzinski; his Bowl repertoire comprised the Brahms Second, Tchaikovsky First, Rachmaninoff Second, Beethoven Fourth, Chopin First and Second, Schumann and Liszt First Concertos, and Rachmaninoff's Rhapsody on a Theme of Paganini. An article about Rubinstein's reputedly troubled relations with the Bowl's administration appeared in *Daily Variety* on August 23, 1946, and it made the pianist so angry that he replied with a letter to the editor that was printed four days later. "The article," he wrote, "states that 'having learned . . . that Heifetz was booked at $5,000, Rubinstein has blown his top and the Bowl forever, he declares, taunted by jibes of fellow artists.' The article also states that I have disclosed that I 'will never again play the Bowl—at any figure' and that I 'condescended' to appear at the Bowl for $2500.00. . . . My next appearance at the Bowl will be on September 2, 1946. . . . I have also indicated to the Bowl management my willingness to appear next year . . . and the amount paid for my appearance there (other than benefit performances for which I do not accept compensation) is in excess of $2500.00. . . ." On the other side of the continent, at the New York Philharmonic's outdoor concerts at Lewisohn Stadium, Rubinstein played repertoire similar to what he played at the Bowl, with Rodzinski, Alexander Smallens, Reiner, and Beecham, between June 1941 and June 1946.

Sometimes, however, summertime relaxation was a little more relaxed. In a cookbook that Nela Rubinstein published after her husband's death, she told the story of a summer expedition with family and friends to catch crayfish in the Los Angeles River. "Rising at dawn, . . . we dressed in our oldest clothes—which for one member of the family meant an elegant outfit worn at daytime rehearsals in the hot summer for outdoor concerts. This included a fine Panama hat [and] a carnation boutonnière. . . . Armed with a jar of bait (horse liver bought at an odd little market) and a motley assemblage of buckets, string, sticks, sieves, strainers, and one real fish net, the adult and teenage members of the household drove off over the hills into the valley. . . . Competition was in the air, and jealousy over each crayfish brought in and 'pailed' made us change places often and tug too nervously on our strings. . . . Arthur, being comfortably placed on the best rock in the shadiest spot, and having the steadiest hands (and the only proper net), invariably caught twice as many crayfish as anyone else. In a few hours, the six or seven of us once caught about 450, enough for a real feast . . ." Nela also remembered a party that she and Arthur gave "the night before our tenth anniversary," in July 1942; it "could have been disastrous," she said, "for the help inexplicably left . . . , our son, Paul, had mumps, and we had invited fifty guests to a sit-down dinner, then more guests for dancing, and a late supper for, as it turned out, everyone!"[38] Labunski remembered a similar "tremendous affair, with a . . . dinner for sixty people, at small tables in all rooms downstairs, sun room and terraces. All the celebrities of Hollywood were there—actors and actresses, directors, producers. I had the privilege of being dinner partner of the great actress and delightful person, Ethel Barrymore, while Wanda was entertaining her partner, Ronald Coleman. Up to the last minute Nela was in the kitchen cooking, directing, and doing the last-minute check. And then she threw away her apron and greeted the guests, looking like a queen. After dinner and champagne, a folding floor was put over the rug of the living room, more guests came, and people began dancing. At the moment when I was waltzing with the charming Loretta Young, burglars entered her house and took away furs, jewelry and other valuables. . . . Toward the end of the party, well after midnight, Cole Porter started playing the piano, Jeannette McDonald and Dinah Shore sang, and Danny Kaye made his unique imitations."

During the same stay, the Labunskis met Stravinsky and his wife at a lunch at the Rubinstein's home, and the Labunskis found the "great composer a delightful person and a very interesting 'causeur.' Being among us Poles he emphasized the fact that he was of Polish ancestry, and told us how in his childhood he spent many months vacationing in the Ukraine, where there was a large Polish population. He understands Polish quite well, but did not speak it that day on account of his wife who did not know it." A frequent visitor *chez* Rubinstein was Oscar Levant, the pianist, wit, and notorious hypochondriac. "He usually came toward the end of the evening," Labunski recalled, "and immediately asked for coffee, which he drank in enormous quantities all evening, simultaneously smoking one cigarette after another."[39]

Typically, the Rubinstein's guests at large and small gatherings during their California years were Hollywood stars or members of the community of exiled European artists and intellectuals. In 1942, Basil Rathbone wrote to Rubinstein: "If I could be such an artist as you are I would not feel one moment[']s unhappiness about my contribution to human happiness. You play great music greatly—I make cheap entertainments often very inadequately."[40] Four years later, Cary Grant wrote to tell Arthur and Nela that he had "had the most enjoyable evening I have spent in months when last I was at your house—after Cole [Porter]'s party. You were telling me then, Arthur, about a book of musicians' letters to each other and I think I told you about the existence of a similar book of painters' letters. I am sending it to you with this note. . . ."[41]

In 1944, Rubinstein had received an entirely different sort of letter from

Franz Werfel. The Austrian-born, Beverly Hills–based novelist asked him to sign a petition in which the American Society of Composers, Authors, and Publishers was requested, in honor of Schoenberg's seventieth birthday, to "double the customary sum of his royalties for the balance of his life," since "the material rewards for Schoenberg's accomplishments have not been at all commensurate with their cultural importance."[42] Rubinstein probably signed it, although in his memoirs he mentioned only having been one of a "group of musicians who decided to help" the composer, and who thought that Schoenberg ought to "obtain a commission . . . to compose music for films"[43]—a project that was never realized. Schoenberg attended at least one chamber music party at the Rubinsteins' house, because thirty years later Monika Mann—Thomas Mann's daughter—recalled having been present with her parents, and having sat "next to Schoenberg, who ate an enormous amount while you played chamber music!!" Rubinstein saw the Manns on several occasions when both families were living in California. "I remember the Santa Monica period, when my father was writing his [Doktor] Faustus," Monika Mann wrote to Rubinstein in 1973. "He was much preoccupied with the nature of musicians—and once, not without 'lighthearted envy,' declared: 'This Rubinstein is a happy man!' "[44] Rubinstein replied: "The recollection of my encounters with your father and his family remains deeply engraved in my memory, I remember every word he said and it was always a joy to make music before him, because he loved and understood it so well."[45]

Eva Rubinstein recalled, "One summer my father wrote a piano transcription of 'Salome's Dance,' and every time I hear that music, even now, it sounds funny played by an orchestra. I see myself in one of the small patios, at the house in Marlboro Street: I'm nine, I'm hearing it through his library wall. Once, he wrote cadenzas for Beethoven's Fourth Concerto, and that would keep him occupied mentally, as well. He would practice, he would play a little, there would be chamber music occasionally, we had dinner parties, and there was their anniversary and my mother's birthday late in July. But toward August he would start to twitch, because he hadn't had an audience for a while. It was like going cold turkey. He would start being uncomfortable. He would say, 'Well, I don't know, maybe this should be the last season'—almost thinking eschatologically of his career; maybe this was it. Which was total nonsense: the first concert got him completely out of it. But he would go through this every single summer."[46]

Edwin Knopf, a Hollywood producer who was the brother of Alfred A. Knopf, the publisher, and Edwin's wife Mildred, got to know the Rubinsteins well during the war years. Mildred remembered meeting Arthur and Nela for the first time at a lunch at the Brown Derby Restaurant, opposite the Beverly Wilshire Hotel; Olivia de Havilland and her sister Joan Fontaine were also present. "Arthur did nothing through the meal but talk to and flirt with these two beautiful young stars, and Nela sat there, grim-faced," Mrs. Knopf recalled. But she and Nela soon became the best of friends. "Nela and I had such good times together in California," she said, "but she was two different people: She was one person when Arthur was there, and another when he wasn't. When he wasn't, she was loving and relaxed and finding dozens of things to do that entertained and amused us; when he was, she was uptight and worried all the time that she might be disturbing or distressing him or doing the wrong thing. Arthur was very much wrapped up in himself and wanted others to recognize whatever he did or said. In some ways you could relax with him, if he was talking about music or art or the theater or famous people or funny episodes in his own life, but you couldn't relax in a silly, easygoing way with him." During the war, when food was rationed, Mildred and Nela kept chickens, in order to have a supply of fresh eggs, but the chicken feed attracted rats and the whole process soon became so complicated that they killed the chickens. Nela decided to make chicken soup, and she invited Mildred over to help her pluck the chickens. They were working, laughing, and gossiping together, "when suddenly the door opened and in walked Arthur, looking very smart in a fedora hat, a brown suit with a vest, a red carnation, and his cane," Mildred said. "He was absolutely *furious* and started *screaming* at Nela: 'You have servants—it's insulting to use your friends for this kind of thing!' The whole situation was so embarrassing that I got up and walked home. He never forgave her for that. He was a self-made man; he had made all this money and was proud of the fact that he could have luxury, including endless servants. To him, the idea that someone on his social level would do the work of a servant was absolutely appalling. He didn't mind the fact that she was plucking chickens, but that she was 'using' a friend like me to help.

"Nela was really something, in those days—so extraordinary, so creative, and such fun to be with," Mrs. Knopf continued. "She had tremendous vitality, tremendous joy in living. The household ran as smooth as silk; she did everything so that he would not be upset or embarrassed about anything—and small thanks she got for it. After a concert, she would go home a little early and make sure that everything was set up for the dinner guests. She loved the people who loved him, hated the ones who didn't, and she lived totally for him. I think it was very hard on the children, because they were always left alone; she never let him go off on his tours without her: she saw that his ruby studs were ready, and an extra starched shirt, because he perspired when he played. She spent her whole life thinking about him. She always believed that her relationship with Arthur was on an even keel. She knew that he flirted with other women, but I don't think it ever occurred to her that he was unfaithful. He said later that she was terribly naive to have believed that he had been faithful; he said he'd never been faithful to her for a week."[47] Fifty years later, Mrs. Rubinstein commented: "As far as other women were concerned, I absolutely trusted him, and he said, 'Je ne t'ai jamais trompée' ['I never cheated on you']. Now I'm not so sure what he meant by that. Louis Bender, his valet, sometimes told me that he had saved Arthur from 'compromising situations.'" Rubinstein told a few intimates about several erotic escapades that he had enjoyed in America during that period: He was allegedly involved with Peggy Korn—the daughter of Governor Herbert Lehman of New York—until Nela became pregnant in 1944, when he brought the story to a close;[48] and he had affairs with a certain Gloria in Houston, with the wife of a well-known conductor in a midwestern city, and with others—probably quite a few others.

During his leisurely wartime summers, Rubinstein began to devote considerable attention to teaching. He did not give piano lessons as such, but rather coached a few promising young pianists who were already far advanced in their studies. One of the first was Laura Dubman, a San Franciscan who had played for him in Paris in 1938, at the age of fourteen, and whom he had coached at Deauville during the summer of 1939. She and her mother traveled to America with Rubinstein and his family in October 1939, and in New York he listened to Laura whenever he had free time. She followed the Rubinsteins to California, lived with them at various times, and eventually became the Rubinstein children's piano teacher. For a while she played in public, but she stopped giving concerts when she was nineteen.[49]

Like Dubman, Patricia Smolen, a Chicagoan, first played for Rubinstein in 1938, at the age of fourteen. The encounter took place at John Alden Carpenter's home in Chicago; he heard her play the first movement of the Tchaikovsky Concerto and "he suggested I come to Paris to work with him," she said, but she was not able to make the necessary arrangements before his immigration to the States. She studied with Egon Petri, a Busoni disciple, then with Artur Schnabel and with the American pianist Leonard Shure. (She said that Rubinstein "winced" when she told him that she had been working with Schnabel but "made no comment" on Shure.) Eventually, she began to take occasional lessons from Rubinstein, at fifty dollars per lesson; Schnabel had charged forty dollars. When he knew that he was going to be in New York for a spell, he would send her a note like the following one, dated May 1, 1945: "Dear Patsy—I am coming to New-York on May 18th or 19th and stay 10 days—so I hope to see you and hear you—I shall stay at the Madison [Hotel] please telephone me and we can make a date—I hope your music is in fine shape! Yours always Arthur Rubinstein." Smolen recalled, in a letter written forty-five years later:

He would listen to me play a complete composition before offering suggestions and criticisms. He would demonstrate by playing different sections himself, tying together what he had previously taken apart. His approach was towards the overall conception of the work itself. . . .

[On Chopin:] I can still hear him imploring, "Sing, sing, sing." In a raspy voice, he tried to demonstrate while he played the music. He would tenderly begin a long melodic phrase relapsing into his own inimitable rubato. I distinctly remember his sumptuous legatos and whispering pianissimos. Playing the big A flat Polonaise, he showed me how to produce the effect of volume without resorting to earsplitting fortissimos.

Rubinstein on several occasions voiced his disapproval of students trying to imitate their teachers. He flatly stated that he wouldn't want an audience to say, "Aha, she studied with Rubinstein." . . . He went on, "Your ears are your best teacher. You must always listen carefully to yourself. Even if you make records, listen very critically to them." . . .

Rubinstein never talked to me about any of his own studies or teachers; made few references to his personal life; did not refer me to managers, orchestras, etc.; never talked about technical problems per se, stressing rather, interpretive aspects almost exclusively. . . .

My studies with Rubinstein ended when I got married and left New York. Although I saw him when we happened to be in the same city, I never played for him again.[50]

Eunice Podis, a pianist from Cleveland who was about the same age as Dubman and Smolen, studied with Rubinstein during the summer of 1942. She recalled, in a 1989 interview: "The lessons really took much of the day; he didn't watch the clock at all. We would work for a while, then we'd listen to some of his recordings, we'd talk, then play some more, then we'd have lunch, then play some more again. He was in no hurry at all. He said, 'You know, I am not a pedagogue, but from working with you I find that I have to analyze things that I normally just do instinctively in the music, so it's very good for me to do this.' I played the Debussy 'Minstrels' for him; he listened to it—always with a big cigar in his mouth—and he said, 'You know, I thought, here's a young American girl, and she's really going to know how to play this piece!' Because after all, minstrel shows were American. 'But it's all wrong,' he said. 'You're playing it like Chopin or a Romantic composer.' We worked on it, and he gave me a much more authentic interpretation of it.

"I studied Rachmaninoff's Third Concerto with him, the whole Op. 119

[three intermezzos and the E-flat Major Rhapsody] of Brahms, and Chopin's
A Minor Etude—the 'Winter Wind'—and he demonstrated for me how he
had played it when he was young, without playing any right notes in the right
hand, but somehow or other it came off anyway. I also did Chopin's G Minor
Ballade and some Scriabin études. But we worked mainly on the 'Appassionata' Sonata. Five years later, when I was making my New York debut at
Town Hall, I decided to play it there. By that time I had realized that I
needed something further in the way of discipline, and I had written to Rudolf Serkin to ask him if he would listen to my Town Hall recital program. At
my first lesson with him, I played the 'Appassionata,' and he said, 'I don't
know if I can teach you. You don't play two bars in the same tempo.' Well,
when I'd played for Rubinstein, that hadn't been necessary. On the first page,
where there are those syncopated chords, Rubinstein just went crazy; Serkin
played them strictly in time. They were two completely different extremes—
which is wonderful, of course, but it was a little unsettling at the time."

In an article published in 1983, Podis said that Rubinstein had "spent
very little time on technical problems—there was no talk of scales, arpeggios
or exercises—for he took these aspects of piano-playing for granted. . . . Never
rigid or authoritarian, he allowed me a great deal of freedom as long as I
played persuasively; 'I would not do it that way, but you have convinced me,'
he would say occasionally, and then he would not change one note. Yet he
could spend two hours on the first page of Beethoven's 'Appassionata,' delv-
ing into the complexities of rhythm, color, proportion, phrasing, character. . . .
Of all Rubinstein's philosophies, the one that most endeared him to me was
his attitude toward practice. 'Never practice more than three or four hours a
day,' he insisted; 'No one can concentrate longer than that, and you must
spend the rest of your time learning about life and love and art and all the
other wonderful things in the world. If a young person sits in the practice
room all day, what can he possibly have to express in his music?' "[51]

"For seven or eight weeks," Podis said in the 1989 interview, "I would
have a lesson whenever I was ready; some weeks I had two lessons. But then I
got appendicitis—had to have my appendix out—and went back home as
soon as I was well enough. After that, whenever he came to Cleveland or
whenever I was in a city where he was playing, I would play for him. He was a
man who loved life more, probably, than anybody else I've ever known.
Many artists find concert tours a terrible drag, but he was at home anywhere
in the world, and I think he always enjoyed himself fully no matter where he
was. He used to play on the Concert Course at the [Cleveland] Music Hall,
and after the concerts the wealthy businessmen who sponsored the series entertained lavishly for the artists, with full-course meals. I remember so many
occasions when Rubinstein would attend these, eat dinner, smoke cigars,

drink champagne, and do what he did better than anything else except play the piano—tell marvellous stories. The fun and joyousness of those occasions is still clear in my mind. He always was a party guy—he loved conviviality. The good life was a very important part of his makeup. He had such a strong personality and was so very lovable. And he wanted to be lovable—it was important to him."[52]

Most of the pianists whom Rubinstein coached were talented, young, and female, and he later told Annabelle Whitestone that he had had an affair with one of them—not named above—when he was in his mid-seventies and the pupil in her early twenties. But he also listened to and encouraged several promising young male pianists, including the brilliant William Kapell, a pupil of Josef Lhévinne. In July 1941, Rubinstein's friend Fredric R. Mann, a music-loving businessman, reported to Rubinstein that the eighteen-year-old Kapell had given a highly successful concert in Philadelphia—where Mann lived—and referred to him as "your protégé."[53] Relations between Kapell and Rubinstein were often plagued by misunderstandings, but the older pianist continued to approve of the younger one's playing. Kapell's extraordinary career ended tragically when he was killed in an airplane crash in 1953.

DURING THE EARLY years of Rubinstein's American residency, many American observers continued to associate him with modern piano music. In March 1940, for instance, Olin Downes gave considerable space in a review in the New York Times to Rubinstein's playing of the polka from Shostakovich's ballet The Golden Age and to Prokofiev's Suggestion diabolique, both of which he brought off "with consummate understanding and probably keen relish of their irony and brilliance."[54] And some months later, the critics in the Times and the Herald-Tribune praised his playing of modern Spanish music (Albéniz, Falla, and Mompou) while castigating what they both described as an excessively cool and "objective" performance of Schubert's "Wanderer" Fantasy.[55] In January 1942, in Cleveland, he gave his first performances of Szymanowski's Fourth Symphony—better known as the "Symphonie Concertante"—with Rodzinski and the Cleveland Orchestra; the work, written ten years earlier, had been dedicated to him, and he played it often in the following years. But by the mid-1940s, most of the modern works in his repertoire had been in it for many years, and all of them were written in idioms that had long since ceased to shock audiences. He had become a thoroughly "safe" pianist— one to be revered and praised for his performances of "safe" repertoire.

So successful did Rubinstein become that from time to time he gave concerts whose programs were not announced in advance; he decided which pieces to play when he sat down in front of the audience, and he relied on his own name, rather than the composers' names, to fill the hall. "The first blow was struck in Carnegie Hall last night in what may shape up to a crusade against printed programs," wrote Louis Biancolli in the *New York World-Telegram* on February 25, 1946. "Artur Rubinstein, lapsing from the stuffy old tradition of the printed word, announced his numbers from the stage."

> The whole program came by word of mouth—Mr. Rubinstein's—and by hand, two hands, in fact—also Mr. Rubinstein's. The only printed matter were the ads and Mr. Rubinstein's manifesto on behalf of the spoken word.
> "I will begin my program with the Chaconne by Bach, transcribed by Busoni." With those words Mr. Rubinstein launched his quasi-impromptu program.
> The celebrated pianist had reserved the right to let the spur of the moment dictate the next number. Also the mood of the house, the acoustics, and the impish little gremlins who might whisper "Bach" into [the] pianist's waiting ears.
> . . . you didn't need a guide at all to Mr. Rubinstein's numbers. What he played didn't matter. It was all fine and poetic, fiery and articulate. Mr. Rubinstein could have saved his breath.
> When a pianist plays like Artur Rubinstein, words, even spoken ones, are superfluous. Bach, César Franck, Chopin become mere labels. All you need know about the next number is that it is more Rubinstein. . . . It was nice to have Mr. Rubinstein divulge titles if you couldn't identify the music unaided. But the man was playing so well, you were half tempted to assure him it really didn't matter what the next number was.[56]

This and similar articles probably made Rubinstein understand how easily listeners could be persuaded that performers were more important than the works they played; before long, he went back to choosing his programs in time to have them announced in print. When Rubinstein gave his first Carnegie Hall recital the following season, Francis D. Perkins remarked in the *New York Herald-Tribune* that "this time . . . it was published in advance that he would play Beethoven's Pathetic Sonata, Chopin's twenty-four preludes and works of Albéniz, de Falla, Milhaud and Brahms." And, he added laconically, "He played them remarkably."[57]

Rubinstein's growing celebrity made him a candidate for approaches from Hollywood, and in the 1940s he agreed to appear and/or play the piano in several movies. One of them—made by RKO—was described by Herbert Kupferberg, in his history of the Philadelphia Orchestra, as "a tear-jerker

. . . about a blind night-club musician with a great concerto racing through his head." In the end, the musician manages to have his work performed by Rubinstein, with Ormandy conducting. Ethel Barrymore, Merle Oberon, and Dana Andrews played in the film, and Leith Stevens, a Hollywood composer, wrote a concerto for it. "The movie underwent a number of vicissitudes, including three changes of title, *Counterpoint, Memory of Love* and *Night Song,*" Kupferberg said. "Reviewing the picture in the New York *Times,* Bosley Crowther termed the music 'a scrappy and meaningless jangle' and commented: 'If Mr. Rubinstein and Mr. Ormandy can swallow it, along with their pride, they must have pretty strong stomachs.' "[58] Rubinstein also recorded parts of the sound track of the film *A Song of Love,* about Robert and Clara Schumann; this experience he enjoyed, because he tried to imagine and reproduce the keyboard styles of the Schumanns, Liszt, and Brahms, all of whom figured in the plot. "He had a great old time making that movie," Eva Rubinstein recalled, and her father said that "Katharine Hepburn did wonders impersonating Clara Schumann, playing . . . as if she were a born pianist. The whole film was made with love and respect for the subject,"[59] and Hepburn remained a friend of Rubinstein and his family. But the best-known of his screen appearances was filmed not in Hollywood but in Carnegie Hall, as Richard Schickel reported in his history of the auditorium. "In July of 1946 a whole trainload of equipment was shipped from Hollywood to New York and installed in Carnegie Hall as Boris Morros, the noted counterspy, began production of his film *Carnegie Hall.* Streets were torn up as heavy cable, capable of handling the electrical load imposed by klieg lights and other equipment, was installed. From then until October, something known as a cast of thousands labored in the unair-conditioned hall to make the film. . . . Included in the cast were Damrosch, Rodzinski, Walter, Stokowski and Fritz Reiner. On the set Piatigorsky, Rubinstein and Heifetz, Risë Stevens, Jan Peerce, Ezio Pinza and Lily Pons rubbed shoulders with Harry James, Vaughan Monroe and his orchestra and hundreds of extras sweltering in dress clothes. . . . The only trouble with the whole thing was the plot. Before beginning work on the picture Rubinstein had cracked, 'I bet it ends up with Harry James playing the trumpet.' Little did he dream how right he was. The plot had Marsha Hunt as a charwoman at the hall taking her son to concert after concert in order to instill in him the desire to be a serious pianist."[60] A single movie assignment could bring Rubinstein as much as $85,000, but in 1946 he denied, in a letter to the editor of Hollywood's *Daily Variety,* that he had been offered $500,000 for a three-year contract with Metro-Goldwyn-Mayer.[61]

In addition to his occasional cinema earnings, by the 1947–48 season, ten years after his "re-debut" in the United States, Rubinstein was making as much as $100,000 a year from recordings and was charging $3,500 each for most of the approximately one hundred concerts that he gave each year in North America.[62] Among the New York Philharmonic's soloists during the 1949–50 season, the only one who received a higher fee than Rubinstein — who was paid $8,000 for performing in three concerts (he played Rachmaninoff's Rhapsody on a Theme of Paganini in all three and, additionally, Mozart's Concerto in A Major, K. 488, in two of them) — was Heifetz, who received $9,500 for a similar service; after them came Myra Hess at $7,000, Robert Casadesus at $4,150, Rudolf Serkin at $4,100 for four performances, Nathan Milstein at $3,800 for three, and then all the others.[63] In 1964, Rubinstein's American fee was either $6,000 per performance or 70 percent of the gross box office take — whichever was higher.

By the mid-1940s, Rubinstein was a wealthy man. And yet, financial security and high living were not the prime movers in his professional life. "You mustn't tell Mr. Hurok," he often joked with interviewers, "but the fact is, I would go on giving piano recitals just for the fun of it, whether I got paid or not."[64] He loved to play for people, loved to give, loved the intoxication of intense communication with others. And at last, musicians and music lovers in the United States as elsewhere had come to understand this aspect of the Rubinstein phenomenon. In an article published in the *Herald-Tribune* in 1949, the composer and critic Virgil Thomson summed up the attitudes of hundreds of thousands of listeners: "Artur Rubinstein, who played a recital of piano music last night in Carnegie Hall, made his first American appearance more than forty years ago," Thomson wrote. "He has long been a great musician and a grand executant; and now, approaching sixty [Rubinstein was already sixty-two), he is king of his profession. Others may be regularly more flashy, though few can dazzle so dependably; and none can match him for power and refinement. He plays very loudly and very beautifully, very softly and thoroughly clean, straightforwardly, elegantly and with a care for both the amenities of musical discourse and the clear transmission of musical thought. He is a master pianist and a master musician. There has not been his like since Busoni."[65]

Other musicians, too, touched Rubinstein with their personal messages. "I want to thank you most warmly for the great treat you gave me last night with your masterly & deeply satisfying rendering of the Beethoven [Fourth] Concerto," the composer and pianist Percy Grainger wrote in 1940, after a Rubinstein concert with the New York Philharmonic under Barbirolli. "It seems unbelievable to me that anyone can play as flawlessly, as gracefully, as euphoniously as you do!"[66] Three years later, after he had played another concerto with the Philharmonic, Rubinstein received a note from Isidor Philipp, an old acquaintance who had been the most celebrated piano professor at the Paris Conservatoire but, because of his Jewish origins, had fled to New

York early in the war. "My dear friend, I want to tell you . . . how much I admired your playing, the sovereign technique, the sound so pliant to every nuance, the musicality, the bravura, the absolute security of your memory," Philipp wrote. "The Symphony of Saint-Saëns"—one of Philipp's teachers— "brought back to me so many fine and tragic moments in my life that I am not ashamed to say that I had tears in my eyes—but as I listened to you play with such joy, dare I tell you that a bit of hope began to comfort the sad exiled man that I am."[67] Early in 1952, after having attended a Rubinstein recital in New York, the eighty-eight-year-old Philipp wrote: "Dear friend, the adoring crowd prevented me from seeing you yesterday. I was going to ask you where you get that sound, that rhythm, that unparalleled technique, that youthfulness and—that kindness, which means that after one has exchanged only a few words with you, one is sure that you are his best friend! One day, after I had played Mozart's Concerto in C Minor at the Conservatoire, Gounod came up to me in the foyer and said: 'My young friend, do you know where this concerto comes from?' 'Where it comes from, Master?' 'It comes from heaven, like everything that the God of music wrote. Yes, Mozart is the greatest.' I shall paraphrase this *mot:* 'Your talent comes from heaven and you are the greatest!' "[68]

DURING THE WAR, Rubinstein's friend Fredric R. Mann maintained contacts with Jewish underground organizations in German-occupied Europe and was one of the people through whom Rubinstein tried to find out what was happening to his family and friends, and to help whenever possible. Thanks to Rubinstein, Mann, and Mann's contacts, Vladimir Golschmann's brother and the composer Alexandre Tansman managed to escape from France to the United States in 1940.[69] Escape from Eastern Europe, however, was much more difficult. In April 1940, Rubinstein's niece Janka Landau Englender—his sister Hela's daughter—wrote to him from Galati, Rumania, to ask for assistance in obtaining a French visa, but the German conquest of France in May and June rendered any such attempt futile, and the spread of the war cut lines of communication. Three and a half years later, Rubinstein tried to contact his nephew Kazimierz Landau through the American Red Cross,[70] but the attempt was fruitless: by then, Himmler's gas chambers and crematoria were working around the clock. Not until February 1946 did Rubinstein learn of the fate of most of his brothers and sisters and their children and grandchildren, through a letter from the same niece, Janka. The letter, written in English, was sent from Slatina Olt, Rumania.

Dear Arthur,
Ever since 1939 the moment when I crossed the Polish-Roumanian
border, I have tried to get in touch with you by letters and tele-

grams. I wrote to concert-offices, but all in vain. - I was in a hell of
despair for except for my brother Jerry [Jerzy] who had to undergo
the whole terror-martyrdom—I have nobody in the world but you,
my dear Mother's only [sic] brother, who used to be everything for
her and for us. - As Jerry saw with his own eyes, Mother was killed
in 1942 in the action in Warsaw, the same fate overtook aunt Jadzia
[Jadwiga, Rubinstein's eldest sister] and Aniela [Jadzia's daughter]
and all our people at Lodz of whom only Pauzio [presumably
Rubinstein's uncle Paul Heiman] and uncle Likiernik [the husband
of Arthur's other sister, Frania] died a natural death; - the rest of the
family died at the hands of the hitlerist hangmen. - By miracle Jerry
and his wife Roma and Hala, Kazio's wife survived. - About Kazio
[Arthur's nephew Kazimierz, whom the pianist had tried to contact
in 1943] we don't know anything as he was a prisoner in Germany,
also Lilka Bernhardt, Aniela's daughter Hala Krukowska and part of
the family Szeminsky [?] were saved and you, who fortunately went
to the other side of this globe. -

Arthur dear, I don't want to bore you with the description of
our 7 years wandering which we spent in continual fear of the hit-
lerists without being able to settle down or earn anything. - We lived
on the relief we got from the government and sold some small
things we had taken along from home. -

But the real tragedy began now, when we don't know what to
do with ourselves. - We wanted to return home but conditions there
are extremely bad for "our" people, hitlerism has poisoned the public spirit so deeply that there is no room for us there. - Here we are
not allowed to stay, Palestine is not yet open to us. - So we are in
great despair, pennyless, without a roof over our heads, badly
clothed as we have only what we ran away with in 1939 and these
things are wearing out. - In Warsaw we lost everything and here we
are helpless. - The letter from Mr. Ignacy Neumark [a son or grandson of one of Rubinstein's mother's sisters], written in your name
cheered me up and gave me again some will to live. - I do hope you
will understand my situation and help me. - I beseech you by the
memory of my unforgettable mother, your sister, to help me. -
Above all I want to come over to you and I implore you to help me
in this direction. - I know it is a long and difficult matter but it cannot be hopeless for a man with your connection. - Till the time,
when that will be possible help me by sending me some money
through "Hicem", whose head office is in New-York and a branch-
office in Bucharest and who do that sort of things. - It will have to be

sent by cable as otherwise it might last months. - First of all I want to buy some clothes, because mine are completely worn out and, besides, if I have some money at my disposal I might manage to get to Palestine and from there perhaps to America. -

Arthur dear, I am sure when you get this letter you will realize my position and help me by doing everything you can as now you are the only person in the world I can count upon. - *The most important thing is to help quickly.* - I suppose you received the telegram I sent directly after getting the letter from Mr. Neumark to his address. - In order to understand my situation let me tell you that I sold a frock in order to pay for this cablegram. - How are you and your family? How is Maryla and Janek?

Write to me soon!

> Best love to you all
> Yours Janka[71]

It is believed that Rubinstein did help (Janka eventually returned to Poland, where she died of cancer in 1981), and he certainly helped Karola Schneck (originally Sznek), the niece of his mother's sister who was the wife of Boleslaw Sznck—the uncle who had taken Arthur to the opera in Warsaw in 1896–97. Karola, her parents, and her brother had lived in Belgium before the war, and the tone of the letter that she sent him from Marseilles in the fall of 1945—although it uses the formal *vous*—demonstrates that he knew them personally and knew about their prewar life. "We left Belgium in May 1940 and came to France," she wrote. ". . . My mother and I had the luck of escaping from the Gestapo and avoiding deportation, but it was not the same for my brother Marcel, who was deported in 1942. I've had no news since. My dear Father died in March 1943 in Marseilles, which means that out of four there are only two of us left. How I lived until the liberation is too long a story to tell you. What I want to say to you is that like many Jews and non-Jews, one had to live under very difficult conditions, like outlaws. My Mother is ill and I don't know whether the state of her health will allow her to return to Belgium. In remembrance of my dear Father and our uncle Boleslaw and in the name of my Mother I ask you whether it would be possible for you to send us a little money. We lost everything in Belgium and the little that we had, we had to sell to survive. . . . You will understand our situation and that if I weren't really in need I would have avoided asking this of you. . . ."[72]

Rubinstein asked others for advice and made a note on Karola's letter: "Bad exchange on money[,] packages may be helpful." He wrote to her: ". . . I am keenly aware of the enormous difficulties that you have had to face during these tragic years, and it was with deep regret that I've read your letter and learned of the fate of your father and brother. I hope that the situation will begin to improve now and that the state of your mother's health is good once again, so that you can return soon to Belgium. The situation in Belgium seems to be a little better than the situation in France. Unfortunately, I am not in a position to send you the little money that you asked for. At the moment the exchange rate isn't good and you would receive very few francs for the dollars that I would send from here. I think it would be more useful and also more advantageous if I send you some packages with provisions. I'll send you some parcels, and please let me know that you've received them and also send me any change of address. Hoping that these parcels will be of use to you and make your life a little easier, I beg you to give your mother my best wishes. . . ."[73]

Alina Rubinstein was only a baby when her father learned of the fate of his family, but she later got the impression from him that "the fact that many members of his family died in the holocaust wasn't a direct emotional experience for him. It was something that reinforced other feelings. Because he never mentioned any one person he lost during the war. He was never close to his family."[74] According to Nela Rubinstein, Maryla Landau, Jadwiga's daughter—the one who had hidden a piece of halvah from Arthur when they were both children (and the one whom Janka Landau Englender asked about in her above-quoted letter)—had managed to get out of Europe before the war. "She had married a baron but she worked as a cook in New York, smoked five hundred cigarettes a day, and played bridge," Nela said. "Arthur couldn't bear her," because of the halvah incident. "His brother Tadeusz's daughter wound up in Tel Aviv, and Arthur helped her there. Her daughter was a gifted violinist—good but not great; Isaac Stern and Henryk Szeryng listened to her. She and her husband, a pianist, came to Paris and Arthur helped to look after them; he said that the husband, too, was gifted but not exceptional. I eventually threw them out of the house because Arthur was giving them hundreds of dollars a month yet still they would malign him to other people and accuse him of neglecting his family in Poland. I didn't have a gun to shoot them, so I said, 'Out!' I can't stand injustice."

Pleas for money from the few survivors among Arthur's siblings' children and grandchildren continued to reach him from time to time and eventually exasperated him. A faded and difficult-to-read draft of his reply to one such request from his nephew Jerzy Landau—Hela's son and Janka's brother—demonstrates his feelings on the subject.

26 October 1953
Dear Jerzy,
This is an answer to your last letter and, at the same time, to the few letters that you have written to me since the end of the war.

I would like to clear up some fundamental misunderstandings between us, such as, first, the difference in our ideas about the importance of relatives. You clearly consider blood ties and feelings separately, but I, unfortunately, am not of the same opinion. Having left my family when I was a ten-year-old boy, and having been educated in Berlin on other people's money, I got used in my very youngest years to thinking and living completely independently of my family, and that's why all through life I've been maintaining [?] brotherly friendships rather than [close relationships?] with so-called "relatives" (the closest ones). You ought to remember that I was living in misery in Warsaw . . . - none of you [came to my aid?] in times that were rather difficult for me, materially and morally. I don't deny [?] of course that I felt, somewhere in my veins, love of family and, to some degree, attachment to my sisters and brothers, but rather from a distance, for we had few *things in common.* [?] They didn't react in a family-type way. *Forgive me for stating this so coldly.* As to more distant relations, I have of course had almost no contact with you.

Forgive me for writing this to you so brutally, but I feel a need to straighten this question out once and for all. [?] On the other hand, in all your letters about all my nieces and nephews, apart from reminding me of our close kinship, I've been getting nothing but demands on my wallet, and probably for about 30 years. I can't remember a letter written to me either out of interest in my life *or my music* or simply out of the need to express a warmer feeling — so don't be surprised that my own family, which I have created myself, completely occupies all my active blood ties. Forgive me for explaining it to you so brutally, but I prefer that our relationship be clarified. I send you [?] Do not decide, as my nephews and nieces often do, whether the sum that you need is or is not a small one for me. I am the only one who can judge that. Let me remind you that once, to please your mother, I offered a large sum in dollars to Jadzia, your sister, as a dowry. The money was lost, I don't know how — nothing came of the marriage, and she and even you tortured me with letters demanding [?] sum ($3,000), considering it a trifle for me — and I was living from one concert to the next at that time. Well, never mind that.

I hope from my heart that the fortunes of all of you will improve so much that you will be able to think of me as a man and not as a close relative with money.

Your old Artur[75]

Rubinstein was occasionally in touch with H. M. Landau, one of his nephews, who lived in Paris after the war and did not ask him for money,[76] but the only member of his family in Europe whom Rubinstein both sought out and regularly helped was his brother Ignacy. Nela Rubinstein recalled that before the war Ignacy had been a radical political agitator but had also been very supercilious and sarcastic; he had gladly accepted whatever money Arthur gave him but had considered himself superior to his younger brother. During the German occupation he had lived with a Frenchwoman who had kept him hidden; thus, at war's end, he was Arthur's only surviving sibling. "I have been to see your brother at the Rothschild Hospital," Germaine de Rothschild wrote to Arthur in October 1945; she had evidently visited Ignacy at Arthur's request. "It was painful to see the poor man. He is very thin and I must say that he looks ill. Besides, he himself complains about being very ill. He seems to have nothing, and if it is possible for you to get some money and clothes to him, you would do him a great favor. He has absolutely nothing to wear. So it would be a matter of your giving him underwear, socks, a suit, and a coat. His wish, as he has let you know, I believe, would be to live in a little pension where he wouldn't be alone and would be released from all responsibilities and domestic worries. . . . [But] I am a little afraid that your brother's health is too bad for him to be able to live in a pension. Maybe a clinic? Food packets each week would be a great delight for him—jam, chocolate, coffee (I suppose he drinks it?), meat spreads, cheese, sardines, honey, cocoa, etc. All this sort of thing arrives in perfect condition. . . ."[77] The brothers met for the last time in Paris in 1947; Ignacy died at the Rothschild Hospital on November 10, 1948, at the age of sixty-eight. Arthur paid all of his brother's outstanding hospital bills, and when he received Ignacy's papers he was surprised to discover that his deceased brother had left a son, Hyacinthe. At sixty-one, Arthur was the oldest surviving member of the once-numerous Rubinstein and Heiman families.

Besides assisting some members of his own family, Rubinstein helped his wife's family. In 1940, when the United States was still a neutral power, Nela Rubinstein and her sister Wanda Labunska had tried to bring their mother to America. Wanda, who was already a U.S. citizen, had even arranged a preferential visa for Mrs. Mlynarska, but, according to Rubinstein, "the Russian authorities refused to give her the required exit permit." In November 1945, he cabled Helmer Enwall, his manager in Stockholm: "Would be infinitely grateful if you could suggest someone important enough in Sweden who would know me well enough to help me getting my wife's mother Mrs. Mlynarska from Kaunas [near the family estate in Lithuania] to Sweden in order to get her to her two daughters in America. I would support financially any possibility. . . ." Enwall promised to help, and a few days later Rubinstein sent him a letter that gave full details about his mother-in-law's background, national status, and whereabouts.[78] The plan worked, but a full year was needed to get Mrs. Mlynarska from Lithuania to California. Rubinstein also provided the money needed to bring Nela's brother, Bronislaw—who had spent part of the war in a Soviet forced labor camp—to the United States. For a time, Rubinstein employed his brother-in-law as his secretary; later, Bronek, who had divorced his first wife—one of Lily Wertheim Radwan's daughters—married the actress Doris Kenyon, a former star in silent films, and he ran an antiquarian bookshop that specialized in books on music. Nela said that Arthur "got along well with my brother and mother" and that "he was very good" to them and to other members of her family, including her sister Alina, who remained in Poland and eventually turned into a religious fanatic.

The atrocities committed by Germany during World War II reinforced Rubinstein's decision—which was thirty years old by the time the war ended—never to play again in the land of Bach, Beethoven, and Brahms, and he extended his boycott to Austria. In the late 1940s, however, he was dragged into a related debate that was then raging in American musical circles. The question was: Should celebrated German musicians who had remained and performed in their country during the war, thereby lending the luster of their names to Hitler's regime, be allowed to perform in the United States and to earn dollars and adulation from the American public? The issue was a complicated one. Many of the musicians in question had already been welcomed back to European countries that had been direct victims of German aggression; why should they be kept out of America, which had known no German occupation? On the other hand, most of the well-known Jewish and anti-Nazi musicians who had had to flee Europe had ended up in the United States, and, in cold percentages, the Jews as an ethnic group had suffered more than any individual nation under the Nazi German onslaught. Among musicians who had escaped from fascist-controlled Europe, feelings on the issue of the German performers ran high in the period that immediately followed the war and the Nuremberg trials.

The pianist Walter Gieseking, who had claimed to be a Nazi enthusiast before and during the war, claimed after the war to have been a victim of Nazi pressure tactics; Rubinstein and many other musicians wanted him kept out of the United States. When he arrived in New York in January 1949 he was arrested by the immigration authorities, and he agreed of his own volition to return to Germany, where he was reported to have said that Americans "evidently believe seventy million Germans should have evacuated Germany and left Hitler there alone." During the same month, Wilhelm Furtwängler was nominated for the conductorship of the Chicago Symphony Orchestra, effective the following season, and his case exploded in the American press. Furtwängler's political history is especially complicated: There is no longer any doubt that the conductor detested Hitler's regime and behaved courageously in trying to save many individual Jews from the Nazis' hands, but there is also no doubt that he remained behind and made the compromises with the regime that were necessary not only for his physical and artistic survival but also to bolster his professional defenses against his young rival, Herbert von Karajan, an authentic Nazi opportunist. Neither Rubinstein nor the other protesters were interested in fine distinctions. "I refuse to be associated with anyone who sympathized with Hitler, Göring, or Goebbels," Rubinstein wrote to the Chicago Symphony's board of directors. "Had Furtwängler been a good democrat, he would have turned his back on Germany, as, for example, Thomas Mann did. Furtwängler remained because he assumed that Germany would win the war. Gieseking behaved in a similar manner. It is said that Furtwängler rescued some people from the Nazis' clutches. This has not been confirmed. At present, he is seeking dollars and prestige in America, and he deserves neither." Other protesters included the pianists Horowitz and Alexander Brailowsky, the conductors Fritz Busch and André Kostelanetz, the violinists Milstein and Heifetz, and the soprano Lily Pons. Milstein eventually withdrew from the protest and remarked that German scientists had been brought to the United States after the war "presumably to benefit us by giving us their know-how. Well, maybe we can obtain some of those benefits from the musical skills of persons like Furtwängler." Rubinstein replied: "German scientists may be considered in the category of spoils of war that belong to the victor. Those who have been imported are being used by our government for specific purposes within laboratory walls. If Gieseking and Furtwängler were brought here on this same basis, I would say use them, not for public appearances where they may exert some influence . . . but in institutions experimenting with musical therapy and other humanitarian projects. The comparison with scientists would then be analogous."[79]

However they felt about the pros and cons of the issue, the Chicago Symphony's administrators knew that if such prestigious artists as Rubinstein, Horowitz, and Heifetz were to refuse to appear with the Chicago Symphony, many of their colleagues would feel compelled to do the same; besides, the orchestra's many Jewish members would find themselves in an untenable position, and many members of the huge Jewish segment of the audience would boycott the orchestra. Furtwängler was not engaged. In one of the notebooks in which he made entries from time to time, the conductor wrote, with respect to the artists who had opposed him: "There is also Arthur Rubinstein, whom I do not know, but who plainly does not know me either, for he should know that I was the one artist who remained in Germany and *emphatically* intervened on behalf of Jews until the very end." Furtwängler also complained about the attitudes of Toscanini, Brailowsky, Stern, and Piatigorsky. Michael Tanner, who edited Furtwängler's notebooks for publication in English, described Rubinstein as "certainly one of the ring-leaders of the protest."[80] Rubinstein himself, however, immediately became the target of accusations of having protested merely in order to keep German pianists out of his territory. Some accusatory letters came from the musical public at large, others from such fellow artists as Artur Rodzinski. But the notion that Rubinstein—who, at a conservative estimate, was offered two or three times as many engagements each year as he could manage to play—believed that he would suddenly find himself unloved or unemployed if the best of his German colleagues returned to America is utter nonsense. One may agree or disagree with his attitude toward these colleagues, but the attitude was sincere. Daniel Barenboim said, "The one time he really was very annoyed with me was when I went to Berlin in 1964 and played a piano concerto for the tenth anniversary of Furtwängler's death. He never forgave me. 'He was a Nazi,' he said. I said it was a very complicated matter, but he was adamant."

Rubinstein's continuing exclusion of Germany from his concert circuit created difficulties and bitterness in various quarters for the rest of his life. In 1962, for instance, he felt obliged to decline an invitation to participate in a World Children's Aid Fund Day program, for the benefit of UNICEF, simply because it was taking place in Düsseldorf, but in a letter he expressed his support for the program.[81] More than once he was quoted (misquoted, he claimed) as having said that he played in every country in the world except Tibet, which was too high, and Germany, which was too low, and the remark always upset many people. He once received a sarcastic note from a man in Hannover who asked him whether the royalties that he received from German sales of his recordings weren't also too "base" for him; the letter included the man's postal savings account number, in case Rubinstein was having trouble disposing of the money. Rubinstein replied that the letter-writer's "ironic reaction" was "perfectly justified. Therefore I am sending you a photostat of the correction to the original article which the most important New York paper printed. I beg you to believe that I have never uttered such a vulgar phrase about a tragedy like the one which happened under Hitler." He did not play in Tibet, he said, because there were "no pianos in that country," and he did not play in Germany "out of respect for the victims of the most cruel persecution the world has ever known of my family and my co-religionists. As to the royalties from the gramophone records sold in Germany . . . I use them chiefly to help in many parts of the world victims of the German holocaust."[82] In a letter to another interlocutor he explained that he was "very sad at not being able to play for the many fine Germans who, I am certain, live, and love music. But, as you know, unfortunately there are still too many of the others alive, and I couldn't face even a single one of the last-named in a concert of mine in their own country."[83]

In 1968, as a token of partial reconciliation, Rubinstein gave a recital in the Dutch town of Nijmegen, which is located on the German border and within a ninety-minute drive of such major German cities as Cologne, Düsseldorf, Dortmund, Essen, and Wuppertal. In some respects, however, this half-gesture only aggravated the situation. He received a critical letter, for instance, from a Jewish lawyer in Stuttgart whose father had been killed by the Germans: "the role of your genius should be that of the conciliator, of being the interpreter of a generous and constructive pardon," the man said,[84] rather than that of keeping old hates alive. Rubinstein replied, "I gather from your letter that although your father was shot by the Germans, you have nonetheless accepted the position of lawyer at the Stuttgart lawcourt, thus your pardon seems a self-interested one, one way or another, inasmuch as it's mixed in with your professional business. As for me, I can tell you that I have been offered signed blank cheques for giving concerts in Germany, and my decision not to play in that country doesn't date, as you seem to believe, from the last war, but all the way from that of 1914–18. You are also mistaken in attributing my attitude to 'hatred.' It's not that, I always play for an audience that I love, and it could not be the same for a German audience because I might find myself face to face with some nazi (and there still are thousands of them), and hear myself told, 'Get out, dirty Jew!!' Given your profession, you don't run the risk of hearing this."[85] Barenboim described the rationale behind the Nijmegen concert as "nonsense. It was not on German soil, but it was for German people. I don't know whether it was hypocritical or not. Then it was a big secret that he went to Salzburg a few years later, when Herbert Kloiber, the Unitel man, took him to hear *Meistersinger*. And then he went to Frankfurt for the Book Fair [to promote his memoirs], and he went to Hamburg a couple of times to choose pianos."

Once, during a return trip from Europe, Rubinstein asked Franz Mohr, Steinway's chief concert technician, who was German, " 'Should I maybe play once more in Germany? I know it would be a tremendous success. But not only that: It would be, I believe, a good sign that I do forgive, and that I love the German people. They are *not* all the same.' " Mohr encouraged him to go back to Germany, but in the end, Rubinstein stood by his earlier decision.[86]

Family Matters

In 1945 and 1946, the years in which Rubinstein learned the details of the annihilation of most of his family in Europe, his own little family in America expanded: on January 17, 1945—ten years less a few days after the birth of Paul—Alina Anna was born. Two months earlier, Nela had gone for a walk in the woods with Mildred Knopf. "She saw a tree that she liked and she climbed to the top of it," Mrs. Knopf recalled. "I screamed at her not to do it, but she said, 'I hate sissy women!' I thought for a minute that she might be trying to get rid of the baby, but it was too late anyway."[87] Nearly two years later, on December 8, 1946, John Arthur was born—eight weeks before his father's sixtieth birthday. The house on Marlboro Street in Brentwood was not large enough to accommodate six Rubinsteins plus Nela's mother (who arrived in America within days of John's birth) and the domestic help; it was sold, a larger place was bought—on Tower Road in Beverly Hills—and the family moved in, early in 1948. For years, Mrs. Mlynarska lived with the Rubinsteins. "My father treated 'Grama' well, I think, though I also think there was some tension," Alina said. "She was only about ten years older than my father, but she had been raised on a big estate in Lithuania that even included a school for the children of the family and of the peasants who worked on the estate; to me, it always sounded like something out of Tolstoy. She was a shy, prudish woman who grew up in a Catholic, patriarchal, late-nineteenth-century society, which taught that men and their needs always come first—and I think this attitude filtered down through generations of our family. I learned later that she had not been happy about my mother's first husband being Jewish, but what I recall about her from my childhood in California is her reserve and her deference to my father as the male head-of-household. They seemed to me to get along well enough, though I know my father was never very comfortable being fussed over on the domestic front—having his slippers brought to him, so to speak."

However pleasant life in California may have been, many of Rubinstein's thoughts were focused on Europe, once the war had ended. Indeed, by the time John was born, his father was making plans for his first postwar European tour. Late in the summer of 1947, Arthur, Nela, Eva, and Paul sailed for Britain; Alina and John were left in California with their grandmother and the domestic staff. They saw many old friends in England, Scotland, the Netherlands, Switzerland, Belgium, France, and Italy for the first time in at least eight years, and in each country Rubinstein—who played more than thirty-five times to sold-out houses—enjoyed artistic and professional triumphs. The London concerts were nearly cancelled because Rubinstein was unhappy about the British government's unenthusiastic attitude toward the creation of a State of Israel, but in the end he did play and was received with the greatest warmth. After an appearance there on October 12, he received a note (in English) from the celebrated Swiss pianist Edwin Fischer, who had been one of his cocompetitors in the Anton Rubinstein competition in St. Petersburg in 1910: "Sir, Let me thank you for your ideal playing this afternoon—It was of the best I heard since d'Albert and Busoni[.] God bless you. . . ."[88]

Rubinstein's four Paris concerts grossed five million francs, but the proceeds from the first one (October 16) went to charity, as Raymond Charpentier reported in *Arts*, a Paris weekly: "his first gesture, on coming back among us, has been to give a dazzling concert for the benefit of *Revivre* [Group for Solidarity with the Orphans of the Resistance], with the valuable participation of the Orchestre National and Charles Munch. The artist comes back to us just as he left us, with the same verve, the same sensitive, fresh, and engaging personality, the same digital finesse—perhaps even more assured, if possible—and in short, the same mastery. From Beethoven's Concerto in G and Chopin's in E [Minor] we learned nothing new about him. But he outdid himself in a little-known [*sic!*] work by Rachmaninoff, the Rhapsody on a Theme of Paganini. . . . With this transcendentally difficult work, Arthur Rubinstein and Charles Munch won . . . the most merited of triumphs."[89] For his first appearance in Rome—a recital at the Teatro Argentina on November 14, under the auspices of the Accademia di Santa Cecilia—a box-office line formed at four o'clock in the morning, and during the following five days he gave two grueling concerts in the same theater, with the Santa Cecilia Orchestra under Giuseppe Morelli: in the first, he played the Brahms Second Concerto and the Rachmaninoff Rhapsody, and at the second he played both of the Chopin concertos and a group of solo pieces, also by Chopin. At La Scala in Milan, his first appearance was greeted by a twenty-minute ovation.

Paris, however, was once again to be his European headquarters, and in addition to dealing with concert arrangements and a seemingly endless number of visits with old friends, the Rubinsteins began to address the matter of repossessing their house in the Square de l'Avenue du Bois de Boulogne. As early as December 1944, Marcel Valmalète, Rubinstein's French manager, had cabled his client: "House intact requisitioned by French Ministry. Germans took away all furniture."[90] Rubinstein said, years later, "The house was taken over by the Nazis—for nothing more brutal than a dental clinic, we've been given to understand, but, of course, people may just be trying to spare our feelings. When we returned after the war, we found that the dentists had stolen everything, including five thousand rare books—first editions of Gogol, Pushkin, and Dostoevski among them—and some pictures that meant a lot to me, such as a drawing of myself by Picasso, with whom I once spent a good many lively evenings in Montmartre, and a self-portrait from his Blue Period, showing him in blue trousers and blouse, holding a knife behind his back as he approaches a bed with a beautiful nude on it. When the Germans moved out, some French civilians moved in, and it took us endless litigation and a lot of money to get our house back."[91] Nela Rubinstein recalled in 1991 that "the Germans completely ruined the house, and that's when all the correspondence and everything disappeared. I miss the portrait by Wozlanska—the most wonderful portrait of Arthur—and one of Kochanski, which were stolen from this house." Not until the early 1950s were the legal problems settled, and not until 1954, when the Rubinsteins sold their house in Beverly Hills and bought an apartment at 630 Park Avenue (at East Sixty-sixth Street) in Manhattan, did they decide to spend a substantial part of each year at the house in the Avenue Foch. "Nela set to work renovating and remodelling," Rubinstein said, "bringing over furniture and carpets that we'd been using in California, putting in new bathrooms, a new heating system, and a new kitchen—a big, modern American one. I think she's as fond of that kitchen as I am of my concert grand."[92] Fifteen years after their escape to America, Arthur and Nela were reassembling their European lives.

In the tranquil enclave of the renamed Square de l'Avenue Foch they visited and were visited by their neighbors, who included the writer Marcel Pagnol and his wife Jacqueline, and Prince Rainier and Princess Grace of Monaco, and they welcomed many old and new friends: Marcel and Julie Achard, the writer Jean d'Ormesson, General Pierre de Benouville, and dozens of other visitors, French and foreign. The house became Rubinstein's base of operations during his increasingly extended European tours, and Mrs. Rubinstein had her hands full managing the additional household. In a profile of the pianist that appeared in the *New Yorker* in 1958, Joseph Wechsberg provided a glimpse of Nela's life when the couple was in Paris: The Rubinsteins "had returned from a short concert tour only two days earlier, and . . . she had spent the better part of the time since then preparing dishes for a supper party they were giving for 'a few intimate friends' immediately after his concert. . . . Mrs. Rubinstein remarked that she had arranged to have the piano movers in at five that afternoon to take his concert grand to the Palais de Chaillot in plenty of time for his performance, which was to begin at nine. She acts as her husband's secretary, accountant, chef, travelling companion, housekeeper, consulting physician and psychiatrist, and musical adviser— the last a role in which she is a knowledgeable and exacting critic. During the preceding two days, in addition to getting ready for the party, she had unpacked their luggage, repacked his for a flight the next morning to keep an engagement in Spain, repacked hers for a flight the next afternoon to see the children in New York, attended to his correspondence (letters, telegrams, and cable), fended off friends pleading for tickets to that evening's concert, which was already sold out, and prodded him often and insistently enough to make him get a haircut. 'I don't know where Nela finds the energy to do all the things she does,' Rubinstein said."

Of her husband's daily schedule when they were in New York, Mrs. Rubinstein told Wechsberg: "Artur likes to stay up fairly late—until one or two in the morning, usually—but unless he's awfully tired he makes a point of getting out of bed in time to see our two youngest off to school in the morning. Then it's two hours for breakfast, followed by work at the piano in pajamas and dressing gown. When Artur's preparing for a recital, there's one thing you can be sure of—he won't practice any of the works on the program. He feels that if he does, it will take the edge off the freshness of his approach. Instead, he may practice some concerto that he's not scheduled to play in public for weeks. He remembers everything he's ever played, and that's practically the entire repertory for piano. . . . Well, after the session at the piano comes lunch, which takes another two hours, with lots of talk and coffee. Then, about four in the afternoon, he announces he's going out for a while." When he is in New York, she said, "Artur loves to walk in Manhattan. He may come back with a few more books to be crowded in somewhere, or maybe he'll stop in at Bloomingdale's for one of his favorite delicacies— smoked salmon, or caviar, or a Pischinger *Torte*. Wherever he goes, he's pretty sure to be home by six-thirty, in time to have early dinner with the children and me. And afterward we see that their homework gets done."[93]

Early in 1953, Nela had become pregnant again. When Mildred Knopf found out, she said to her, " 'You've got four children. Will you explain to me why you want to go through this all again?' Nela said to me, 'I want to show the world that Arthur can still do it.' "[94] Or, perhaps, that he was still "doing it" with her, after more than twenty years of marriage. The baby—a boy—was born prematurely; he was given the name Feliks, after Nela's long-dead brother, but he survived only twenty-four hours. Anna Mlynarska, Nela's mother, moved from Beverly Hills to New York with the Rubinsteins, but she was frightened of the city and of living on the twelfth floor of an apartment building. She spent her last years in Kansas City, Missouri, with Wanda and Wiktor Labunski, her daughter and son-in-law, and there she died in 1960, at the age of eighty-three. In 1961, the Rubinsteins moved from 630 Park Avenue to a larger apartment at 941 Park Avenue. Four years later, they acquired a summer home at Marbella, on Spain's Costa del Sol, and in 1969 they bought an apartment in Geneva, Switzerland, thus rendering the logistics of their lives even more complicated. Once the younger pair of children had left home, however, the second Park Avenue apartment was sold, and during stays in New York the Rubinsteins rented a suite at the Hotel Drake.

Whenever his career allowed, Rubinstein followed his children's activities. To his old friend Roman Jasinski in Warsaw, Rubinstein wrote in 1967 that twenty-year-old John was having much success as an actor; Rubinstein *père* was pleased, but he wished that the boy would concentrate more on music in general and conducting in particular.[95] Nine years later, a journalist asked Rubinstein about his children. " 'Brilliant! Enormous talent!' " he exclaimed. " 'You know my son's a famous actor? He played the lead in a hit musical on Broadway for two years. *Wonderful!* Composes too. He's composed film scores for . . . what's his name? Robert Redford, that's it! My eldest daughter used to be an actress but now she's an extraordinary photographer. Sent all over the world! My other daughter was a *brilliant* scholar in comparative languages. But now she's enrolled at Columbia University as a doctor. Can you imagine? She's already helping out with operations. I've a horror of all that! I've always tried to think that my insides are like a garden, but doctors tell me we're made the same way as rats. It's not very flattering, is it?"[96]

WHETHER THEIR NATURES are easygoing or difficult, international celebrities have out-of-kilter relationships with their families, whose other members cannot help being aware, throughout their lifetimes, of being "daughter of," "son of," "husband of," or "wife of" the Important Person. To what degree the relationships are out of kilter depends on the personalities not only of the celebrities but also of their family members. Growing up in the family of a world-famous performing artist made the lives of all four Rubinstein children abnormal, in some respects, and each of them has strong opinions on the subject. Eva, the oldest, seems to have had the most complicated psychological relationship with her father, and she certainly had the toughest things to say about him. She said that her father had difficulty in getting along with most of the people close to him, and she surmised that his childhood experiences were responsible. "He was not a normal child in his own house, among other children, among his own brothers and sisters; he immediately felt above them because he had a talent. The other children suddenly became inferior beings vis-à-vis their four-year-old brother, which is a very skewed sort of image of who's in charge," she said. Thus, for the rest of his life, "he had to be the center of attention, in control. This he could do: he was talented not only at music but also at storytelling, at getting everyone's attention. He had a tremendous amount of charm, *huge* charm; he could be killing you and charming you at the same time."

Eva also felt that her father's need to have others focus on him contributed to what she described as his exceptionally low tolerance for others' points of view. "Things had to go the way he saw them; when people didn't fit into his scheme of things, they became aliens or even enemies. If you disagreed about a book or a film, all of a sudden you were an idiot, having fifteen minutes before been the best, the most loved, the most intelligent: 'Ach, you're just like me, darling!' Which meant only, 'You agree with me,' even if you're just sitting there nodding because you don't dare say anything. I don't think he ever really asked me a question—*and* waited for an answer—other than, 'Do you have enough money?' He would say, 'Well you know, my dear,' and then there would be this very hard index finger pressing on your arm or on your knee. He would do this with anybody, rather patronizingly. And of course you get little bits of revenge here and there. I married a minister—the first man who had ever talked back to my father, who didn't kowtow, who would say, 'No, I don't think that all Germans are bad.' Or, 'There will be a bloodbath in South America and South Africa.' My father was livid. 'What do you mean, my dear fellow? They've built roads and schools in South Africa.' You knew you couldn't talk him out of his version, so he would think that everybody agreed with him because people just gave up. He wasn't used to having a thirty-two-year-old like Bill argue with him. I married Bill not only because he seemed the antithesis of my father—someone who was 'good,' whom I could trust—but also because he was the first touch of reality in my life. It may have been another kind of romanticizing on my part, but it was also getting away from this pervasive mythology, theater, unreality, which I felt I had to do." (Eva and her former husband, the Reverend William Sloane Coffin—the former chaplain of Yale University and a well-known activist in the civil rights and antiwar movements of the 1960s—were married in 1956 and had three children: Amy, born in January 1958; Alexander, born in December 1958; and David, born in March 1960. The Coffins were divorced in 1968; Eva moved to New York to work as a photographer, and the children stayed with their father and his second wife. Alexander died in a car accident in January 1983.)

Alina's experience was somewhat different. "Life was easier when Johnny and I came along than when Eva and Paul were born, because my parents were living comfortably in California," she said. "They were more settled. Also, by the time one has one's third and fourth children, one probably gets the hang of it." But she, too, had problems. "I found it difficult to express myself in the rather intense family milieu, which was so dominated by my father's larger-than-life presence—when he was there." John agreed that he and Alina "had an easier early youth than my older sister and brother," but he felt that his father's demand for "a big display of 'respect' from his children" had "nothing to do with his being a celebrity. It had to do with the European tradition, and maybe even the Jewish tradition: Children were to be seen and not heard, children were the extensions of the father and the mother and were meant to reflect them, respect them, almost kowtow to them. It was very, very different from what emerged in the Dr. Spock/Freud–influenced era in America, after the war. When I visited my friends, whose parents were mostly American-born and younger than mine, I was always astounded to see the way the kids were allowed to talk to their parents. They could say 'Oh, go to hell, Dad,' and Dad would laugh. In our family, an enormous amount of respect was required."[97] Alina remembered her father "demonstrating to Johnny and me at the dinner table how 'a *real* Jewish father would say SHAH!! QUIET!!'—dramatically pounding his fist on the table. He would tell us this to indicate how lucky we were that he allowed us to talk, but the real message was that only *he* could talk. Sometimes, he would eat a piece of chicken with his fingers while telling us, 'Quod licet Jovi, non licet bovi!' (What is permitted to Zeus is not permitted to the cattle): 'This is what you must *never* do!' he would say."

Nela Rubinstein said that her husband simply "didn't know how to bring up children. There he was, spoiling them on the one hand and too strict on the other—not quite understanding what they went through. Because he didn't know very well how to get into the skin of somebody else, to understand the feelings of another person. It was always from his point of view, and what it did to him. But there was also the fact of me being younger than him and in a way closer to the children than he was; and I was there more with them. There was a jealousy [on his part]." She added, "Arthur was too European and too German, in a way," to know how to deal with American children. John said, "We were given love and acceptance—because there's always that underlying paternal and maternal love that was simply there—but beyond that, we were mostly given love and acceptance in proportion to the correct behavior and image that we showed our parents. A lot of what you really did, said, and were, good or bad, could be passed over if you behaved properly toward adults, toward your parents. If one had the correct behavior, the proper manners—table manners, societal manners, the expected deference—one could be forgiven all sorts of other character flaws and be talked about with admiration and affection. Whereas if one breached some of those codes and were in every other respect a good person, one might well be reprimanded, ignored, or severely criticized for not fulfilling the image one was supposed to fulfill. That was a burden for me, and from my observation it was a burden for my brother and sisters, too. There was a lot of pressure, and it made us all—in very different ways—behave strangely sometimes, and feel strange about ourselves."

In his memoirs, Rubinstein said that he had wanted a daughter so that he could possess her love entirely—an expectation that proved to be a formula for trouble. "You can imagine how much of that I heard all my life: A daughter *is* this, a daughter *does* this," Eva recalled. "When I was about twenty-one, I moved out of my parents' home, although I really wasn't independent enough, either financially or personally, to handle it. Once, while I was living in a little walk-up in New York, my father said, 'Ah, but are you comfortable up there?' I said, 'I'm fine, I sleep quietly. . . .' My father kept saying, 'But are you *really* comfortable? Because I *want* you to be *comfortable.*' I said, 'Yes, it's fine, it's home, it's comfortable, it's nice—the bed becomes a couch in the daytime.' Again he said, aggressively, 'But you don't understand!'—more and more angrily. I finally said, 'Daddy, you're not listening to me, I can't even talk to you. One can't discuss anything with you.' I said it really just off the top of my head, because he was not allowing himself to hear that I was saying 'I'm fine,' which I really meant. *That* he never forgave me. At the time, I hadn't understood the subtext, which was, 'Don't leave me—you are leaving me!' He reminded me of it the last time I ever saw him.

"He very often said, 'Ach, a daughter always understands that an artist is a child forever.' I think he was really saying, 'I'm going to be a child forever.' The child*like* qualities are fine—the capacity for joy and wonder and astonishment and all the rest of it—but the child*ish* side is the impatience, the petulance. He had absolutely no self-knowledge, and this is why he never understood other people."

Alina's opinion coincided with Eva's in some ways and diverged from it in others. She described her father's attitude toward his daughters as a "typical, nineteenth-century patriarchal position. I think he wanted us all, including the boys, to love and adore him but felt he had a better chance with a daughter. He did say to me that he thought a woman, especially a daughter, could better appreciate his artistic nature, whereas a son would be disappointed that he couldn't play baseball. He actually expressed to me the notion that daughters never really leave a father because of the shared blood tie—as if this didn't also apply to sons! This fantastic idea made more sense to me after I had read the early chapters of his autobiography. I think he deeply *wanted* to believe it, as a reaction to the separations from his parents at an age when he still really needed them. I remember being surprised when I heard him say with genuine emotion, on a *Sixty Minutes* television segment, that he had suffered from having lived away from his family when he was so young. It was the first time I'd ever heard him reflect on his relationship with them. It must have been difficult for his parents to know what to do with him—a prodigy with a talent they couldn't really appreciate in musical terms—and they necessarily deferred to the advice of more knowledgeable people. It's not easy to be the parents of a child who knows so much more than you do in some area. I think he was always looking for someone who would never leave him even if he left her.

"I certainly did feel, as I think my sister did before me, that he wanted me to be his admirer," Alina said. "But there was another side to his attitude toward women to which I also responded. He always encouraged me to have my own career, never pushed me to 'just' get married and become a housewife, although when he was growing up it was much less common for women to pursue careers. He envisioned me as a pianist and, later, a writer. Interest-ingly, I have always had trouble 'performing' as both, though I love to play the piano and write. So I felt he was simultaneously possessive toward me and supportive of my independence. But he certainly was taken aback when I told him I wanted to pursue medicine, although he had always admired doctors for their dedication. He immediately questioned whether I had the capacity for that kind of dedication, and didn't take me seriously for quite a while. He had never had a formal education, although he was an impressively well-read man, and I think the idea that I was going to earn a professional degree in a field that he shied away from was very distressing. He fully supported me financially through medical school and training, but he and I hardly ever talked about the training until I was far along in it. He also knew that becoming a doctor takes a huge amount of time and energy, which would keep me from seeing him as much as I had been able to do before—and that was certainly borne out."

When they were small, all of the children must have consciously or unconsciously resented their father's long absences from home, especially when their mother accompanied him. Eva said that when her father returned from his tours, "this very strong force would appear and the energy would change. You would hear whispers: 'Shhh, Daddy's working, Daddy's sleeping, Daddy's reading.' It's not that my mother neglected our needs—never! But it was hard for her, too. She was trying not to lose this wild man by having him float around loose all over the world, but at the same time she was very home-loving and maternal, wanting to be with us. She wanted both, but maybe you can't have both. And he wanted both, but he was a man who never should have had children. Perhaps he should have had his wife and a merry old time all over the world, but once there are children it's not so easy. He saw himself as the paterfamilias and Jewish patriarch, but he didn't know what that involved."

Alina recalled that when her father would return home from one of his extended European tours, "it was always a big event for us. Johnny and I hadn't seen him for months. Johnny would run down to the garden to pick a red carnation for my father's lapel—this was in pre–Légion d'Honneur days—and my father would be laden with Christmas presents. He always used to say that he was bringing the sun back with him in his suitcase. In retrospect, I realize that my father's long and frequent absences when we were young children made it hard to feel close to him, as did the large generation gap between us. It was not necessarily more difficult than having a father who comes home every night, turns on the TV, and doesn't talk to his kids, but my father—and often enough my mother, too—would be away so long that when he'd come back I'd feel somewhat distant for some time. It felt like starting from scratch again. I still have the postcards that they would send us, written in big block letters, so we could read them, with Xs on their hotel windows: "THIS IS WHERE I AM STAYING." I couldn't even conceive of where that was, then. So that was tough, I guess. When they were both gone, we had our grandmother, our nurse, and a housekeeper holding down the fort."

John recalled that his father "expected to be loved, demonstrably, when he entered the room, even if he hadn't been home for three months. My parents were very warm and affectionate, both of them—at least to me. They were both kissing and hugging, warm people—*never* cold. But having said that, I must add that there was a *ferocity*, a burning ferocity to my father's demand for adoring behavior; it was tough, possessive. I feel that this, too, is much more a psychological matter than a celebrity-related one. I think that it had to do with how his mother and father had treated him, more than with how many people had heard his name or had written about him in the newspapers. In the only photo of my father's parents that I ever remember seeing, they look sort of bewildered. That's my one image of them. And perhaps he had some bewilderment in him, too—a feeling that 'no matter how much I surround myself with success, admirers, luxury, excitement, something is definitely *missing*.' For him, I believe, what was missing was a trust, a sense of being loved for himself, not for what he did or said: the kind of love that parents usually give you, and, ironically, the kind that children usually give you. The public's love, no matter how much it translates itself into hordes of adorers or millions of dollars, never penetrates that basic need for real, unfettered, unconditional love, and I think that a performer who's really in it for that alone will never be satisfied. My father may have been one of those; I really don't know. You couldn't love him enough for him to truly feel that trust. It was always subject to re-evaluation."

Eva said that her father "had an image of himself *providing* and inspiring, with everybody sitting there in wonderment, admiring and listening and accepting and agreeing. The best times I had with him, when I was a child, were when he did things his way, which I sometimes enjoyed very, very much. He would play records to me and talk to me about music. He didn't tell me musicological stuff; he was simply feeding me music, which was delicious, and I loved it. I remember the *Bachianas Brasileiras* of Villa-Lobos, with Bidú Sayão, and *Romeo and Juliet* of Prokofiev, and Mahler's *Songs of a Wayfarer*; these are among the earliest pieces of music that I remember loving. As a serious student of dance, in those days, I also knew tons of Tchaikovsky, but the music he would play me was very special. He would explain to me what was going on in the music, what was happening. I remember his acting out for me Schubert's *Erlkönig*, and I'm still incapable of hearing that without falling apart. And besides the music, there were the paintings and the books in the house. My father adored reading, and he gave me books as birthday and Christmas gifts; to me, they were the most special presents, and I always opened them last. (He gave us all kinds of lavish presents—sometimes too lavish—and he supported me financially, *almost* to the end. Generous is a small word—he was kingly. But he was a very, very difficult person to give anything *to*, because he was the official giver.) We also met painters and saw museums where he knew every single thing. We'd arrive somewhere by train, and even before we'd go to the hotel, sometimes, we'd go to the museum—in case it was closing or he had a concert. I remember him telling me that the breast of a nude in the museum in Florence would fall if she moved her hand, it was so real. And when my parents had the big house in California, they were buying paintings by contemporary Americans, by Israelis, by people whose work they simply liked. There was Reuben Rubin, an Israeli friend and one-time diplomat, and Lutz, an American who did a lot of racehorses; his work had great charm and energy, and they wanted it *not* because it was valuable but because they liked it. My father's passion for books, paintings, travel, his curiosity about places and languages—these things were contagious, and they did rub off on me tremendously. We were always inspired to learn languages, because my father and mother spoke so many. My father always made us feel that any kind of education, any knowledge, can only be good. He left us with a sense of tremendous curiosity toward life."

Alina and John agreed that one of the most important educational advantages that their father gave them was a familiarity with a variety of European cultures, and with Paris in particular. "I was very excited and happy when we moved to Paris in 1954, for the better part of a year, when I was nine and Johnny seven," Alina said. "It really changed my life because it allowed me to form more of a connection to my father, being with him, finally, on his home turf in Europe, going to his concerts really for the first time, meeting people from their prewar life. I soon fell in love with Paris, seeing it through his eyes, and I still cherish a wonderful picture-book of Paris that he inscribed to me. Learning to love what he loved made me feel closer to him, and he *loved* to share his passions with us." John said that after that year, and until he graduated from high school in 1964, "we would join our parents in Paris in May, about two weeks before school was over, and we would follow whatever our father's tour was that summer. There were periods when he would do one-nighters through Italy and Spain; we wouldn't always go on those—my mother and sister and I would sit in Deauville for a month, or Ischia or Abano, where my mother took radioactive mud-bath cures for her arthritis, or in Venice, where we rented a house on the Giudecca. My father would come and go, staying with us as long as he could between concerts. Then, late in September, Lali [Alina] and I would go back to school in New York; a couple of weeks after school had started. The rest of the time we stayed in New York. Those years were mostly wonderful for me. I got to live in Venice and Paris, to know what European life is like, and it has informed my whole life. Of course, there were many times in my teenage life when I said to myself, 'I come back here in late September and all my friends have spent the whole summer at the beach with other kids our age! They know who all the rock 'n' roll groups are, they can all play baseball better than I can, they talk about sports cars, they've necked in the backseats of cars: they have a life that I have no idea about!' I often felt like an outsider, and I still do, occasionally; you never quite get over that."

How did a nonpracticing-Catholic-turned-Lutheran mother and a non-practicing Jewish father educate their children with respect to religion? "We did not really give them any religious upbringing," Nela said. "We discussed it for a long time. He thought it would be awful if we impressed on them one thing or another, so we let it go. Sometimes I think it may have been a mistake. Some of them may have missed it." Eva recalled, "My father would say, 'There is no God but maybe there is a Providence'—high-flown verbiage, but it didn't really mean much to me. For my father, a profound moment was when he challenged God to prove that He was there: he would say terrible things and wait for punishment; nothing happened, ergo there was no God. I suppose you might do that when you're seven, but not when you're twenty! He had fairly negative views on anything that had to do with religion, with organized observance. The idea was that we children were going to be free to choose our own paths. Once, in Argentina, my parents and Paul and I—I was eighteen, Paul was sixteen and a half—were invited to the Israeli ambassador's house for lunch. September was approaching, they were talking about Yom Kippur, and Paul said, 'What kind of fish is a yum kipper?' My father used to eat kippered herrings for breakfast, a habit he'd picked up in his English days. Well, it was funny—unless you're Arthur Rubinstein sitting with the Israeli ambassador, and this is your eldest son, who doesn't even know what Yom Kippur is! The ambassador looked at my father and at Paul, and there was an awful silence. Who was going to explain what to whom? But the fact is that we didn't know! You get to an age when you're embarrassed to ask, because people assume that you know." Alina said that when she and John were very small, they "knew nothing of being half Jewish. We celebrated Christmas because my mother's mother, a religious Catholic, was living with us."

One might expect that a man whose reputation for high living was as great as Rubinstein's would have tried to inculcate his tastes in his children, but this was not the case—and indeed, the reputation was greatly exaggerated, according to his wife. "He was self-educated, and there were things that his parents didn't teach him, like basic manners, which he had to learn from watching others," she said. "He was overly sensitive about such things. He liked good things, definitely, but he learned about them little by little. He didn't especially care for wine, but he felt always a little bit forced by the restaurants, by the people [around him]. To live in France and not drink wine—people think that you have a sickness! But it wasn't an essential part of his life; he was very satisfied with a glass of water. Sometimes he drank things just to live up to people's opinion of him. He knew all these wine produc-ers—the Rothschilds, Polignacs, and others—and visited them and tasted, and they would teach him. But he did enjoy very good champagne—only very good champagne, not half-good. And he did like fine clothes. Before the war, he used to have his clothes made in England, then after the war England became sort of shabby so he went to Italy. And Buenos Aires had excellent tailors. He was impeccably dressed, always. His tie was always a model of how it should be done. I often think that today's artists could take lessons from him."

Eva said that her father "could be full of charm and delight, and he had an irresistibly contagious laugh. Once, he and Bronek [Bronislaw] Kaper [a Polish-born, Hollywood film composer] were fooling around on two pianos at the house in Beverly Hills; Bronek was playing "Ochi Chorniye" while my father was playing the Chopin Fantasy-Impromptu. They made them mesh—it was wonderful! I was laughing so hard, and they were both laugh-ing with delight as they played. Once, at the house in Paris, when my mother and father and Roman Polanski and I were having dinner, my father started to read a verse on Jewish names, by Julian Tuwim, who had been a dear friend and a very funny man. My father loved to read it aloud to people, but I never saw or heard him get to the end of that poem, because he would always crack up with laughter. Polanski started to laugh, too, and the two of them had tears rolling down their cheeks. There were charming times—wonderful lunches, going to the movies, going to the opera. But then all of a sudden, from one minute to the next, he could change completely and do disastrous, demonic things. During the most delightful times, there was always a little bit of fear hovering in the back—you were never sure when it was going to break through."

In what ways was his behavior "disastrous" and "demonic"? One of the worst things he did to Eva, when she was still very young, was to make her privy to his extramarital love-life, past and present. On the one hand, she said, "he once told me, 'You know, all those stories about my being a great lover— they were greatly exaggerated.' Maybe he was trying to tell me that some of this was just mythology. The pursuit certainly happened, and women were attracted to him because he did have a very potent personality—he exuded a kind of warmth and incredible magnetism." But he also told her about specific affairs, and "this could be devastating," she said. "He would tell me things that I really didn't want to know—things that my mother couldn't possibly be told and mustn't know—and he thereby made me a kind of accomplice. When you give someone knowledge of that kind, it's not a present, not a trust. It's an imposition; it feels like a weight. And it means shifting the roles of the family members. He simply needed his coterie and he tried to make some of us into that. It was destructive beyond belief. It's one thing to tell kids not to do something because you've suffered from it; but with my father it wasn't so that I would understand, it was so that I would be on his side, in his circle. My mother was never suspicious, even when he would try to talk her out of going on trips: 'You've heard this program so often, you'll be bored.' Or, 'It's such a tiring trip.' " And yet, Eva said, her father was "terribly possessive" toward her mother. "The fact of his being so much older than my mother often made him a little paranoid. She was and is very attractive and charming—people just adored her—so men would act a little flirtatious with her. But *she* didn't do anything! She adored my father and she was faithful for all those years. But my father, who was carrying guilt problems around from the day they were married, projected this onto everyone, especially my mother. If anyone, including men of dubious sexual persuasion, so much as looked at her, it upset him. She could have had her choice, but I think her behavior had a lot to do with how she saw herself: she believed in him, she was the faithful wife."

His feelings of guilt sometimes combined with his suspicious nature and made him explode in uncontrollable rage at Nela, who recalled that "he would become completely hysterical. It was a rage that would carry him too far. He would say such things to me, and that was very painful. Arthur was a complex figure, full of taboos, very ambitious, proud. He never wanted anyone to know that he didn't know something. He had a little bit a feeling of inferiority; he would get revenge by poking at me, and he had a very mean streak." Eva remembered that on an overnight train ride, during her father's first postwar European tour, when she was fourteen, "for the first time I heard my father shouting at my mother in ways I didn't know people ever talked to each other. Paul was on the bunk above, I was below, and I remember hearing all this at two in the morning and just going into total shock. I have no idea what it was about, but I heard my mother constantly saying, in Polish, 'Don't upset yourself, it's not worth it. Why are you getting so upset?' And he used words that I barely understood, but that were insulting and demeaning and horrible. I could hardly believe it—hearing my father off guard for the first time, unwittingly overheard, doing this to my mother. My parents had a rule never to quarrel in front of the children, but the trouble with that is that the children get an illusion of what the family is, and it's only when the illusion is dispelled that you begin to see your parents as real people." Alina's recollections are less dramatic but not at odds with those of her older sister. "My father's attitude about conflict in his marriage was that it should be kept private," she said, "and I had no awareness of conflicts until I was a teenager. He would occasionally have a temper tantrum and say something mean to my mother, and she would not fight back strongly. He would get into quite a rage, and it would be intimidating because he was capable of being really pointed and hurtful in a fight. I rarely if ever had the nerve to disagree with him about anything substantial, let alone talk back!"

Eva said that when, as an adult, she would hear her father verbally attack her mother, she would ask her, " 'Why do you let him? How can you take it?' At a certain age I started to stand up for my mother a little bit, and practically got decapitated every time. She would whisper, 'Don't risk it, don't make him angry.' On my wedding day there was something very unpleasant between them, and I asked her, 'How can you take it? How long will you take it?' She said, 'Ach, I always knew it would be difficult, but I loved him and I swore to myself that I was going to do everything to help his career. And I *know* he's faithful — that's the only thing that *really* matters to me.' I was sitting there, and my mother was saying that the one thing that was keeping her alive with this man was the one thing I *knew* she didn't have. I was getting married and leaving; how could I cut her lifeline?"

But Rubinstein's anger was not always directed at his wife. "If he got into one of his rages," Eva said, "he would hurt and insult people and say anything that came into his head — and forget about it immediately afterwards. On the other hand, he would never forget the slight, real or imagined, that had enraged him in the first place. My father called me names I'll never forget. I would say to him, 'Don't say that, because *you're* going to forget about it in fifteen minutes but *I'm* going to remember it for the rest of my life.' A lot of people were offended by my father, despite all of his charm and gentlemanliness. My mother spent half her time mending fences after him." Nela remembered that Arthur would "say terrible things to people. It's strange — he was not good, basically. For instance, Marcel Achard, who was a very great friend, came to visit when he was already ill and having a hard time breathing. Arthur started telling one of his long, long stories; he saw that Achard was getting tired, and Arthur was furious: 'How come he's not all ears and not reacting as he should?' I said, 'But think a little bit, what an effort he is making.' He got very impatient. He wanted always to be the one to talk and to be admired — very much so. The more I look back, now, the more I recognize this. Yes, he was a performer, but it wasn't just that. For instance, we once had a big, big row that marked me. We were in Sicily, in Palermo, in the

1950s or '60s, and the people who had arranged the concert—a couple—
nice, modest little people—asked us for lunch the next day. Arthur said, 'No,
no, you come and have lunch with us.' They accepted, innocently; they
thought he had really meant it, when obviously he had meant it only halfway.
So they came, and for them it was a big deal—Sunday lunch with Arthur. He
was so cruel, so impatient—he didn't want to forgive them for having accepted. I said, 'Why did you ask them?' He gave me hell: 'You're always defending the others!' On those occasions when I opened my mouth, I was his
Enemy No. 1. He didn't realize that his sense of humor was very funny but
also a little bit on the 'pinchy' side, always, and sometimes he went too far. Or
he did not understand the class of people he was dealing with and their men-
tality. He wasn't subtle enough."

The memories of Rubinstein that Nela and her children all seem to
cherish most are the memories of him playing music—similar memories to
those that hundreds of thousands of other people have of him, but more complicated ones. Eva remembers him "marching out on stage with his back very
straight, like a grenadier. He would confront the piano like a worthy rival, as
if it were a duel in which you didn't want to kill your opponent but you certainly wanted to perform the music properly. Then he would sit down to play,
and he would become *himself*. I absolutely adored going to rehearsals, when
he played with orchestra, and secondly to actual concerts, because there I saw
my father's real face and I felt my father's real self. It was only then that I
really felt that I knew who he was and that I could love him completely. All
his awareness was concentrated in music, and there, he became his other
self, he became everything about him that was best. There was understanding, calm, sanity, patience, generosity—toward the music, toward the instrument, toward the audience. He would give and give. And of course the
audience fed back to him. I know what it's like to be on the stage: you feel it,
it's palpable. It works in two directions."

Nela said, "His musicianship was part of him. He didn't have to work at
it, as all of the others did. He was amazing, in that sense—the way he felt the
structure of a piece, all together, right away. He did study, naturally, but less
than others, because he was a little distracted and he liked other things. He
practiced the difficult places in each piece—never too much, because it
bored him. He didn't want to go out and play something which was not quite
fresh and a little dangerous. Actually, that was his inspiration—to expose
himself to danger, like people who like to climb one step too high. It was the
danger that gave a sort of electricity in his concerts. People were electrified by
the fact that when he walked on the stage something was happening already,
before he even touched the piano. And when he played he became the real
Arthur. There was no hysteria; the whole beauty of what he had inside was

coming out. That was always amazing, and the children felt it and I felt it, always. His face changed, from making silly faces and clowning and all of that, all of a sudden he looked like an inspired, wonderful person."

Eva said that even when her father talked about music, "everything he said suddenly made perfect sense. He would talk about the length, the shape of a piece of music, its breadth, the sense that he would make out of it. And all of the things that he said about music seemed to me relevant to a life situation: that something shouldn't last too long, that it should have a form—a beginning, a middle, and an end. His relationship to work—his absolute respect for what he did: in a way, he treated his musicianship with more respect than he ever treated any human being, as if it were something precious he'd been given and had to take care of. I don't think that many other musicians really respected the *music* as much as my father did. It was something wonderful—you knew he had it in him. He was *capable* of respect, love, distance, judgment. He was also terribly proud of being humble: 'I don't understand why there's all this fuss about my music,' he would say. He was humble for all the wrong reasons! The one thing he *didn't* have to be humble about was his piano playing, his musicianship. But there were other things in his life that he might well have been extremely humble about and wasn't."

With respect to his own comfort and soul-state, too, his attitude varied, depending on whether or not he had a professional commitment. "If he had a stomachache when he *didn't* have a concert, the whole world knew about it," Eva said, "but vis à vis anything connected with his professional life, he would be right there like a little soldier. In the 1930s he flew in airplanes over the Andes, and when no one else would go, he would go with the mail plane! He could also be very brave about pain. He had shingles, for instance, and he was absolutely amazing—he just never complained. He would talk himself out of it. He had tremendous willpower—playing concerts when he had food poisoning, and even with pneumonia. Once, in Israel—I was with him there for a month, when I was eighteen—he badly smashed two fingers in a bureau drawer. He was playing twenty concerts in twenty-two days in three cities, driving up and down the length of Israel, and the roads were still quite bad; this was 1951. It was a madhouse: there was total adoration of him, and he hadn't been there since before the war. Very often in his programs he was playing the Bach-Busoni [Chaconne]—without being able to use the fourth finger of his right hand. He would hold it in hot water, then cold water—and I would throw up in the bathroom backstage while he was playing, because I knew how much it hurt him. But sure enough, he refingered it somehow, and you could hardly tell, if you could tell at all, that anything was wrong.

"I was nervous during concerts, when he hit a difficult place. My mother and sister and I would give each other blue marks on our hands, at the end of the Mephisto Waltz or whatever. Will he make it? When I was fourteen, we were in Brussels and he was playing a Beethoven sonata; and all of a sudden he absolutely garbled a scale—it sounded as if he had played it with his elbows. I thought the world had just ended. I went out of the box, ran to the nearest ladies' room, and threw up, and I was thinking, it's over, my father has died. Not one of the critics even mentioned it!"

Alina observed, "My father focused all of his concentration and energy into the keyboard; there was no humming, no making faces, no extraneous gestures. He was a showman, but not in the way some pianists are: he walked onto the stage, did his business, and left. Every once in a while he'd rise off the piano bench or bring his hand down from a great height, as in Falla's 'Fire Dance.' But that was to create a certain strong sound necessary for the music. He was not self-conscious about his playing—he was totally immersed in the music; every movement was made only to communicate something. He was giving them back his gift. I often think that in our family we expressed a lot of feelings toward and about my father most effectively through music and in our various attitudes to music. It was a special, nonverbal, but fluent language that we had with each other. I *still* feel close to my father when I hear a recording of his—it stirs up such a range of feelings toward him, as if it were a private, personal communication from his heart to mine. The irony and paradox of it is that, although I'm his child, I've always shared that most private, 'intimate' connection to him with his entire public."

And John said, "It was really something to observe how my father worked, how real his work was, how much more important to him than anything else, when it was taking place. By osmosis, over the years, hearing him play the same pieces five hundred times had a big effect on me: hearing how a piece would change according to his mood or the weather or the audience or the rest of the program, how my awareness of it changed, how I changed, how much I could glean about him as a human being through how he played Schumann's *Carnaval* on one night as opposed to the way he had played it the night before. I feel tremendously advantaged for having experienced all that. I don't stand out in my profession as my father did in his, but I do feel a kinship with him. It's not a matter of the 'mantle' being passed on, or any such thing. But when I stand in front of an audience or a camera, or when I direct actors or write music for a film, I try to give of my heart—to let it show, as I always saw him show his when he played the piano. I try to do what I do in a way that resembles the way he did what he did. And it's important to me to remember his humility as a musician. When he was working, whatever that needy, greedy, narcissistic thing of his was, it was at its *minimum*, if it was there at all. The moment he stepped away from the keyboard it could come flooding back. *Then* he needed the praise and the acceptance, and wanted it all desperately. But whenever he was playing—I'm sure that if I could have looked inside his mind, he would have been like a little angel. He was always giving, giving, giving; his tone was generous and unadorned. His music-making was the true center of who he was."

Conspicuously absent from this family view of Rubinstein is his son Paul, who was not on speaking terms with his father for the last thirteen years of Arthur's life and has since had infrequent contacts with his mother, sisters, and brother. (He thought about contributing his opinions to this book but decided not to when he learned that the book's author had refused to do military service in the United States armed forces during the Vietnam War and had become a Canadian citizen.) Nela said that "Paul was very much like Arthur, and that was why they couldn't get together at all," even when Paul was very young. "Paul was obsessed with the idea of being an American, and Arthur would say, 'The only ugly thing in this house is you'—because Paul was wearing an undershirt and sneakers." Alina commented that "Paul was very young when my parents moved to the United States. He remained confused and fearful of the Nazis, who he believed had chased the family out of their home in Europe. He and my father ended up rejecting everything about each other, as my father used to say a son inevitably would. It was a self-fulfilling prophecy, perhaps." Eva added, "Paul had a very hard time of it. All of his energies went into disappearing in the crowd, becoming as totally American as possible, forgetting everything from Europe. He was sent to boarding school because he was very difficult at home—no one knew how to deal with him." John, too, felt that his father "was especially rough on Paul. He wasn't terribly interested in trying to figure out what made a young mind go in a given direction. To him, kids of any age were really expected to react and behave like adults, as he had been made to behave when he was a boy. During a tour of South America, around 1949 or 1950, Paul, who was fourteen or fifteen, was tired or perhaps even ill, and he remained in my father's dressing room during a concert. When my father came off the stage he found Paul there, asleep, with his feet up on the table; he hadn't gone into the hall to hear the concert. My father took great offense at that—he never forgot it. This incident became one of the many refrains in the story of my father's estrangement from Paul. That story served me as a warning of how unreasonable my father could sometimes be, and how long his memory was, and how fragile his ego was. It helped to shape my behavior. I didn't want to have too much of that sort of thing on my record."

The break between Arthur and Paul came in 1969. "We were in Rome," Eva recalled, "at the Excelsior Hotel, and my father was to record Schubert's Posthumous Sonata" in B-flat Major, D. 960. "It was his third try; he had a lot of trouble with it. As usual, my mother, father, and I, in our bathrobes, had had a long breakfast, and then came a telephone call from

Paul, who was in New York. It was one of the most ghastly and desperate phone discussions that I've ever heard: accusations, probably just and unjust, were flying back and forth, with neither my father nor Paul giving an inch or really listening to what the other was saying. With the exception of a letter later that year, it was their last communication ever." (In 1970, however—according to statements made by Rubinstein in correspondence—he contributed one hundred thousand dollars to Paul's second divorce settlement. Paul, who has been married and divorced three times, has one son, Jason, born in 1967.) "But afterward, my father was to go to lunch and to the recording session. I went back to my room to get dressed, and I suddenly heard my father start to play the upright piano in the living room of our suite. He played the opening theme of the first movement of the sonata, and I heard that something was different. I put on a robe, grabbed my camera, and went toward the living room. Through the doors I saw him sitting with his back to me, in shirtsleeves, with the back of his neck looking like a little boy's—which it always did, till the day he died—with his little innocent curly hair and his slopy shoulders. He played for a while, and I knew that the sound was different; this was not what he had been practicing for days. I *felt* the difference. Suddenly he stopped playing and put his hands on one knee, one on top of the other, which is something he did rather often—it was a sort of gathering himself together. He leaned off to his right, looked out the window, took a *very* heavy breath, then turned back to the piano and started to play again. He didn't know I was there, so I risked taking several frames, feeling very guilty, as though I were stealing. But it was as if something said to me, 'Do it, do it—you have to.' He made the recording that afternoon, and that's the one he released.

"I've always felt that at that moment, when I heard him through the bathroom vent and went to the doors, he was telling Schubert to help him through something he could not go through with Paul. He was using the music to get him out of it, to express what he couldn't to his own son. And this is the agony of someone like this, who can tell more to and through the music than he can to his own kin and kind. You cannot blame him for this, because this is how he was. My father had a relationship with music which was unique. It was different from any other relationship in his life. There was no woman, no friend, *nobody*, whom he ever loved and understood as much, or cared about as much, or gave as much to. You were put in your place, always, by Chopin, by Brahms, by Schumann, and it was hard, sometimes."

The Years of Maximum Celebrity

In 1956, Khrushchev's denunciation of Stalin at the twentieth congress of the Soviet Communist Party and the return to power, in Warsaw, of the relatively moderate Wladyslaw Gomulka seemed to indicate a slight loosening of the USSR's grip on Poland. Rubinstein began to consider a return visit to his native country, which he had not seen since 1938. Plans were formed, and early in June 1958, Arthur, Nela, Alina, and John traveled to Cracow, the first stop on what proved to be one of the most memorable of the family's many trips. Rubinstein's first significant act, on arrival, was a visit to Szymanowski's tomb in Skalka, the Polish pantheon. Then came his recital. The writer Eva Hoffman, who was then a twelve-year-old music student in Cracow, has set down her recollections of the event in her book, *Lost in Translation*.

In 1958 . . . , a musical event takes place that has the symbolic meaning of transcending immediate politics. For the first time since the war, Arthur Rubinstein comes to play in Poland—and his arrival provokes an outbreak of high excitement, patriotism, nostalgia and pure sentiment that art still has the power to induce here. His long absence was a protest against anti-Semitism, but now he is awaited as a native son. He is the greatest in the world, he is Polish, and he plays the piano in the high Romantic tradition—as it really should be played. In Cracow, people spend the night on makeshift beds in front of Symphony Hall, so they can beat others to the tickets when the box office opens in the morning. My father, who as always prefers short-cut methods, waits until the evening, and then somehow maneuvers us through the onrush of the crowds, past the ticket takers, so that we are propelled into the auditorium, whose aisles are filled with people crowding right up to the stage and being squeezed ever tighter as more people arrive.

The hall is so overheated that two people faint during the concert and have to be carried out. But nothing interrupts the audience's breathless attention to Rubinstein's every note. His tone—warm, pliant, utterly "natural"—is the real stuff. It bespeaks an empathy that never violates the music—never interrupts its fluidity with a harsh or a wooden sound. As for me, I am fascinated by the way he raises his eyes, a beatific smile on his face, as if to focus on some point in his mind and breathe the music in, receive it from some outside source. The concert progresses through tiers of excitement. When, at the end of the first half, he plays the A Major Polonaise, with its heroic, revolutionary echoes, the audience spontaneously breaks out into a shout of "Wiwat! Wiwat!"—which is simultaneously a toast and a salute of camaraderie and celebration.

After the official program is finished, there are two or three of the usual encores—but the audience doesn't have any intention of letting Rubinstein go. People begin shouting out names of pieces they want him to play and, inclining his elegant head, the pianist stands on the stage listening to the requests, and then sits down and plays again and again and again, as if this were a family reunion, and he too didn't want to leave this packed and overheated hall. But finally he indicates by a gesture of the hands that this is the end, that he can't go on anymore—and then the audience, as if moved by some unanimous impulse, rises and starts up the song "Sto lat, sto lat," which means "May he live a hundred years," while the pianist stands there, visibly moved, bowing his head and blowing kisses. Then, exhausted and exhilarated, the crowd moves slowly out. We've had our moment of collective euphoria; we've had our catharsis.[98]

"It was a miracle that everybody survived that concert," Nela Rubinstein said, "because there was absolutely no place even to walk, let alone to leave if something had happened. There was such enthusiasm, and Arthur was in such a mood, so moved. Ach, it was beautiful!" The Rubinsteins then went on to Warsaw, where "Arthur caught such a cold that I thought he would die there," Nela recalled. "He had such a bronchitis that when he coughed the children and I couldn't sleep. I don't know how he survived those nights. And yet he didn't postpone anything. In that respect he was fantastic, always. He never gave in; he always exacted the utmost from himself. He had no respect for all those artists who change like marionettes: you blow on them and they cancel."

The Polish Press Association covered Rubinstein's Warsaw performances as if they had been events of major international importance, and there was no official mention of the celebrated guest's Jewish origins or United States citizenship. An emotional article by A. M. Rosenthal described the events in the New York Times issue of June 13, after Rubinstein's final appearance in Warsaw:

> . . . the members of the audience stood for Rubinstein. They stood when he walked onto the stage, under the great chandeliers of the Philharmonia Concert Hall. They rose again with a surge with the last chords of Chopin's "Polonaise." They stood and cheered and shouted and sang "May He Live a Hundred Years" and ten times they brought him back from the wings.
>
> This is not simply a story of a triumphal concert by a great pianist. It is a story of the reunion of a man and a city and of the emotions that swept them.
>
> Artur Rubinstein was born in the shabby textile-manufacturing city of Lodz. . . . He is an American now, but a Polish writer said with a shrug, "He is the best so he is a Pole."

In the old days Rubinstein came back again and again to Poland from tours that made his one of the great names in music. But he never came back after 1938. There was World War II and occupations and the murder of his family in Lodz by the Germans. ("They wanted him to play in Lodz this time," said Mme. Aniela Rubinstein . . . , "but he couldn't. That was too much. That he couldn't do.")

During the long, icy years after the war, Rubinstein felt he could not come back. But the pull of old friends and old memories never left him. After 1956 the Rubinsteins were able to see some of their friends and relatives abroad, and he felt that things had changed enough in Poland for him to come back.

The Rubinstein concerts—the three that had been scheduled grew to six, including a rehearsal at which 1,200 people showed up—meant a variety of things in Poland. For the young musicians who crowded around him and for a whole new generation of music lovers it meant a chance to hear a man they had known only through records. For musicians and writers who were Rubinstein's friends it was an almost painfully poignant link with youth and memories. They kissed him and hugged him and asked delightedly, "You really do remember me?"

For the Rubinsteins these days in Warsaw have been an experience both joyous and wracking. Friends and relatives unseen for two decades crowded into the couple's rooms all day long to talk, to cluck admiringly at their 11-year-old son and 13-year-old daughter or just to sit a while, drink tea and look.

The sight of old friends brought Rubinstein to tears and so did the sight of Warsaw. It was not just stretches of wrecked streets, but the rebuilding of beloved squares and churches and other old and dear things. "They asked me what I thought of Warsaw now," said Rubinstein before he left today. "And I said, 'Divinely impractical!' Oh, Poles!"[99]

Rubinstein's second postwar visit to Poland, in 1960, attracted almost as much attention as the first. He headed the jury of the Sixth International Chopin Competition in Warsaw and, between February 16 and 24 he gave concerts in Poznan, Bydgoszcz, Warsaw, Katowice, and even Lodz. Why had he refused to play in his hometown during his first visit? "I have a terrible sentiment for Lodz," he explained several years later. "Here the Germans killed off all of my family. We were 70, 80, an enormous clan. They desecrated the synagogues. They desecrated my father's grave. I was frightfully bitter after the war and never wanted to come back here. I was afraid I would break down. It was an alien city, a city of nothing but strangers. There was no one here that I knew, no one who would say, 'remember?' "[100] But once he was back, he immediately felt at home. "I was moved that so many people had come so far from Cracow, from Warsaw, and the audience in Lodz is my audience," he said on the day after his concert. "I consider all the people from the audience my relatives. . . . When I played yesterday I was very moved that this was the town where I had been born, here were my first steps, my first thoughts, my first feelings—after all, this happened here."[101] Before long he had overcome his emotion and was telling reporters anecdotes from prewar days. One of the stories involved a Mr. Strauch, an impresario who had cheated him in Lodz. Times were bad, Strauch had said to him, and he implored him to cut his fee in half. Rubinstein agreed to do it, but only if the hall were less than half full. Just before the concert was to start, he peeked out from the wings and saw that the auditorium was completely empty. He was so upset that he began to feel badly for Strauch as the impresario duly counted out half the fee. But when Rubinstein walked onto the stage, a full house greeted him warmly: Strauch had kept the audience locked in the foyer until the last minute. In telling the story, Rubinstein added that he had indignantly reported the occurrence to a Warsaw impresario, whose only comment was, "Unfortunately, our Philharmonic Hall here doesn't have a large enough foyer." And this story reminded Rubinstein of a more generous Polish impresario who had kindly provided a piano for him to use in his hotel room. The good man visited Rubinstein in his room after the first of his concerts in the town and asked whether he was satisfied with the instrument. "Oh yes, it is excellent. When I play it, I immediately know what time it is," Rubinstein said. The impresario looked puzzled; Rubinstein sat down and began to play, and a few seconds later someone in the next room banged on the wall and shouted, "Don't you know that it's two A.M.?"[102]

A month later, during a stop in Amsterdam, Rubinstein told Harry Gilroy of the *New York Times* that he had found the Poles more interested in music than they had been before the war. " 'They are unhappy, they are hungry, they are working very hard and they need music,' he explained. . . . Mr. Rubinstein said that he was greatly impressed with the style in which the Chopin contest was presented and that he was deeply touched that the Polish regime had arranged that he be made an honorary citizen of Lodz. . . ."[103]

In September 1966 Rubinstein was back in Warsaw to give a mammoth recital: Schubert's last sonata (B-flat Major) and Schumann's *Carnaval* in the first part, and two pieces by Debussy, one by Chabrier, and three by Chopin (the G Minor Ballade, two études, and the B Minor Scherzo) in the second. A year and a half later, however, he fell into official disfavor in Poland as a result of a letter of his that had appeared in the *New York Times*:

To the Editor:

Some days ago the world observed the 25th anniversary of the Warsaw ghetto uprising, when 40,000 Jews took up arms in a doomed effort to combat the Nazi forces. This was surely one of the glorious chapters in the annals of martyrdom and heroic resistance to tyranny. What irony and tragedy that at this moment virulent anti-Semitism is being revived on Polish soil soaked with the blood of millions of Jews. The wave of anti-Jewish hysteria in Poland is being whipped up by potent reactionary forces in the regime and exploited as a weapon in a power struggle, a scapegoat for popular discontent, a smoke-screen for economic and political ills, an instrument to stifle progressive reforms demanded by the intelligentsia and students. The close link between anti-intellectualism, antiliberalism and anti-Semitism is once again tragically demonstrated.

On March 8 thousands of Warsaw University students demonstrated for freedom of expression, fair trials and an end to censorship. These demonstrations spread swiftly to other universities throughout the country, and were met by police violence and arrests. It is universal knowledge that the outbreak of students' demonstrations was due to the suppression by the authorities of public performances of "Dziady," the masterpiece of Mickiewicz, Poland's greatest poet. Will the music of Chopin be next to be prohibited from being heard in public? The political ideology of Chopin and his friend Mickiewicz was identical.

Since then Poland has been undergoing a massive systematic course of purge and propaganda whose central feature has been its undisguised anti-Semitism. The Jewish community of 18,000, many elderly or ill, is accused of disloyalty and browbeaten into self-abasement. Dozens of distinguished Jewish academics, artists, writers and intellectuals of international repute are called alien to Poland, charged with being spiritual instigators of the student movement, expelled from the Communist party and dismissed from their positions. Scores of students are arrested. All, intellectuals and students alike, are named and are pointed out as Jews. Many hundreds of others less prominent are also being purged more quietly but not less efficiently.

Most shocking is that all this is being done to the accompaniment of a vast propaganda campaign which has charged the country's atmosphere fearfully. Jews are accused of being "cosmopolitans, national nihilists, members of an international Zionist conspiracy,

Zionist lackeys of Western imperialism." Jewish philanthropic organizations which have poured millions of dollars into the economic
and social rehabilitation of war-torn Poland are accused of conspiracy, sabotage and espionage at the behest of international Zionism
and Western imperialism.

The moral nadir of this campaign is the falsification and dis-
tortion of the facts of Jewish martyrdom at the hands of the Nazis,
the obscene denigration of the Jewish victims of mass murder.

This is the brutal lexicon used by Stalin and his anti-Semitic
purges of 1948–52 and in the infamous doctors' plot he concocted in
January 1953. It is, tragically, the very language that has been
revived in the Soviet Union since the Arab-Israel War last June, in
an ominous propaganda campaign against the Jewish people. This
is the policy and the propaganda now taken over and carried further
by the Polish authorities.

I appeal to the leaders of Poland to cease this outrage. I appeal to world public opinion to rally to the defense of the Polish intelligentsia and Polish Jewry.

Arthur Rubinstein
Paris, April 16, 1968

The letter caused Rubinstein to be " 'denounced as a demagogue in the
Polish press,' " he told the *New York Times* in 1975, during his first return visit
to Poland in nine years. " 'It was a great honor, but I wouldn't come back
after that, to be arrested or molested.' Mr. Rubinstein thinks the new leadership of Poland changed its mind about him after the publication of his book
'My Young Years' two years ago," the *Times* report continued. " 'They saw in
it that I am terribly fond of this country, that I love this country very deeply,'
he said." Rubinstein hoped that Edward Gierek, the new Polish leader,
would be " 'a little different' " from his predecessors, and he said that he had
accepted requests from his Polish publisher "that he allow the removal of
passages that speak of his experience of Polish resentment of Russian rule,
which appear to him relevant to this day. 'I told them to go ahead,' he said.
'Everybody knows it anyway.' "[104]

Rubinstein gave what proved to be his last concert in Poland on May
30, 1975, when he played Chopin's Second and Beethoven's "Emperor"
Concertos with the Lodz Philharmonic, which was celebrating its sixtieth
anniversary. He played to a full house at the Grand Theater, and the *Times*
reporter chronicled the event. "He was greeted by a standing ovation before
he had played a note, a rare tribute even in Mr. Rubinstein's career. . . . At the
end, with flowers in the national colors, red and white, covering the stage,

with the public roaring and the orchestra applauding behind him, with the young people in the balcony singing the Polish equivalent of 'He's a Jolly Good Fellow,' with the elderly concertmaster dabbing at his eyes, Mr. Rubinstein finally stopped acknowledging the cheers with smiles, bows and lifting his hands from his heart toward the public in embracing gestures. He sat down again at the piano and, speaking in Polish, said what they wanted to hear: 'I have been asked to play Chopin's "Polonaise." ' There was no need to specify which of the many Polonaises he would dedicate to the occasion. It had to be the 'Grand ["Heroic," A-flat] Polonaise,' which in this intensely national-minded country expresses love of Poland even more than does the national anthem. The result was the predictable outpouring of emotion on both sides of the stage lights and a rush toward the front, which the pianist escaped by locking himself in the artist's room and receiving only a handful of carefully screened visitors. . . . Despite the enthusiasm of the concertgoing public, Mr. Rubinstein's homecoming received scant publicity in the Government-controlled information media, and few of the people of Lodz know that he was born here. He walked unrecognized in the crowded streets of his native city, one of the few cities in the world where this is likely to happen."[105]

No, RUBINSTEIN CERTAINLY did not lack recognition in most parts of the world, and the recognition was not limited to public applause and esteem among colleagues; it sometimes took official forms. Considerable portions of his papers consist of announcements of awards that had been or were about to be given him, invitations to receive honorary degrees and to attend state banquets, and thank-yous for having contributed his services to charitable organizations. Over the years, he accepted honorary doctorates from Yale (where he was inducted together with President John F. Kennedy), Columbia, Tufts, Brown, Wake Forest, Southwestern, University of California, and several other American universities and music schools. He attended numerous charity dinners in honor of various celebrities, including himself, and he dined with U.S. diplomats—Clare Boothe Luce and Ellsworth Bunker, among many others—at their postings around the world. On January 9, 1957, President Dwight D. Eisenhower sent him a letter of thanks for having participated in a special concert in Washington the previous evening; Rubinstein's personality had made so strong an impression on the unmusical president and his wife that they invited him to play at the White House four months later, during a state visit of the president of South Vietnam, Ngo Dinh Diem—of whom a great deal more was to be heard during the following few years. Steinway & Sons wanted Rubinstein to use the piano that they had renovated the previous year for the East Room of the White House, as a gift to the nation, but Rubinstein found its tone dull and insisted on having another piano brought in.

In France, President Charles de Gaulle and his wife invited Rubinstein to receptions at the Elysée Palace in 1962 and 1963. The pianist was made a commander of the Legion of Honor in 1970, and the following year President Georges Pompidou sent him a letter to inform him that he had been elected to the Académie des Beaux-Arts of the Institut de France; among all the official honors that Rubinstein received, this was probably the one that pleased him most. "Mr. Rubinstein, in tails and white tie as tradition has it, was guided to his seat by the academy's secretary, the composer Emmanuel Bondeville," the New York Times reported on December 12, 1971, of the previous day's ceremony. "Then there was a welcoming speech by Jacques Carlu, the architect who is president of the Academy, and finally the great pianist's own speech," which was dedicated, as tradition required, to his predecessor, "the late Swiss animal sculptor Edouard Sandoz. Mr. Rubinstein innovated by praising his predecessor's predecessor, his fellow pianist, Ignace Paderewski, who was Poland's first president after World War I. This led to Mr. Rubinstein's own field and a discussion of the relationship between composers and virtuosos—'Vampires,' as he called them. . . . The Academy of Fine Arts has 50 full members and 10 associate members, including nonartist benefactors." As a foreigner, Rubinstein was an associate member of the academy, and after his death, his place was taken by Richard Nixon, whose induction speech, in 1987, revolved around a trite reminiscence of a post-concert handshake with the pianist in Washington thirty-five years earlier. (In 1968, in one of the few partisan political acts of his life, Rubinstein had joined the Committee of Arts and Letters that was supporting Vice President Hubert H. Humphrey in his ultimately unsuccessful campaign against Nixon for the presidency of the United States.)

In his later years, Rubinstein enjoyed the friendship of the Belgian royal family and a particularly cordial relationship with the Dutch royal family. In 1971, Queen Juliana of the Netherlands made him a commander in the Order of Orange Nassau,[106] and in 1975 he and Nela dined twice, in private, with the sovereigns. Rubinstein was pleased to have been elected an Academico de Honor in Spain's Real Academia de Bellas Artes de San Fernando in 1974, at the time of his eighty-seventh birthday.[107] Later that year, he received a touching letter from Vassos Vassiliou, the Greek undersecretary of state. "Now that political freedom has returned to Greece," Vassiliou said, "I am writing to thank you for the sympathy and moral support you have given to the people of Greece during the past seven years. We are all deeply grateful for your help to us in refusing to perform in our country throughout the repressive regime of the military junta and we hope that in the near future you will honor us again by visiting our country and giving your great music to the people of Greece."[108] (Six years earlier, the Czech conductor Rafael Kubelik had written to Rubinstein to thank him for his "support of the Czechoslovak cause" following the Soviet invasion, but he did not specify what form the support had taken. "You have helped to confirm the unanimity among the Czechoslovaks at home, and helped also to unify, among people all over the world, the strength to stand in the search for the truth," Kubelik said.)[109]

On April 1, 1976, in a ceremony at the White House, President Gerald R. Ford gave Rubinstein the Medal of Freedom—"the highest civilian honor that it is within the power of a President of the United States to bestow," Ford said. "I feel deeply privileged today to act on behalf of all Americans in presenting that medal to one of the giants of our time. . . . Arthur Rubinstein has shared his singular and deeply personal mastery of the piano throughout the world. For over seven decades, his ceaseless vitality, his luminous spirit and his profound depth of mind have brought a fresh sparkle to the lives of people everywhere. His audiences love him; his colleagues and friends revere him; and his country, the United States of America, is proud to proclaim him as a giant among artists and men." Rubinstein replied: "I blush orally because my old age doesn't allow me to blush on my face. I am touched deeply. . . . due to the Second World War I brought my wife and children with me [to America] and have never left the country since." Rubinstein obviously meant that he had never given up his residency in the United States. "And this country began to spoil me—to love me, to give me such long, long years of affection. I cannot express it in words, really. Millions of people are my friends. Well, my feeling toward the United States is one of *great* gratitude and the continuation of a long, beautiful love affair. Thank you, Mr. President, for giving me the best sign of anything I could receive in this country."[110] He did not mention that he had never bothered to vote in an election in the United States or that earlier in 1976 he had inquired about the possibility of taking out Swiss citizenship. Swiss law, however, required twelve years of official residency in the country before naturalization could be considered; as he had been officially resident in Geneva only since 1969, he was not eligible. Thus, after having spent his first thirty years as a subject of the tsars of all the Russias and the following twenty-nine as a citizen of Poland, he remained a citizen of the United States for the last thirty-six years of his life.

The many generous tributes that Rubinstein received, especially during the last third of his long life, were balanced by the generosity with which he gave to others, and not only by moving people through his playing. Often, he gave benefit performances to assist foundations and individuals, or shared with outsiders some of the economic bounty that his work had brought him.

Apart from his already-mentioned contributions to war-related and specifically Polish enterprises, he contributed, during his American years, to many other organizations. The biggest of his charitable undertakings was probably the dedication, to various nonprofit organizations, of the box-office receipts from his historic series of ten recitals at Carnegie Hall in the fall of 1961. (At the same hall, in a two-week period five years earlier, to mark the fiftieth anniversary of his American debut, he had given a five-concert cycle in which he had played eighteen different piano concertos. "It is not really so difficult," he had told the pianist, teacher, and writer Abram Chasins. "After all, I've played these works all my life. Never well enough. Now, before it is too late, I want to play them all together, and perhaps more decently. I won't make a penny of course. But maybe I'll be able to feel that I've accomplished something better than just pounding keys for fifty years.")[111] A letter from Hurok's office to Mrs. Rubinstein listed the beneficiaries for each of the events: October 30, Musicians Emergency Fund; November 1, Musicians Foundation; November 3, Big Brothers; November 6, Collegiate School and Nightingale-Bamford School; November 10, United Jewish Appeal of Greater New York; November 19, the Mannes College of Music in New York; November 24, the National Association for the Advancement of Colored People; December 4, the National Association for Mental Health; December 8, the United Hospital Fund of New York; and December 10, the Polish Mutual Assistance fund.[112]

Rubinstein's contributions to the civil rights movement in the United States are particularly gratifying when one recalls his diatribe, in the 1920s, against jazz and what he had described as "Negromania." In addition to the 1961 benefit performance for the NAACP, he played, in November 1962, to raise funds for the same association's Legal and Defense and Education Fund,[113] and in April 1964 he was thanked by the National Council of the Churches of Christ for a contribution of one thousand dollars to the Commission on Religion and Race; the money was to be applied toward "the cost of bail bonding and legal expenses arising out of the arrests occurring in St. Augustine, Florida," the Commission's letter said. "The struggle for racial justice is often a costly one. . . . it will take considerable litigation before those rights are vindicated. . . ."[114] During the same month, Ralph J. Bunche—the first African-American to win the Nobel peace prize—wrote to thank Rubinstein for having agreed to join the Committee of Sponsors for the Convocation of the NAACP Legal Defense and Educational Fund, the following month.[115] And in 1965 Rubinstein was a member of the honorary committee of the "Once in a Lifetime Tribute to the Negro Performer," sponsored by the Negro Actors Guild of America.[116]

Rubinstein also contributed to music-related enterprises. In 1964 he gave one thousand dollars toward the establishment of the Toscanini Memorial Archive at New York's Library and Museum of the Performing Arts at Lincoln Center, for "the creation . . . of an extensive photographic Archive of the manuscript scores and sketches of the master composers, reproduced from the originals in the great libraries and private collections of the world." In 1968, he approved the use of a photograph of himself and an accompanying message in support of the Musicians' Benevolent Fund in England, and he almost certainly donated money to the Fund, whose Honorary Treasurer was Lesley Jowitt. And in 1971 he donated the one-thousand-dollar Rubinstein Piano Award to Raymond Kendall's Young Musicians Foundation in Los Angeles.[117] Again, these examples are but a few among a great many.

Of his private generosity, the violinist Henri Temianka told a story that is representative of Rubinstein's behavior: "a great European pianist was in financial distress following his wife's catastrophic illness. Knowing that Artur Rubinstein was an admirer and friend of his, I phoned Rubinstein long-distance. Although Rubinstein, already past seventy, was due home very late that night after a concert and a strenuous flight, he invited me to an early breakfast the next morning. He wrote out a four-figure check in our friend's name, and handed it to me, saying, 'If the situation were reversed, I know he would do the same for me.' "[118]

Rubinstein's kindness did not take only musical and monetary forms. Steinway's Franz Mohr described the pianist as "very easy to work for. He was extremely appreciative of whatever you did for him. He always thanked you. Horowitz could blow up if the piano was not in the right position, but not Rubinstein." Even with respect to his choice of piano for his most important concerts during any given season, Rubinstein was easy to deal with. "One year when he came in to make a selection, I had lined up four or five pianos I thought he'd like. He sat down at the first piano and immediately fell in love with it. He turned and said to me, 'Oh, that is so beautiful. This one I take.' . . . He didn't even look at [the others]. He said, 'Either I have a relationship with an instrument immediately, or I don't. . . .'"[119]

Many composers who were aware of Rubinstein's fundamental decency wrote to him during the 1940s and '50s, to request that he perform or at least look over or listen to their music: Mario Castelnuovo-Tedesco, Henri Barraud, David Diamond, Ernst Křenek, Goffredo Petrassi, Daniele Amfiteatroff, Federico Mompou, Isidor Philipp, and Ernesto Halffter all approached him by letter on this subject. Although Rubinstein rarely wanted to play the compositions sent for his inspection, he tried to help by making recommendations in appropriate places—if he felt that a composer demonstrated real talent. Typical is a letter that Lukas Foss sent him from the Music Department of the University of California at the end of 1953, to thank him for having given a warm recommendation for the revised version of his Second Piano Concerto, which won the New York Music Critics' Award the following year. "I can't tell you how grateful I am to you," Foss wrote. "This is the best Christmas present of all. Ah, if only there were other great musicians as generous as you are, composers' lives would be less difficult."[120] But few composers bothered to write to Rubinstein after he passed his seventieth birthday; they probably assumed that to place their hopes on a man whom they viewed as a holdover from the Romantic era was absurd. Indeed, one can hardly imagine what prompted the cellist Paul Tortelier to suggest, in October 1971, that Rubinstein commission the French composer Henri Dutilleux to write a piano concerto for him—as if Rubinstein, at eighty-four, were up to learning a new work in a modern idiom! But he sometimes showed authentic interest in music that was not fundamentally to his taste. "I saw [Schoenberg's] very controversial opera, *Moses und Aron*, in Paris and I was deeply impressed by its emotional impact," he told a British journalist in 1962. "I didn't understand the music well; but 'understand' is a word one shouldn't apply to music; there's nothing to *understand*—for me, music must be *felt*."[121] More often, however, he defended his lack of interest in the latest musical developments on the grounds of having done his part for the new music of his own day. "In my young years, I'm proud to say I was a violent fighter for the music of my contemporaries, which I was incredibly eager to bring to the public so that they could understand and appreciate it as I did," he told Robert Jacobson in 1968. "Often I fought against strong public opposition . . . when I played works of Scriabin, Debussy, Ravel, Szymanowski, Villa-Lobos, Shostakovich and Prokofiev. I was hissed in Milan for playing a Shostakovich prelude and in Warsaw when I played Debussy there in 1904, for these were then novelties. I did this for half of my life, but more recently new names have not appeared on my programs. . . . I do not feel able to fight now for Stockhausen or Boulez or Nono—this I leave to the young people. I feel out of touch with new developments of music and so I dare not criticize it either; one has no right to do this about what one does not understand."[122]

Performing musicians, more often than composers, applied to Rubinstein for assistance; he listened to many of them, and when he was positively impressed he did his best to help. The pianists William Masselos, Moura Lympany, Jacob Lateiner, and Maria Tipo, and the conductor Antonia Brico, all received advice and various sorts of help from him, but in the long run the most successful of Rubinstein's protégés was Daniel Barenboim. "He always said that he knew my parents when my mother was pregnant with me," said Barenboim, who was born in 1942, and whose father, Enrique, was a well-known piano teacher. "I first heard Rubinstein in Buenos Aires, sometime between 1948 and 1951. When he would come, the whole city would go crazy:

the queues started days before. My family took turns—one would stand in line for a few hours, then someone else stood patiently. I met him then; he came to my parents' house. I vividly remember hearing him play two pieces—one was the Schumann *Carnaval* and the other was the 'Appassionata.' I don't remember whether they were on the same concert or on different concerts. The first time I played for him was in Paris, at his house on Avenue Foch, in 1954 or '55. We were living in Paris—I was studying harmony with Nadia Boulanger. A common friend of ours, Alexandre Tansman, took me. I remember my father and mother not wanting to go with me, because they had known him in Argentina—not very well, but they didn't want him to feel that they were trying to push their talented son. So when Tansman took me there, Rubinstein didn't make the connection at all; he was just listening to a child whom Tansman was bringing him. He was very embarrassed because he was over an hour late—he had been to some lunch. And then for a couple of hours I played everything I knew. Whenever he listened to me, he was always positive and he liked a lot of things, but he always had criticisms to make about other things. I was always very happy about that because I felt that the positive remarks were sincere.

"I went a couple of times to play for him, and then one evening Nela phoned and asked my mother whether she could bring me over. She said that Arthur thought it was important that I come. I was taken out of bed and I went there. There had obviously been a very nice party, and they had just finished dinner. Sol Hurok, Ernesto de Quesada, and some other people were there. Rubinstein asked me to play, and he practically told Hurok what to do with me: 'You should take him to America, on a tour, and you should not exploit him; he shouldn't play too much. You won't make much money on him at first.' He basically negotiated my contract, as it were, and that's how I went to America for the first time, in December 1956. Rubinstein definitely helped to launch my career. Quesada also gave me a few concerts in Spain.

"I always kept in touch; I always played for him whenever he came to Israel or wherever else I was. When I got married, Jackie [the cellist Jacqueline du Pré] and I spent our honeymoon [at the Rubinstein's place] in Marbella." In January 1967, the concertmaster of the Israel Philharmonic attended Barenboim's unanticipated conducting debut in London, and he told Rubinstein about it the next time they met. Rubinstein said that he wanted to play with Barenboim, and their first collaboration took place later that year, in Tel Aviv. "He was my first major soloist!" Barenboim recalled. "He played the Schumann Concerto and the Chopin F Minor Concerto"— the latter is an especially tricky piece to conduct—"and after that he played all over with me, in Israel, in London several times, with the New York Philharmonic, and two or three times in Paris, also. We recorded all the Beethoven concertos together—although in concert we did only the last three to-gether—and we did both Brahms concertos on several occasions. So he was very helpful to me in my professional career as a conductor as well as in my career as a pianist.

"There was something very Polish—gentlemanly, I suppose—about him. He was correct and polite until you got really very close, which was very rare. And in spite of his formality, he was always able to show great warmth. It was not a cold formality. You always felt you were in the presence of a great person to whom you didn't dare get too close, but who managed to show great, great warmth. I think he had genuine affection for me—he had known me since I was a child—and he absolutely adored Jacqueline. We were very, very close to him; we used to go once a week, I think, to lunch with him when we were in Paris. As soon as there were three or four people, he was a differ-ent person: He told stories, he was the entertainer, and he had a good sense of humor. But he would talk not just about personal things, but also about litera-ture and theater and opera. He was a much more erudite person than people who knew him only from parties were led to believe."

Rubinstein continued to coach young pianists occasionally until very late in his life. Ann Schein, his principal disciple during the early 1960s, was a pupil of Mieczyslaw Münz at the Peabody Institute in Baltimore. Rubin-stein had first heard about her through Halina Lilpop Rodzinska, who thought highly of her; Schein had then written to him, and he had replied kindly and honestly but not entirely encouragingly, in a letter that outlined his attitude toward advanced study:

> Frankly I do not believe that a pianist of your accomplishment
> needs any help from me. My feeling is that when one becomes the
> master of the keyboard with well obeying fingers he ought hence-
> forth to be his own professor.
>
> I am sure that when you listen to the first tape of a new re-
> cording of yours you discover, as I always do, a lot of shortcomings,
> a lot of disappointing phrasing, wrong tempo, etc. I call my records
> the only real teachers I ever had. I am afraid that pianists like myself
> cannot resist the temptation of imposing their personalities upon
> anyone who asks them for an opinion. Your goal should now be to
> develop your own personality. This you can do listening to your rec-
> ords with a critical ear; this you can do listening to many pianists
> and adopting what you like in their interpretations and rejecting
> what you dislike.
>
> This approach will make you feel sure of your own approach
> to music and will help you create your own musical personality.

With Artur Rodzinski, 1950s.

With Pablo Casals, Zürich, 1951.

A caricature by Giuseppe Damiani, 1957.

Rubinstein the raconteur, during his first postwar visit to Poland, 1958.

With Indira Gandhi, 1960s. (City News Bureau, Washington, D.C.)

Typical between-concert activity: playing cards with Nela and Alina, 1960s.

With Picasso, in the south of France, 1960s.

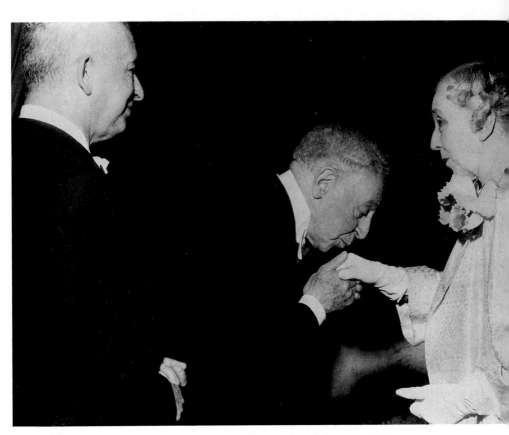

With Vladimir Golschmann and Queen Elisabeth of Belgium, c. 1960.

In the courtyard of what had been his family's home in Lodz, 1960.

With Igor Stravinsky in front of the Teatro la Fenice, Venice, c. 1962.

Receiving an honorary doctorate at Yale University, June 1962, from the president, Whitney Griswold. President John F. Kennedy is visible at left.

Tokyo, 1966.

A gala concert in Tel Aviv, November 1967, to celebrate the tenth anniversary of the Mann Auditorium. From left to right: Nela, the conductor Paul Paray, Rubinstein, Paul Tortelier, Isaac Stern.

Lucerne, 1968.

With Nela, c. 1970.

Rubinstein, c. 1970.

Conducting (or trying to conduct)
the Israel Philharmonic, c. 1970.

With the dancer Serge Lifar in Nice, 1972. (Keystone, Paris)

With Krystian Zimerman, c. 1975.

With Bernard Haitink, London, c. 1975.

Making a point during a 1975 rehearsal with the Lodz Philharmonic, before his last concert in Poland.

Dancing with Eva at a Polish ball, New York, March 1976.

With Svyatoslav Richter at Rubinstein's home in Paris, c. 1979. (Photograph by and property of A. Weidenfeld)

The last photograph of Arthur and Nela together, 1977.

Rubinstein with (from left to right) Shlomo Mintz, Nelson Freire, Marta Argerich, and Paul Ostrowski, Geneva, 1982. (Photograph by and property of A. Weidenfeld)

The last photograph of Rubinstein, with Annabelle Whitestone; taken by Zubin Mehta, Geneva, December 1982. (Collection of A. Weidenfeld)

The butterfly* flies from flower to flower and tries to find the best mixture in creating her honey, - so try to make your musical honey the same way.

Now then, if you would like to play for me and discuss some interpretations with me, I shall be delighted to see you and hear you any moment when I am free. . . .

Wishing you all the success you deserve, I am

Cordially yours,

Arthur Rubinstein

*my foolish secretary took *bees* for butterflies!

His interest in Schein increased when Mrs. Rodzinska forced him to listen to the young woman's recording of Rachmaninoff's Third Piano Concerto; he suggested that she visit, with Münz. After Rubinstein had heard Schein, he contacted Hurok, who put her name on his very select roster and sent her on a tour of the Soviet Union the following season. Rubinstein coached her in Paris during the summer of 1961, attended her Carnegie Hall debut the following March, and coached her again in Paris and Lucerne the following summer. She recalled that she had played Schumann's *Humoreske* at their first session, and that Rubinstein had "seemed curiously moved, and asked me to stay for lunch. He asked if I could come the next day so that I could play the Humoreske again for his wife, and for their friend Fela [Krance], who was Halina Rodzinska's sister. I did, and after this experience, I was generally there twice a week for several hours, including luncheon afterward." She played many major compositions of Beethoven, Schubert, Chopin, Schumann, and Brahms for Rubinstein. "He sat not far away, on a small chair, always smoking a cigar. . . . His whole demeanor was alert, comfortable and full of anticipation. He made you *want* to play." Schein was impressed by Rubinstein's aversion to hearing a piece played in his own style. " 'I want you to *convince* me with your playing of each piece,' " he told her. " 'You see, my legs, my knees will begin to shake impatiently if I feel it is not convincing me, or going in the wrong direction.' . . . His knees shook often." In his coaching, he emphasized "keeping the momentum and the direction of the piece, being totally expressive in phrases, understanding the style of fine Chopin playing, the drama and mood of each work," Schein said. "I remember aspects of the first movement of Les Adieux [Beethoven's Sonata in E-flat Major, Op. 81a], the mood and kaleidoscopic harmonies in the opening Adagio, and the impetus and arch of the joyful octaves once the Allegro began. He would sing, go to the other piano to play a phrase, his arms moving widely and expressively in an indication of the shape. . . . Rather than belabor difficulties, he would always leave you with new ideas and go on to something fresh. He knew when to shift moods and gears, and he never allowed a negative atmosphere to remain."

When Schein played Mozart's Concerto in G Major, K. 453, Rubinstein told her that performing Mozart " 'is a test of our directness. We must be simple. It is almost impossible to be simple. I have struggled all my life to be simple, and it should be the goal of our musical lives, to achieve this simplicity.' " He asked her to read through Schubert's B-flat Sonata, D. 960, at the following lesson, "and when I got to the end of the slow movement, he looked very grave," she recalled. " 'Schubert is the only composer who could look straight at death,' " Rubinstein told her. " 'This movement is like death. There is nothing else as close as his music that shows us what death feels like. I think when I die, I do not want to be around anyone. I would like to do like the animals that go off into the woods to die with dignity—alone.' " Schein said that on one stormy day, when it had taken her two hours to get to the Rubinsteins' house from where she was staying in the Paris suburbs, "he cheerfully bounced down the stairs to greet me. . . . I was tired and soaked and depressed by the dark day. 'Ah, I am *never* depressed by the weather! I am *much* stronger than the weather!' And he rarely expressed another mood than that in all the times I saw him. . . . There would be a fleeting shadow in his voice lasting only a measure or two, like a Mozart harmony; then it was gone." On one occasion, "he showed me a little pouch he carried with him on every trip. It was full of tiny stuffed animals. 'These are for good luck,' he said, looking like a child himself, suddenly. 'It is important to stay like a child, you know.' " (According to Annabelle Whitestone, "the bag Arthur carried around with him when giving concerts and which was always with him in his bedroom . . . contained sentimental mementos, a very old unrecognizable baby's cuddly toy, which I think belonged to Alina, letters which were precious to him . . . , some wafer-thin dark Lindt chocolates or Bahlsen wafers covered in dark chocolate which one was offered while travelling or sitting and waiting at airports, the Penhaligon's Hammam toilet water which he always used since José Antonio Gandarillas gave him some in 1915, and the Elnet hairspray which served for the hair and the keyboard. Arthur, perhaps only late in life, suffered from very dry hands—he never perspired, and he felt that it helped to make the keyboard slightly sticky with hair lacquer.")

Not only did Rubinstein refuse payment for Schein's lessons: he also gave her presents. One was "a pin, a pure carved ivory daisy with white petals and a yellow center," she said. " 'I bought one for Alina, and I thought you might like one, too,' " he told her. "Another day, he came to the piano store where I practiced in Lucerne before my lessons. I had a rather large, utilitarian alarm clock on top of the piano. The next day, he appeared with a package. It was a small, black, incredibly elegant alarm clock from Piaget. 'For your trips and practicing,' he said, always with a mock look of wonder and surprise!" And he gave her "two of his recordings he particularly liked. One was the Schumann Carnaval and the other was the Brahms Sonata in f minor. We listened to them together." In later years, Rubinstein attended Schein's performances whenever he could.[123]

COACHING AND ENCOURAGING young pianists seemed to Rubinstein an excellent means of giving back some of the bounty that his art had brought him, but through his sixties, seventies, and eighties his main means of giving to others remained his concert appearances. He could easily have chosen to restrict himself to a few public performances a year—for which he would have been able to charge exceptionally high ticket prices and sell radio, television, and recording rights—or to withdraw altogether from the stage and live comfortably on record royalties and the interest on his previous earnings. Instead, each year he retraveled the length and breadth of North America and Western Europe, performing in small towns as well as great capitals, and on occasion he returned to South America, to Eastern European countries besides Poland (he even revisited the Soviet Union in 1964 and was able to see his dying friend Harry Neuhaus),[124] and to Asia and the Pacific. During the 1966–67 season, in the course of which he turned eighty, Rubinstein gave 114 concerts and made many recordings. Thus, his playing and his persona continued to make a profound impression on the imaginations of hundreds of thousands of people around the world, and his audiences' enthusiastic reactions continued to keep him going. "I cannot tell you . . . how much I love to play for people," he told an interviewer in the mid-1960s. "Would you believe it—sometimes when I sit down to practice and there is no one else in the room, I have to stifle an impulse to ring for the elevator man and offer him money to come in and hear me? I am happy to play to a crowded Carnegie Hall. But I am just as happy to play for a thousand people, for three hundred, for a hundred, indeed for anyone who cares to listen."[125] He did not have to pay others to listen to him: by the early 1970s he was earning up to twenty-four thousand dollars for a single concert,[126] and he loved the tributes of esteemed admirers. "We once attended a concert of Arthur's in Lucerne," Mildred Knopf recalled. "Afterward, a short, energetic, Jewish-looking man burst into his dressing room and said, 'Ah, if only I could paint the way you play!' Arthur said, 'Don't worry about it, my old friend!' It was Chagall."[127]

From the early 1950s to the end of Rubinstein's career, Israel was one of his favorite performing locations. Unlike his feelings toward Poland and the other countries in which he had lived, his enthusiasm for Israel—which he visited only as an outsider—was virtually unquestioning. "I have the feeling that through the terrible 1930s and the beginning of the '40s and the Holocaust, he must have had a terrible shock," Barenboim said. "Because he had tried to be very assimilated. And I think that that's the reason for his extreme generosity toward Israel—going there every year, not taking any money, and playing day and night." Among the memorable Israeli events in which Rubinstein participated, one of the most significant was the opening of the Mann Auditorium—the Israel Philharmonic Orchestra's new home in Tel Aviv—on October 2, 1957. He played Beethoven's "Emperor" Concerto with the Philharmonic under Leonard Bernstein. Other soloists on the same concert were the violinist Isaac Stern and the cellist Paul Tortelier, a Gentile who was so devoted to Israel that he had learned to speak Hebrew. The hall was named after Fredric R. Mann, its principal benefactor and Rubinstein's old friend.

Rubinstein apparently believed that Israel could do no wrong, and in 1975, when the United Nations Educational, Social, and Cultural Organization (UNESCO) took sides in the Arab-Israeli dispute by cutting off funds for Israel, he joined several pro-Israel protests and spoke out on the subject during one of his Carnegie Hall concerts and on other occasions. To the Italian pianist Guido Agosti, who had headed a protest by Italian musicians over the same issue, he wrote: "The moral contribution of Italy, which is so cultivated and civilized, has given me great pleasure. I must say that the intellectual world has expressed its disgust for UNESCO's procedures against Israel. First, this selfish world sold Israel for gasoline and since then it has completely isolated it. But I have enough faith in the character and courage of the Jews to know that once again they will be able to defend themselves against the selfishness and wickedness of this cowardly world."[128] On October 2, 1975, Rubinstein performed at a Paris concert "in honour of Israel's Ambassador to France, Asher Ben-Natan, who was ending his tour of duty," according to the *Jerusalem Post*. "The 88-year-old pianist played Schumann's Piano Concerto with the Cleveland Orchestra, with proceeds going to providing scholarships in memory of the Ben-Natans' son, Amnon, who fell in the Yom Kippur War. Almost 3,000 people, including political leaders, packed the Paris Congress Palace for the occasion."

An even stronger connection between Rubinstein and Israel had been created in September 1974, at the time of the first running, in Tel Aviv, of the Arthur Rubinstein International Piano Master Competition; the event was the brainchild of Jan J. Bistritzky, a Pole who had been involved in the administration of the Chopin Competition in Warsaw before he immigrated to Israel. Since 1910, when Rubinstein had tried unsuccessfully to win the Anton Rubinstein Prize in St. Petersburg, he had been leery of music competitions—although he had sat on the juries of several important ones during the intervening decades—and he hesitated to lend his name to Bistritzky's project for fear that it might not live up to the standards of the most prestigious international competitions. But once the competition's first heat was underway, his worries were allayed. "NEVER, NEVER, NEVER have I met such a concentration of talent before," he told the *Jerusalem Post* while the event was still in progress; "everyone, at a lesser contest, would easily have won first prize."[129] The formidable jury consisted of Arturo Benedetti Michelangeli and Guido Agosti from Italy; Enrique Barenboim (Daniel's father), Mindru Katz, Pnina Salzman, and Michal Smoira-Cohn from Israel; Jacques Février and Alexandre Tansman from France; Henri Gagnebin from Switzerland; Dieter Weber from Austria; and Eugene Istomin, Irving Kolodin, and Rubinstein himself from the United States.

Emanuel Ax, a brilliant, Polish-born American pianist, won the first prize—a gold medal and $5,000; Eugene Injic, another American, won the second—a silver medal and $3,000; and the Canadian Janina Fialkowska and Austrian Seta Tanyel tied for third—bronze medals and $2,000. Rubinstein took a special interest in Fialkowska's playing, and she later recalled that if he had not had his way she would not have won any prize at all. "One of the jurors had a wife in the competition, another had two pupils in it, and it seems that I was marked very low because I was expendable—the only Canadian," she said. "Arthur had a rough time pushing me through; he said that he would take his name away from the competition if I didn't make the finals." He told her that he didn't " 'allow injustices in competitions' " and that he had similarly defended the Polish pianist André Tchaikovsky at the Queen Elisabeth Competition in Brussels in 1956 and the Belgian pianist Michel Block at the Chopin Competition in Warsaw in 1960.[130] (Block bore a slight physical resemblance to Rubinstein, and Rubinstein's defense of his playing led to false and malicious rumors to the effect that Block was Rubinstein's illegitimate son.) At the prize distribution ceremony, Rubinstein told the audience, which included Golda Meir, the prime minister, that Israel "has so many things to face, so many more difficult [problems] than any country in the world just now, and yet, the pride of my heart is that it has never lost sight of culture, of music, of art, of love of life, of high spirit, of magnificent humanity. This is the pride of this country. This is one of the reasons why I love it so dearly, and so much, and so deeply."[131]

BY THE END of the 1940s the era of magnetic sound tape and long-playing records had begun. Rubinstein spent more time than ever in the recording studio, and he continued to make many records throughout the last three decades of his career. In 1948, twenty years after his first HMV recording sessions, for which he had been guaranteed a modest $144 per 78 rpm side, he earned the extraordinary sum of $110,000 in royalties from RCA—probably as a result of a special initiative undertaken by the company. His royalties dropped to the still-substantial figure of $35,000 in 1949—the year in which he became the No. 1 foreign recording artist in Great Britain—but his annual average recording income for the following seven years was over $81,000; between 1957 and 1962, inclusive, the average was $134,500.[132] In the early 1960s, RCA guaranteed Rubinstein $110,000 a year in royalties; by the late 1960s, the guarantee was $120,000. In 1968, his earnings exceeded the guarantee by more than $65,500, and his five best-selling records in the United States that year were the Chopin Waltzes, the Chopin Nocturnes, Mozart's Concerto in A Major, K. 488, Beethoven's "Moonlight" Sonata, and the Grieg Concerto. By 1965, approximately three million copies of his recordings had been sold worldwide. "In his time," said Max Wilcox, who produced most of Rubinstein's recordings from 1959 to the end of the pianist's career, "he was probably RCA's best-selling instrumentalist. . . . Of course, we're talking about a time when there weren't dozens of versions of all the great works in the catalogue. When he recorded, say, the Rachmaninoff Second Concerto, with Reiner [in 1956], he was able to sell 350,000 copies. But [fifteen] years later, when he was even more famous, he recorded the work again with Ormandy and sold only 20,000 copies, just because there were so many versions around by then."[133]

Wilcox described a typical Rubinstein recording session, in the summer of 1965 at RCA Italiana's headquarters near Rome. Rubinstein began by telling funny stories to the producer, engineer, and piano tuner, then entered the recording studio. "The work for that morning is a continuation of the complete recordings of the Chopin Nocturnes that he had begun a few days earlier. Now it is the time for the Nocturne Opus 48, No. 2. . . . After he makes the first take he comes into the control room and says, 'Now I will take my lesson.' And this is literally what he does, for he listens with completely objective ears. If he is pleased with the first performance, he will almost always do one or two more, which will be even more beautiful and simple. In the case of this particular Nocturne, Rubinstein found his whole approach a little too elaborate and decided that it must be played in a more simple and subtle manner. Ten takes later this great musician had achieved what he wanted; the final performance was a totally different conception from the first performance. . . . This . . . is an extreme example, for Mr. Rubinstein usually finds two or three takes sufficient to record his performance, but I mention it because, rather than being satisfied, he became constantly more inspired until he achieved what the music was saying to him that day. . . . He must play the music as it speaks to him, and since it speaks to him in ever new ways, he is happy with his recordings for several months or even, in rare instances, a few years, but, as he has often told me, 'The records don't change, but I do.' "[134]

A few years after Rubinstein's death, his son John talked with Wilcox about the Rubinstein approach to recording:

JR: He was not a complainer in any sense of the word when it came to work. He would always feel very sorry for himself and want a lot of compassion and pity, but when it really came down to showing up and doing the job, he would make it great for everybody around him. . . . He had to have everybody attuned and enthusiastic about what he was going to do before he could really do it. And he was terribly sensitive if that weren't the case. [About listening to the test pressings of his recordings:] . . . he played those lacquers more than he played anything else, ever. By the time the record came out, he had heard the lacquers so many times that he hardly even listened to the record. . . . It was a very exciting time when those things came in the plain brown wrappers. We put them on, and he would tense up. . . . You had to tell him the truth, so you would always have to say good things first, and of course that was easy because there were always good things. But, boy, he would *watch* people. . . .

MW: There's a certain kind of nervous tension to concert performances that is thrilling at the time, but sometimes I felt that there was a solidity and nobility in the recorded performances that didn't always come over into the concert performances.

JR: Yes. There was a thoughtfulness that he sometimes didn't allow himself when he was playing in concerts, especially when he would get nervous—and he would, like any other performer. . . . I found really that the big difference between his concerts and his recordings was that he would pay more attention to tempos. He tended to rush in concerts. He would rush from nerves and enthusiasm and just for effect. And in the recordings he wouldn't. He would rein in and take that passage with its full gusto, and so it would be much stronger. . . . But he didn't really alter the spontaneity of his playing or his inspiration. He didn't get crazy to play correct notes and let the inspiration go. He couldn't play that way. . . .

MW: You were the page turner for the famous recording in Rome of the Chopin waltzes [on June 25, 1963]. I remember that he started recording the waltzes and got up to ten of them. Normally we'd do five or six and come back the next night to finish them up. But he was making only two takes each, and sometimes one. We had started at about seven at night, I think, and it was about 10:30 when he'd gotten through ten of them. And I never have known to this day if he was teasing us or not when he said, "Oh well, I think that's enough." And everybody screamed, "No, no, keep on going, keep on going!" . . . And about an hour and a half later, he had finished all 14 Chopin waltzes—in four and a half hours. And then, since he had a lot of energy left, we all went to the Via Veneto and partied until two o'clock in the morning. . . . I loved all that excitement of the great food and the great cigars and all the things that I learned from him. But what I remember most about him is the serious musician who sat beside me during a playback and listened to himself play.[135]

Wilcox was fascinated by Rubinstein's way of transforming himself "from a flamboyant public personality into a scholarly intellectual" when he got to work. "He was a prodigious worker, and he would say of some of the people who worked with him, 'All they want to do is get rid of me at five o'clock and drink martinis.' He worked quickly but carefully, and he didn't want to be told, 'Oh, that was fantastic!' We had a good rapport—it was instinctive more than anything else—and he trusted me to choose the takes" that were used in the final, published recordings.[136]

With respect to his recorded repertoire, one question plagued Rubinstein more than any other. "You asked me why I hadn't yet recorded Chopin's Etudes," he wrote, in response to a fan letter from California in 1962. "Quite a few music lovers request this recording. My answer is simple. To do them justice is a most difficult task, which I haven't yet had the courage to attempt. However, it has never left my mind, and I hope to be able to do it in the nearest future."[137] In 1968 he told the music critic Robert Jacobson that he was "scared to death" of the études, "technically and musically. But, maybe before I die I will do them. I have heard some very musical performances of the Etudes, but it is very rare for both to happen together. Records are different from a concert in the ultimate product. If I were dishonest, I could record them bar by bar: I could tape three bars and have coffee, then play three more and have tea, and then three more and lie down. Then the producers could splice all these together and have it all of a piece."[138] Monika Mann wrote to Rubinstein, in 1973: "There is much happiness in my cellar in Capri and in me when Chopin's waltzes, nocturnes, sonatas, and concertos are played by your hands—unfortunately I haven't yet been able to hunt up the mazurkas, etudes, and preludes, haven't they been recorded?" Rubinstein replied: "I'll try to send you the records of the Chopin Mazurkas, my Preludes [recorded in 1946] aren't good enough, and I've never dared to record the Etudes."[139] In the end, Rubinstein's authorized recordings included only the Trois nouvelles études and none of the canonical twenty-four études of Op. 10 and Op. 25, but unauthorized live recordings of a few of them have been published.

During his last active decades, Rubinstein recorded three of the ten Beethoven violin and piano sonatas, and all three of Brahms's, with the Polish-Mexican violinist Henryk Szeryng, as well as several trios with Szeryng and the French cellist Pierre Fournier. And he took special pleasure in making a series of records with the New York–based Guarneri String Quartet. The matchmaker was Wilcox, who, in 1965, had persuaded the pianist to listen to one of the first tapes made by the young ensemble, which had been formed the previous year. Rubinstein was impressed. "He asked to meet with the Quartet and said that now perhaps he could make the recordings of piano quintets and quartets of which he had so long dreamed," Wilcox reported.[140] In isolated enterprises, Rubinstein had recorded Brahms's G Minor Piano Quartet with members of the Pro Arte Quartet in 1932 and the Fauré C Minor Quartet with members of the Paganini Quartet in 1949, and in the 1950s he and the Juilliard String Quartet had sounded each other out about working together but had not reached an agreement.[141] Rubinstein met the members of the Guarneri Quartet on December 26, 1966; together, they rehearsed the Brahms Quintet in F Minor, Op. 34, and they agreed to begin to record it two days later. "Everything went exceptionally well," Wilcox said, "and by noon on December 29, the Brahms quintet was completed. . . . When the last note . . . had sounded and we all gathered together in the playback room, Mr. Rubinstein casually announced that if the members of the Guarneri Quartet were available, he would love to record the Schumann quintet the next day!" The quartet was available, but—as Arnold Steinhardt, the first violin, recalled—"We thought, 'Oh my God! You can't record it!' He hadn't played some of these pieces in a quarter-century or half a century. At first he would play a fistful of wrong notes, but he was unflappable. He wouldn't say, 'I missed those notes—I'm so sorry.' He would say, 'Listen to this passage over here—isn't this wonderful!' The little concerns obviously had to be met and overcome, but he was interested in something far beyond them."[142] Late on the evening of December 30, "the Schumann quintet was on tape, and champagne in paper cups was being held high in the air," Wilcox said.[143] One month before his eightieth birthday, Rubinstein had found "his" string quartet.

The results of these sessions made a deep impression on listeners, including some extremely exacting ones. Glenn Gould, whose reclusive personality and dislike of public performances made him Rubinstein's pianistic opposite, interviewed his older colleague for *Look* magazine in 1971 and told him that he considered the Rubinstein-Guarneri recording of the Brahms Quintet "the greatest chamber-music performance with piano that I've heard in my life. . . . my notion of what Brahms represents has been changed by your recording." (In other respects, the two pianists' conversation revealed nothing new about either of them: they agreed to disagree about the relative virtues and failings of live concerts and recordings, until Rubinstein finally allowed, "Well, you begin to persuade me. I was born in another epoch, you see. I trail the old things that hang all around me like—well, like the tin cans they hang on the wedding car, you know. They stay with me. But you were born into another world. . . .")[144] Rubinstein and the Guarneri members eventually recorded the two Mozart and three Brahms quartets, the Dvořák Second and Fauré First Quartets, and the Dvořák Quintet, in addition to the Brahms and Schumann quintets. Steinhardt said, "I think I can speak for the whole quartet when I say that it was an extraordinary experience, a joyful experience, and for me, personally, a great learning experience, just to let it go and enjoy the music. Rubinstein had a great intellect but he was not an intellectual. He had a beautiful balance between intellect and emotion, and there was a carefree abandon to his personality. The marriage of that to a powerful mind and real musicianship was a wonderful thing. These days, you hear people who are either out of control in their playing or so in control that it's like hearing their own record of a piece. With Rubinstein it was always fresh: he would treat every piece as if he were playing it for the first time. He could mold a phrase with great freedom, but it was never excessive or in bad taste. It was magical, because you never knew how he did it: he'd do those little rubati, but with an eyedropper—just a little bit with a note here or there. You got an overwhelming feeling of fluidity and elasticity, and it was always aristocratic.

"The spirit of chamber music was evident in his whole approach," Steinhardt recalled. "We were a young and largely unknown quartet at the beginning of our career. Just by dint of his age and fame, he had tremendous power over us." (The members of the quartet were thirty-eight to fifty years younger than Rubinstein.) "He could have run the show; he could have told us to play louder here and faster there. But the feeling was really one of true equals, and this was quite a marvelous thing. I've played with elderly musicians who have said, 'I want you to do what you feel you have to do, but I've learned my part this way.' What they're really saying is 'Follow me.' But Rubinstein was not like that *in any form*." Steinhardt's recollections are corroborated by an article that appeared in *Time* in January 1968:

> The old man sat at a table in an RCA Victor recording studio in Manhattan and listened to a playback. The cello came on with a rhapsodic, throbbing solo. "Very beautiful," sighed the old man, and tapped Cellist David Soyer approvingly on the knee. Then, a gnarled passage for piano and strings. "No," said the old man, "that's not so good. Here Brahms makes a trap, and we fell in. What shall we do?"
> Violist Michael Tree offered a suggestion. "Maybe," he told

the old man, "you could come in a little slower, maybe more quietly." Violinist John Dalley agreed with a nod. "Fine," said the old man, "let's try it." And Arthur Rubinstein, a month short of his 81st birthday, led three members of the Guarneri Quartet, whose average age was 36, back to the microphones for another try at Brahms's *Piano Quartet in G Minor*.[145]

Rubinstein's energy impressed Steinhardt almost as much as the pianist's music-making and openness to suggestion. "He exhausted me," the violinist said. "In Paris, once, we got together with him in the morning and we played; then we broke for lunch, and Arthur had his cigar and told stories; then we rehearsed all afternoon. Then Nela prepared a wonderful sausage dish, and we had dinner. Then *more* stories, *more* wine, *more* cigars. After dinner, I was reeling, but Rubinstein said, 'Well, how about another piano quartet?' I was the odd man out in that quartet—John Dalley and I alternated in the piano quartets—and I remember saying to myself, 'Thank God I don't have to play this piece! I couldn't lift my violin!' I was just wiped out. But Rubinstein was raring to go. There I was, a guy in my early thirties, and he was in his eighties. It was like food for him: he was living off the experience of making music. He wasn't expending energy; he was getting energy. He said to us, 'I'm old now, and I must tell you frankly that before I go out to start a recital, when I'm standing in the wings, I say to myself, "How on earth am I going to get through this?" But when I finish the concert, I know I could go out and play the whole program again.' " (Although most of the Guarneri Quartet's work with Rubinstein took place in the recording studio, they gave three joint concerts—one each in New York, Paris, and London—and Steinhardt said that Rubinstein "was quite nervous beforehand because he wasn't accustomed to playing chamber music in public.")

Many of the stories that Rubinstein told his young colleagues involved the chamber music sessions at the Drapers' in Edith Grove more than half a century earlier. "He would get a faraway look in his eyes and tell us that some of the pieces we were playing together he had last played with Ysaÿe, Thibaud, and Casals," Steinhardt recalled. In general, Rubinstein avoided talking about other pianists' playing, but he enjoyed recounting anecdotes about his colleagues and himself. "Rudi Serkin used to play every year for the Philadelphia Orchestra's pension fund," Steinhardt said, relating one of Rubinstein's best stories. "He would donate his services, and they were very grateful for this yearly event. On one such concert, after he had done this many times, as he was bowing at the end of the concerto, a farm tractor was brought out on the stage—because Serkin lived on a farm up in Vermont. The people in charge had thought it would be an appropriate and funny present, and sure enough, the incident made the national news as a human interest story. A short while later, Rubinstein was playing a concert somewhere or other, and a woman came backstage afterward and said, 'Oh, Mr. Rubinstein, I loved the performance—congratulations! And isn't it wonderful that the Philadelphia Orchestra gave you a tractor!' Rubinstein said, 'Madam, you're confusing me with Rudolf Serkin. He's the farmer; I'm the concert pianist.' "

In summing up the impression that Rubinstein made on the ensemble, Steinhardt said, "We've played almost all the pieces we played with Rubinstein many, many times since then, but he put his handprints all over them. There are passages that I can't hear played by any other person because he made them his own in such a powerful way. And yet, as great a musician as Rubinstein was—and he certainly was a great musician—what I treasure most is the lesson in life that his being was: the love of life, the enthusiasm. And this made itself felt in his music-making. I miss him on the concert stage. We have a lot of great musicians, great pianists, but his ardor and love of life communicated themselves immediately when he played."

IN THE MIDST of his first sessions with the Guarneri Quartet, Rubinstein remembered to send a ninetieth birthday telegram to one of his favorite chamber music partners from Edith Grove days, the violist Lionel Tertis.[146] The two musicians remained devoted to each other until Tertis's death in February 1975, at the age of ninety-eight; Rubinstein attended the special memorial service that was held for Tertis the following May. The violinist Sylvia Sparrow Caunter, another of Rubinstein's Edith Grove chamber music partners, had died in 1969; Arthur and Nela had visited her when she was ill. Rubinstein was sometimes put out by requests for attention from other old friends in England, but he did what he could to satisfy them. "I really do not know anything about the letter you mention about the Fund for Puff [Anthony Asquith]," he wrote to Lesley Jowitt in 1968. "Of course, I am with all my heart for it. As to Juanita [Gandarillas] I am rather upset and do not understand why she should have no money, after having had so much, but if I can help I will heartily, as I do not forget how nice she was to me. I too look forward to seeing you in December and will explain, verbally, why it is impossible for me to play for the Musicians Benevolent Fund Concert. As always, my old love." Rubinstein eventually made £200 available to Juanita on the first of every month until her death, in 1971.[147] José Antonio Gandarillas, her husband, had died long since ("I think he was drug-crazy," Nela Rubinstein said); his aunt, the generous Eugenia Errazuriz, had died in a road accident in Chile in 1951.[148]

Precisely in those years—the late 1960s and early 1970s—Rubinstein had plenty of opportunity to think about these and other old friends, because he was spending much of his free time writing his memoirs. Thirty years earlier, Alfred and Blanche Knopf had asked him to undertake the project and had even given him a token advance against royalties, but he had procrastinated. A letter, dated March 6, 1942, from Blanche Knopf to Rubinstein extended the delivery date for the manuscript to January 15, 1943. Although he set the project aside, he did express himself in print, in English, a few times during the following few years—notably in a substantial foreword to the American edition (published in 1949 by Simon & Schuster) of a biography of Chopin by the Polish poet Casimir Wierzynski, and in a highly critical review, published in 1950 in the *New York Times Book Review,* of the American edition of André Gide's *Notes sur Chopin.* When an interviewer raised the matter of the memoirs, in the early 1960s, Rubinstein said, "I am so busy living my life that I can't seem to find time to write about it. If I ever do an autobiography I shall call it *A Fairy Tale,* because that is what it has always been."[149] But he finally set to work. " 'Yes, I am writing my memoirs—autobiography is a rather big word,' " he told another interviewer, in 1968.

> I have a good memory and I want to tell a truthful life story. What I don't want is a eulogistic book; that I find nauseating. I am old enough not to worry what people will think. . . . Already I've written over 500 pages and I'm still 20 years old! Because my mind is filled with musical things during the season, I can write only in the summer. Last summer I wrote 150 pages in Marbella in Spain, and I never touched the piano. . . . To help my English I have ten dictionaries all around me to find the right words. People tell me to use a dictaphone or a tape recorder to tell the story—and actually I do like to talk—and then let someone else put it into a book. But writing must have a certain style and movement, otherwise it is sloppy. With an editor, it would have a foreign style with his shape, not with mine. My style may be primitive, but it is mine.
>
> I think the first volume will be of my young years, when I was poor, always in trouble—I was no good. In this volume I will open the window on hope: something *might* happen to a no-good bum! Later the writing will become more difficult, in my 40's and 50's. I face the choice of suppressing some feelings or hurting others. It is also difficult to criticize—can I criticize Horowitz, Richter or Gilels as I can speak my mind about Nikisch, d'Albert, Schnabel and all the others of my past? I will treat my later life as an epilogue to remind the public of what they know of me. What can I tell?—that I signed with Sol Hurok and made a lot of money? Or that I made many records and again a lot of money?[150]

The following year, Nela Rubinstein informed a New York journalist of her husband's progress on the book. " '. . . he has total recall. He . . . writes on those large notepads in small writing. I built for him [in Marbella] one large room completely separated from the house. It has a piano and a desk; it is just really a sacred place. There he writes seven or eight hours a day, only taking his meals with us, and then he plays the piano sometimes till 2 in the morning. He has an immense capacity for work. . . . What bothers me is that it is mentally exhausting because he relives it all, he completely gets absorbed.' . . . Mrs. Rubinstein said that to finish the book her husband should have arranged to suspend his concerts entirely this year. 'On the other hand, he really needs . . . his public. . . . Playing refreshes him, cures him. . . . I am slowing down and I am 22 years younger. Sometimes I am really amazed.' "[151]

Rubinstein eventually decided to "draw the curtain," as he put it, after the story of his Spanish triumphs during World War I, and to postpone to a later date a decision on whether or not to write a second volume. The manuscript of the first volume—to be called *My Young Years*—was turned over to Judith Jones at Knopf in 1972; it was expertly edited (blatant errors in Rubinstein's English were corrected and awkward usage was tidied up, but the slightly foreign individuality of his language was preserved), and it was published in the spring of 1973. On May 29, the *New York Times* reported that the Book-of-the-Month Club had chosen *My Young Years* as its Book-of-the-Month for June, "which meant a windfall of more than $120,000 to Rubinstein and his publishers . . . which they split 50-50. A Book-of-the-Month vice president, Edward E. Fitzgerald, happily said, 'It's a good book about a man worth knowing.' " And Rubinstein said, " 'Now I am a man of letters.' " The book became a best-seller in the United States and was soon published in most of the major European languages and many of the minor ones, as well as in Hebrew and Japanese. Garson Kanin, the well-known American playwright and all-around man of the theater, and an old friend of the Rubinsteins, wrote to Nela and Arthur: "To be on the best seller list for such a period of time is remarkable. Last year, over forty six thousand new titles were published in the United States, two thirds of them non-fiction, so you can see what a nonpareil, what a nonesuch [sic], what an exception a book has to be to break through. I for one am not in the least surprised. It deserves what is happening to it. Incidentally it will make one day a tremendous film in the tradition of those marvelous musical films Hollywood used to do in its golden days. I know that if I were still in the film business I would be knocking on many doors in an attempt to put it together. . . ."[152] Rubinstein was pleased to learn Kanin's opinion, but when Thomas Mann's daughter wrote to Rubinstein, to tell him that she was looking forward to reading his memoirs, he became a bit worried. "I very much fear that you'll be disappointed when you read my book," he wrote to Monika Mann, "but don't forget that I'm not a writer and that only the exceptional memory that I possess made me reveal my youth, which isn't a very good example."[153]

According to Max Wilcox, Rubinstein "actively promoted" his memoirs and "made countless television appearances and granted a multitude of interviews in conjunction with the book."[154] Well-known book reviewers like Hubert Saal in *Time* magazine, Joseph Wechsberg in the *Chicago Tribune*, and Richard Freedman in the *Washington Post Book World* were enthusiastic about *My Young Years*, but some music critics were perplexed by it. Harold C. Schonberg wrote, in the *New York Times Book Review*: "There are . . . some sharp and delightfully bitchy vignettes of famous musicians in 'My Young Years.' . . . If Rubinstein does not like somebody, he twists the knife, sometimes cruelly. . . . But once he leaves his own appetites, musical or otherwise, it is surprising how successfully he manages to steer away from musical insights. And that's a pity. . . . Aside from a few musical allusions, Rubinstein has regrettably concentrated on being an entertainer. . . . Perhaps a companion book, from 1916 to the present, will be stronger in musical conception, and a little less insistent on proving the pianist's lust for life."[155] As has been pointed out at various times in the previous chapters, Schonberg's qualms—and those of many others as well—were only too justified.

During the period in which Rubinstein was working on his book, François Reichenbach, a French film director, was shooting many miles of footage of him in various parts of the world. The result, which captured Rubinstein playing, traveling, and reminiscing, was called *Arthur Rubinstein, ou l'amour de la vie*; in its American version—*Love of Life*—it won an Academy Award in 1970, and a few months later Gregory Peck hand-delivered an Oscar to the Rubinsteins' home in Paris. NBC Television made a ninety-minute adaptation of the film and broadcast it to a vast audience. But five years later, Rubinstein wrote to a casual interlocutor from New York: "To be honest I must confess that I never liked my motion picture very much, it was made up [hap]hazard and I would have preferred to express my thoughts a little more clearly and solidly, even my playing was most improvised and never prepared. Strangely enough I discovered also that people appreciate my movie finding it so 'naturelle', but personally I do not like to be caught in my underwears [sic], morally speaking."[156]

The Last Seasons

"I shall go on playing as long as anyone wants to hear me," Rubinstein had told an interviewer in the early 1960s, "or until my fingers fail me and my heart dries up, or until I am attacked by dry-as-dust doctrinairism. . . . I hate musical straitjackets and I never shall put one on."[157] A few years later, at the age of eighty, he wrote to Roman Jasinski that he would stop playing when people whose opinions he trusted began to tell him that he was no longer up to the task. And shortly after his eighty-seventh birthday Rubinstein said, in another letter to Jasinski, that his latest American tour had gone well and had proved to him that he could continue to make public appearances for a while, although he confessed that he had begun to prefer playing concertos to giving full-length solo recitals.[158] "No farewell recitals, that's the main thing!" he told an interviewer. "People send you flowers, they applaud you for an hour. Then, if you don't die, they feel cheated."[159]

" 'I only regret that it is so late in the day,' Artur Rubinstein was saying, although he did not sound truly regretful at all," reported John Corry in the *New York Times* on January 30, 1974. " 'Ah, 87—a large number,' he said. 'I should respond to it.' He was talking about his 87th birthday, which was on Monday. He celebrated by taking his wife to lunch. Rubinstein jumped from his chair, bent his back, extended his arm, and mimed a man with a cane, doddering around the living room. The great pianist was in his apartment in a hotel on Park Avenue, and clearly he was enjoying himself. . . . Rubinstein brandished a cigar. He said that he could no longer get No. 3 Montecristos, but that this cigar, an Upmann, was even better. He said that he liked Iranian caviar better than Russian caviar, and that above all, he liked his wife's cooking. 'She is a genius,' he said. 'She is a much better cook than I am a musician. . . . I am a fellow in incredible luxury—incredible luxury.' "

Rubinstein spent part of the day on which Corry's article appeared coaching the 1973 winners of the National Piano Competition, sponsored by the American Music Scholarship Association, in works of Chopin; an audience was present at Alice Tully Hall. He arrived early and chatted with the three young musicians—aged eighteen to twenty—to put them at their ease, then sat down on a chair at the bass end of the keyboard. "Mr. Rubinstein found something good to say of each performer's effort; but when something didn't go so well, he queried: 'That wasn't so good, was it?' And he proceeded to explain, with humor and to the point, how it could be improved. . . . When one [player] aroused a burst of applause, and didn't know quite how to respond, Mr. Rubinstein urged: 'Stand up and bow—we all love applause, no matter what our age is.' "[160]

This encounter was a casual one, but during the same period Rubinstein had begun to take a serious interest in the talent of François-René Duchable, a young French pianist. He had read reviews of a concert given by Duchable in Paris in November 1973, had inquired about him, and had arranged for Duchable to play for him, toward the end of that month, at the house in Avenue Foch. Duchable recalled that he had been very nervous but that Rubinstein had quickly put him at his ease; the young man played Brahms's Paganini Variations—the first work that Rubinstein had played for Paderewski at Riond-Bosson, seventy years earlier—and some Chopin pieces, and Rubinstein invited him to come back and play for him again, several times. They exchanged opinions and even argued, and Duchable found Rubinstein remarkably open to others' views. Rubinstein had his pianistic prejudices, Duchable said, but he also expressed great admiration for Richter, Gilels, and—among those of the younger generation—Maurizio Pollini. In February 1974, in a letter to Jasinski, Rubinstein praised Duchable highly; he mentioned having heard him play the "Paganini" Variations, Chopin's Ballade in F Minor, and Ravel's "Alborada del gracioso," and he called him the best of the young pianists, excepting Pollini.[161] The following summer, Rubinstein invited Duchable to play for him and some friends in Marbella; he paid for his flight and even gave him a token fee, saying that a professional should never play without a fee. Rubinstein's interest helped Duchable to secure concert engagements in Spain, England, Holland, and Japan.[162]

Three days before he wrote to Jasinski, Rubinstein had sent a letter to the conductor Stanislaw Skrowaczewski. "I have decided to stop my concert activities, except but a few in Europe and, of course, on the condition that I can cancel any concert shortly before the date set," he said. "At my ripe age of 87 I have no right to plan a year ahead for anything. . . . Frankly I believe that the time has come when I ought to cede my place to the younger generation who shows so much talent."[163] But two months later, in an "Artist Status Report" to his bosses at RCA, Max Wilcox set out a more positive view of Rubinstein's condition and plans.

> At this point in his career Mr. Rubinstein does not commit himself to any set repertoire plan for a recording season. His most recent recordings have been concertos with Ormandy (Brahms B-flat and Rachmaninoff No. 2) and chamber music with the Guarneri Quartet and Szeryng and Fournier. He nearly retired after a serious bout with shingles a year ago, and it was only after his incredible concerts in America this year that he decided he would still maintain a limited concert career.
>
> In essence the current situation is that when he feels like recording he lets us know. He has spoken seriously with me within the past few weeks about doing such solo repertoire as selected Chopin Etudes and Preludes (something we have been asking him to do for the last 16 years) and the Beethoven Sonatas Op. 28, Op. 31, No. 2 and Op. 31, No. 3.

He had considered doing some of this music in Geneva during the trio sessions, but wisely reconsidered since his fantastic energy has begun to taper off to that of a mere mortal. I will be trying to confirm arrangements for forthcoming solo sessions when we meet in Geneva.

Mr. Rubinstein would also like to record the Beethoven "Archduke" Trio with Szeryng and Fournier at some future date in Geneva. . . .

. . . Mr. Rubinstein now feels he must decide the time and repertoire for any future recording sessions. He has been extremely flexible and cooperative during his long recording career and this has a great deal to do with the longevity of his catalog of recordings. A Rubinstein recording is almost never cut from our catalog.

We can only hope for his continued health. When he is feeling fit he plays as well as ever, and his playing at Carnegie Hall this January made it the best New York recital (among his many great ones) that he has given in several years. . . .

Mr. Rubinstein's contract expires in February of 1975. He has long since produced all of the records required under that contract. His current credit balance is $818,000. During the last five domestic quarters he earned $120,000 in royalties and during the last approximately 18 months he earned $206,000 in royalties on foreign sales. Since he receives half royalty on foreign sales, this means that about 75% of the total world-wide units sold are sold in foreign countries. . . .[164]

Rubinstein made plans for the 1974–75 season—and brought them off. In the middle of the season, on February 3, 1975, he played Beethoven's Fourth and Brahms's First Concertos with Barenboim and the New York Philharmonic, to raise money for the orchestra's pension fund. (He had played the same works with the same conductor and orchestra on a pension fund concert in 1971, and in 1972 he had played the Brahms Second with Karel Ančerl at yet another Philharmonic Pension Fund concert.) A few days before the concert, Vladimir Horowitz had told Barenboim that he needed to talk to him. "I really couldn't imagine what Horowitz wanted," Barenboim recalled. "I went to his house; he opened the door, he was correct, he was formal. I sat down, and we talked and talked about everything under the sun. I asked him about his Berlin days, and he told a lot of stories—very one-sided versions, I'm sure, but it was still a lot of fun. Then he said, 'Tell me, you know Clementi sonatas?'

" 'Not really.'

" 'Do you want me to play for you?' He got up, he got the music out, and he started going through I don't know how many Clementi sonatas, showing me this, showing me that—'Look at this figuration here.' Fascinating, obviously. Then we sat down again, and it was one of those situations where you think, this is all very nice, but why am I here? Why have I been summoned? I remember looking at my watch and saying, 'It's late, you must want to go to bed, and I have a rehearsal tomorrow. I've had a lovely evening, and thank you very much.'

" 'No, no, no. Stay. We're having a nice time and Wanda [Horowitz's wife] is not here; she's playing cards.' Suddenly there was a lull in the conversation, and I had the feeling that now, *now* I would find out why I was there. In a sort of forced, intimate tone of voice, he said, 'Tell me, I read in newspaper that you are conducting with Rubinstein, with Phyilharmonyik. What he plays?'

"I said, 'He's playing Beethoven G Major and Brahms D Minor.'

" 'Oh, in one evening. He's an old man now, no? He doesn't forget?'

"I said no.

" 'But wrong notes he plays, no?'

"I said, 'Look, I played with him in London, the 'Emperor' Concerto, a few months ago, and it was note-perfect.' I lied!

"He said, 'How much strength? You know, an old man, he has strength? These are big pieces!'

"I said, 'Yes, you can't cover him with the orchestra.'

"He said, 'This is very strange: an old man; no memory lapse, no wrong notes, lots of strength. [Long pause.] But a little bit dry, no?'

"It had all been for this! Not much later, I had lunch with Rubinstein and told him the story, in great detail. He was very amused."

The concert—Rubinstein's last with the Philharmonic—was an outstanding personal success for the pianist and raised eighty-three thousand dollars for the orchestra. "By the time the Brahms was over, with Rubinstein even adding some unwritten chords to help out the orchestra at the very end, the concert had gone almost a half-hour beyond the usual two-hour length of such events," wrote Leighton Kerner in the *Village Voice*. "But the audience by now had gone understandably crazy, and perhaps so had Rubinstein, because he sat down and played as an encore the . . . A-flat Polonaise of Chopin. . . . This was slightly messy at the beginning, but Rubinstein, as of yore, pulled himself up and built the ceaselessly rolling left-hand octaves of the long middle section into an ever-rising thunder that rivaled the biggest sonorities one could recall having heard from the whole orchestra that night. And when that was over, his repeated 'Thank you' could be heard bellowing right through the roar of the crowd. He seemed not a whit tired."[165]

Barenboim remembered, however, that Rubinstein had been "upset and very nervous" before the concert because "Nela was having an operation in Los Angeles. He had had a little memory lapse during the rehearsal—really nothing—but afterward, when we were in the car (I was going to have lunch with him at the Drake), he said, 'You know, I've come from Paris and I forgot to bring my music. I made that stupid mistake; I'm nervous. Do you mind if we stop at the music shop? I want to buy the music—I want to look at it.' So we stopped at Patelson's and he told me to wait in the car. He came back a few minutes later with no music. He said, 'They didn't have the edition I'm used to playing from, and I have such a photographic memory: I know where there's a coffee stain on the page, and I have to see the coffee stain. I have to have the same edition.' But I was with him the whole day: in the morning there was the rehearsal, then I had lunch with him—then obviously not in the afternoon," when Rubinstein was resting, "but then the concert, and afterward there was a supper with Kloiber, the man from Unitel [television corporation], and we had a very nice talk. So I was with him the whole day, and he was really very upset and nervous about Nela. He was not putting that on."

Eva Rubinstein had a different slant on the story. "For nine months my mother had had serious symptoms; she had seen a doctor in Paris, but he hadn't seemed very concerned." In California, however, where Nela went to visit John, his wife (Judith West), and their two children (Jessica, born in 1972, and Michael, 1973),* she had some tests done. " 'Sometimes I feel like an old dog who wants to go home to a familiar tree to die,' " she told Eva. "Not many days later," Eva remembered, "she called and said that she had colon cancer. 'This can't happen to me,' she said, 'because I have to take care of everybody.' The surgery was on a Monday morning, very early; my father that night had his concert in New York, and my sister had an interview at the medical school she most wanted to get into. My mother had said to me, 'Try not to let him come before the surgery, because if he comes into the hospital he'll start making dramatics and everyone will start taking care of *him*. It happened even when you were born: I was in labor for twenty-four hours without medication, and he practically fainted—and everybody dropped me and just looked after him. I've had enough of that.' So we told him, 'Look, there's nothing you can do, she'll be in surgery for hours, there's no point, you have the concert. We'll call you immediately afterward; come the next day with Alina.' She had the operation; the cancer turned out to be localized and she

---

*With his second wife, Jane Lanier, John Rubinstein has one son, Peter, born in 1994.

didn't have to have chemotherapy. She had a wonderful doctor, and Johnny and I were there.

"My father and Alina flew in the next day, and by then we knew that things were under control. But he went right ahead and did his number. 'I can't take it! I can't stand this!' It became his thing, all of a sudden. I was going to drive him back to his hotel that evening, and having seen my father talking to my mother and never asking her, 'How do you feel? What do you want to do afterwards? Where do you want to go? What can I do to help *you*?' instead of 'I will do this and we will do that,' I had one of my little attacks of 'God, I've got to say something to him!' I said, 'You were very sweet to tell Mummy this and that, but why don't you ask her what she wants and needs?' Already I'm getting The Look. We were in front of the hospital elevator—I remember that another couple was coming to the elevator as we were standing there—and he looked at me and said, 'Be careful of what you say!' I said, 'Daddy, I've never been so careful in my life of what I'm saying. I'm saying that you have to think a little bit of why she was so negligent of her own well-being when she certainly knew something was very wrong.' He said, 'You're accusing me of giving Mama cancer!' I said, 'No I'm not. You can't give somebody cancer.' Louder, 'YOU ARE ACCUSING ME OF GIVING YOUR MOTHER CANCER!' By then, we were in the elevator, going down, and I said to myself, 'This is it—it's all over now.' And from then on, from the elevator to the hall to the parking lot to the car, he was in such a rage that there was no point in my saying anything else. I got him into the car, and fortunately I got our seat belts on. We were driving on Sunset Boulevard, which is very dangerous, and he started screaming and howling and pounding on the dashboard: 'You're a viper! Everything that's ever been wrong with this family is your fault! I've hated you since the day you were born! Poor little Paul—that was all your fault! You always sided with your mother! Why is it that the whole world adores me and only my family is critical?' The whole routine. When we got to the hotel I unbuckled him and he got out and slammed the door.

"I know that I called him before he left, and I said, 'Daddy, I'm really sorry that we had this thing.' I don't remember exactly what he said, but it was like from another planet—something like, 'Well! Someday we can discuss it again.' And he left; I didn't see him. I didn't tell my mother any of this until years later." Rubinstein claimed in private that he was upset not only because Eva had accused him of giving Nela cancer—this was indeed his version of the story—but also because friends of theirs in California had told him, "Now you'll be nice to her, won't you?" He returned to New York, where an interviewer asked how his wife was. " 'Fine—or I would not be talking to you,' he said. 'It was a serious operation. For cancer. But now she has no pain. We had a little supper with champagne before I left.' " The reporter asked about Rubinstein's future plans. " 'Look here,' Rubinstein says, laughing, 'I don't like making plans for my death. I am too lazy.' "[166]

The rest of the season went well, but Rubinstein did not know whether he ought to schedule concerts for the following one. He decided to try to make more records, as the *New York Times* reported on June 10, 1975: "Artur Rubinstein has signed a new five-year recording contract with RCA Records. The 89-year-old [*sic*] pianist, who has just finished recording all five Beethoven concertos [with Barenboim and the London Philharmonic Orchestra], has been an RCA artist since 1940; his records released on RCA in this country in the nineteen-thirties were made by the Gramophone Company, Ltd., of Britain. Mr. Rubinstein is the top best-selling classical pianist on records, with over eight million disks sold." (This meant that five million had been sold in the previous ten years; in the United Kingdom alone, three hundred thousand copies of his RCA Red Seal records were sold between 1968 and 1975.) By September he had decided to confirm his concert plans for the 1975–76 season, and he wrote to the violinist-conductor Alexander Schneider, "Unfortunately I doubt if I can learn concertos which I had not played nor recorded before, as I imposed upon myself rather too big a tour both in Europe and in America. Your so colourful and enticing description of your famous Christmas concerts [for young string players, at Carnegie Hall and Washington's Kennedy Center] is of course most attractive but the old man, aged 89 in January, has to rest in Marbella during Christmas unless he collapses [i.e., lest he collapse] altogether. So you must continue your precious work without me unfortunately. I must tell you before I finish this letter that I don't enjoy making music with anybody more than with you."[167]

One of Rubinstein's reasons for deciding to take on another season was his wish to help Janina Fialkowska's career: he insisted that she be given an engagement by every concert organization with which he played that season. "It was pretty tough for me," she recalled. "I'd never in my life played for money. A lot of people resented the fact that he was helping me, or they were suspicious. But it was very exciting, and my entire career was based on that first season. I gave about forty concerts, and before that I had been totally unknown. First, there were six concerts with Zubin Mehta and the Israel Philharmonic, then a lovely tour of Spain. I had a Hollywood Bowl engagement; I did the Cleveland Orchestra with Lorin Maazel, the Philadelphia Orchestra with Leonard Slatkin, an Orchestra Hall recital in Chicago, and recitals in Houston, Boston, San Francisco, San Diego, Vancouver, and Montreal. Typically, it took Rubinstein to get me to play in Canada, my country. In England, I had one of the nicest concerts I've ever played, with Bernard Haitink and the London Philharmonic." But the English tabloids confused Fialkowska with another woman and put out the story that she was Rubinstein's "companion." "Arthur thought it was hilariously funny, but my career in England came to a dead halt for three or four years. But eventually England became 'my place'—one of the places where I play most."

For Rubinstein, however, a major—indeed decisive—problem arose that season. As early as 1968, he subsequently told an interviewer, he had begun to see double from time to time. " 'Two trees instead of one. Two beautiful women instead of one. It didn't disturb me. . . .' He could still focus clearly on anything close by. But six months ago, the focus went completely in both eyes."[168] That was in the late fall of 1975. Arthur and Nela had been in Los Angeles, and he had visited a specialist at a local hospital. Janina, who was staying at their hotel, recalled that "when he came back from the hospital he was with his old friend Bronek Kaper, who was one of the all-time great jokers. Arthur was coming in to tell us that the diagnosis was that he would never see right again"—he had lost his central vision, but not his peripheral vision—"and Bronek led him in, pretending to be a seeing-eye dog. Arthur was crashing into the furniture, on purpose. That same day, we went to a rehearsal that Zubin was conducting with Igor Oistrakh, then to a dinner, then to a concert, then to another dinner. Then Mrs. Rubinstein was driving us back to the hotel; I was in front with her, and he was in the back seat. We were all exhausted, and Mrs. Rubinstein was in shock" because of the report on her husband's vision. "He was humming and smiling, and suddenly he said, 'Why don't we go to a movie?' That was the guy: you could never get him down!'"

" 'It's a funny thing,' " Rubinstein told a journalist. " 'What I look at, I cannot see. If I look directly at your face I can't see your face at all. I see your hands instead. But if I look at your hands—there! I see your face. . . . Well, I know where the keys are by now, you see. In any case, I've always played without looking, back very straight.' " And yet, although he did not have to focus steadily on the keyboard when he played, he did have to look at it from time to time, and this he could no longer do. " 'Still,' he added cheerfully, 'if I look at the black keys I can see the white. I can live with it very well.' " The journalist thought that Rubinstein might have had a premonition about his eyes, because the previous year he had decided to read all of Proust for the first time, as well as books about Proust, Joyce's *Ulysses*, and two novels by Thomas Mann. He had also read part of Curtis Cate's biography of George Sand, but "when he got to the great meeting with Chopin, he could no longer see."[169]

And still he kept playing. His last New York appearance—although it was not billed as such—took place at Carnegie Hall on March 15, 1976, seventy years and two months after his American debut in the same hall. Before the concert, he had been "in a bitter mood" about the piano he had chosen, he told a reporter the next day. "I thought I chose the wrong one." Then Alina came by and told him how much she was looking forward to hearing him play Schumann's *Carnaval.* "I thought, even if it's only for her, I will play everything out, and I did."[170] He performed Beethoven's Sonata in E-flat Major, Op. 31, No. 3; Schumann's *Fantasiestücke*—after *Carnaval*; and Chopin's Preludes in C Major, A Major, F-sharp Minor, and D-flat Major, and Scherzo in B-flat Minor. Harold Schonberg wrote, in the *New York Times*, that only in the last part of the *Fantasiestücke* did Rubinstein seem "perceptibly tired." Elsewhere, "the old lion" demonstrated that he could "still tear the piano apart when he so desires." He played the Scherzo "at regulation tempo, with thunderous sonorities and infinite attention to detail. That detail included the opening triplets, so mushed up by many pianists. . . . His sound, too, is as mellow, penetrating and colorful as ever. . . . There was a rising ovation on the pianist's entrance, and a rising ovation at the end of the concert. Carnegie Hall was awash with love in all directions last night—love from pianist to audience, love from audience to pianist."[171] The last of Rubinstein's three encores was the Polonaise in A-flat, and when he had finished it, "he raised his hand and said: 'For 40 years I came every year. [He was counting, of course, from his grand return to New York during the 1937–38 season.] You listened with marvelous affection for me. I love you.' "[172] The next day, a journalist observed a dialogue between Mr. and Mrs. Rubinstein.

Nela: *"What is it, darling?"*

Artur: *"I am saying that yesterday I play less wrong notes. . . ."*

Nela: *"Fewer."*

Artur: *". . . fewer wrong notes without eyes than I used to play with my big, big eyes wide open. Eh?"*

Nela: *"Possibly."*

At this, Artur roars with laughter.

Nela: *"I didn't count them."*

Artur roars louder.

Nela: *"I was ready with a basket to catch them."*

Artur's face is now on the table, his shoulders shaking with glee.[173]

Before he left New York, Rubinstein attended an annual Polish ball, which, that year, was held in his honor. "I remember him dancing the mazurka and the krakowiak with me, like a madman," said Eva, who was temporarily reconciled with her father. "And I thought, well, if he's going to have a heart attack, this is a pretty good way to go. When he finally got tired, I walked him out to the car, through the big hall where cocktails had been served before the ball. There were just the two of us, alone in this huge room. He had his cane, and all of a sudden, he sang out, 'YA-DA-DA DA DA-DA-DA!' and took two or three steps of the dance again."

His final North American recital took place in Cincinnati. Franz Mohr was there, and he recalled that when Rubinstein had tried out the piano, on the afternoon prior to the performance, he had said, "Something is wrong with the piano. I don't know . . . it doesn't sound right. I don't feel comfortable." While Rubinstein was taking a preconcert rest at his hotel, Mohr checked the piano thoroughly but found nothing wrong with it. That evening, Rubinstein played a brief first piece and then, instead of remaining on stage to play the second piece, as was his custom, he walked off the stage to have a word with Mohr. " 'Franz, there is nothing wrong with that piano. I just didn't feel right [earlier]. I do thank you so much. The piano is just fine.' It shows you what kind of a person he was," Mohr said, "considering that explanation to me of such importance that he would leave the stage to come back and reassure me, before going on with the second number." And at the age of eighty-nine, and with his vision impaired.[174]

Rubinstein fulfilled a series of scheduled engagements in Europe, and it may have been on the occasion of what proved to be his last performance in Paris that he was visited by Eliette von Karajan, the beautiful wife of Herbert, with whom Rubinstein had always refused to perform because of the conductor's Nazi past. "She came backstage and told him what a wonderful concert it had been," according to Barenboim. "She said, 'My husband has achieved everything that he has wanted, but only one wish remains unfulfilled, and that is to make music with you.' And Rubinstein said, 'Madame, when you come to see me—such a beautiful and attractive lady—how do you expect me to talk about your husband?' "

ON THE EVENING of Monday, May 31, 1976—the exact seventy-fifth anniversary of the first concert ever performed in London's Wigmore Hall—Arthur Rubinstein stepped onto the auditorium's stage, walked cautiously but steadily to the piano, bowed with dignity, as always, to the packed-to-the-rafters audience, sat down, and began to play. A month earlier, in the same hall, he had played what had been billed as his last London appearance, but he had been prevailed upon to return for the anniversary event, although he was on medication for stomach ulcers and under "unbelievable stress"—according to Janina Fialkowska—because he could not see the keyboard. The program was similar to but not identical with his final Carnegie Hall recital of eleven weeks earlier. He began with Beethoven's Sonata in E-flat Major, Op. 31, No. 3, which he had recorded late in April. (This piece plus Schumann's *Fantasiestücke*, taped at the same sessions, were the last works that he recorded; appropriately enough, the last piece of the *Fantasiestücke* is called "Ende vom Lied" — "End of the Song.") Max Harrison, in the next day's *Times*, said that the interpretation combined "the clear-eyed enthusiasm of youth with the distilled, unrepentant wisdom of maturity. . . . For the record it must, I suppose, be noted that in the finale, *Presto con fuoco*, and elsewhere throughout the programme there were various wrong notes. Yet while it is musically important to recognise discrepancies, it is still more so to realise when they do not matter. Mr Rubinstein was born in 1887, and his sight, and, one suspects, his hearing, are not quite what they were. The pieces he plays are as meaningful to him now as in his youth or middle years, and he in the fullest sense maintains the music's line despite any mishaps: when great works are being relived, indeed recreated, as vividly as on this occasion, small keyboard accidents mean little."

Schumann's *Carnaval*, which the twenty-five-year-old Rubinstein had played on his London debut recital in the same hall sixty-four years earlier, followed the Beethoven sonata. "The sheer beauty of the sound that he draws from his instrument and the skill which he dispenses in probing the innermost secrets of his chosen composers made this an unforgettable occasion," wrote D.A.W.M. (David Money) in the *Daily Telegraph*. "So complete is his mastery of Schumann's textures in the more intimate moods of 'Eusebius' and 'Chopin' from *Carnaval* that in his hands they became perfectly conceived musical images. Two characteristic features of his performance were the very slow tempo in 'Estrella' and the whirlwind account of the final 'Marche.' " Dominic Gill, in the *Financial Times*, noted "a sudden ray of the deepest tenderness in 'Chiarina' and 'Aveu;' an electrifying hush at the change, in the 'Davidsbündler,' to *più vivo*." And he said that "for all its technical shortcomings" the performance was "a remarkable account, galvanised with astonishing reserves of energy in the 'Davidsbündler' march, stretched taut as a drumhead right to the point of the last, wholly forgivable, splashed final chord." Harrison, too, found that some of *Carnaval*'s movements, "such as 'Eusebius,' had a magical, almost eery freshness."

The second part of the concert, after the intermission, began with Ravel's *Valses nobles et sentimentales*, which had been an integral part of Rubinstein's repertoire for so many years. His performance made these pieces "the epitome of civilized refinement," said Harrison. "The smallness of the Wigmore Hall heightened the impact and warmth of Mr Rubinstein's playing." Then there was Chopin—the Etude in F Minor, Op. 25, No. 2

(*Presto*), "every note of whose triplet melody, played slowly, almost deliberately, but very beautifully, was made to sing," said Gill, and the Etude in C-sharp Minor, Op. 10, No. 4 (*Presto*), which "dazzled" Money. Harrison described Rubinstein's playing of the celebrated Nocturne in D-flat Major, Op. 27, No. 2, which followed, as "profoundly melancholy yet devoid of stress, conveying infinite sadness recollected from afar." In the midst of what Edward Greenfield, in the *Guardian*, described as a "world-shaking performance" of the Scherzo No. 2 in B-flat Minor, with which the programme came to an end, Rubinstein's vision clouded, and Gill reported that he played "several handfuls of wrong notes" before he regained control; but "it was a performance, for all its passing and forgettable inaccuracies, of satanic energy and force," Gill said, full of "lyrical flights" and communicating the "utmost joy." Rubinstein silenced the thunderous applause and bravos that followed to apologize for his "dreadful performance," and a woman in the audience shouted, "We love you anyway!" which brought on more applause. But Rubinstein said that he wanted "to excuse my faults" by playing an encore—Chopin's C-sharp Minor Waltz. And then, as the applause and cheers thundered on, he surprised everyone by launching into Villa-Lobos's comical *Polichinelle*—a brilliant performance that "had one registering every shimmer of every clattering chord," Greenfield said. Afterward, Rubinstein thanked everyone again and "announced sadly for his large and adoring audience that this concert was to be his last in London," according to Money. "Whatever thoughts of abdication he may have in mind, he must be persuaded back again, and soon," Greenfield admonished. But that evening— eighty-one years, five months and seventeen days after his first public performance, in Lodz—Arthur Rubinstein, pianist, made his way from stage to artist's room for the last time in his life.

7

To Thine Own Self Be True

In the summer of 1969, Rubinstein had been in London to play a solo recital and a chamber music concert with the Guarneri Quartet. After the recital, he made the acquaintance of a young Englishwoman, an assistant to Wilfrid Van Wyck, his British manager. "I'd *implored* Van Wyck to introduce me to him," the assistant later recalled. "Van Wyck was a difficult man; he was very possessive about his artists, and he wouldn't let me get anywhere near Rubinstein, although he let me do all the work." On that occasion, however, Van Wyck relented. The assistant was tall, blond, and twenty-four years old; Rubinstein looked at her, then looked back at Van Wyck and asked whether this was the young lady who would turn pages for him during his concert with the Guarneri.

"Oh no, no, no," Van Wyck said.

"What a pity!" Rubinstein exclaimed. The assistant recalled: "He kissed my hand, and he made an overwhelming impression on me. I remember coming home and saying to my mother, 'My goodness, that man has got something.' "[1]

Annabelle Whitestone had been educated in a convent and had had musical training. She had first heard Rubinstein play—Beethoven's Fourth Piano Concerto, with Barbirolli—in London in 1961, when he was awarded the gold medal of the Royal Philharmonic Society. Her career in concert management had begun with the firm of Ingpen & Williams, and she had also worked for Ibbs & Tillett before she joined Van Wyck's forces. Not many weeks after her first encounter with Rubinstein, she left Van Wyck, at the suggestion of Henryk Szeryng—one of the artists whom she had managed—and went to Madrid to work for Ernesto de Quesada's son Ricardo, who was gradually taking over the direction of the Spanish branch of the Daniel agency. A year later, in November 1970, Rubinstein flew to Madrid to give a Chopin recital. "Ricardo and I went by car to the airport, to meet him, and I remember Ricardo saying, 'I hope he comes alone. He's always so nervous when he's with Nela,' " Annabelle reported. "And he was alone—she came a little later. He arrived carrying a *panettone*"—a Milanese Christmas cake.

"There was a photographer taking photos of people as they arrived. Arthur showed me his and said, 'Am I *guapo* [handsome]?' And I said, 'Yes, very *guapo*.' He dedicated the photo 'to lovely Annabelle.' I always remember that Madrid arrival, and the incredible magnetism and charm he had. It was absolutely irresistible," she said. "Then he went to Bilbao, accompanied by Ricardo, and when Ricardo came back he said that Rubinstein had been asking all sorts of questions about me: What was my surname? How had I come to work in Madrid?"

What Annabelle did not know was that Rubinstein's interest in her had begun a year earlier, in December 1969. "He played in Madrid at the Teatro Real," Quesada recalled. "Annabelle and I went that morning to the Hotel Palace to accompany him to the hall for a short rehearsal. . . . I had lunch with him alone and he asked me quite a lot of questions about Annabelle and expressed his admiration for her and how beautiful she was. So, definitely it was Rubinstein who was interested in her already. . . . He left Spain . . . without letting Annabelle know anything yet—and when he came back in 1970 he had asked me previously that he wanted that Annabelle would accompany him on his tour."[2] After his November 1970 recital in Madrid, Rubinstein went home to Paris, Annabelle said, "but a few days later he returned to Spain, to play in Valencia and in Palma de Mallorca, and I accompanied him, along with Ricardo and his wife, Tola. After the concert, Ricardo and Tola went on ahead to Palma, and I stayed with Rubinstein in Valencia. We talked till about four in the morning." He asked her everything about her life, told her about his (*My Young Years* had not yet been completed), and described his family situation as very difficult. "I felt that in spite of his being a father and grandfather he was essentially a lonely man," she recalled. They went on to Palma the next day, and after the concert they visited Valldemosa, where Rubinstein played on Chopin's piano. "Then he left," said Annabelle, "and I was absolutely miserable, because I realized what had happened. I realized that I was absolutely lost. And I thought, it just had to be not only a man of eighty-three, not only a grandfather, not only a much-publicized married man, but also Arthur Rubinstein, who was known everywhere. Before he left, he had said to me, 'You'll see a lot of me,' but I couldn't imagine it. Where? How? It seemed to me impossible. I was in tears at the airport; Ricardo and Tola could do nothing with me—they couldn't understand what was the matter.

"That was towards the end of November. On the sixteenth of December—I remember, because it's my mother's birthday—he suddenly phoned me. I had just had a Mexican lunch with Ricardo and Tola, and I had drunk quite a lot of tequila. I had got back to my little pension thinking I would have a siesta, so I was not quite in my senses when Arthur's call came. 'Can you come to Geneva the day after tomorrow?' I thought I was hearing things. But it was true. I went, and I was with him there for a few magical days. And that was the beginning. Then he left for the States, for a tour of forty-six concerts and recordings. I thought that was it—that would be the end of him." But the affair went on, despite the logistical difficulties and the fifty-eight-year age difference between the protagonists. He went to Spain as often as possible, without Nela, and he happily played in towns like Saragossa, La Coruña, Bilbao, and San Sebastián for whatever fees the local concert organizers were able to pay. "Dear Maestro," Annabelle wrote him, on August 28, 1971, in an official letter from the Quesadas' office:

> Needless to say, everyone is utterly delighted that you have agreed to come and play in Bilbao, Pamplona and San Sebastian during the period *December 6 to 10 1971.* The actual distribution of places and dates could be arranged according to your wishes but it seems that the most convenient would be
>   Bilbao Dec. 7th
>   San Sebastian Dec. 9th
>   Pamplona Dec. 10th
> The next point I should raise before we go any further is the financial side of things, which I am afraid is not frightfully bright. As these recitals would be for the Philharmonic Societies in each place, with no backing from the Comisaria de la Música or the Ministerio it means we are limited to their absolute maximum fee which is 175.000 ptas (2,500 old dollars) per concert. I do not like asking you to accept a lower fee, and in fact have kept putting it off, but knowing how badly these societies want to hear you, I must give it a try. . . .
>
> With warmest affection from the Quesada family and myself,
>   Annabelle Whitestone,
>   CONCIERTOS DANIEL.[3]

Rubinstein's French secretary sent her boss's acceptance "with the conditions that you have indicated."[4]

It was natural for manager and client to stay in the same hotel during these tours; thus, Rubinstein and Annabelle were able to be together without attracting attention. Once, in Valencia, as they were walking down a hotel corridor, he must have been asking himself how he, a small old man, looked as a partner for a tall young woman. She recalled, "He looked at me, sort of sideways, and said, 'You know, Annabelle, most of the great men were small.

Beethoven was small, Napoleon was small, Nelson was small.' It just sort of came out, à propos of nothing. I said, 'Oh yes, of course!' And I've often laughed about it since." The Quesadas, who had befriended Annabelle and who were eager to please their most celebrated client, assigned her to look after him during his Spanish trips and allowed her to disappear at a moment's notice when he summoned her: she would fly to Paris or elsewhere, whenever he was alone and free for a day or two. "I had a full-time job in Madrid, and a very serious one," she said. "We dealt with all the biggest artists—Arrau, Menuhin, everybody—and they were very much my responsibility; they would arrive, and I would suddenly say to Ricardo, 'Look, I'm going to Paris the day after tomorrow.' He never made any objection. I don't know what I would have done without the Quesadas as friends." According to Annabelle, the only person besides the Quesadas who knew what was going on was Louis Bender, the trusty Hurok employee who looked after Rubinstein during his American tours.

"What haunted me was the fear that each time I saw him would be the last. If you start a relationship with a man of eighty-three, however marvelous his condition seems to be, you think, well, any day. . . . And I'm simply going to read the news in the paper or hear it on the radio or see it on the television. The thought really made a terrible impression on me. When he had an attack of shingles, I found out about it through the papers," she said, and she was "terrified that he would become really ill with something prolonged, and that I would have no access to him, wouldn't be able to see him. It's funny, now, that whenever I dream about Arthur my dreams go back to those days, when I was separated from him and never knew when I would see him again."

For six years, the situation continued in much the same way. Annabelle said that Rubinstein never even mentioned the possibility of separating from Nela, let alone divorcing her. "Arthur was terrified of a scandal; he was terrified of upsetting the way things appeared to be. Not because he was a hypocrite who wanted to pretend he was something that he wasn't, but because that was really the way he would have loved it to be. I would stay at the Hôtel Claridge in Paris, and we would walk separately—one behind the other—to wherever we were going, so that no one would see us together. He tried to choose restaurants where he wouldn't be known, but of course he always was. The headwaiter would say 'Ah oui, Maître,' and we knew right away that we were finished." But the story remained private.

One Sunday, in Paris, when the Rubinsteins' domestic staff was not home, Annabelle came over. "Arthur was playing me the test pressing of his record of the Fauré Quartet, with members of the Guarneri Quartet. We were in the middle of it, sitting and listening, when the key turned in the lock and in came Adam, Arthur's Polish valet," Annabelle recalled. "Normally, he

didn't come back till Monday morning, but since there was going to be a
Métro strike that Monday, he had come back early. Arthur took Adam aside
and told him not to say a word, and Adam felt that he was keeping a privileged secret. Sometimes Nela would stay in the States longer than Arthur did;
she would do a slimming cure or a health cure." (She suffered from severe
arthritis and occasionally went to a spa.) "He would come back to Europe
alone, and we always took advantage of that." Once, at the end of a pleasant
day together in Paris—they had seen four films and had had meals in between—Rubinstein said, "Ah, who knows, Annabelle? I might end up with
you."

FROM THE START, the Rubinstein-Whitestone relationship was more serious
than most or probably any of his previous extramarital affairs had been. Nevertheless, only when he realized that his career was about to end abruptly did
the possibility of a break with Nela take shape in his mind. One day, in November 1975, he phoned Annabelle from Seattle to tell her that he was losing
his vision. "I hope you won't mind having a blind friend," he said.

"Of course I don't mind, but you won't let it get in the way of us being
together?"

"We'll manage somehow," he answered. But Annabelle couldn't imagine how they would manage. "I right away saw the whole picture: his concerts are finished and we'll never be alone," she said. "I imagined that he
would be completely blind—thank goodness it never came to that. He came
back to Paris, alone, early in December; we saw each other right away, and I
realized that he could still walk in the street and live a fairly normal life,
thank God. In January he played in Spain—Barcelona, Madrid, all over the
place—and then I went to London to hear him play the Schumann Concerto
in his last concert with orchestra. But then the concerts stopped and a change
in existence started for him. And he decided to write the second volume of
his autobiography."

Nela and Annabelle had rarely met. "Nela absolutely dominated the
situation at home: who came, who saw Arthur, who didn't," Annabelle said.
"And that, in my story, is a very important part. Because if people said, later
on, that I wheedled myself into the house, the fact is that I *had* to be on good
terms with Nela if I ever wanted to see Arthur again. My one objective—and
I could put both hands in the fire on this point—was to be able to have access
to him, to have tea with him from time to time, to see him. My obsession was
to not be cut off completely from Arthur. I could take never seeing him alone
again, but I had to be sure that I would be able to see him." (Eva Rubinstein
said, however, that her mother did not "dominate the situation" but simply
ran the household, because her husband had never wanted to be bothered

with such duties.)[5] "At that time," Annabelle said, "I was helping Janina Fialkowska and François Duchable with their careers, and I was in touch with Arthur over that. Nina [Janina] was giving a recital in Marbella while Arthur and Nela were staying there, in April 1976, and Arthur begged me to go to that. I stayed in a hotel, but I saw a lot of them. And Nela softened to me, little by little." (Nela said that she didn't have to soften to Annabelle, because she genuinely admired her. "Annabelle was efficient and well-organized," she said, and she mentioned that the two of them used to go shopping together.)[6] "I took great care," Annabelle recalled. "With all that Arthur had told me about Nela, I felt that I knew her very well—much better than she knew me—and it was very easy for me to cope with her."

Tony Madigan, the grandson of Estrella Boissevain, an old friend of the Rubinsteins', had started to work with Arthur on the autobiography, but by the end of Annabelle's stay in Marbella the Rubinsteins had asked her to come back in August, to type up the results of Tony's interviews. She also managed to spend a day in July with them, in Paris, and afterward she sent Nela a long note to thank her for the delicious supper—especially the borscht—and to chat about the things she had done in the intervening days. "Please tell the Maestro how I loved listening to the first pages of the book and I am looking forward to hearing the next instalments," she wrote. "Certainly he and Tony are doing a fantastic job and it was so good to see the Maestro in such wonderful form, putting up with the heat better than anyone, with the rest of us wilting around him! . . . I hope by now you and the Maestro are at last getting some peace and relaxation in Marbella, where I am *longing* to join you! With any luck I should be with you by about 5 oo pm on August 7th. Should you want to contact me or need anything from London, I shall be there until the 5th in the evening. . . ."[7] Annabelle did indeed arrive in Marbella. "I typed, and I jolly well made sure that nothing went wrong, so that I could always go back to see Arthur," she said. Observing him at home, she was struck by what an "emotional person" he was. He had been working on some Beethoven with Janina, and he had lent her a book about Beethoven's relations with his nephew, Carl. One morning, he reread Beethoven's tormented Heiligenstadt Testament, and the reading left him "in a terrible state," Annabelle recalled. "There were floods of tears. He could be easily and at the same time deeply moved."

In the fall, Ricardo de Quesada agreed to let Annabelle go to Paris, to stay with the Rubinsteins and continue the project. Tony was there, too, and when he would go out in the evening Annabelle would stay with Rubinstein, reading back to him what he had dictated to Tony or reading to him from other books, since he could no longer read to himself. Tony soon withdrew from the project for reasons of his own; Annabelle and Arthur proceeded alone, and their relationships to each other and to Nela began to change radically.

This is the point in the Rubinstein story at which the Pirandello Factor or *Rashomon* Effect becomes operative: As told by different people, the story is really a collection of stories that diverge from each other in many details. Each story is entirely logical and convincing until it is set beside the others. Annabelle, who heard only Arthur's side of the story, and only in his last years, has expressed the opinion that the Rubinsteins' marriage was largely a mistake from the start, and that most of the difficulties within the Rubinstein family were of Nela's and the children's making. "In any case, I think that if a marriage is solid it can take a third person, in general, and that sometimes the third person even improves it," she said. "I do not believe that a third person coming in from the outside can break up a good marriage." In her role as the third person, she was, in her opinion, as much a result of previous difficulties as she was a cause of what was to be the final, irreparable crisis between Nela and Arthur. The problems were all "well known in the family," according to Annabelle. "The children, the people who were near him, knew that things weren't easy, and that in fact by the time he met me the marriage was only a façade—a façade which I think she [Nela] believed in, all the same." From the start of their affair, Annabelle said, Rubinstein "was always very honest with me about how difficult things were" within his family, and he described himself as "really a lonely man at home." Eva said, "If he was lonely, it was because he had alienated each of us in one way or another. He said to me that we had all 'abandoned' him." But she agreed with Alina and John that their parents' marriage had known plenty of difficulties. Even Nela, although she stressed the view that "for years and years we were absolutely like one person" and that they "usually agreed on everything," admitted that there had been dissension between her and her husband. Whether the marriage was "only a façade," however, or was, instead, merely subject to vexations of a sort common to many long-term relationships—vexations exacerbated, in this case, by the celebrity of one of the partners—cannot be determined by anyone except the participants.

Annabelle recognized that the termination of Rubinstein's career had made life "very difficult for Nela, too," because Nela "suddenly had Arthur at home, instead of having the business of concerts and tours and everything else: he was suddenly *there*. She obviously felt that, too, because she was always inviting people to stay." But Eva said that her mother had been "*longing* for the day when my father's life would calm down, when he would stop playing, and all the attendant nerves and problems would stop, and they could both head toward old age with books and theater performances and concerts—other people's!—and films and the visits of admiring and eager younger musicians. She spoke of this so often. But when the time for him to stop came, Annabelle became the mistress/wife/daughter/worshipper/confidante cum secretary he had wanted us all to be—and in addition, my father didn't feel either the weight of fifty years of guilt toward Annabelle—which he did feel toward my mother—or the familiarity." Annabelle's view is that Nela and Arthur "were each of them lonely, and I would go out with Nela, too, accompanying her to do this and that. At first, that was fine." Elzbieta Jasinska Libera, Roman Jasinski's daughter, stayed with the Rubinsteins in Paris in the fall of 1976, and recalled later that Nela had been full of praise for Annabelle, whereas she herself had felt that something was going on between Annabelle and Arthur. Eva also began to "put together the pieces of the puzzle," she said, later; many of her father's actions at the time "astonished me a lot less than they astonished my mother, who made a tremendous effort not to know many, many things." Eva took an immediate dislike to Annabelle.

In a letter that Nela wrote to Alfred Knopf in October 1976, she described Arthur's doings matter-of-factly: His eyesight continued to be poor, he was continuing to dictate his memoirs, he was spending four or five hours a day listening to records, and he was also listening to young pianists who came to play for him.[8] Gradually, however, she began to suspect that something was seriously amiss, and "things started to deteriorate," Annabelle said. "But even when Nela was still fairly well-disposed toward me, she used to tell me, 'You spoil him!' I didn't at all. If he felt like listening to something at eleven o'clock in the evening, and I was there, I put the record on. She would say, 'No, it's bedtime, we've had enough of this!' When the test pressings of his recordings came, she would never have the time to listen with him—he was always alone—and he loved sitting and listening to music *with* others, feeling their reactions, feeling how they felt. She didn't have the patience. Later on, when she saw us [listening], she'd join us. There was a lot of tension in the house, because she suddenly felt that she was in competition with me." But Nela, who had known Arthur for half a century and had been married to him for forty-four years, could not seriously compete against Annabelle, who had never before spent more than a few days at a time with him, whose admiration for him was fresh, and who did not find his demands boring or unreasonable. Alina recalled, for instance, that during her father's active years, "when he would make a record and get the test pressing, we would have to listen to it—and God forbid that you breathed at the wrong time, or that the phone rang and you looked around to see if you should answer it. He wanted total fixation on whatever he was doing. This could become very exhausting after a while, especially for my mother, who was with him most of the time. I think that he wanted more than she or any of us could give him—and that hurt him, no doubt. She went out of her way to take care of him, but he wanted a kind of care that was admiration and devotion; she tended to take care of him in other ways—ways that made him feel not so good about himself. He was narcissistically vulnerable, and that was the source of whatever problems there were. I think that when he became really old, he just wanted to get away from someone who knew his insecurities so well, which made him feel dependent and childlike."[9]

And yet the contest ran on. "Sunday mornings, when there was no help around to prepare breakfast, I would get up to prepare it," Annabelle said, "so she would get up, too. We'd both be preparing breakfast in the kitchen. The atmosphere—you could have cut it with a knife! There came a time when he'd be having his breakfast downstairs with me, and she would be alone upstairs. Later, in order to avoid this weekend tension and proximity, Arthur and I would go to Versailles, to the Hôtel Trianon." Arthur, however, squeezed more than a little enjoyment out of the tension and out of being, at eighty-nine, the object of contention between two women—the first one young enough to be his daughter, the second younger than the first one's daughters. Janina, who was in Paris during part of the crisis, reported that although "things were getting him down," he stopped her from trying to cheer him up. " 'You're very sweet,' he told me, 'but you don't realize that I'm *loving* being depressed!' "[10]

In November 1976, Nela went to Geneva for a weekend. When she returned, Arthur told her that he had taken Annabelle to a matinée at the Comédie Française: he had phoned Pierre Dux, the director, who had given him his own special seats. According to Annabelle, "Nela's reaction was, 'People *saw* you at the Comédie Française with her?'

"Arthur said, 'Of course they did.'

" 'So I suppose you'll make her your heiress, now!' And little by little, Arthur began to see things in a different light. He felt those were the things she cared about. She left us alone in the house, where we could do whatever we liked, but she was upset about him being seen with me, and about the money side." Or so he persuaded himself. At that point, he began "to care much less, scandal or no scandal," according to Annabelle—and for once, Eva's and Annabelle's opinions coincide: "Once my father was no longer giving concerts," Eva said, "he didn't care so much about his public persona. Until then, his discretion had been legendary." But Eva also believed that her father was provoking her mother "into doing and saying things that would justify him in going ahead with what he wanted to do."

Annabelle said, "there came a moment when [Nela] absolutely wanted me out of the house, and he put his foot down. This was around Christmas 1976. I understand her point of view. She thought she'd had a faithful husband all her life, which she hadn't." As to Arthur, Annabelle said, "it was only when he felt, in his own self, that Nela was giving him the right to leave, by her attitude to me, that all his inhibitions left, and that he told her, 'Look, you can do what you like. I can't stop you from coming over, but I need Annabelle, I can't live without her.' Of course he couldn't throw Nela out: she'd been living in the house as long as he had, and it was in both their names. And she was absolutely determined to be there." Nela's determination is not surprising: She was already sixty-eight years old; she had spent nearly two-thirds of her life as Rubinstein's wife; and she did not want to become part of a triangle, as the rival of a woman thirty-seven years her junior. Besides, she thought at first that the problem would disappear all by itself. "After Annabelle had taken over," Eva recalled, "my mother was convinced that my father was in a sort of geriatric parenthesis, and that it would end and he would come back to her. I knew bloody well that he wasn't going to do any such thing. And I knew that she needed to face this because Annabelle and my father were going to do everything possible to wipe her out. I called my mother from New York and said, 'I'm going to tell you something that you're going to hate me for, but I have to tell you because nobody else will, and you have to protect yourself. This is not a geriatric aberration or a sudden, old-age twitch. He's been doing this for years. Get a lawyer—someone who will protect your rights.' She said, 'What do you mean?' I was in agony—I kept trying to make her understand, without saying too much. Suddenly, she said to me, 'Ach, why didn't you tell me all this twenty years ago? Why are you telling me now? I could have married somebody else and been happy.'

"If only my father had said to my mother, when he went off with Annabelle, 'Look, we've had a great marriage, we've certainly enjoyed ourselves, traveling all over the world, and now I just want to run off and play!' But no. What he said to her was, 'You never loved me.' Now, that is a horrendous thing to tell a woman who has given her life to being your wife and nothing else. She'll never get over it." Nela said, ten years after Arthur's death, that what she resented even more than his rejection of her was his mendacity. "I will never recover from the fact that he was not truthful to me; it belittles him so much. For so many years we were together, and he pretended—at least he *pretended*—that it was fine, it was wonderful, it was lovely. How could he? He was running around with Annabelle, for God's sake!" Nela kept a suitcase full of love-letters and letters of praise for her as wife and mother—letters that her husband wrote to her while he was having affairs with other women, she later realized. She felt that when he left her, he may have "wanted to create some sort of sensation"—wanted, in other words, to remain in the public eye for a new reason, since he could no longer hold the limelight as a pianist—although in other respects he had accepted his withdrawal from concert life "pretty well, on the whole," she said.

In January 1977, the Rubinsteins and Annabelle were in New York, all staying at the Hotel Drake, to celebrate Arthur's ninetieth birthday. "Things were already pretty bad," Annabelle recalled. "Nela wanted me put on a completely different floor of the hotel. They wouldn't speak with each other for days on end, but then a photographer would arrive and right away she'd be lovey-dovey." But Arthur, too, tried to make visitors think that all was well. On March 3, after they had returned to Paris, Nela and Arthur were visited by Svyatoslav Richter, who noted later, in his diary: "Artur Rubinstein played me his favorite records. It was very interesting and enjoyable. Anyway, with him it was always very fine. He was a positive, happy, simple, humorous, and charming man. I remember his stories—you could have died laughing, he had such a talent for telling them. His wife Nela had created her own special style, simple and elegant. I think it is a typically Polish trait. Our talks together were lively and sharp. I felt very good at their place. As to the program, the disks were really unique. I especially remember Artur's praising Gabriella Besanzoni (he said that in all his life he had never heard a better Carmen, and, what is more, it seems that she was a beauty). [Chopin's] mazurkas played by him in a good old concert tradition, positively and without the least trace of sickliness—and so that evening he convinced me. He was almost blind by then, but he was absolutely not depressed. On the contrary, [his poor sight] was even the subject of some of his anecdotes."[11]

Arthur and Nela were together again in Israel the following month, for the second running of the Rubinstein Competition, which was won by Gerhard Oppitz. According to a *Jerusalem Post* journalist, Rubinstein "made it a point in his speech at the festive awards dinner to note that a German was awarded the first prize in the State of Israel, among the people who had suffered at the hands of his nation in a way the civilized world had never seen before. In that competition, Rubinstein attended every session. . . . At times the master looked as though he would wander off with his thoughts or even fall asleep. To my astonishment, when we met after the finals, he poured out an exhaustive analysis of the performance of each and every contestant. He sang particular phrases to make a point about phrasing peculiarities, while marking the notes with his fingers on the table in front of him. He had heard, and remembered, every tone and intonation, every inflexion, every strong and weak point in the musical make-up of these young artists."[12] During the summer, the Rubinsteins were once again together—with Annabelle—at Marbella, and Janina also arrived for coaching sessions with Arthur. He told her a little about Barth, for whom "he had a grudging affection," she said. One of Barth's fixations had been sitting still at the keyboard, and Rubinstein became annoyed with Fialkowska for moving around too much while she played the Tchaikovsky Concerto for him. "Arthur said, 'I'll bet you ten dollars that you can't play it all the way through without moving,' " she recalled. "I said, 'Well, you're wrong.' I won the bet, but the point had been made. He never talked about technique, but he said that the most important thing was to project the sound: 'When you want to play a *piano* sound that projects, use the soft pedal and play loud.' He would also say that Picasso had told him, 'I paint with my stomach, with my gut,' and Arthur said, 'That's where you have to feel your rhythm—in your stomach.' "

Through the following months, Arthur traveled with Annabelle and without Nela. He wanted to show his new, young companion places that she had never seen before, as he had wanted to show them to Nela nearly half a century earlier and to other lady friends earlier still. On again and off again, Arthur and Annabelle were together with Nela in Paris. Later in 1977, Nela, Arthur, and Annabelle were to go to Venice together, but just before they were scheduled to depart, according to Annabelle, the Rubinsteins "had a *terrible* row that went on until all hours of the morning. Afterwards, Arthur thought he was going to have a heart attack. And the two of us left, alone, for Venice. That was really when the break came." Janina was to have met Arthur and Nela in Venice, but when she got there, "What did I see? Arthur and Annabelle, with no Mrs. Rubinstein," she said. He was scheduled to talk about his life, that evening, before an audience, and Janina was to play during the second half of the program. "He was terribly nervous about talking in Italian, which he spoke with great abandon but not very well. I was backstage, waiting to play, and he talked on and on and on; the audience lapped it up. I'm sure I was the grand anticlimax." Janina had hoped that Rubinstein would show her around Venice, as he had shown her around other places, but he and Annabelle were taken up with each other and left for Rome without her.

WHATEVER ONE MAY think of the story as a whole, there can be no doubt that during the early part of Annabelle's membership in the Rubinstein household, in Marbella and Paris, she and Arthur had one advantage over Nela: The two "conspirators" knew what was going on between them; Nela did not. Moreover, when Nela found out, she did not know how to cope with the situation. To her, Annabelle was a troublemaker who, after having had affairs—Nela and some people close to her have alleged—with other famous musicians, without being able to get them into her clutches, finally found someone foolish and selfish enough to let himself be manipulated by her. Eva's opinion was even tougher. "All my father had to do was keep spending the money, and Annabelle was there," she said. "She did have some affection for him, I think, but it was organized around everything else." But Nela and Eva's accusation that Annabelle's goal was to put her hands on Arthur's money does not hold up under close scrutiny. Arthur and Annabelle's affair—which he had initiated—began long before she could possibly have imagined that she might inherit a substantial fortune from him someday: he was eighty-three in 1970 and his wife was only sixty-two; there was no sign that he was ever going to be anything less than solidly married, and it is extremely unlikely that an attractive woman in her twenties whose profession gave her the opportunity to travel far and wide with interesting people—including gifted young men who were not poor—would have thrown herself into the arms of an octogenarian merely in order to be treated, once in a while, to a weekend at a fine hotel or a meal at a fine restaurant. Although Alina and John Rubinstein express mixed feelings about Annabelle, they do not join their mother and sister in accusing her of greed.

The pianist Nikita Magaloff, who had been friendly with the Rubinsteins for many years, and who remained on good terms with both Nela and Arthur after the break, said that Annabelle "did an extraordinary job. She helped him in every way. She was like a nurse, and she made him happy in his last days. It is very natural that a wife, whom he left to live with another person, cannot accept it."[13] Barenboim refused to comment on the matter, "not to evade giving an answer, but because you never really know what happens between two people," he said. "And then you run the danger of saying, 'Such a great man, such a great artist who gave so much to so many thousands of people—there's something special about him. Hasn't he, maybe, earned the right to this special moral condition, at some point in his life?' I don't know whether I would answer that positively or negatively." Barenboim had conducted some performances of *Parsifal* shortly before we discussed Rubinstein, and he mentioned that Wagner's last work "deals with the question of sensuality versus loyalty. I don't think Rubinstein ever solved it."[14] For that matter, has anyone faced with the problem ever solved it satisfactorily?

Alina Rubinstein pointed out that forty-five years before her father went off with Annabelle, he had intentionally married someone young enough to be his daughter, and that he had always wanted a daughter of his own. "I think this meant to him that somebody would always be there for him—would look up to him, respect him, admire him, love him," she has said. Certainly, there is a striking resemblance between his reasons for marrying Nela and wanting a daughter, on the one hand, and, on the other, his reasons for going off with Annabelle. But there is an even more striking analogy to be drawn between his affair with Annabelle and the earliest of all the loves he could remember—the infatuation with his cousin Noemi Heiman, who had died when she and Arthur were still children. Rubinstein's late-in-life recollection of his relationship with little Noemi was a retrospective fulfillment of the relationships that he might have liked to have had with all the women who had played important parts in his adult life—wife, daughters, and lovers: "we loved each other so passionately that we were inseparable. . . . [She] particularly liked playing husband and wife with me. She would obey me blindly, leaving the choicest morsels of food for me, and easily bursting into tears whenever she saw me in trouble. My piano playing made her gasp with admiration."[15] More than eighty years after Noemi's death, Rubinstein began to live with someone else who was willing to accept him entirely on his own terms—as one accepts a child, in some respects. As always, the force that drove his actions was the strong instinct for protecting his exceptional musical talent—an instinct that had led him, over the decades, to abandon parents, teachers, lovers, and a succession of cities and countries that he had called home. Now that he had retired, he no longer required the talent; the instinct, however, remained intact, and it led him, once again and for the last time, to abandon home and hearth. He made his choice, and in such cases, in Western society—and in most other societies—all possible choices are wrong: someone, often everyone, gets hurt. Rubinstein, who never overcame his resentment of his parents' abandonment of him when he was a child, felt that whatever advantages he later managed to wrest from life were his due, no matter what consequences others had to pay. In December 1919 he had described himself to a Spanish journalist as a "perfect egotist." Now he was in love with Annabelle, he wanted the sort of attention that only Annabelle was willing to give him, and by God, he was going to spend his last years with Annabelle.

FOR THREE YEARS, Annabelle and Arthur did a good deal of traveling together. They visited Holland at tulip time (a new strain of tulip was named after him), went to Jerusalem for more than one of Annabelle's birthdays, and made trips to New York, Los Angeles, Venice, Switzerland, Deauville, and elsewhere. They also made what was to be his last visit to Poland, in 1979. In Lodz, Rubinstein told the conductor Henryk Czyz that there had been a grocery store near the gate to the building in which he had passed much of his childhood, and that the grocer would sometimes plunge his hand into a sack of colorfully wrapped, fruit-flavored candies and give them away to the children who were playing nearby. Rubinstein said that at the time, his dream had been to own a similar shop when he grew up and to give away similar candies to children. "I grew up and earned much money," he told Czyz, "but somehow I never did buy a shop like that. I wasted my life."[16] It was also in 1979, during a visit to Berne, that Arthur and Annabelle stopped to see his cousin Fania Meyer—Aunt Salka's daughter from Berlin, who was even older than he—at the Mon Repos rest home; they had a warm chat (his German was still better than serviceable), and he gave some money to her daughter so that Fania could have a private room and be well looked after. He was extremely happy to have seen her—the occasion was his last contact with anyone who remembered him from the nineteenth century—and to have been able to make her last days a little easier for her. On another occasion, Britain's former Prime Minister Edward Heath invited Arthur, Annabelle, and Isaac Stern to lunch in London, where he tried to persuade the two musicians to go to Germany, as a gesture of reconciliation. "I think he wanted Stern to play and Arthur to be present," Annabelle said. "Stern got out of it by joking that his wife would divorce him if he played in Germany, and Arthur said, 'For me, it's out of the question.' The lunch was very embarrassing, because Heath kept trying to convince them both and neither of them would give in."

During a stay in New York, Rubinstein gave a cocktail party at the Waldorf-Astoria, where he was staying. He had been told that the same morning, the *New York Times* had advertised that Ann Schein—who was to attend the party with her husband, Earl Carlyss, of the Juilliard String Quartet—would give a year-long series of concerts dedicated entirely to Chopin's music. She later recalled that when she entered the room, "his voice called out to me, 'Is that Ann? Come here, I want to tell you how wonderful this is, how excited I am that you are doing this—*that's* the way to do it, *that's* the spirit!' He went on, incredibly, 'I do not have my piano here, but I will *send* for one from Steinway, and you can come and play me these pieces! We will do them together!' For the next two weeks, I went to play the repertoire for him. He wanted to hear the First Sonata, which he had not heard performed since his youth. He wanted to hear the songs. I played eight of them, and he sang each one with haunting intimacy, the tears running down his cheeks. I played ballades, nocturnes, mazurkas, scherzos. He pulled the music out of me, as he always had, he was demanding, he was relentless, and he was upliftingly confident."[17]

Rubinstein made a series of half-hour films, produced by Emilio Azcarraga for Televisia, the Mexican television network, and directed by François Reichenbach. The films, in which he expounded and reexpounded his philosophy of life—simplistic and Panglossian, at least as it came across—were described by Gail Williams, in the *Hollywood Reporter*, as "slow-moving, poorly organized," and lacking in focus. "How deeply Rubinstein revered the music of Chopin is the strongest impression one receives of the great pianist in [the first] production."[18] Meanwhile, he continued to chip away at his autobiography. "We were working very hard," Annabelle recalled. "He was dictating to me during the day, and I was typing half the night or in the morning, to keep up. When Roman Jasinski came for visits, they would speak together for a long time, in Polish, and I would catch up on the typing."

There was plenty of other business to deal with, too. Now that he had become a piece of living history, Rubinstein was frequently asked for information on the past. "You want to know what I did with the two works which Stravinsky dedicated to me," he said, in a letter to an interlocutor from Radio Hilversum in the Netherlands, toward the end of 1976. "Well, I still dislike the Piano Rag Music and I did say so frankly to Stravinsky himself. Of course I never played it in public, but nevertheless I am proud of owning the manuscript by this great composer. As to Petrushka, I have performed it always in my own way, with the verbal permission of Stravinsky, but I never dared to make a record of it because I was afraid that he might have forgotten his permission and might get angry with my very personal approach to it. In his later years he became rather pedantic."[19] Dozens of similar requests reached him, and so did requests from pianists for professional assistance in one form or another. A young, London-based artist, for instance, wrote to him at the end of 1977, after having met him at Covent Garden some months earlier, and included a copy of a recording that he had made of Szymanowski's music. Rubinstein replied that when he had met the young man in London, the latter's enthusiasm "gave me the wish to hear you play. . . . But it was a mistake to have sent me your record. I listened to both sides with great attention and must confess sadly that the Szymanowski disappointed me very much. You played out all the notes, you showed that technical problems do not exist for you, your trills sound very well but there was no trace of the real meaning of all three pieces. They all sounded to me like vague improvisations with the accent on unimportant technical incidents, neglecting the melodic line completely and so the total absence of any rhythmical hold on the pieces distorted them completely. . . . If you still feel like wanting to play for me, I might be able to give you a better insight into the true character of Szymanowski's beautiful pieces."[20] Rubinstein's appraisal was severe but honest, and the offer of assistance was generous.

Awards and other forms of homage accumulated ever more rapidly, especially in the weeks immediately before and after his ninetieth birthday. On December 30, 1976, Nicholas Henderson, the British ambassador to France, wrote to tell Rubinstein that "Her Majesty the Queen has been pleased to make you an Honorary Knight Commander of the Most Excellent Order of the British Empire," and Rubinstein, in his reply, described Henderson's letter as "the loveliest present for my ninetieth birthday."[21] The birthday was also the occasion for tributes from around the world, including the publication, in the *New York Times*, of excerpts from an interview that Rubinstein had granted to the Public Broadcasting System in the United States. Rubinstein claimed, in the interview, to have discovered an advantage in his loss of vision. "When I was seeing, I was reading too much. Some books which I shouldn't have read because they were not intelligent enough, I lost my time on it." And because he had played and traveled too much, he hadn't had time to go to others' concerts—thus he had missed out on a lot of wonderful music, he said. "Now . . . I spend all my money on records. I listen to— Mahler symphonies, beautiful performances by my colleagues . . . [also to music played] by violins, by pianos, by quintets. . . . I get angry, I discuss it with them, when they play badly. I mean, I discuss inside, of course. They are not here." Asked whether he believed people who called him the greatest pianist of the century, he replied: "I get very angry when I hear that because it is absolute, sheer, horrible nonsense. There isn't such a thing as the greatest pianist. . . . Nothing in art can be the best. It is only different. . . ." While demolishing one generalization, however, he managed to air another that was more to his taste and that he had often repeated: Although he did not play as well, technically, as many other pianists, he said, when he heard young pianists, "I have my little question for them. I ask them, when will you start to make music?"[22]

Colleagues often visited, and Annabelle recalled "the last time Richter came to see him. He came to tea and very sweetly brought a little bouquet of orchids. We'd been to his recital the night before, at the Salle Pleyel in Paris, but we'd been sitting rather far away, and Arthur had had difficulty hearing and assimilating the Ninth Sonata of Prokofiev. Arthur asked him to play it again, and Richter was like a child: He sat down at the piano rather shyly— this great, big, bulky man—and he started to play. Then he stopped and started again. I shall never forget that. Arthur sat right near him—he took it in, listened to the whole sonata. Richter played some other Prokofiev for him, too—the *Romeo and Juliet* arrangement and, I think, some extracts from *War and Peace*. Arthur was very touched. He was very fond of Richter. He sometimes didn't agree with the tempi or the programs—'Why did he play a whole program of Schubert sonatas, and not the best ones?' he'd ask—but he used to say that Richter always held your attention. He had tremendous admiration for him."

Other well-known musicians kept in touch with him. In April 1977, Rubinstein sent thank-you notes to Lorin Maazel and Isaac Stern, who had made him gifts of their recordings. At some point—the date is unclear—a telegram arrived: "Just heard your tape of [Chopin's] four ballads and four scherzi[;] bouleversé as always you are still the greatest much love Lenny Bernstein."[23] In June, Annabelle sent a promised photo of Rubinstein to the soprano Kiri Te Kanawa. "You gave him immeasurable joy with your wonderful performance in the Magic Flute," Annabelle wrote.[24] James Galway, the flutist, wrote to him, in January 1978, to thank him for his records and a signed photograph, which had made his stay in hospital in the aftermath of a car accident "more bearable."[25] In April of that year, Paul Tortelier wrote: "Dear Master, I often think of you, of your magnificent wife and of Annabelle, a rare secretary with so much sensitivity for all the things of life."[26] (Like many of Rubinstein's other acquaintances, Tortelier was hedging his bets with respect to the Master's domestic situation.) And in August 1978, the violinist Alexander Schneider wrote, simply and movingly, although somewhat ungrammatically: "I do hope dear Arthur, that you are well and enjoying life more than ever. You have given so much of yourself to everybody and I am one of them."[27]

Despite all the attention he received, "sometimes he would be sitting with Annabelle and myself," Janina Fialkowska recalled, "and he would say, 'You know, it's really quite sad. I have no friends anymore.'

"We would say, 'What do you mean?!'

" 'When I say friends, I mean men friends.' He always liked the idea of having a buddy. Apart from his best friends, Paul Kochanski and Karol Szymanowski, I think he most missed the Paris crowd between the wars— Pagnol, Cocteau, and so on. He liked Roman Jasinski very much, but he thought he was a bit flighty and had funny tastes in music—and he was also Mrs. Rubinstein's friend. Bronek Kaper was a buddy of his, but more for joking around than for serious things. So there was great excitement when they invited over Joseph Kessel, the author of *Belle de jour*." Kessel, born in Argentina, was of Russian Jewish extraction, had lived most of his life in France, and was only eleven years younger than Rubinstein. "Arthur was really counting on this man to be his new best friend, with whom he could discuss things," Janina said. "He felt that he couldn't do that with women; he did it, anyway, but he had this idea. I think Kessel turned out to be a bit of a disappointment—and then he went and died," in 1979. Annabelle said that although "in general Arthur didn't particularly like the company of men, there were a few he just adored talking and listening to: Jean d'Ormesson, Roman Jasinski, and Teddy Kollek, the mayor of Jerusalem—they were intelligent, and they stimulated him. There weren't many musicians who were as widely read as Arthur. Claudio Arrau was one, but they didn't have much contact— their careers didn't allow it, and I suppose they didn't have that much in common, musically." (In 1927, however, Rubinstein had been one of the judges—the others were Cortot, Ernest Schelling, José Vianna da Motta, and Joseph Pembauer—who had awarded the twenty-two-year-old Arrau first prize in the competition of the Concours International des Pianistes in Geneva.)

In September 1978, Rubinstein watched Horowitz—another musician with whom he had little in common—on television, when Horowitz gave a concert with the New York Philharmonic to mark the fiftieth anniversary of his American debut. "Horowitz was changing tempi all the time, and I don't know how Zubin Mehta managed never, never to let him go for one second," Annabelle recalled. "Arthur thought it was quite a feat." But afterward, Rubinstein cabled Horowitz: "Dear Volodya, I just heard your Rachmaninov Concerto No. 3 which absolutely enchanted me and want to congratulate you on your immense success so long overdue." Success long overdue—for *Horowitz?* Perhaps Rubinstein was impishly suggesting that Horowitz would have an easier time now that he, Rubinstein, had retired; Horowitz, however, cabled his thanks.

Rubinstein's relations with most other musicians were good, but with a few they were openly hostile, and not always for musical reasons. When he attended the Lucerne Festival in 1979, for instance, he refused, again, to have anything to do with Herbert von Karajan because of the conductor's early membership in the Nazi party. The situation was particularly difficult inasmuch as Karajan, his wife, and their two daughters were staying at the Hotel Palace, where Rubinstein and Annabelle were also staying. "We had neighboring tables at the hotel's restaurant," Annabelle said. "Sometimes we would arrive first, sometimes they would, but in any case there were our tables, cheek by jowl, with no communication between them."

Janina, who spent some time in Lucerne with Annabelle and Arthur, remembered the tension between the Karajan and Rubinstein tables, but she also remembered Rubinstein's somewhat too barbed teasing of her in front of another celebrated conductor, Georg Solti, who stayed at the Palace Hotel. Rubinstein knew that Janina greatly admired Solti and his Chicago Symphony Orchestra, and he "was very jealous of Solti because I thought he was so great," Janina said. "We were in the hotel restaurant on the day that Solti was to arrive, and Arthur would say to me, 'Swallow your food! I think he's coming in!' Finally, Solti did come in. He very sweetly rushed over and embraced Arthur, who said, 'I'd like you to meet a young pianist who absolutely *detests* you.' No sooner had I turned purple than Arthur said, 'No, I'm kidding—she's madly in love with you!' Poor Solti didn't know where to look. Years later, when I did play with Solti, his wife remembered the episode. Arthur was also jealous of my friend, Jeffrey Swann, the pianist. Jeff wasn't my boyfriend, but Arthur didn't like my having such a good friend. I once told Arthur that Jeff could play by heart anything Wagner had written. By then, Arthur was partly deaf and blind—he was in a world of his own—and you could watch his face, watch him thinking. There was a long silence while a whole range of emotions battled for supremacy in his facial expression, and then he looked up and said, very softly, almost shyly, 'I used to be able to play some Wagner by heart, too.'"

***

AT LAST, IN 1979, the typescript of *My Many Years*, the second and final volume of Rubinstein's memoirs, was completed and turned over to Knopf. *My Young Years* had taken Rubinstein's life up to 1917, fifty-six years before it was published; by making a few judicious omissions and name-changes, he had been able to describe his early life with considerable frankness—from his point of view, of course. "I had the luck with my first book to have practically all the personalities I wrote about dead," he joked with Peter J. Rosenwald, who had interviewed him in 1976 for the British magazine, *Records and Recording*. *My Many Years*, however, took his story right up to the day of its completion. "It's not so easy for me this time. I can't invent a novel about my life. It must be exactly what happened. It's all I can do. I have a fantastic memory which is not so good for me because I remember very bad things. Like the first book, this one is almost a diary. I hardly omit anything. At the ripe age which I have, I don't fear so much. If I were condemned to prison, it . . . wouldn't be for ten or twenty years. I couldn't make it."[28] But, as Pirandello demonstrated long ago, to relate "exactly what happened" is not possible—and even if it were, no one would do it. Like other autobiographers, Rubinstein exercised various forms of self-censorship to protect himself and others. "Arthur felt terribly inhibited about the second volume," Annabelle recalled. "He didn't feel he could write freely about family, about friends still living, or about his own successes. He felt he would be accused of boasting."

The writing of *My Many Years* was rendered exceptionally difficult by Rubinstein's near blindness. As Jean-Paul Sartre discovered in his sightless last years, to hear someone read back what one has dictated is no substitute for rereading one's own text. And even a superficial check of all the dates, personalities, and events would have required months of research—for which assistants would have had to be engaged—followed by weeks of cross-questioning, with which the nonagenarian Rubinstein could not have coped. As his age advanced and his strength waned, he and everyone else involved in the project must have understood that the text had to be rushed into print or abandoned. Judith Jones, the senior Knopf editor who was in charge of the book, reported later, with apparent bitterness: "*My Many Years* had practically no editing because by then Arthur had decided that Annabelle Whitestone was the only editor he needed and would listen only to her. Conveniently he did not hear very well at that point so any criticism fell on deaf ears. . . ."[29] But Annabelle described Jones's accusations as "TOTALLY false. Arthur did not want changes in *content* but neither he nor I, who had no time nor pretensions to edit, considered me the editor. We went to New York in March 1979 with the completed manuscript (I think [Jones] had already received some large chunks previously) and the book was published in January 1980. What the hell were they doing all that time at Knopf's when they should have been editing the thing? With hindsight I realise they sat back and took advantage of the situation to blame me for non-existing editing—*their* job. It was all I could do to keep abreast of the typing—early morning, late at night, when not with Arthur, and *always* exhausted!"[30] In any case, one reads with astonishment sentences like the following one, about Heifetz: "He was wildly interested in the shops where I bought my ties and shoes and in the golden chain which held my keys safely in my pocket, not to speak of my valet and Besanzoni herself."[31] Or, "Chicago had ups and downs but was not able to keep a foothold in the Midwest."[32] Under the circumstances, however, Annabelle did a good job of patching the complicated story together. The fact that the book exists at all is largely a result of her efforts, and she herself has said that *My Many Years* did not turn out as well as *My Young Years.*

Much of Rubinstein's account of his life has been discussed earlier in this book, and many errors have been pointed out. But the weaknesses in *My Many Years* are not merely factual, structural, or syntactical. Rubinstein was capable of deep insights and generous behavior, but the superficial and vindictive sides of his nature occupy center stage in the book. He huffs and puffs over the state of the world as a whole and art in particular, but his remarks are too generic to be interesting. And, at the end of a remarkably long and full life and a fabulously successful career, he demeaned himself by dwelling on petty slights, personal or professional, from the distant past. *My Many Years* is fundamentally ungenerous. In some ways it is probably more honest than Rubinstein realized, but it is also unfair to his better side. Most book reviewers either did not notice or pretended not to notice this aspect of *My Many Years*: they were too busy titillating their readers with summaries of Rubinstein's erotic revelations or grappling with the question of Annabelle's role in the ancient pianist's life. (The book is dedicated "To Annabelle, my devoted friend and companion, with my love and gratitude," and in the epilogue Rubinstein stated that "my dear deus ex machina has provided me with the most beautiful last years of my life.") The harmonica virtuoso Larry Adler said, in his own memoirs, that he had reviewed the British edition of Rubinstein's book: "I disapproved of the way he named his many affairs and suggested he could have subtitled the book, *The Lay of the Last Minstrel*," Adler recalled.[33] When the French edition of *My Many Years* appeared, it provoked a nasty exchange between Rubinstein and Bernard Gavoty, a well-known Paris music critic. Gavoty had been Cortot's friend and biographer, but he was also a longtime acquaintance and admirer of Rubinstein, who had been the subject of one of the critic's series of illustrated booklets, *Les Grands interprètes*. In an article in *Le Figaro*, Gavoty apostrophized Rubinstein in the second person and complained that *My Many Years* consisted of "nothing but dinners, bedroom scenes, travels, lobsters, caviar, and champagne!"

You present yourself in a not very flattering light: that of an unregenerate pleasure-seeker. There is liveliness, certainly, but it is the liveliness of vanity! I look through your pages for some general ideas that are yours, and all I see are frivolity, the desire for money at any cost, one-night adventures, intolerable fatuousness, the acknowledgement of your incurable laziness about overcoming your technical weaknesses!

I find you unpardonably guilty of frying all your colleagues in a spicy sauce. Be their names Schnabel, Hofmann, Gieseking, Heifetz, Horowitz, Cortot—and on and on—each one is described as having small virtues, entirely unequal to yours!

This is full-fledged megalomania.

How dare you write that Cortot gives us a "weak tubercular" Chopin? Have you listened to Cortot's recordings of the *Twenty-four Etudes* and the *Twenty-four Preludes*? They are miracles of technique, consistent elegance, and virile élan.

Haven't you told me many times that you were unable to realize these marvelous pieces completely? And you always held against me my great admiration for Cortot! As if I ought to have praised only you.

How sad, vain, small-minded, and nasty this story is![34]

Although the article reveals that Gavoty could be at least as high-handed as Rubinstein, many of the criticisms hit the mark. They angered Rubinstein, of course, and some of his friends, in their haste to demonstrate their solidarity with him, fanned the flames. "By chance, a few days ago I came upon an article by Gavoty," wrote Jean d'Ormesson, the *Figaro*'s former editor, in an undated letter. "It was distressing—for what it said about him, however. Rest assured that I am entirely on your side. . . . I am one of the people—and there are many of us—who never tire of listening to you."[35] Gavoty well knew how Rubinstein would react to his article, and a few weeks later he sent the pianist a letter that mixed apologies with further offenses.

Dear Arthur,
I don't want to let the year end without having told you how much I regret having caused you pain by allowing an article about you to be published in the *Figaro*.

It is true that I don't appreciate at all the tone and the contents of your *Mémoires*. . . . You justly dedicated the first volume to Nela, to whom you owe so much, but whom you abandoned in the declining years of your life. This is worse than an error: it is an act of cowardice, committed late in life. I respect and I love Nela: like her, I am mortified.

There remains the Cortot "case". You didn't like my dividing my admiration between him and you. It was my absolute right as a strictly independent and sincere critic. Have you listened with open ears to Cortot's recordings of the 24 *Preludes* and 27 *Etudes* of Chopin? [The twenty-four Etudes mentioned in Gavoty's article have become twenty-seven in the letter because the critic was including the *Trois nouvelles études.*]

Have you listened in the same way to Horowitz's *Kreisleriana* and *Fantasy* of Schumann? They make one fall on one's knees. We are not alone in the world. . . .

Having said that, [I must add that] you have enriched me in a singular way. And I don't believe that I have stinted in my enthusiasm for your art and your sparkling wit. Nothing can erase this from my memory. Thus, without the least hypocrisy or any sort of contradiction, I allow myself to send you, at this year's end, my wishes for your health and happiness, as well as the homage of a heart that hasn't forgotten what it owes you.[36]

Rubinstein dictated a reply:

Bernard,
Your article has angered me. You are intent upon reproaching me for having participated in the wild living and parties of the 1920s, after the victory, although you well knew about my long and fine world-wide career, whose success continued unabated through my last concert. . . .

As to your letter, . . . it offended me. What right do you have to mix into my marriage? If my wife had the bad taste to complain to you about my behavior, you—who are supposedly a friend— should have made it your duty to hear my side. Besides, your insinuations about my jealousy of Cortot or Horowitz are absurd. I have always expressed my admiration for the art of these two artists, by word of mouth and in my books, but I swear that I feel only hatred for the behavior of Cortot and Vuillermoz [a French music critic] under Vichy [the German-controlled puppet government of much of France during World War II], and your good will toward these two betrayers of the true France has often given me food for thought. As to Horowitz, I didn't like his encores in bad taste, and don't forget that it was your bad review that prevented him from returning to France.

Finally, the word "cowardice", which you have dared to use on me, is unpardonable.

That is all.

Arthur Rubinstein[37]

But Gavoty's assessment of Rubinstein's opinions of Cortot and Horowitz was not incorrect: in *My Many Years*, Rubinstein had described Cortot's Chopin playing as "too delicate" and had complained of "Cortot's treatment of Chopin as the weak tubercular artist."[38] In private conversation, too, he was "quite negative about Cortot," according to Daniel Barenboim. Rubinstein's last expression of "admiration" for Horowitz, in the book, was: "Horowitz returned to the concert life as the great virtuoso he always was, but in my view does not contribute anything to the art of music."[39] He had every right to his devastating criticisms of his colleagues, especially since, in the same volume of his memoirs, he gave high and intelligent praise to Rachmaninoff's playing and a well-balanced description of the strong and weak points in the playing of Hofmann, Gabrilowitsch, and others. He could better have defended himself from Gavoty's attack by using the simple and unopposable argument that his expertise and conviction were precisely the qualities that made his opinions of other pianists valuable, rather than by claiming to admire people whom he obviously did not admire. Indeed, had there been more strong musical opinion in it, the book would have had greater value. John Rubinstein said, "Whenever I stood around watching and listening to my father play—not at a concert but in a living room—if I would ask, 'What about that G-flat major theme?' he would have *volumes* to say, about a theme or a phrase: why he played it that way, how he had played it before, how he wished he could play it, how Rachmaninoff had played it. He would have so much to say about the images that were in his mind, or that had been in it but had changed, or about the history and background of the piece."[40] But very little of this found its way into either volume of the memoirs.

Gavoty's words continued to sting, and Rubinstein dictated an addendum to his earlier letter. Among other things, he said: "In my youth, my greatest admiration was for Busoni and Eugène d'Albert and my great love was for Edouard Risler, and not for Paderewski, whom the world adulated but who, in my opinion, was a bad pianist. Besides, it was his style of playing Chopin that created the stylistic exaggerations and the lack of rhythm that were in vogue through the long years during which I was harshly criticized for my way of playing him simply, like Mozart. Let me remind you that in the early years of our acquaintance, you judged me with plenty of harshness. Nowadays, my greatest admiration is for Richter, despite the fact that his ideas are very different from mine, and this is because he is the greatest musician of all of us. I myself launched the career of the marvelous Gilels, and I myself gave the

Chopin prize in Warsaw to the young Pollini, who even then was showing that he had the claws of a lion. I don't need to listen to anyone's records, because I know from personal experience that the [technical] perfection is fake."[41] The following September, Gavoty wrote a highly complimentary review of Rubinstein's recently released recording of Schumann's Fantasy and the Novelettes Nos. 1 and 2. It was his last article: he died on October 24, 1981, and Rubinstein sent his widow a telegram of condolences.

Judith Jones reported that *My Many Years* "sold poorly compared to the first volume."[42] It is not surprising that Nela Rubinstein's feelings about the book were far from positive; her versions of some of her husband's stories have been cited earlier in this book. Eva and Alina have claimed not to have read *My Many Years* in its entirety, and John said that he hadn't read either volume. "That's the horrible truth. My father read a lot of the first one aloud to me while he was writing it, but the second one I haven't even cracked," he said. Eva commented, "To dictate to your mistress the book about your marriage! It was just so awful!" Emanuel Ax said that reading *My Many Years* gave him the biggest disappointment that he had ever had in an individual. "Until then, I had idolized Rubinstein—I had wanted to have a life like his. The book changed all that." But Magaloff said, of both volumes of Rubinstein's memoirs, "A lot of people have criticized those books, saying that they are not profound, but I think this is a big error. Those books are exactly like him. His personality comes through sincerely. He wasn't like Busoni, for instance—he was as far from him as anyone could be! Why look for philosophy? Rubinstein hadn't that kind of mind!"

THE PUBLICATION OF *My Many Years*, in January 1980, coincided with the beginning of a serious and ultimately fatal decline in Rubinstein's health. Well over a year earlier, he had begun to experience pains in the back, groin, and right leg; at first, the pains were mild, but before long walking had become difficult. "Arthur had prostate cancer, and it was not diagnosed in time," Annabelle said. "I fault the American Hospital in Paris and the doctor who saw him. I used to go with Arthur, but if I had a query—whether or not he should carry on with the pills he was taking, for instance—I felt I was just spoiling their fun. Instead of any serious talk, Arthur and the doctor used to crack jokes together. Arthur's symptoms showed that the prostate was not in order. I learned after the event that any medical student ought to have known that, but the hospital never did any elementary tests or biopsies. At the end of December 1979, his right leg swelled up tremendously. I kept telephoning the doctor—I thought there might be something wrong with the hip or the leg, because it was so swollen—and he said, 'Well you know, you can't make a young man out of an old man, Annabelle. Make him walk, make him take exercise.'

"I said, 'He *can't* walk! The leg hurts him!'

"He said, 'The only thing you have to watch out for is that the other foot doesn't swell, because if that happens it could be the heart. But this swelling—it's his age. There's nothing to be done, and nothing to worry about.' We tried acupuncture, we tried God knows what. In May 1980, we went to New York for the promotion of the book and to see Johnny playing in *Children of a Lesser God*, for which he got the Tony Award. Arthur was in a bad way, and I asked Alina to find a doctor."

In those years, Alina was first an intern and then a resident in psychiatry. "My father showed me his leg, and I was shocked," she recalled. "It was so swollen that it was twice as big as the other. I knew it had to be a bad thing." In a letter, Alina wrote: "I described it to my supervising resident. He said it sounded as if there might be a risk of spinal cord compression (an emergency) if it was not treated, and gave me Dr. [Peter H.] Berczeller's name. Dr. Berczeller diagnosed lymphatic obstruction probably due to metastases from a primary prostate cancer (advanced stage)." Annabelle described Berczeller as "marvelous—he took one look at that leg and said, 'We have to operate right away. There's no doubt about it.' They did a CAT scan; I was with them in the room where you see the images coming out, and they were saying, 'Oh God! Oh God!' The cancer had already spread pretty far. And it needn't have done. If he had started treatment two years earlier, it would have made all the difference. But he had the operation."

Berczeller, in his charming book, *Doctors and Patients*, described his first encounter with Rubinstein—not the "bubbly raconteur" whose tale he had read in *My Young Years*, but a "silent, pale, very old little man wearing a voluminous coat, scarf, and hat . . . [and] sitting immobile in a wheelchair. . . . He was obviously quite deaf, but after Annabel[le] had introduced me, not speaking too loudly but enunciating each word very clearly, he did open his eyes and say, 'Bonjour.' . . . I quickly realized that he was completely alert and that, if I imitated the way she spoke to him, he understood everything I told him. What's more, even though he had very poor eyesight, I was astonished to hear him pick out the name of the artist (Chagall) responsible for the original of the Metropolitan Opera poster advertising *The Magic Flute* that was hanging on the far wall of the office." Berczeller went on to describe the examinations that were performed on Rubinstein, and then said:

> Over the years, I should not have been so contemptuous of the 'celebrity doctors' who were known to spend large chunks of time with their Very Important Patients, because I found myself doing the same thing. Now that he knew that something definitive was to be done for him, whatever the diagnosis, Rubinstein was very cheerful, and each time I saw him, he wore a beautiful silk dressing gown

with a matching pocket handkerchief, his feet encased in embroidered velvet slippers, and he smelled of an unfamiliar cologne,
which he said was a special fragrance made for him by Chanel. He
was very talkative and so witty that his book, which I had found to
be so extraordinary, had to be rated a distant second behind his actual presence.

It was my custom to see my hospital patients once a day, and
twice if they were seriously ill. I found myself seeing Arthur three or
four times a day and staying about half an hour each time. The frequent visits were not necessary medically . . . but I was so fascinated
by him, and had begun to like him so much, that I felt physically
drawn to see him as often as I could. Yet he was unlike any VIP I had
ever heard of. He made no demands, went along with all my suggestions, and left the choice of doctors entirely up to me.[43]

The surgery took place at New York University Hospital. "My father
had a 'TURP' (transurethral resection of the prostate) under general anesthesia," Alina wrote. "They wanted to use a spinal block . . . to avoid the higher
risks of general anesthesia, but due to his advanced age his spine was so stiff
that they couldn't do it." Annabelle said, "Of course, one was terrified that he
wouldn't come round. He was already ninety-three. The night before, alone
in his room, we held hands and listened to Mozart piano quartets—his recordings with the Guarneri Quartet. Eva visited him and upset him in her
usual way." On the day of the operation, Berczeller "woke up very early," he
said. Rubinstein "was the first case, and I wanted to be sure to check him one
more time before he went to the operating room. When I arrived, Annabel[le], who slept on a cot in his room, was already up, but our star patient
was sleeping peacefully. . . . When Arthur woke up, though, he immediately
made us laugh as he imitated Vladimir Horowitz, who had been the principal player in the dream from which he had just awakened." Before the operation, Rubinstein requested that someone play him a tape of Mozart's String
Quintet in G Minor as he was coming out of the anaesthetic; if, instead, he
heard the Adagio from the Schubert String Quintet in C Major, he would
know that he had died and gone to heaven, he joked. Berczeller was "very
anxious all the while that Arthur was lying there unconscious with a breathing tube down his throat. But the monitor showed a normal rhythm, the
blood gases were excellent, and the surgeon was whistling . . . , so I was reassured to some degree." John, who visited his father immediately afterward,
recalled: "For the first time in his life, he looked like a poor, sick old man. He
had tubes and I.V.s sticking out all over, and he couldn't talk. When I came
in, I probably asked him something dumb, like 'How are you feeling?' He

looked at me, and his eyes twinkled, and he *sang* quite a long section of a Mozart quintet—a jaunty little theme, not a sad one. To me, it was a validation of what had come to seem a pat declaration, on his part, about his unconditional love of life."

"We sacked the night nurse the first night," Annabelle said, "because she was making light of the fact that he was having so much pain. After that, I stayed with him all the time—I never budged from the hospital." According to Berczeller, Rubinstein's postoperative progress was so good that he could be discharged from the hospital after only five days. At the hotel, Annabelle said, "Arthur seemed so tired after the operation that one evening I phoned the doctor, who said he would stop over—it was before or after a formal dinner, and the doctor was all dressed up. Well, Arthur just sparkled. He was telling stories to the doctor, and he really perked up." (Four years earlier, when an interviewer had asked him whether he was tiring him, Rubinstein had replied: "No! But I will be tired when you leave. As long as anything lasts, I'm happy to keep going. If there's a party after a concert I'm always the last to leave. They can't get rid of me.")[44] Once Rubinstein's condition had improved sufficiently, Berczeller invited him and Annabelle to a "victory lunch" at a Park Avenue restaurant. "Arthur looked splendid," the doctor recalled. "I began with a champagne toast to his recovery, and he then took over with a toast to Doktor Leben ["Doctor Life"—Rubinstein's German-Yiddish nickname for Berczeller], then one to the 'faithful' Annabel[le], then one to the 'beautiful' Adrienne (my wife). At my request, he imitated Horowitz again, and then he was off and running with several other imitations, among them Toscanini and Stokowski." Rubinstein was still walking with difficulty and could not negotiate stairs; at one point, he had to urinate, and Berczeller remembered with alarm that the men's room was downstairs. Eventually, he led his patient to a closet in the restaurant's cloakroom and gave him an empty wine carafe to use for the purpose, to the amusement of both of them.[45]

Annabelle and the Rubinstein family agreed that Arthur was not to be told that he had cancer. "I knew that the moment he heard the word 'cancer', he'd think, 'My God, this is it,' " Annabelle said. "Luckily, most of the things that went wrong with him could have been attributed to his age." For that matter, he had never wanted to know anything about how his body functioned, and perhaps this form of willful ignorance helped to lengthen his life. Alina believed that her father was given a brief course of radiation therapy before he was started on DES (diethylstilbestrol, anti-testosterone) therapy. When he had regained some of his strength, he returned to Paris with Annabelle. "For a while he was much better," she recalled, "but he had awful eczema. At all hours of the night or day he would suddenly have terrible attacks of itching. We tried various creams and medications, but nothing really worked." Eventually, the eczema developed into *mycosis fungoides*.

The attention of old friends helped Rubinstein to keep his spirits up. Marlene Dietrich, for instance, who lived in Paris, wrote him a note (apparently in response to receiving a copy of his memoirs from him) in gigantic block letters, so that he might be able to read it himself: "DEAREST I LOVE YOU AND ALL MY THANKS! PLEASE TELL ME BY PHONE WHAT I CAN DO FOR YOU? WHO COOKS FOR YOU? I CANNOT DO ALL THE TERRIFIC COOKING YOU DESCRIBE [in *My Many Years*] BUT I MAKE THE *BEST BOUILLON* THAT YOU SHOULD *DRINK*! JUST HAVE SOME ONE TELL ME WHEN YOU WANT IT (EXCEPT MONDAYS) AND I WILL SEND IT OVER. NO WORK FOR ME JUST LOVE FOR YOU. AS EVER MARLENE."[46] Such attention would have made anyone feel good. And Rubinstein could hardly have been saddened by a message from his lawyers in New York, in June 1980, to the effect that RCA was depositing a check for $822,201.73—the accumulation of several months' royalties and advances—in his account in the First National City Bank of New York.[47] By the end of August, his RCA record sales had earned him an additional $196,542.07 for the previous six-month period.[48] Early the following year—according to an RCA interoffice memo—Seth Frank, one of Rubinstein's lawyers, had informed the company that "in his view Mr. Rubinstein would be offended at the prospect of RCA releasing any of his recordings on Gold Seal"—a mid-price label. "Frank, therefore, has rejected our request to so release the Beethoven concertos [conducted by Erich Leinsdorf] and suggests we refrain from making any other similar plans involving Mr. Rubinstein's recordings while Mr. Rubinstein is alive."[49]

On the evening of July 29, 1980, after having watched the news on television, Rubinstein stood up and experienced what Annabelle described as "a frightful, excruciating pain at the top of his left leg. I called the doctor in New York—we no longer had any faith in the doctor in Paris—and asked, 'What do I do? Is it anything to do with the illness?' He found a colleague of his who came round right away, and we took Arthur to the Hôpital Foch; X rays were taken, and they discovered that he'd simply broken the neck of the femur—a spontaneous break. There was a long operation, again with general anaesthetic, and an artificial neck of the femur was inserted. I thought it was the cancer that had gotten through to the bones, but the surgeon said that it was a very strong bone which he'd cut through with great difficulty." Although the operation was successful, Rubinstein's hospital stay weakened him considerably. "We were in that hospital for a month, and I never moved from his room," Annabelle said. "Then they threw us out—they said they couldn't do anything more. We decided to go to Zurich, to the Dolder Hotel—a marvelous hotel where we'd stayed several times while writing the book, and which we loved. We had an ambulance take us to the airport; on the plane, three seats were removed, and Arthur made the flight on a stretcher. There was an ambulance waiting for us in Zurich, to take us to the hotel. Arthur was at his worst point: he wasn't moving—he had terrible pain in his back, especially when he sat up, from being in bed so long. We had a very good doctor"— Christian Funk—"and a marvelous, German-trained physiotherapist. She worked on Arthur, and she got him walking. On my birthday, October 21, he was able to walk the length of the corridor. We went down in the lift, with no wheelchair, and we went to the restaurant. That was a real feat! We stayed at the Dolder for seven months, and lots of people came to visit us there at different times—Roman, Johnny, Alina." Nela, too, went to see her husband at the Dolder. "They had a very serious talk—I left them alone," Annabelle recalled; she added that Rubinstein was determined to divorce Nela, but that he gave up the idea when his lawyers said that he would have to face a terrible battle. Nela, however, later claimed that Arthur had never raised the issue of divorce with her—neither during her visit to the Dolder nor at any other time. And a few years earlier, before the crisis in his marriage, Rubinstein had told Barenboim, 'No matter what happens—other women and this and that—I will never divorce. I am a Jewish family man.' He liked to see himself that way, and I think that must have been one of his key problems in his relations with his children."

Little by little, the cancer was advancing, and Rubinstein began to be afflicted by bouts of acute septicemia. "Toward the end of our stay at the Dolder, Arthur had started to have sudden, very frightening, very high fevers, with strong shivering," Annabelle said. "That was quite terrifying, but we got used to it. It happened often, and he had to be given antibiotics right away." Eventually, he and Annabelle left the Dolder and moved to his apartment in Geneva, at 9 Avenue Krieg. There, the septicemia continued to afflict him. "It always happened at around eleven o'clock in the evening. He'd start shivering like mad, and I knew what I was in for. The first few times, we'd go to the hospital in the middle of the night, but then I got a stock of antibiotics and I would give some to him right away; we stayed home. But his appetite wasn't what it should have been: he got thinner and thinner, as the pictures taken then show. Yet he never lost his incredible optimism. He was *marvelous*—he never complained." When Alina came to visit, she, too, marveled at her father: "I thought he was amazingly uncomplaining and at peace about being sick and infirm," she said. "When he was a little younger, even if he hurt his finger he would act like it was all over. And here he was dying of cancer, and in a lot of pain—I know from having taken care of patients who had what he had: the skin cancer that was secondary to the prostate cancer is incredibly painful. But he never complained about it. He was too busy listening to music or watching some Fred Astaire film on TV, with what little peripheral vision he had. That was better than any painkiller for him."

Annabelle said that even more than listening to music, "what really took him out of himself and made him forget his pain was listening to the Maigret novels of Georges Simenon. We read every one that I could lay my hands on, and I'd read to him until I was completely hoarse. He could listen to Maigret for hours. I would see his eyes go off into the Maigret world, and he would be happy and content. Then we read all the other novels of Simenon." The author, who lived nearby, came to visit Rubinstein and gave him a copy of what he said was his own favorite among his novels, *Le Petit saint*. Annabelle also read Arthur the books of another occasional visitor, Jean d'Ormesson. "Arthur loved to hear all those books, and I'd love to see him being transported, to see that little twinkle, to see him actually in the world of the book we were reading. We read Albert Cohen's *Belle du Seigneur*—a big, fat book—from beginning to end. Sometimes, I would start to reread a passage we had read the day before, and he would say, 'Yes, yes, that we read yesterday.' He would always remember exactly where we'd left off. He was like that with doing sums, too—he'd do them in his head in two seconds. His brain was absolutely clear, right up to the end. One was conscious of him being ill, but not old."

Musicians continued to visit him frequently. "Marta Argerich lived in Geneva and used to come and see us; we would have dinner together," Annabelle said. "Once, at dinner after a wonderful recital of hers in Lucerne, he said, 'Marta! Why did you play the last movement of the Chopin sonata so fast? How *could* you do it like that?' She said, 'I know, I know! But I can't help it!' But she fascinated him. He used to love to talk and listen to her, and he admired her very much, although there were lots of things in her playing that he didn't agree with. He also admired Maria Tipo and Nikita Magaloff a lot." Magaloff recalled, "Until a few months before he died, Rubinstein would sometimes have my wife and myself to lunch at his Geneva apartment, and he would even ask me to play something on the piano. It was very sad that at the end of his life he was so ill. I saw this wonderful person, whom I knew when he was so full of life, at his very weakest. He couldn't hear very well, either. But his head was always there—not like Kempff," who was ill with Parkinson's and senile in extreme old age. "And he always insisted on a good meal," Magaloff said.

Another musician whose visits Rubinstein enjoyed, in his last months, was the young violinist Shlomo Mintz, whose playing reminded Rubinstein of the artistry of Paul Kochanski. They met after Rubinstein had heard Mintz play the Brahms Concerto in a televised concert. "Arthur was just in tears, he was so moved by his playing," Annabelle recalled. "I saw that Shlomo was due to come and play a recital in Geneva, but Arthur wasn't well enough to go—he was already quite ill, by then. I found out where Shlomo was staying, and I phoned him. I explained that Mr. Rubinstein had heard him on the television. 'He would love to meet you, but unfortunately he can't come to your concert,' I said. 'Would you perhaps come to the apartment?'

"He said, 'Of course! I can come with my pianist—we can play the whole program we're playing tonight!'

" 'Fine, come to lunch!'

" 'May I bring my fiancée?' I said yes, gave him the address, and set a time; and then he said: 'Do you mind if I ask you one question? It is *the* Rubinstein, isn't it?' He suddenly thought that maybe it was a banker! Shlomo was very warm, and Arthur adored his playing and adored *him*. Whenever Shlomo was anywhere near, he would come over; once, he even got a helicopter from somewhere to come to Geneva. He would play for him before concerts or after concerts, and he became very close to Arthur in those last two years."

Rubinstein introduced Annabelle to the opera repertoire, of which she had known very little, and she introduced him to certain areas of the chamber music repertoire that he had not previously cultivated. Other areas he knew thoroughly, however, and "he used to get very irritated at the way certain quartets played," Annabelle reported. "He would say that you couldn't hear the first violin playing the melodic line. If he heard music that he thought was not being treated well, he could get into a terrible rage. 'How can they play like that?' He would complain that certain groups played the first movement of the Mozart G Minor Quintet as if it were a little scherzo, and he would say, 'What are they thinking of?' I found him a recording of the old Griller Quartet with William Primrose playing the Mozart quintets, and that he adored."

Another matter that frequently enraged Rubinstein was the world's attitude—or his interpretation of it—toward Israel. In his last years, he was not merely benevolent toward Israel: he was a right-winger, certain that Israel could do no wrong. The territories that Israel had occupied in 1967 were Israel's by right, he believed, and he said that the Palestinians were nomads in whom Lawrence of Arabia had unfortunately implanted the notion of being a people—after which they had done nothing but procreate. They ought to be settled on Jordanian soil, he declared on more than one occasion. Since the Soviet Union had become the major supporter of Israel's opponents, Rubinstein even suggested that the United States bomb the Kremlin. When the Labor party governed in Israel, Rubinstein was friendly with its leaders, and Annabelle remembered a visit from Golda Meir, during one of Rubinstein's stays in Tel Aviv: "Near the Dan Hotel there was a little coffee shop that made a very good cheese cake; I went and bought a whole one, and she lapped up the entire thing. She used to say to him, 'Arthur, there are only two pianists in the world: you and Menachem'—her grandson." When the conservative Likud party came to power, Rubinstein became friendly with the new leadership. He often visited Prime Minister Menachem Begin—whom he described, in *My Many Years*, as "a great statesman"—and they occasionally phoned each other and exchanged letters. In March 1982, for instance, Rubinstein said, in a note dictated to Annabelle: "Why is [sic] America, West Europe and Israel itself so silent about Jordan which is the real home of the Palestinians as it was under the Turks, until Hussein went from house to house killing them all to get the last of them out of their country? Why is this very historic fact absolutely ignored by all the countries including Israel? Now it seems taboo to mention it. Excuse me, my dear Prime Minister, for daring to mention politics, but if I were young I would make a colossal campagne [sic] to remind the world of it."[50]

Rubinstein carried on a running debate with Yehudi Menuhin over the Israeli question. In 1977, he had attacked Menuhin in the press over what he perceived as the violinist's soft stand vis-à-vis UNESCO's censure of Israel. Shortly thereafter, Menuhin sent him a gentle letter in which he did not even mention the matter: he thanked him for making a "personal gesture" in favor of Yitkin Seow, who had been a contestant in the Rubinstein Competition in Tel Aviv, because Seow was a student "from my own School," and he continued: "I heard from Annabelle that she is helping you with your new book. I am sure it will be a splendid one. I am also taking the liberty of sending you my autobiography and I hope that you and Nella [sic] will enjoy it." Rubinstein replied: "Cher ami: Your nice letter and the gift of your book overwhelmed me. After my severe criticism of your un-Jewish attitude at UNESCO, you respond like a good Christian; I admire you for it and thank you very much for the book which I shall have read out to me as I cannot any more read or write."[51]

As in earlier years, Rubinstein continued to take a special interest in the development of educational and cultural facilities in Israel. In December 1980, for instance, Harold Hill, executive vice president of the American Committee for the Weizmann Institute of Science in Rehovot, sent him a letter of thanks for a donation of $100,000 to the Institute.[52] Earlier that year he had given $50,000 to the Israel-America Cultural Foundation in honor of Isaac Stern, on the violinist's sixtieth birthday, and, with Annabelle's encouragement, he left $500,000 in his will to the city of Jerusalem, with instructions that the money be used by the Jerusalem Foundation for cultural purposes. Had Rubinstein's health allowed, he would have gone to New York in October 1982 to be guest of honor at a $500-a-plate banquet at the Waldorf-Astoria, for the benefit of the Weizmann Institute. John Rubinstein, who stood in for him at the dinner, said that his father's doctor had ruled against the trip, and that his father had told him, on the phone, " 'Can you imagine how frustrating it feels to be boxed up in an armchair in Geneva instead of being among you to join the fun?' "[53]

ONCE IN A while, even during the last year of his life, Arthur Rubinstein would go to the piano and play for a few minutes — as long as he could bear to sit. "He wouldn't play a Chopin nocturne or something else out of his repertoire," Annabelle recalled, "but a Polish melody by Pankiewicz or Moniuszko—something he hadn't played for years and years, and which would suddenly come back to him, just like that. He would sit down and play them beautifully. Or he would feel out some interesting harmonies from different parts of *Aida*." These were his last contacts with the keyboard.

Nela went to Geneva for Arthur's ninety-fifth birthday party, on January 28, 1982. According to a newspaper report, the guests changed the traditional Polish toast, "May you live to be a hundred!" to "May you live to be a hundred and fifty!"[54] Annabelle gave Arthur a videocassette recorder, and everyone present—including Marta Argerich—watched an old film of the Rubinstein-Heifetz-Piatigorsky Trio. In April, the television host David Frost interviewed Rubinstein in Geneva. "I just now am living the happiest years of my life," Rubinstein said. He spoke of his love for Annabelle: "She keeps me alive, she makes my life divine. . . . I don't want to die at all."[55]

Another visitor in April 1982 was Janina, who hadn't seen Rubinstein in two years, although she wrote to him "at least once every ten days," she said. Her career, which he had launched so spectacularly, had taken a plunge immediately after his retirement, and he could not get used to the fact that agents and conductors who had tried to satisfy his every whim as long as he was active now turned down his requests for further assistance for his protégée. "It was a shock to him," Janina said. "After that, I wasn't even able to talk to him about my career. We talked about museums, good books—anything except career matters. But this time I was able to show him that things were working out—that what he had started was really beginning to gather momentum and fly on its own. Right away, he wanted to hear me. I played Bach's Second Partita and Prokofiev's Sixth Sonata, which he had asked me to learn; he really loved the Prokofiev sonatas, even though he didn't play them, and he once made me a present of a bound volume of them. I don't particularly love the Sixth, but I had learned it for him, and he had me replay, over and over, the passages he especially liked. Then I did Book Two of Debussy's *Images*; he said that he'd loved *Poissons d'or* but that he'd had 'a nice

nap' during the first two pieces. Thank you very much! I knew he had enjoyed what I was playing if he stopped smoking and his cigar went out. If he
kept smoking, it was bad news for me. I played the First Ballade of Chopin,
and he had a lot to say about the rhythm of the opening. 'Would you *please*
stop doing those rubatos all over the place?' he said. I didn't do tremendous
rubatos, but he was so straight about it—and of course he was right: it's a
matter of inflection, more than anything else. He talked about structure,
rhythm, and projection—the three things he was always after me about.

"The session was punctuated by meals. He looked as if he weighed sixty
pounds—it was hard, to see him so emaciated—but did he eat! I had brought
him some real Canadian maple syrup, so we had waffles with maple syrup;
then we had some halvah that had been sent him by one of his fans in Turkey; we had caviar and vodka; and then Annabelle made steak au poivre with
French fries, and an apple tart to follow it. All this in a seven-and-a-half-hour
period. Annabelle had to feed him, because he couldn't see, but he was just
loving it. He told me about Shlomo Mintz—he showed me a video of him—
and he started to cry and became very sad. I think his attachment to Shlomo
was tied in with his love of Israel. But he perked up—because even as a very
sick old man, he never stayed sad for long. Then my manager phoned to ask
me to go to Edinburgh the next day, to give a recital in place of someone who
had cancelled. I felt miserable, because I only had two days to spend in Geneva, and I knew it was the last time I would see Arthur. So I said no—but
when Arthur found out, he said, 'You should go, absolutely! Edinburgh is
terribly important—I played there with my future father-in-law.' So I phoned
back and accepted. When I left him, there were tears in his eyes."

A month later, on May 22, he was visited by the entire Juilliard String
Quartet. "We tried to conceal our shock at the sight of how much Rubinstein
had physically deteriorated since our last meeting [1977] in Paris," Earl Carlyss, the second violin, recalled, in a letter. But "in spite of his appearance I
was amazed at how sharp his mind was. He could still tell a great story and
seemed to have a firm grasp [of] what was happening in the outside world."
Rubinstein was told that his visitors had brought along the parts for all of the
Beethoven quartets and was asked which one he wanted to hear.

> He said, "I remember sitting on a window sill in Germany listening
> to the Joachim Quartet play Opus 18, No. 2. That's the 'Gentle-
> man's' quartet, you know." He began to sing the opening theme,
> pretending he was tipping his hat to a lady in time with the music.
> "I would like to hear that one." After playing it we said, "What
> else?" "You choose," he said. "Do you want to hear a late quartet?"
> Bobby Mann [the first violin] asked. "No," he replied, "but how

about the F Major, Opus 59." We played the work in its entirety.
During the slow movement, I glanced over at him. His head was
leaning back, his eyes were closed, he seemed to be concentrating
intensely. After we finished playing, we waited. He said nothing for
a while. [Then he said,] "You know, the slow movement of this
quartet must be the most tragic piece that Beethoven ever wrote."

"Would you like to hear anything else?" we asked. "You are
so kind," he said. "If you have the energy I would like to hear a little
of the F minor, Opus 95." We played three of the four movements
for him and by this time it was clear to us that he was really tiring
and that it was probably time for us to leave. "Please come again
when you are in the area. I would love to see you," he said. We bid
our fond farewells, wishing him stronger health, but we knew in our
hearts that we would never see him again. The ride back to the train
station was silent—each of us in his own private world of recollections. I thought of his strange comment to me in Paris. . . . "I am really not a very nice person. I have a bad character. Just ask my
family—they will tell you. But when it comes to the music, *the
music*—ah, that is where I have total integrity."[56]

Eva visited her father occasionally until the spring of 1981, when she
had a final falling-out with him. "That last time, I said the things that I had
been wondering about all those years," she recalled. "I asked him, 'How
could you have done this?' and 'Why did you do that?' and 'How could you
sleep at night?' The things that both he and I brought up at that last meeting
were probably *the* things in both our lives that we felt most unhappy or insecure about—he vis-à-vis himself and I vis-à-vis him. He didn't accuse me of
anything, that time; all the things he said were in defense of himself and accusing other people. He would say, 'Ach, well you know, when your mother
did this or that. . . .' He mentioned, again, the fact that she had gone ahead
and married poor Miecio Münz: 'Why didn't she understand?' he said. I said,
'Well, you didn't write to her for three months, while you were off with one of
your mistresses! She was eighteen—what do you expect? She was proud.' But
I couldn't get through to him. 'Then she trapped me into marrying her,' he
said. 'Why couldn't she have left things the way they were? We were happy—
everything was fine.' The next morning, Annabelle was screaming at me: 'All
those accusations! Why didn't you just comfort him?' But comfort him about
what? That he destroyed his family? That he made a bunch of neurotics out
of all his children, who then went on to do the same to others? The last thing
I ever heard him say was, 'Throw her out, throw her out.' " Immediately after
their final encounter, Rubinstein cut Eva out of his will, and she said that this

was done with Annabelle's encouragement. But Eva's portion of her father's legacy went directly to her children, not to Annabelle. And Annabelle said that she had thrown Eva out "to keep Arthur's fever from going up. It had nothing to do with the will. His fevers almost always came in the evening, but when Eva was there his fever went up even during the day." In a letter dictated several months later, Rubinstein said, "Eva came here full of love, got a lovely 3,000 dollars in her pocket and at the end insulted me in a way which is and will be impardonable [sic]."[57]

John wrote that his father, in his last years, "became more and more fixated on his will, and on 'righting the record' of his relationships with his children. He suffered, I believe, a great deal; feeling guilt for all kinds of different unhappy events, but also nurturing most of his old resentments about past perceived slights and injustices. He worked it all around and around." Once, when John was visiting him in Zurich, Arthur told him that he had decided to write Paul back into his will. " 'But you must never tell him while I'm alive, because he might then come and be nice to me, and I would suspect him of doing it just for the money!' " John was "very moved by his obvious sincerity, and overjoyed," he said. "In his secretive, strange, and defensive way, he desperately wanted to make peace with Paul, at least in his own heart. I promised that I would say nothing, and I felt jubilant." But the next day, "he told me curtly, 'I couldn't sleep all night. I've changed my mind! I won't leave anything to Paul. And it's your fault.' I was stunned. 'Why?' I asked. 'Because I can't trust you not to run to him and tell him, first thing. You never could keep a secret!' I argued and insisted and promised, but he didn't waver." Before long, he was expressing the notion that Paul was not his own son—an absurdity, according to the other children, not only because the idea seems not to have occurred to their father until Paul was in his mid-forties, but also because Paul, in his youth, looked even more like their father than any of the rest of them did—and they all bear striking resemblances to him.

Rubinstein seemed surprised that his children did not see Annabelle in the same light in which he saw her, and he occasionally accused them of being interested in his money but not in him; the two issues merged, in his mind. There were some ugly exchanges on these subjects, face to face and by telephone and letter, but, in the cases of John and Alina, he usually calmed down quickly. John, who was working on Broadway and raising two young children, was unable to visit his father often. They saw each other for the last time early in the summer of 1982, in Geneva. "I listened to music with him—a recording of the Rachmaninoff Third Concerto played by Joey Alfidi, who, as an eleven- or twelve-year-old kid, back in 1961, had sat in the front row center of most or all of my dad's ten Carnegie Hall recitals. My dad was very impressed with the recording," John said. (Three years earlier, Rubinstein had persuaded the conductor Emmanuel Krivine to engage Alfidi as soloist with Radio France's Nouvel Orchestre Philharmonique.) "We also watched television—he would sit very close, to be able to make something out. He had no appetite—he said so himself—and I remember discussing that with Annabelle. I took some pictures of him making his 'pig-face' "—one of the funny, rubbery grimaces that he had always been good at; "it moved me that as he approached his death, he still had that desire and ability to bring smiles and joy from me."

Alina, too, had complicated relations with her "escaped" father and with Annabelle, but she visited him several times, despite the awkwardness of the situation. "One of the last times I was in Europe when my father could still walk around, he insisted on taking me to the Richard Wagner house/museum in Lucerne, even though he had recently been there and was already almost completely blind from the senile retinal degeneration," she said in a letter. "It reminded me of how he had played practically the whole score of *Die Meistersinger* for Johnny and me as children, before the first time he took us to see it. He would get us so enthusiastic! He did the same before we heard for the first time the Brahms Requiem and the Mahler First Symphony during the Lucerne festival. I'll never forget those 'previews,' or hearing the music for the first time with my father." When she went to Geneva to see him in October 1982, "he spoke a lot about wanting to write a book—a little monograph, or something of the sort—about Chopin, to show that Chopin really wasn't a weakling, as he was usually portrayed," she said. "It was a burning issue, and he regretted that he might not be able to do it. My speculation is that he identified with Chopin and wanted to 'set the record straight' on Chopin, to show him as a strong man. I wonder if my father's wanting to write about Chopin, as he was dying, could have been motivated in part (unconsciously) by trying to deal with his old disappointment in his father's 'weakness' of character as well as his own weaknesses. He often said that he felt guilty about having survived so many years when geniuses like Mozart, Chopin, Schumann, Schubert died so prematurely. I'm sure my father spent a great deal of time in his last years replaying and reevaluating his whole life, his family, our family, his musical 'gods,' et cetera, as everyone probably does at the end.

"During that particular visit," Alina continued, "he had Annabelle make a lobster dinner, as if we were having a celebration; he was barely able to get two spoonfuls of soup down, but he still wanted to give me a good time. He didn't want it to be a horrible experience for me, coming to see a dying man—and that's the way he was, till the end. He gave me a book by Albert Cohen, *Le Livre de ma mère*, which I think he had read not long before. It is a son's eulogy for his dead mother, and he encouraged me to read it; I'm sure there's a message in there for me, somewhere, but I haven't been able to read it yet, for emotional reasons rationalized as lack of time. Somehow, as I was leaving, rushing to get my flight, I forgot to take the book. I realized it when I got downstairs; I went back to get it, and I found him already asleep on the couch. That was how I saw my father for the last time." It was the last time that any of his children saw him alive.

Although Rubinstein's strength continued to wane, he was never completely bedridden, and he continued to take an interest in world events. "When Brezhnev died, in November, he said he was sure that there was going to be a big, big change in Russia," Annabelle said. "'You'll see, Annabelle—take my word. You'll tell me about it!'—which he used to say about lots of things. He saw things incredibly clearly, right up until the end." Zubin Mehta visited him early in December, and on Sunday, December 19, Paul Tortelier and his wife came to see him. "Arthur played them a recording of the Double Concerto of Brahms with Rostropovich and Perlman," said Annabelle. "They clearly didn't like it—they were looking at each other and making faces—but Arthur thought it was marvelous." This work, which was written the year Rubinstein was born, and which he had heard Joachim and Hausmann—for whom Brahms had composed it—play in Berlin circa 1900, was the last piece of music he listened to.

The next morning, he awoke in the throes of another attack of septicemia. "I took his temperature; it was very high, so I immediately gave him antibiotics orally and called two doctors. They weren't available—as always happens, when you want a doctor—but then the fever started to go down, and I told him: 'It's marvelous—it's going down!' He still couldn't speak, but in the afternoon he pointed to his side. I asked, 'What is it? Is it hurting or is it itching?' And he made a motion, as much as to say that he didn't know. I said to him, 'Well you know that I love you.' And he just smiled." Annabelle paused for several seconds, in telling the story, then continued: "That I'll never forget, because it was the most incredible smile. His whole face just lit up. But I didn't even think the situation was serious. He had had fifty, sixty, a hundred of those fevers. Then, towards the evening, he started to have terrible difficulty in breathing." The Spanish couple who worked as domestic help for Arthur and Annabelle didn't speak French; thus, Annabelle "had to leave Arthur for a minute, to telephone the doctor and the ambulance," she said. "I told them to bring oxygen. Then I tried to put him on his side—I tried to change his position—something to make the breathing easier—but nothing worked. And then he suddenly stopped breathing. The ambulance came, with oxygen, and I said, 'Try, at least try artificial respiration. Try anything.' They did, but there was nothing to be done."

Rubinstein died at 6:30 P.M. on Monday, December 20, 1982, one month and eight days before his ninety-sixth birthday. His death was front-page news throughout the world, and tributes from colleagues and other celebrities were reported in the next day's newspapers and on radio and television. Although he had known that his desire to have his ashes spread over the Jerusalem forest would be difficult to fulfill, as Jewish religious law does not permit cremation, he had had so great a horror of the decomposition of the body that he had given John a slip of paper on which he had written his wish to be "incinerated"—just as the dying Chopin had written out instructions to have his veins opened after he died, so that he could not be buried alive, by accident. Nela, Eva, Alina, and John flew to Geneva; Paul was "unable to attend," according to the *New York Times*.[58] "I always remember the terrible moment when Arthur's body was taken out of the flat," Annabelle said. Alina "came over to me in front of the rest of the family and put her arms around me." The body was cremated on December 22. Eva told Reuters news agency that her father had left "strict instructions forbidding any ceremony . . . and so the gathering was short and informal, with no speeches and little music."[59] His ashes were eventually transferred to Israel, where the rabbinate had ruled that realizing the pianist's request would have meant placing the public park "under religious laws governing cemeteries," the Associated Press reported. But Rubinstein's friend Teddy Kollek, the mayor of Jerusalem, had made "a yearlong effort . . . to fulfill Rubinstein's wishes. . . . A compromise was reached under which a small plot was set aside for Rubinstein's grave."[60] The "Rubinstein Panorama," located within the city limits, in a pine forest planted in Rubinstein's honor seventeen years earlier, is where the ashes were interred on December 21, 1983, a year and a day after his death, in the presence of Nela, Eva, Alina, and Annabelle, while Shlomo Mintz played music by Bach.

I have always thought of myself as a musical instrument—neither violin nor piano—but "essence" of music. I never walk or dream or go to sleep without having music in my head. Music is "my form."[61]
—Arthur Rubinstein

Part II

The Recorded Legacy

The Recorded Legacy

In 1993, Alina Rubinstein went into a major Manhattan record store to buy one of her father's recordings. When she did not find the compact disc in the appropriate composer's bin, she asked a sales clerk whether the disc was out of stock and was told that she had been looking in the wrong place: "Rubinstein is in our 'Legends' section," he said.

One doesn't have to be a member of Rubinstein's family to be jolted by the "legendary" denomination. For most musicians and music lovers born before 1960, Rubinstein remains a real presence—a performing artist who was, or at least could have been, experienced firsthand—and the over-thirty-five-year-olds of the mid-1990s may have difficulty in grasping the significance of the fact that Rubinstein's last concerts took place two decades ago. To today's twenty-five-year-olds, Rubinstein is as historical a figure as Rachmaninoff to the fifty-year-olds and Busoni to the seventy-five-year-olds.

A generation ago, there was nothing historical about Rubinstein. He was a flesh-and-blood human being with a big, warm personality. For me, the musical year revolved around his appearances in Cleveland, where I grew up. Thanks to his friendship with George Szell, he came to the city virtually every season to play a special concert or two at Severance Hall with the Cleveland Orchestra, of which Szell was musical director, and he sometimes gave a solo recital under the auspices of the Cleveland Opera Association at the Public Music Hall. I first heard him in January 1959, when I was twelve; I was sitting with my mother near the center of the very last row of Severance Hall's balcony. During the first half of the concert, he played Beethoven's "Emperor" Concerto, and during the second half he played the Rachmaninoff Second. I won't pretend that I remember the performances, but the impression that Rubinstein's sound made was enormous, and the palpable excitement that his presence stirred in the audience was contagious. Afterward, I raced backstage and was taken to the pianist's dressing room by Maurice Wolfson, a violinist in the orchestra and a friend of my parents; John Rubinstein, who is exactly six months younger than I, was with his father. Like any self-respecting twelve-year-old, I asked Rubinstein for his autograph, which he gave me. A moment later, however, a horde of adult fans arrived en masse; when the first of them asked for an autograph, Rubinstein excused himself by telling her that he suffered from arthritis and wasn't able to move his fingers very well. She and the people behind her fell for his ploy and left him in relative peace.

During the following five years, I heard Rubinstein perform, with Szell and the Cleveland Orchestra, three Beethoven concertos (the Second, Third, and—two more times—the "Emperor"), the Brahms Second, the Chopin Second, the Liszt First, and the Mozart G Major (K. 453) and D Minor (K. 466), and I attended rehearsals at which he played the Beethoven First, Second, and Fourth, the Mozart D Minor, and the Schumann concertos. The concert of January 28, 1961, included the Liszt Concerto, and I remember Rubinstein rising slightly off the bench in the big octave scale passages toward the end of the last movement. I also recall that during a break in a rehearsal that included the Beethoven First Concerto, in January 1962, Rubinstein remained on stage for a few minutes to practice one of the cadenzas. When he had finished, he got up and, as he was walking off the stage, entertained the few people seated in the auditorium by singing the second subordinate theme (A Minor) of the finale as if it were a Latin American dance tune, while shuffling a few more or less appropriate steps. At another rehearsal—probably the following day—I handed Rubinstein a copy of a photograph of himself that Peter Hastings, the orchestra's photographer, had taken the previous year, and I asked him to sign it for me. "How old I look!" he said with dismay, as he glanced at the photo. (He does, in fact, look tired in the picture.) But he signed it, and I was thrilled. At twelve, fourteen, sixteen, one is concerned with questions of championship—Who is the biggest? the fastest? the strongest? the greatest?—and there was no doubt in my mind about Rubinstein's being the greatest living pianist. Vladimir Horowitz, who did not play in public between 1953 and 1965, was little more than a name to me, and the other celebrated pianists I heard in those years—Rudolf Serkin, Robert Casadesus, Emil Gilels, Svyatoslav Richter, Rudolf Firkušný, Van Cliburn, Gina Bachauer—did not have the extramusical aura that Rubinstein had, and that evidently appealed to me at that age. When Laszlo Krausz, a violist in the Cleveland Orchestra and a wise and witty man, told me that he much preferred Serkin's playing to Rubinstein's, I thought that he was joking, mad, or deaf, or all three. The only pianist who fascinated me almost as much as Rubinstein was Glenn Gould, but I only saw him twice; he, too, had extramusical appeal, although his could hardly have been less like Rubinstein's brand.

I have a fairly clear memory of an evening rehearsal of the Schumann Concerto during the 1963–64 season. Rubinstein arrived at the last minute, deposited his overcoat on a seat in the front row of the auditorium, and walked onto the stage; again, he looked tired. After a brief, whispered conference between pianist and conductor, the two of them and the orchestra went through the concerto virtually without stopping, as I recall, up to the tricky E Major passage in the last movement; there, at the piano's entry, Szell stopped to fix a few untidy orchestral details, but Rubinstein continued to play. "Artur, I must just clean this up a little," Szell said, but Rubinstein pressed on, beyond the piano's lyrical, eight-bar solo into the extended arpeggiated passage in which the piano "accompanies" the orchestra. Many of the orchestra members smirked behind their music stands, because the autocratic Szell was unaccustomed to opposition. Szell eventually shrugged, called out a rehearsal letter or number, and brought the orchestra in. There were no further stops until the end, when—after another whispered conference between soloist and conductor—Rubinstein left the stage while Szell cleaned up the orchestral passage that had bothered him. As Rubinstein, waiting for Szell to finish, paced up and down one of the aisles in the auditorium, another young music student and I walked boldly up to him and made standard, silly remarks about how much we were enjoying the rehearsal. "Do you call this a rehearsal?" Rubinstein asked, with mock indignation. "I was up very late last night—there was the annual Polish charity ball in New York and I was out dancing—and I had to fly out of Newark today, in the snow, on Allegheny Airlines." His right arm described terrifying aerial zigzags and figure eights. "Of course the flight was late. I came here right from the airport, and *he*"—pointing to Szell—"wants me to rehearse!" A moment later, Szell came down from the stage, walked over to Rubinstein, and grinned at him. "Come, old man," he said, "we take you home and put you to bed." (Szell was ten years younger than the seventy-seven-year-old Rubinstein.) A few moments later, as I walked across the Severance Hall parking lot, I saw Szell brushing snow from the windshield of his aging Cadillac while Rubinstein looked on, amused, his arms folded across his chest; he seemed to be saying, "My chauffeur is doing his duty."

The next morning, there was to have been a rehearsal of the "Emperor" Concerto for the evening's concert; I didn't want to miss it, so I generously gave myself permission to skip a few high school classes. When I got to the hall, I was disappointed to hear Szell announce that Rubinstein was still exhausted and that they would play the concerto that evening without rehearsal; the morning rehearsal was used for preparatory work on a subsequent program. Of course I went to the concert, and I was astonished to observe— from the front-row seat to which one orchestra member or another had kindly given me a ticket—that Rubinstein split what sounded like seamless arpeggios between his two hands and covered the breaks with the pedal. Afterward, I was pestering Szell with a technical question when a member of the orchestra's board of directors interrupted to declare that he had never heard such a wonderful performance of the "Emperor." In a serious tone of voice, Szell told him that it had gone so well because of all the rehearsal time that everyone had put into it. After the edified board member had departed, Szell chuckled and then admitted that sometimes, when artists knew each other as well as he and Rubinstein did, and when an orchestra knew a work as well as the Cleveland knew the "Emperor," a performance could gain from not being rehearsed. "But very rarely!" he added, emphatically.

During the 1965–66 season, Rubinstein made a number of Carnegie Hall appearances in conjunction with the sixtieth anniversary of his American debut in the same auditorium. I was a student at the Mannes College of Music in New York at the time, and I attended a concert in which he played three Mozart concertos—the G Major (K. 453), D Minor (K. 466), and A Major (K. 488)—with a rather good pick-up orchestra under the direction of Alfred Wallenstein. With an enlarged version of the same ensemble, again under Wallenstein's direction, he was to play both Brahms concertos on a single concert. The previous evening, a Mannes classmate and I went to Carnegie to hear the first New York recital in nearly twenty years of the pianist Arturo Benedetti Michelangeli, and we found ourselves sitting across the aisle from Rubinstein and his wife. With the boldness of my nineteen years, I went up to Rubinstein, during the intermission, and asked if my classmate and I could attend his rehearsal the following morning. He kindly gave his permission. Two details of the rehearsal of the Second Concerto are fixed in my memory. Before the second movement, which begins with three quick bars for the piano alone, Rubinstein waited for a moment, looking expectantly at Wallenstein; when nothing happened, he asked the conductor, "Aren't you going to give them a downbeat?" The piano enters on the second beat of a bar in ¾ time, and Rubinstein, who had had the piece in his repertoire for many decades, knew that if a conductor fails to indicate all three bars of rest to the orchestra, some players may make wrong entrances later on. Wallenstein seemed not to understand what Rubinstein was getting at. "Give them a beat," Rubinstein said. Wallenstein still looked confused. "Like this!" Rubinstein said. He stood up, gave a vigorous downbeat with his left arm, and continued to punch out the downbeats of the following three bars while his right hand played the piano's opening passage. After that, everything went smoothly. Then, at the end of the third movement, which contains long, sustained solo cello passages, Rubinstein stood up and told the principal cellist that in all the years in which he had played this concerto, he had never heard the solo done so beautifully. Some time later, I related this to a musician from another orchestra and was told that Rubinstein made this moving declaration to the first cellist of every orchestra with which he played this concerto, to ensure maximum dedication to the task at hand during the performance; I do not know whether or not this is true.

During the intermission in the rehearsal, my classmate and I walked over to Rubinstein, who was sitting in the auditorium, smoking a cigar and chatting in Russian with Alexander Schneider. We thanked him for letting us attend, and then, to my horror, my classmate asked him for his opinion of the Benedetti Michelangeli recital that we had all heard the previous evening. Fortunately, Rubinstein was in an expansive mood. "You know," he said, "we pianists aren't like conductors and singers who are always slamming each other. We are gentlemen. But you're music students, not journalists, so I don't mind telling you what I think." And with that, he handed down what amounted to a death-sentence for his colleague. The only detail I remember had to do with Debussy's *Poissons d'or*, about which Rubinstein said, more or less, "I've been playing that piece almost since it was written. There's not a lot of meat on its bones, but you have to find what there is. Well, what does this fellow do? He punches a few keys down there" (Rubinstein gesticulated as if he were playing a piano's bass keys with both hands) "and then he punches a few keys up here" (Rubinstein pretended to reach for the highest keys), "and what's it all for? It's to show you what a man named Michelangeli can do to the piano." Gentlemen, indeed!

Through the 1960s, in Cleveland, New York, and, later, Toronto, I also heard Rubinstein play a fair sampling of his recital repertoire: only one Beethoven sonata (C Major, Op. 3, No. 2) and none of the Brahms *Klavierstücke*, but four pieces by Debussy ("Hommage à Rameau," "Ondine," *Poissons d'or*, and one of the Preludes—but I've forgotten which one), Rubinstein's own arrangement of the "Ritual Fire Dance" from Falla's *El amor brujo*, Liszt's Twelfth Hungarian Rhapsody, Ravel's *Valses nobles et sentimentales*, Villa-Lobos's *Polichinelle*, and, above all, a great deal of Chopin—the Andante spianato and Grande Polonaise Brillante; the Ballades in G Minor and A-flat Major; the C-sharp Minor and E Minor Etudes; the Fantasy in F Minor; the Impromptu in G-flat Major; a mazurka (I don't remember which one); the Polonaises in F-sharp Minor and A-flat Major; the Preludes in D-flat, F, and A-flat Major and D Minor; the Scherzos in B Minor and B-flat Minor; the Sonata in B-flat Minor; the Tarantella; and the Waltzes in A Minor, F Major, C-sharp Minor, and A-flat Minor. I heard him play several of these pieces two, three, or even four times, and I still remember—or have fooled myself into thinking that I remember—how he phrased and pedalled certain passages in some of the pieces. Above all, I remember (of this I am certain) Rubinstein's deep, generous sound and magnetic presence. About the sound, more will be said in due course. As to magnetic presence, the entire concept now holds for me little of the fascination that it held when I was an adolescent, because I know more than I knew then about audience behavior and about the potential effects of magnetic presences on crowds of human beings. And yet Rubinstein did exude dignity, composure, and concentration when he played; his whole being communicated with remarkable force his love of music and his pleasure in re-creating it.

My other contacts with Rubinstein were epistolary and, with a single exception, one-way. In going through his papers, in 1990, I was first astonished, then embarrassed, and finally moved to find two letters that I had sent him. One was a fan letter written after the first time I heard him, when I was twelve. The second item, written three years later, was a request for an opinion on a textual question in the last movement of Beethoven's First Piano Concerto, which I was learning. Neither letter received an answer, and some-one—not Rubinstein—had written the words "nothing requested" on the second one. I wrote to Rubinstein again, when I was nineteen, to ask whether he would let me interview him for a radio series on Toscanini that I wrote and announced for WCLV-FM in Cleveland. This letter he answered. He would be delighted to participate, he wrote, because he and his older musician friends knew each other so well that they had nothing more to say to each other, and he would enjoy talking to a young musician for a change. But the interview was never arranged, and I have lost Rubinstein's letter.

I suppose it was inevitable that such intense admiration be followed by a period of rejection. By 1972, when I last heard Rubinstein—in a recital at Toronto's Massey Hall—I had fastened onto some fairly dogmatic ideas about music-making and had become disenchanted with Rubinstein's approach. As he was not at his best that evening I assumed that he had begun an irreversible decline (he was eighty-five years old, after all), and I made no effort to hear him again. This was exceedingly stupid of me: I now know that when he was "on," in his very last seasons, Rubinstein delivered some of his most memorable performances. Although I cannot claim to have become wise, musically or in other respects, on reaching middle age, I believe that my current attitude toward Rubinstein's music-making, as his work has been preserved through recordings, is far removed from both the nearly unquestioning adoration with which I listened to it in my adolescence and the partial antagonism that I felt toward it during the following decade or so.

THIS SURVEY OF some of Rubinstein's recordings is a highly personal one, and it requires a few explanations and general comments. Like most other musicians of his generation, Rubinstein was not much interested in using "clean," musicologically correct editions of the works he played, although his papers demonstrate that during the 1960s and '70s he encouraged Günter Henle and other original-text publishers and editors in their work. Late in Rubinstein's life, Eunice Podis visited him in Marbella and was "surprised," she said, that "there in his living room, piled up on the nine-foot Steinway grand, was a bunch of Schirmer editions, which he did not hesitate to use. By that time, we were hiding Schirmer editions in brown paper covers—you didn't dare be seen with one." The G. Schirmer company published editions that had been heavily edited by nineteenth-century musicians who were considered specialists in one composer or another—Hans von Bülow's Beethoven, Karl Mikuli's and Rafael Joseffy's Chopin, and so on. Thus, certain phrasings, dynamics, pedalings, embellishments, and even notes, here and there in Rubinstein's recordings, do not correspond to current notions about what is correct and what is not. In some cases the differences are substantial; in others they are insignificant. With respect to embellishments (grace notes and the like), Rubinstein was a man of his generation, inasmuch as he played most of them before the beat rather than on it, regardless of whether they were written as acciaccaturas, appoggiaturas, mordents, or anything else. Having said this, I will not refer to the matter again in my comments on individual recordings, and only in a few significant cases will I point out wrong notes, other major and minor keyboard accidents, or the frequent, stray sounds of clicking fingernails and clogged sinuses. Although most of Rubinstein's recordings were made in the magnetic tape era, and although he was not averse to judicious editing, he preferred a flawed take that captured the feeling he wished to convey to a flawless one that did not.

My first realization, on listening to the Rubinstein recordings en bloc as I prepared to write this section, was that they have truly become historical recordings, inasmuch as they reveal a directness of approach, a nonfussiness, that has become uncommon—although not impossible to find—nowadays. A few years ago, James Levine voiced the opinion that the trouble with many contemporary performances of traditional repertoire is that they are either eccentric or anonymous. Rubinstein's performances were neither: His playing had strong individual character, but his goal was not to do "something different," at any cost. From the 1940s until the end of his career, he was often labelled by music critics and newspaper feature writers with such epithets as "the last of the Romantic pianists" and "the Romantic poet of the piano," but these commentators were reading his public persona into his playing. To the extent that "Romantic" implies impassioned and communicative, Rubinstein's playing was Romantic, but it did not have the self-absorbed and self-indulgent characteristics that this adjective has also come to represent. In this sense, although in few others, he was closer to his German-school contemporaries Schnabel, Fischer, and Kempff than to such Eastern European contemporaries (albeit somewhat older contemporaries) as Rachmaninoff and

Hofmann, let alone to Horowitz, who was seventeen years younger than Rubinstein but stylistically closer to the old-timers. Listeners who wish to hear an unfettered, Romantic approach to Chopin, for instance, should turn to the recordings of Paderewski, Vladimir de Pachmann, Rachmaninoff, or, to some extent, Horowitz; Rubinstein's Chopin—even as heard in the more freewheeling pre–World War II recordings—is thoroughly modern.

My survey moves in a loosely chronological way, composer by composer, but without separating composers whom I wished to group by national schools or for other, equally obvious reasons. To avoid turning this chapter into an encyclopedia, I will not compare Rubinstein's versions of specific works with the versions of other pianists, except in a few special cases. Technically speaking, BMG's and EMI's transfers of Rubinstein's recordings to CDs (they were originally issued on 78, 45 or 33⅓ rpm records) seem to me excellent, on the whole; in particular, the Chopin recordings produced by Max Wilcox in the late 1950s and the 1960s emerge with a warm, natural sound. Among the recordings discussed in this chapter, those that are currently (1995) out of print will be marked with an asterisk (*), but I will not bore readers by repeatedly mentioning those recordings that I have *not* heard. (Exact dates and other information about in-print and out-of-print recordings, including those not discussed here, can be found in Donald Manildi's discography, which follows this chapter.) Nor will I discuss Rubinstein's piano roll performances—1919–25—some of which have been released on Italian and Australian CDs; they differ strikingly from the performances heard on the later 78 and 33⅓ rpm recordings: on the whole, they are more brilliant and more erratic, but they are also strangely mechanical and jerky— qualities that are probably attributable to the rolls themselves. (Readers may recall, from chapter 4, that Rubinstein disliked the medium and expressed shame at having participated in the producing companies' promotional campaigns.) I do not trust the accuracy of piano rolls.

A final caveat: I am an opinionated man. For many years, I have refused to review concerts or opera performances, except in a few special cases, because I know that my tastes, like everyone else's, are restricted, and that I would later regret most of the opinions, positive and negative, that I handed down. To discuss recordings is a somewhat different matter, because one can listen to a recording as many times as one pleases—and when one is in the right frame of mind—before one tries to formulate an opinion. I have learned, however, to mistrust my opinions of recordings, too, because—as I wrote in an earlier book—a mysterious virus causes certain recorded performances to change, as they sit, unplayed, on my shelves; when I return to recordings that I have set aside for several years, I discover details that I would have sworn were not there before. So take these opinions for what they are—

temporary assessments—and then listen to the recordings and draw your own conclusions.

RUBINSTEIN CONSIDERED **Bach** one of the greatest of all keyboard composers (Play " 'Bach, Bach, and again Bach,' Rubinstein used to say," according to Moura Lympany),[1] but he performed Bach's music only in nineteenth- and early-twentieth-century arrangements. On the other hand, he was highly critical of Romanticized performances of Bach. Speaking about Casals, Rubinstein told Eric Lipmann: "He transformed Bach into Schumann! He played him with so much Romantic exaggeration that the audience was in heaven. My God, people wept! Bach, this severe gentleman who composed 'Ta, ta-ta-ta-ta-ta-ti-ti-ti-ta-ta.' With Casals, this became 'Taaaa! - tah-tah-tah——tah-taaaaah! titititi! TAAAAH! TAAAA! Nanananiaaaaaah!' "[2] Rubinstein's 1970 version of Busoni's arrangement of the Chaconne from Bach's Partita No. 2 in D Minor for unaccompanied violin is beautiful; he plays the work as Busoni apparently intended—as a masterpiece of Romantic expression, in other words—but there is no bombast and no huffing and puffing in his introspective, sometimes despairing, occasionally forceful, and always strictly controlled playing. Whatever one may think of the arrangement, this performance was a remarkable achievement for the eighty-three-year-old pianist.

E. T. A. Hoffmann considered **Haydn** a Romantic composer, and the Variations in F Minor (also called Sonata, Piccolo Divertimento, and Andante and Variations)—written in 1793, when Haydn was sixty-one—comprise one of the composer's most intensely personal works as well as one of his last pieces for the keyboard. The restrained but profound expressiveness of Rubinstein's only recording (1960) of the piece is exemplary. He plays the theme in surprisingly understated tones and at a natural basic tempo—sober but not slow—from which he makes logical and convincing departures in the individual variations. Once in a while the pedal is overemployed, but on the whole the performance is clear-voiced and beautiful.

Although **Mozart**-Rubinstein is not a pairing that springs to mind as readily as Chopin-Rubinstein, Mozart was one of Rubinstein's great musical loves. And yet, so far as I have been able to determine, Rubinstein played only six of Mozart's twenty-seven piano concertos, and one of these six—the last, in B-flat Major, K. 595—he played rarely and did not record. Of the solo piano works, only the Rondo in A Minor, with which the ten-year-old Rubinstein had made so profound an impression on Joachim, appeared in the adult Rubinstein's programs and was recorded by him. He played the E Minor Violin and Piano Sonata, K. 304, in public with Kochanski and possibly also with others, but he did not record it. The two piano quartets that he recorded with members of the Guarneri Quartet did not figure in his concert repertoire. One wonders in vain why he did not perform such works as the Concerto in C Major, K. 503; the Sonata in A Minor, K. 310; the Sonata in D Major, K. 576; and at least half a dozen other compositions related in expressive content to those that he did play.

To my ears, his Mozart concerto recordings are a mixture of great virtues and easily explainable defects. His only recording (1961) of the Concerto No. 17 in G Major, K. 453, with the RCA Victor Symphony Orchestra under Alfred Wallenstein, is beautifully conceived but too carefully executed. The tempi all feel natural and the rapid Mozartian transitions from lightheartedness to dead seriousness are perfectly grasped and never overplayed, but many individual phrases are heavily overlaid with nuances that seem too self-conscious. I wish that I could recall the two live performances of the work that I heard Rubinstein give, but I cannot. I do, however, remember the impact of his playing of the Concerto No. 20 in D Minor, K. 466, and I find that his 1961 recording of the work, again with Wallenstein and the RCA Symphony, renews and strengthens the impression. Rubinstein's tempi are brisk, and his poise and elegance are perfectly matched by his intensity and sensitivity to the work's drama—whereas most pianists play this work either elegantly and undramatically or dramatically and inelegantly. It is hard to imagine a better performance of the jaunty subordinate theme in the finale—but then, it is hard to imagine a better all-around performance of most of the concerto. We have become unaccustomed to hearing great pianists play Mozart so straightforwardly; thus, this recording leaves one feeling both elated and nostalgic. (I have heard a live 1963 performance of the concerto by Rubinstein, Carlo Maria Giulini, and the Philharmonia Orchestra of London, on various "pirate" labels, but it is much heavier and less gripping than the authorized RCA recording.) The same sort of direct, refreshing music-making is to be heard in the first two movements of the Concerto No. 21 in C Major, K. 467, recorded by the same forces in the same year. I was not surprised by Rubinstein's completely satisfying rendering of the playful first movement, but I was surprised—pleasantly surprised—by the lack of Romantic inflation in his playing of the second movement, which, since it was used in the sound track of the film *Elvira Madigan*, has been the victim of various moonstruck interpretations. Once again, Rubinstein plays with profound but restrained emotion. The performance of the last movement is not up to the standard of the rest: The energy flags a little, here and there, and the verve seems somewhat forced.

The Concerto No. 23 in A Major, K. 488, which Rubinstein had first played under Joachim's baton during the 1899–1900 school year in Berlin, figured in his concert and recorded repertoires more often than any other piece by Mozart. His 1949 version, with Golschmann and the St. Louis Symphony, is beautifully played and full of life. A 1955 radio broadcast (available on a pirate CD), with Otmar Nussio and the Italian Swiss Radio Orchestra of Lugano, is pedestrian by comparison, but it is better than Rubinstein's final authorized recording of the piece, made in 1961 with Wallenstein and the RCA Symphony. This version is disappointingly scaled-down with respect to sound and overly cautious with respect to tempos; there seems to be little muscle and nerve in the performance, and the same is true of Rubinstein's 1958 recording of the Concerto No. 24 in C Minor, K. 491, again with the RCA Symphony but this time under the baton of Josef Krips. Here, too, the pianist may have been concentrating too hard on not making mistakes in the passagework, and the results are often pale or heavy-handed. Similar criticisms apply to Rubinstein's 1959 recording of the Rondo in A Minor, K. 511: Although the performance is well thought out, it is miniaturized—overly delicate and, at the same time, over-pedalled.

To my way of thinking, Rubinstein's 1971 recordings of the Mozart piano quartets with members of the Guarneri Quartet are well-brought-off realizations of fundamentally wrongheaded concepts of the works; they are the least successful of Rubinstein's collaborations with the Guarneri and the least successful of his Mozart recordings. Most of the tempi are on the slow side, but this is not the essence of the problem. Rubinstein seems to be trying to demonstrate that these works are charged with deep emotion—as indeed they are—but the lightness of touch with which he successfully achieves a similar demonstration in the D Minor Concerto, for instance, is missing here. There is an exaggeratedly legato quality to the melodic lines, and the result of the attempt to make each phrase pregnant with significance is a loss of coherence. Despite all the players' best efforts, the phrases often sag in the middle. And one notices for the first time a problem that occurs in some of the other recordings made during Rubinstein's last half-dozen active years: His playing is often too loud. The problem almost certainly stemmed from his deteriorating hearing and is therefore understandable and excusable, but it is still a problem.

In a 1962 newspaper interview, Rubinstein expressed his view of the musical-historical transition from Haydn and Mozart to **Beethoven**. "I call Beethoven the greatest romantic because he is the one who dared to break the line of that severe classicism which was Mozart and Haydn," he said. "You see, Mozart and Haydn have just as much emotion in them . . . as any Beethoven had. For me Mozart can express in a few bars more than Beethoven in a whole movement of a sonata. I *adore* Mozart; he is my great, great, great, deep love. The thing is simply that Mozart was able to put all his heart and soul, his musical talent, his genius, into the forms, into the mould. . . .

But Beethoven was the first one who risked [showing his personal feelings]. . . ."[3] In interviewing Daniel Barenboim, I expressed the opinion that Beethoven wasn't "Rubinstein's composer," and that his feelings about Beethoven were ambivalent. "I know what you mean, but I don't know that I agree with you," Barenboim said. "Rubinstein had innumerable qualities, but two of them stand uppermost. One was his sense of rhythm: It was like a backbone, and I think that this is what made his playing of a lot of heroic pieces by Chopin so unique—the element of pride that comes out in this music. And of course for Beethoven rhythm is capital. The other quality was the unique, full-bodied sound. But for Beethoven, I think the problem of interpretation was solved, for him, by his fantastic sense of rhythm, and— whenever there was a transition or something of the sort—the problem was always solved from the point of view of the sound. From that point of view, I suppose you could say that Beethoven was not especially his composer; I think he must have known this, because although he never [in later years] played late Beethoven, he knew those sonatas inside out. I remember that he talked to me about the 'Hammerklavier.' But a lot of the heroic pieces, like the 'Waldstein,' had a wonderful structural sanity to them, and obviously also the more lyrical pieces, like the G Major Concerto."[4]

I began to listen with special interest to Rubinstein's Beethoven recordings, after a hiatus of quite a few years, and I found, here as in most of Rubinstein's other recordings, a degree of directness that is becoming increasingly difficult to find. There is no posturing, no monumentalizing, no excess rhetoric. But I also had the feeling, especially in the concertos but to some extent also in the solo and chamber music, that Rubinstein's Beethoven lacked the remarkable combination of instinct and conviction that his Chopin and Brahms recordings demonstrate. The issue has nothing to do with liking or not liking his performances of specific works: I agree with Rubinstein's approach to some of Beethoven's works more than I agree with his approach to certain pieces by Chopin or Brahms. In the music of Chopin and Brahms, however—and to a considerable degree also in the music of Schumann, Rachmaninoff, Ravel, and the Spanish composers—I nearly always feel that Rubinstein is absolutely sure of his concept of the piece *at that moment* and that he *must* communicate it in that way and no other. His Beethoven does not usually convey to me such security and urgency.

For most of his professional life, Rubinstein played only the Fourth of Beethoven's five piano concertos with any frequency, but in his last active decades all five were part of his standard concerto repertoire. His live, 1944 broadcast-performance of the Third with Toscanini and the NBC Symphony Orchestra was issued on records, and in 1947 he recorded the Fourth with Sir Thomas Beecham and the Royal Philharmoic Orchestra of London.* He later recorded all five concertos three times: in 1956 with Josef Krips and the Symphony of the Air; between 1963 and 1967 with Erich Leinsdorf and the Boston Symphony Orchestra; and in 1975 with Daniel Barenboim and the London Philharmonic Orchestra.* The Krips set presents Rubinstein's most dandyish Beethoven performances, replete with fussy phrasings and prettified dynamics and articulations; in addition, Krips's conducting is for the most part humdrum. The Barenboim set bears witness to the undiminished verve and intelligence of Rubinstein at eighty-eight and—thanks to advanced technology—comes closest to reproducing Rubinstein's rich sound, but the exaggeratedly slow tempi that the aged pianist often had to adopt in order to manage the fast passages, and the exaggerated accentuations that the slow tempi occasioned, are a major drawback. The middle set, with Leinsdorf, seems to me the best of the three.

In all three versions of the Concerto No. 1 in C Major, Op. 15, and the Concerto No. 2 in B-flat Major, Op. 19, Rubinstein seems in his element only in the rondo finales, which he plays wittily and in which he gives pungent individuality to each theme. The first movements are flawed by a somewhat slack, two-to-the-bar pulse, instead of the four-to-the-bar pulse that must characterize them, regardless of whether they are taken at very quick or only moderately quick tempos; otherwise, they fall into a repetitive STRONG-weak, STRONG-weak rut. If the pulse weakens—and it often does in all three of Rubinstein's recordings of both first movements—the loud parts become heavy rather than robust and the soft parts dainty rather than expectant; the overall structure feels more episodic than it really is, and the sixteenth-note scales and arpeggios in the C Major Concerto emerge as filler material rather than brilliant flourishes. In the second movements of both works, and indeed of all the concertos except the Fourth, the sustained, silvery sound that Rubinstein often adopted seems to me more appropriate to Chopin than to Beethoven.

In the 1944 recording of the Concerto No. 3 in C Minor, Op. 37, Rubinstein and Toscanini were ill-matched, and the result is an unsuccessful compromise between two musicians with good intentions but highly dissimilar musical personalities. And yet, in this performance, as in the 1947 Rubinstein-Beecham* recording of the Concerto No. 4 in G Major, Op. 58, there is a dynamism in Rubinstein's playing that his later recordings of these works do not have. All the later versions of the concertos, one suddenly realizes, are more cautious—too cautious, for the most part—and have fewer emotional high and low points, and less color. There is a note-to-note and bar-to-bar tension in the 1944 recording of the Third that is largely absent from the later versions, which include—besides the performances in the three complete sets—a pirate recording of a 1967 performance with Antal Dorati and the

London Philharmonic. And the Fourth, with Beecham, seems to me the most natural and the most successful of all of Rubinstein's Beethoven concerto recordings. To satisfy my own curiosity, I timed six Rubinstein recordings of this concerto (there are pirate recordings with Dimitri Mitropoulos and Dorati, in addition to the four official versions), subtracting the duration of the variable cadenzas from the first and last movements. Here are the results:

- Beecham, Royal Philharmonic, 1947: first movement, 13:56; second movement, 4:51; third movement, 8:24
- Mitropoulos, New York Philharmonic, 1951: 13:52, 4:43, 8:24
- Krips, Symphony of the Air, 1956: 14:58, 4:42, 9:08
- Leinsdorf, Boston Symphony, 1964: 14:50, 4:38, 9:06
- Dorati, Royal Philharmonic, 1967: 15:01, 4:47, 9:09
- Barenboim, London Philharmonic, 1975: 16:26, 5:25, 9:49

Although Mitropoulos's approach to the piece was more erratic than Beecham's, and the New York Philharmonic's playing more slovenly than that of the Royal Philharmonic, Rubinstein's concept was essentially the same in both performances. (In both, Rubinstein played his own cadenzas, which contain touches of Chopin, Liszt, Debussy, Rachmaninoff—and even Beethoven; in all the later recordings, he played Beethoven's cadenzas with Busoni's revisions.) In the following three versions, only the tempi of the second movement remain fundamentally the same as in the earlier recordings, whereas the first and third movements are not only slower but also more warily played than in their predecessors. In the last of the six recordings, the basic tempi of all three movements are much slower than in any of the others. And yet the faster tempi are not what make the 1947 recording more beautiful and involving than the later versions. The sharper contrasts between the work's lyric and dramatic elements and the greater degree of *apparent* impulsiveness in the playing—seconded by a conductor who, by his own admission, was not an enthusiastic Beethovenian, but who seems to have understood this work very well and who had character to burn—are the qualities that make this the most gripping performance. I don't agree with some of the radical tempo modifications in the first movement or with quite a few details of phrasing, dynamics, and articulation in various places, but I love this recording for its freshness and communicativeness.

Memory of things heard tends to be even more empirical, subjective, and quirky than memory of things seen, but I would swear that the performances of the Concerto No. 5 in E-flat Major, Op. 73 ("Emperor"), that I heard Rubinstein play in 1962 and 1964 with Szell and the Cleveland Orchestra were more boldly delineated and sharper in dynamic contrasts than any of Rubinstein's published recordings of the work. (These include not only the three authorized versions but also a 1967 pirate recording of a live performance with Dorati and the London Philharmonic.) There is a great deal to admire, however, in each of these recordings, and especially in the 1965 version with Leinsdorf, who may not have been an inspiring partner but who gave Rubinstein firm and intelligent support. Whereas the Fourth is the most personal of the five concertos, the "Emperor" is the most assertive, and Rubinstein realizes the propulsive force of the first movement, the anticipatory stillness of the second, and the wild joyousness of the third.

Rubinstein recorded only seven of Beethoven's thirty-two piano sonatas. In general, I find the sonata recordings that I have heard more satisfying than his recordings of the concertos, although I disagree with two aspects of his approach. Sometimes—especially in melancholy themes in the early-period sonatas—he used the damper and una corda pedals simultaneously and overplayed the melody; and for *sforzati,* arrowhead accents, and loud staccato octaves he tended to use the same big, round sound that he used in "regular" forte passages, so that some of the jagged rhythms and wild salvos that characterize much of Beethoven's writing sound too tame. My guess is that Rubinstein softened the violence because it was at odds with his ideal piano sound, which was melodic rather than percussive; but Beethoven requires both. These tendencies are very much in evidence in the second theme and development section of the first movement of the Sonata No. 3 in C Major, Op. 2, No. 3ᵃ—the earliest Beethoven sonata that Rubinstein recorded (He recorded it only once, a few days before his seventy-sixth birthday.) On the other hand, he beautifully captured the impish nonchalance of the movement's first theme and the dreamy quality that dominates the second movement. The main part of the third movement (scherzo) seems overly deliberate, but Rubinstein evidently sought a tempo that he could also use in the tempestuous trio section—which he plays excellently—without losing control. His pianism is perfectly tailored to the finale, with its whimsical principal and first subordinate themes and its soaring, almost Brahmsian second subordinate theme (F Major), and he brings the movement off with naturalness and verve.

The noble restraint that characterized Rubinstein's playing of Haydn's Variations in F Minor also characterizes his playing of the first movement of Beethoven's Sonata No. 8 in C Minor, Op. 13 ("Pathétique"), in the 1962 recording. In the introduction, the pedal is used too much, but the overall tone is sober and dignified. The second theme, as Rubinstein plays it, is extremely subtle, even understated, especially in comparison with most of his colleagues' versions, but its quiet lyricism builds gradually until the beginning of the *decrescendo*. The dynamic range of the development section, too, is scaled down, but its impact is not. The second movement's melodic line sings—in accordance with Beethoven's cantabile indication—and its classic proportions are rendered with great freedom but also with great clarity. Rubinstein builds the last movement's tension skillfully, from the subdued first statement of the main theme to the final, wild outburst of the twenty-eight-year-old composer's youthful anger.

Rubinstein made his sole recording of the Sonata No. 14 in C-sharp Minor, Op. 27, No. 2 ("Moonlight"), in 1962, at the age of seventy-five. Its first movement is somewhat slower than the composer's alla breve indication seems to prescribe, but the pianist's strong rhythm keeps the performance from languishing. He focuses the listener's attention not only on the intensity but also on the dignity of this music's sadness; the expressive swells are contained within the reduced dynamic scale that the score demands. The second movement also feels a little too slow here, but it is remarkably graceful. Even more remarkable, however, is his management of the left hand in this movement's trio section: One hears the tenor and bass lines as distinct entities, but each is expressed with great simplicity and blends wonderfully with the other. This is music that any third- or fourth-year piano student ought to be able to play, but only a master can make such exquisite sense of it. One is accustomed to hearing the opening of the fiery finale played as a sequence of three two-bar crescendos and two one-bar crescendos, but Rubinstein plays the passage as Beethoven wrote it: quietly until the *sforzato* outburst on the last beat of each two- or one-bar phrase. I have occasionally heard more impassioned performances of this movement, but I have more often heard jumbled, clattering, out-of-control versions, even from celebrated keyboard artists. Once again, Rubinstein's approach to Beethoven is classical in its restraint.

The first movement of the Sonata No. 18 in E-flat Major, Op. 31, No. 3, is too affected and fussy in Rubinstein's 1954 recording of the work; he even takes the bizarre liberty of ending the first crescendo and its various repetitions on a piano instead of giving the *sforzato* that Beethoven indicated (bars 6, 15, etc.). This is not an insignificant detail: it changes the character of the main theme. In the second movement—Scherzo: Allegretto vivace—Rubinstein emphasizes the "allegretto" at the expense of the "scherzo" and the "vivace" and plays too carefully. And in the minuet, which is marked "Moderato e grazioso," he opts for a cantabile quality that seems too emphatic; he raises the tempo by two or three notches in the trio section, and the body of the movement would probably have benefited from being played at the same tempo. For the finale, however, Rubinstein finds and maintains just the right tone of lighthearted abandon. He rerecorded this sonata in April 1976,* at what proved to be his last recording sessions; the negative characteristics of the first and third movements are even stronger in the later version than in the earlier one, but so are the positive qualities of the fourth movement. And the second movement, in the 1976 recording, is the true "Scherzo: Allegretto vivace" that it was not in 1954: it tears along humorously at a pace that would have required remarkable virtuosity in a pianist in the prime of life, let alone one in his ninetieth year whose eyes could no longer focus on the keyboard.

I imagine that if Rubinstein had recorded the Sonata No. 21 in C Major, Op. 53 ("Waldstein"), in the 1930s or the 1960s he would have left a more intense and more convincing version than his sole, 1954 recording proves to be. Of course this performance has some outstanding characteristics, notably its strong rhythm and the distinct shape of its every phrase. But Rubinstein's tendencies to soften *sforzati* and staccatos and to pedal through rests are seriously detrimental to the piece's overall impact, especially in the first movement: he plays within so restricted a dynamic range and with such weak contrasts in accentuation that this magnificent music sounds bland. Similar defects plus some heavy overpedaling mar the brief second movement (which Beethoven described as an "introduction" to the finale). The last movement comes off better than its predecessors because Rubinstein at last makes some strong dynamic contrasts, but even here he is not at his best. Perhaps he was exaggerating the much-discussed "Apollonian" qualities of this work, to heighten the contrast with the "Dionysian" piece that came next, chronologically, in his Beethoven sonata repertoire.

"The left hand should be your Kapellmeister, while your right hand plays 'ad libitum,'" Rubinstein told Lipmann.[5] In other words, as long as the left hand maintains the basic pace, the right hand can take rhythmic liberties. But in the first movement of Beethoven's Sonata No. 23 in F Minor, Op. 57 ("Appassionata"), Rubinstein sometimes interrupts the flow of the left hand's eighth-note triplets—in the passage that runs from bar 26 to bar 42, for instance—in order to give freer rein to the right hand, and the result is extremely unnatural. For the rest, however, this recording, made in 1963, is much more convincing than that of the "Waldstein": Rubinstein is not afraid, here, of dramatic outbursts or strong dynamic contrasts, although even in the whirlwind finale he never makes a harsh or ugly sound. The second movement is especially beautiful, and Rubinstein's non-legato approach to the main theme of the last movement feels right and works splendidly. I cannot imagine that he would have wanted the banging, disjointed, and sloppy version of the "Appassionata" that was videotaped in Pasadena, California, in 1975, during a live benefit recital for Israel, to be released, but released it was, on videocassette and CD, ten years after his death. I shall not comment further on this or the other performances contained in that recital.

One wonders in vain how Rubinstein approached the Sonata No. 27 in

E Minor, Op. 90, and the Sonata No. 29 in B-flat Major, Op. 106 ("Hammerklavier"), both of which figured frequently in his concert repertoire during the first half of his career. In the latter half, the last of the Beethoven
sonatas that he played was No. 26 in E-flat Major, Op. 81a ("Les Adieux"),
which he recorded in 1940* and 1962; I know only the latter version, and I
consider it the finest of all of Rubinstein's Beethoven sonata recordings that I
have heard. He plays the poetic introduction to the first movement—which
Beethoven called "The Farewell"—with great warmth and intense but contained expressiveness. For the body of the movement, he takes a moderate
tempo but propels it forward through the drive of his rhythm and, even more,
the sweep of his phrasing. In addition to giving the title "Absence" to the
second movement, Beethoven took the trouble to write out a German elabo-
ration of the Italian indication "Andante espressivo": "At a walking pace, but
with much expression." Rubinstein's realization of this movement's tender
longing and quiet ambiguity is very fine indeed, and equally wonderful is his
exuberant and exhilarating playing of the last movement—"The Return"
("At the quickest tempo," Beethoven commanded)—in which he even refrains from pedalling through rests.

     Max Wilcox's 1974 report to RCA, quoted in chapter 6, mentions that
Rubinstein wanted to record two other Beethoven sonatas—No. 15 in D
Major, Op. 28 ("Pastorale"), and No. 17 in D Minor, Op. 31, No. 2 ("Tempest")—toward the end of his career, but he did not manage to do so. Thus,
the only other compositions by Beethoven in his recorded repertoire are
chamber works. In the early 1950s, Rubinstein met Henryk Szeryng, a young
Polish violinist, in Mexico, where Szeryng was living. He was impressed with
Szeryng's playing, and between 1958 and 1961 the two musicians made a series of sonata recordings that helped to launch a major international career
for Szeryng. (Rubinstein also recommended Szeryng to Hurok and other
managers and persuaded RCA to engage the violinist to record the Brahms
Concerto with Monteux; the result was one of the finest recordings of that
work ever made.) Among the pieces that they recorded together were three of
Beethoven's ten sonatas for violin and piano: No. 5 in F Major, Op. 24
("Spring"); No. 8 in G Major, Op. 30, No. 3; and No. 9 in A Major, Op. 47
("Kreutzer"). All three are exceptionally beautiful and bear witness to a true
partnership rather than a marriage of convenience. Szeryng's sound is less
rich than Rubinstein's, but a fine balance is maintained without any apparent
sacrifice on the part of either musician. The two artists allow the "Spring"
Sonata to unfold its charms in as natural a way as I have ever heard; they play
the G Major with a combination of effervescence and charm reminiscent of
the old Kreisler-Rachmaninoff recording of the piece; and they bring to the
"Kreutzer" all the vigor, poetry, and diabolical virtuosity that it demands. I

wish that the two musicians had recorded the A Minor, Op. 23; the C Minor, Op. 30, No. 3; the G Major, Op. 96; and—why not?—the other four sonatas, too.

Beethoven's Trio in B-flat Major, Op. 97 ("Archduke"), was one of the three works that Rubinstein recorded in September 1941 with Heifetz and Feuermann; the background to these recordings was discussed in chapter 6. The most immediately striking quality of this "Archduke" is its anti-monumentality, its absolute lack of rhetorical emphasis. This is not a reverent performance of Beethoven-as-Milestone-in-Western-Civilization, but rather a vital performance of one of Beethoven's most noble—and also most playful—works. The recordings that these three master players made together do not have the unity of conviction that the best permanent ensembles acquire, but this does not mean that the participants go off in three different directions: they have made their joint interpretive decisions, and they stick to them—and the playing, individually and together, is glorious. Basic tempi are brisk and steady, but wonderful things happen *within* those tempos—as, for instance, in the last fourteen bars of the first movement, which swirls and drives to a powerful climax without losing its underlying rhythmic pulse. The second movement may be a trifle too fast, but the jaunty articulation is marvelous. To hear the third movement played as Beethoven indicated—"Andante cantabile: semplice"—is a wonderful experience, since it is usually treated as a High Romantic adagio; I cannot remember ever having heard the intense part of the coda, in which the violin and cello "sing" quietly over the piano's triplet chords, played with greater simplicity or greater effectiveness. The phrasing of the last movement has been brilliantly thought out; Rubinstein botches a few passages in the whirlwind coda, but who cares? Not long before his retirement, he wanted to rerecord the "Archduke" with Szeryng and Pierre Fournier; the recording would have had a more up-to-date sound and the interpretation would almost certainly have been more carefully worked out and more deliberate, but I doubt that it would have been as enjoyable as this version.

Like Mozart, **Schubert** is not one of the composers whose names immediately spring to mind when one thinks of Rubinstein. Rubinstein adored Schubert as he adored Mozart—and played even less of Schubert's music than of Mozart's. He performed the Fantasy in C Major ("Wanderer") in public from the age of fifteen onward, and the G-flat Major and A-flat Major Impromptus (Op. 90, Nos. 3 and 4) were staples of his repertoire for decades, as was Tausig's arrangement of the *Marche militaire*. But—apart from a few chamber works played at occasional private gatherings but rarely if ever in public—he kept few if any other pieces by Schubert in his active repertoire until late in his life.

His recording of the "Wanderer" Fantasy astonished me the first time I listened to it. Perhaps I was subconsciously expecting to hear a beautiful but somewhat too legato, overpedalled version of this masterpiece, and to find that the work's stormy and stressful sections had been underplayed. Instead, the seventy-eight-year-old Rubinstein explodes into the Fantasy's first section, articulating staccato notes and chords with a sharpness that he generally refused to use even in Beethoven. He puts maximum emphasis on the contrast between vigor and delicacy in this section, and the refinement of his voicing of chords is truly remarkable. The third and final sections of the work come off beautifully for similar reasons, but Rubinstein's most wonderful achievements are to be heard in the second section, which is the Fantasy's heart. Schubert took the theme (which is closely connected to the themes of the other sections) from his own song "Der Wanderer," written in 1816, six years before the Fantasy, and specifically from the melody with which he set the verse that begins "Die Sonne dünkt mich." ("The sun seems to me so cold here, / my blood parched, my life old, / and people's talk empty noises; / I am a stranger everywhere.") Rubinstein captures the theme's loneliness and longing for warmth, the fearfulness of the crystalline sixty-fourth-note scale passages, and the deathly chill of the tremolos with a mastery that I cannot imagine bettered. His playing of the whole section reflects his comment, reported by Ann Schein, to the effect that Schubert was the only composer who could unflinchingly contemplate death. In short, this is one of Rubinstein's great recordings.

Of his 1961 recording of the two impromptus, the G-flat Major is beautiful—although the tempestuous parts are somewhat understated—and the A-flat Major is noteworthy for the silvery sound of the melodic line and for the way in which the pianist fashions each group of descending arpeggios into a gentle cascade pulled downward by the force of gravity, rather than a series of pretty notes with no particular reason for existing.

Although Rubinstein recorded the minuet movement of Schubert's Sonata in G Major, Op. 78, in 1936,* he did not play a whole Schubert sonata in public—as far as I have been able to determine—until the 1963–64 season, when he included the Sonata in B-flat Major in several of his recitals. He had recorded it the previous summer but had been dissatisfied with the recording and did not allow its release. Two years later, he rerecorded the sonata, but he eventually decided against releasing this version, too. Finally, in 1969, he recorded it again (in chapter 6 of this book, Eva Rubinstein described the circumstances under which the recording was made) and approved the version for release. I listened to that recording shortly after it was issued, and I found it strangely disjointed and unconvincing. Max Wilcox, who produced all three versions, wrote about the released one: "The critical reaction was unusually mixed for a Rubinstein recording, and it seemed possible that this most natural of musicians and recording artists had allowed himself to 'over-worry' his approach to this music." A few years after Rubinstein's death, Wilcox compared the 1969 to the 1965 recording, and reported that "about two minutes" into the earlier version he realized that this was "the performance I had been carrying around in my head all these years. The phrasing was beautifully natural; Rubinstein's tone was its usual golden self, and the great pianist sounded as if he were raptly playing for a few close friends in his living room."[6] With Nela Rubinstein's permission, the 1965 version was released on a compact disc in 1987, and it is indeed a fine recording of this elusive, ambiguous work, which was composed only a few weeks before Schubert's death, at the age of thirty-one. Rubinstein's playing of the first movement is as introverted a performance of this music as I have ever heard, but he maintains the "very moderate" pace prescribed by the composer, rather than wallowing in an adagio or lento tempo, as many pianists do. My only major quibble is with his decision to pedal through many of the rests in the coda, thus destroying the poignant, irregular rhythmic effect that Schubert evidently wished to achieve. The second movement, with its tone of tragedy beyond grief, is more adagio than andante in this version, but Rubinstein beautifully sustains his chosen tempo; he lets the pathos speak for itself, with no underscoring, and his performance makes one think of T. S. Eliot's "This is the way the world ends / Not with a bang but a whimper."[7] At the top of the third movement, Schubert wrote "Allegro vivace con delicatezza," and Rubinstein follows the indication exactly: this is a fleet-footed (although subtly fluctuating) version of the scherzo, in which the pianist's tendency to soften the impact of staccato notes works to excellent effect. In the trio section, however, Rubinstein again pedals through the rests and in so doing eliminates some of the feeling of menace implicit in the left hand's line. But in the finale, he beautifully balances the forlorn and angry elements against the element of forced merriment that struggles for supremacy to the very end of the piece, when it wins a Pyrrhic victory.

One is tempted to speculate that Rubinstein succeeded with Schubert because of his ability to sustain a melodic line exceptionally well. In general, however, the performers (including singers) who are least successful with Schubert are those who give more attention to the composer's melodies than to his highly personal, meandering forms and their strong rhythmic underpinnings. In a rare moment of musical self-analysis in his memoirs, Rubinstein said, "my own talent as an interpreter is mainly based on my need for understanding the structure of a musical work."[8] And Annabelle Whitestone recalled: "In listening to music—records, concerts, or pianists who came to play—nothing upset Arthur more than 'false' rhythm or lack of rhythmic intensity."[9] These are the factors that provide the biggest clue to Rubinstein's fine Schubert recordings, and I wish that he had made more of them. The only other works that he committed to disc are the Trios in B-flat Major, Op. 99, and E-flat Major, Op. 100. The 1941 version of Op. 99, with Heifetz and Feuermann, has virtues similar to those of the "Archduke" recording made by the same players during the same period. Although some of Heifetz's rubatos and other inflections in the second movement strike me as more suitable to Tchaikovsky than to Schubert, the performance as a whole is remarkable for its spontaneity, verve, impeccable phrasing, and forward momentum. Nearly thirty-three years later, Rubinstein rerecorded the work with Szeryng and Fournier. In every moment, the later recording is not only slower but also more deliberate and often more emphatic than the earlier one; that Rubinstein could play the piece as beautifully as he did at the age of eighty-seven is astonishing, but this performance lacks the naturalness, the impetuousness, the sense of fun, and, above all, the daring of the earlier one. It is pleasant and comfortable, but it cannot bear comparison with its exuberant predecessor. I have not heard the Rubinstein-Szeryng-Fournier recording of Op. 100,* but I have been told by more than one musician that its virtues and defects are similar to those of the same group's Op. 99 recording, made during the same days.

RUBINSTEIN MADE MORE recordings of pieces by **Chopin** than of pieces by all other composers combined, and to comment in detail on all of his Chopin recordings would require a volume in itself. Thus, although I like the piano concertos, the Fantasia on Polish Airs, the Berceuse, the Boléro, the *Trois nouvelles études*, and indeed most of Chopin's other works—and Rubinstein's performances of them—I shall limit my remarks to those pieces that I consider more central to the Chopin repertoire. In addition to his authorized recordings for HMV and RCA, some pirate CDs made in Italy from tapes of 1969 and 1970 recitals in Milan, Bologna, and an unidentified location include several works of Chopin, but these performances do not provide substantially new views of any of the pieces, and in addition their sound is poor; for these reasons, they will not be discussed here.

For those of us who heard Rubinstein only in his last decades, he seemed—by virtue of his age and national origins—a closer link to Chopin than anyone else alive. (If Chopin, Mendelssohn, Schumann, and Liszt—all born in the years 1809–11—had lived to the age that Rubinstein reached, they would have been able to hear him perform their works.) Early in the compact disc era, BMG Classics released many of the Chopin recordings that Rubinstein had made for RCA from the 1940s to the 1970s, and in 1992 and 1993 EMI released CDs that contain most of the Chopin recordings that he had made for HMV in the 1920s and 1930s. Thus, anyone who would like to study the evolution of Rubinstein's Chopin playing over a forty-year period can now do so. The HMV recordings disprove, once and for all, Rubinstein's often-repeated statements about the faultiness of his technique until his summer of hard work, in 1934; they support, instead, the remarks of those observers of his early work who described his technique as brilliant. He sometimes glossed over difficulties out of laziness, but not because he was incapable of mastering them. On the whole, his pre–World War II Chopin playing was more dazzling, more freewheeling, and more original than his post–World War II playing. (In the early 1990s Nela Rubinstein heard some of the early recordings, for the first time in many years, in a Pearl Gemm CD transfer, and exclaimed to Eva, *"That's* how he played when I first knew him and fell in love with him!") But his playing was also more careless, and not only with respect to textual accuracy. The earlier recordings are more episodic; each section of a given piece has something delectable to offer, but the sections don't always mesh convincingly, and the rhythmic underpinnings sometimes collapse—a fault that hardly ever mars the later versions, in which the use of rubato is more subtle. My guess is that when Rubinstein made the later recordings, he was profoundly concerned about the responsibility that his reputation as the elder statesman of Chopin interpreters placed on him, and that he was determined to impress on future generations of musicians the primary importance of understanding and revealing the structural logic behind Chopin's music.

In his 1959 recordings of the four scherzos and four ballades, for instance, structural clarity is the determining characteristic. He was very much attuned to the works' narrative quality, and in these performances he *appears* to allow the wordless stories to unfold by themselves. Not only does he take great pains to hold some of his energy in reserve until the coda of each piece: he also draws the listener's attention—conscious or unconscious—to the fact that each section of each piece has a beginning, a climax, and an ending (although the climax and the ending sometimes coincide). It is true that in some of these recordings Rubinstein was overly cautious. One would have liked him to take riskier tempos and to cut himself loose from his moorings a little more often in, for instance, the C-sharp Minor Scherzo, which seems to me much too slow as he played it in 1959. And yet, despite the many, many details in the 1932 version of the scherzos that I find more striking and more beautiful than in the 1959 version, the latter usually provides more satisfying overall realizations. Thus, although the accusation of blandness that some musicians and critics have made against the later recordings is understandable, it is also inaccurate.

Those of the early recordings that seem to me clearly superior to the later ones are usually of pieces that are either shorter or less tightly knit than the ballades and scherzos. The 1928 recording of the lovely, meandering **Barcarolle,** for instance, is amazing in its mixture of quiet intimacy, melodic splendor, mounting eroticism, and dazzling explosions of joy; the 1962 recording, although beautiful, pales beside it. (The 1946 version, which has also become available on compact disc, cannot quite match its predecessor in gracefulness and lyricism.) Above all, the recordings of fifty-one **mazurkas** that he made in 1938–39 have a fresher, more improvisational charm than most of the 1965–66 versions of the same pieces; their élan is wilder, their melancholy more profound, their overall expressive variety greater. To me, these early versions of the mazurkas comprise the most beautiful individual group of Rubinstein's Chopin recordings, and one of the most important parts of his recorded legacy.

In the case of the nineteen **nocturnes,** both the 1936–37 English set and the 1965 "American" (but recorded in Rome) set give so much pleasure and are so full of insights that I would not want to be without either of them. In general, there is a greater range of tempo and dynamic variation in the 1936–37 recordings, whereas the 1965 versions are stronger with respect to structural cohesion and give a more accurate idea of Rubinstein's sound. The first five nocturnes, for instance, seem to coalesce better in the later version, although the *con fuoco* middle section of the fourth (F Major, Op. 15, No. 1) is bolder and more charged with drama in the earlier version. (A 1949 version* of No. 1 in B-flat Minor, Op. 9, No. 1, is similar to the earlier version in its free use of rubato but similar to the later one in its slow tempos.) The older recording of No. 6 (G Minor, Op. 15, No. 3) seems to hang together better than the later one, and its basic tempo is reasonably close to the metronome mark of dotted half-note = 60; but perhaps Rubinstein was right to slow down and loosen up for the later recording, since Chopin's indication, under the initial "Lento," is "languido e rubato." In No. 7 (C-sharp Minor, Op. 27, No. 1), as in No. 4, the tempestuous middle section is better realized in the earlier version, but the intense sadness of the beginning and ending is heard to better effect in the later one. Rubinstein excessively underplays the dramatic contrasts in his recordings of the remarkable ninth nocturne (B Major, Op. 32, No. 1), and in its successor (A-flat Major, Op. 32, No. 2) he presses forward too quickly at several points in the earlier recording (which, however, has a marvelously impassioned middle section) and to drag in the later one. I prefer the steadier later version of No. 11 (G Minor, Op. 37, No. 1) to its predecessor, but the earlier recording of No. 12 (G Major, Op. 37, No. 2) has a slight edge over the later one—beautiful, nevertheless. Tempi match better in the later performance of No. 13 (C Minor, Op. 48, No. 1), and Rubinstein's playing of the first fourteen bars of the middle section *(poco più lento)* is itself worth the price of the whole set: the voicing of the chords is subtle to a degree that I have rarely heard matched by any pianist in any work. Nothing is deliberately brought out—the parts are exquisitely integrated—but every voice in the chord progression has a life of its own; the damper pedal sustains everything but covers nothing. This is magisterial pianism. The remaining nocturnes "speak" more naturally in the 1936 versions (No. 17—B Major, Op. 62, No. 1—is particularly stunning, and so is the agitato section of No. 18—E Major, Op. 62, No. 2), but how could one not fall under the spell of Rubinstein's tone in those of 1963?

The meditative quality that Rubinstein brought to the nocturnes is surprisingly strong once again in his 1963 recording of fourteen of the sixteen **waltzes;** two of the posthumous waltzes were not in his repertoire. When Herbert Weinstock, who wrote the introductory notes for this set, reminded Rubinstein of Schumann's statement to the effect that Chopin's waltzes ought to be danced by countesses, at the very least, the pianist "vigorously shook his head. 'No,' he said, 'or at best true of only some of the waltzes. They are almost as varied as the preludes or the etudes, and it's no use trying to say just one thing to describe them all. They range all the way from echoes of Lanner and Schubert and Johann Strauss the elder to almost-Waldteufel Parisian dances for countesses and their gentlemen. . . .' " About the "Grande Valse Brillante" in E-flat Major, Op. 18, Rubinstein told Weinstock that "despite all its glitter and dash, it is of the type that Schubert composed shyly." This gentle quality is present even in Rubinstein's somewhat erratic 1953* recording of the piece, and more strongly in the 1963 version. One of the EMI compact discs includes quite a messy recording (1929) of the Waltz No. 2 in A-flat Major, Op. 34, No. 1; the 1963 version is superior in every way. Rubinstein's recording of the Waltz No. 3 in A Minor, Op. 34, No. 2, is remarkable for its simplicity and lack of bathos, and the same is true of No. 7 in C-sharp Minor, Op. 64, No. 2, of which there is an equally beautiful 1930 version on EMI. Rubinstein told Weinstock that his favorite waltz was No. 8 in A-flat Major, Op. 64, No. 3, " 'as it is the most original.' He went over to the Steinway to play it, calling my attention particularly to the fourteen measures beginning with the right-hand trill and leading up to the section in C. 'That, of course,' he commented, 'is not a waltz for dancing. . . . Nor is it a "salon piece." . . . No . . . it is a thing directly from Chopin's heart and soul.' "[10] And Rubinstein plays it accordingly. The three waltzes from Op. 70—G-flat Major, F Minor, and D-flat Major—are even more charming and poised in the 1953* than in the 1963 versions, but there is nothing wrong with the latter!

Rubinstein plays the three **impromptus,** the **Fantasy-Impromptu,** and the **Fantasy in F Minor** with extraordinary poise and tonal beauty in the RCA versions that date from the 1960s. Taken as a group, his recordings of the six **polonaises** and the **Polonaise-Fantasy** (the other, posthumously published polonaises were not in his repertoire) seem to me less striking than his recordings of the previously mentioned groups of Chopin's works. The 1934–35 HMV/EMI versions bring many brilliant details to the listener's attention, but they are not as well thought out as their 1964 RCA/BMG counterparts—which, however, seem to lack much of their predecessors' vitality. In particular, the basic tempo of the 1964 version of the C Minor Polonaise, Op. 40, No. 2, is so slow (more a largo than the allegro maestoso that Chopin indicated), and its articulation so ponderous, that I find the whole performance unnatural—a word that rarely describes a Rubinstein recording. Of the 1950–51 RCA set* I have heard only the Polonaise No. 1 (C-sharp Minor, Op. 26, No. 1); the performance combines the boldness of the earlier version with the coherence of the later one, and if it is representative of the rest of the set, the whole group ought to be released on a compact disc.

"My preludes aren't good enough," Rubinstein wrote to Monika Mann in 1974, in a letter that was more amply quoted in chapter 6. He recorded all of Chopin's **Twenty-four Preludes,** Op. 28, only once, in 1946, and although the set contains some gems, on the whole I agree with Rubinstein's assessment. The first two preludes (C Major and A Minor) are nicely played but strangely uninvolving. No. 3 (G Major) is too fast and sloppy, but No. 4 (E Minor) is very fine—poetic but unexaggerated. The D Major Prelude, No. 5, sounds too abrupt, even perfunctory, but the B Minor, No. 6, is as excellent as No. 4, to which it is closely related. Rubinstein's playing of No. 7, in A Major, is beautiful, but I wish that he had brought the piece to a climax on the seventh-chord in bar 12, as Chopin indicated, rather than lowering the volume. He presses ahead too roughly at bars 23 and 24 of No. 8 (F-sharp Minor); otherwise, he brings the piece off well. No. 9 (E Major), on the other hand, is simply too erratic: instead of establishing a basic tempo and departing from it when he sees fit, Rubinstein moves apparently at random from one tempo to another. The tenth (C-sharp Minor) and eleventh (B Major) preludes are played gracefully and with delicate poise, respectively, but the twelfth (G-sharp Minor) is pounded out and laced with wrong notes. Rubinstein's recording of No. 13 (F-sharp Major)—one of Chopin's masterpieces—is far better than Cortot's absurdly mannered 1926 recording but far less subtle and sensuous than either of Vladimir Ashkenazy's recorded versions. The performance of No. 14 (E-flat Minor) is unsatisfactory: Chopin's tempo indication is "allegro," but he also wrote "pesante" (heavy) at the top of the page; in his desire to maintain the allegro, Rubinstein sacrifices the pesante. No. 15 (D-flat Major), too, is on the fast side, but the tempo works well, especially in the middle section; this is an uninflated, direct, and beautiful performance. Rubinstein's wild approach to the wild Sixteenth Prelude (B-flat

Minor) is just right, but he seems to tire in the second half, and he uses the pedal to cover many misdemeanors. The Seventeenth (A-flat Major) begins well but quickly becomes mannered, and remains so to the end; and Rubinstein, who tended to neglect *sforzato* indications in Beethoven, bangs them out mercilessly in the last twenty-five bars of this piece. His performance of No. 18 (F Minor) is alternately perfunctory and brutal, and Nos. 19 (E-flat Major) and 20 (C Minor) are oddly characterless; they fall flat. The next three, however, are very fine: the cantabile quality of No. 21 (B-flat Major) is beautifully brought out without sacrificing the clarity of the complicated accompaniment; No. 22 (G Minor) is full of rage; and No. 23 (F Major) is elegant and refined. There are good moments and bad in No. 24 (D Minor), but Rubinstein ends the piece, and the set, as they ought to end—in despair and doom. It is too bad that he did not rerecord the whole set in the 1960s, because it would almost certainly have been better thought out than this version was.

Among the three Chopin **sonatas**, Rubinstein did not play the early and rarely performed No. 1, but the other two were staples of his repertoire. There are two recordings of No. 2 in B-flat Minor, Op. 35. In the first version (1946), the first movement is beautifully conceived but often carelessly executed; the body of the second movement is uncontrolled and messy, but the trio section is exceptionally beautiful; the pacing of the celebrated funeral march is natural and even and the sound glows, especially in the D-flat Major section; but the finale, as in Rachmaninoff's recorded version, is so fast as to be unintelligible. Perhaps Rubinstein listened to this recording fifteen years later, before he rerecorded the sonata, because the erratic playing in the first and second movements of the earlier version were replaced by overly cautious playing in 1961. Fortunately, the trio of the second movement is as beautiful here as it was in 1946, and the recorded sound is better. The funeral march is much slower in the later version—too slow to be a march—but its phrasing is as beautiful as it was in the earlier recording and its sound even more glowing. The finale is almost but still not quite intelligible. In Rubinstein's only recording of the Sonata No. 3 in B Minor, Op. 58—begun in 1959 and completed in 1961—every movement is brilliantly conceived and beautifully realized. One could quibble that in the last movement the main theme starts a little too tamely, or that preoccupation with making the right-hand scale passages (bars 54 to 99, etc.) as dazzling as possible evidently led Rubinstein to underplay the left hand's line, but otherwise this is an outstanding recording—one of Rubinstein's greatest.

THE 1950 RUBINSTEIN-Heifetz-Piatigorsky recording of **Mendelsohn**'s Trio in D Minor, Op. 49, is exhilarating, but more as an exhibition of truly amazing virtuosity than as a musical experience. Rubinstein's recordings of works by Liszt have the emotional range, technical brilliance, and gargantuan energy that the music demands, but in the B Minor Sonata Rubinstein could not match Horowitz's diabolical fury.

Schumann's music, like Chopin's, was heard at Rubinstein's debut concert in 1900 and at his last recital in 1976, and it accounts for a noteworthy portion of his recorded repertoire. His 1963 version of *Carnaval*, Op. 9, is as charming a performance as I have ever heard, despite some annoying departures from the text: In the "Préambule," the *più moto* that is supposed to begin at the end of bar 24 is delayed nearly four bars and the fortissimo at bar 40 is ignored; the staccato arpeggio in bars 44–45 of "Pierrot" is not differentiated from its legato predecessor and successor; the septuplet figurations in "Eusebius" are too conveniently divided into groups of three and four; and so on. These divergences are not trivial—they alter the character of segments of the piece—and yet the character of most of this performance could not feel righter. The same is true of Rubinstein's 1962 recording of the *Fantasiestücke*, Op. 12: Had he recorded the piece in the 1930s, he might have played the waltz theme in "Grillen" (bars 18–44, etc.) more exuberantly, and one could quibble that "Traumes-Wirren" lacks a touch of irony at the little ritardandos (bars 8 and 46, for instance) and needs stronger left-hand motor-rhythm in bars 17–35 and the subsequent parallel passage. But the rest of the performance is beautifully and movingly realized. Rubinstein recorded the *Fantasiestücke* again in April 1976,* at the age of eighty-nine, during his last recording sessions. The articulation in this version is often heavier than in the previous one, made when he was a youth of seventy-five, but the results, as a whole, would have been remarkable for a pianist one-third his age.

Rubinstein's sole recording of Schumann's *Etudes en forme de variations*—better known as the *Etudes symphoniques*—Op. 13, is a rare example of a concert tape that he authorized for release; it was made during one of the ten recitals that he gave at Carnegie Hall in the fall of 1961. The performance begins solemnly—although there is a bit of Chopinesque rubato in and around bar 9 of the theme—and it continues beautifully, with the exception of some blurred chordal passages in the heftier études. In the Finale Rubinstein seems to become increasingly nervous, and there is a fair amount of banging and overpedalling, but the good parts far outweigh the bad in the performance. The other solo pieces by Schumann that are available on compact discs as of this writing are all essential items in the Rubinstein discography: the 1964 recording of *Kreisleriana*, Op. 16; the 1965 recording of the Fantasy, Op. 17; the 1969 recording of *Arabeske*, Op. 18; the 1963 recording of the Romance in F-sharp Major, Op. 28, No. 2; and the 1969 recording of the strange and haunting "Vogel als Prophet" ("Bird as Prophet") from *Wald-*

szenen (Forest Scenes), Op. 82, No. 7. Once again, I imagine that in his forties Rubinstein played certain passages more boldly or more brilliantly than he does in these recordings, but the readings offered by the septuagenarian and octogenarian Rubinstein are unsurpassed for their assurance and coherence and for the poetic beauty of the playing.

I have heard four Rubinstein recordings of Schumann's Piano Concerto in A Minor, Op. 54; all of them contain sturdy, straightforward readings, with the ritardandos, accelerandos, and caesuras that, rightly or wrongly, have become traditional in this work. An authorized version made in 1958 with Krips and the RCA Victor Symphony Orchestra is more fleet in the first movement and more lightly articulated throughout than another authorized version made in 1967 with Giulini and the Chicago Symphony Orchestra, but the playing—Rubinstein's and the orchestra's—is clearer in the Giulini version. The first movement of a tinny-sounding 1964 pirate version with the Alessandro Scarlatti Orchestra of the RAI of Naples conducted by Franco Caracciolo, is a little more fiery than either of the authorized recordings, and a better-sounding 1968 pirate recording (with Mehta and the Montreal Symphony Orchestra) is similar, overall, to the Giulini recording, but less accurately played. I cannot imagine a more glowing, delightful version of the Quintet in E-flat Major for Piano and String Quartet, Op. 44, than Rubinstein's 1966 recording with the Guarneri Quartet. The basic tempo of the second movement is much more dirgelike than the composer indicates ("a bit broadly," half-note = 66), but this, too, has become a "tradition" in Schumann interpretation—and Rubinstein and the Guarneri sustain their slow tempo well. The other movements, and the other sections of the second movement, are played warmly, lightly, passionately, or brilliantly, as the music requires. The only other piece of chamber music by Schumann in Rubinstein's catalogue of recordings is the Trio in D Minor for Piano, Violin, and Cello, Op. 63, with Szeryng and Fournier. The late date (1972) of this interpretation led me to guess that the moderately paced first movement and the slow third would be more interesting than the quick second and fourth movements, but I was *precisely* wrong: Some dissimilarity in phrasing and articulation among the players, along with occasional out-of-tune playing on Fournier's part, cause the slower movements to give at the seams, whereas the quicker ones are played with charm, power, and unity of intent.

The idea that a composer's disciples can possess an authentic performing tradition for the master's works, and that successive generations of disciples can pass the traditions on, is absurd. And yet there is no doubt that Rubinstein's frequent contacts, throughout his formative years, with such important Brahmsians as Joachim and his quartet, Barth, Emma Brandes Engelmann, and various members of Clara Schumann's circle helped him to immerse himself in the world of **Brahms**'s music as few if any other musicians of his generation were able to do. When I told Barenboim that I considered Rubinstein even finer, overall, in Brahms than in Chopin, he said, "I think he thought so himself. He always said that Brahms was his favorite composer." Emanuel Ax told me that he loved Rubinstein's Brahms even more than his Chopin, and several other fine pianists of my acquaintance are of the same opinion. One hopes that BMG will eventually rerelease all of the recordings of the various *Klavierstücke* from Opp. 76, 79, and 116–119 that Rubinstein made for RCA during the 1940s and early '50s, especially inasmuch as there are some that he did not rerecord in later years. Fortunately, however, a fair amount of material is already available on compact discs.

The first-written of Brahms's works in Rubinstein's concert repertoire seems to have been the Sonata in F Minor, Op. 5, which he was playing at least as early as 1904—only seven years after Brahms's death. Ax described Rubinstein's 1959 recording of the piece as an example of "complete identification with the young Brahms" on the part of the aging pianist, and he added, "I wish that he had also recorded the F-sharp Minor Sonata, Op. 2, and many of the other early works." In the first movement of Op. 5, the directness with which Rubinstein plays the transitional *fest und bestimmt* (steady and determined) passages and the glowing, unpompous character that he brings to the second theme are particularly noteworthy. There is no undue emphasis in his *espressivo* playing in the second and fourth movements, no lack of vigor in the main part of the third movement and no excess rhetoric in the trio section of that movement, and the finale exudes wonderfully youthful verve. Finer still, however, is his 1970 recording of the Four Ballades, Op. 10. These pieces are all in clear-cut three-part form and are therefore tighter, structurally, than Chopin's ballades; and unlike the Chopin pieces, they were all written in the same year—1854, when Brahms was twenty-one—and benefit from being heard as a group. The eighty-three-year-old Rubinstein brilliantly captured the grim essence of the first piece, the dreaminess of the second (but also the severity of its middle section), the nervousness of the third, and the lied-like lyricism of the fourth.

Although Rubinstein's 1928 recording of the Capriccio in B Minor, Op. 76, No. 2, displays beautiful staccato playing, it feels much too fast, especially in view of the *Allegretto non troppo* indication that Brahms set atop it, and the rhythm is exceptionally uneven, by Rubinstein's standards. His 1970 RCA recording of the piece is much better integrated and thoroughly charming. In his 1941 recording* (the only one he made) of the Intermezzo in A Minor, Op. 76, No. 7, he achieves an outstanding balance between the sober simplicity of the opening and closing bars and the quietly expressed but intense longing of the rest of the piece. He is not at his best in the 1970 recording of the Two Rhapsodies (B Minor and G Minor), Op. 79; in particular, the obsessively repeated triplets that haunt so much of No. 2 (end of bar 20 through bar 31, for instance) are often more ponderous than ominous, as heard here, and the rubato effects detract from the cumulative impression. One would like to hear the earlier versions* of both pieces. In his 1970 recording of the Intermezzo in E Minor, Op. 116, No. 5, he pedals through most of the eighth-rests that are an essential feature of the piece, but the 1959 recording of the E Major Intermezzo, Op. 116, No. 6, is lovely in every respect: pace, voicing of the chords, melodic tension, and expressive naturalness. The same is true of Rubinstein's 1941 recording of the Intermezzo in E-flat Major, Op. 117, No. 1, whereas the Intermezzo in B-flat Minor, Op. 117, No. 2, is too nervous in the 1941 version and too stodgy in the 1970 version; the 1953 version* synthesizes the best qualities of the other two. The 1953 recording of the Intermezzo in C-sharp Minor, Op. 117, No. 3, is amazingly beautiful; oddly, however, Rubinstein's left hand plays two D-sharps instead of D-naturals in bars 48 and 68; he had evidently misread the notes, and as both bars are repeated, there are eight jarringly incorrect D-sharps within a very short period. Both the 1941* and 1953 recordings of the Intermezzo in A Major, Op. 118, No. 2, and the 1959 recording of the Intermezzo in F Major, Op. 118, No. 5, are also gems in the Rubinstein discography. I am not sure that it is possible to play the E-flat Minor Intermezzo, Op. 118, No. 6, in a thoroughly satisfactory way: its beginning and end are exceptionally introverted and mysterious, whereas its middle section is an almost unbearably strong cry from the heart; the subtleties of rhythm, dynamics, and articulation that this range of expression requires are daunting, and to find a tempo that can accommodate all the soul-states, without opting for distentions that border on distortions, is nearly impossible. Rubinstein's 1941 recording* of the piece is strangely perfunctory, and in the 1970 version many passages are too resounding or too deliberate; the 1953 version—despite its slightly too skittish basic tempo—comes remarkably close to communicating this elusive work's essence. The 1953 recording of the Intermezzos in E Minor and C Major, Op. 119, Nos. 2 and 3, are outstanding, whereas the 1941* recording of the latter is nervous to the point of unsteadiness. But the 1941* recording of the Rhapsody in E-flat Major, Op. 119, No. 4, is brilliantly thought-out and realized.

Rubinstein and Szeryng recorded all three of Brahms's violin sonatas in 1960–61. The tempo of the first movement of No. 1 in G Major, Op. 78, is on the slow side, but it is supported by strong melodic tension. No. 2 in A Major, Op. 100,* is given a glowing performance throughout, and one wonders why, alone among the three, it has not been released on a compact disc. Likewise, EMI ought to rerelease the 1932 recording of the Sonata No. 3 in D Minor,

Op. 108, that Rubinstein made with Kochanski.* I prefer the more severe first movement and the simpler second movement in the later version, with Szeryng, but the third movement is much lighter and more charming in the Kochanski version, and each version of the fourth movement offers special virtues: The earlier one is more rhapsodic and natural, the later one stronger in its cumulative effect. With Piatigorsky, Rubinstein recorded both of Brahms's cello sonatas—the first, in E Minor, Op. 38, by itself in 1936, and the first and second (F Major, Op. 99), thirty years later. In the 1936 recording, Rubinstein seems to be playing within a restricted dynamic range, as if he had been cautioned not to overpower the cello's sound; the performance also sounds underrehearsed. Piatigorsky's playing in 1966 was not as good as it had been three decades earlier, and there are moments in the finale of the E Minor Sonata and the third movement of the F Major in which the articulation of both artists seems overly deliberate, even bombastic. But the later recordings have their glorious moments: In No. 1, the glow of the closing theme of the first movement and the yearning quality of the waltz-like trio in the second movement; and in No. 2, the entire second movement.

The Trio No. 1 in B Major, Op. 8, was recorded twice by Rubinstein— in 1941 with Heifetz and Feuermann,* and in 1972 with Szeryng and Fournier. The earlier version is superior in every movement—the radiantly exuberant first, the brilliant and rhythmically impetuous second, the quietly intense third, and the fatefully lilting finale. The 1972 Rubinstein-Szeryng-Fournier recording of the Trio No. 2 in C Major, Op. 87, is overly cautious and somewhat pallid, like the recording of No. 1. Rubinstein recorded the Piano Quartet No. 1 in G Minor, Op. 25, in 1932 with members of the Pro Arte Quartet; his playing is lively and intelligent throughout, but the string players make a hash of the piece in several important places. He may be slightly more reserved, here and there, in his 1967 recording of the same work with members of the Guarneri Quartet, but his playing is no less intelligent than in the version of thirty-five years earlier—and his young partners play beautifully. Indeed, there are passages in this recording that are quintessential Rubinstein: the *Animato* section of the third movement, for instance, which he begins by playing piano but articulating forte, like a great singer, and then attacks (at the change of key signature) as if the piano were a whole battery of trumpets and drums; or the wild opening, precipitous scale passages, and soaring melodies of the finale. Equally fine are the Rubinstein-Guarneri recordings of the Quartet No. 2 in A Major, Op. 26,* and No. 3 in C Minor, Op. 60. And the finest of their whole series of collaborative efforts may well be the Quintet in F Minor, Op. 34—the recording that Glenn Gould described as "the greatest chamber-music performance with piano that I've heard in my life" and that had changed his "notion of what Brahms represents."[11]

There is little to say about Rubinstein's 1954 recording of Brahms's Concerto No. 1 in D Minor, Op. 15, with Reiner and the Chicago Symphony Orchestra, or his 1958 recording of the Concerto No. 2 in B-flat Major, Op. 83, with Krips and the RCA Victor Symphony Orchestra, except that they are musts among the various recorded versions of these works and among Rubinstein's recorded legacy. The unemphatic grandeur, the drama, lyricism, and humor, the overall musical coherence, and the richness and variety of piano sound make these performances classics in their genre. Even poor old Krips rises to the occasion. At various times over the years, I have heard Rubinstein's other recordings of these concertos—the First with Leinsdorf and the Boston Symphony (1964*) and with Mehta and the Israel Philharmonic (1976*); the Second with Munch and the Boston Symphony (1952*) and with Ormandy and the Philadelphia Orchestra (1971*)—but I did not like any of them as well as the versions that are currently available. The very earliest of his Brahms concerto recordings, however—and indeed the earliest of all his concerto recordings—is worth mentioning.

In *My Many Years*, Rubinstein described the depressing conditions under which he had recorded the Second Concerto with Albert Coates and the London Symphony Orchestra in October 1929. "It was . . . impossible to [meet with] Mr. Coates before the recording, as I had hoped. We were given only two days for this longest of all concertos with its four movements, and the result was completely unsatisfactory. . . . the piano had a good sound but it was slightly out of tune and the tuner was not able to fix it. Mr. Coates conducted at the opposite end of the room, far away from me, so of course I had as neighbors the percussion and brass instruments at the back of the orchestra."[12] Rubinstein plays fistfuls of wrong notes in the recording, the orchestra is a mess, and the coordination between piano and orchestra is poor. And yet this version is worth hearing, inasmuch as most of its tempi are shockingly fast compared to those that have become the norm in our day. Brahms did not often put metronome numbers in his works, but in this case he took special care to do so. If one were to follow his indications inflexibly—which, of course, was not his intention—the first movement would last about 16:30, the second and third about 7:30 each (including the repeat in the second and allowing a great deal of leeway for the slower parts of the third), and the finale about 8:50. Here are the timings for two thoughtfully and beautifully played modern recordings: Alfred Brendel with Claudio Abbado and the Berlin Philharmonic (Deutsche Grammophon)—17:52, 9:20, 12:15, 9:21; Vladimir Ashkenazy with Bernard Haitink and the Vienna Philharmonic (Philips)—18:40, 9:26, 13:07, 9:29. The timings for every movement of Rubinstein's 1958 recording are also slower (16:53, 9:05, 12:39, 9:02) than Brahms indicated but not as broad as Brendel's or Ashkenazy's—except the third movement, which is slightly shorter in Brendel's version. If one listens to the well-known Horowitz-Toscanini-NBC Symphony recording of 1940, one hears a performance that is closer still to Brahms's indications (the timings are 16:15, 8:06, 11:05, 8:25) and—in the case of the first and fourth movements—a jot faster than the composer's guidelines suggested. But to contemporary ears, Rubinstein's 1929 recording (timings: 14:35, 8:10, 9:09, 7:54) sounds rushed in every movement except the second, and absurdly so in the third, which, however, is not played nearly as quickly as Brahms indicated.

Is there a lesson to be drawn from this? Probably not, apart from the already well-known one, to the effect that trends in musical performance change from generation to generation. When one listens, today, to recordings of the Brahms symphonies conducted by Felix Weingartner or Toscanini, one hears tempos that are considerably faster, on the average, than those to which we have become accustomed in recent decades. And yet Weingartner had conducted Brahms *for* Brahms (and had received the composer's praise), and Toscanini had modeled his approach on that of Fritz Steinbach, who was one of Brahms's favorite conductors. Barth, Rubinstein's teacher, had played Brahms's music in the composer's presence, and the young Rubinstein had heard Brahms played by many other proto-Brahmsians. I would be willing to bet that, despite its defects, Rubinstein's 1929 recording of the concerto was closer to what Brahms had in mind when he wrote the work than is Rubinstein's 1958 recording or any of the later ones by other pianists. Which does not mean that it is easy to love.

RUBINSTEIN'S 1942 RECORDING of the **Grieg** Piano Concerto, with Ormandy and the Philadelphia Orchestra—a best-seller in its day—presents a livelier and more dramatic reading of the work than either his 1961 recording with Wallenstein and the RCA Victor Symphony or a 1963 concert performance, available on a pirate CD, with Giulini and the Philharmonia Orchestra. The poetic 1953 recordings of the Ballade, Op. 24; the Album-leaf, Op. 28, No. 4; and excerpts from the Lyric Suites Opp. 12, 38, 43, 47, 54, and 68 are thoroughly delightful. Equally beautiful and engaging are the Rubinstein-Guarneri recordings of **Dvořák**'s Piano Quartet No. 2 in E-flat Major, Op. 87 (1970), and Piano Quintet in A Major, Op. 81 (1971). And his 1953 recordings of Anton **Rubinstein**'s once-popular and still-charming Barcarolles Nos. 3 (G Minor) and 4 (G Major) and Valse-Caprice in E-flat Major are pleasant to hear.

Anton Rubinstein was as much a cosmopolite as Arthur, but as a teacher he exercised most of his influence in Russia, where he founded the St. Petersburg Conservatory. Among the many Russian musicians who admired, feared, and learned from him, **Tchaikovsky** is the best known. Arthur Rubinstein recorded only two of Tchaikovsky's works: the Concerto No. 1 in

B-flat Minor, Op. 23, and the Trio in A Minor, Op. 50. He was justifiably proud of his first (1932) recording of the concerto, with Barbirolli and the London Symphony: it is dynamic and virtuosic—even vertiginous—and it demonstrates, once again, that Rubinstein, especially during the first two-thirds of his career, had little reason to envy Horowitz's or anyone else's keyboard technique. A 1946 broadcast performance (available on a pirate CD) with Rodzinski and the New York Philharmonic is similar in most respects to the 1932 version, but the basic tempo of the second movement is faster. In comparison with either of these versions, Rubinstein's 1963 recording of the concerto, with Leinsdorf and the Boston Symphony, sounds bombastic and rhetorical. His single recording of the trio (which was written in memory of yet another accomplished and influential musician named Rubinstein, Anton's younger brother Nikolai) was made in 1950, with Heifetz and Piatigorsky, and it is altogether less hectic and better integrated than the same musicians' recording of the Mendelssohn trio mentioned above. Among the many noteworthy details of the performance, Rubinstein's playing of the "Mazurka" variation in the second movement is particularly striking—which ought to surprise no one.

Rubinstein regarded **Rachmaninoff** more highly as a pianist than as a composer, and only the Concerto No. 2 in C Minor, Op. 18, and the Rhapsody on a Theme of Paganini, Op. 43, among all of Rachmaninoff's piano works, figured frequently in Rubinstein's repertoire. His 1956 recording of the concerto, with Reiner and the Chicago Symphony, is beautiful and warm, but I suspect that a younger Rubinstein, or a Rubinstein performing in concert, would have played the brilliant passages more daringly than the sixty-nine-year-old Rubinstein chose to do as he sat before the microphones. The same comment applies to his 1956 recording of the rhapsody, also with Reiner and the Chicagoans, but in this case my hunch was verified by an off-the-air recording made in 1950 with Victor De Sabata and the New York Philharmonic: Despite the poor sound, one has no trouble hearing that this performance is far bolder and livelier in the fast variations and far freer and more lyrical in the slow ones than is the official version. De Sabata, a brilliant conductor, was better attuned than Reiner to this work, and the Philharmonic matches Rubinstein nuance for nuance—and plays with much greater verve than the Chicago Symphony. Rubinstein's authorized recordings of **Prokofiev**'s music amount to only a studio version of the March from *The Love for Three Oranges* and live concert performances of twelve of the twenty *Visions Fugitives*, Op. 22. These interpretations are masterly and thoroughly enjoyable, and they make one regret that Rubinstein did not play more of Prokofiev's music.

Rubinstein's recorded repertoire of works from the French school begins with music of the Belgian César **Franck**. There are fine recordings of the Prelude, Chorale, and Fugue (1970) and the Symphonic Variations (1958, with Wallenstein and the Symphony of the Air, in addition to a pirate recording of a 1953 performance with Mitropoulos and the New York Philharmonic), and, with Heifetz, a stunning one of the Violin and Piano Sonata (1937); indeed, this richly varied and astonishingly executed interpretation of the sonata makes one wish that Heifetz and Rubinstein had set aside their differences and recorded all the masterpieces of the Romantic violin and piano repertoire.

When Rubinstein recorded the **Saint-Saëns** Concerto No. 2 in G Minor with Ormandy and the Philadelphia Orchestra in January 1969, the work had been in his active repertoire for over sixty-eight years, and yet the performance is fresh and high-spirited. A pirate recording of the piece, made at the same Mitropoulos–New York Philharmonic concert at which the Franck Symphonic Variations were recorded, is musically more incisive but technically sloppier than the 1969 version. Rubinstein's 1963 recordings of **Chabrier**'s Scherzo-Valse and **Fauré**'s Nocturne, Op. 33, No. 3, are both charming, and his 1970 recording of Fauré's Piano Quartet No. 1 in C Minor, Op. 15, with members of the Guarneri Quartet, is a truly magnificent rendition of a first-rate work.

"If you wanted to be critical, you could say that in Rubinstein's Debussy you sometimes wanted a more disembodied sound," Barenboim said in 1992. "I think his Ravel playing was much more interesting than his Debussy playing. The *Valses nobles et sentimentales* he played wonderfully. But this is slightly dry music, isn't it?" It is possible, however, that Barenboim knew only the **Debussy** performances and recordings of Rubinstein's last two decades. The excerpts from the 1945 and especially the 1952 Debussy recordings that have been reissued on CDs—and those that have not yet been reissued—present a very different image of Rubinstein's Debussy. Exemplary, in this respect, are the 1945 versions of "Reflets dans l'eau" and "Hommage à Rameau" and the 1952 versions of "La Cathédrale engloutie,"* "La Fille aux cheveux de lin,"* "Ondine,"* and "La Terrasse des audiences du clair de lune."* And even the 1929 HMV recording of "La Cathédrale engloutie," which is exceptionally fast (4:24, as compared with 5:57 in 1952, and 6:32 in Gieseking's 1953 version), is calm and vaporous in a way that the 1961 version (5:41) is not. (I suspect that the high speed of the 1929 version may have been induced by a producer's request to fit it onto one side of a 78 rpm disc.) But there is no question that Rubinstein's recordings of **Ravel**'s "La Vallée des cloches" from *Miroirs*, "Forlane" from *Le Tombeau de Couperin*, and especially *Valses nobles et sentimentales* all represent playing of the highest order. Ax, who studied the *Valses nobles* with Rubinstein, reported that the older pianist was very much against a "wispy" sound for these pieces, and that he was more concerned with achieving a proper voicing of the chords than with pursuing the melodic line. Finally, the 1950 Rubinstein-Heifetz-Piatigorsky recording of Ravel's Trio in A Minor documents a truly exhilarating performance.

Three *Mouvements perpétuels* and two Nocturnes (A-flat Major and D-flat Major) of Poulenc, all charmingly played by Rubinstein in 1963 recordings, complete the part of his French recorded repertoire with which I am familiar. I am not expert enough with respect to **Szymanowski**'s or **Villa-Lobos**'s music, or the music of Spanish composers (**Albéniz, Falla, Granados,** or **Mompou**), to voice an opinion of Rubinstein's recordings of their works, except to say that I have enjoyed listening to every one of them in my possession — and that they are all listed in the discography that follows.

I HAVE BARELY referred to the various Rubinstein video cassettes and videodiscs that have been published in recent years: concerto performances with André Previn (on the Decca/London label) and Bernard Haitink (Philips), a solo recital that was taped in California in 1975 (RCA), bits of pieces by Mendelssohn and Chopin (in the Philips compendium *The Golden Age of the Piano*), and other items as well. On the whole, the performances are not especially interesting, musically, but they show Rubinstein as he is remembered by most of the people who saw him: the dignified bearing, the absence of extraneous body movement and facial contortions, the absorption in the music, and the occasional surreptitious, canny glance at the conductor, to assist with or take a cue. Barenboim said that even Rubinstein's way of sitting at the piano "exemplified naturalness," and remarked that "there was something so self-evident about everything he did." When I mentioned that most of Barth's pupils sat calmly at the piano and played from the back and the shoulder, Barenboim said, "I have a feeling that this was very much the general way of the different schools. When you see photos of Busoni and d'Albert and Schnabel and so on, you don't see anything of the Glenn Gould sort, which is an extreme, of course. Not that this is of any artistic value, in the end; but I think that the physical idiosyncrasy is a phenomenon that must have started after the war."

On a broader matter, I mentioned to Barenboim that Rubinstein seemed to me fundamentally healthy, musically speaking. His playing was almost always thoughtful but not picky. "Yes, he saw the forest first — absolutely," Barenboim said. "He was negative about anything that had to do with exaggeration. What was interesting for me was that all the concertos I conducted for him, except the Chopin F Minor, I had played myself, many, many times, but when I conducted for him he made me forget that there could be any other way of playing them. There was something so unerring—there's no other word for it." About Rubinstein's healthy musical intellect, Ax commented: "After having worked with Rubinstein, I concluded that if you want to sound inspired you have to work very hard, and that if you sound too drily intellectual you probably haven't given enough thought to what you're doing."[13]

Eunice Podis said, "Rubinstein's playing had a very natural quality to it. Much of it was so moving that you got the impression that it was very free, but actually it wasn't. He was fairly strict in his tempi and he didn't take great liberties. There were certain little mannerisms that distinguished his music-making—as is true of all great artists—but they were by no means flagrant violations of tempo or rhythm. His vision of the music was so absolutely convincing that whatever he did came out sounding right, somehow. I've never heard another pianist whose music is as 'horizontal' as his was: he was always shaping a long line. This is something that you don't hear anymore, and it was what made his playing so compelling. You were often carried along on a very long, legato line—in Chopin, especially. He had a fabulous technique—every bit as virtuosic as Horowitz's, I think—but it was a means to an end. He used it for the effects that he wanted to make, rather than as something to be admired in itself. When Rubinstein was playing well, you walked away from his concert in an altered state of being. It was more than just a satisfying musical experience—it was on a different level from most performances. You thought the world was a better place and you were a better person."[14]

A Rubinstein Discography

Compiled and Edited by Donald Manildi

(Curator, International Piano Archives, University of Maryland)

Rubinstein's earliest recordings were apparently made around 1910 in Poland for the Favorit label. Only one such release has been traced, although it is certainly possible that others exist. In 1928 Rubinstein began recording in earnest for the Gramophone Company (HMV) of London, moving in 1940 to its then-affiliate, RCA Victor (though there were a few additional HMV releases after World War II). He continued this association until his final recording sessions in April 1976 (with the sole exception of the Brahms Concerto No.1 with Mehta and the Israel Philharmonic, made for Decca/London). Fortunately the majority of his recordings have been reissued in the compact disc format.

This discography lists every commercially issued Rubinstein recording (whether "authorized" or not) as of April 1995. All current American catalog numbers are included; for recordings not available at present, I have supplied the number under which the given item was most recently, or most widely, available. At a future date it may be possible to publish a comprehensive study of the Rubinstein recordings with session-by-session information, recording venues and producers, matrix and take numbers, all release numbers for all countries, and details of unissued material. Such a project, of course, would require a sizable volume by itself. It is hoped that the listing which follows will enable most listeners to identify and locate each item with minimum difficulty. Appended to the discography is information on commercially released video material and on Rubinstein's reproducing piano rolls.

Special thanks go to Bernadette Moore of RCA/BMG Classics, to A. R. Locantro, formerly of Electric & Musical Industries Ltd. (EMI), and to Jon M. Samuels for their assistance in providing necessary data.

Key: CD = compact disc
     LP = 33⅓ rpm vinyl disc
     45 = 45 rpm vinyl disc
     78 = 78 rpm shellac disc
     # denotes a recording made at a public performance

* means that one or more performances of the work thus marked have also been released in video format (see Appendix I)

Albéniz, Isaac

Córdoba, Op. 232, No. 4
(1-23-1929) LP: Electrola C027-1435551
(10-22-1953) CD: RCA Victor 61261

Evocación (*Ibéria*, No. 1)
(1-23-1929) LP: Electrola C027-1435551
(12-27-1955) CD: RCA Victor 61261

Navarra (completed by Séverac)
(1-23-1929) CD: Pearl GEMM 9464; Grammofono 2000 AB-78539
(6-17-1941) CD: RCA Victor 61261
#(12-10-1961) CD: RCA Victor 5670; RCA Victor 61445

Sevillanas (*Suite española*, No. 3)
(1-23-1929) CD: Grammofono 2000 AB-78539
(11-6-1953) CD: RCA Victor 61261

Triana (*Ibéria*, No. 6)
(12-15-1931) LP: Electrola C027-1435551

Bach, Johann Sebastian

Chaconne (Violin Partita No. 2 in D Minor, BWV 1004, arr. by Busoni)
(6-1970) CD: RCA Victor 5673; RCA Victor 62590

Toccata, Adagio, & Fugue in C, BWV 564 (arr. by Busoni)
(11-26, 28-1934) LP: Electrola C027-1435551

Beethoven, Ludwig van

Concerto No. 1 in C, Op. 15
(12-16-1956) Josef Krips/Symphony of the Air
CD: RCA Victor 61260
(10-20, 21-1967) Erich Leinsdorf/Boston Symphony Orchestra
CD: RCA Victor 5674
(4-9 to 11-1975) Daniel Barenboim/London Philharmonic Orchestra
LP: RCA Victor ARL1-1416; RCA Victor CRL5-1415

Concerto No. 2 in B-flat, Op. 19
(12-14-1956) Josef Krips/Symphony of the Air
CD: RCA Victor 61260
(12-21-1967) Erich Leinsdorf/Boston Symphony Orchestra
CD: RCA Victor 5675
(4-9 to 11-1975) Daniel Barenboim/London Philharmonic Orchestra
LP: RCA Victor ARL1-4711; RCA Victor CRL5-1415

Concerto No. 3 in C Minor, Op. 37*
#(10-29-1944) Arturo Toscanini/NBC Symphony Orchestra
CD: RCA Victor 5756; RCA Victor 60261
(12-6-1956) Josef Krips/Symphony of the Air
CD: RCA Victor 61260
(4-5, 6-1965) Erich Leinsdorf/Boston Symphony Orchestra
CD: RCA Victor 5675
#(12-7-1967) Antal Dorati/London Philharmonic Orchestra
CD: Hunt 567
(4-9 to 11-1975) Daniel Barenboim/London Philharmonic Orchestra
LP: RCA Victor ARL1-1418; RCA Victor CRL5-1415

Concerto No. 4 in G, Op. 58
(9-30-1947) Sir Thomas Beecham/Royal Philharmonic Orchestra
LP: Electrola C137-1544273
#(4-22-1951) Dimitri Mitropoulos/New York Philharmonic-Symphony
CD: AS Disc 532; Legend LGD 102
(12-6, 7-1956) Josef Krips/Symphony of the Air
CD: RCA Victor 61260
(4-20-1964) Erich Leinsdorf/Boston Symphony Orchestra
CD: RCA Victor 5676
#(12-7-1967) Antal Dorati/London Philharmonic Orchestra
CD: Hunt 567
(3-10, 11-1975) Daniel Barenboim/London Philharmonic Orchestra
LP: RCA Victor ARL1-1419; RCA Victor CRL5-1415

Concerto No. 5 in E-flat, Op. 73 (Emperor)
(12-14-1956) Josef Krips/Symphony of the Air
CD: RCA Victor 61260
(3-4-1963) Erich Leinsdorf/Boston Symphony Orchestra
CD: RCA Victor 5676
#(12-7-1967) Antal Dorati/London Philharmonic Orchestra
CD: Hunt 567

(3-10, 11-1975) Daniel Barenboim/London Philharmonic Orchestra
LP: RCA Victor ARL1-1420; RCA Victor CRL5-1415

Piano Sonata No. 3 in C, Op. 2, No. 3
(1-24-1963) LP: RCA Victor LSC-2812

Piano Sonata No. 8 in C Minor, Op. 13 *(Pathétique)*
(8-26, 27-1946) LP: RCA Victor LM-1072
(12-28-1954) LP: RCA Victor LM-1908
(4-1962) CD: RCA Victor 61443; RCA Victor 62561

Piano Sonata No. 14 in C-sharp Minor, Op. 27, No. 2 *(Moonlight)*
(4-6-1962) CD: RCA Victor 5674; RCA Victor 61443; RCA Victor 62561

Piano Sonata No. 18 in E-flat, Op. 31, No. 3
(5-23-1945) [third movement only] 78: RCA Victor M/DM-1018
(8-27, 28-1946) LP: RCA Victor LM-1071
(12-29-1954) CD: RCA Victor 61260
(4-21 to 23-1976) LP: RCA Victor ARL1-2397; RCA Victor ARL1-4711

Piano Sonata No. 21 in C, Op. 53 *(Waldstein)*
(12-28, 30-1954) LP: RCA Victor LM-2311

Piano Sonata No. 23 in F Minor, Op. 57 *(Appassionata)**
(5-22, 23-1945) LP: RCA Victor LM-1071
(12-30-1954) LP: RCA Victor LM-1908
(1-25, 30-1963) CD: RCA Victor 61443; RCA Victor 62561
#(1-15-1975) CD: RCA Victor 61160

Piano Sonata No. 26 in E-flat, Op. 81a *(Lebewohl)*
(12-31-1940) 78: RCA Victor M/DM-858
(4-1962) CD: RCA Victor 61443; RCA Victor 62561

Violin Sonata No. 5 in F, Op. 24 *(Spring)*
(12-31-1958) Henryk Szeryng, violin
CD: RCA Victor 61861

Violin Sonata No. 8 in G, Op. 30, No. 3
(1-3-1961) Henryk Szeryng, violin
CD: RCA Victor 6264; RCA Victor 61861

Violin Sonata No. 9 in A, Op. 47 (*Kreutzer*)
    (12-30-1958) Henryk Szeryng, violin
        CD: RCA Victor 61861

Piano Trio in B-flat, Op. 97 (*Archduke*)
    (9-12, 13-1941) Jascha Heifetz, violin; Emanuel Feuermann, cello
        CD: RCA Victor 60926; RCA Victor 61778

Brahms, Johannes

Ballades (4), Op. 10
    (6-10 to 12-1970) CD: RCA Victor 5672; RCA Victor 61862

Ballade in G Minor, Op. 118, No. 3
    (6-17-41) 78: RCA Victor 11-8622

Capriccio in B Minor, Op. 76, No. 2
    (3-9-1928) CD: Pearl GEMM 9464; Grammofono 2000 AB-78539
    (8-6, 7-1953) LP: RCA Victor LM-1787
    (6-10 to 12-1970) CD: RCA Victor 61263

Concerto No. 1 in D Minor, Op. 15*
    (4-17-1954) Fritz Reiner/Chicago Symphony Orchestra
        CD: RCA Victor 5668; RCA Victor 61263
    (4-21, 22-1964) Erich Leinsdorf/Boston Symphony Orchestra
        LP: RCA Victor LSC-2917
    (4-1976) Zubin Mehta/Israel Philharmonic Orchestra
        LP: London CS 7018; London JL 41069

Concerto No. 2 in B-flat, Op. 83
    (10-22, 23-1929) Albert Coates/London Symphony Orchestra
        CD: Claremont GSE 78-50-41
    (8-11-1952) Charles Munch/Boston Symphony Orchestra
        LP: RCA Victor LM-1728
    (4-4-1958) Josef Krips/RCA Victor Symphony Orchestra
        CD: RCA Victor 5671; RCA Victor 61442
    #(2-22-1960) Witold Rowicki/Warsaw Philharmonic Orchestra
        LP: Muza SX 1862/4 (with rehearsal); Fonit Cetra DOC 10
    #(5-4-1962) André Cluytens/RAI-Turin Symphony Orchestra
        LP: Fonit Cetra LAR 30

(11-22, 23-1971) Eugene Ormandy/Philadelphia Orchestra
LP: RCA Victor LSC-3253

Hungarian Dance No. 4 in F-sharp Minor
(3-12-1947) 78: RCA Victor MO-1149

Intermezzo in A Minor, Op. 76, No. 7
(6-17-1941) 78: RCA Victor M/DM-893

Intermezzo in E Minor, Op. 116, No. 5
(6-10 to 12-1970) CD: RCA Victor 5671; RCA Victor 61442

Intermezzo in E, Op. 116, No. 6
(12-31-1959) CD: RCA Victor 5672; RCA Victor 61862

Intermezzo in E-flat, Op. 117, No. 1
(11-5-1941) 78: RCA Victor M/DM-893

Intermezzo in B-flat Minor, Op. 117, No. 2
(11-19-1941) 78: RCA Victor M/DM-893
(8-3-1953) LP: RCA Victor LM-1787
(6-10 to 12-1970) CD: RCA Victor 5671; RCA Victor 61442

Intermezzo in C-Sharp Minor, Op. 117, No. 3
(8-3-1953) CD: RCA Victor 62592

Intermezzo in A, Op. 118, No. 2
(5-26-1941) 78: RCA Victor M/DM-893
(8-5-1953) CD: RCA Victor 62592

Intermezzo in E-flat Minor, Op. 118, No. 6
(5-26-1941) 78: RCA Victor M/DM-893
(8-7-1953) CD: RCA Victor 62592
(6-10 to 12-1970) CD: RCA Victor 61263

Intermezzo in E Minor, Op. 119, No. 2
(8-10-1953) CD: RCA Victor 62592

Intermezzo in C, Op. 119, No. 3
(6-17-1941) 78: RCA Victor M/DM-893
(8-7-1953) CD: RCA Victor 62592

Piano Quartet No. 1 in G Minor, Op. 25
    (10-10, 11-1932) Pro Arte Quartet members (Alphonse Onnou, violin;
        Germain Prévost, viola; Robert Maas, cello)
        CD: Biddulph LAB 027
    (12-27 to 30-1967) Guarneri Quartet members (John Dalley, violin;
        Michael Tree, viola; David Soyer, cello)
        CD: RCA Victor 5677

Piano Quartet No. 2 in A, Op. 26
    (12-27 to 30-1967) Guarneri Quartet members (Arnold Steinhardt,
        violin; Michael Tree, viola; David Soyer, cello)
        LP: RCA Victor LSC-6188

Piano Quartet No. 3 in C Minor, Op. 60
    (12-27 to 30-1967) Guarneri Quartet members (Arnold Steinhardt,
        violin; Michael Tree, viola; David Soyer, cello)
        CD: RCA Victor 5677

Piano Quintet in F Minor, Op. 34
    (12-28, 29-1966) Guarneri Quartet (Arnold Steinhardt, John Dalley,
        violins; Michael Tree, viola; David Soyer, cello)
        CD: RCA Victor 5669

Rhapsody in B Minor, Op. 79, No. 1
    (6-6-1941) 78: RCA Victor M/DM-893
    (8-5-1953) LP: RCA Victor LM-1787
    (6-10 to 12-1970) CD: RCA Victor 61263

Rhapsody in G Minor, Op. 79, No. 2
    (4-3-1937) CD: Grammofono 2000 AB-78539
    (3-12-1947) 78: RCA Victor MO-1149
    (8-4-1953) LP: RCA Victor LM-1787
    (6-10 to 12-1970) CD: RCA Victor 5671; RCA Victor 61442

Rhapsody in E-flat, Op. 119, No. 4
    (6-6-1941) 78: RCA Victor M/DM-893
    (8-10-1953) LP: RCA Victor LM-1787

Romance in F, Op. 118, No. 5
    (12-31-1959) CD: RCA Victor 5672; RCA Victor 61862

Cello Sonata No. 1 in E Minor, Op. 38
    (7-6-1936) Gregor Piatigorsky, cello
        CD: Biddulph LAB 086; Music & Arts 674; Pearl GEMM 9447
    (10-11-1966) Gregor Piatigorsky, cello
        CD: RCA Victor 62592

Cello Sonata No. 2 in F, Op. 99
    (10-11-1966) Gregor Piatigorsky, cello
        CD: RCA Victor 62592

Piano Sonata No. 3 in F Minor, Op. 5
    (6-17-1949) LP: RCA Victor LM-1189
    (12-17-1959) CD: RCA Victor 5672; RCA Victor 61862

Violin Sonata No. 1 in G, Op. 78
    (12-28, 29-1960) Henryk Szeryng, violin
        CD: RCA Victor 6264

Violin Sonata No. 2 in A, Op. 100
    (12-30-1960) Henryk Szeryng, violin
        LP: RCA Victor LSC-2619

Violin Sonata No. 3 in D Minor, Op. 108
    (6-15-1932) Paul Kochanski, violin
        CD: Biddulph LAB 086; Pearl BVA 1
    (12-30-1960; 1-3-1961) Henryk Szeryng, violin
        CD: RCA Victor 6264

Piano Trio No. 1 in B, Op. 8
    (9-11, 12-1941) Jascha Heifetz, violin; Emanuel Feuermann, cello
        CD: RCA Victor 61778; Biddulph LAB 086
    (9-4 to 10-1972) Henryk Szeryng, violin; Pierre Fournier, cello
        CD: RCA Victor 6260

Piano Trio No. 2 in C, Op. 87
    (9-4 to 10-1972) Henryk Szeryng, violin; Pierre Fournier, cello
        CD: RCA Victor 6260

Piano Trio No. 3 in C Minor, Op. 101
    (9-4 to 10-1972) Henryk Szeryng, violin; Pierre Fournier, cello
        LP: RCA Victor ARL3-0138

Wiegenlied (Cradle Song), Op. 49, No. 4 (arr. by Rubinstein)
(3-12-1947) 78: RCA Victor MO-1149
(10-1-1947) LP: Electrola C151-03244/5

Chabrier, Emanuel

Scherzo-Valse (*Pièces pittoresques*, No. 10)
(4-3-1963) CD: RCA Victor 5665; RCA Victor 61446

Chopin, Frédéric

Andante spianato and Grand Polonaise in E-flat, Op. 22
(2-7, 8-1935) CD: EMI 64697; EMI 64933
(12-14-1950) LP: RCA Victor LM-6109; RCA Victor LM-6802
(1-20-1958) Alfred Wallenstein/Symphony of the Air
CD: RCA Victor 60404
#(2-1-1960) LP: Paragon LBI 53001; Discocorp BWS 740
(3-23-1964) CD: RCA Victor 5617; RCA Victor 60822

Ballade No. 1 in G Minor, Op. 23
(4-28-1959) CD: RCA Victor RCD1-7156; RCA Victor 60822
#(2-16-1960) LP: Paragon LBI 53001; Discocorp BWS 740

Ballade No. 2 in F, Op. 38
(4-29-1959) CD: RCA Victor RCD1-7156; RCA Victor 60822

Ballade No. 3 in A-flat, Op. 47
(4-29-1959) CD: RCA Victor RCD1-7156; RCA Victor 60822
#(1969) CD: Ermitage 101
#(11-5-1970) CD: Arkadia 918.1
#(11-7-1970) CD: Ermitage 127

Ballade No. 4 in F Minor, Op. 52
(4-28-1959) CD: RCA Victor RCD1-7156; RCA Victor 60822
#(11-5-1970) CD: Arkadia 918.1

Barcarolle in F-sharp, Op. 60
(4-18-1928) CD: EMI 64697; EMI 64933; Pearl GEMM 9464
(8-28-1946) CD: RCA Victor 60047; RCA Victor 60822
(c. 1957) LP: RCA Victor LM-2277
(11-26-1962) CD: RCA Victor 5617; RCA Victor 60822
#(10-1-1964) LP: Melodiya C10 21327; CD: Fonit Cetra CDE 1024

Berceuse in D-flat, Op. 57
>   (7-22-1932) CD: EMI 64697; EMI 64933; Pearl GEMM 9464
>   (6-20-1946) CD: RCA Victor 60047; RCA Victor 60822
>   (4-21-1958) LP: RCA Victor LM-2277
>   (11-26-1962) CD: RCA Victor 5617; RCA Victor 60822
>   #(1969) CD: Ermitage 101
>   #(11-5-1970) CD: Arkadia 918.1
>   #(11-7-1970) CD: Ermitage 127

Boléro, Op. 19
>   (11-27-1962) CD: RCA Victor 5617; RCA Victor 60822

Concerto No. 1 in E Minor, Op. 11
>   (4-5-1937) John Barbirolli/London Symphony Orchestra
>   CD: EMI 64491; EMI 64933
>   #(2-9-1947) Bruno Walter/New York Philharmonic-Symphony
>   CD: AS Disc 411
>   (12-12-1953) Alfred Wallenstein/Los Angeles Philharmonic
>   LP: RCA Victor LM-1810
>   (6-8, 9-1961) Stanislaw Skrowaczewski/New Symphony Orchestra,
>   London
>   CD: RCA Victor 5612; RCA Victor 60822
>   #(4-29-1964) Franco Caracciolo/RAI-Naples Scarlatti Orchestra
>   CD: Arkadia 515.1; Hunt 515; Virtuoso 2697102

Concerto No. 2 in F Minor, Op. 21*
>   (1-8-1931) John Barbirolli/London Symphony Orchestra
>   CD: EMI 64491; EMI 64933
>   (3-25-1946) William Steinberg/NBC Symphony Orchestra
>   LP: RCA Victor LM-1046
>   (1-20-1958) Alfred Wallenstein/Symphony of the Air
>   CD: RCA Victor 5612; RCA Victor 60822
>   #(2-22-1960) Witold Rowicki/Warsaw Philharmonic Orchestra
>   LP: Muza SX 1861; I Grandi Concerti GCL-27
>   #(5-16-1960) Carlo Maria Giulini/Philharmonia Orchestra
>   CD: Hunt 567
>   (10-1-1968) Eugene Ormandy/Philadelphia Orchestra
>   CD: RCA Victor 60604

Etude No. 4 in C-sharp Minor, Op. 10, No. 4*
>   #(10-1-1964) LP: Melodiya C10 21327
>   #(1-15-1975) CD: RCA Victor 61160

Etude No. 5 in G-flat, Op. 10, No. 5 *(Black Key)*
#(2-1-1960) LP: Paragon LBI 53001
#(10-1-1964) LP: Melodiya C10 21327

Etude No. 6 in E-flat Minor, Op. 10, No. 6
#(2-1-1960) LP: Paragon LBI 53001

Etude No. 8 in F, Op. 10, No. 8
#(2-1-1960) LP: Paragon LBI 53001

Etude No. 9 in F Minor, Op. 10, No. 9
#(2-1-1960) LP: Paragon LBI 53001

Etude No. 13 in A-flat, Op. 25, No. 1 *(Aeolian Harp)*
#(10-1-1964) LP: Melodiya C10 21327

Etude No. 17 in E Minor, Op. 25, No. 5*
#(10-1-1964) LP: Melodiya C10 21327
#(1969) CD: Ermitage 101
#(11-5-1970) CD: Arkadia 918.1
#(11-7-1970) CD: Ermitage 127
#(1-15-1975) CD: RCA Victor 61160

Etudes, Trois Nouvelles (1839)
(4-21-1958) LP: RCA Victor LM-2277
(11-28-1962) CD: RCA Victor 5617; RCA Victor 60822

Fantasy in F Minor, Op. 49
(2-11-1957) LP: RCA Victor LM-2277
(11-27-1962) CD: RCA Victor 5616; RCA Victor 60822
#(1969) CD: Ermitage 101
#(11-5-1970) CD: Arkadia 918.1
#(11-7-1970) CD: Ermitage 127

Fantasy on Polish Airs, Op. 13
(10-1-1968) Eugene Ormandy/Philadelphia Orchestra
CD: RCA Victor 60604

Fantasy-Impromptu in C-sharp Minor, Op. 66
(5-21-1951) LP: RCA Victor LM-1153
(3-11-1957) LP: RCA Victor LM-2277; RCA Victor LM-6802
(3-25-1964) CD: RCA Victor 5617; RCA Victor 60822

Impromptu No. 1 in A-flat, Op. 29
    (2-12-1954) LP: RCA Victor LM-2277; RCA Victor LM-6802
    (3-23-1964) CD: RCA Victor 5617; RCA Victor 60822

Impromptu No. 2 in F-sharp, Op. 36
    (11-1953) LP: RCA Victor LM-2277; RCA Victor LM-6802
    (3-23-1964) CD: RCA Victor 5617; RCA Victor 60822

Impromptu No. 3 in G-flat, Op. 51
    (3-26-1946) 78: RCA Victor M/DM-1075
    (11-3-1953) LP: RCA Victor LM-2277; RCA Victor LM-6802
    (3-24-1964) CD: RCA Victor 5617; RCA Victor 60822
    #(10-1-1964) LP: Melodiya C10 21325

Mazurkas (51)
    (11-13-1938) [Op. 6, Nos. 1–2; Op. 17, No. 4; Op. 24, No. 2; Op. 41, No. 2;
        Op. 50, Nos. 1–2; Op. 63, Nos. 2–3]
    (12-12-1938) [Op. 6, No. 3; Op. 7, Nos. 1–5; Op. 17, No. 3; Op. 30, No. 1;
        Op. 33, No. 4; Op. 50, No. 3]
    (12-13-1938) [Op. 6, No. 4; Op. 17, Nos. 1–2; Op. 24, Nos. 1 & 3; Op. 30,
        Nos. 2–4; Op. 33, Nos. 1 & 3; Op. 41, Nos. 1 & 4; Op. 56, No. 2; Op.
        59, No. 1; Op. 67, Nos. 2–4; Op. 68, Nos. 3–4; "Gaillard" in A
        Minor]
    (12-14-1938) [Op. 41, No. 3; Op. 56, No. 1; Op. 59, Nos. 2–3; Op. 67, No.
        1; Op. 68, Nos. 1–2; "Notre temps" in A Minor]
    (5-10-1939) [Op. 24, No. 4; Op. 33, No. 2; Op. 56, No. 3; Op. 63, No. 1]
        CD: EMI 64697; EMI 64933

    (7-14-1952) [Op. 6, Nos. 1–4; Op. 7, Nos. 3–5; Op. 17, Nos. 1–4; Op. 24,
        No. 2; Op. 30, Nos. 1 & 3]
    (7-15-1952) [Op. 30, No. 4; Op. 33, Nos. 1–2, 4; Op. 41, Nos. 1–4; Op. 50,
        Nos. 1–3; Op. 56, Nos. 1–3; Op. 59, Nos. 1–3; Op. 63, Nos. 1–2]
    (7-16-1952) [Op. 63, No. 3; Op. 67, Nos. 1–4; Op. 68, Nos. 1–4; "Notre
        temps" in A Minor; "Gaillard" in A Minor]
    (7-24-1952) [Op. 24, No. 3]
    (9-5-1952) [Op. 7, No. 1]
    (2-5-1953) [Op. 7, No. 2; Op. 24, Nos. 1 & 4; Op. 30, No. 2; Op. 33, No. 3]
        LP: RCA Victor LM-6109

    (12-27-1965) [Op. 6, Nos. 1–4; Op. 7, Nos. 1–4; Op. 17, Nos. 1–4; Op. 24,
        No. 1]

(12-28-1965) [Op. 6, No. 1; Op. 7, No. 5; Op. 17, Nos. 3–4; Op. 24, Nos. 1–4; Op. 41, Nos. 1–4; Op. 50, Nos. 1–3; Op. 56, No. 1]

(12-29-1965) [Op. 30, Nos. 1–4; Op. 33, No. 1; Op. 56, Nos. 2–3; Op. 59, No. 1]

(12-30-1965) [Op. 59, Nos. 2–3; Op. 63, Nos. 1–3]

(1-3-1966) [Op. 33, Nos. 2–3; Op. 67, Nos. 1–4; Op. 68, Nos. 1–4; "Notre temps" in A Minor; "Gaillard" in A Minor]
  CD: RCA Victor 5614; RCA Victor 60822

Mazurka No. 23 in D, Op. 33, No. 2
  (7-22-1932) CD: Pearl GEMM 9464
  #(1969) CD: Ermitage 101

Mazurka No. 35 in C Minor, Op. 56, No. 2
  (7-22-1930) LP: Electrola C027-1435551
  #(2-1-1960) LP: Paragon LBI 53001
  #(1969) CD: Ermitage 101

Mazurka No. 39 in B, Op. 63, No. 1
  (7-22-1932) CD: Pearl GEMM 9464

Nocturnes (19)
  (5-28-1936) [Op. 55, No. 2]
  (5-29-1936) [Op. 48, No. 2]
  (10-19-1936) [Op. 15, No. 2; Op. 27, No. 1]
  (10-20-1936) [Op. 37, No. 2; Op. 55, No. 1; Op. 62, No. 2]
  (10-30-1936) [Op. 9, No. 2; Op. 27, No. 2; Op. 32, No. 1]
  (2-12-1937) [Op. 15, No. 3]
  (2-13-1937) [Op. 9, No. 1; Op. 32, No. 2; Op. 37, No. 1; Op. 62, No. 1]
  (2-14-1937) [Op. 9, No. 3; Op. 15, No. 1; Op. 48, No. 1; Op. 62, No. 1]
  (4-2-1937) [Op. 72, No. 1]
    CD: EMI 64491; EMI 64933

  (6-29-1949) [Op. 9, No. 2; Op. 15, No. 2; Op. 27, Nos. 1–2; Op. 48, No. 1]
  (6-30-1949) [Op. 37, No. 1; Op. 55, No. 1]
  (7-28-1949) [Op. 15, No. 3; Op. 32, Nos. 1–2]
  (7-29-1949) [Op. 48, No. 2; Op. 55, No. 2; Op. 62, Nos. 1–2]
  (9-26-1950) [Op. 9, Nos. 1 & 3; Op. 15, No. 1; Op. 37, No. 2; Op. 72, No. 1]
    LP: RCA Victor LM-6005; RCA Victor LM-6802

(8-30-1965) [Op. 9, Nos. 1–3; Op. 15, Nos. 1–3; Op. 27, No. 1]
(8-31-1965) [Op. 27, No. 2; Op. 32, Nos. 1–2; Op. 37, Nos. 1–2; Op. 48, No. 1]
(9-1-1965) [Op. 48, No. 2; Op. 55, No. 1; Op. 62, Nos. 1–2]
(9-2-1965) [Op. 72, No. 1]
(2-21-1967) [Op. 55, No. 2]
     CD: RCA Victor 5613; RCA Victor 60822

Nocturne No. 5 in F-sharp, Op. 15, No. 2*
#(5-8-1961) CD: Ermitage 127
#(1-15-1975) CD: RCA Victor 61160

Nocturne No. 8 in D-flat, Op. 27, No. 2
#(10-1-1964) LP: Melodiya C10 21325; CD: Fonit Cetra CDE 1024

Polonaise No. 1 in C-sharp Minor, Op. 26, No. 1
(2-6, 8-1935) CD: EMI 64697; EMI 64933
(5-21-1951) LP: RCA Victor LM-1205; RCA Victor LM-6802
(3-4-1964) CD: RCA Victor 5615; RCA Victor 60822

Polonaise No. 2 in E-flat Minor, Op. 26, No. 2
(2-7-1935) CD: EMI 64697; EMI 64933
(9-27-1950) LP: RCA Victor LM-1205; RCA Victor LM-6802
(3-4-1964) CD: RCA Victor 5615; RCA Victor 60822

Polonaise No. 3 in A, Op. 40, No. 1 (Military)*
(12-5-1934) CD: EMI 64697; EMI 64933
(9-28-1950) LP: RCA Victor LM-1205; RCA Victor LM-6802
(3-4-1964) CD: RCA Victor 5615; RCA Victor 60822

Polonaise No. 4 in C Minor, Op. 40, No. 2
(12-6-1934) CD: EMI 64697; EMI 64933
(9-27-1950) LP: RCA Victor LM-1205; RCA Victor LM-6802
(3-4-1964) CD: RCA Victor 5615; RCA Victor 60822

Polonaise No. 5 in F-sharp Minor, Op. 44
(1-29-1935) CD: EMI 64697; EMI 64933
(5-12-1951) LP: RCA Victor LM-1205; RCA Victor LM-6802
(3-5-1964) CD: RCA Victor 5615; RCA Victor 60822
#(10-1-1964) LP: Melodiya C10 21325
#(1969) CD: Ermitage 101

Polonaise No. 6 in A-flat, Op. 53 *(Heroic)**
    (2-6-1935) CD: EMI 64697; EMI 64933
    (9-28-1950) LP: RCA Victor LM-1205; RCA Victor LM-6802
    #(2-22-1960) LP: Muza SX 1862/4; CD: Fonit Cetra CDE 1024
    (3-6-1964) CD: RCA Victor 5615; RCA Victor 60822
    #(10-1-1964) LP: Melodiya C10 21327
    #(11-5-1970) CD: Arkadia 918.1
    #(1-15-1975) CD: RCA Victor 61160

Polonaise-Fantasy in A-flat, Op. 61
    (12-5-1934) CD: EMI 64697; EMI 64933
    (12-13-1950) LP: RCA Victor LM-6109; RCA Victor LM-6802
    (3-12-1964) CD: RCA Victor 5615; RCA Victor 60822

Preludes (24), Op. 28
    (6-10-1946) [Nos. 1–10, 14–15]
    (6-11-1946) [Nos. 16–24]
    (6-20-1946) [Nos. 11–13]
        CD: RCA Victor 60047; RCA Victor 60822
    #(1969) [Nos. 8, 15, 23–24] CD: Ermitage 101
    #(11-5-1970) [Nos. 8, 15, 24] CD: Arkadia 918.1
    #(11-7-1970) [Nos. 8, 15, 23–24] CD: Ermitage 127

Scherzo No. 1 in B Minor, Op. 20
    (10-12-1932) CD: EMI 64697; EMI 64933; Pearl GEMM 9464
    (6-28-1949) LP: RCA Victor LM-1132
    (3-26-1959) CD: RCA Victor RCD1-7156; RCA Victor 60822

Scherzo No. 2 in B-flat Minor, Op. 31
    (10-12, 17-1932) CD: EMI 64697; EMI 64933; Pearl GEMM 9464
    (6-28-1949) LP: RCA Victor LM-1132
    (3-26-1959) CD: RCA Victor RCD1-7156; RCA Victor 60822
    #(1969) CD: Ermitage 101
    #(11-5-1970) CD: Arkadia 918.1

Scherzo No. 3 in C-sharp Minor, Op. 39*
    (10-16-1932) CD: EMI 64697; EMI 64933; Pearl GEMM 9464
    (6-28-1949) LP: RCA Victor LM-1132
    (3-26-1959) CD: RCA Victor RCD1-7156; RCA Victor 60822

Scherzo No. 4 in E, Op. 54
    (10-16-1959) CD: EMI 64697; EMI 64933; Pearl GEMM 9464
    (6-29-1949) LP: RCA Victor LM-1132
    (3-25-1959) CD: RCA Victor RCD1-7156; RCA Victor 60822
    #(2-16-1960) LP: Paragon LBI 53001

Sonata No. 2 in B-flat Minor, Op. 35 *(Funeral March)*
    (3-11, 18, 29-1946) CD: RCA Victor 60047; RCA Victor 60822
    (1-9 to 11-1961) CD: RCA Victor 5616; RCA Victor 60822
    #(5-8-1961) CD: Ermitage 108
    #(10-1-1964) LP: Melodiya C10 21325

Sonata No. 3 in B Minor, Op. 58
    (5-1, 2-1959; 1-5-1961) CD: RCA Victor 5616; RCA Victor 60822

Tarantelle in A-flat, Op. 43
    (9-2-1965) CD: RCA Victor 5617; RCA Victor 60822

Waltzes (14)
    (11-6 to 13-1953) [Op. 64, No. 2; Op. 69, No. 2]
    (11-25-1953) [Op. 34, Nos. 1 & 3]
    (11-27-1953) [Op. 42; Op. 64, Nos. 1 & 3; Op. 69, No. 1; Op. 70, Nos. 1–2]
    (12-12-1953) [Op. 18; Op. 34, No. 2; Op. 70, No. 3; Op. Posth. in
        E Minor]
        LP: RCA Victor LM-1892; RCA Victor LM-6802

    (6-25-1963) [all] CD: RCA Victor 5492; RCA Victor 60822

Waltz No. 2 in A-flat, Op. 34, No. 1
    (3-29-1929) CD: EMI 64697; EMI 64933; Grammofono 2000 AB-78539
    #(10-1-1964) LP: Melodiya C10 21327

Waltz No. 3 in A Minor, Op. 34, No. 2
    #(10-1-1964) LP: Melodiya C10 21327; CD: Fonit Cetra CDE 1024

Waltz No. 7 in C-sharp Minor, Op. 64, No. 2*
    (12-17-1930) CD: EMI 64697; EMI 64933
    #(2-1-1960) LP: Paragon LBI 53001
    #(   ) CD: Ermitage 101
    #(11-5-1970) CD: Arkadia 918.1
    #(11-7-1970) CD: Ermitage 127

Debussy, Claude

La cathédrale engloutie (*Préludes*, Book I: No. 10)
  (1-24-1929) CD: Pearl GEMM 9464; Grammofono 2000 AB-78539
  (5-13-1952) LP: RCA Victor LVT-1042
  #(12-4-1961) CD: RCA Victor 5670; RCA Victor 61445

La fille aux cheveux de lin (*Préludes*, Book I: No. 8)
  (5-13-1952) LP: RCA Victor LVT-1042

Hommage à Rameau (*Images*, Book I: No. 2)
  (1-4-1945) CD: RCA Victor 61446
  (5-14-1952) 45: RCA Victor ERA-86
  #(10-30-1961) CD: RCA Victor 61445

Jardins sous la pluie (*Estampes*, No. 3)
  (1-11-1945) CD: RCA Victor 61446

Masques
  (5-14-1952) LP: RCA Victor LVT-1042

Minstrels (*Préludes*, Book I: No. 12)
  (5-13-1952) CD: RCA Victor 61446

Ondine (*Préludes*, Book II: No. 8)*
  (5-13-1952) LP: RCA Victor LVT-1042
  #(11-3-1961) CD: RCA Victor 5670; RCA Victor 61445
  #(10-1-1964) LP: Melodiya C10 21327

La plus que lente (Valse)*
  (1-11-1945) CD: RCA Victor 61446
  (12-11-1950) LP: RCA Victor LM-1153
  (6-1970) LP: RCA Victor ARL1-3850
  #(1-15-1975) CD: RCA Victor 61160

Poissons d'or (*Images*, Book II: No. 3)
  (1-11-1945) CD: RCA Victor 61446
  (5-14-1952) LP: RCA Victor LVT-1042
  #(10-30-1961) CD: RCA Victor 5670; RCA Victor 61445

Prélude in A Minor (*Pour le piano*, No. 1)*
    (12-14-1931) CD: Grammofono 2000 AB-78539
    #(1-15-1975) CD: RCA Victor 61160

Reflets dans l'eau (*Images*, Book I: No. 1)
    (1-11-1945) CD: RCA Victor 61446

Soirée dans Grenade (*Estampes*, No. 2)
    (1-11-1945) CD: RCA Victor 61446

La terrasse des audiences du clair de lune (*Préludes*, Book II: No. 7)
    (5-14-1952) LP: RCA Victor LVT-1042

Dvořák, Antonin

Piano Quartet No. 2 in E-flat, Op. 87
    (12-28-1970) Guarneri Quartet members (Arnold Steinhardt, violin;
        Michael Tree, viola; David Soyer, cello)
        CD: RCA Victor 6256

Piano Quintet in A, Op. 81
    (4-5, 8-1971) Guarneri Quartet (Arnold Steinhardt, John Dalley, violins;
        Michael Tree, viola; David Soyer, cello)
        CD: RCA Victor 6263

Falla, Manuel de

Andaluza (*Pièces espagnoles*, No. 4)
    (6-30-1949) CD: RCA Victor 61261

Dance of Terror (*El Amor Brujo*)
    (7-22-1930) CD: Grammofono 2000 AB-78539
    (5-8-1947) CD: RCA Victor 61261

Miller's Dance (*El Sombrero de Tres Picos*)
    (2-12-1954) CD: RCA Victor 61261

Nights in the Gardens of Spain
    (11-14-1949) Vladimir Golschmann/Saint Louis Symphony Orchestra
        CD: RCA Victor 61261
    (3-25-1957) Enrique Jorda/San Francisco Symphony Orchestra
        CD: RCA Victor 60046

#(4-27-1960) Ernest Ansermet/Orchestre de la Suisse Romande
LP: I Grandi Concerti GCL 61
(1-2-1969) Eugene Ormandy/Philadelphia Orchestra
CD: RCA Victor 5666; RCA Victor 61863

Ritual Fire Dance *(El Amor Brujo)*
(7-22-1930) CD: Grammofono 2000 AB-78539
(5-8-1947) CD: RCA Victor 61261
(3-23-1961) CD: RCA Victor 5666

Fauré, Gabriel

Nocturne No. 3 in A-flat, Op. 33, No. 3
(11-13-1938) 78: HMV DB 3718; RCA Victor 15660
(4-5-1963) CD: RCA Victor 5665; RCA Victor 61446

Piano Quartet No. 1 in C Minor, Op. 15
(8-26, 27, 29-1949) Paganini Quartet members (Henri Temianka, violin; Robert Courte, viola; Adolphe Frezin, cello)
LP: RCA Victor LM-52
(12-28-1970) Guarneri Quartet members (John Dalley, violin; Michael Tree, viola; David Soyer, cello)
CD: RCA Victor 6256

Franck, César

Prelude, Chorale, and Fugue
(1-3, 4-1945) 78: RCA Victor M/DM-1004
(9-8, 10-1952) LP: RCA Victor LM-1822
(6-1970) CD: RCA Victor 5673; RCA Victor 62590

Violin Sonata in A
(4-3-1937) Jascha Heifetz, violin
CD: Biddulph LAB 025; EMI 64929; RCA Victor 61778

Variations Symphoniques
#(4-14-1953) Dimitri Mitropoulos/New York Philharmonic-Symphony
CD: Music & Arts 655; AS Disc 508
(1-15-1958) Alfred Wallenstein/Symphony of the Air
CD: RCA Victor 5666; RCA Victor 61496

Gershwin, George

Prelude No. 2
    (3-11-1946) 78: RCA Victor 11-9420

Granados, Enrique

The Maiden & the Nightingale (*Goyescas*, No. 4)
    (7-22-1930) CD: Pearl GEMM 9464
    (6-30-1949) CD: RCA Victor 61261
    (10-22-1952) LP: RCA Victor LM-2181
    #(5-8-1961) CD: Ermitage 108

Spanish Dance No. 5 in E Minor (*Andaluza*)
    (2-12-1954) CD: RCA Victor 61261

Grieg, Edvard

Album Leaf, Op. 28, No. 4
    (11-9-1953) CD: RCA Victor 60897

Ballade in G Minor, Op. 24
    (11-6-1953) CD: RCA Victor 60897

Berceuse, Op. 38, No. 1
    (8-11-1953) CD: RCA Victor 60897

Concerto in A Minor, Op. 16*
    #(1939?) [first movement only] Donald Voorhees/orchestra
        LP: Melodram 304
    (3-6-1942) Eugene Ormandy/Philadelphia Orchestra
        CD: RCA Victor 60897
    (8-22-1949) Antal Dorati/RCA Victor Symphony Orchestra
        LP: RCA Victor LM-1018
    (2-11-1956) Alfred Wallenstein/RCA Victor Symphony Orchestra
        CD: RCA Victor RCD1-5363
    (3-10-1961) Alfred Wallenstein/RCA Victor Symphony Orchestra
        CD: RCA Victor 6259; RCA Victor 61262
    #(11-25-1963) Carlo Maria Giulini/Philharmonia Orchestra
        CD: Intaglio 7101

Cradle Song, Op. 68, No. 5
    (11-4-1953) CD: RCA Victor 60897

Elfin Dance, Op. 12, No. 4
Folk Song, Op. 12, No. 5
Folk Song, Op. 38, No. 2
Little Bird, Op. 43, No. 4
    (8-11-1953) CD: RCA Victor 60897

March of the Dwarfs, Op. 54, No. 3
    (11-4-1953) CD: RCA Victor 60897

Papillon, Op. 43, No. 1
    (12-12-1953) CD: RCA Victor 60897

Shepherd Boy, Op. 54, No. 1
    (8-11-1953) CD: RCA Victor 60897

Spring Dance, Op. 38, No. 5
    (11-4-1953) CD: RCA Victor 60897

Spring Dance, Op. 47, No. 6
    (8-11-1953) CD: RCA Victor 60897

Haydn, Franz Josef

Andante & Variations in F Minor
    (4-19-1960) CD: RCA Victor 7967

Liszt, Franz

Concerto No. 1 in E-flat
    #(1947) Eugene Ormandy/Philadelphia Orchestra
        LP: Melodram 304
    (2-11-1947) Antal Dorati/Dallas Symphony Orchestra
        CD: RCA Victor 60046
    (2-12-1956) Alfred Wallenstein/RCA Victor Symphony Orchestra
        CD: RCA Victor 6255; RCA Victor 61496

Consolation No. 3 in D-flat
    (2-14-1937) CD: Grammofono 2000 AB-78539
    (10-23-1953) CD: RCA Victor 61860

Funérailles (*Harmonies poétiques et religieuses*, No. 7)
    (11-6 to 11-1953) CD: RCA Victor 61860

Hungarian Rhapsody No. 10 in E
    (4-3-1937) CD: Grammofono 2000 AB-78539
    (11-6 to 11-1953) CD: RCA Victor 61860

Hungarian Rhapsody No. 12 in C-sharp Minor
    (c. 1910) [abridged] 78: Favorit 1-74612
    (11-6 to 11-1953) CD: RCA Victor 61860

Liebestraum No. 3 in A-flat*
    (11-7-1935) CD: Grammofono 2000 AB-78539
    (12-12-1950) LP: RCA Victor LM-1153
    (11-6 to 11-1953) CD: RCA Victor 61860
    (c. 1969) LP: RCA Victor LS 10319-M; RCA Victor OPO 1001

Mephisto Waltz No. 1
    (12-28-1955) CD: RCA Victor 61860
    #(5-8-1961) CD: Ermitage 108

Sonata in B Minor
    (4-19-1965) CD: RCA Victor 5673; RCA Victor 62590

Valse-Impromptu in A-flat
    (10-23, 27-1953) CD: RCA Victor 61860

Valse Oubliée No. 1
    (3-18-1946) 78: RCA Victor 10-1272
    (12-11-1950) CD: RCA Victor 61860
    (3-23-1961) LP: RCA Victor LSC-2566

Mendelssohn, Felix

Spinning Song, Op. 67, No. 4*
    (12-12-1950) CD: RCA Victor 62662
    (c. 1969) LP: RCA Victor LS 10319-M; RCA Victor OPO 1001

Piano Trio No. 1 in D Minor, Op. 49*
    (8-25-1950) Jascha Heifetz, violin; Gregor Piatigorsky, cello
        CD: RCA Victor 7768; RCA Victor 61778

Milhaud, Darius

Saudades do Brasil Nos. 5, 9, 11
(8-26-1946) 78: RCA Victor 11-9420

Mompou, Federico

Cancó i Danza No. 1
(12-28-1955) CD: RCA Victor 61261

Cancó i Danza No. 6
(2-12-1954) CD: RCA Victor 61261

Mozart, Wolfgang Amadeus

Concerto No. 17 in G, K. 453
(3-30, 31-1962) Alfred Wallenstein/RCA Victor Symphony Orchestra
CD: RCA Victor 61859

Concerto No. 20 in D Minor, K. 466
(4-1-1961) Alfred Wallenstein/RCA Victor Symphony Orchestra
CD: RCA Victor 7967
#(11-25-1963) Carlo Maria Giulini/Philharmonia Orchestra
CD: Intaglio 7101

Concerto No. 21 in C, K. 467
(4-1-1961) Alfred Wallenstein/RCA Victor Symphony Orchestra
CD: RCA Victor 7967

Concerto No. 23 in A, K. 488
(1-9-1931) John Barbirolli/London Symphony Orchestra
LP: Electrola C137-1544273
(11-14-1949) Vladimir Golschmann/Saint Louis Symphony Orchestra
CD: RCA Victor 61859
#(5-12-1955) Otmar Nussio/Swiss-Italian Radio-Television Orchestra
CD: Ermitage 127
(3-30, 31-1961) Alfred Wallenstein/RCA Victor Symphony Orchestra
CD: RCA Victor 7968

Concerto No. 24 in C Minor, K. 491
    (4-12-1958) Josef Krips/RCA Victor Symphony Orchestra
        CD: RCA Victor 7968

Piano Quartet No. 1 in G Minor, K. 478
    (4-8, 9-1971) Guarneri Quartet members (John Dalley, violin; Michael
        Tree, viola; David Soyer, cello)
        CD: RCA Victor 60406

Piano Quartet No. 2 in E-flat, K. 493
    (4-20-1971) Guarneri Quartet members (John Dalley, violin; Michael
        Tree, viola; David Soyer, cello)
        CD: RCA Victor 60406

Rondo in A Minor, K. 511
    (12-22-1959) CD: RCA Victor 7968

Poulenc, Francis

Intermezzo in A-flat
    (4-3-1963) CD: RCA Victor 5665; RCA Victor 61446

Intermezzo No. 2 in D-flat
    (4-3-1963) CD: RCA Victor 5665; RCA Victor 61446

Mouvements perpétuels (3)
    (11-13-1938) 78: RCA Victor 15660; HMV DB 3718
    (4-5-1963) CD: RCA Victor 5665; RCA Victor 61446

Napoli Suite
    (10-1-1947) 78: HMV DB 6614

Prokofiev, Serge

March, Op. 33 (The Love for Three Oranges)
    (3-23-1961) CD: RCA Victor 5666
    #(5-8-1961) CD: Ermitage 108

Visions Fugitives, Op. 22, Nos. 1–3, 12, 6–7, 10–11, 18, 9, 16, 14
    #(11-6-1961) CD: RCA Victor 5670; RCA Victor 61445

Rachmaninoff, Sergei

Concerto No. 2 in C Minor, Op. 18
    (5-27-1946) Vladimir Golschmann/NBC Symphony Orchestra
        LP: RCA Victor LM-1005
    (1-9-1956) Fritz Reiner/Chicago Symphony Orchestra
        CD: RCA Victor RCD1-4934; RCA Victor 61851
    (11-23-1971) Eugene Ormandy/Philadelphia Orchestra
        LP: RCA Victor ARL1-0031

Prelude in C-sharp Minor, Op. 3, No. 2
    (10-29-1936) CD: Grammofono 2000 AB-78539
    (12-11-1950) CD: RCA Victor 62662

Rhapsody on a Theme of Paganini, Op. 43
    (9-16, 17-1947) Walter Susskind/Philharmonia Orchestra
        LP: Electrola C137-1544273; RCA Victor LM-1744
    #(3-26-1950) Victor de Sabata/New York Philharmonic-Symphony
        CD: Nuova Era 2232
    (1-16-1956) Fritz Reiner/Chicago Symphony Orchestra
        CD: RCA Victor RCD1-4934; RCA Victor 61851

Ravel, Maurice

Forlane (*Le Tombeau de Couperin*, No. 3)
    (2-23-1934) CD: Grammofono 2000 AB-78539
    (3-23-1961) CD: RCA Victor 5665; RCA Victor 61446

Piano Trio in A Minor
    (8-28-1950) Jascha Heifetz, violin; Gregor Piatigorsky, cello
        CD: RCA Victor 7871; RCA Victor 61778

La vallée des cloches (*Miroirs*, No. 5)
    (4-5-1963) CD: RCA Victor 5665; RCA Victor 61446

Valses nobles et sentimentales
    (1-31-1963) CD: RCA Victor 5665; RCA Victor 61446

Rubinstein, Anton

Barcarolle No. 3 in G Minor, Op. 50, No. 3
Barcarolle No. 4 in G
    (8-20-1953) CD: RCA Victor 61860

Valse-Caprice in E-flat
    (11-7-1935) CD: Grammofono 2000 AB-78539
    (11-3-1953) CD: RCA Victor 61860

Saint-Saëns, Camille

Concerto No. 2 in G Minor, Op. 22*
    #(4-14-1953) Dimitri Mitropoulos/New York Philharmonic-Symphony
        CD: Music & Arts 655; AS Disc 508
    (1-14-1958) Alfred Wallenstein/Symphony of the Air
        CD: RCA Victor 61496
    (1-2-1969) Eugene Ormandy/Philadelphia Orchestra
        CD: RCA Victor 5666; RCA Victor 61863

Schubert, Franz

Fantasy in C, Op. 15 (D. 760) (Wanderer)
    (4-20, 21, 24-1965) CD: RCA Victor 6257

Impromptu in G-flat, Op. 90 (D. 899), No. 3
    (3-29-1946) 78: RCA Victor DM-1371
    (3-23-1961) CD: RCA Victor 6257

Impromptu in A-flat, Op. 90 (D. 899), No. 4
    (4-18-1928) CD: Grammofono 2000 AB-78539
    (12-11-1950) LP: RCA Victor LM-1153
    (3-23-1961) CD: RCA Victor 6257

Sonata in G, Op. 78 (D. 894)
    (10-29-1936) [third movement only] CD: Grammofono 2000 AB-78539

Sonata in B-flat, D. 960
    (4-22-1965) CD: RCA Victor 6257
    (6-11-1969) LP: RCA Victor LSC-3122

Piano Trio No. 1 in B-flat, Op. 99 (D. 898)*
  (9-13-1941) Jascha Heifetz, violin; Emanuel Feuermann, cello
    CD: RCA Victor 60926; RCA Victor 61778
  (4-13 to 19-1974) Henryk Szeryng, violin; Pierre Fournier, cello
    CD: RCA Victor 6262

Piano Trio No. 2 in E-flat, Op. 100 (D. 929)
  (4-13 to 19-1974) Henryk Szeryng, violin; Pierre Fournier, cello
    LP: RCA Victor ARL2-0731

Schumann, Robert

Arabeske in C, Op. 18
  (3-11-1947) 78: RCA Victor MO-1149
  (10-1947) LP: Electrola C151-03244/5
  #(11-19-1961) CD: RCA Victor 5670; RCA Victor 61445
  (6-16-1969) CD: RCA Victor 61444

Carnaval, Op. 9
  (10-27 to 29, 11-2-1953) LP: RCA Victor LM-1822
  (12-3, 4-1962; 1-23-1963) CD: RCA Victor 5667

Concerto in A Minor, Op. 54
  #(1947) Eugene Ormandy/Philadelphia Orchestra
    LP: Melodram 304
  (5-9, 10-1947) William Steinberg/RCA Victor Symphony Orchestra
    LP: RCA Victor LM-1050
  (4-5, 6-1958) Josef Krips/RCA Victor Symphony Orchestra
    CD: RCA Victor 61444
  #(4-29-1964) Franco Caracciolo/RAI-Naples Scarlatti Orchestra
    CD: Fonit Cetra CDE 1024; Virtuoso 2697102
  (3-8-1967) Carlo Maria Giulini/Chicago Symphony Orchestra
    CD: RCA Victor 6255
  #(2-11-1968) Zubin Mehta/Montréal Symphony Orchestra
    CD: Music & Arts 655

Etudes Symphoniques, Op. 13
  #(11-19-1961) CD: RCA Victor 61444

Fantasiestücke, Op. 12*
  (6-16-1949) LP: RCA Victor LM-1072
  (4-19, 12-3-1962) CD: RCA Victor 5667

#(10-1-1964) [No.1 only] LP: Melodiya C10 21327
#(1-15-1975) CD: RCA Victor 61160
(4-21 to 23-1976) LP: RCA Victor ARL1-2397

Fantasy in C, Op. 17
(9-2-1965) CD: RCA Victor 6258; RCA Victor 61264

Kreisleriana, Op. 16
(12-28, 29-1964) CD: RCA Victor 6258; RCA Victor 61264

Nachtstück in F, Op. 23, No. 4
(10-27-1953) 45: RCA Victor ERA-203

Novelette in F, Op. 21, No. 1
(10-23-1953) 45: RCA Victor ERA-203
(4-24-1965) CD: RCA Victor 6255

Novelette in D, Op. 21, No. 2
(4-24-1965) CD: RCA Victor 6255

Piano Quintet in E-flat, Op. 44
(8-25, 26-1949) Paganini Quartet (Henri Temianka, Gustave Rosseels,
    violins; Robert Courte, viola; Adolphe Frezin, cello)
    LP: RCA Victor LM-1095
(12-30-1966) Guarneri Quartet (Arnold Steinhardt, John Dalley, violins;
    Michael Tree, viola; David Soyer, cello)
    CD: RCA Victor 5669

Romance in F-sharp, Op. 28, No. 2
(4-2-1937) CD: Grammofono 2000 AB-78539
(12-12-1953) 45: RCA Victor ERA-203
(3-23-1961) CD: RCA Victor 5667

Träumerei (Kinderscenen, Op. 15, No. 7)
(3-12-1947) 78: RCA Victor MO-1149
(10-1-1947) LP: Electrola C151-03244/5

Piano Trio No. 1 in D Minor, Op. 63
(9-4 to 10-1972) Henryk Szeryng, violin; Pierre Fournier, cello
    CD: RCA Victor 6262

Vogel als Prophet (*Waldscenen*, Op. 82, No. 7)
    (3-29-1946) 78: RCA Victor 10-1272
    (3-23-1961) CD: RCA Victor 5667
    (6-16-1969) LP: RCA Victor LSC-3108

Widmung (Dedication) (arr. by Liszt)
    (3-12-1947) 78: RCA Victor MO-1149
    (10-1-1947) LP: Electrola C151-03244/5

Strauss, Johann, Jr.

On the Beautiful Blue Danube [abridged] (arr. by Rubinstein?)
    (c.1910) 78: Favorit 1-74612

Szymanowski, Karol

Mazurkas, Op. 50
    (3-15-1946) [Nos. 1–4] 78: RCA Victor 11-9219
    #(11-1-1961) [Nos. 1–3, 6] CD: RCA Victor 5670; RCA Victor 61445

Symphonie Concertante, Op. 60
    (12-19-1952) Alfred Wallenstein/Los Angeles Philharmonic
        CD: RCA Victor 60046

Tchaikovsky, Peter Ilyich

Concerto No. 1 in B-flat Minor, Op. 23
    (6-9, 10-1932) John Barbirolli/London Symphony Orchestra
        CD: Claremont GSE 78-50-41
    #(3-24-1946) Artur Rodzinski/New York Philharmonic-Symphony
        CD: AS Disc 519; Legend LGD 237
    (11-16-1946) Dimitri Mitropoulos/Minneapolis Symphony Orchestra
        LP: RCA Victor LM-1028
    (3-5-1963) Erich Leinsdorf/Boston Symphony Orchestra
        CD: RCA Victor RCD1-5363; RCA Victor 6259; RCA Victor
        61262

Piano Trio in A Minor, Op. 50
    (8-23, 24-1950) Jascha Heifetz, violin; Gregor Piatigorsky, cello
        CD: RCA Victor 7768; RCA Victor 61778

Villa-Lobos, Heitor

Alegria na horta (*Suite floral*, Op. 97, No. 3)
    (11-4-1941) 78: RCA Victor M/DM-970

Prole do Bébé, Book I
    (12-14-1931) [Nos. 2, 6, 7] LP: Electrola C027-1435551
    (5-16, 21-1941) [Nos. 1–3, 5–8] 78: RCA Victor M/DM-970
    (3-23-1961) [No. 7] LP: RCA Victor LSC-2566
    #(10-30-1961) [Nos. 1–2, 5–8] CD: RCA Victor 5670; RCA Victor 61445
    #(10-1-1964) [No. 7] LP: Melodiya C10 21327

Appendix I:
Commercially Issued Video Recordings of
Rubinstein

Kultur V1102 (VHS)

Three half-hour black-and-white programs, recorded 1949–50. They feature Rubinstein at a recording session and in his Los Angeles home. Conversational segments are included. Repertoire performed: **Schumann:** Fantasiestücke, Op. 12, Nos. 2 and 4; **Mendelssohn:** Spinning Song, Op. 67, No. 4; **Liszt:** Liebestraum No. 3; **Chopin:** Waltz No. 7 in C-sharp Minor, Op. 64, No. 2; Polonaise No. 3 in A, Op. 40, No. 1; Prelude in F-sharp Minor, Op. 28, No. 8; Mazurka No. 21 in C-sharp Minor, Op. 30, No. 4; Scherzo No. 3 in C-sharp Minor, Op. 39; Nocturne No. 5 in F-sharp, Op. 15, No. 2; Polonaise No. 6 in A-flat, Op. 53. Also included are a brief rehearsal and performance with Heifetz and Piatigorsky of **Schubert:** Trio No. 1 in B-flat, Op. 99 [first movement]; **Mendelssohn:** Trio No. 1 in D Minor, Op. 49 [first, second, and third movements].

Video Artists International 69045 (VHS)

Rubinstein Remembered. An hour-long Peter Rosen production with host and narrator John Rubinstein. Color and black-and-white. A multifaceted portrait of Rubinstein the man and the musician.

London LD 071 200-1 (Laserdisc); VHS 071 200-3 (VHS)

Grieg: Concerto in A Minor, Op. 16; **Chopin:** Concerto No. 2 in F Minor, Op. 21; **Saint-Saëns:** Concerto No. 2 in G Minor, Op. 22. André Previn/London Symphony Orchestra. Recorded 1975.

London LD 071 209-1 (Laserdisc); VHS 071 209-3 (VHS)

Beethoven: Concerto No. 3 in C Minor, Op. 37; **Brahms:** Concerto No. 1 in D Minor, Op. 15. Bernard Haitink/Concertgebouw Orchestra of Amsterdam. Recorded August 1973.

RCA 61160-6 (Laserdisc); 61160-3 (VHS)

Beethoven: Sonata No. 23 in F Minor, Op. 57; **Schumann:** Fantasiestücke, Op. 12; **Debussy:** Ondine; La plus que lente; Prélude in A Minor; **Chopin:** Scherzo No. 3 in C-sharp Minor, Op. 39; Etude No. 17 in E Minor, Op. 25, No. 5; Etude No. 4 in C-sharp Minor, Op. 10, No. 4; Nocturne No. 5 in F-sharp, Op. 15, No. 2; Polonaise No. 6 in A-flat, Op. 53; Waltz No. 7 in C-sharp Minor, Op. 64, No. 2; **Mendelssohn:** Spinning Song, Op. 67, No. 4. A benefit recital for the International Cultural Center for Youth in Jerusalem, given at Ambassador College Auditorium, Pasadena, California, January 15, 1975.

Appendix II
Reproducing Piano Rolls by Rubinstein

Albéniz	El Albaicin (*Ibéria*, No. 7)	Duo-Art 6204 (issued 12-1919)
	Córdoba, Op. 232, No. 4	Ampico 57446H
	Evocación (*Ibéria*, No. 1)	Duo-Art 6378; D-491 (issued 12-1920)
	Sevillanas (*Suite Española*, No. 3)	Duo-Art 6298; D-489 (issued 6-1920)
	Triana (*Ibéria*, No. 6)	Ampico 57556H
Brahms	Capriccio in B Minor, Op. 76, No. 2	Duo-Art 65969; D-99 (issued 2-1923)
	Intermezzo in A, Op. 118, No. 2	Duo-Art 6971-3 (issued 2-1926)
	Rhapsody in B Minor, Op. 79, No. 1	Duo-Art 6744-4 (issued 4-1924)
Chopin	Ballade No. 3 in A-flat, Op. 47	Duo-Art 6252-4 (issued 3-1920)
	Barcarolle in F-sharp, Op. 60	Duo-Art 6542-3 (issued 7-1922)
	Etude No. 3 in E, Op. 10, No. 3	Ampico 57775H
	Nocturne No. 5 in F-sharp, Op. 15, No. 2	Duo-Art 6162-4; D-85 (issued 7-1919)
	Polonaise No. 3 in A, Op. 40, No. 1	Ampico 57296H
	Polonaise No. 5 in F-sharp Minor, Op. 44	Duo-Art 6505-4 (issued 2-1922)
	Preludes, Op. 28, Nos. 1, 4, 10, 21, 24	Duo-Art 6811-4 (issued 11-1924)

Debussy	La Cathédrale engloutie	Ampico 57667H
	Danse	Duo-Art 63549
		(issued 11-1920)
	L'Isle joyeuse	Duo-Art 6834-4;
		D-779 (issued 1-1925)
	La plus que lente (Valse)	Duo-Art 6182-3
		(issued 10-1919)
Falla	Ritual Fire Dance	Duo-Art 6755; D-239
		(issued 5-1924)
Liszt	Hungarian Rhapsody No. 12	Ampico 58087H;
		70543
Prokofiev	Suggestion diabolique, Op. 4, No. 4	Duo-Art 6922-4
		(issued 10-1925)
Rimsky-Korsakov	Selections from *Le Coq d'or* (arr. by Rubinstein) (Introduction; Hymn to the Sun; Dances from Act 2; Conclusion)	Duo-Art 6857-4; D-355 (issued 3-1925)
Anton Rubinstein	Barcarolle in A Minor, Op. 93	Ampico 57516H
Schumann	Fantasiestücke, Op. 12 [No. 1]	Ampico 57304K
	[No. 5]	Ampico 57384K
	Papillons, Op. 2	Duo-Art 6560-4
		(issued 10-1922)

NOTE: The Ampico rolls were probably recorded in 1919.

Notes on the Sources

Legend: Y = *My Young Years* by A. Rubinstein; M = *My Many Years* by A. Rubinstein; RA = Rubinstein family archives, originally located at the Rubinstein home in Paris but now found partly there, partly in the Library of Congress, Washington, D.C., and partly at the City of Lodz Historical Museum in Poland; AR, ER, JR, NR, and AW = author's conversations (held between 1990 and 1995, and sometimes supplemented by phone conversations, letters, and faxes) with, respectively, Alina Rubinstein, Eva Rubinstein, John Rubinstein, Nela (Aniela) Rubinstein, and Annabelle Whitestone (Lady Weidenfeld); RyE = *Rubinstein y España* by various authors; NYT = *New York Times*; CBC? = unidentified transcript (found in RA) of an interview whose text *seems* to indicate that it was done by a Canadian radio journalist in Paris circa 1960; EMI = EMI Archives, Hayes, Middlesex, England; RCA = RCA files, Bertelsmann Building, New York.

Preface

1. G. Astruc, *Le Pavillon des fantômes*, 17
2. JR
3. Y166–7
4. Y4
5. *Times Literary Supplement*, London, November 6, 1994, 29

Chapter 1

1. RA
2. J. Tuwim (trans. A. Gillon), *The Dancing Socrates and Other Poems*, 50
3. B. Horowicz, *Musiques et Paroles*, 14–15
4. Y3
5. Y3
6. Y3
7. Y18
8. RyE, 59

9. Ibid., 59
10. Horowicz, op. cit., 13
11. Y8
12. Y4
13. *Spotkania z Arturem Rubinsteinem*, 1975 Poltel documentary transcript, 2
14. Y4
15. *Spotkania*, op. cit., 1
16. H. Kamm, "Flowery and Forgetful, Lodz Cheers Rubinstein," NYT, June 1, 1975
17. Y4
18. D. Brandes, "Fantasia for Virtuoso Voice," *Fugue*, March 1978, 26
19. S. Chotzinoff, *A Little Nightmusic*, 126
20. Y6
21. RyE, 19
22. Y6–7
23. CBC? 8–9
24. RA, letter, April 4, 1962
25. RA, letter, March 2, 1968
26. Brandes, op. cit., 26
27. RA, letter, June 14, 1978
28. JR
29. Y9
30. Y9
31. Chotzinoff, op. cit., 125–6
32. *Spotkania*, op. cit., 3
33. Y9
34. RA, letter, January 7, 1977
35. Y10
36. CBC?, 8–9
37. Y7
38. Y46
39. Y18 & 46
40. Y46–7
41. F. Mohr, *My Life with the Great Pianists*, 56
42. JR
43. AW
44. JR
45. A. Blyth, "Arthur Rubinstein Talks to Alan Blyth," the *Gramophone*, November 1968, 650
46. Y10
47. NR (and subsequent quotations of Nela Rubinstein in this chapter)
48. Y8
49. Y10
50. Author's conversation with Josef Kanski, Warsaw, 1991

51. Y15
52. Y15
53. Y15
54. Y15
55. Y20
56. Y23

Chapter 2

1. F. Gaisberg, *Music on Record*, 187
2. Author's conversation with Daniel Barenboim, Berlin, 1992
3. RA
4. Y23
5. RA
6. Y24
7. Y24
8. RyE, 20
9. W. Kempff, *Unter dem Zimbelstern*, 51
10. Y24
11. Y24
12. Y24
13. Y27
14. JR
15. Kempff, op. cit., 58
16. Ibid., 54
17. Y63
18. Kempff, op. cit., 59
19. Ibid., 54
20. Y27–8
21. Kempff, op. cit., 59
22. Gaisberg, op. cit., 1919
23. B. Erdely, letter to author, November 28, 1990
24. Y28
25. Y58
26. Y25–6
27. RA
28. M. Campbell, *The Great Violinists*, 79
29. Y32
30. Y400
31. Y32
32. Y35
33. Y32
34. Y33
35. A. Moser, *Joseph Joachim, ein Lebensbild*, 317–8

36. B. Litzmann, *Clara Schumann, ein Künstlerleben*, 241
37. Moser, op. cit., 317–8
38. Y34
39. Y31
40. Y31
41. Gaisberg, op. cit., 187
42. M. Wilcox, "An Afternoon with Artur Rubinstein," *High Fidelity*, July 1963, 28
43. Y31
44. Gaisberg, op. cit., 187
45. Y31
46. Wilcox, op. cit., 29
47. Y38
48. Wilcox, op. cit., 29
49. Y41
50. M159
51. Barenboim conversation
52. H. Temianka, *Facing the Music*, 103
53. Y46–7
54. Y36
55. Y39–40
56. RA
57. Y41
58. Y49
59. Y49–50
60. RA
61. RA, letter, November 7, 1949
62. Y41
63. Y51–2
64. RA, letter, January 1, 1901
65. Y57
66. P. J. Rosenwald, draft of article for *Records and Recording*, attached to letter to Rubinstein, December 13, 1976
67. Y61
68. Y51
69. Staatsarchiv, Senat der Freien und Hansestadt Hamburg, letter of Ms. or Mr. Möhring to author, July 9, 1993
70. I. Newton, *At the Piano—Ivor Newton*, 153
71. Y55–6
72. Y61
73. Y61
74. Y62
75. Y62–3
76. Y63

77. Y64
78. Y64-5
79. AR
80. Y47
81. Y64-5
82. Y51
83. Y67
84. Y67
85. Y69
86. Y69
87. AR
88. Y71
89. Y73
90. H. Modjeska, [Modrzejewska] *Memories and Impressions*, 466-8
91. I. J. Paderewski and M. Lawton, *The Paderewski Memoirs*
92. Gaisberg, op. cit., 175-6
93. Y74-5
94. Y76
95. Y78
96. H. Kissel, interview in *Women's Wear Daily*, May 23, 1973
97. Y78
98. Y81
99. Barenboim conversation
100. Y86
101. Y86
102. Y91
103. Y86
104. Y86-7
105. W. Niemann, *Meister des Klaviers*, 205
106. *Gazeta Warszawska*, February 19, 1919
107. Y88
108. Y88
109. Y92
110. Y96
111. Author's conversation with Maria Kempinska, Warsaw, 1991
112. Y95, 97
113. S. Spiess, *Ze wspomnien melomana*
114. M. Fuks, *Zydzi w Warszawie*
115. Y100

Chapter 3

1. Y109
2. Y110

3. A. Buchwald, *Bravo*, January–February 1962, 15
4. Y112
5. Y106
6. Y114
7. ER
8. RA
9. RA
10. RA
11. RA
12. Astruc, op. cit., 233
13. F. Lesure & R. Nichols (eds.), *Debussy Letters*, 279
14. M. Martin du Gard, *Carte rouge*, 85
15. Y124
16. Y124
17. Lesure & Nichols, op. cit., 279
18. Y126
19. AW
20. RA, letter, September 29, 1969
21. Astruc, op. cit., 209
22. Y131
23. Y129
24. Astruc, op. cit., 215
25. *Le Figaro*, December 14, 1904
26. Y132
27. *Le Figaro*, December 17, 1904
28. Y132, 134
29. CBC?, 13
30. Y134, 136
31. Y135
32. *Le Figaro*, January 19, 1905
33. Ibid., January 28, 1905
34. Astruc, op. cit., 215
35. Y143
36. Y144–5
37. Janina Fialkowska, conversation with author, New York, 1991
38. Y140, 142
39. RA, letter, undated
40. RA, telegram, May 5, 1905
41. Astruc, op. cit., 217
42. Y157
43. Y158
44. Y164
45. Y164
46. RA

47. Y174
48. "Arthur Rubinstein, Polish Pianist, Is Here," *Musical America*, January 6, 1906, 7
49. Y176
50. RA
51. Y178
52. A. Loesser, "Arthur Rubinstein," *Fine Arts*, 14/716, February 26, 1968, part 2
53. R. Schickel, *The World of Carnegie Hall*, 116–7
54. Ibid.
55. Loesser, op. cit.
56. RA
57. Y185
58. Y185
59. RA
60. Y195
61. Y203
62. RA
63. RA
64. Warsaw Philharmonic program book, September 13, 1966
65. Y208
66. Y207
67. Y209
68. Kempinska conversation
69. Y213
70. Astruc, op. cit., 216
71. Y215
72. J. Freeman, letter to the author, November 16, 1993
73. Y217
74. Y222
75. Lesure & Nichols, op. cit., 179
76. Y222
77. RA
78. Y220
79. RA
80. RA
81. RA
82. RA
83. CBC?, 11, 13
84. Y239
85. ER
86. Y248
87. A. Schein, manuscript sent to the author, 1994, 32
88. NR
89. Y249

90. Y252
91. Y254–5
92. P. Johnson, A History of the Jews, 359, 361
93. NR
94. B. M. Maciejewski, Karol Szymanowski, 34
95. Y281
96. Y287–8
97. Kempinska conversation
98. Y256
99. NR
100. M534
101. Kempinska conversation
102. RA
103. RA
104. NR
105. Neue Freie Presse, December 12, 1909
106. Y310
107. Y301
108. NR
109. Y299
110. Vossische Zeitung, March 17, 1910
111. Y339
112. Y340–1
113. Y353
114. Y357
115. P. I. Tchaikovsky, Letters to His Family, 186
116. Y358
117. Johnson, op. cit., 363
118. Y363–4
119. Y366
120. W. Labunski, typescript of unpublished memoirs, 256
121. B. Gromadzki, "Wspomnienia o mlodosci Karola Szymanowskiego," in Ruch Muzyczny, 1948/2
122. Neue Zeitschrift für Musik, Leipzig, 79 (1912) 6, 75; Signale für die musikalische Welt, Berlin, 70 (February 7, 1912) 6, 186; Allgemeine Musikzeitung, Leipzig, 39 (February 9, 1912) 6; all from Leipzig's Gewandhausarchiv, Pressedokumentation, with letter of Claudius Böhm to author, July 27, 1993
123. "Spotkania z Karolem Szymanowskim," Muzyka, 1955, 9/10, 39–43
124. T. Chylinska, Szymanowski, 55
125. Y375
126. J. Nicholas, Godowsky, the Pianist's Pianist, 84
127. D. Godowsky, First Person Plural, 14–17
128. Y378
129. D. Godowsky, op. cit., 153

130. NR
131. *Times* (London), May 2, 1912
132. Ibid., May 17, 1912
133. Y383
134. *Times* (London), May 24, 1912
135. Ibid., June 6, 1912
136. Ibid., June 5, 1912
137. M. Luhan, *Intimate Memories*, 2/257
138. Ibid., 268–9
139. M. Draper, *Music at Midnight*, 33
140. Ibid., 35–7
141. Y388–9
142. Luhan, op. cit., 255
143. M. Draper, op. cit., 32
144. Ibid., 44
145. J. Iwaszkiewicz et al., *Begegnung mit Karol Szymanowski*, 117
146. Ibid., 118
147. Y396
148. Y397
149. RA
150. Y397–8
151. Y399
152. K. Szymanowski (T. Chylinska, ed.), Korespondencja, I, 1903–19, 370–1
153. *Times* (London), May 21, 1913
154. M. Gorky, *Chaliapin*, 182
155. Gaisberg, op. cit., 191
156. Draper, op. cit., 66
157. E. Goossens, *Overtures and Beginners*, 98
158. L. Tertis, *My Viola and I*, 45
159. Draper, op. cit., 93–4
160. Ibid., 95
161. Goossens, op. cit., 99
162. Y412
163. Y414
164. Y414
165. Draper, op. cit., 119
166. Ibid., 124
167. Y414–5
168. Y413–6
169. Chylinska, *Szymanowski*, 60
170. Iwaszkiewicz, op. cit., 123
171. Szymanowski, *Korespondencja*, I, letter, October 14/27, 1919, 594–5
172. Ibid., letter, November 27/December 12, 1913, 400–1
173. Y419

174. Chylinska, *Szymanowski*, 62
175. Y photo pages
176. Draper, op. cit., 142–3
177. Ibid., 150–1
178. R. Craft (ed.), *Stravinsky: Selected Correspondence*, II/293
179. V. Stravinsky and R. Craft, *Stravinsky in Pictures and Documents*, 603
180. E. Lipmann, *Arthur Rubinstein*, 91
181. *Times* (London), May 7, 1914
182. Draper, op. cit., 193
183. Luhan, op. cit., 272
184. Y430
185. Draper, op. cit., 85–6
186. Ibid., 202–8
187. Ibid., 162
188. Ibid., 173
189. R. Elkin, *Queen's Hall, 1893–1941*, 77
190. Y431
191. Draper, op. cit., 230
192. Y433
193. Y440–2
194. Y442
195. Tertis, op. cit., 45
196. Draper, op. cit., 227
197. Tertis, op. cit., 45
198. Ibid., 40
199. Y459
200. Draper, op. cit., 233–7
201. Y446
202. RyE, 21

Chapter 4

1. RyE, 93–8
2. RyE, 31
3. H. Wood, *My Life of Music*, 301
4. RyE, 96
5. RyE, 31
6. Y461
7. Labunski, op. cit., 253–4
8. RyE, 87
9. RyE, 31–2
10. RyE, 20
11. Y471

12. RyE, 68
13. RyE, 70
14. Chotzinoff, op. cit., 122
15. Y471
16. RyE, 53–4
17. G. Casadesus & J. Muller, *Mes noces musicales*, 74
18. RyE, 68
19. RyE, 21
20. RyE, 68
21. CBC?, 16–17
22. Chotzinoff, op. cit., 1–2
23. R. Jacobson, *Reverberations*, 170
24. CBC?, 1–2
25. Mohr, op. cit., 49
26. Chotzinoff, op. cit., 122
27. RyE, 68
28. Z. Jachimecki, *Karol Szymanowski*, 33
29. M12
30. Y470
31. Y478
32. M70
33. *Buenos Aires Herald*, July 3, 1917
34. M19
35. *El Día*, Montevideo, July 21, 1917
36. Ibid., July 23
37. Ibid., July 24
38. Ibid., July 25
39. Ibid., August 8
40. Ibid., October 10
41. Ibid., October 2
42. V. Perlis, transcript of interview with Rubinstein, 1979, 5
43. M19–20
44. Craft (ed.), op. cit., II/183
45. Ibid., II/162
46. Ibid., I/144
47. Ibid., II/452
48. M85
49. Lipmann, op. cit., 88–9
50. F. Sopeña, *Vida y obra de Manuel de Falla*, 115
51. S. Demarquez, *Manuel de Falla*, 117–9
52. Ibid., 119
53. Sopeña, op. cit., 117, and M200, 228
54. J. Pahissa, *Manuel de Falla*, 107
55. M229

56. Draft in Archivo Manuel de Falla, Granada
57. Letter, February 1, 1929, in Archivo Manuel de Falla, Granada
58. Draft in Archivo Manuel de Falla, Granada
59. M20
60. Y251
61. M20–1
62. M21
63. B. Tosi, *Pertile*, 65
64. M22
65. M35
66. Author's telephone conversation with Manuela Pertile, February 16, 1994
67. L. Rasponi, *The Last Prima Donnas*, 171
68. Ibid., 128
69. Ibid., 301
70. *Jornal do Commercio*, Rio de Janeiro, June 11, 1918
71. Ibid., June 12
72. Ibid., June 14
73. Ibid., June 16
74. Ibid., July 1
75. *Correio da Manha*, Rio de Janeiro, July 1, 1918
76. M31
77. M29–30
78. G. Antoine, *Paul Claudel, ou l'enfer du génie*, 191
79. M34
80. M34
81. M32
82. M45–6
83. R. Draper (N. Warren, ed.), *The Letters of Ruth Draper*, 75
84. M326
85. RA, included with letter, February 28, 1956
86. R. Aldrich, *Concert Life in New York, 1902–1923*, 590–1
87. A. T. Schwab, *James Gibbons Huneker*, 253
88. Notes to Fonè compact disc 90 F 08
89. Chotzinoff, op. cit., 132
90. CBC?, 17
91. M58
92. M52
93. M47
94. Lina Prokofieva conversation with the author, 1982
95. M500
96. D. Henahan, "This Ageless Hero, Rubinstein," NYT Magazine, March 14, 1976
97. M47–8
98. H. Robinson, *Sergei Prokofiev*, 101

99. Chotzinoff, op. cit., 121
100. M65
101. M68
102. H. Greenfield, *Caruso*, 229
103. M74
104. M75
105. M75–6
106. RyE, 59–62
107. M100
108. J. Harding, *The Ox on the Roof*, 209–10
109. Undated letter in Archivo Manuel de Falla, Granada
110. I. Newton, op. cit.
111. Wigmore Hall archive
112. AW
113. Lipmann, op. cit., 106–7
114. AW
115. M84–5
116. AW
117. Rasponi, op. cit., 171
118. R. de Quesada, letter to the author, November 11, 1993
119. NR
120. M92
121. Chotzinoff, op. cit., 132
122. A. Rubinstein, "Villa-Lobos," in *Muzyka*, Warsaw, 1928/12, 577–80
123. M252
124. M94
125. M97
126. M99
127. R. M. Schafer (ed.), *Ezra Pound and Music*, 234–40
128. M80
129. Chotzinoff, op. cit., 132
130. Gaisberg, op. cit., 189
131. M102
132. Craft (ed.), op. cit., I/150
133. M138
134. Szymanowski, op. cit., II/168
135. Iwaszkiewicz, op. cit., 156
136. Szymanowski, op. cit., II/168–74
137. Ibid.
138. Ibid., II/175 et sego
139. Ibid, 108–9
140. M113
141. Iwaszkiewicz, op. cit., 156
142. S. Golachowski et al., *Begegnung mit Karol Szymanowski*, 55–7

143. Szymanowski, op. cit., II/199 et sego
144. Boston Symphony Orchestra archives (information sent with letter to author from Bridget P. Carr, January 27, 1994)
145. Szymanowski, op. cit., II/238–9
146. Craft (ed.), op. cit., I/149
147. Szymanowski, op. cit., II/258–61
148. Ibid.
149. Ibid., II/268
150. S. Hurok and R. Goode, *Impresario*, 155
151. D. Henahan, op. cit. (see note 96 to this chapter)
152. Perlis, op. cit., 2–3
153. M168
154. M165
155. Hurok & Goode, op. cit., 269–71
156. CBC?, 17
157. Szymanowski, op. cit., II/356–7
158. Chotzinoff, op. cit., 123–4
159. M122
160. *Le Figaro*, May 1, 1923
161. J. Marnold, "Musique: Concerts Rubinstein," in *Mercure de France*, July 1, 1923
162. H. Prunières in *La Revue musicale*, IV/8, June 1, 1923, 159
163. Madeleine Milhaud, conversation with the author, 1991
164. M115
165. JR
166. NR
167. R. Draper, op. cit., 75
168. M116, 208
169. Szymanowski, op. cit., II/222–3
170. NYT, January 28, 1972
171. *Wiadomsci Literackie*, Warsaw, October 19, 1924
172. Labunski, op. cit., 253
173. Szymanowski, op. cit., II/2/214–27
174. RyE 77–9
175. M176 and letter to author from L. Oswald, December 30, 1994
176. Labunski, op. cit., 391–2
177. M255–6
178. E. Schwarzkopf, *On and Off the Record*, 143
179. M281
180. M297
181. EMI, letter, January 11, 1930
182. Chylinska, op. cit., 169
183. N. Slonimsky, *Perfect Pitch*, 128–9
184. R. Draper, op. cit., 151–2
185. D. Godowsky, op. cit., 152–3

Chapter 5

1. RyE 60–2
2. M247–8
3. NR (also subsequent quotations of Nela Rubinstein in this chapter)
4. H. Rodzinski, *Our Two Lives*, 22–3
5. Ibid., 23
6. Ibid., 27
7. M248
8. M250
9. M253–4
10. Labunski, op. cit., 354–5
11. M259
12. M258, 260–1
13. M271–4
14. Labunski, op. cit., 354–5
15. Ibid., 480
16. M292
17. Rodzinski, op. cit., 41–2
18. M303–4
19. M305–7
20. M318
21. M308
22. M309
23. AW
24. M309
25. M310
26. M310
27. AW
28. N. Rubinstein, in *Arturo Rubinstein 1887–1982: Recuerdos de España*, 7–9
29. J. Piatigorsky, *Jump in the Waves*, 87–8
30. RA, letters of March 16 and 26, 1964
31. M320
32. R. Draper, op. cit., 152–3
33. M320–2
34. M322
35. ER
36. R. Draper, op. cit., 152–3
37. F. M. Eckman, interview with Rubinstein in *New York Post*, February 22, 1975
38. M201
39. N. Rubinstein, *Nela's Cookbook*, xiii
40. EMI, letters of January 28 and 31 and April 26, 1933
41. Chotzinoff, op. cit., 133
42. M250

43. M334
44. M342–3
45. A. Bliss, *As I Remember*, 102
46. J. Wechsberg, "Metamorphosis," in *New Yorker*, November 1, 1958
47. M354
48. Labunski, op. cit., 253–4
49. Ibid., 256–7
50. M358
51. C. B. Lyon, letter to the author, September 7, 1990
52. EMI, letter of May 2, 1935
53. EMI, letters of May 29 and June 14, 1935
54. M382
55. M397
56. M399
57. Gaisberg, op. cit., 191
58. Szymanowski, op. cit., II/2/459–63
59. Hurok & Goode, op. cit., 273–4
60. Schickel, op. cit., 302–3
61. NYT, January 8, 1938
62. Schickel, op. cit., 302–3
63. RA, letter, March 27, 1965
64. Hurok & Goode, op. cit., 273–4
65. Gaisberg, op. cit., 188–90
66. R. Draper, op. cit., 212
67. Gaisberg, op. cit., 190–1
68. *Warszawski Dziennik Narodowy*, September 20, 1938
69. M460
70. EMI, letters, October 3 and 9, 1939
71. M466

Chapter 6

1. R. Draper, op. cit., 220
2. RA
3. RA, letter, April 23, 1942
4. RA, letter, July 9, 1942
5. RA, letter, April 20, 1944
6. RA, letter, May 24, 1944
7. M510–11
8. NR (also subsequent quotations of Nela Rubinstein in this chapter)
9. Buchwald, op. cit., 15
10. Ibid.
11. RA
12. RA, letter, February 18, 1944

13. RA, letter, January 15, 1952
14. M546
15. K. G. Roy, *Not Responsible for Lost Articles*, 187
16. D. Barenboim, conversation with the author, 1992 (also subsequent Barenboim quotations in this chapter)
17. RA
18. M585
19. C. Reid, *John Barbirolli*, 102
20. D. Walter, letter to the author, October 19, 1990
21. E. Ax, conversation with the author, Milan, 1994
22. M. Bookspan and R. Yockey, *André Previn*, 357
23. M. Bookspan and R. Yockey, *Zubin*, 94
24. EMI, letter, September 24, 1935
25. EMI, letters, December 2, 1937, and early January 1938
26. EMI, letters, April 9 and 12, 1940, and August 25, 1941
27. A. Weschler-Vered, *Jascha Heifetz*, 109–10
28. M494
29. W. Primrose, *Walk on the North Side*, 143
30. RA
31. Weschler-Vered, op. cit., 111
32. Ibid., 123–4
33. I. Newton, op. cit., 152–3
34. RA
35. RA, letters, June 15 and August 16, 1942
36. A. Steinhardt, conversation with the author, New York, 1994 (also subsequent Steinhardt quotations in this chapter)
37. RCA, May 17, 1963
38. N. Rubinstein, *Nela's Cookbook*, xiv
39. Labunski, op. cit., 781–3
40. RA, letter, November 8, 1942
41. RA, letter, July 31, 1946
42. RA, letter, August 11, 1944
43. M493
44. RA, letter, November 21, 1973
45. RA, letter, February 15, 1974
46. ER (also subsequent quotations of Eva Rubinstein in this chapter)
47. Taped conversation between Mildred Knopf and her daughter, Wendy Knopf Cooper, early 1980s
48. AW
49. L. Dubman Fratti, conversation with the author, New York, 1991
50. P. Smolen, letter to the author, December 27, 1990
51. E. Podis, "Rubinstein Recalled," in *Clavier*, December 1983, 35–6
52. E. Podis, conversation with the author, Cleveland, 1989
53. RA, letter, July 31, 1941

54. NYT, March 12, 1940
55. NYT and *New York Herald-Tribune*, November 25, 1940
56. *New York World-Telegram*, February 25, 1946
57. *New York Herald-Tribune*, October 28, 1946
58. H. Kupferberg, *Those Fabulous Philadelphians*, 147–8
59. M530
60. Schickel, op. cit., 352–3
61. *Daily Variety*, Hollywood, August 27, 1946
62. W. Sargeant, "Arthur Rubinstein," *Life*, April 5, 1948, 101
63. H. R. Axelrod (ed.), *Heifetz*, 12
64. Sargeant, op. cit., 114
65. *New York Herald-Tribune*, February 14, 1949
66. RA, letter, November 17, 1940
67. RA, letter, no date, but December 1943
68. RA, letter, March 3, 1952
69. RA, letter, July 31, 1941
70. RA, letter, November 18, 1943
71. RA
72. RA, letter, August 27, 1945
73. RA, letter, November 21, 1945
74. AR
75. RA
76. RA, letter, December 12, 1956
77. RA, letter, October 9, 1945
78. RA, letters, November 17 and 28, 1945
79. S. Shirakawa, *The Devil's Music-Master*, 351
80. W. Furtwängler, *Notebooks 1924–1954*, 190
81. RA, letter, April 16, 1962
82. RA, letters, March 30 and April 16, 1964
83. RA, letter, April 6, 1964
84. RA, letter, October 9, 1968
85. RA, letter, October 21, 1968
86. Mohr, op. cit., 57
87. M. Knopf tape (see note 47, this chapter)
88. RA, letter, October 12, 1947
89. "Le Retour d'Enesco et d'Arthur Rubinstein," *Arts*, Paris, October 24, 1947
90. RA, letter, December 23, 1944
91. J. Wechsberg, op. cit.
92. Ibid.
93. Ibid.
94. M. Knopf tape (see note 47, this chapter)
95. R. Jasinski's papers, Warsaw: Rubinstein letter, September 3, 1967
96. J. Heilpern, "A Musical Soul," *Observer*, London, May 23, 1976
97. JR (also subsequent quotations of John Rubinstein in this chapter)

98. E. Hoffman, *Lost in Translation*, 72–4
99. NYT, June 13, 1958
100. NYT, June 1, 1975
101. Found in Peter Rosen's material; source untraced
102. RA, articles from *Express Poznanski*, February 2, 1960
103. NYT, March 20, 1960
104. NYT, June 1, 1975
105. Ibid.
106. RA, letter, June 17, 1971, from consul-general of the Netherlands in New York
107. RA, letters, February 5 and 12, 1974
108. RA, letter, October 2, 1974
109. RA, letter, September 11, 1968
110. E. K. Kirk, *Music at the White House*, 334
111. Schickel, op. cit., 378
112. RA, letter, October 27, 1961
113. RA, letter, November 13, 1962
114. RA, letter, April 15, 1964
115. RA, letter, April 20, 1964
116. RA, telegram (Rubinstein's), January 21, 1965
117. RA, letters, March 25 and 29, 1971
118. Temianka, op. cit., 102
119. Mohr, op. cit., 50–1
120. RA, letter, December 31, 1953
121. *Sunday Times* (London), February 11, 1962
122. Jacobson, op. cit., 167–8
123. Schein, op. cit., 10–43
124. RA, letter of Astrid Schmidt-Neuhaus to Rubinstein, April 24, 1966
125. Chotzinoff, op. cit., 120
126. *New York Sunday News*, March 14, 1971
127. M. Knopf tape (see note 47, this chapter)
128. RA, letter, March 25, 1975
129. *Jerusalem Post*, September 13, 1974
130. Fialkowska, conversation with the author
131. Program book, Seventh Arthur Rubinstein International Piano Master Competition, Israel, March–April 1992
132. RCA, May 17, 1963
133. "Arthur Rubinstein at 100," *Keynote*, July 1987, 16
134. R. Kennedy, untitled and undated RCA pamphlet
135. *Keynote* (see note 133), 8–13
136. M. Wilcox, conversation with the author, 1989
137. RA, letter, April 6, 1962
138. Jacobson, op. cit., 172
139. RA, letters, November 21, 1973, and February 15, 1974
140. M. Wilcox, notes to booklet accompanying RCA compact disc 5669-2-RC

141. RA, telegram from R. Hillyer to Rubinstein, February (?) 19, 1956
142. A. Steinhardt, conversation with the author, 1994; also subsequent quotes
143. See note 140
144. *Look*, March 9, 1971
145. *Time*, January 12, 1968
146. RA, letter, December 27, 1966
147. RA, letters, October 21, 1968, and December 28, 1970
148. Stravinsky and Craft, op. cit., 615
149. Chotzinoff, op. cit., 125
150. Jacobson, op. cit., 170–1
151. H. Duder, "Her Husband the Pianist," in *New York Post*, August 30, 1969, 27
152. RA, letter, August 23, 1973
153. RA, letter, February 15, 1974
154. RCA, report, April 10, 1974
155. NYT, June 3, 1973
156. RA, letter, July 1, 1975
157. Chotzinoff, op. cit., 134–5
158. Jasinski papers, letters, September 3, 1967, and February 18, 1974
159. Lipmann, op. cit., 29
160. I. K. (presumably Kolodin), Avery Fisher Hall program book, New York, March 1974
161. See note 158, February 18, 1974
162. F. Duchable, telephone conversation with the author, 1990
163. RA, letter, February 15, 1974
164. RCA, April 4, 1974
165. *Village Voice*, New York, February 17, 1975
166. F. M. Eckman, *New York Post*, February 22, 1975
167. RA, letter, October 9, 1975
168. Heilpern, op, cit.
169. Ibid.
170. *Time*, March 29, 1976
171. NYT, March 16, 1976
172. *Time*, March 29, 1976
173. Ibid.
174. Mohr, op. cit., 57–8

Chapter 7

1. AW (also subsequent quotations in this chapter)
2. R. de Quesada, letter to the author, November 5, 1993
3. RA, letter, August 28, 1971
4. RA, letter, September 9, 1971
5. ER (also subsequent quotations in this chapter)
6. NR (also subsequent quotations in this chapter)

7. RA, letter, July 4, 1976
8. RA, letter, October 23, 1976
9. AR (also subsequent quotations in this chapter)
10. Fialkowska, conversation with the author, 1990 (also subsequent quotations in this chapter)
11. S. Richter, diary entry, March 3, 1977 (photocopy given to the author)
12. Y. Boehm, A. Zvielli, article in *Jerusalem Post* (no date on copy in author's possession, but published shortly after Rubinstein's death)
13. N. Magaloff, conversation with the author, Florence, 1990 (also subsequent quotations in this chapter)
14. Barenboim, conversation with the author, 1992
15. Y8
16. J. Cegiella, in program book, Seventh Arthur Rubinstein International Piano Master Competition, Israel, March–April 1992, 52
17. Schein, op. cit., 49–51
18. *Hollywood Reporter,* August 9, 1982
19. RA, letter, November 8, 1976
20. RA, letter, January 3, 1978
21. RA, letter, December 30, 1976
22. NYT, January 28, 1977
23. RA, telegram
24. RA, letter, June 30, 1977
25. RA, letter, January 17, 1978
26. RA, letter, April 6, 1978
27. RA, letter, August 8, 1978
28. Rosenwald, op. cit.
29. J. Jones, letter to the author, December 6, 1990
30. AW, letter to the author, March 24, 1990
31. M5a
32. M497
33. L. Adler, *It Ain't Necessarily So,* 240
34. B. Gavoty, "Le piano refermé," *Le Figaro,* undated copy from RA
35. RA, undated letter
36. RA, letter, December 21, 1980
37. RA, undated letter
38. M123
39. M602
40. JR (also subsequent quotations in this chapter)
41. RA, letter, January 15, 1981
42. See note 29
43. P. H. Berczeller, *Doctors and Patients,* 190–2
44. Heilpern, op. cit.
45. Berczeller, op. cit., 192–7
46. RA, letter, July 23, 1980

47. RCA, June 10, 1980
48. RCA, January 9, 1981
49. RCA, February 2, 1981
50. RA, letter, March 18, 1982
51. RA, undated letter
52. RA, December 1, 1980
53. NYT, October 20, 1982
54. *Miami Herald*, January 31, 1982
55. NYT, September 23, 1982
56. E. Carlyss, letter to the author, March 27, 1994
57. A. Rubinstein, letter to J. Rubinstein, January 31, 1982
58. NYT, December 21, 1982
59. *Boston Globe*, December 23, 1982
60. Associated Press, December 22, 1983
61. Lipmann, op. cit., 39

The Recorded Legacy

1. M. Lympany and M. Strickland, *Moura*, 22
2. Lipmann, op. cit., 58
3. H. Brandon, article in *Sunday Times* (London), February 11, 1962
4. Barenboim, conversation with the author (also subsequent quotes in this chapter)
5. Lipmann, op. cit. 57
6. M. Wilcox, notes to RCA compact disc 6257-2-RC
7. T. S. Eliot, "The Hollow Men," *Collected Poems 1909–1935*, 105
8. M252
9. AW
10. H. Weinstock, notes to RCA compact disc RCD1-5492
11. *Look*, March 9, 1971
12. M296
13. Ax, conversation with the author
14. Podis, conversation with the author

Bibliography

Books

Adler, Larry. *It Ain't Necessarily So*. London: Collins, 1984.

Aldrich, Richard. *Concert Life in New York, 1902–1923*. New York: Putnam's, 1941.

Antoine, Gérald. *Paul Claudel, ou l'enfer du génie*. Paris: Robert Laffont, 1989.

Astruc, Gabriel. *Le Pavillon des fantômes*. Paris: Belfond, 1987.

Axelrod, Herbert R (ed.). *Heifetz*. Neptune City, N.J.: Paganiniana, 1981.

Baldock, Robert. *Casals*. London: Gollancz, 1992.

Barenboim, Daniel. *A Life in Music*. New York: Scribner's, 1991.

Begegnung mit Karol Szymanowski (includes Golachowski, Stanislaw: *Karol Szymanowski*; Iwaszkiewicz, Jaroslaw: *Begegnungen mit Szymanowski*; Szymanowski, Karol: *Briefe und Aufsätze*). Leipzig: Philipp Reclam, jun. 1982.

Berczeller, Peter H. *Doctors and Patients*. New York: Lisa Drew/Macmillan, 1994.

Bliss, Arthur. *As I Remember*. London: Faber & Faber, 1970.

Bookspan, Martin, and Ross Yockey. *André Previn*. New York: Doubleday, 1981.

——. *Zubin*. New York: Harper & Row, 1978.

Buckle, Richard. *Diaghilev*. London: Weidenfeld & Nicolson, 1993.

Campbell, Margaret. *The Great Violinists*. London: Granada, 1980.

Casadesus, Gaby, and Jacqueline Muller. *Mes noces musicales*. Paris: Buchet/Chastel, 1989.

Chasins, Abram. *Leopold Stokowski*. New York: Hawthorn Books, 1979.

Chissell, Joan. *Clara Schumann, a Dedicated Spirit*. London: Hamish Hamilton, 1983.

Chotzinoff, Samuel. *A Little Nightmusic*. New York: Harper & Row, 1964.

Chylinska, Teresa. *Szymanowski*. Cracow: PWM, 1981.

Craft, Robert (ed.). *Stravinsky, Selected Correspondence*. New York: Knopf 1982 (Vol. I), 1984 (Vol. II), 1985 (Vol. III).

Demarquez, Suzanne. *Manuel de Falla*. Barcelona: Editorial Labor, 1968.

Draper, Muriel. *Music at Midnight*. New York and London: Harper & Bros., 1929.

Draper, Ruth (ed. Neilla Warren). *The Letters of Ruth Draper*. New York: Scribner's, 1979.

Dubal, David. *Conversations with Menuhin*. London: Heinemann, 1991.

Eliot, T. S. *Collected Poems 1909–1935*. New York: Harcourt Brace, 1936.

Elkin, Robert. *Queen's Hall, 1893–1941*. London: Rider & Co., n.d.

Furtwängler, Wilhelm (ed. Michael Tanner). *Notebooks, 1924–1954.* London and New York: Quartet, 1989.

Gaisberg, F. W. *Music on Record.* London: Robert Hale, 1947.

Gallego, Antonio. *Manuel de Falla.* Madrid: Alianza, 1990.

Giazotto, Remo. *Quattro secoli di storia dell'Accademia nazionale di Santa Cecilia.* Rome: Accademia nazionale di Santa Cecilia, 1970.

Gillis, Daniel. *Furtwängler and America.* Palo Alto, Calif.: Ramparts Press, 1970.

Godowsky, Dagmar. *First Person Plural.* New York: Viking, 1958.

Golachowski: see *Begegnung.*

Goodman, Virginia. *Isador Goodman, a Life in Music.* Sydney: Collins, 1983.

Goossens, Eugene. *Overture and Beginners.* London: Methuen, 1951.

Gorky, Maxim. *Chaliapin.* London: Columbus, 1988.

Graffman, Gary. *I Really Should Be Practicing.* New York: Avon, 1981.

Greenfield, Howard. *Caruso.* New York: Putnam's, 1983.

Haendel, Ida. *Woman with Violin.* London: Gollancz, 1970.

Harding, James. *The Ox on the Roof.* New York: Da Capo, 1986.

Hoffman, Eva. *Lost in Translation.* New York: Penguin, 1990.

Horowicz, Bronislaw. *Musiques et Paroles.* Paris: France-Empire, 1979.

Horowitz, Joseph. *Conversations with Arrau.* New York: Knopf, 1982.

Hurok, Sol, and Ruth Goode. *Impresario.* Westport, Conn.: Greenwood Press, 1975.

Itzkoff, Seymour W. *Emanuel Feuermann.* University, Ala.: University of Alabama Press, 1979.

Iwaszkiewicz: see *Begegnung.*

Jachimecki, Zdzislaw. *Karol Szymanowski: Rys dotychczasowej tworczosci.* Cracow: 1927.

Jacobson, Robert. *Reverberations.* New York: William Morrow, 1974.

Johnson, Paul. *A History of the Jews.* New York: Harper & Row, 1987.

Kaiser, Joachim. *Great Pianists of Our Time.* New York: Herder & Herder, 1971.

——. *Wie ich sie sah . . . und wie sie waren.* Munich: Piper, 1987.

Kehler, George. *The Piano in Concert.* Metuchen, N.J., and London: Scarecrow Press, 1982.

Kempff, Wilhelm. *Unter dem Zimbelstern.* Munich: Piper, 1985.

Kennedy, Michael. *Barbirolli.* London: MacGibbon & Kee, 1971.

Kirk, Elise K. *Music at the White House.* Urbana, Ill.: University of Illinois Press, 1986.

Kupferberg, Herbert. *Those Fabulous Philadelphians.* London: W. H. Allen, 1970.

Labunski, Wiktor. Untitled and unpublished memoirs, written in the early 1960s, and in possession of University of Missouri Library, Kansas City, Missouri.

Lesure, François, and Roger Nichols (eds.). *Debussy Letters.* London: Faber and Faber, 1987.

Lewinski, Wolf-Eberhard von. *Arthur Rubinstein.* Berlin: Rembrandt-Verlag, 1967.

Lipmann, Eric. *Arthur Rubinstein.* Paris: Editions de Messine, 1980.

Litzmann, Berthold. *Clara Schumann, ein Künstlerleben.* Leipzig: Breitkopf & Härtel, 1908.

Luhan, Mabel Dodge. *Intimate Memories,* Vol. II. New York: Harcourt, 1935.

Lyle, Wilson. *A Dictionary of Pianists*. London: Robert Hale, 1985.

Lympany, Moura, and Margot Strickland. *Moura*. London: Peter Owen, 1991.

Mach, Elyse. *Great Pianists Speak for Themselves*. New York: Dodd, Mead, 1980.

Maciejewski, B. M. *Karol Szymanowski*. London: Poets' and Painters' Press, 1967.

Martin du Gard, Maurice. *Carte rouge: Le théâtre et la vie, 1929–1930*. Paris: Flammarion, 1930.

Menuhin, Diana. *Fiddler's Moll*. London: Weidenfeld & Nicolson, 1984.

Michalski, Grzegorz, Ewa Obniska, Henryk Swokien, and Jerzy Waldorff. *Geschichte der polnischen Musik*. Warsaw: Interpress, 1988.

Milstein, Nathan, and Solomon Volkov. *From Russia to the West*. New York: Holt, 1990.

Modjeska, Helena. *Memories and Impressions*. New York: Macmillan, 1910.

Mohr, Franz. *My Life with the Great Pianists*. Grand Rapids, Mich.: Baker Book House, 1992.

Moser, Andreas. *Joseph Joachim, ein Lebensbild*. Berlin: Verlag der deutschen Brahms-Gesellschaft, 1910.

Neugaus, G. G. (Neuhaus, H. H.). *Razmishleniya, vospominaniya, dnevniki*. Moscow: Sovyetskii Kompozitor, 1975.

Newton, Ivor. *At the Piano—Ivor Newton*. London: Hamish Hamilton, 1966.

Nicholas, Jeremy. *Godowsky, the Pianist's Pianist*. Wark, Hexham, Northumberland: Appian Publications and Recordings, 1989.

Niemann, Walter. *Meister des Klaviers*. Berlin: Schuster & Loeffler, 1919.

Noye, Linda J. (ed.). *Pianists on Playing*. Metuchen, N.J.: Scarecrow Press, 1987.

Paderewski, I. J., and Mary Lawton. *The Paderewski Memoirs*. London: Collins, 1939.

Pahissa, Jaime. *Manuel de Falla*. London: Museum Press, 1954.

Palmer, Christopher. *Szymanowski*. London: BBC, 1983.

Piatigorsky, Jacqueline. *Jump in the Waves*. New York: St. Martin's Press, 1988.

Pietraszczyk, Bozenna (ed.). *Artur Rubinstein, 1887–1982*. Lodz: Muzeum Historii Miasta Lodzi, [1990?].

Plaskin, Glenn. *Vladimir Horowitz*. New York: William Morrow, 1983.

Primrose, William. *Walk on the North Side*. Provo, Utah: Brigham Young University Press, 1978.

Rasponi, Lanfranco. *The Last Prima Donnas*. New York: Knopf, 1982.

Rattalino, Piero. *Da Clementi a Pollini*. Milan: Ricordi/Giunti Martello, 1983.

———. *Pianisti e fortisti*. Milan: Ricordi/Giunti, 1990.

(Regia Accademia di Santa Cecilia.) *I Concerti dal 1895 al 1933*. Rome: Manuzio, 1933.

Reid, Charles. *John Barbirolli*. London: Hamish Hamilton, 1971.

Ritchie, Lady. *Blackstick Papers*. London: Smith, Elder, & Co., 1908.

Robinson, Harlow. *Sergei Prokofiev*. New York: Viking, 1987.

Rodzinski, Halina. *Our Two Lives*. New York: Scribner's, 1976.

Roy, Klaus G. *Not Responsible for Lost Articles*. Cleveland, Ohio: Musical Arts Association, 1993.

Rubinstein, Arthur. *My Many Years*. New York: Knopf, 1980.

——. *My Young Years.* New York: Knopf, 1973.

Rubinstein, Nela. *Nela's Cookbook.* New York: Knopf, 1983.

Rubinstein y España (various authors). N.p.: Banco Santander, [1987].

Samson, Jim. *The Music of Szymanowski.* New York: Taplinger, 1981.

Schafer, R. Murray (ed.). *Ezra Pound and Music.* New York: New Directions, 1977.

Schickel, Richard. *The World of Carnegie Hall.* Westport, Conn.: Greenwood Press, 1973.

Schonberg, Harold C. *The Great Pianists.* New York: Simon & Schuster, 1963.

Schwab, Arnold T. *James Gibbons Huneker.* Stanford: Stanford University Press, 1963.

Schwarzkopf, Elisabeth. *On and Off the Record.* New York: Scribner's, 1982.

Shirakawa, Sam H. *The Devil's Music-Master.* New York and Oxford: Oxford University Press, 1992.

Slonimsky, Nicolas. *Perfect Pitch.* Oxford: Oxford University Press, 1988.

Sopeña, Federico. *Vida y obra de Manuel de Falla.* Madrid: Turner, 1988.

Spiess, Stefan. *Ze wspomnien melomana.* Cracow: 1963.

Stern, Richard (ed.). *Was muss der Musikstudierende von Berlin wissen?* Berlin: [Stern], 1909.

Stravinsky, Vera, and Robert Craft. *Stravinsky in Pictures and Documents.* New York: Simon & Schuster, 1978.

Szymanowski, Karol (ed. T. Chylinska). *Korespondencja.* Cracow: PWM, 1982 (Vol. I), 1994 (Vol. II).

Tagliaferro, Magdalena. *Quase tudo (memórias).* Rio de Janeiro: Nova Fronteira, 1979.

Tchaikovsky, Piotr Ilyich. *Letters to His Family.* New York: Stein and Day, 1981.

Temianka, Henri. *Facing the Music.* Sherman Oaks, Calif.: Alfred, 1980.

Tertis, Lionel. *My Viola and I.* London: Paul Elek, 1974.

Thomson, Virgil. *Virgil Thomson.* New York: Da Capo, 1966.

Tillis, Malcolm. *Chords and Discords.* London: Phoenix House, 1960.

Tosi, Bruno (ed.). *Artur Rubinstein, una vita nella musica.* Venice: Malipiero, 1986.

Tosi, Bruno. *Pertile, una voce, un mito.* Venice: C.G.S., 1985.

Tuwim, Julian (trans. Adam Gillon). *The Dancing Socrates and Other Poems.* New York: Twayne, 1968.

Vospominaniya o Sofronitzkom (various authors). Moscow: Sovyetskii Kompozitor, 1970.

Weschler-Vered, Artur. *Jascha Heifetz.* London: Robert Hale, 1986.

Wierzynski, Casimir. *The Life and Death of Chopin* (with foreword by Rubinstein). New York: Simon and Schuster, 1949.

Wood, Henry. *My Life of Music.* London: Gollancz, 1938.

Pamphlets and Magazine Issues Dedicated Wholly or in Large Part to Rubinstein

(Arthur Rubinstein International Music Society, The.) *The Seventh Arthur Rubinstein International Piano Master Competition, March–April 1992, Israel.*
(City of Lodz History Museum.) *To the Memory of Artur Rubinstein.* N.d.
(Concurso Internacional de Piano Paloma O'Shea.) *Arturo Rubinstein 1887–1982, Recuerdos de España.* Santander: Fundación Isaac Albéniz 1987.
(Fundación Isaac Albéniz.) *Una pagina per a Rubinstein.* Barcelona: 1987.
Gavoty, Bernard. *Arthur Rubinstein.* Geneva: Krister 1956.
Loesser, Arthur. *Artur Rubinstein.* [Cleveland]: Fine Arts, Vol. 14, No. 716, February 26, 1968, Part II.
Musica. Milano: February–March 1988, No. 12/48.
(Poltel [Polish Television].) *Spotkania z Arturem Rubinsteinem,* unpublished English translation of transcript of 1975 documentary.
Quaderns Fundació Caixa de Pensions. [Barcelona?]: September 1987, No. 37.
S. Hurok has the honor to present Artur Rubinstein (souvenir booklet for a Rubinstein tour in the United States). New York: Hurok Artists, Inc., [1961].
Symphonia. Bologna: December 1992, III/22.

Some Substantial Articles (in chronological order)

"Artur Rubinstein," by Winthrop Sargeant, in *Life,* April 5, 1948.
"Rubinstein: Evolution of an Artist," by Howard Taubman, in the *New York Times Magazine,* ?, 1956.
"Metamorphosis" (Profiles), by Joseph Wechsberg, in the *New Yorker,* November 1, 1958.
"He Remains King," by Harold C. Schonberg, in the *New York Times,* October 29, 1961.
"A Visit with Artur Rubinstein," by Joseph Roddy, in *Look,* ?, 1961.
"A Conversation between Henry Brandon and Artur Rubinstein," by Henry Brandon, *Sunday Times* (London), February 11, 1962.
"Rubinstein Ruminates," by Art Buchwald, in *Bravo,* January–February 1962.
"An Afternoon with Artur Rubinstein," by Max Wilcox, in *High Fidelity,* July 1963.
"The Rubinstein Touch, Untouched at 75," by Harold C. Schonberg, in the *New York Times Magazine,* January 26, 1964.
"The Undeniable Romantic," by Ray Kennedy et al., in *Time,* February 25, 1966.
"Artur Rubinstein Talks to Alan Blyth," by Alan Blyth, in the *Gramophone,* November 1968.
"Rubinstein," by Glenn Gould, in *Look,* March 9, 1971.
"The perennial prodigy," by Phil Santora, in *New York Sunday News,* March 14, 1971.

"Rubinstein at 85: Still a Fresh Outlook," by Donal Henahan, in the *New York Times*, January 28, 1972.

"This ageless hero, Rubinstein," by Donal Henahan, in the *New York Times Magazine*, March 14, 1976.

"A Musical Soul," by John Heilpern, in the *Observer*, May 23, 1976.

"TV: At 90, Rubinstein Plays On," by John J. O'Connor, in the *New York Times*, January 26, 1977.

"Fantasia for Virtuoso Voice," by David Brandes, in *Fugue*, March 1978.

"Rubinstein Recalled," by Eunice Podis, in *Clavier*, December 1983.

"Arthur Rubinstein at 100," by Max Wilcox and John Rubinstein, and "The Rubinstein Legacy," by Allan Kozinn, in *Keynote*, July 1987.

"Un adorabile infedele," by Egidio Ortona, in *Amadeus*, March 1992.

"In viaggio con Artur," by Nela Rubinstein, in *Amadeus*, August 1992.

"Rubinstein/Gould, les deux menteurs," by Alain Lompech, in *Le Monde*, December 10, 1992.

Items of Related Interest

(38 Festival de Musica y Danza.) *España y los Ballets Russes.* Granada: 1989.

(Fundación Archivo Manuel de Falla.) *Manuel de Falla: Dialogos con la cultura del S. XX.* Granada: 1991.

(Institut de France.) *Discours prononcés dans la séance publique tenue par l'Académie des Beaux-Arts . . . pour la réception de M. Richard Nixon élu associé étranger en remplacement de M. Arthur Rubinstein.* Paris: 1987.

Krynski, Magnus J. "Politics and Poetry: The Case of Julian Tuwim," in the *Polish Review*, New York, 18/4, 1973.

Levine, Madeline G. "Julian Tuwim: 'We, the Polish Jews . . . ,' " in the *Polish Review*, [1972?].

Poesia. Madrid: 1991, Nos. 36 and 37 (in one volume).

Wigmore Hall, 75th Anniversary, 1901–1976. London: 1976.

Index